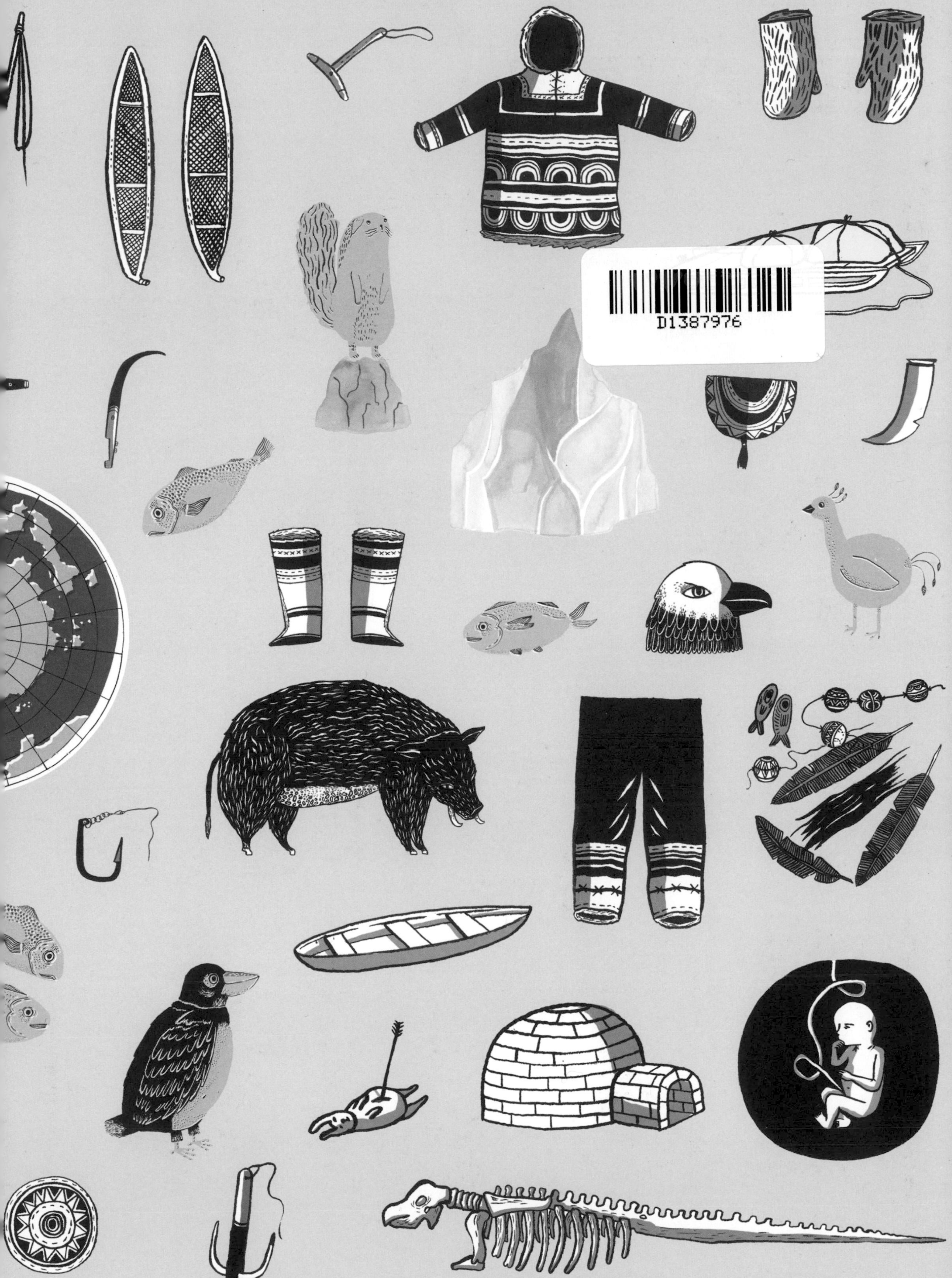

The ENCYCLOPEDIA
of
EARLY EARTH

A Graphic Novel by Isabel Greenberg

JONATHAN CAPE

LONDON

LOVE IN A VERY COLD CLIMATE

When the Nord man and the South Pole woman first paddled their canoes alongside each other in the icy seas of the South Pole, it was clear to them both within seconds, that they were soulmates.

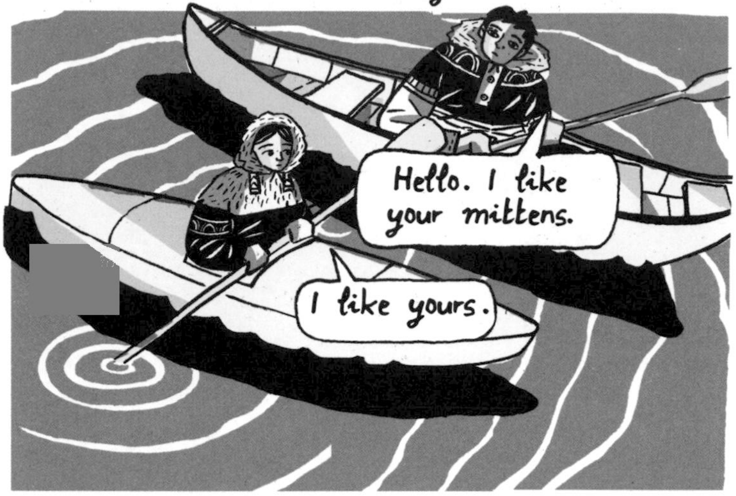
Hello. I like your mittens.
I like yours.

He was the First Nord to ever circumnavigate Early Earth and land on the shores of the South Pol

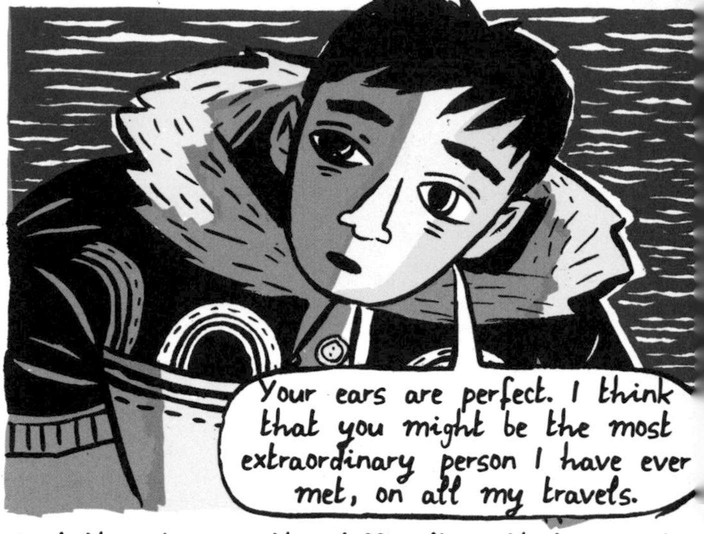
Your ears are perfect. I think that you might be the most extraordinary person I have ever met, on all my travels.

Which is why they had no idea about the strange and perverse reaction this would have on the magnetic field of Early Earth.

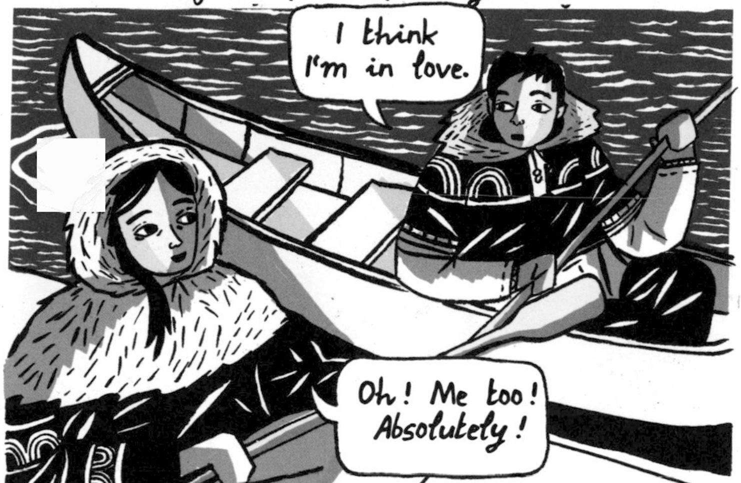
I think I'm in love.
Oh! Me too! Absolutely!

Had they known the difficulties that were to befall them, they might not have been so rash in falling in love.

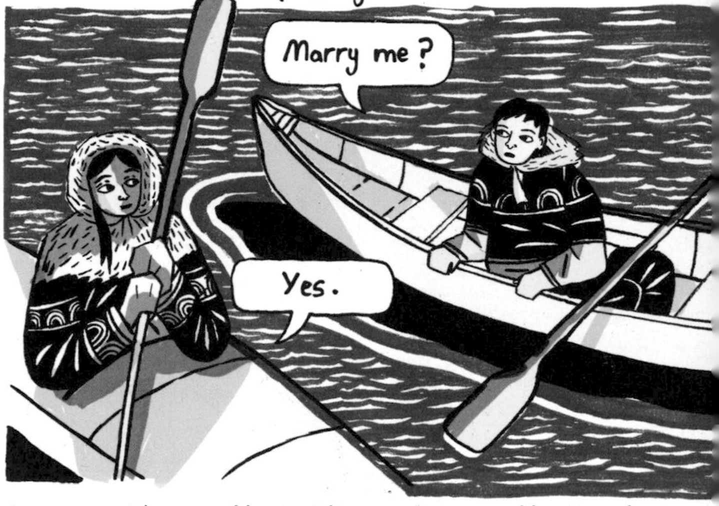
Marry me?
Yes.

But perhaps there was no way of avoiding it. Fate, karma, the will of the Gods... call it what y like, it was surely meant to happen. After all, in all the vastness of the Universe they had been thrown together.

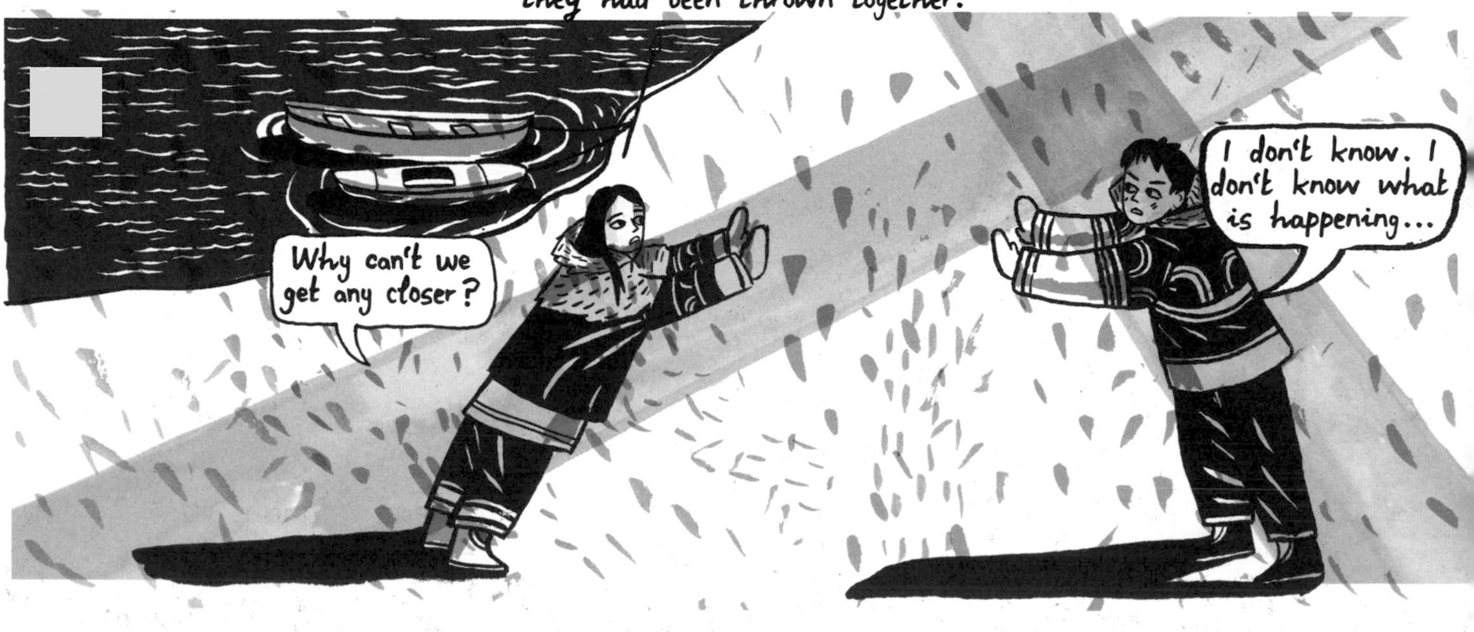
Why can't we get any closer?
I don't know. I don't know what is happening...

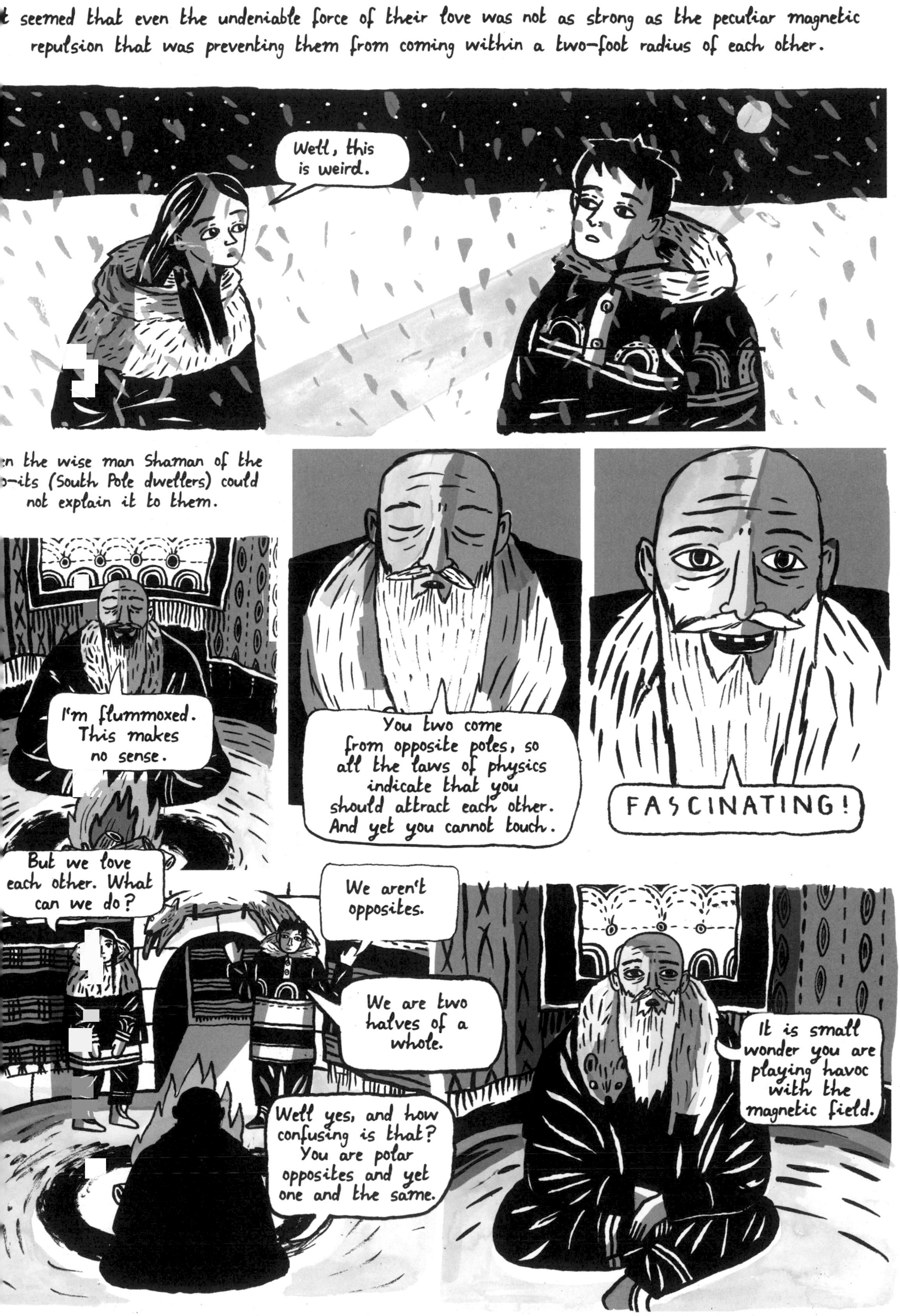
t seemed that even the undeniable force of their love was not as strong as the peculiar magnetic repulsion that was preventing them from coming within a two-foot radius of each other.
Well, this is weird.
n the wise man Shaman of the -its (South Pole dwellers) could not explain it to them.
I'm flummoxed. This makes no sense.
You two come from opposite poles, so all the laws of physics indicate that you should attract each other. And yet you cannot touch.
FASCINATING!
But we love each other. What can we do?
We aren't opposites.
We are two halves of a whole.
Well yes, and how confusing is that? You are polar opposites and yet one and the same.
It is small wonder you are playing havoc with the magnetic field.

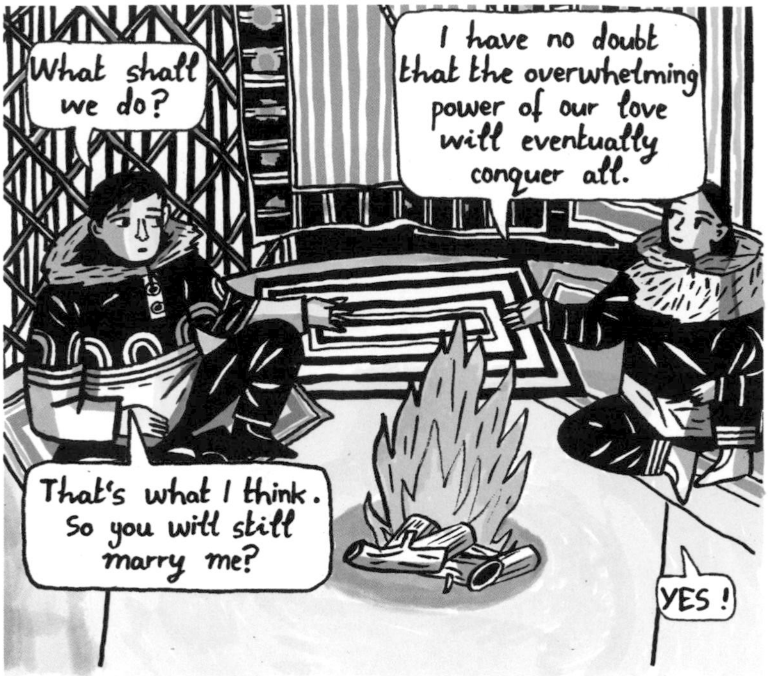
What shall we do?
I have no doubt that the overwhelming power of our love will eventually conquer all.
That's what I think. So you will still marry me?
YES!

So they were married. Two feet apart of course.

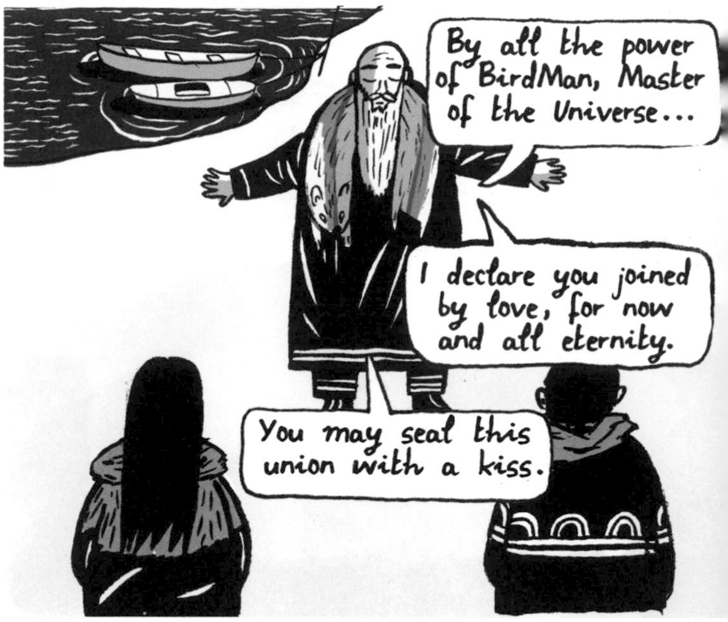
By all the power of BirdMan, Master of the Universe...
I declare you joined by love, for now and all eternity.
You may seal this union with a kiss.

But of course they could not. So they kissed scraps of paper and blew them to each other. (In fact many historians believe this to be the first recorded instance of anyone blowing a kiss.) Like most newlyweds, they wanted to kiss each other all the time, and in those early years the skies of the South Pole were alive with hundreds and hundreds of paper kisses, mingling with the snow flakes as they were swept away on the icy winds.

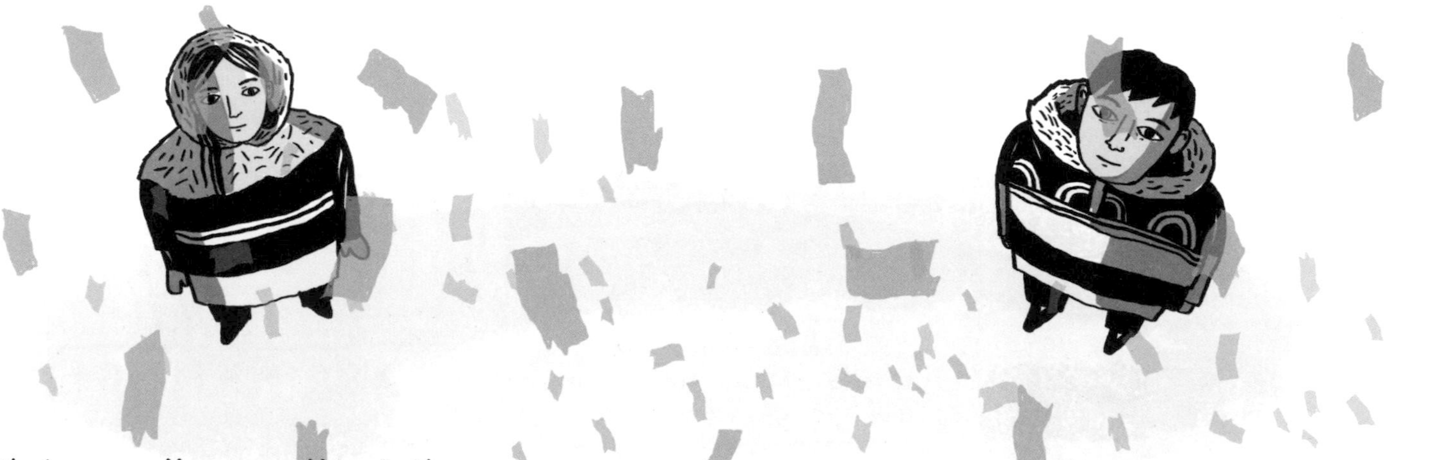

That was all very well, but there was only one way that they could ever feel the warmth of the other.

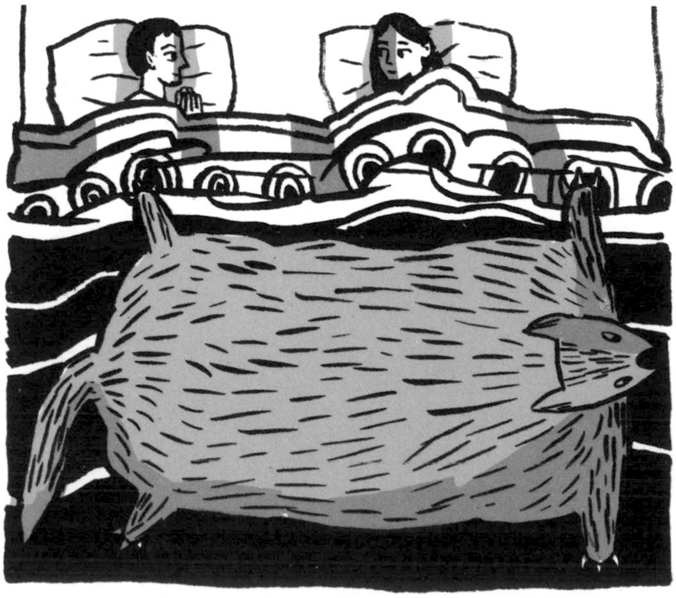

Each morning they would get up and swap sides of the bed. That way they could lay their heads in the impression the other had made in the pillow. And for a few fleeting moments, until the pillows cooled and the warmth faded, it was almost as though they were holding each other.

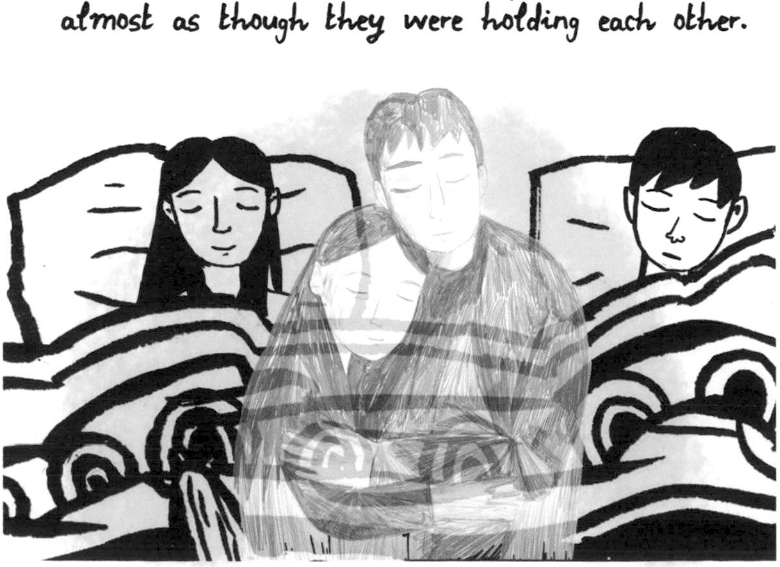

So the days became weeks, and the weeks became years,
and still the magnetic force did not relent. They spent hours staring into each other's eyes.
And yet still they could not so much as brush fingertips.

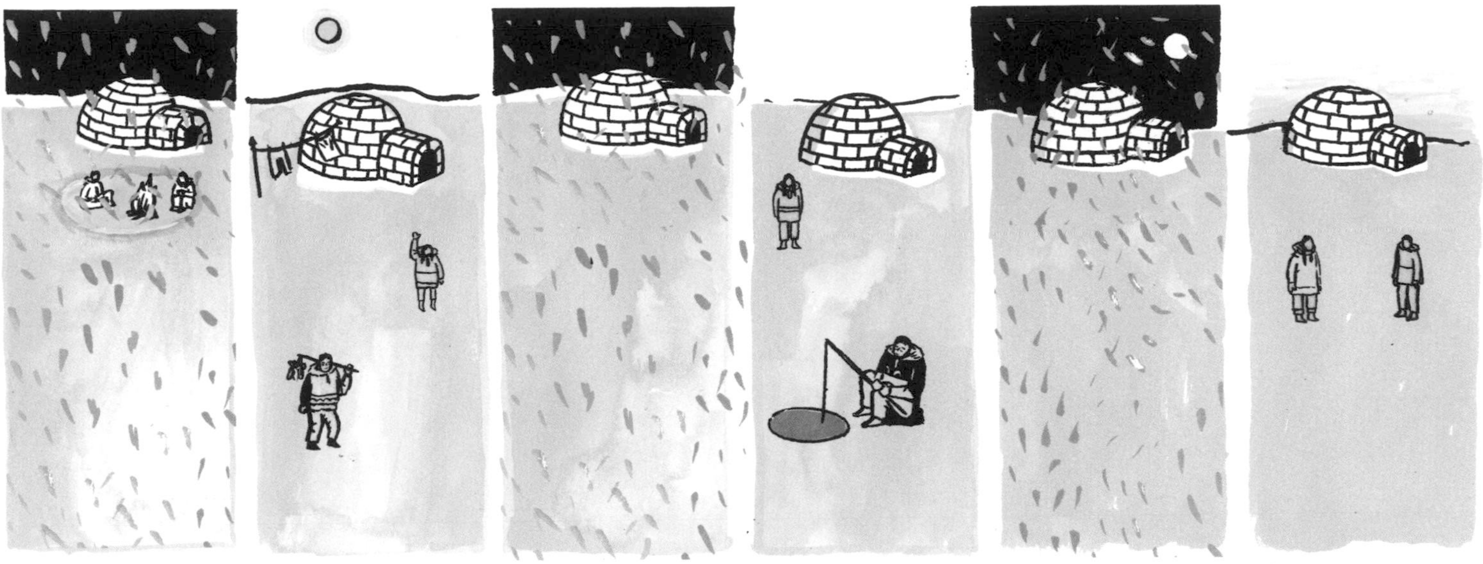

And so instead, all through the deep night of the South Pole winter they told each other stories.
All through those huge, bright, star-flung nights, nights that stretched on and on, they sat and told each other stories.

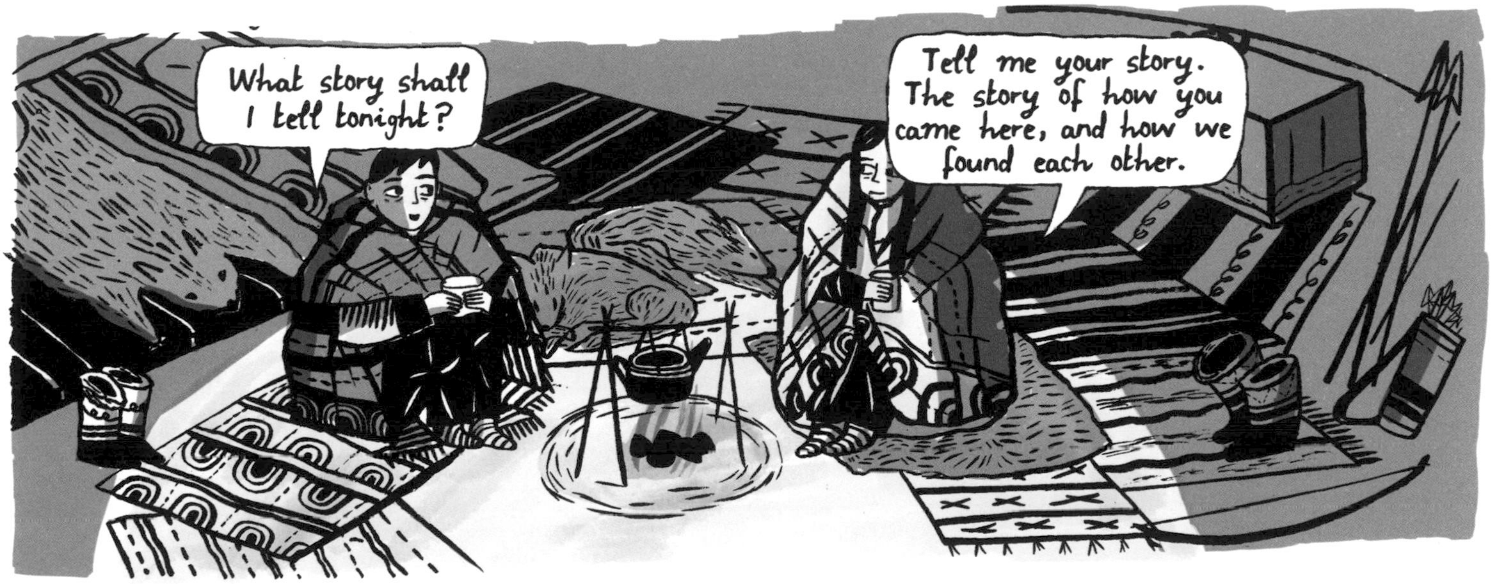
What story shall I tell tonight?
Tell me your story. The story of how you came here, and how we found each other.

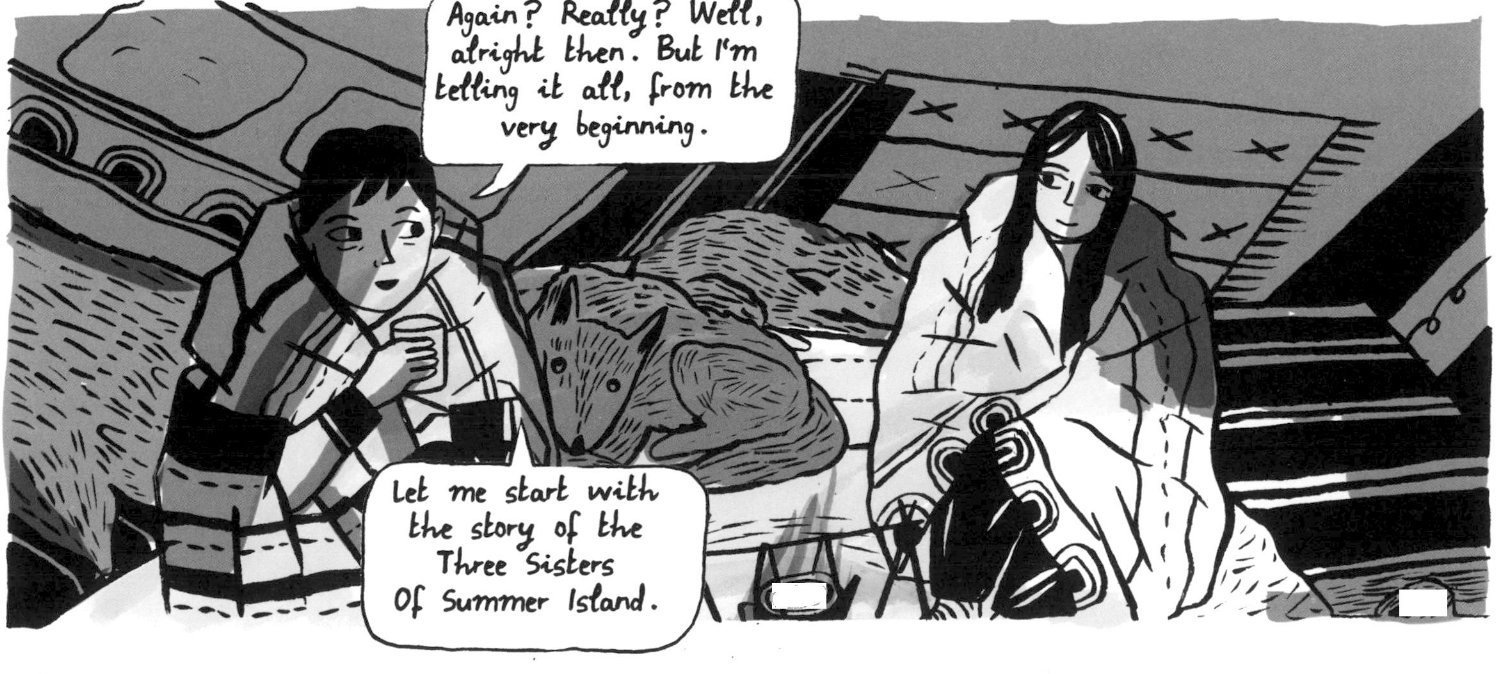
Again? Really? Well, alright then. But I'm telling it all, from the very beginning.
Let me start with the story of the Three Sisters Of Summer Island.

Part The First:

The LAND OF NORD

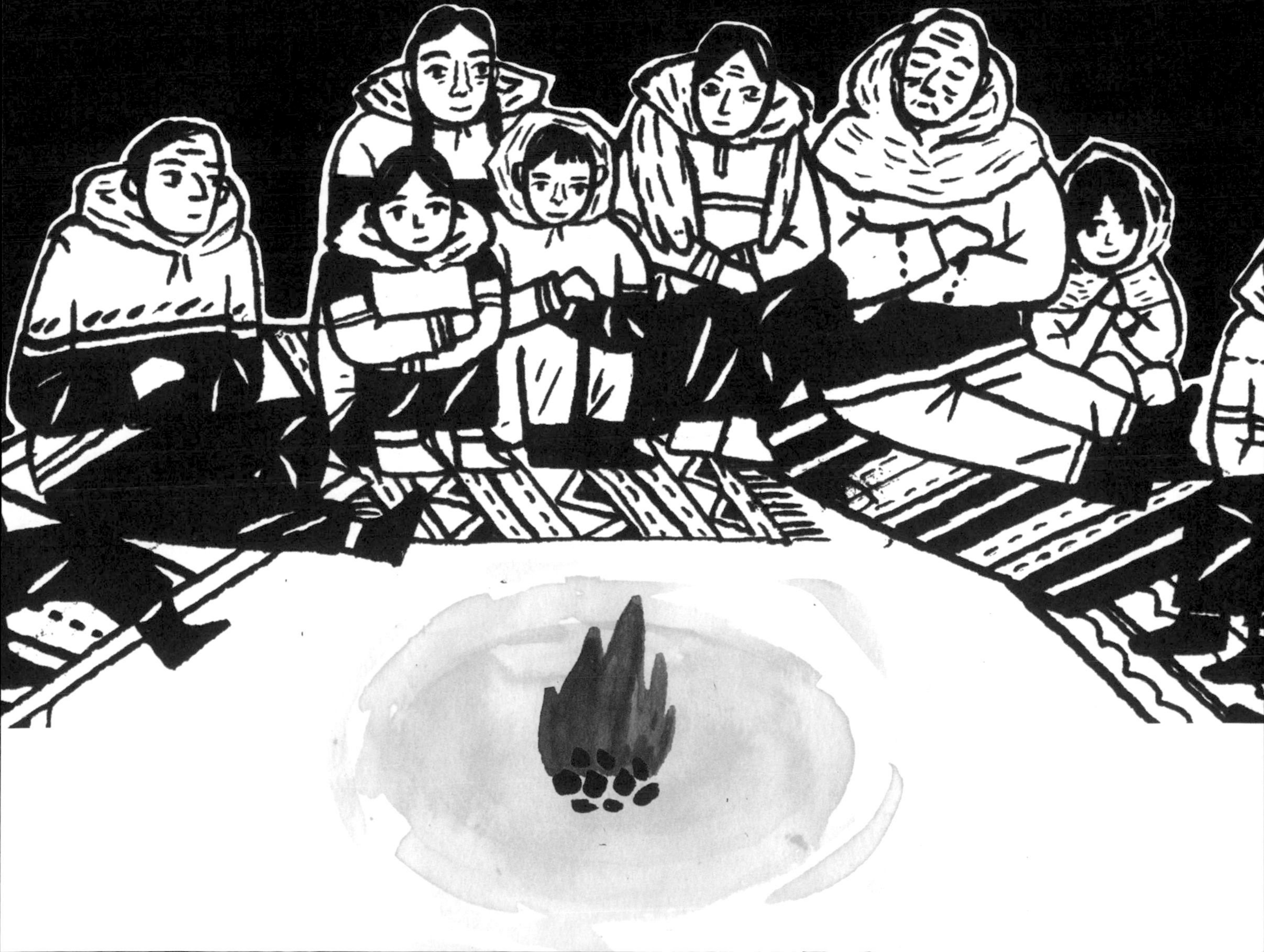

THE THREE SISTERS OF SUMMER ISLAND

In the heart of the land of Nord, the ice and snow never melt. But head south and you come to Summer Island. There the temperature rises enough for trees to grow. In winter, bent as they are under the weight of the snow, they are a forest of old men. But in the summer, they stand tall.

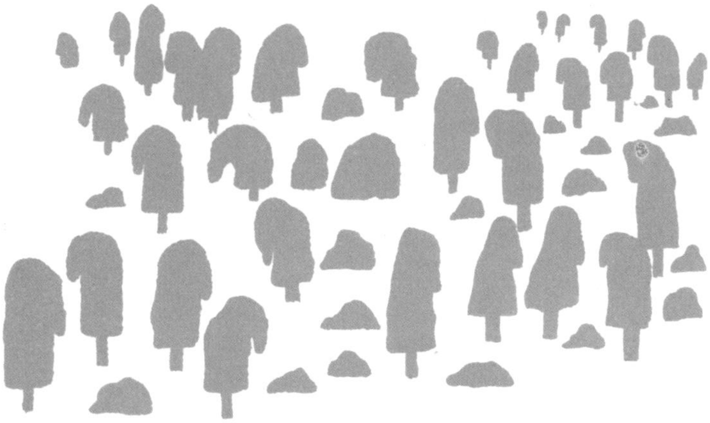

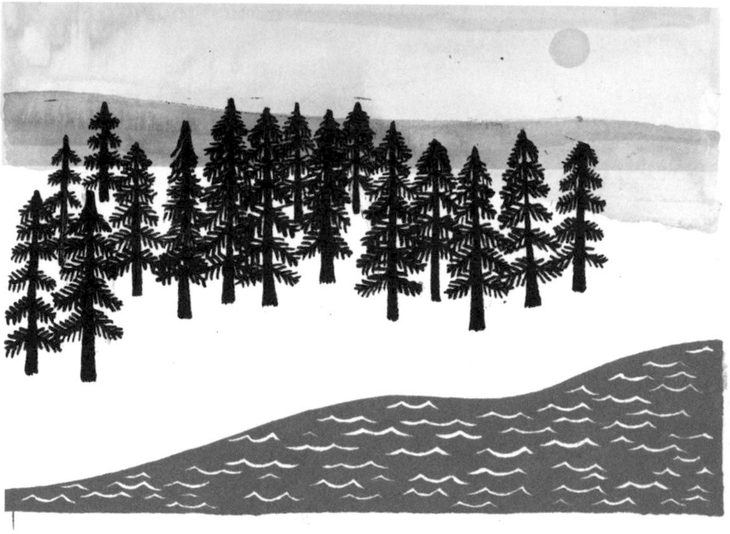

Summer Island is a place of tall pine forests and endless rushing tundra, of huge wide skies and dark glacial lakes. These lakes, deep and blue and still as a mirror, reflect the sky so absolutely, that looking into their depths you feel dizzy with vertigo.

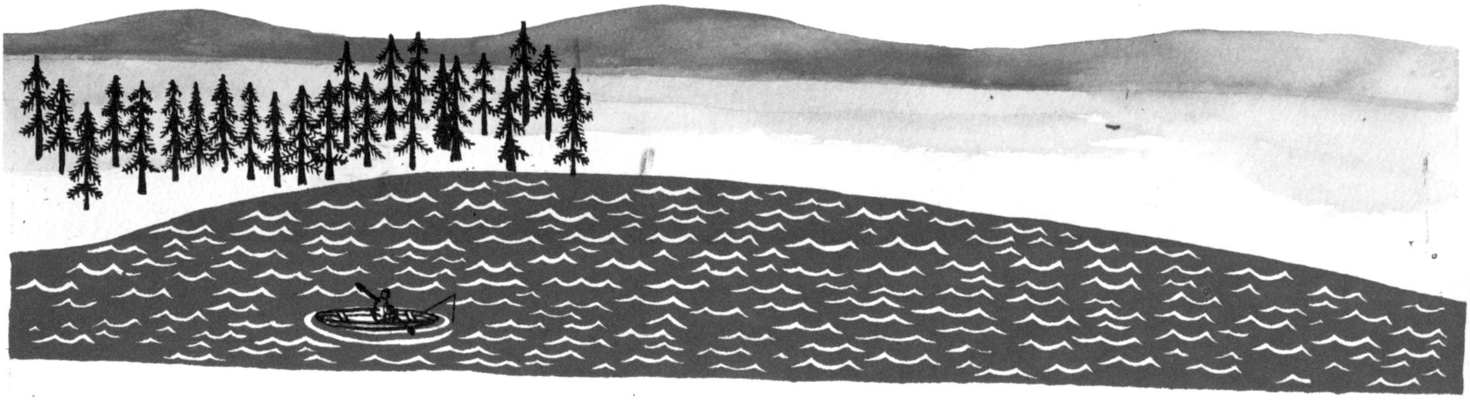

The biggest lake is at the centre of the island and every spring the rushing glaciers melt and pour down the valleys into it. It is called the Sky Lake, and on its shores is a village, and in the village live three sisters.

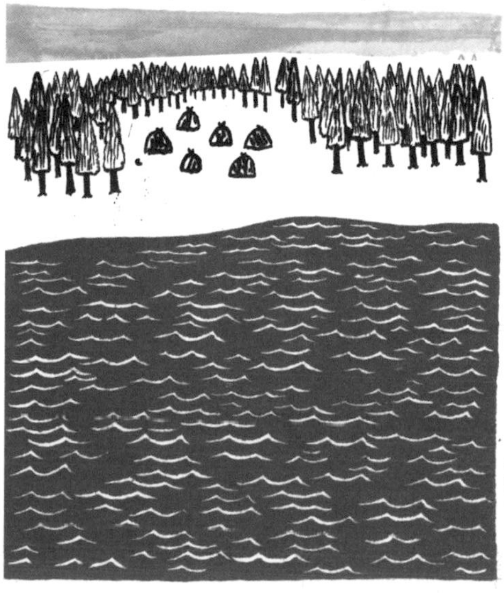

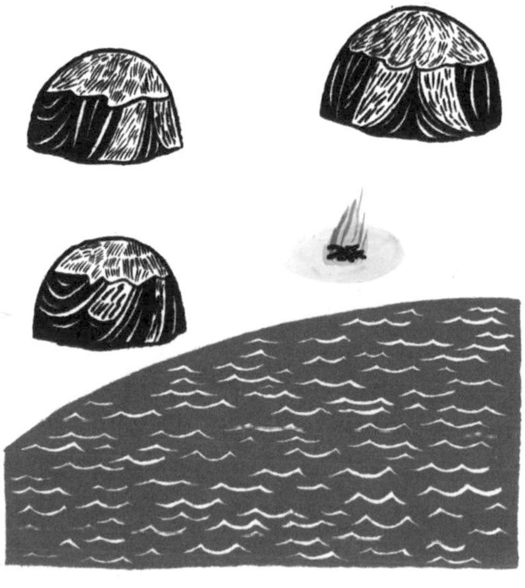

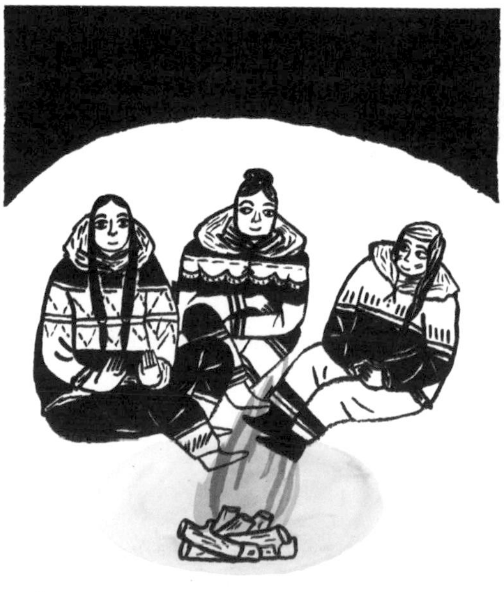

Their names are not easily translated, but roughly they could be called Gull-Wing, River-Reed and First-Snow. They loved each other as much as sisters can, and were as competitive as only sisters can be.

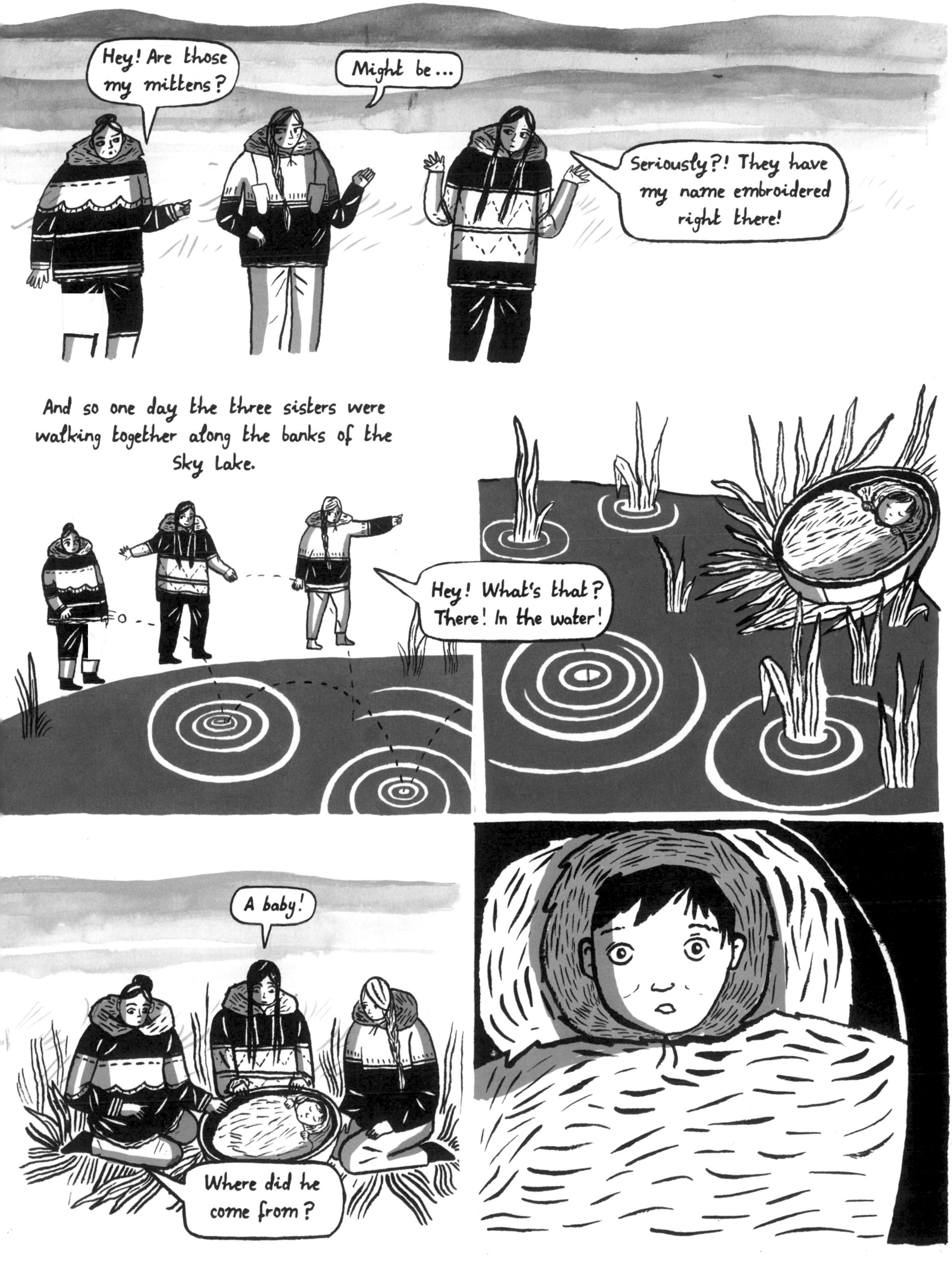
Hey! Are those my mittens?
Might be...
Seriously?! They have my name embroidered right there!
And so one day the three sisters were walking together along the banks of the Sky Lake.
Hey! What's that? There! In the water!
A baby!
Where did he come from?

Not knowing what else to do, they took the baby home, intending to keep him only until they had found out where he came from, and returned him. But although they sent out word with the travelling storytellers and the traders and the nomadic herders, no one claimed him. It was a mystery. He had come from nowhere, and now he was in their lives.

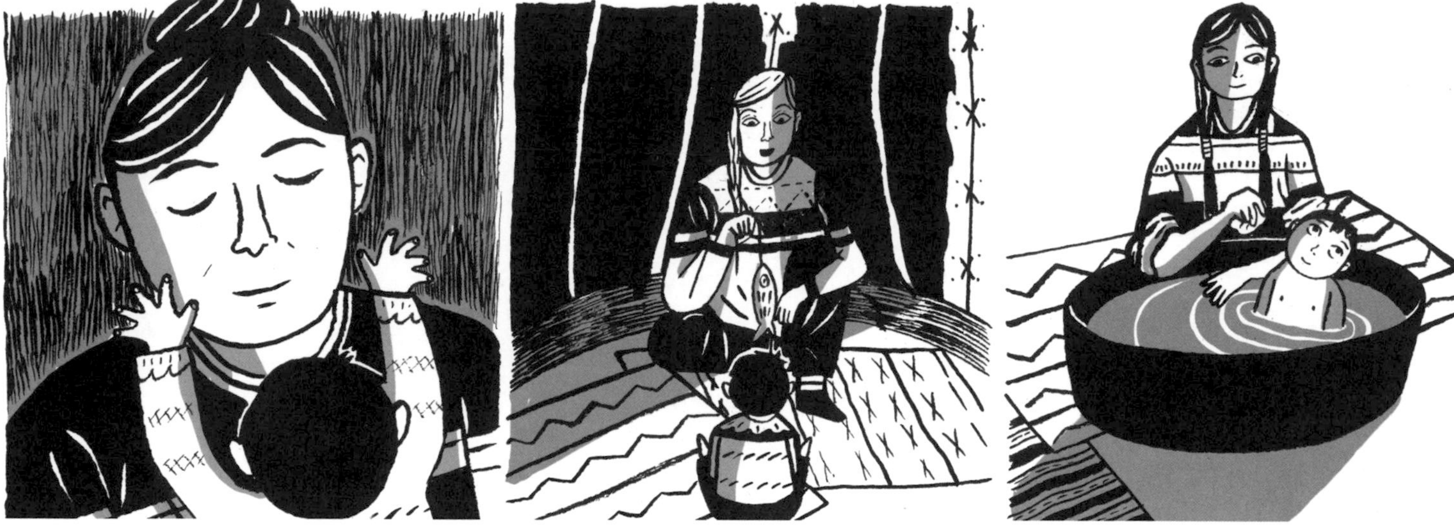

Well, gradually they grew fonder and fonder of the little boy, and soon the competitive sisters began to bicker about who loved him the most, and who should raise him as their own...

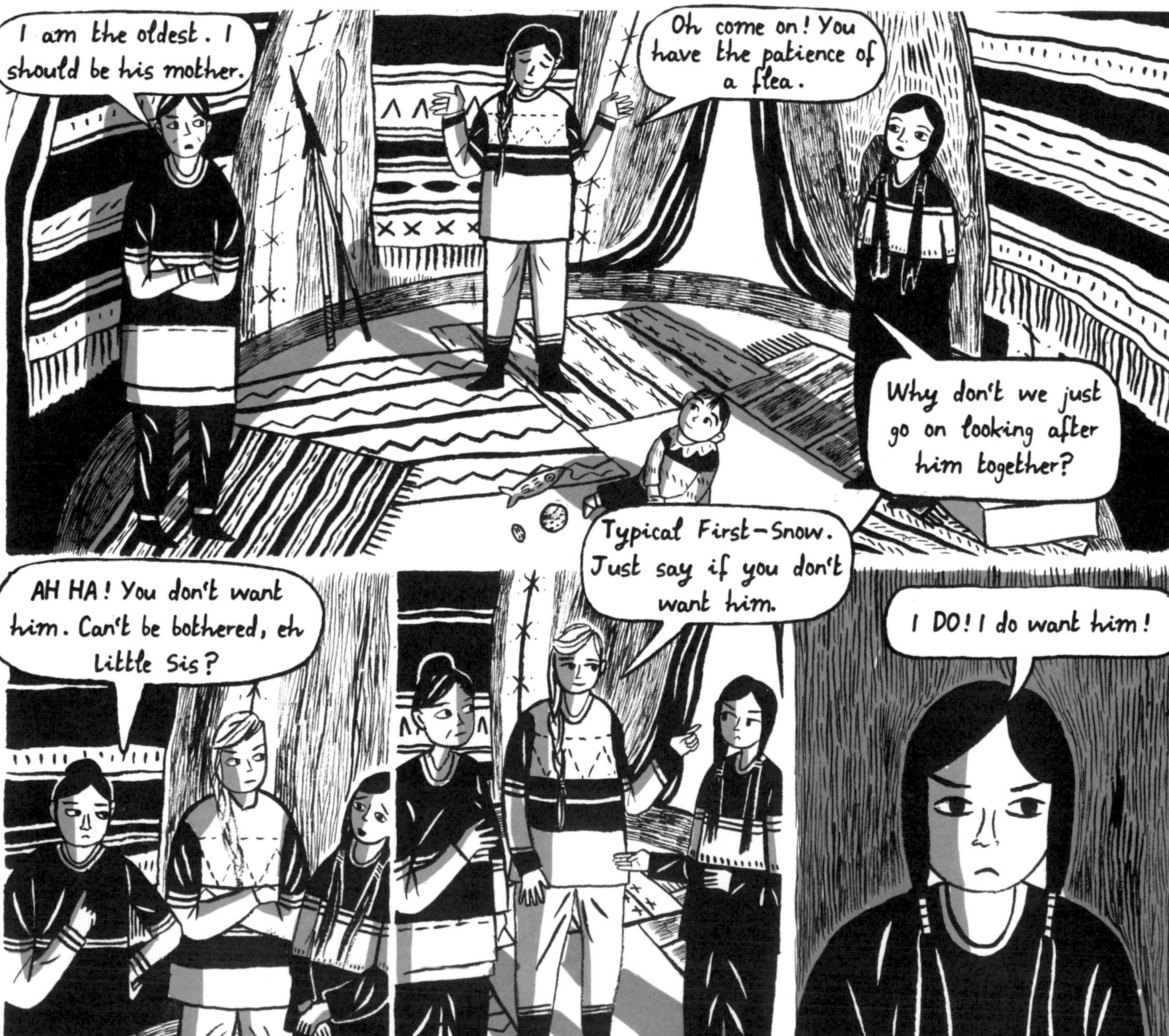
I am the oldest. I should be his mother.
Oh come on! You have the patience of a flea.
Why don't we just go on looking after him together?
Typical First-Snow. Just say if you don't want him.
AH HA! You don't want him. Can't be bothered, eh Little Sis?
I DO! I do want him!

Their quarrels raged on and on, and they could find no way of agreeing. So they took the little boy and went to see the Medicine Man. He lived alone on the far side of Summer Island, on an iceberg, and the Nords deferred to him in all matters of importance.

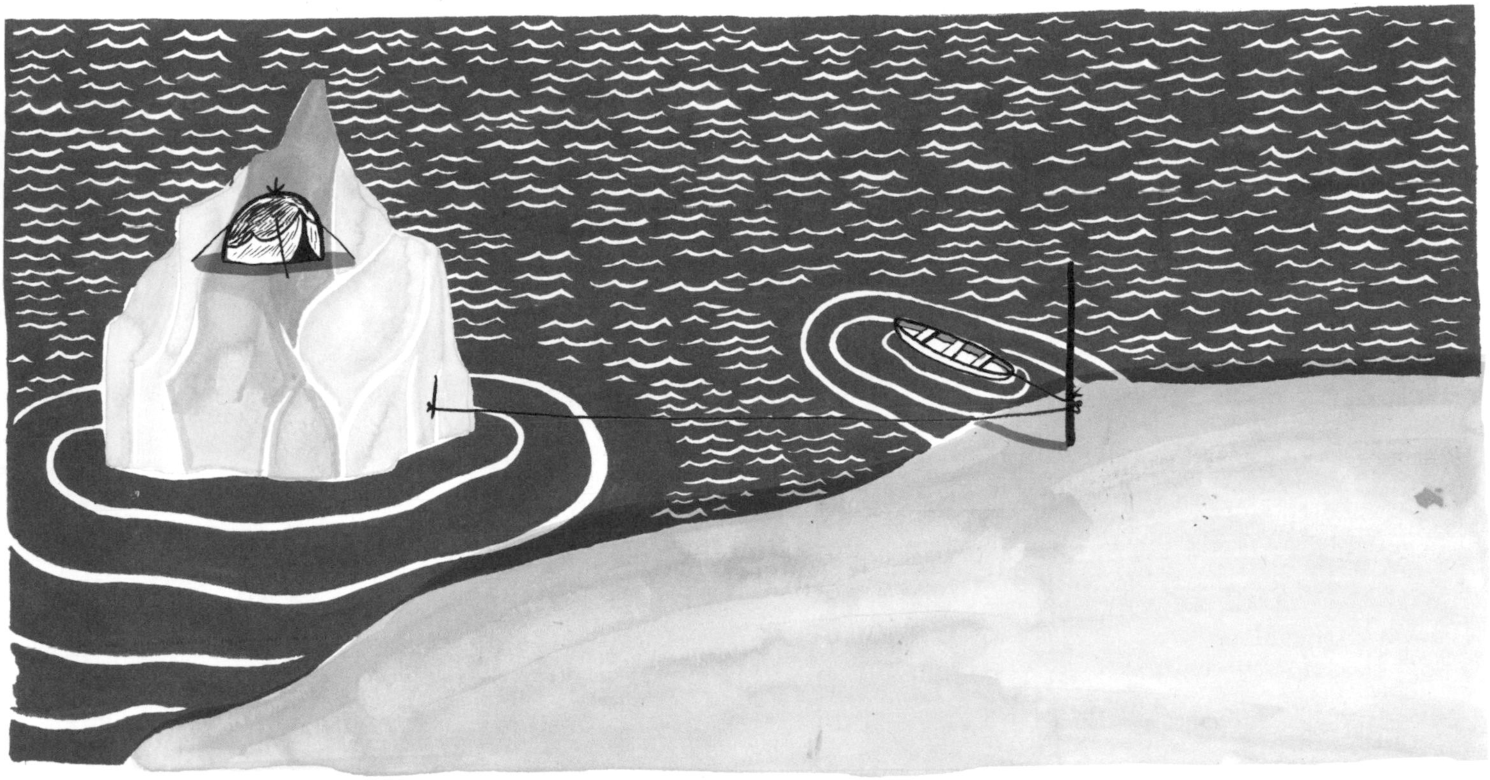

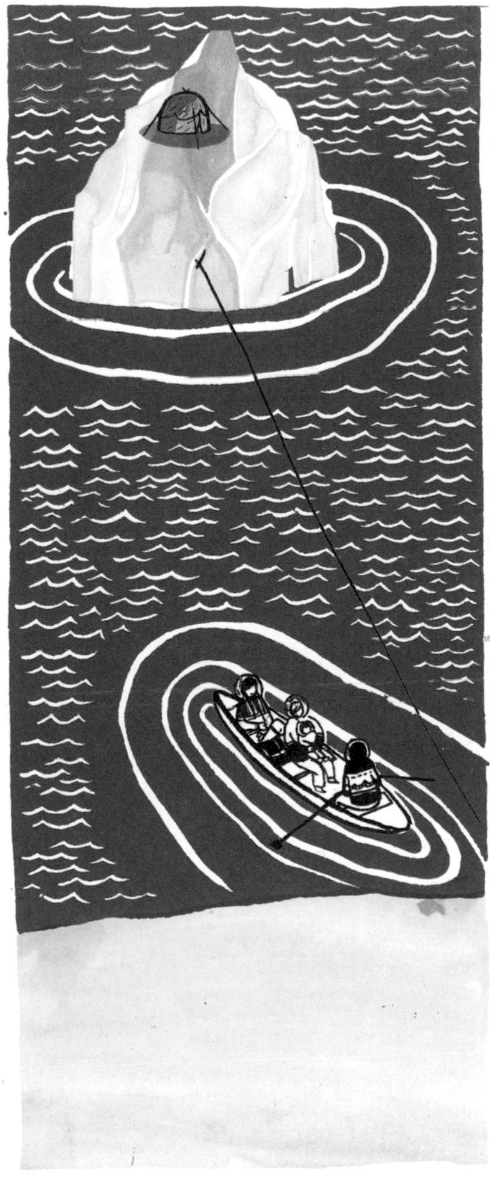

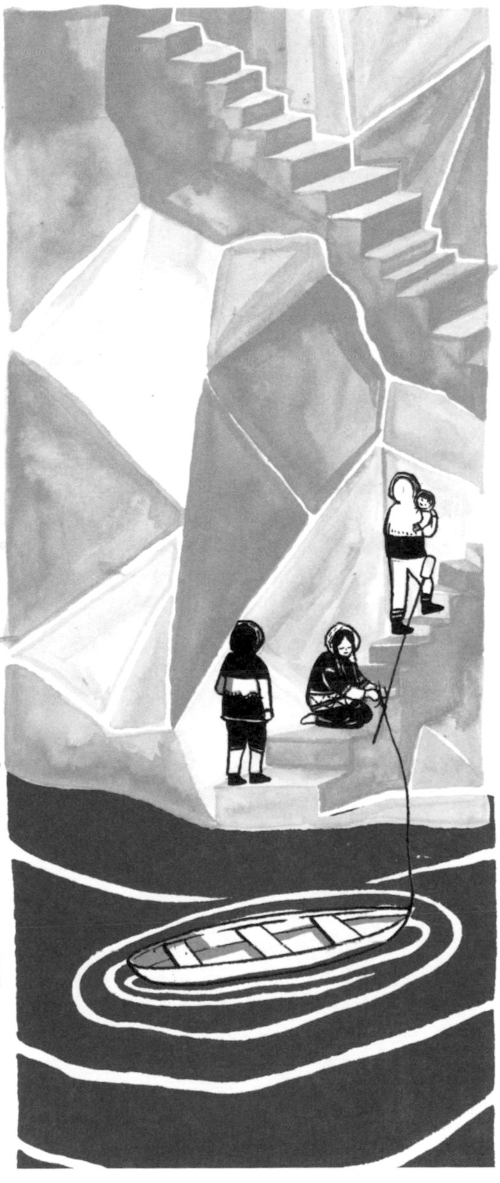

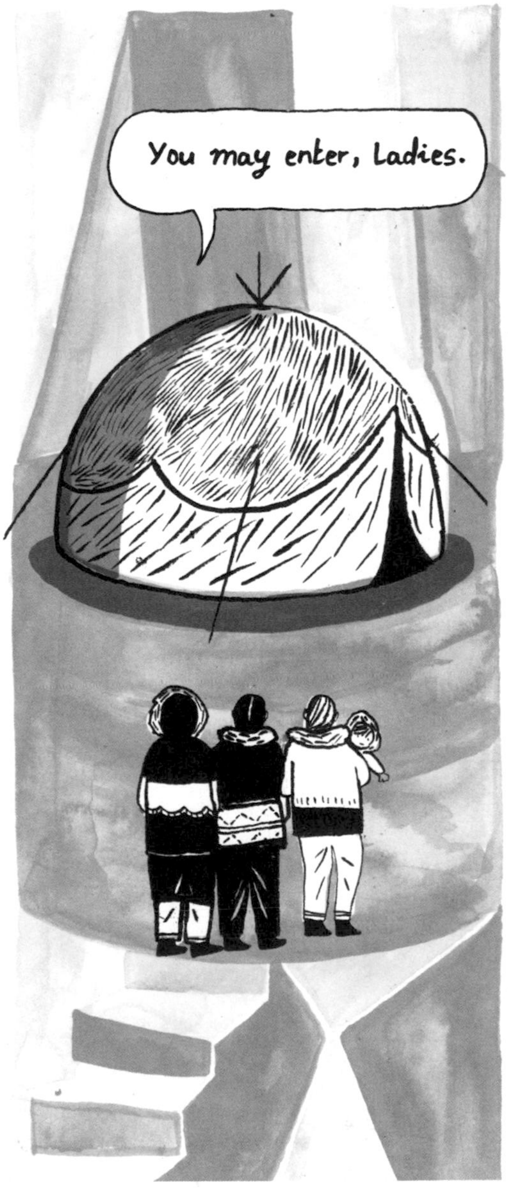
You may enter, Ladies.

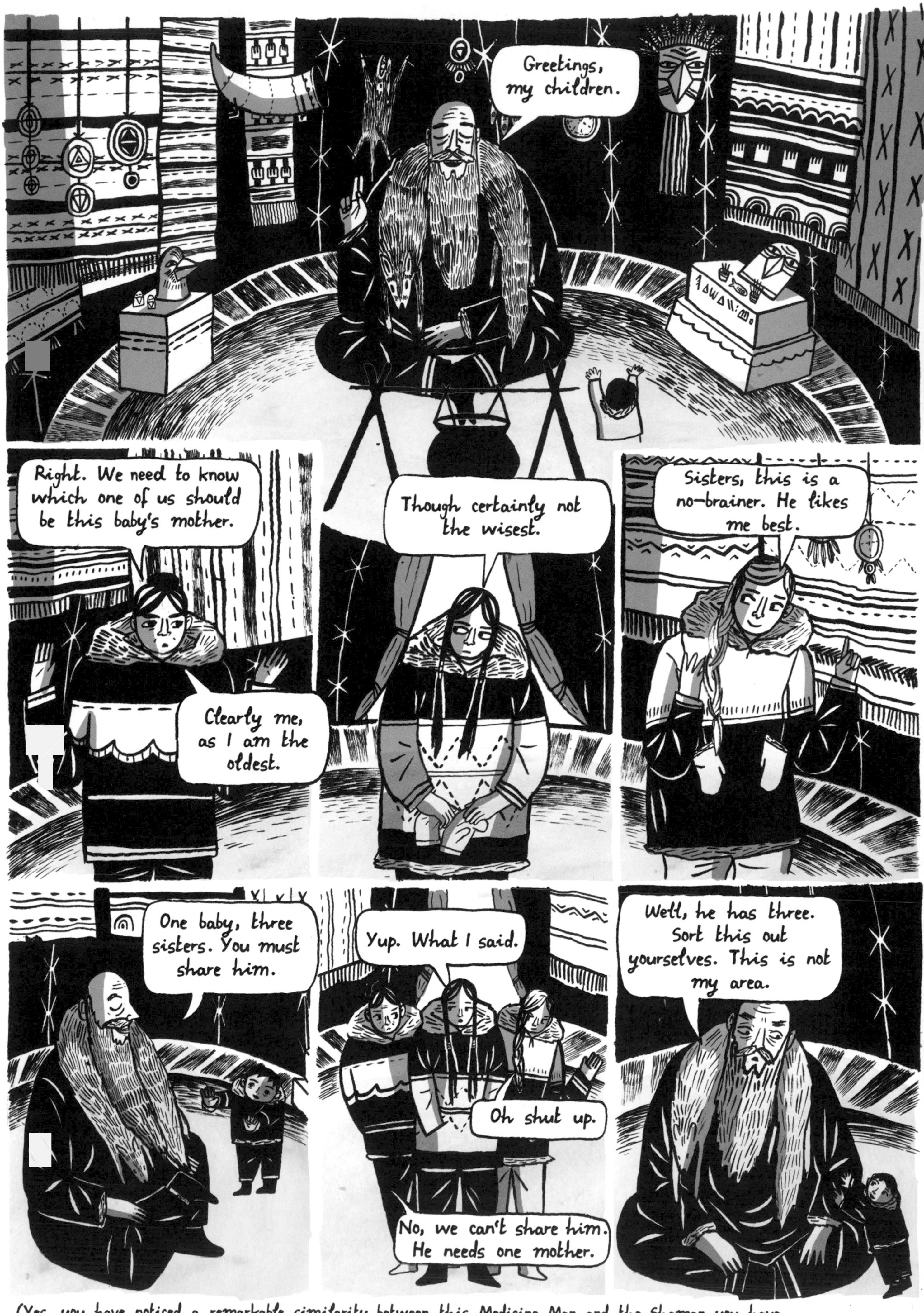
Greetings, my children.
Right. We need to know which one of us should be this baby's mother.
Clearly me, as I am the oldest.
Though certainly not the wisest.
Sisters, this is a no-brainer. He likes me best.
One baby, three sisters. You must share him.
Yup. What I said.
Oh shut up.
No, we can't share him. He needs one mother.
Well, he has three. Sort this out yourselves. This is not my area.

(Yes, you have noticed a remarkable similarity between this Medicine Man and the Shaman you have already met! Well spotted. This is a plot device that will never be explained, so deal with it!)

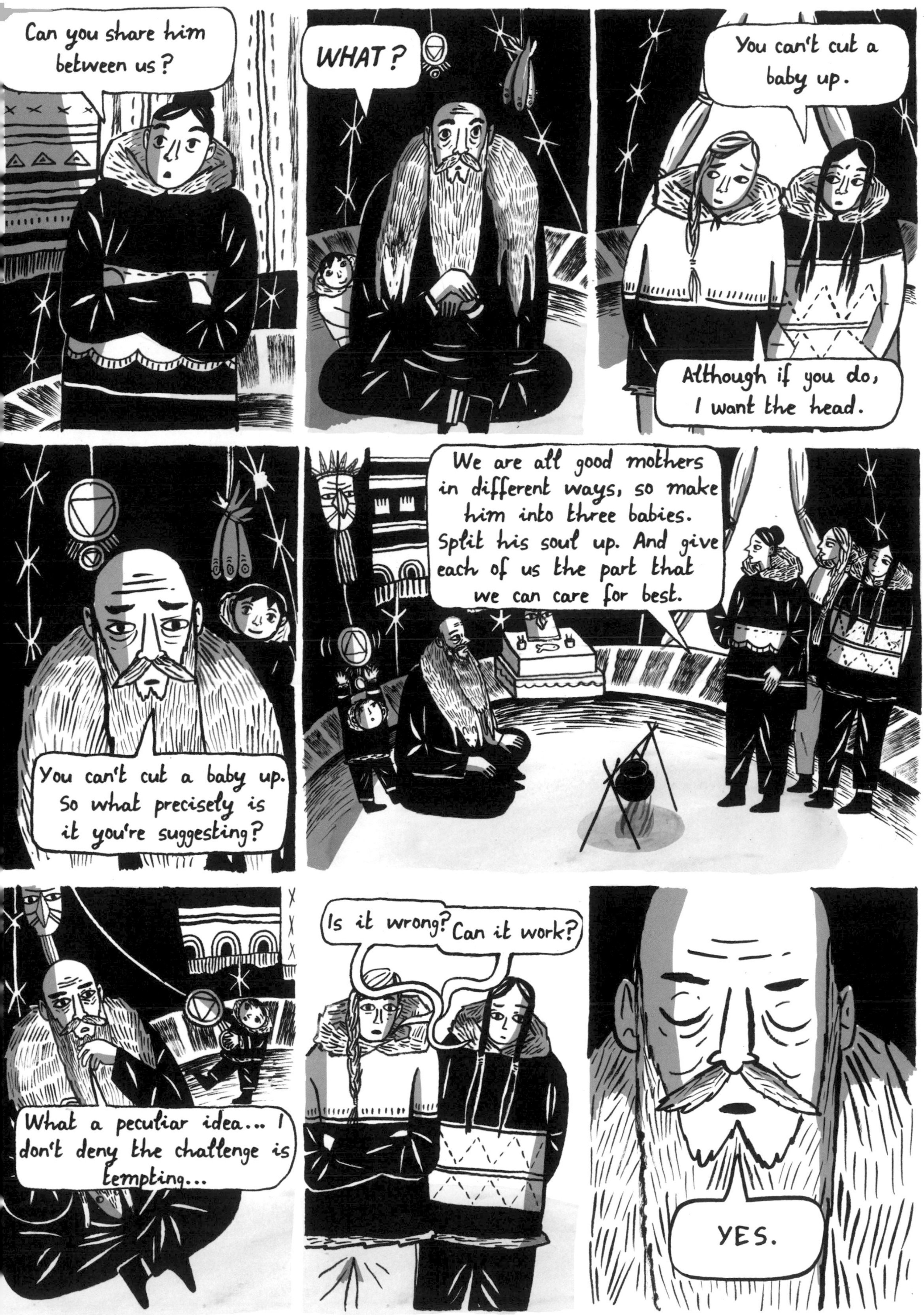

Can you share him between us?
WHAT?
You can't cut a baby up.
Although if you do, I want the head.
You can't cut a baby up. So what precisely is it you're suggesting?
We are all good mothers in different ways, so make him into three babies. Split his soul up. And give each of us the part that we can care for best.
What a peculiar idea... I don't deny the challenge is tempting...
Is it wrong?
Can it work?
YES.

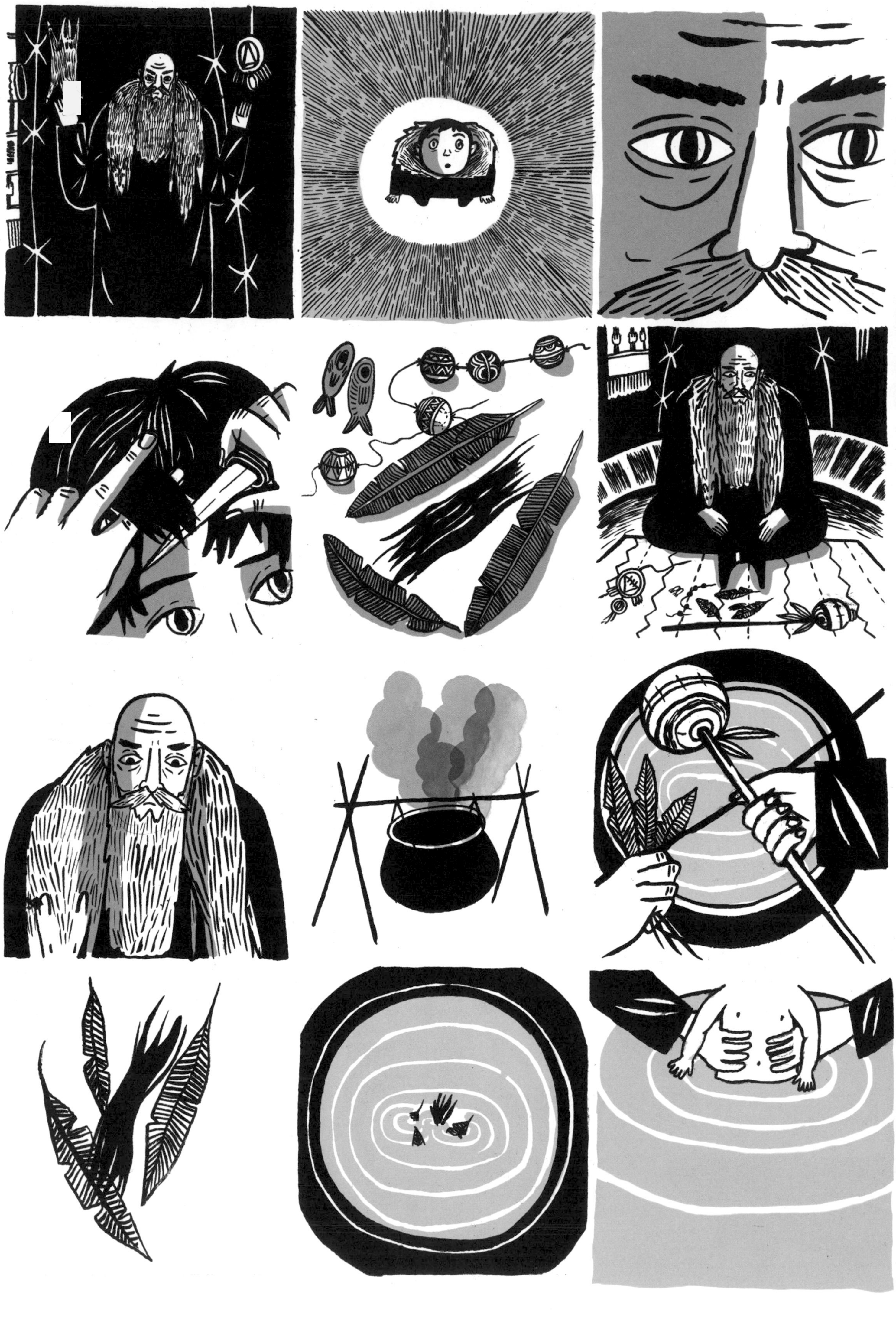

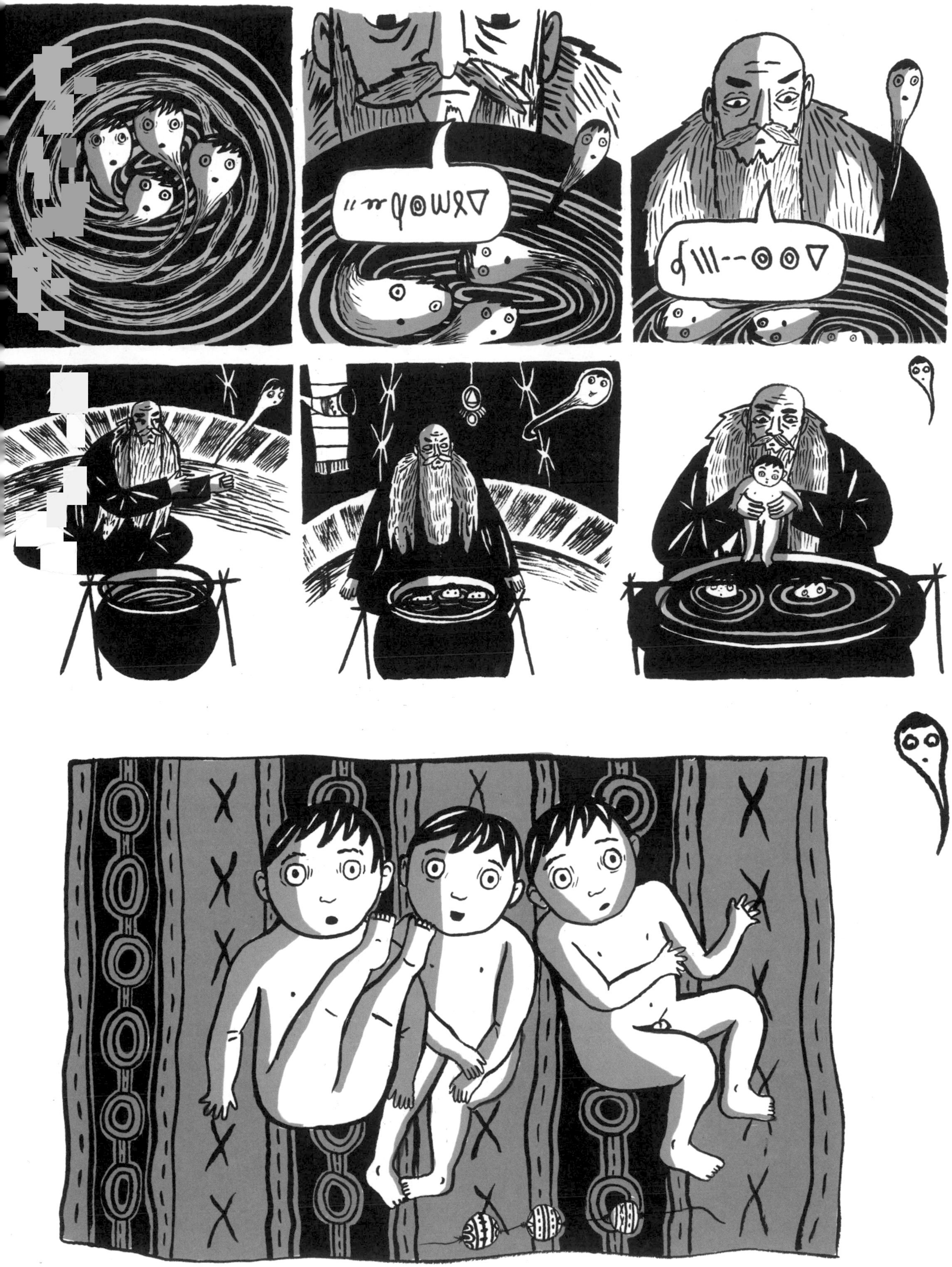

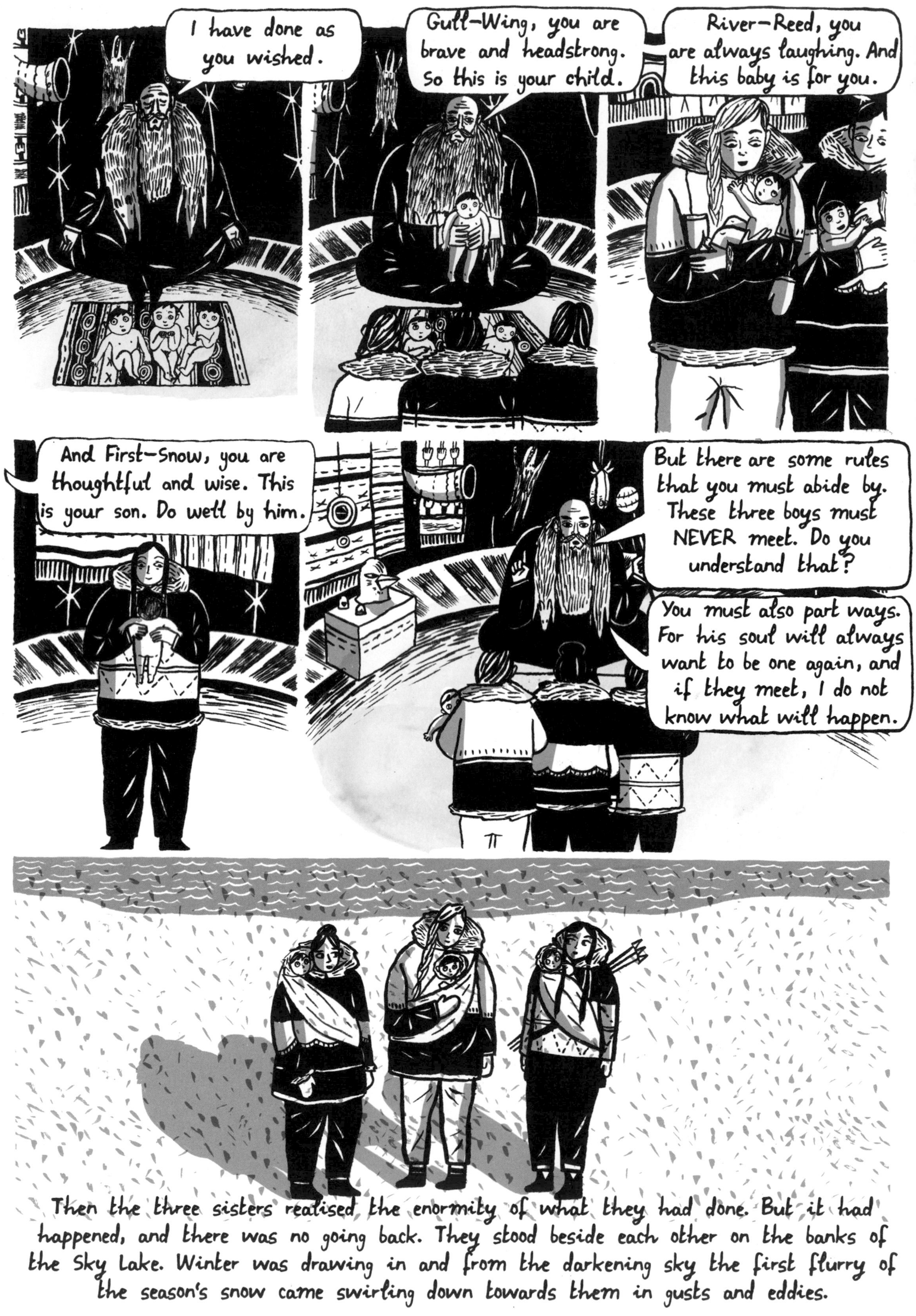
I have done as you wished.
Gull-Wing, you are brave and headstrong. So this is your child.
River-Reed, you are always laughing. And this baby is for you.
And First-Snow, you are thoughtful and wise. This is your son. Do well by him.
But there are some rules that you must abide by. These three boys must NEVER meet. Do you understand that?
You must also part ways. For his soul will always want to be one again, and if they meet, I do not know what will happen.
Then the three sisters realised the enormity of what they had done. But it had happened, and there was no going back. They stood beside each other on the banks of the Sky Lake. Winter was drawing in and from the darkening sky the first flurry of the season's snow came swirling down towards them in gusts and eddies.

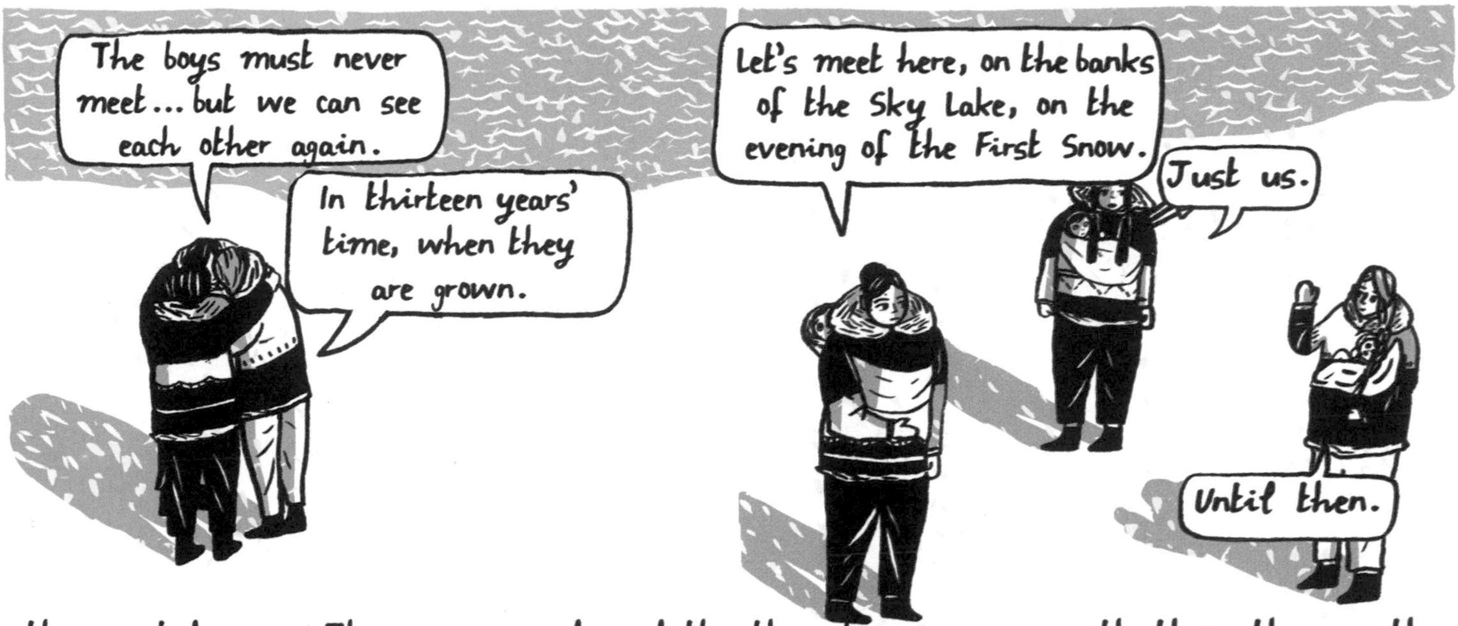
The boys must never meet... but we can see each other again.
In thirteen years' time, when they are grown.
Let's meet here, on the banks of the Sky Lake, on the evening of the First Snow.
Just us.
Until then.

o they parted ways. The years passed, and the three boys grew up with their three mothers. Gull-Wing had been right, they were all good mothers. But they were not happy. No place felt like home after Summer Island, and so they found themselves always on the move.

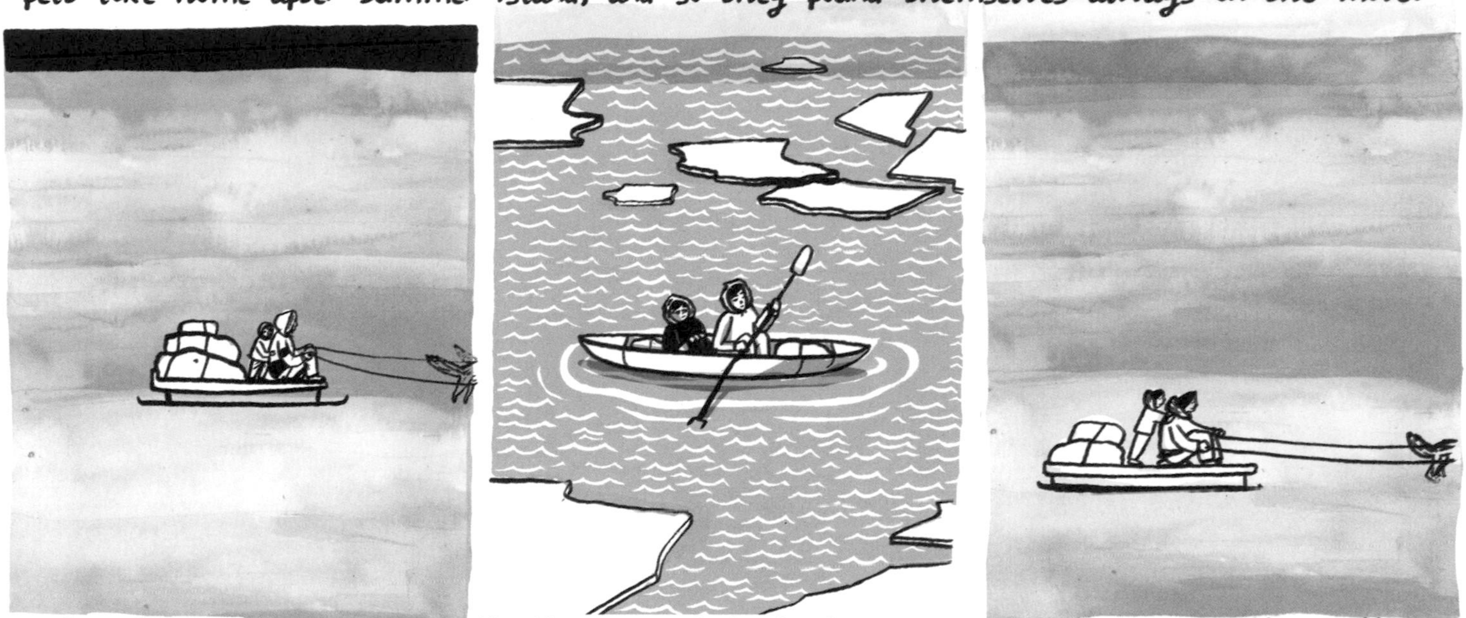

There was nothing wrong with the boys, at first glance anyway. They were all small for their age, and in some light they seemed strangely insubstantial. But on the whole they were happy, and all three loved their mothers more than anything else. It was only as they grew that problems began to appear.

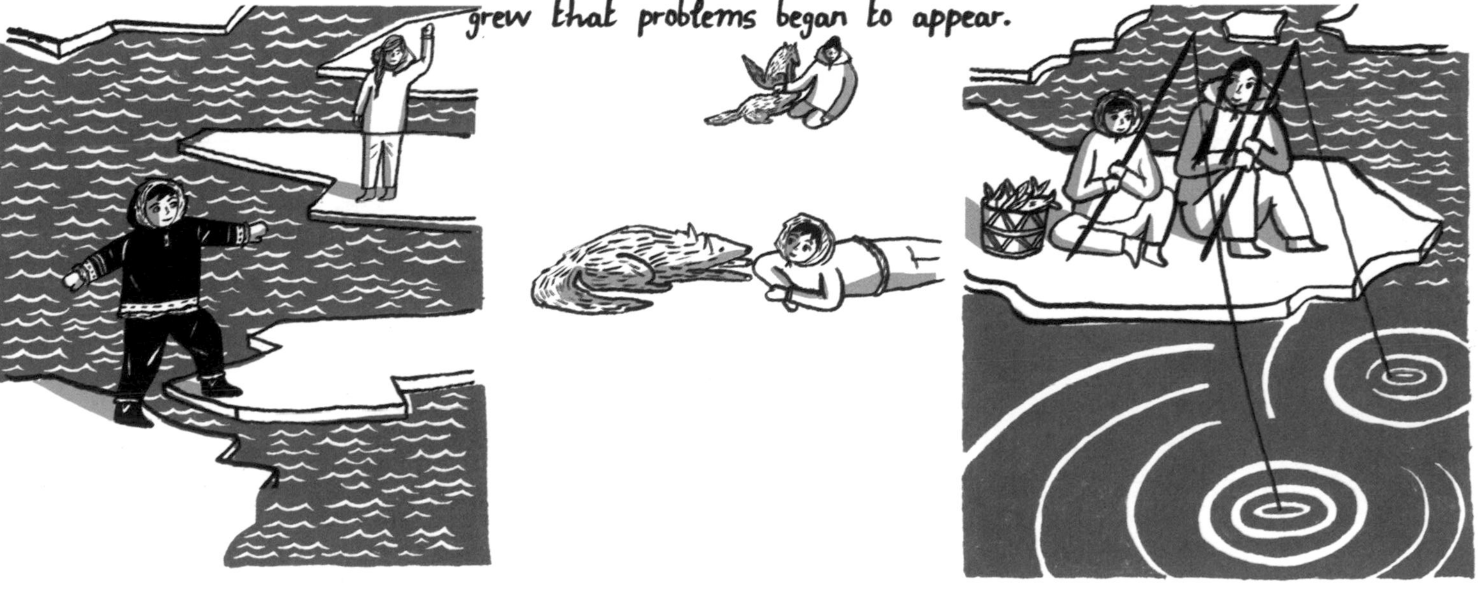

Gull-Wing's boy was just as the Medicine Man had predicted; fierce and brave but also fiendishly argumentative. And the older he got, the more quarrelsome he became. Sometimes he would wake raging against the whole world, and he could do nothing but shout. Gull-Wing would watch him standing and screaming, as his voice was snatched away on the northern winds. And she worried.

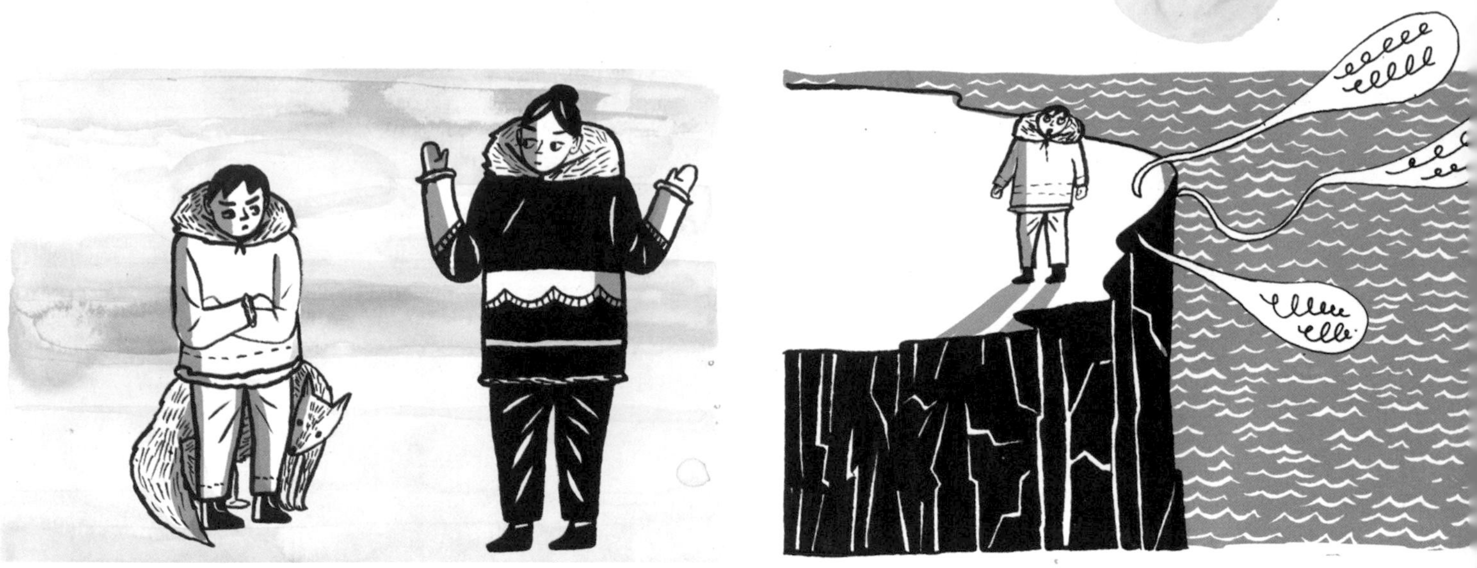

River-Reed's boy was always laughing and when he was young he seemed like the happiest chil that had ever been. But if he could not laugh or make light of the situation, he would ignore i River-Reed began to suspect he was shallow or, worse, heartless.

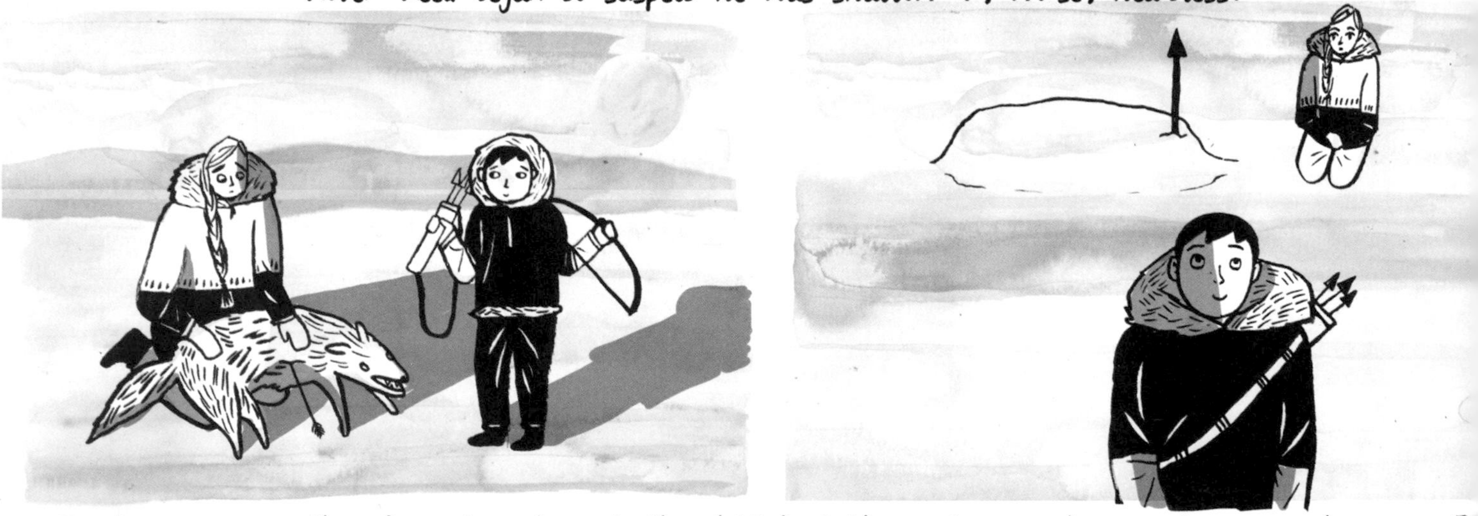

First-Snow was the cleverest and most thoughtful of the sisters, and so in turn was her son. B he too grew up a little oddly. He became withdrawn and silent, he lay for hours on his back staring up at the three moons of Early Earth and the bright arctic stars. Sometimes First-Snow thought he had guessed everything, but how could that be?

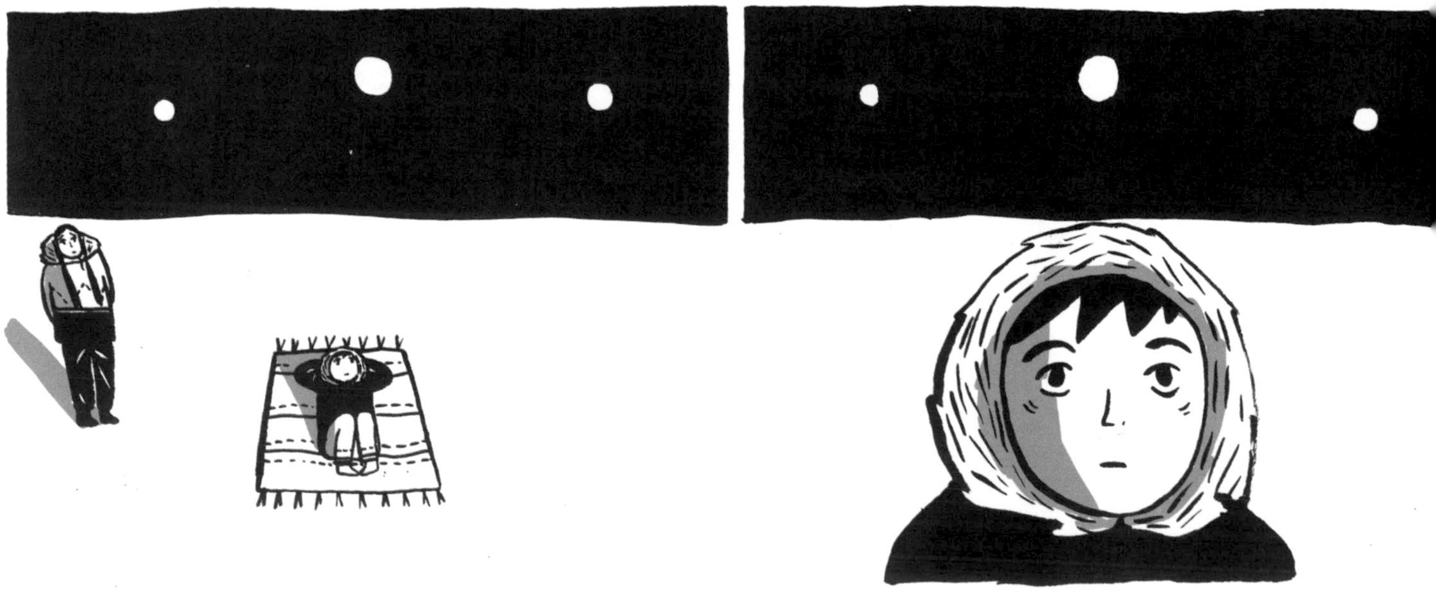

Separately the three sisters worried more and more, and as the years went by and they drew closer to the day when they would meet again, they began to dread it. For they knew that something had gone terribly, terribly wrong.

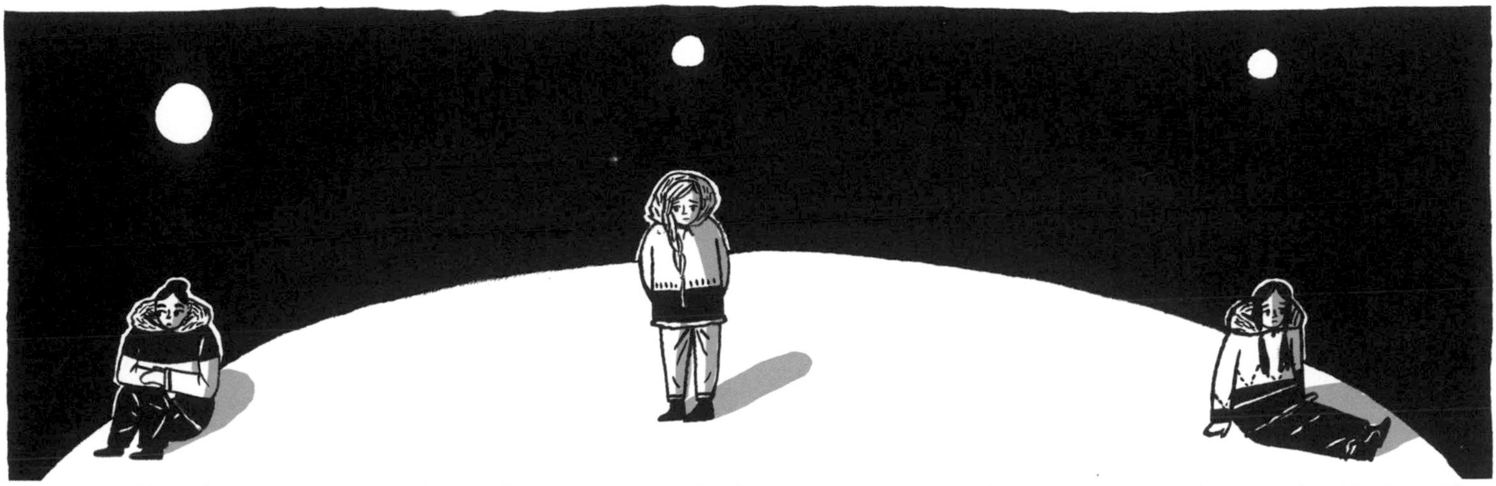

But finally the day came when the boys turned thirteen. It is tradition among the Nords that all children, when they reach thirteen, set off for a winter alone. It's a rite of passage, journey into adulthood sort of thing.

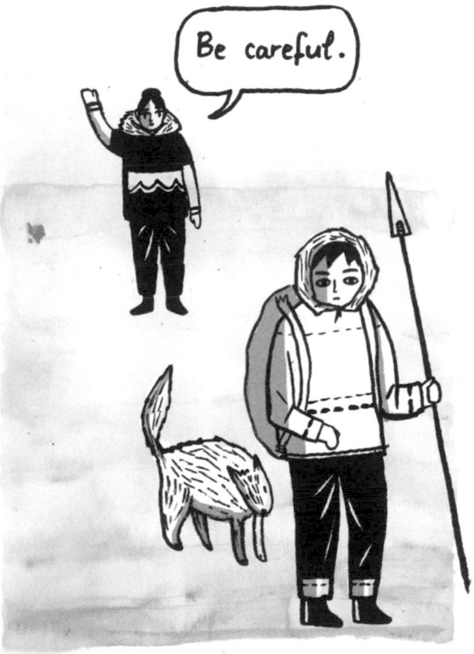
Be careful.

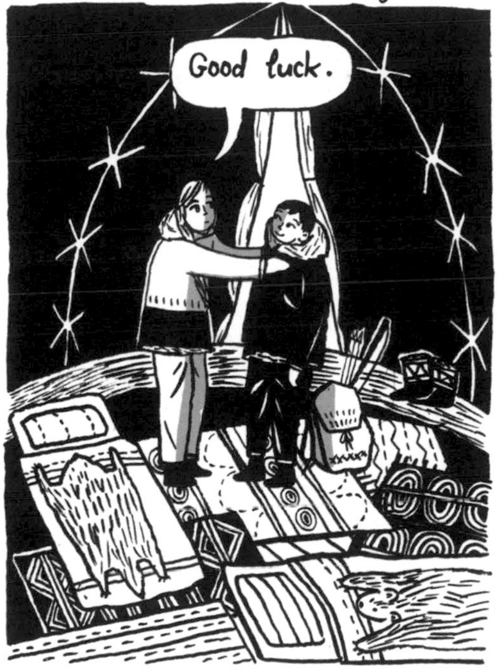
Good luck.

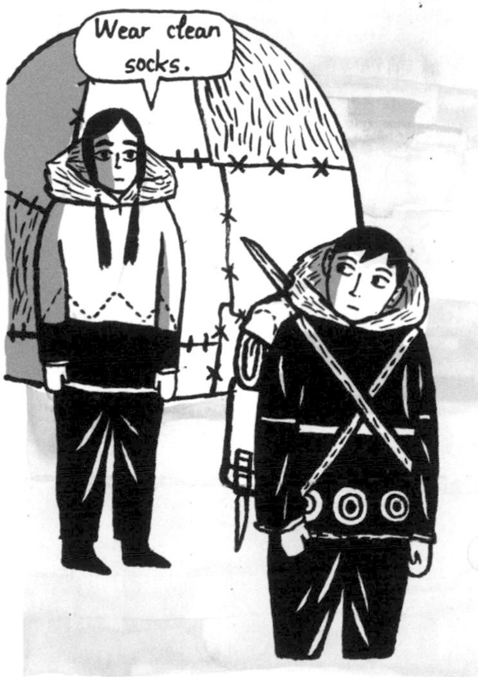
Wear clean socks.

The boys set off into the Nordish winter, and the three sisters packed up their boats and made for Summer Island.

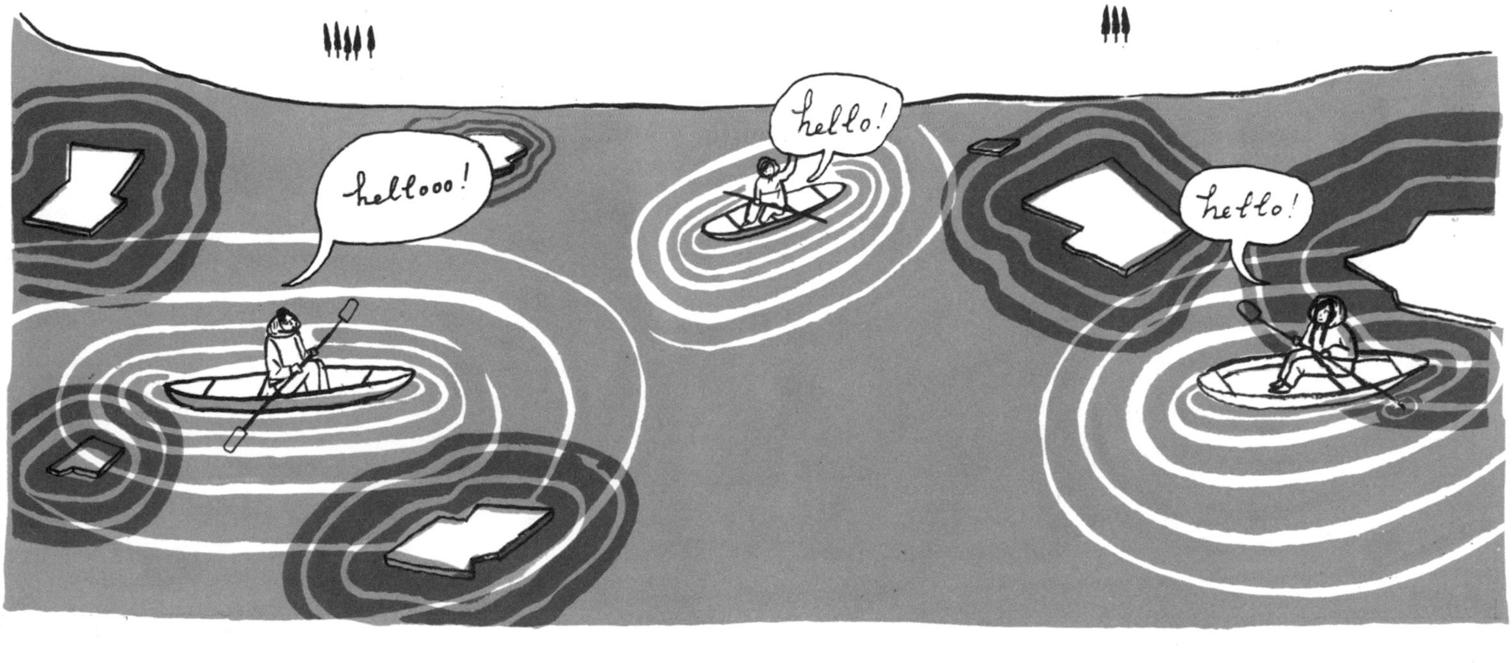
helloo!
hello!
hello!

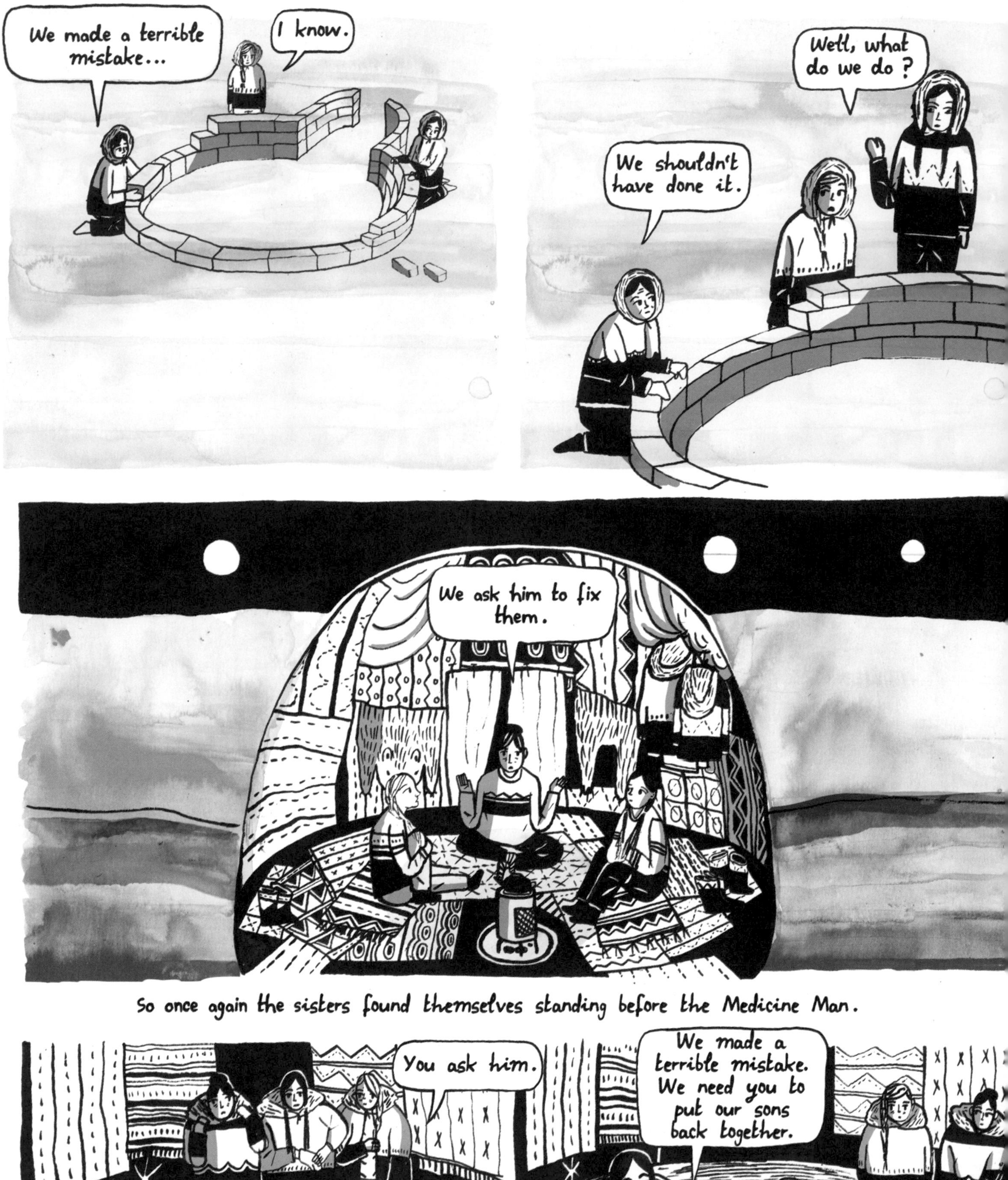
We made a terrible mistake...
I know.
Well, what do we do?
We shouldn't have done it.
We ask him to fix them.

So once again the sisters found themselves standing before the Medicine Man.

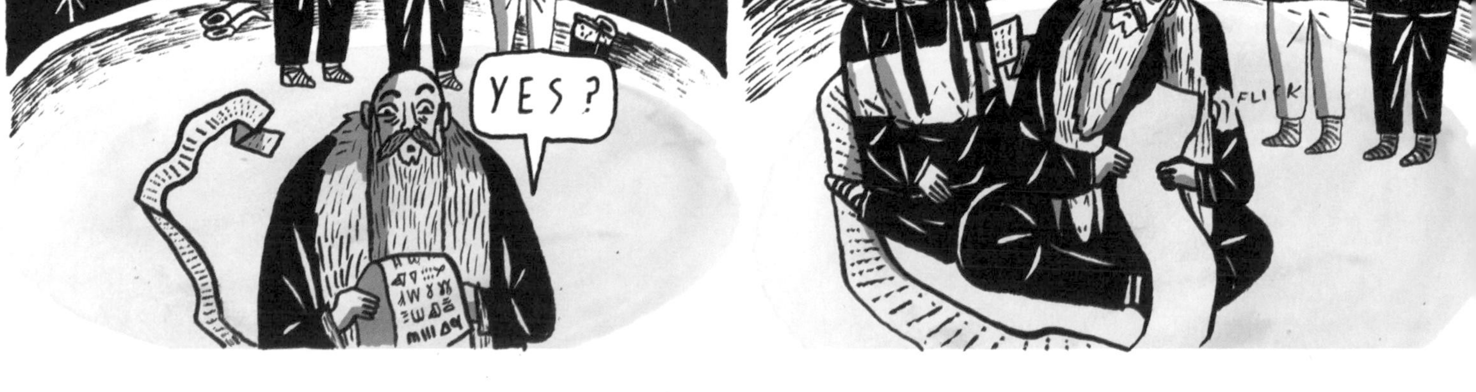
You ask him.
YES?
We made a terrible mistake. We need you to put our sons back together.
FLICK

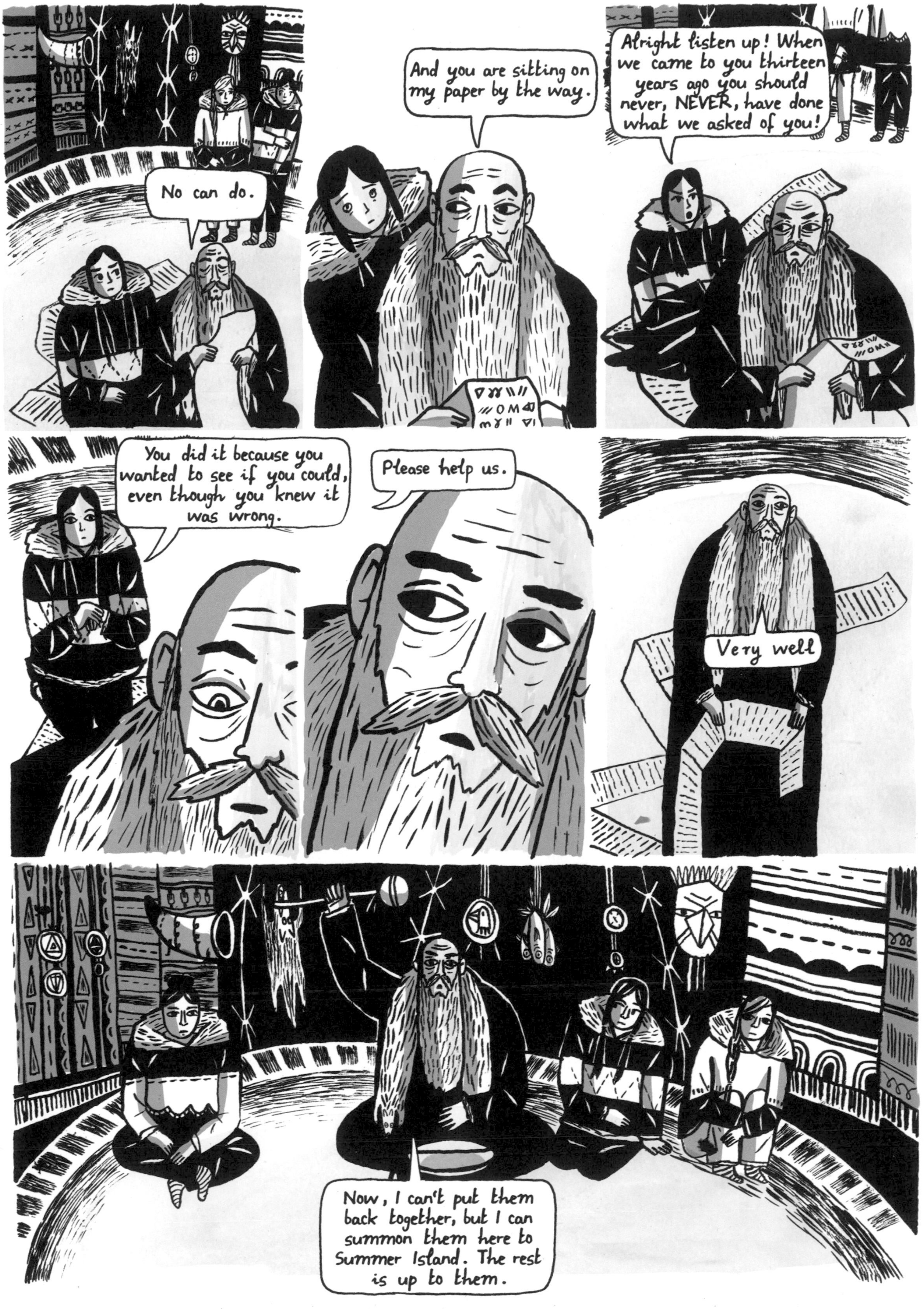
No can do.
And you are sitting on my paper by the way.
Alright listen up! When we came to you thirteen years ago you should never, NEVER, have done what we asked of you!
You did it because you wanted to see if you could, even though you knew it was wrong.
Please help us.
Very well
Now, I can't put them back together, but I can summon them here to Summer Island. The rest is up to them.

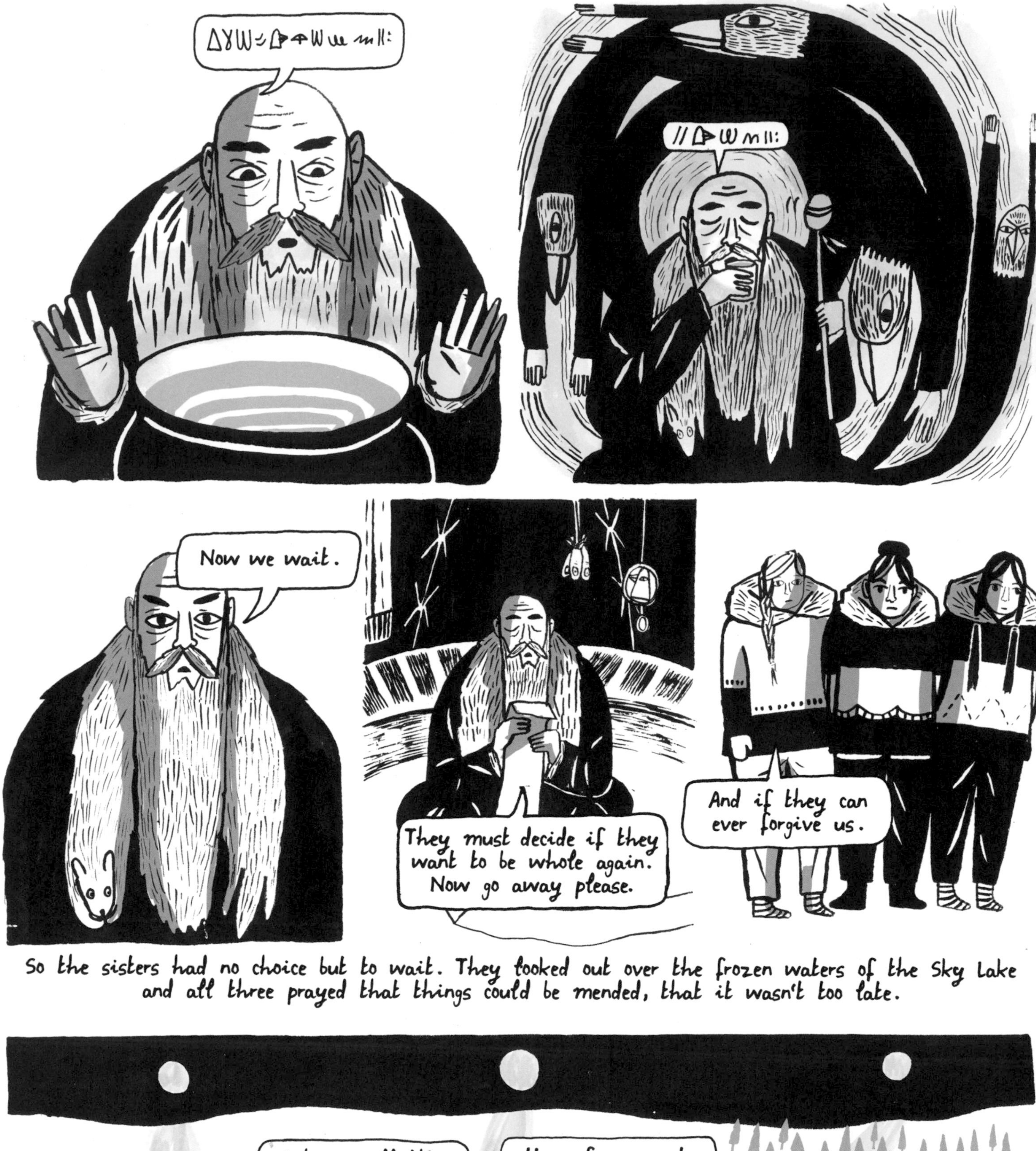
Now we wait.
They must decide if they want to be whole again. Now go away please.
And if they can ever forgive us.

So the sisters had no choice but to wait. They looked out over the frozen waters of the Sky Lake and all three prayed that things could be mended, that it wasn't too late.

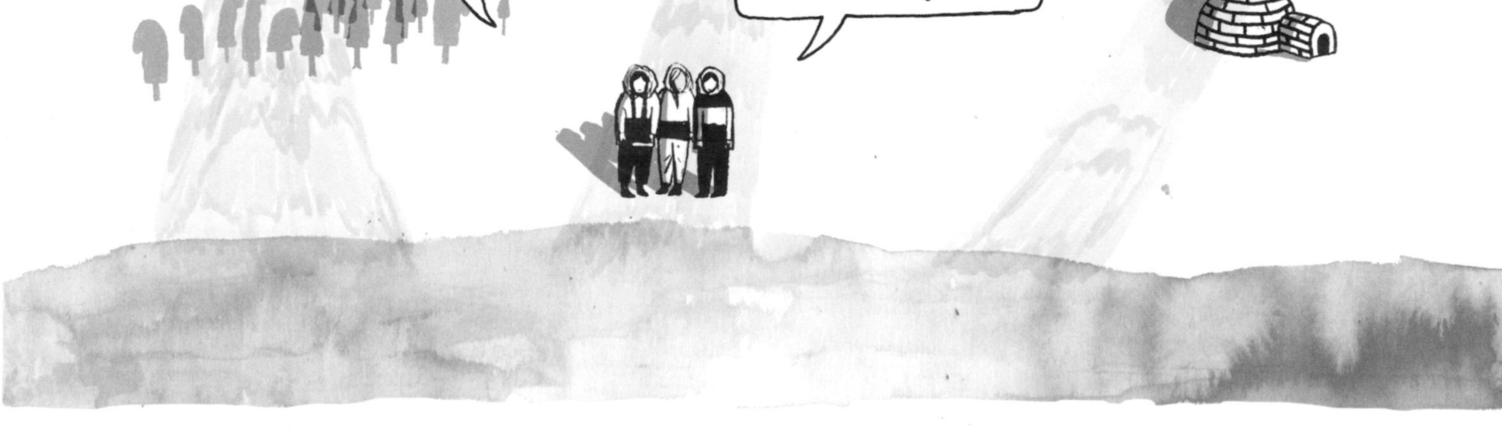
Where will they come?
Here of course, to the Sky Lake, where it all began.

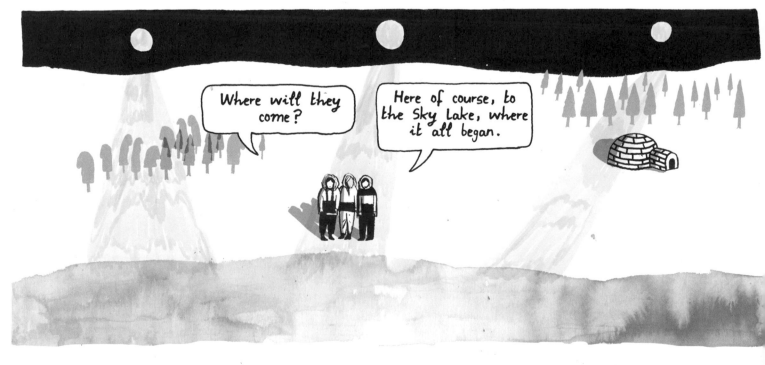

d meanwhile the three boys, scattered all over the Land of Nord, found themselves heading towards ummer Island. It was a strange and irresistible pull that seemed to be leading all three, and they urged their dogs on faster and faster, though they did not know what they were racing towards.

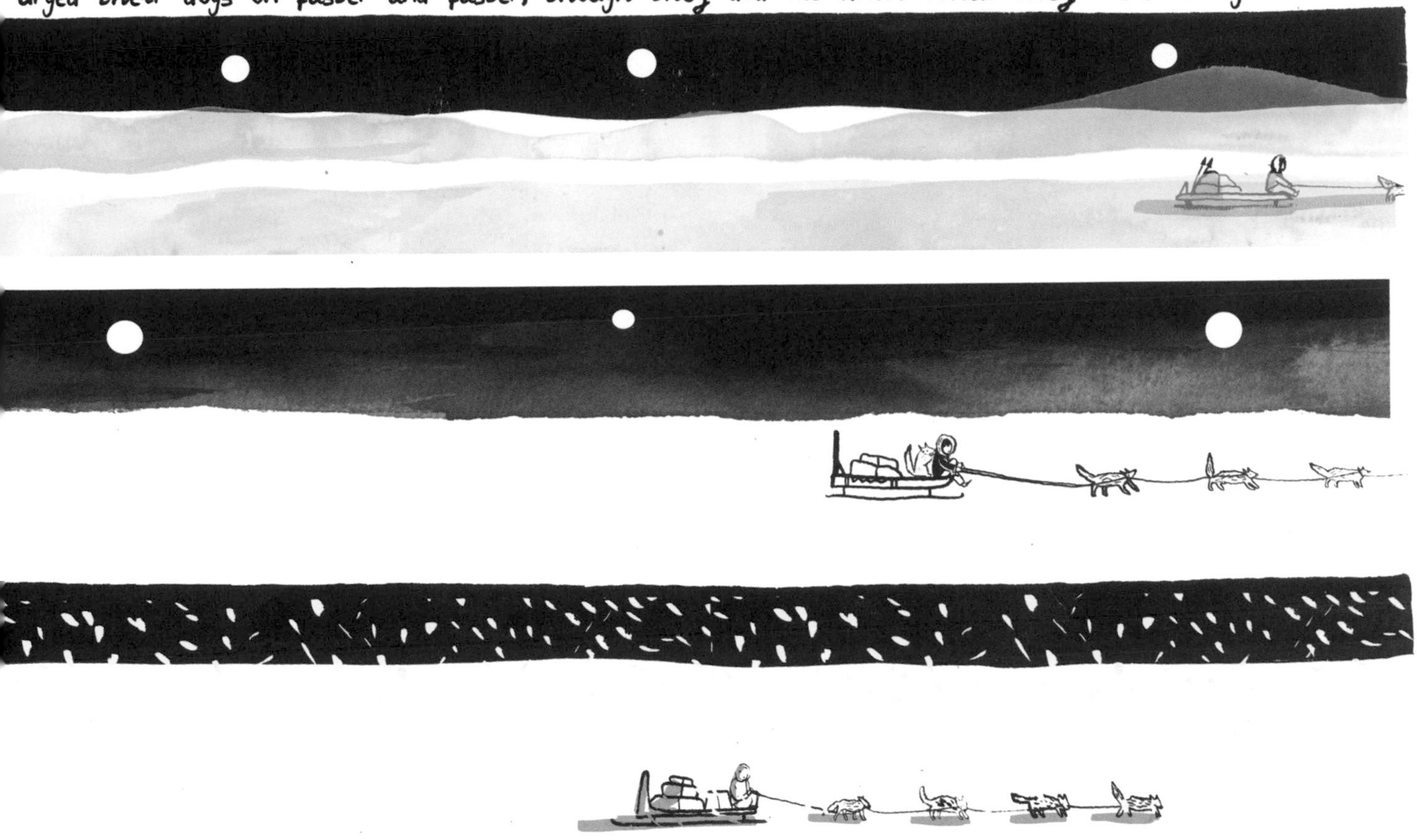

The closer they came to Summer Island the stronger the force seemed to be, until finally they were by the shores of the Sky Lake, and it was so strong it was almost unbearable. They stood looking at each other, beneath the vast winter sky under the silver light of the three moons, and they did not speak. Would you recognise yourself, if you saw yourself standing before you? They did, they knew in an instant.

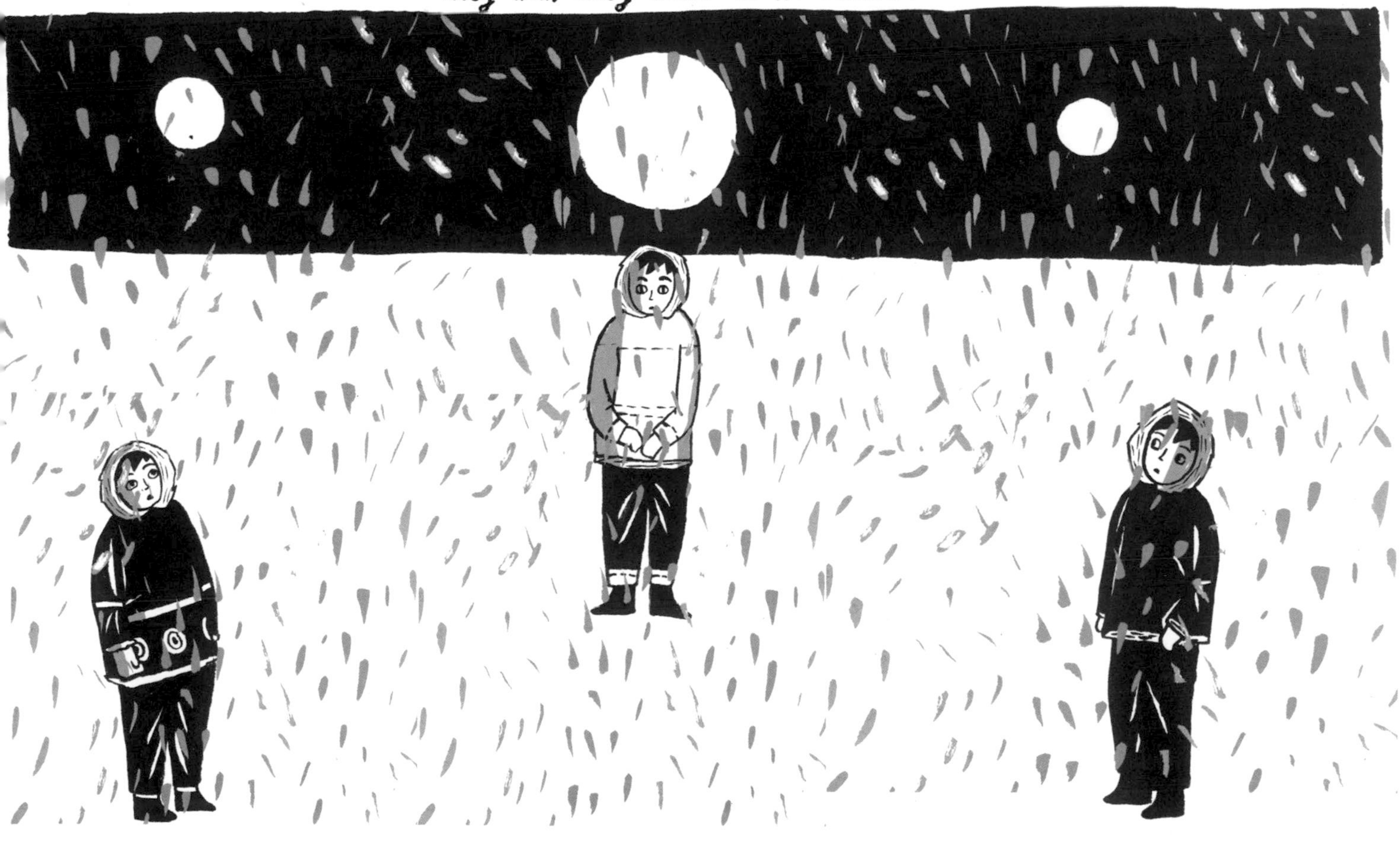

There was no time to greet each other, no time to marvel at what they were seeing, because before any of them knew what was happening they were running towards each other.
And then there was a pull.

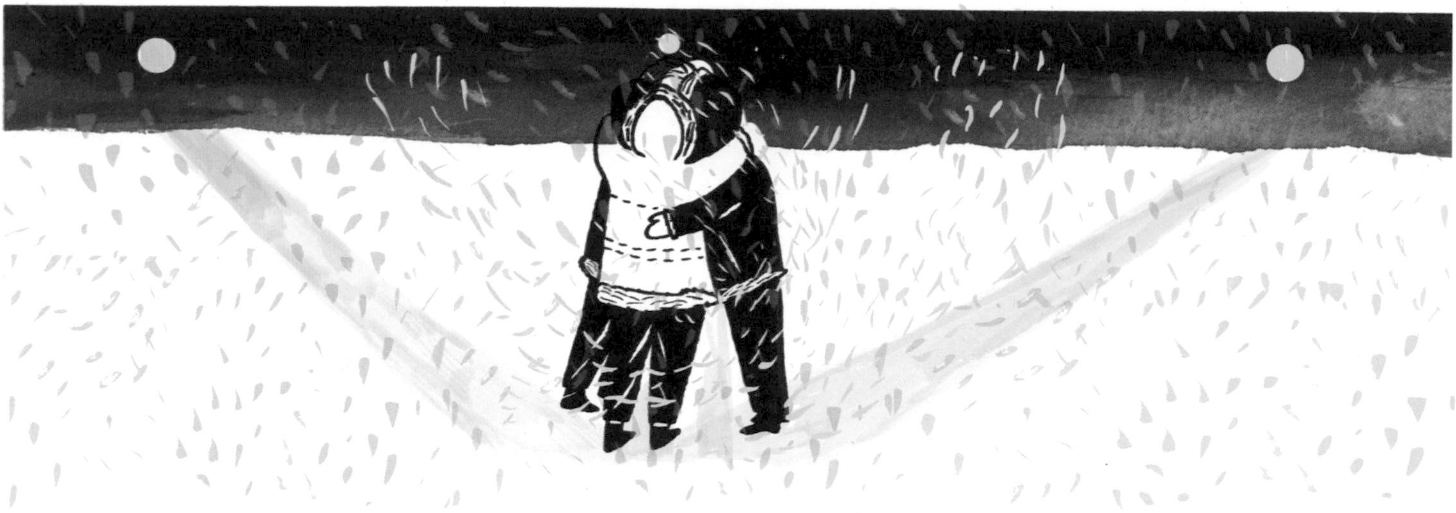

It was a pull that squeezed at each of their hearts and screamed in each of their heads. And then a moment of pure elation.

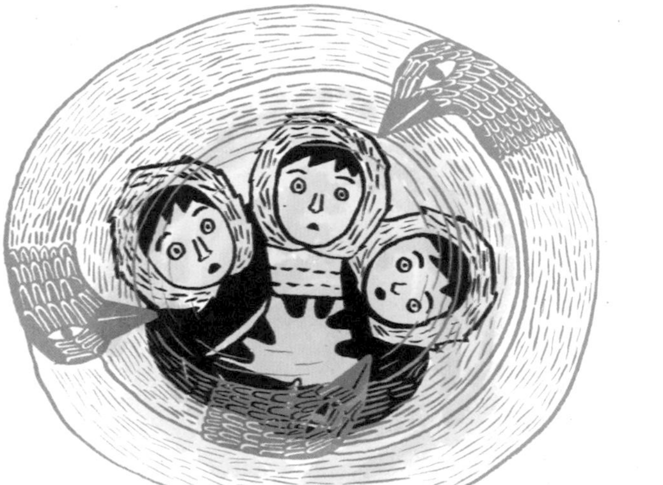

And they were one boy again. One boy looking up at the bright stars and laughing and crying.

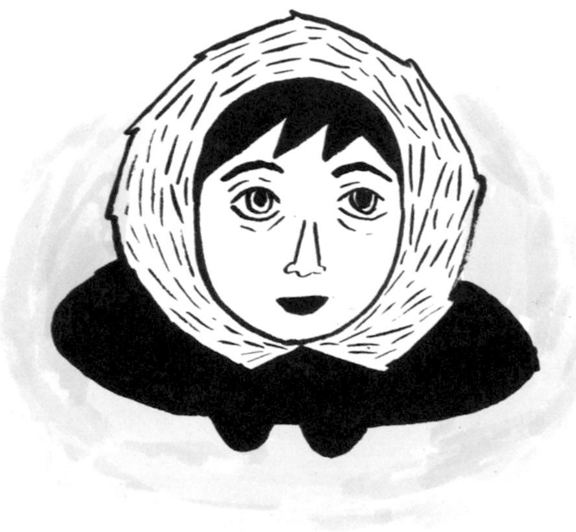

And what happened next? Well the Three Sisters, reunited, went back to behaving how they always had; to bickering and teasing and generally behaving exactly how sisters who love each other have always and will always behave.

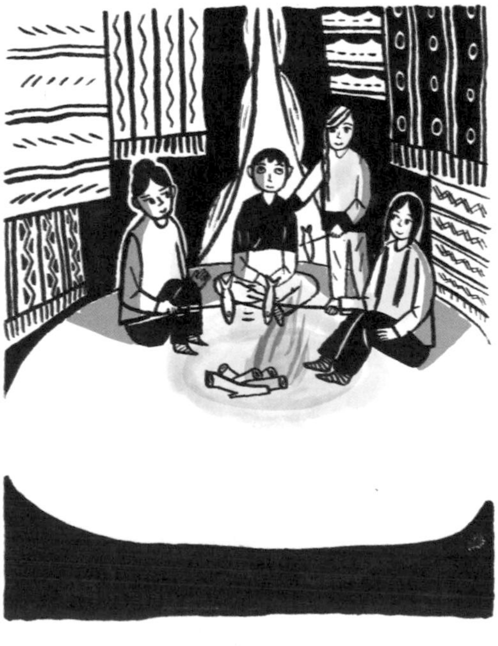

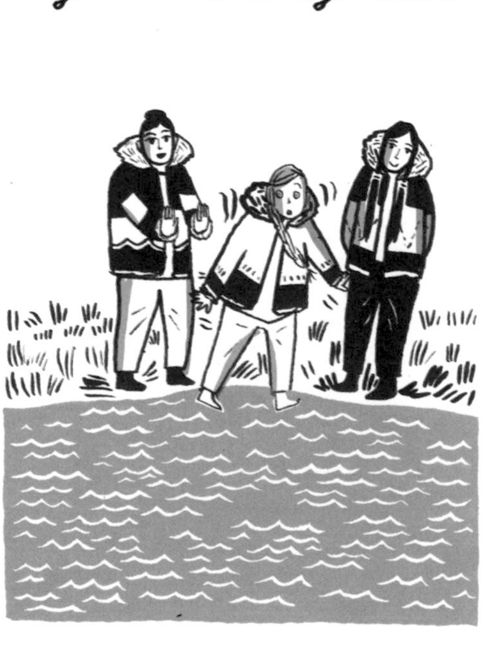

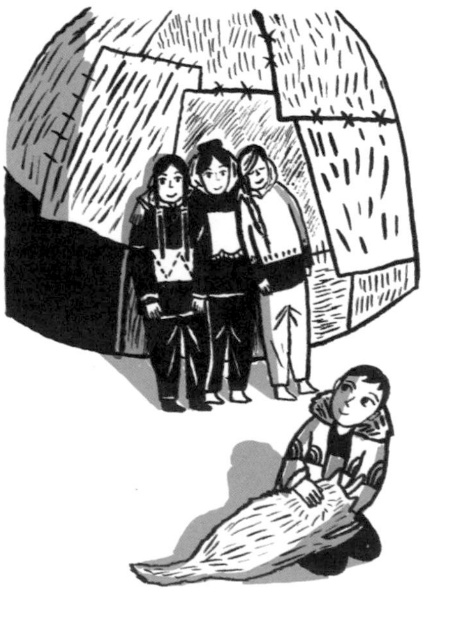

And the boy? Well instead of being three unhappy half people, he was suddenly one person, with far too much personality. Because it is not, of course, so easy to simply piece a person back together. The three different parts of himself were very often at odds with each other. Even the smallest decision was agony. And most troubling of all were his three sets of memories, that ran alongside each other, fighting all the time for supremacy.

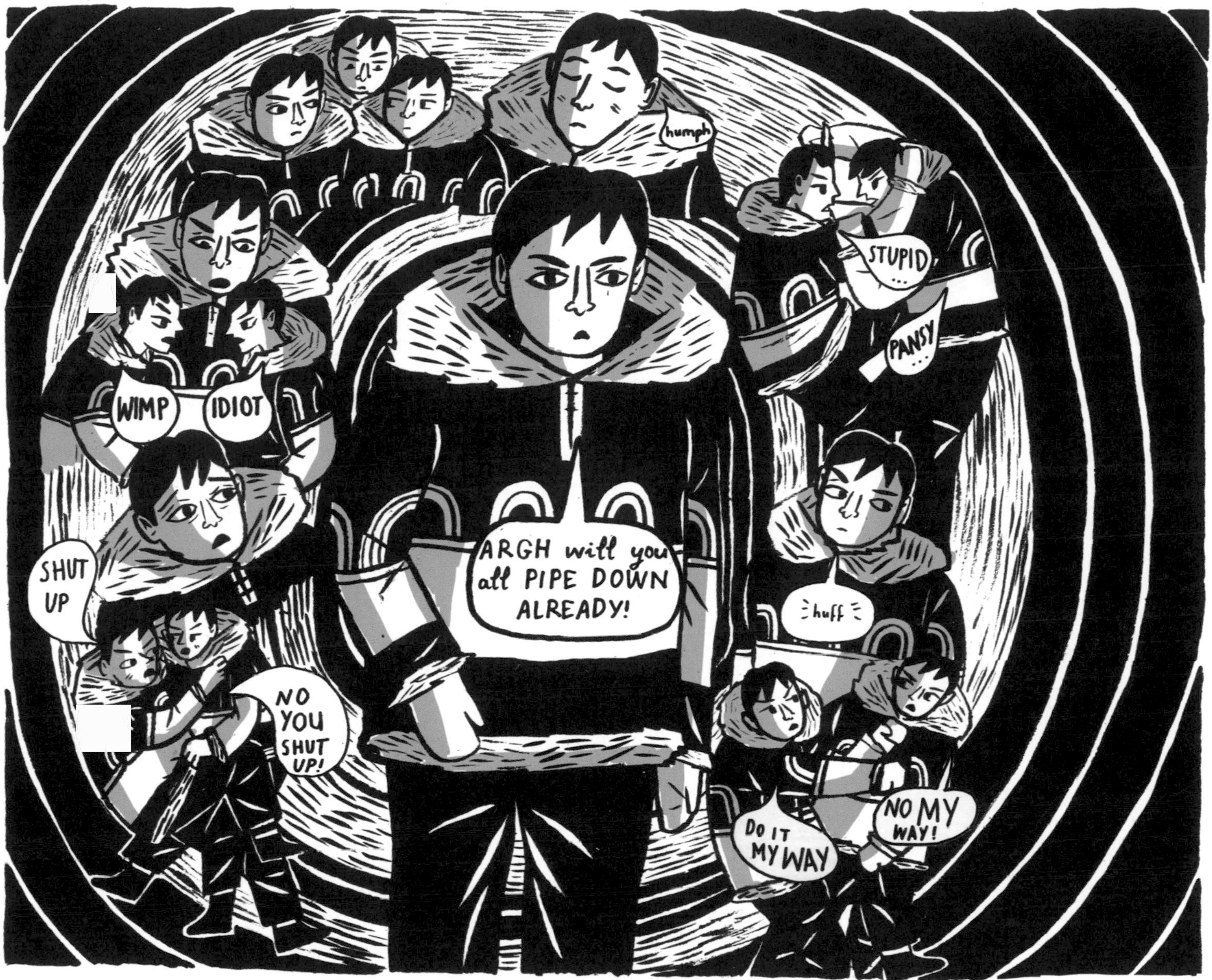
humph
STUPID ...
PANSY ...
WIMP
IDIOT
SHUT UP
NO YOU SHUT UP!
ARGH will you all PIPE DOWN ALREADY!
huff
DO IT MY WAY
NO MY WAY!

Of course having three sets of experiences has some upsides, and he was a really excellent storyteller. In fact he was so good that he became the Storyteller for his clan.

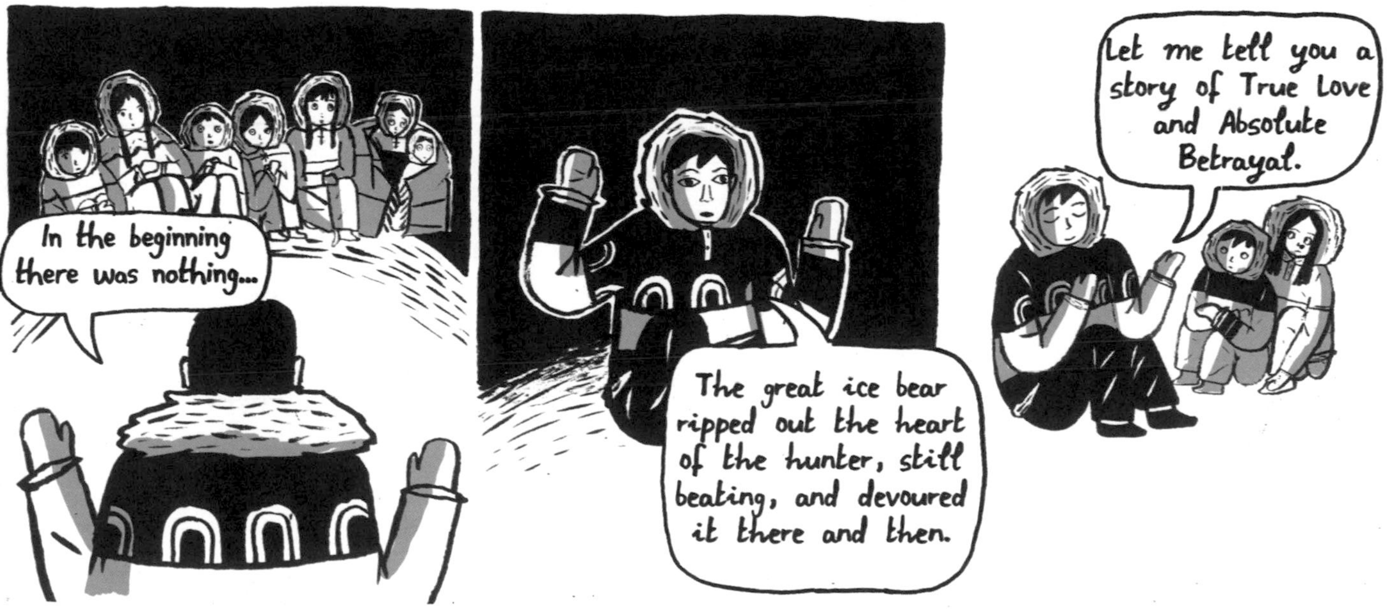
In the beginning there was nothing...
The great ice bear ripped out the heart of the hunter, still beating, and devoured it there and then.
Let me tell you a story of True Love and Absolute Betrayal.

But more and more he found himself discontent. He became convinced that there was a part of him still missing, and that if only he could find it, he might silence the clamour in his head.

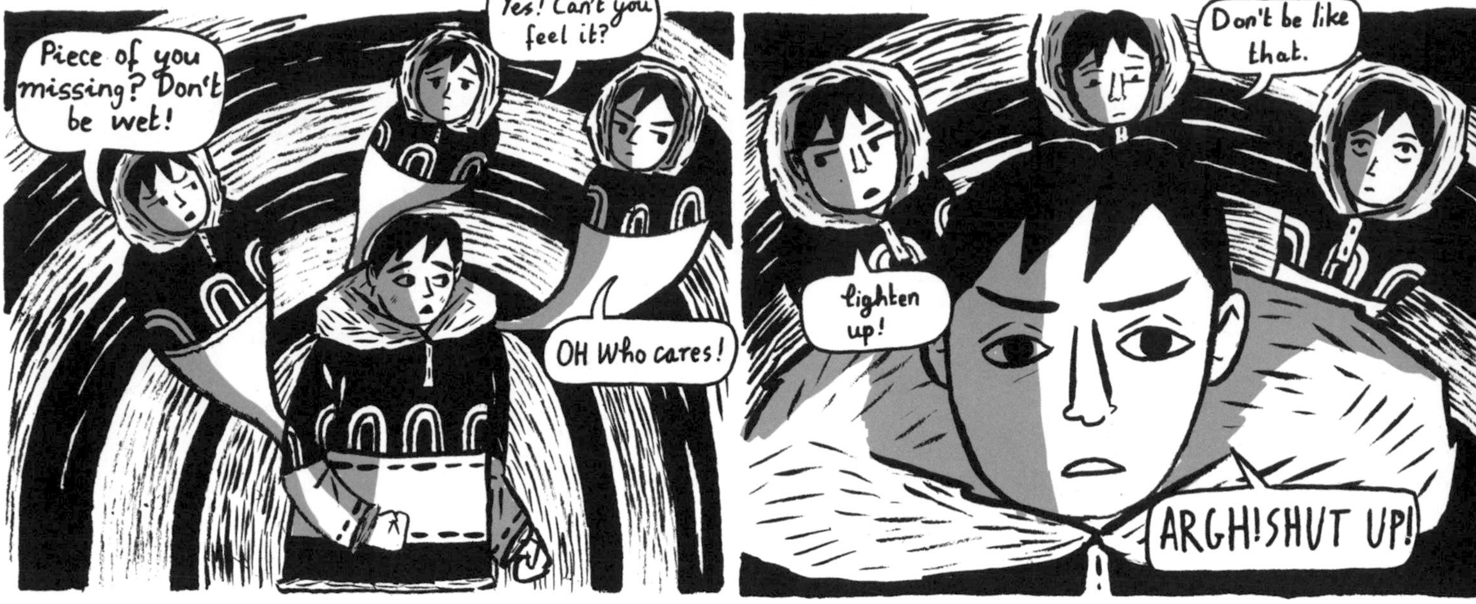
Piece of you missing? Don't be wet!
Yes! Can't you feel it?
OH Who cares!
Don't be like that.
lighten up!
ARGH!SHUT UP!

So he went back to the Medicine Man, who had, after all, been the architect of the whole mess.

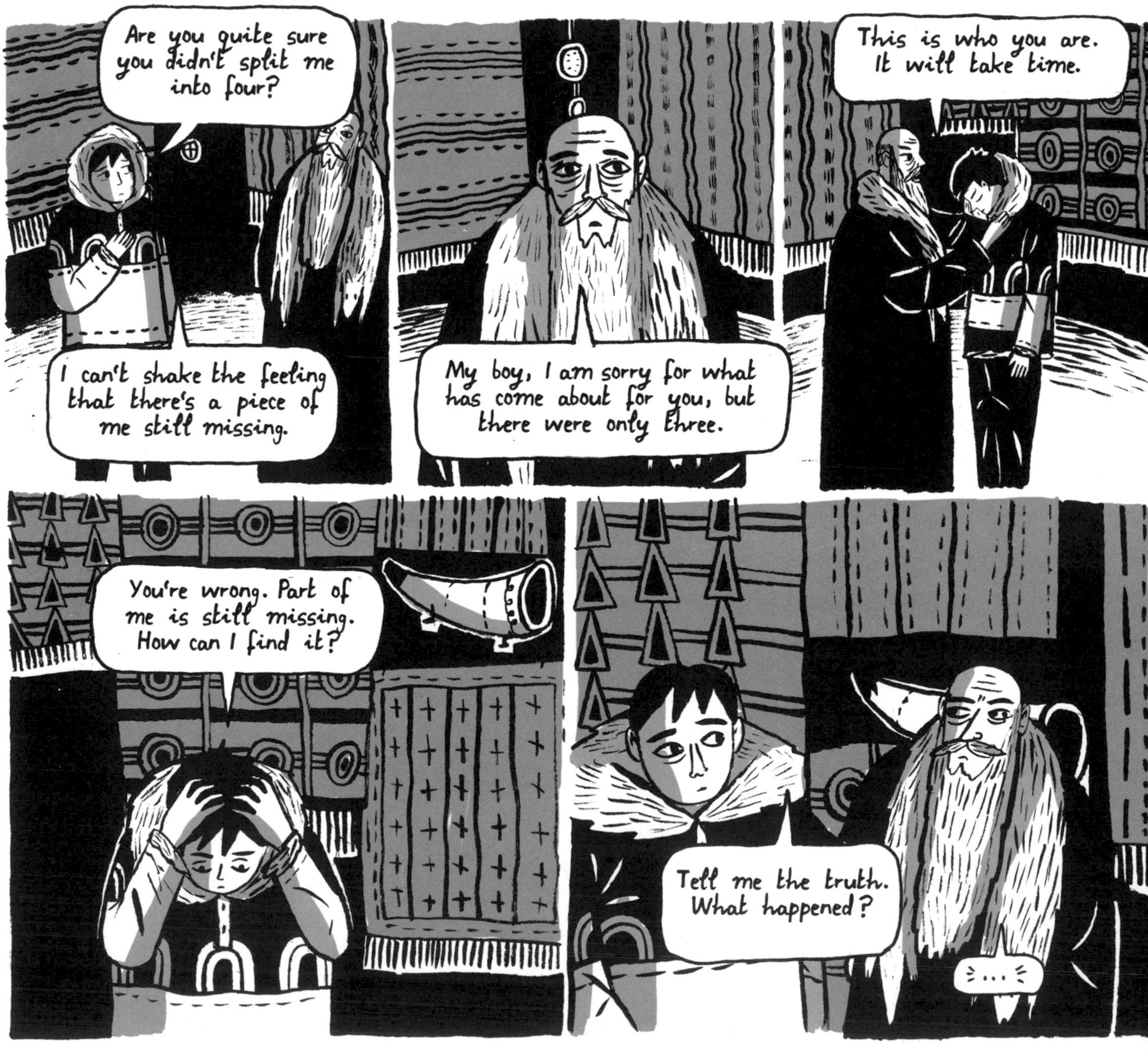
Are you quite sure you didn't split me into four?
I can't shake the feeling that there's a piece of me still missing.
My boy, I am sorry for what has come about for you, but there were only three.
This is who you are. It will take time.
You're wrong. Part of me is still missing. How can I find it?
Tell me the truth. What happened?
...

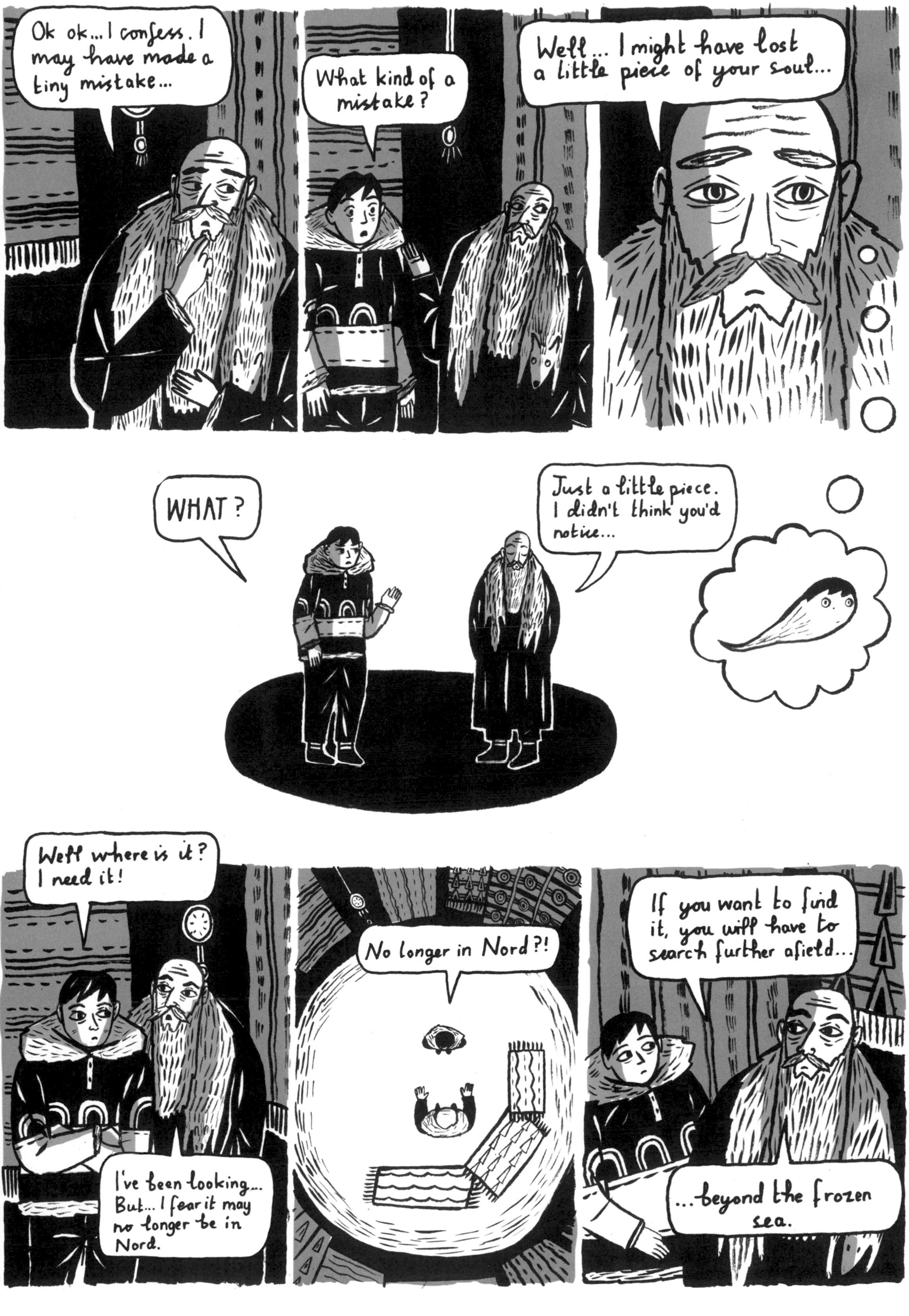
Ok ok... I confess. I may have made a tiny mistake...
What kind of a mistake?
Well... I might have lost a little piece of your soul...
WHAT?
Just a little piece. I didn't think you'd notice...
Well where is it? I need it!
I've been looking... But... I fear it may no longer be in Nord.
No longer in Nord?!
If you want to find it, you will have to search further afield...
...beyond the frozen sea.

BEYOND THE FROZEN SEA

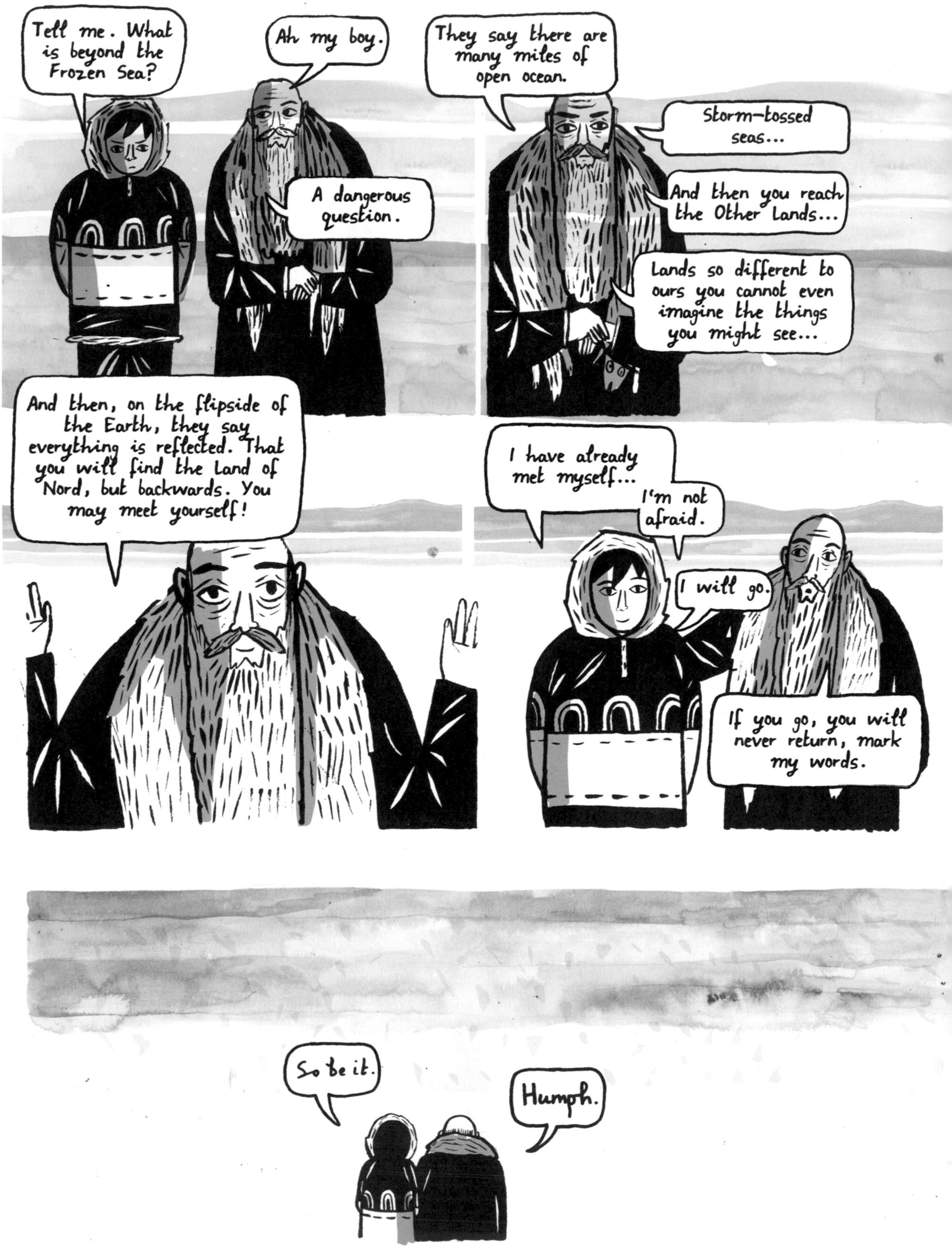

Tell me. What is beyond the Frozen Sea?
Ah my boy.
A dangerous question.
They say there are many miles of open ocean.
Storm-tossed seas...
And then you reach the Other Lands...
Lands so different to ours you cannot even imagine the things you might see...
And then, on the flipside of the Earth, they say everything is reflected. That you will find the Land of Nord, but backwards. You may meet yourself!
I have already met myself...
I'm not afraid.
I will go.
If you go, you will never return, mark my words.
So be it.
Humph.

So our Storyteller said goodbye to the Medicine Man, and to his three mothers, who naturally disagreed with each other over the whole endeavour.

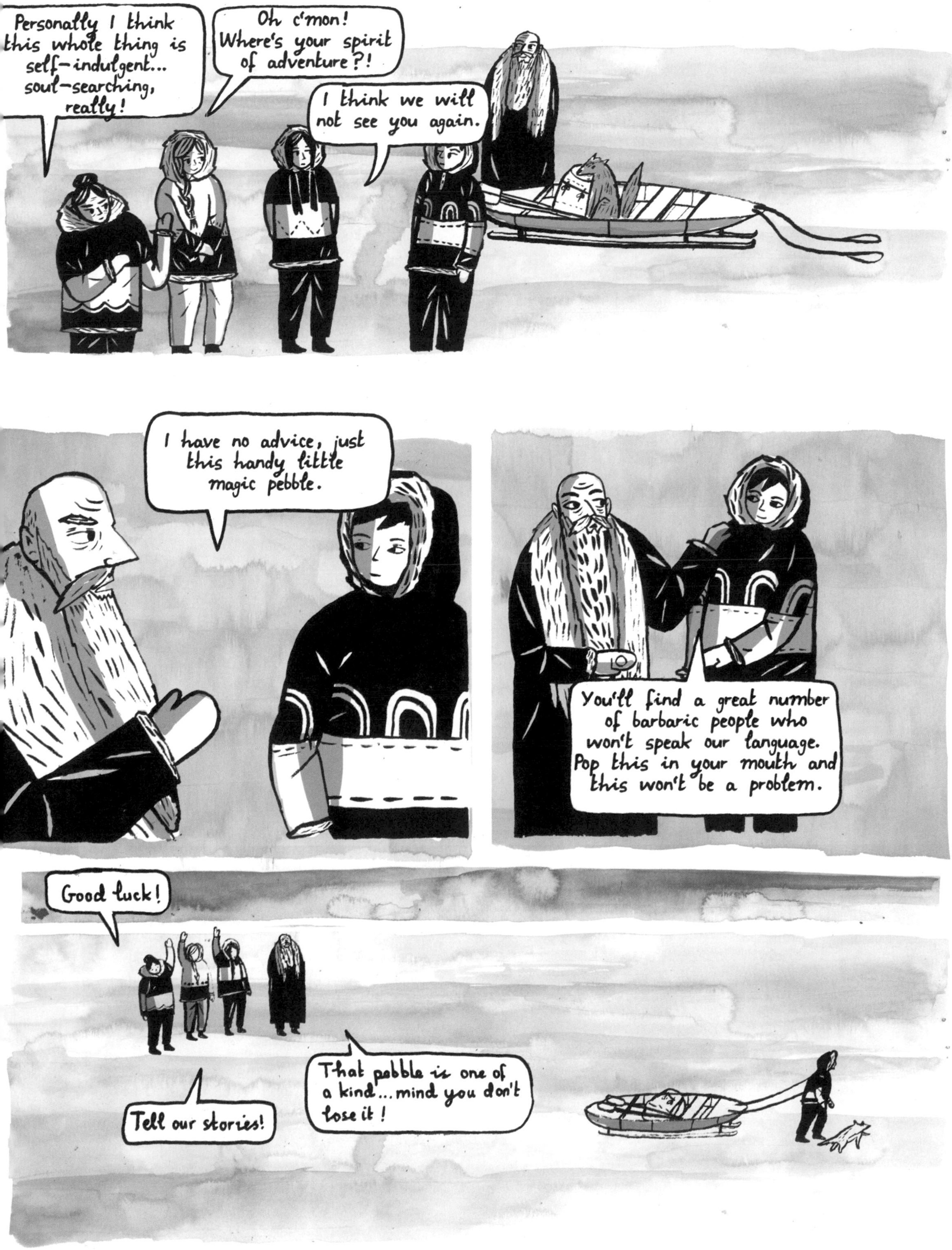

Personally I think this whole thing is self-indulgent... soul-searching, really!
Oh c'mon! Where's your spirit of adventure?!
I think we will not see you again.
I have no advice, just this handy little magic pebble.
You'll find a great number of barbaric people who won't speak our language. Pop this in your mouth and this won't be a problem.
Good luck!
Tell our stories!
That pebble is one of a kind... mind you don't lose it!

THE GODS

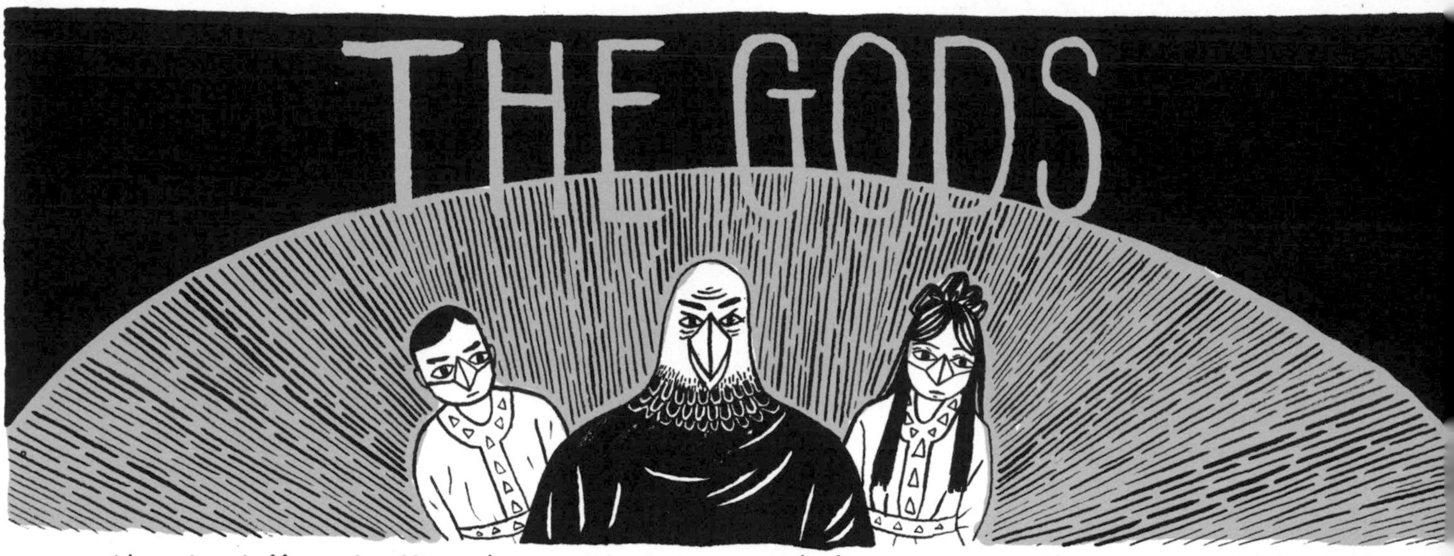

So the Storyteller set off on his quest, but meanwhile it is time that you meet the Gods. Beyond the Aurora, in the fourth (or maybe fifth) dimension, is the Cloud Castle. There the Eagle God BirdMan dwells, with his two children, The Ravens, Kid and Kiddo. For Gods, the fabric of the worlds is thin, and they pass through it as easily as parting a curtain, and high up in the Cloud Castle they spend their days watching the lives of the humans down on Earth.

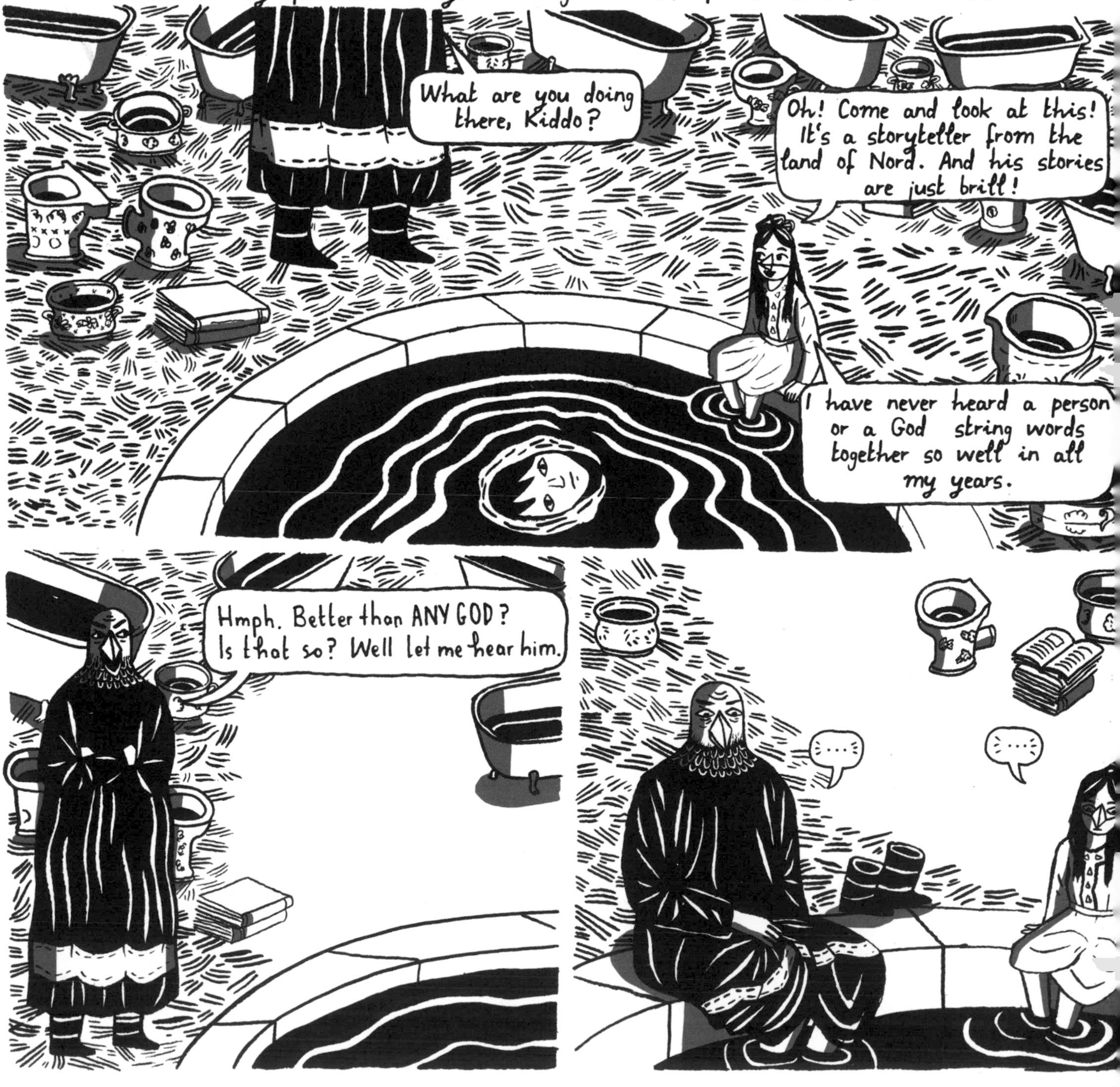

What are you doing there, Kiddo?
Oh! Come and look at this! It's a storyteller from the land of Nord. And his stories are just brill!
I have never heard a person or a God string words together so well in all my years.
Hmph. Better than ANY GOD? Is that so? Well let me hear him.
...
...

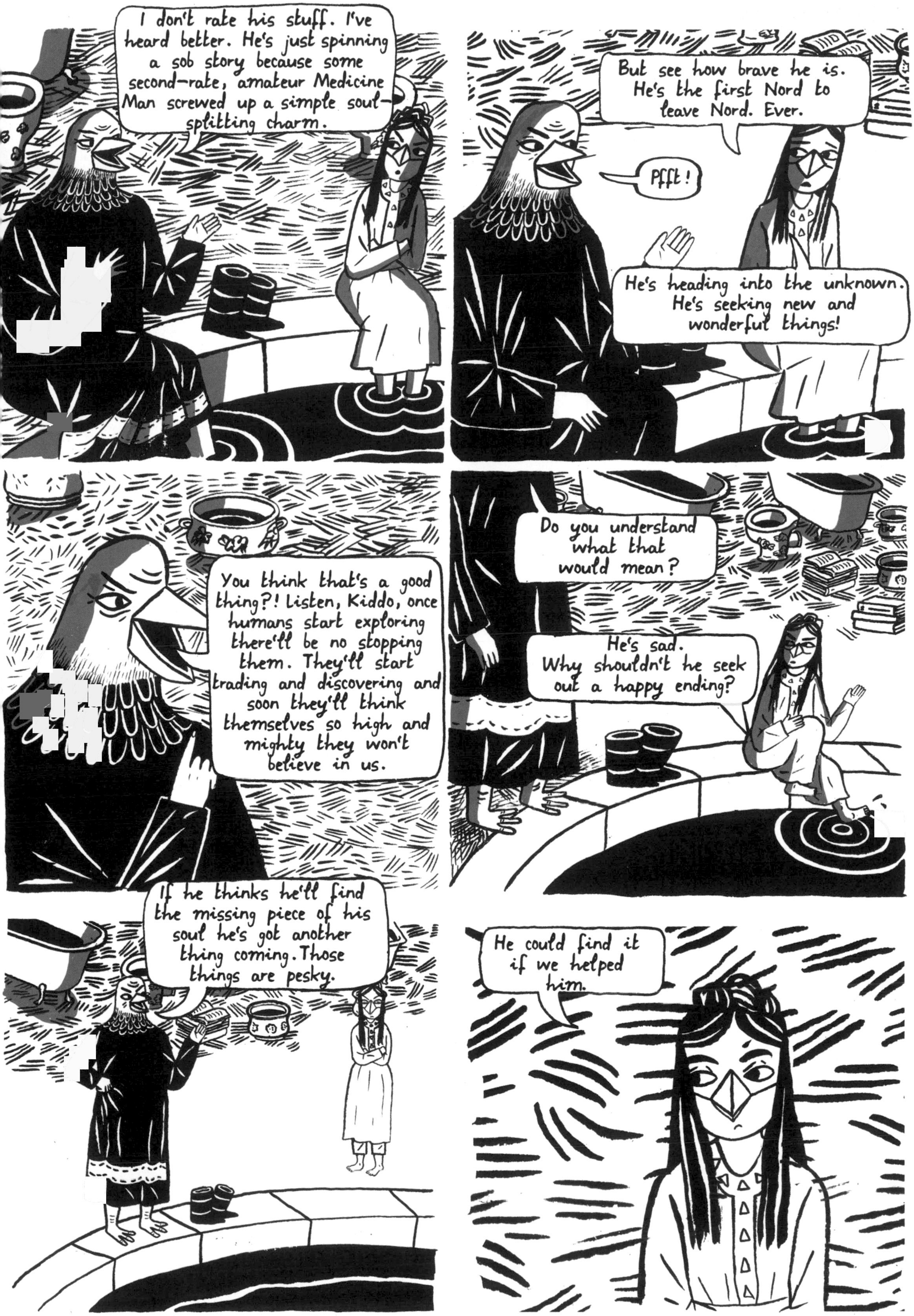
I don't rate his stuff. I've heard better. He's just spinning a sob story because some second-rate, amateur Medicine Man screwed up a simple soul-splitting charm.
But see how brave he is. He's the first Nord to leave Nord. Ever.
Pfft!
He's heading into the unknown. He's seeking new and wonderful things!
You think that's a good thing?! Listen, Kiddo, once humans start exploring there'll be no stopping them. They'll start trading and discovering and soon they'll think themselves so high and mighty they won't believe in us.
Do you understand what that would mean?
He's sad. Why shouldn't he seek out a happy ending?
If he thinks he'll find the missing piece of his soul he's got another thing coming. Those things are pesky.
He could find it if we helped him.

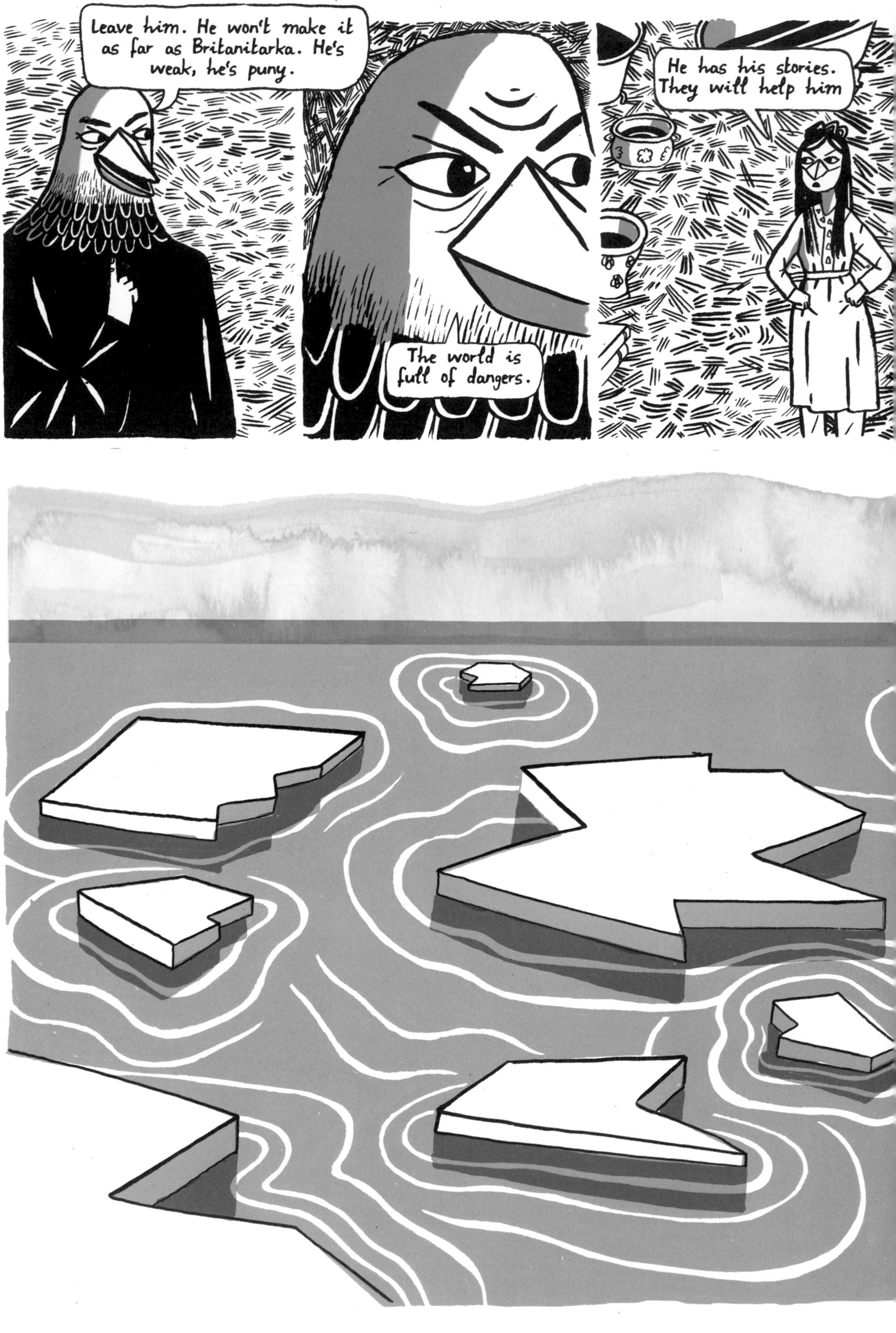
Leave him. He won't make it as far as Britanitarka. He's weak, he's puny.
The world is full of dangers.
He has his stories. They will help him

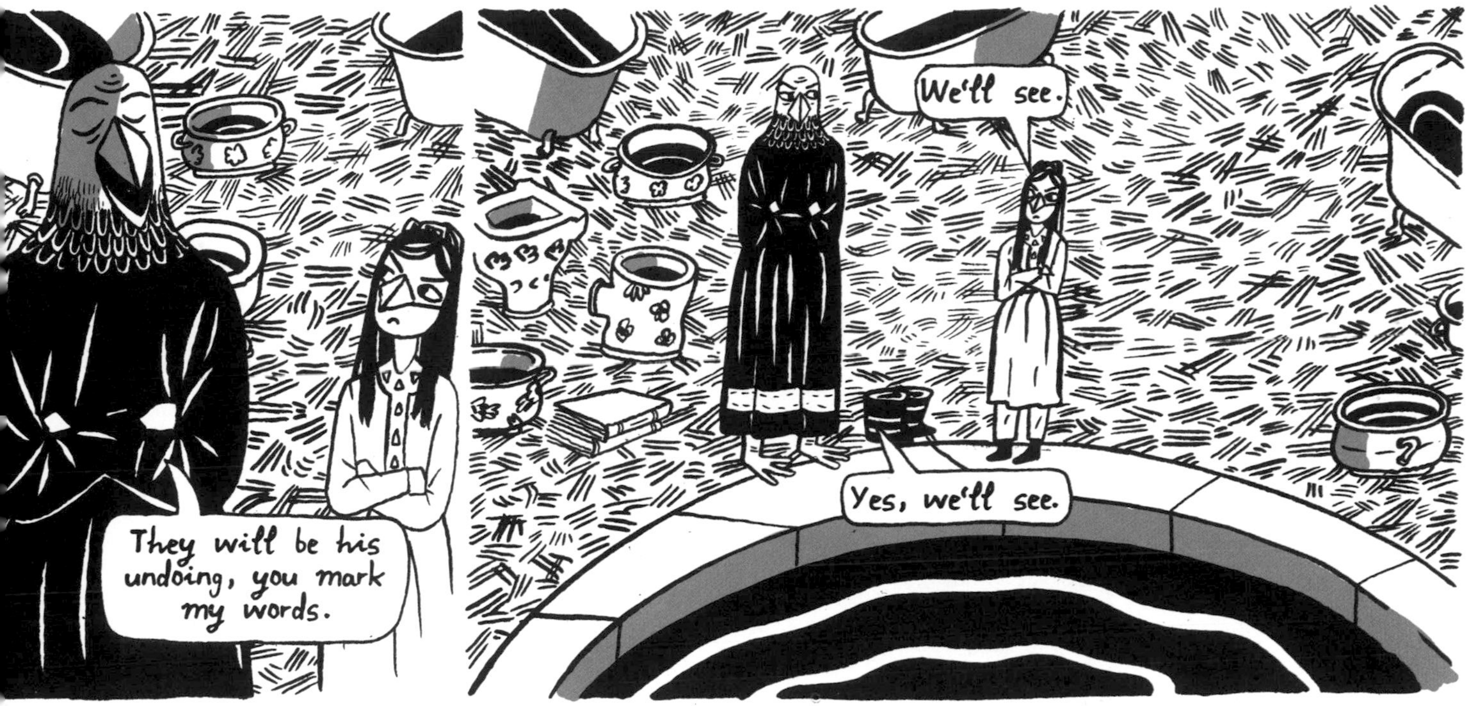
They will be his undoing, you mark my words.
We'll see.
Yes, we'll see.

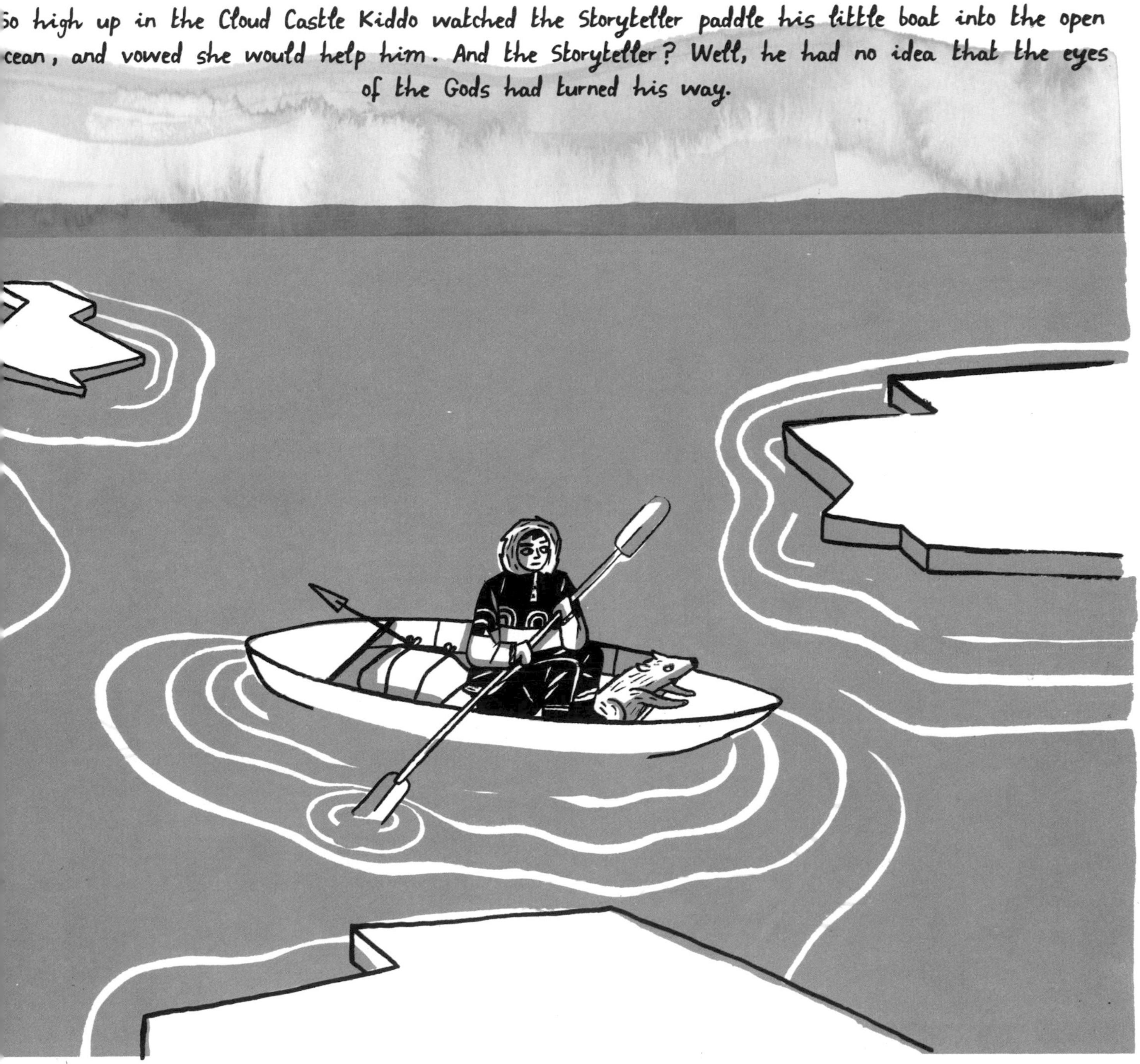
So high up in the Cloud Castle Kiddo watched the Storyteller paddle his little boat into the open
cean, and vowed she would help him. And the Storyteller? Well, he had no idea that the eyes
of the Gods had turned his way.

THE ODYSSEY BEGINS

As the Frozen Sea gave way to open ocean, and the Land of Nord had long been eaten up by the horizon, the Storyteller felt his heart soar. Behind him lay the old and sacred stories of his people. But in front were new stories, to be lived and learned.

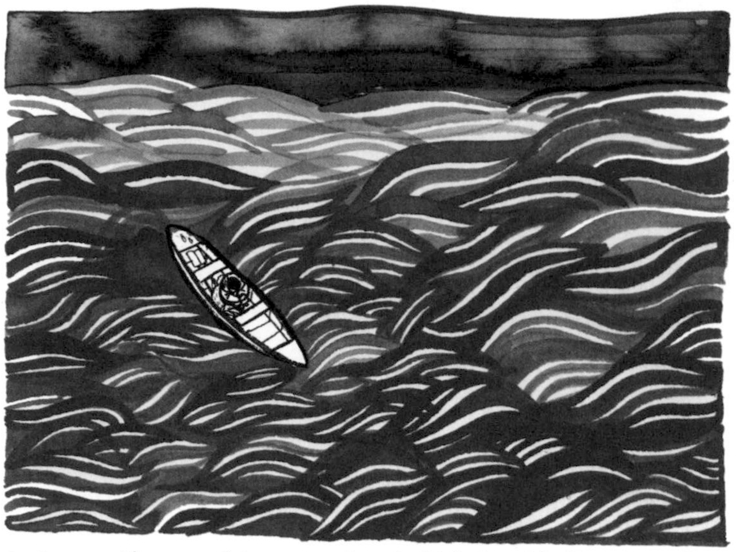

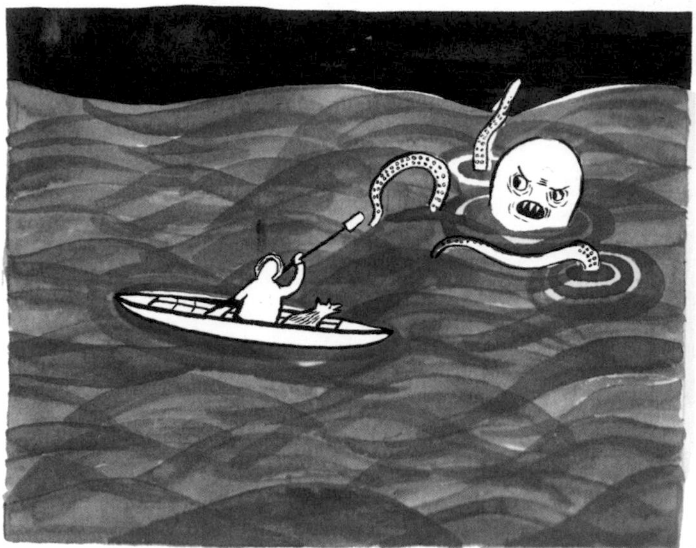

Out on the wild ocean he battled all the perils of the sea; fearsome storms, terrible winds and, of course, wildlife! He found himself in all manner of strange and lonely places, including what cartographers later learnt to call the Archipelago of No No No...

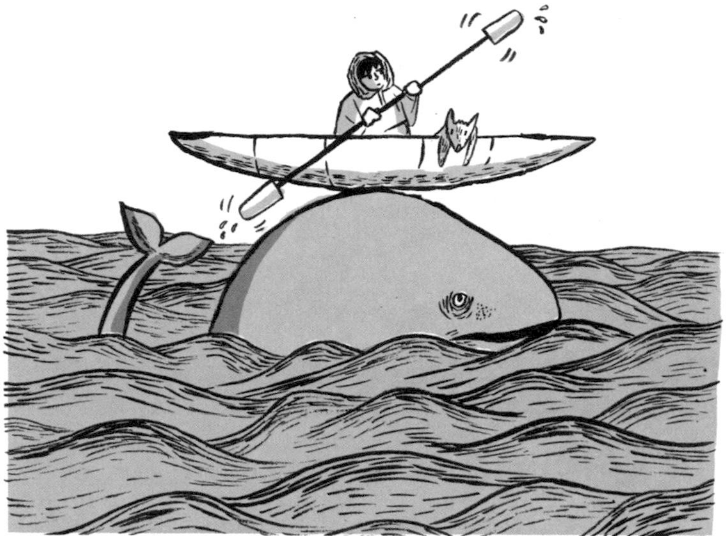

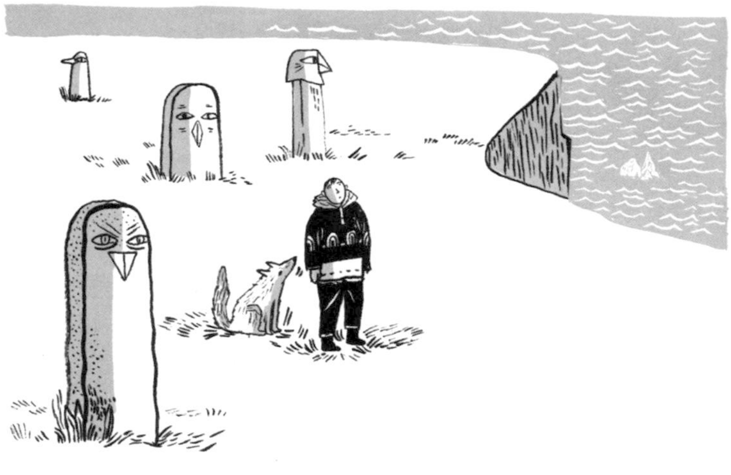

There he walked on its deserted shores, the first human to stand there in over a thousand years. All that dwelt there now were the sea birds and the fierce winds, and the ruins of a long abandoned civilisation.

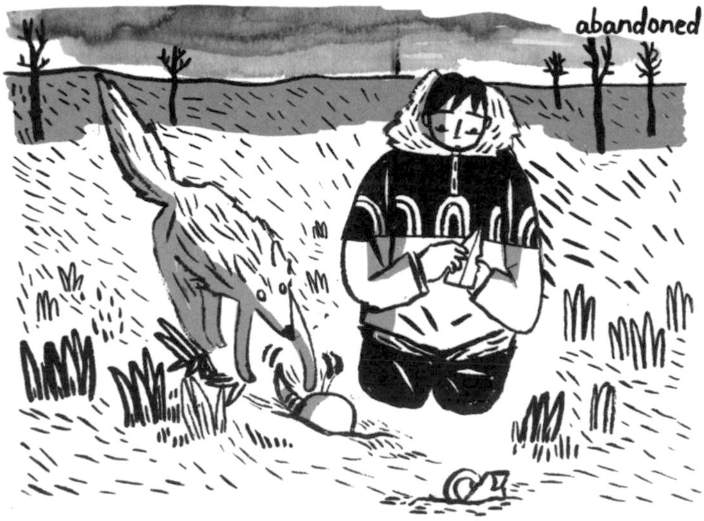

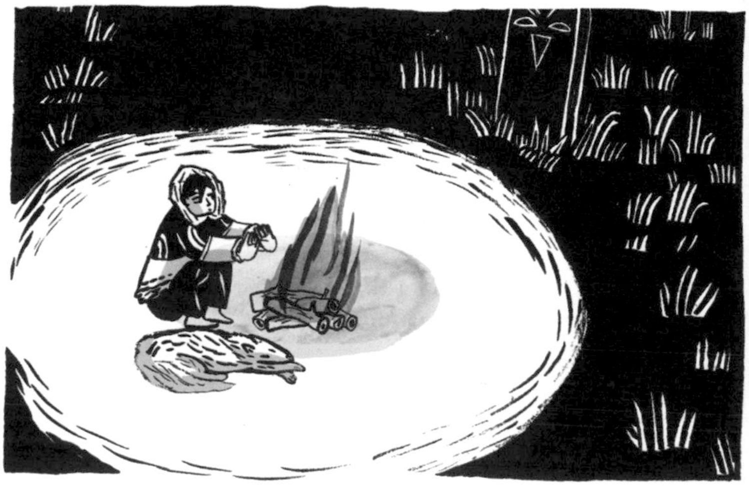

He came upon an island that had once been a volcano and among the craters and boulders and naked trees he met a cyclops. Whom of course he bravely defeated.

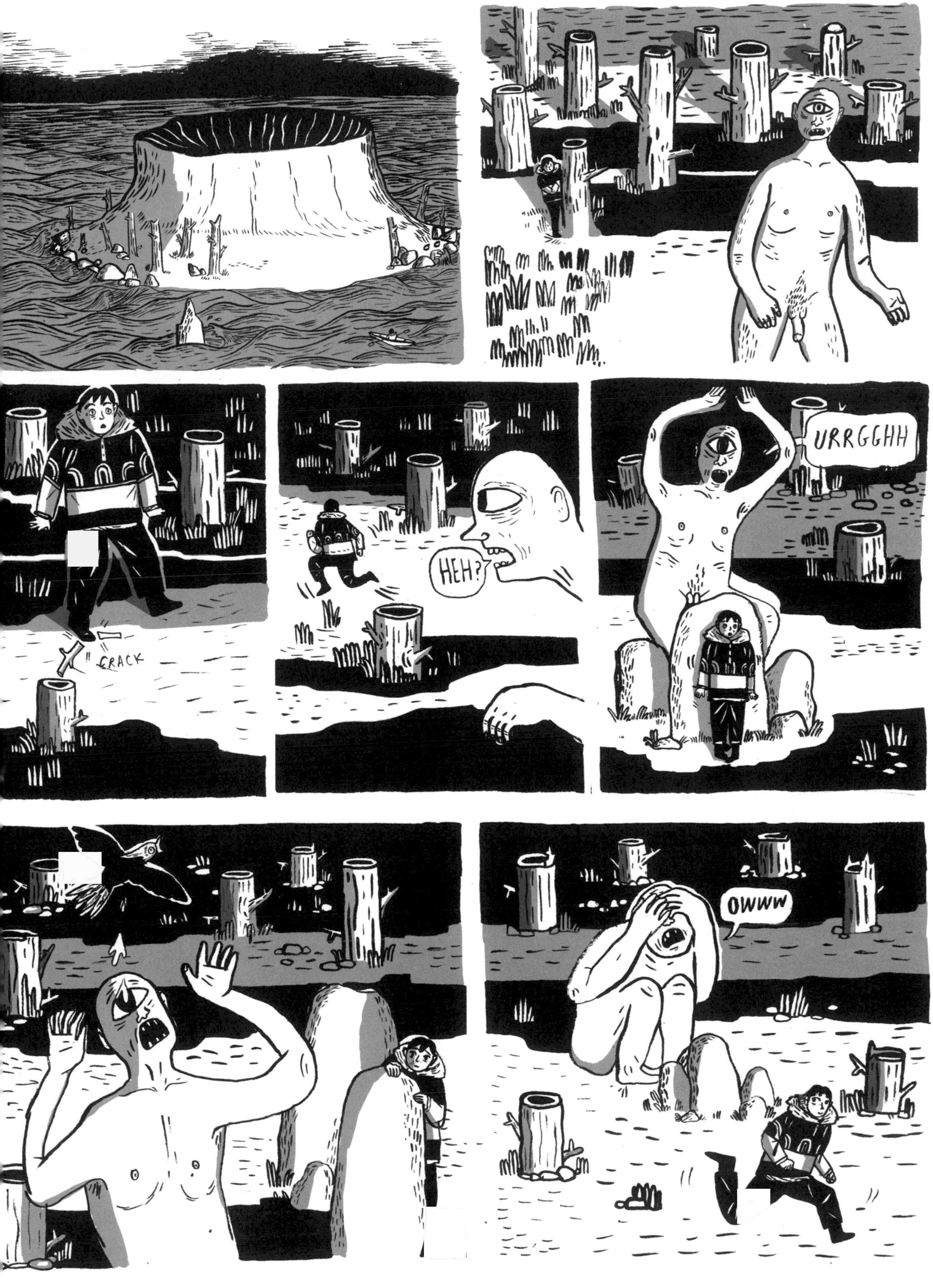
CRACK
HEH?
URRGGHH
OWWW

Passing by the mountainous island of Sor-Tum, he nearly faced untimely death at the hands of the enchanting Sirens. The dangerous temptresses wished to entice him onto the rocks with their strange and beautiful songs and have their wicked way with him.

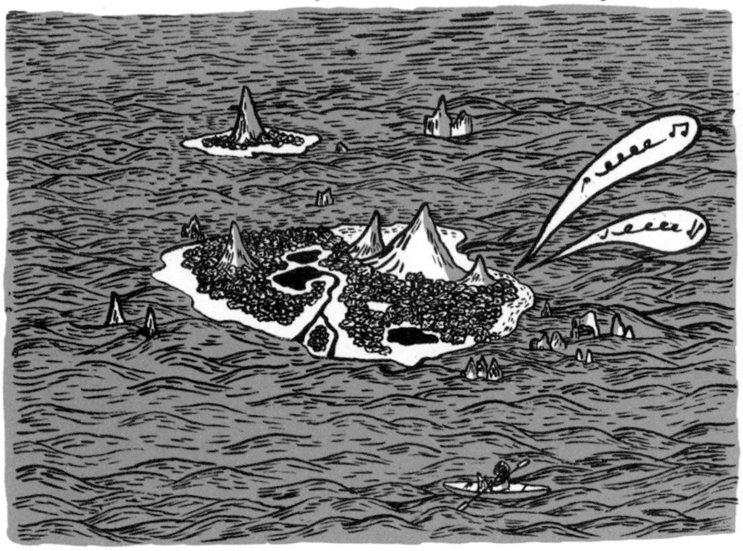

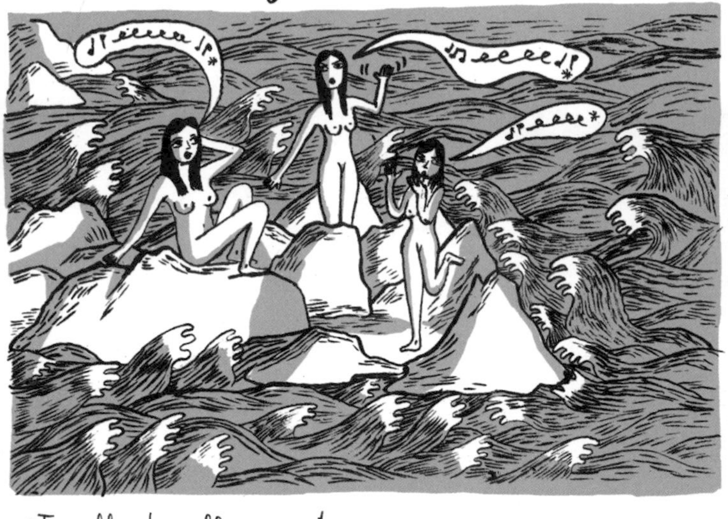

*Traveller, traveller come to us...

* You can't resist our womanly ways... * Come a little closer, closer...

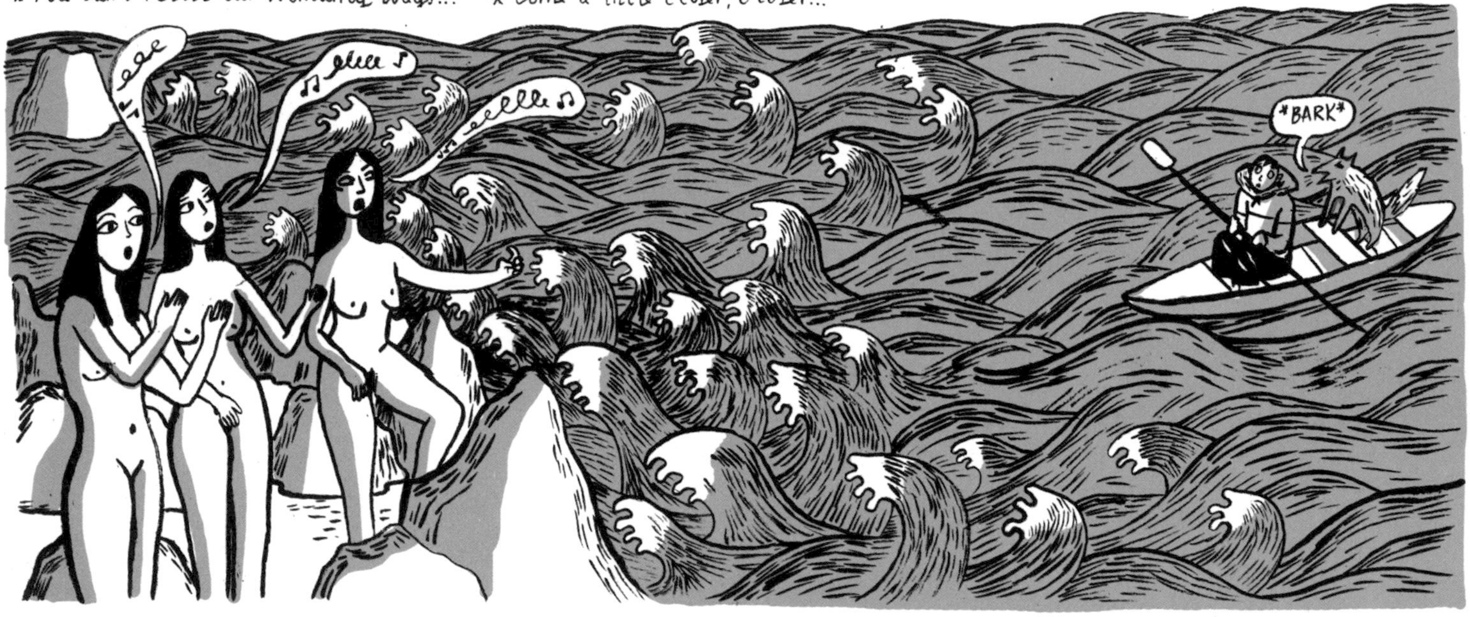
BARK

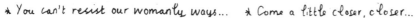

Luckily at the last moment, he came to his senses, and turned around.

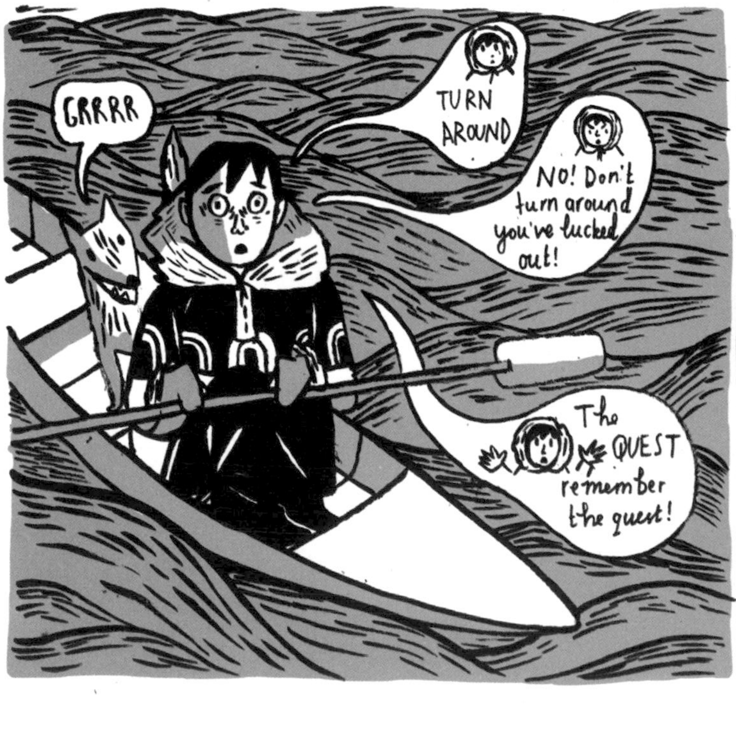
GRRRR
TURN AROUND
NO! Don't turn around you've lucked out!
The QUEST remember the quest!

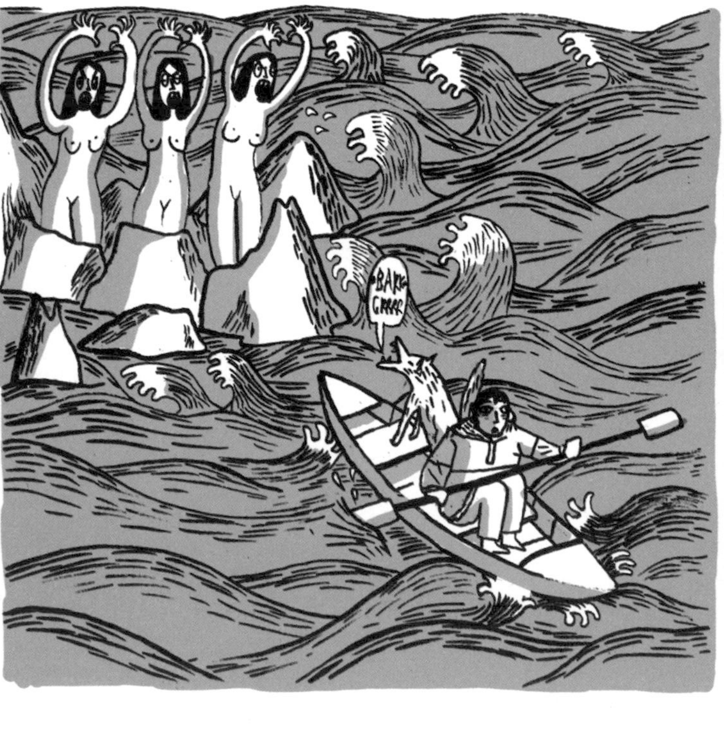
BARK GRRR

And so for many days and nights, the Storyteller sailed the seas.

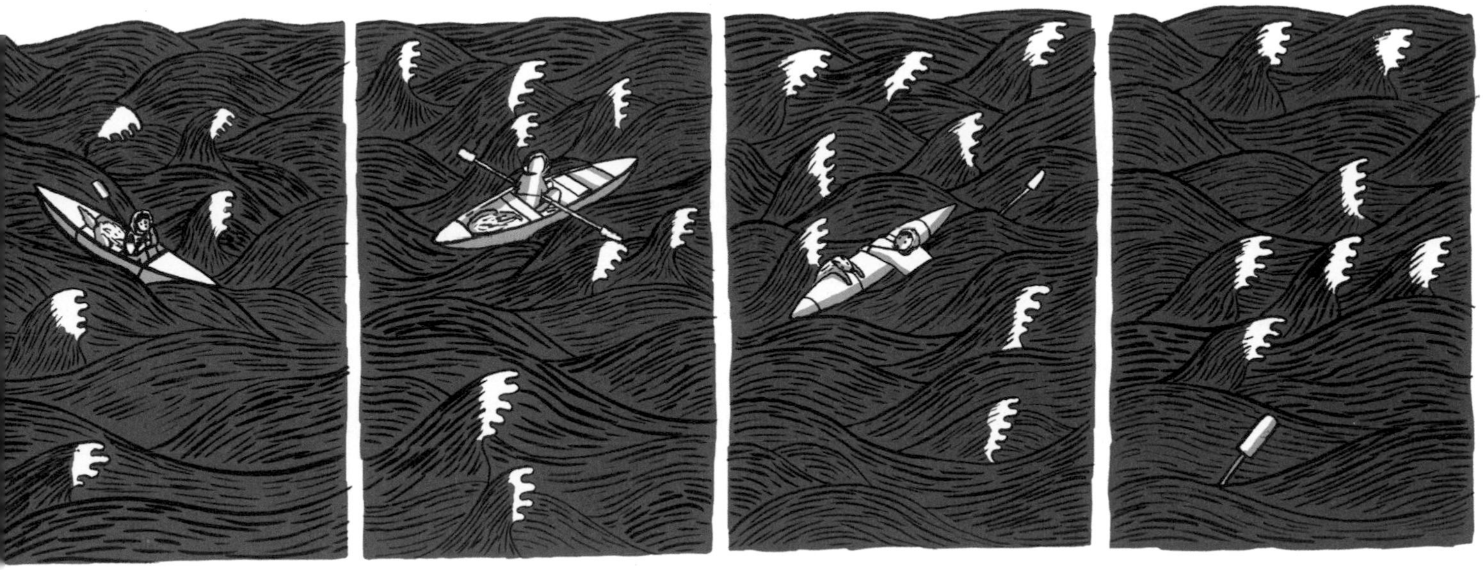

But at length he was washed up on the shores of a grey, unfamiliar land.

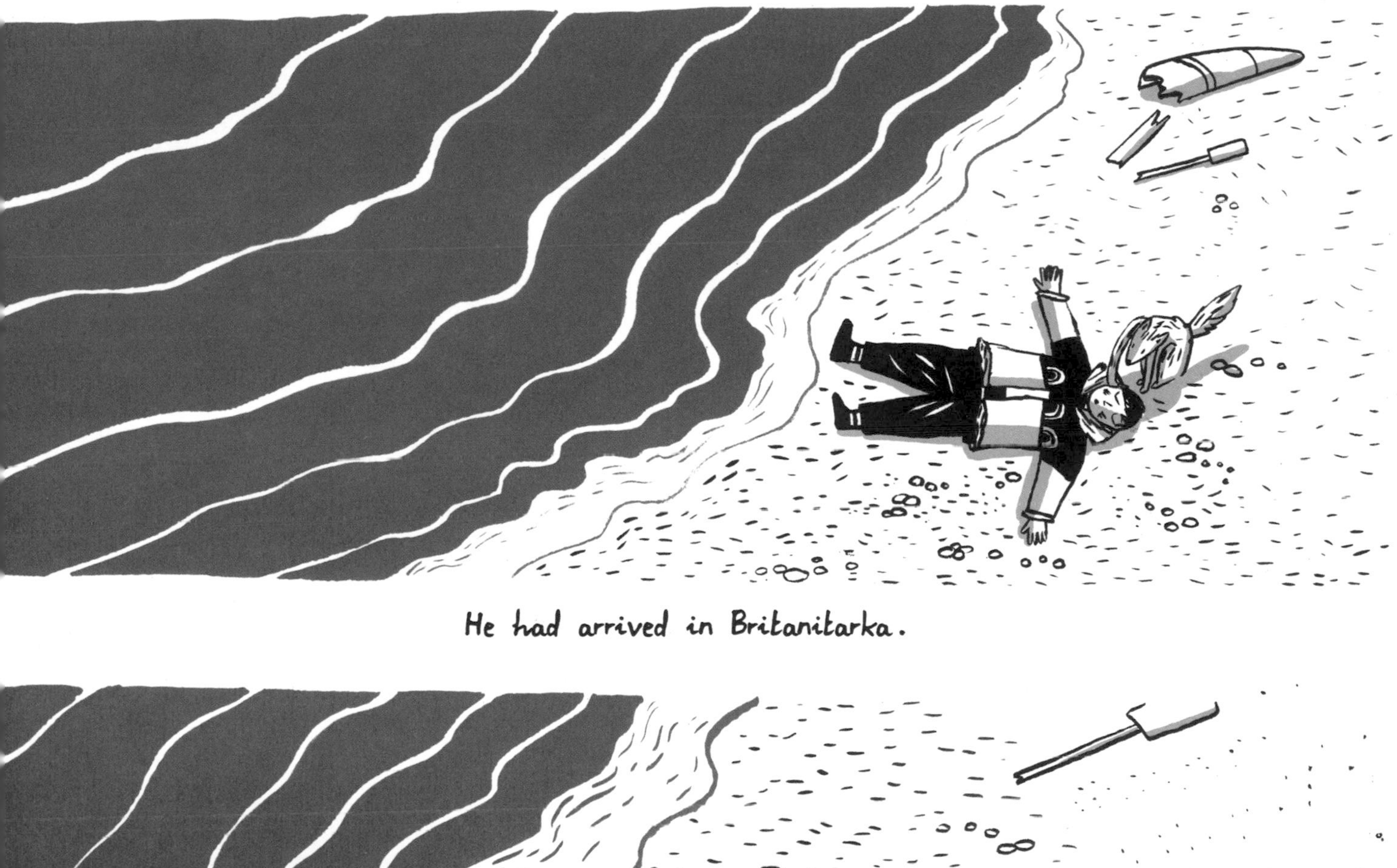

He had arrived in Britanitarka.

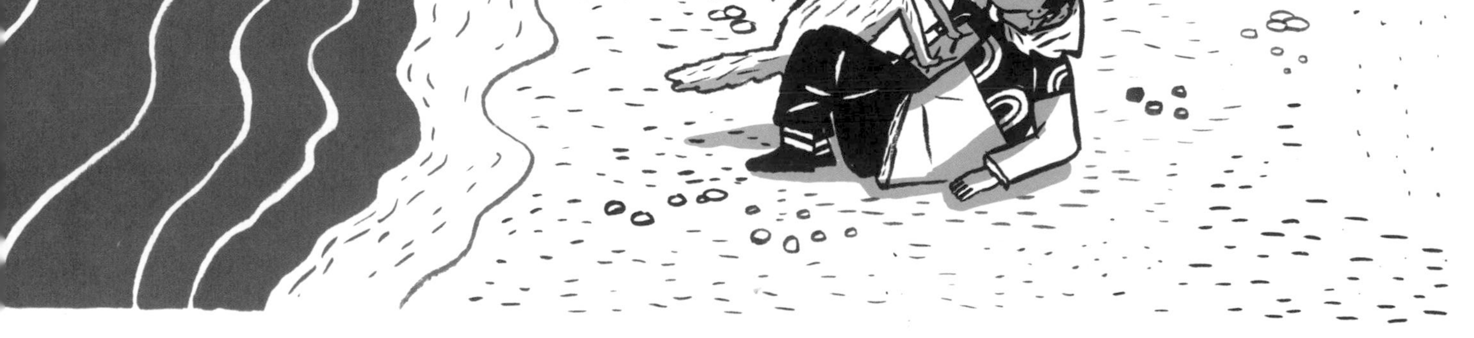

Part The Second:

BRITANITARKA

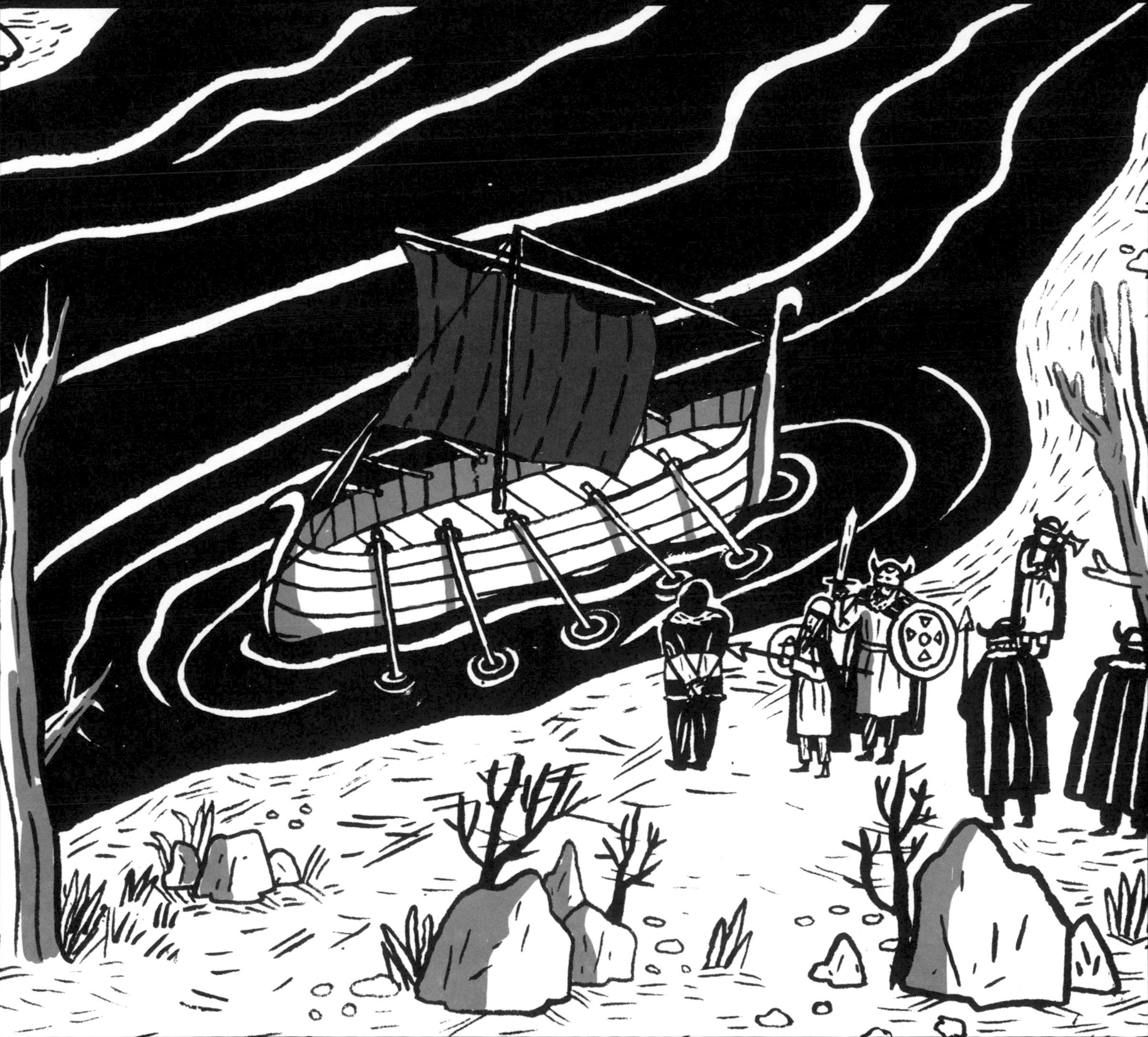

The Storyteller had never felt more alone or further from home in all his life. Standing on the unfamiliar shores of Britanitarka, he doubted his quest for the first time. But it was too late for that. He had left Nord to seek adventure, new stories and, of course, that missing piece of himself.

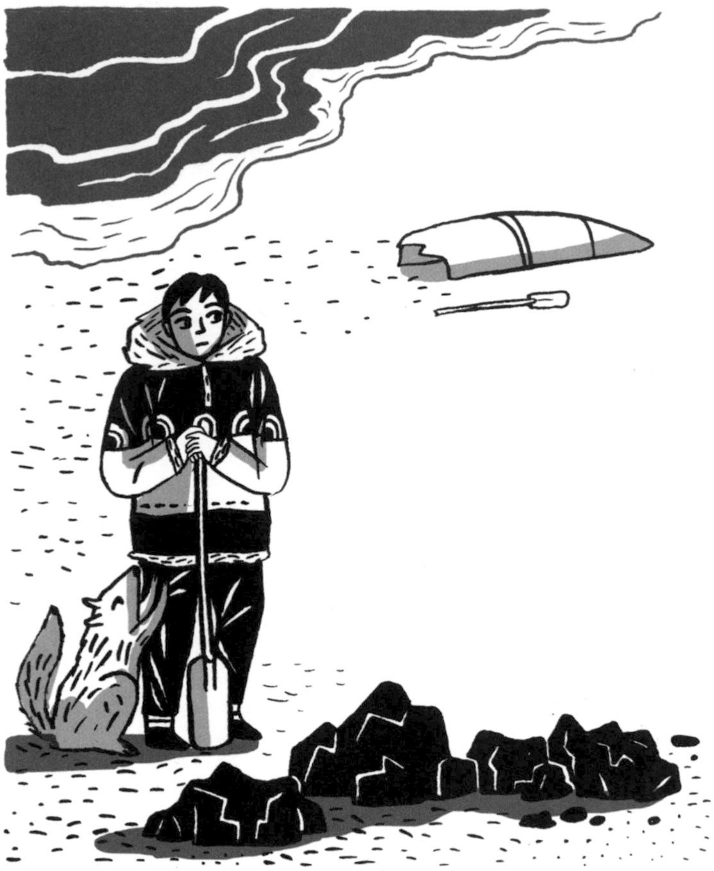

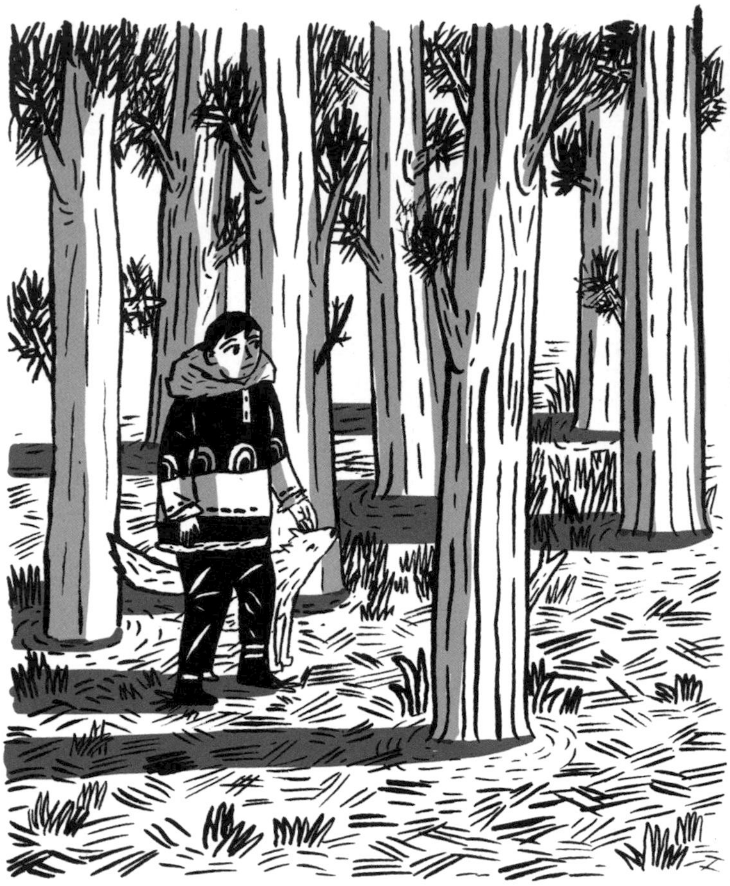

So he did the only thing he could do; he started walking.

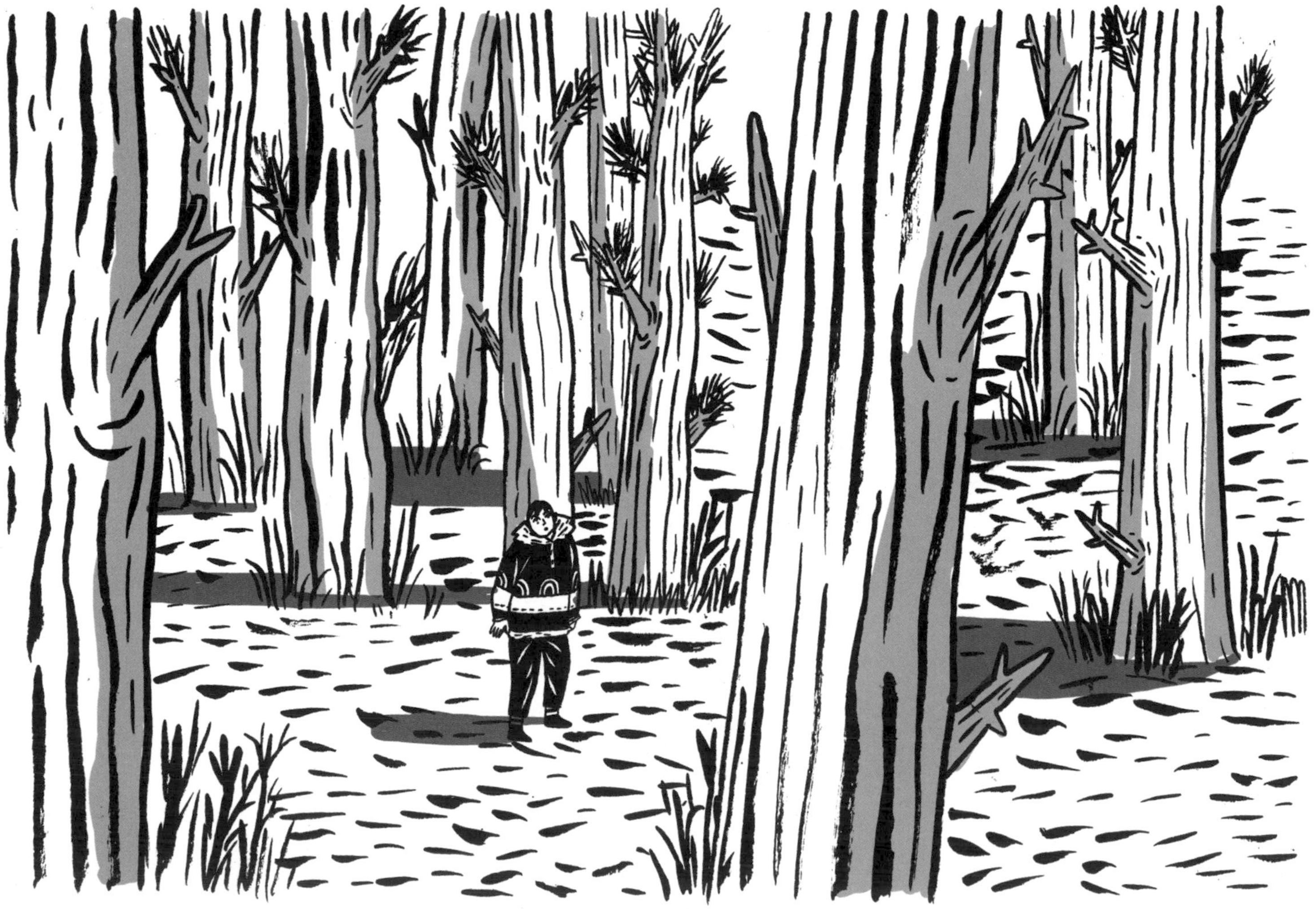

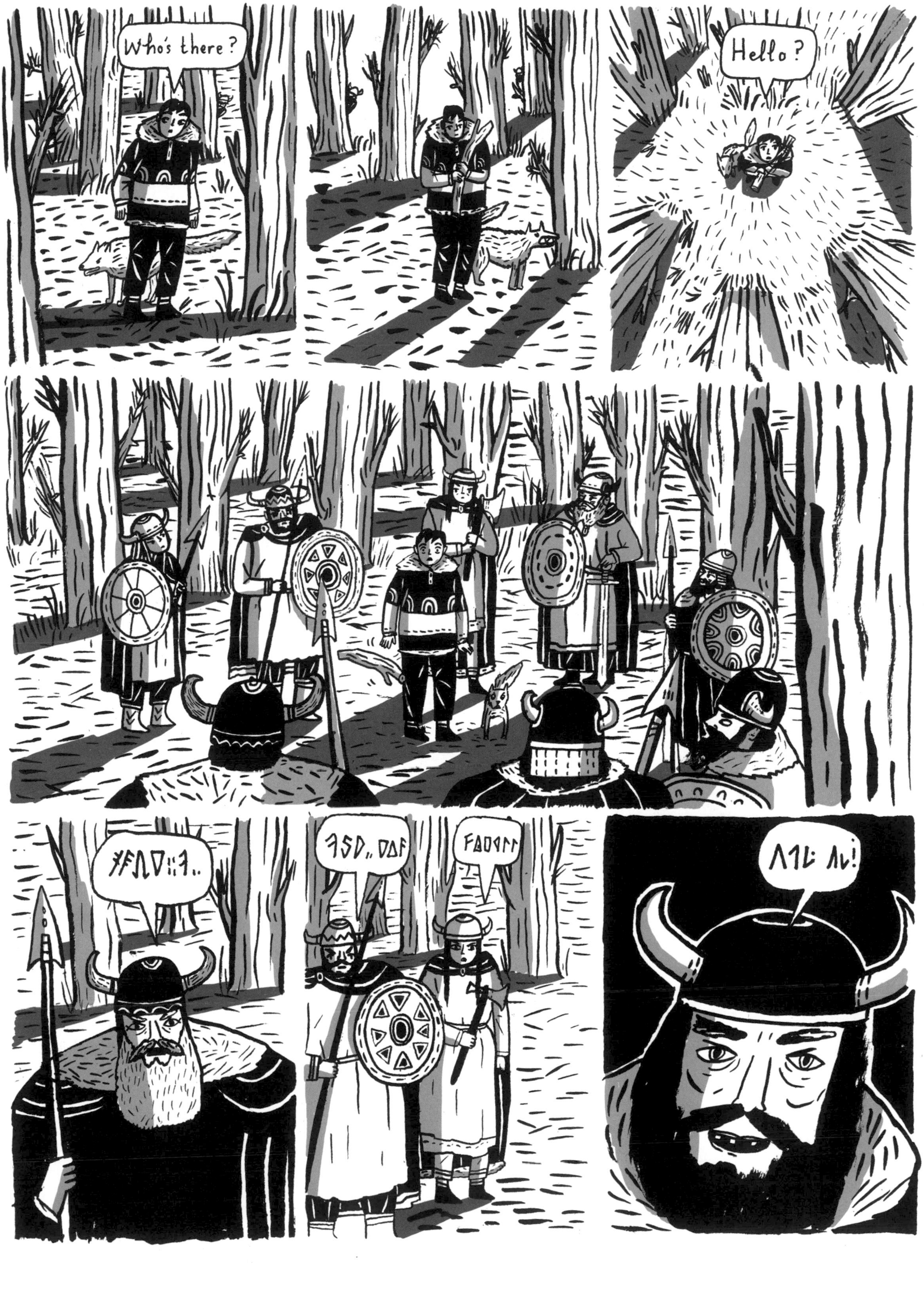
Who's there?
Hello?

Luckily he remembered the Medicine Man's magic pebble.

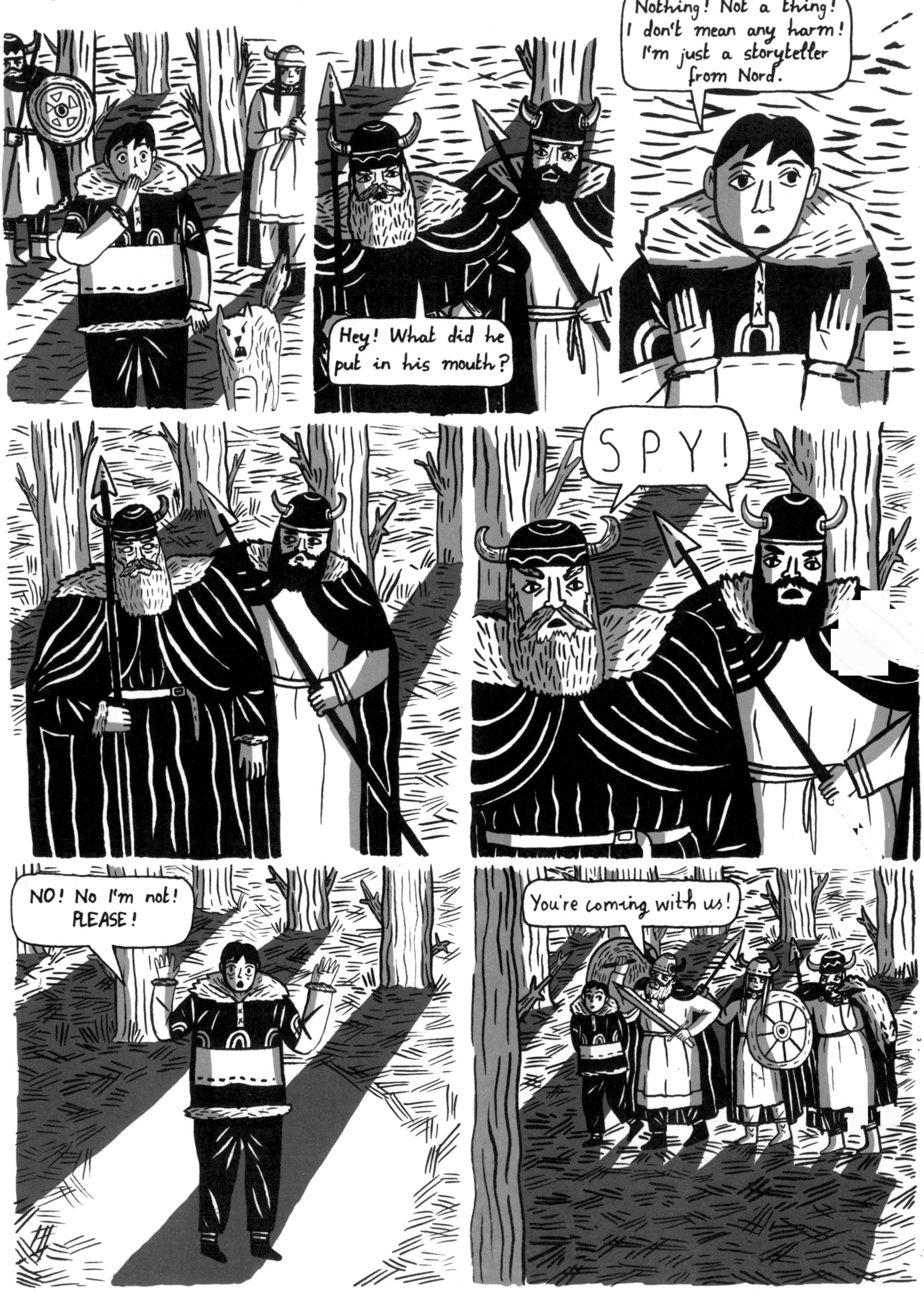

Hey! What did he put in his mouth?
Nothing! Not a thing! I don't mean any harm! I'm just a storyteller from Nord.
SPY!
NO! No I'm not! PLEASE!
You're coming with us!

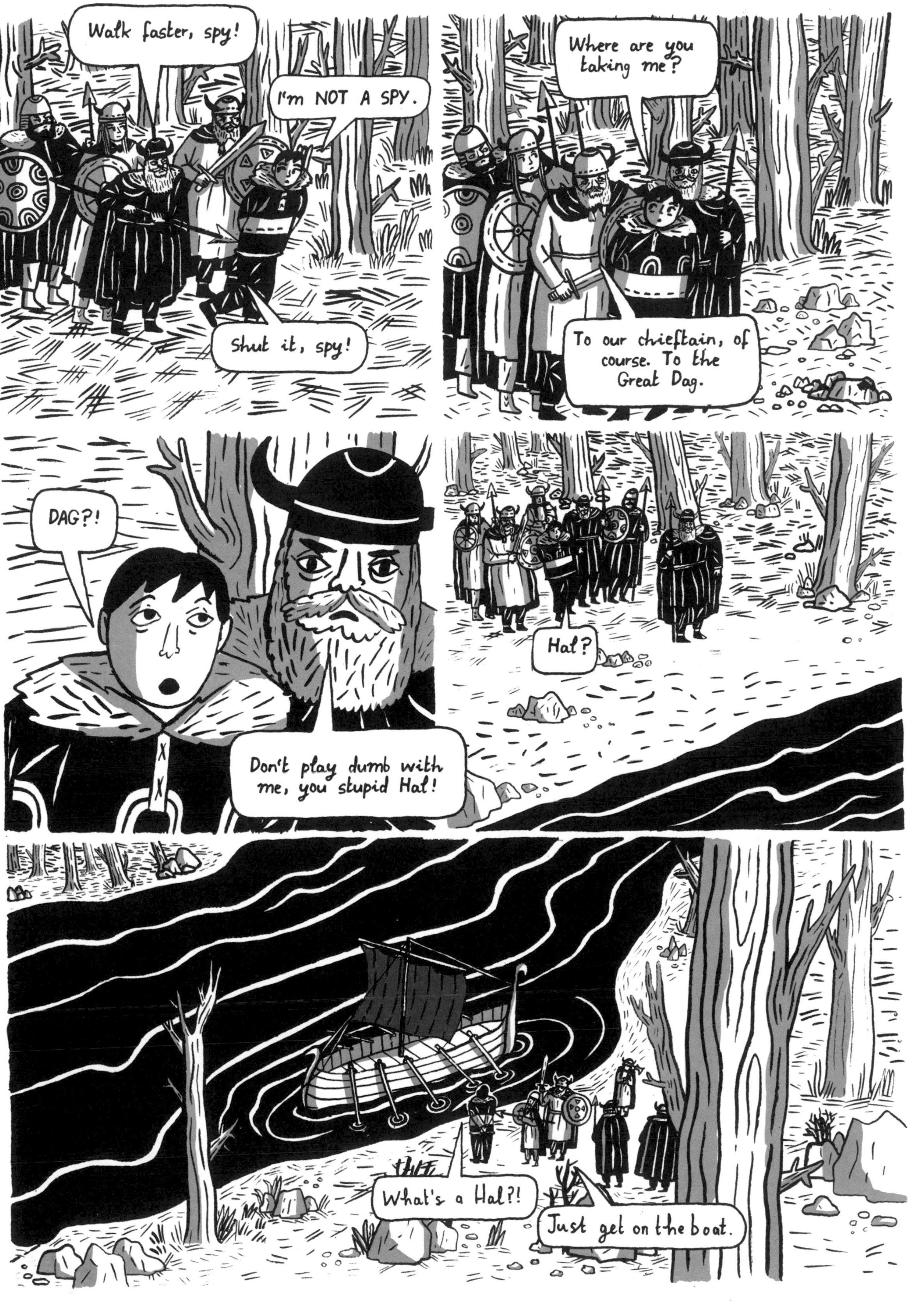
Walk faster, spy!
I'm NOT A SPY.
Shut it, spy!
Where are you taking me?
To our chieftain, of course. To the Great Dag.
DAG?!
Don't play dumb with me, you stupid Hal!
Hal?
What's a Hal?!
Just get on the boat.

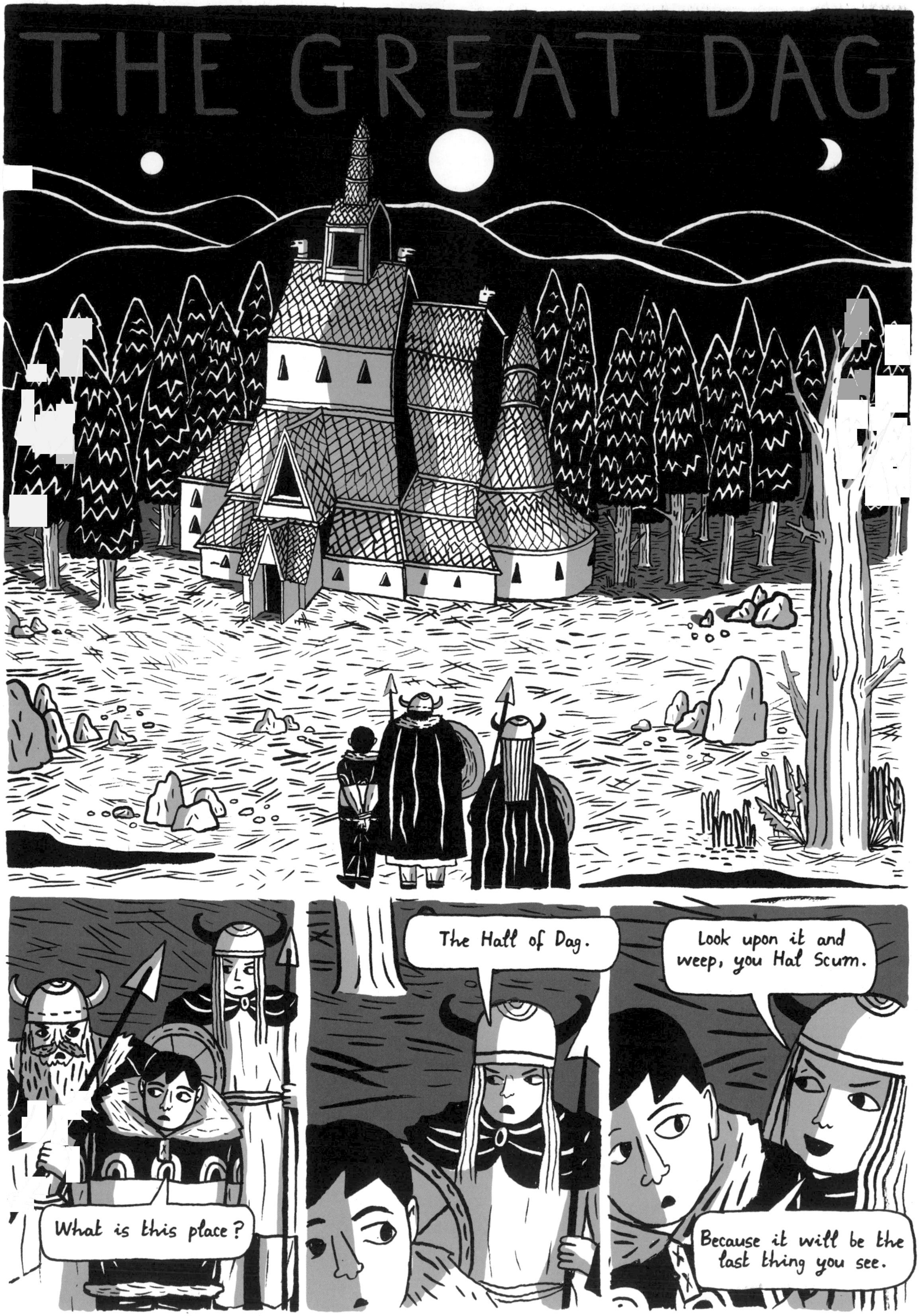
THE GREAT DAG
What is this place?
The Hall of Dag.
Look upon it and weep, you Hal Scum.
Because it will be the last thing you see.

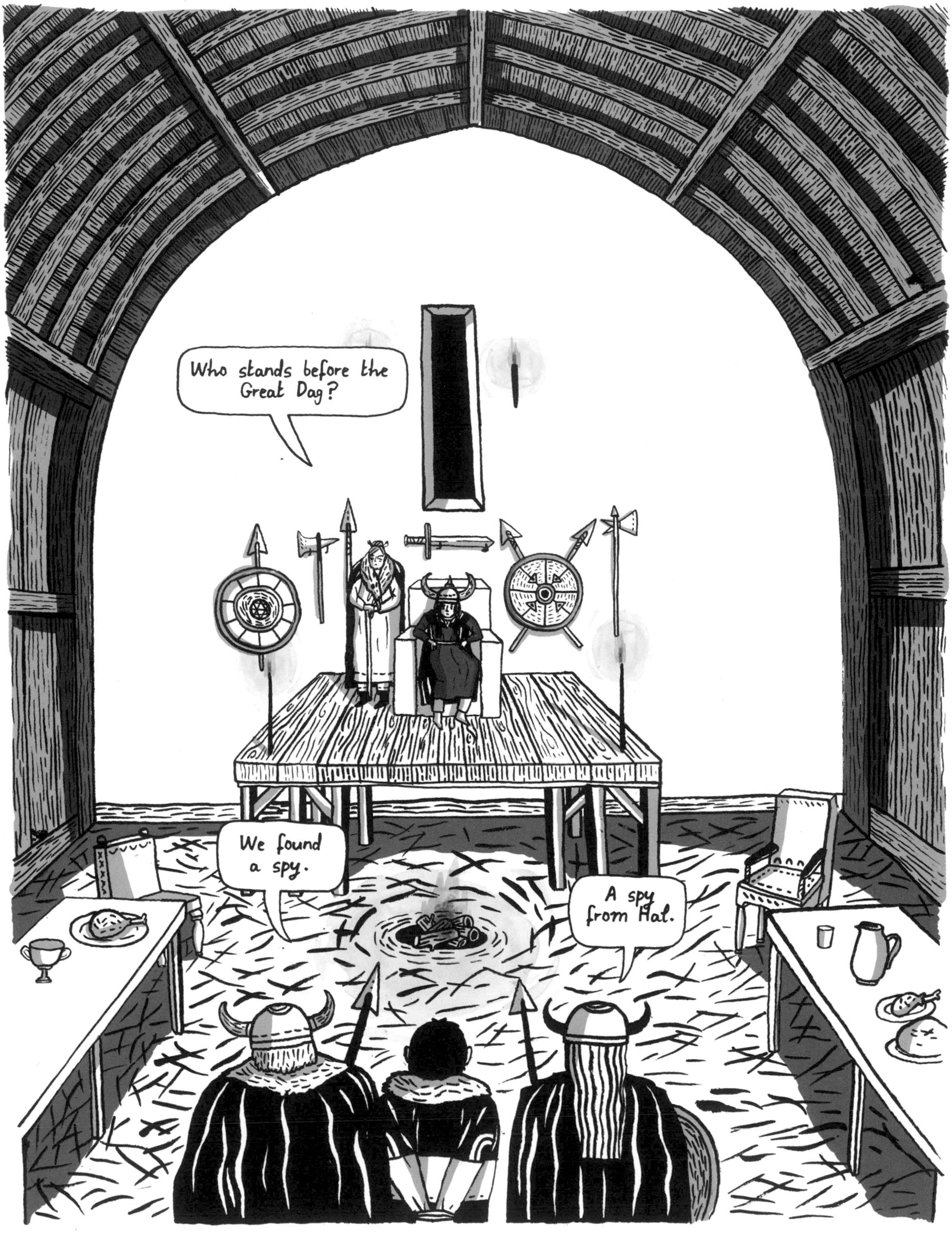
Who stands before the Great Dog?
We found a spy.
A spy from Hal.

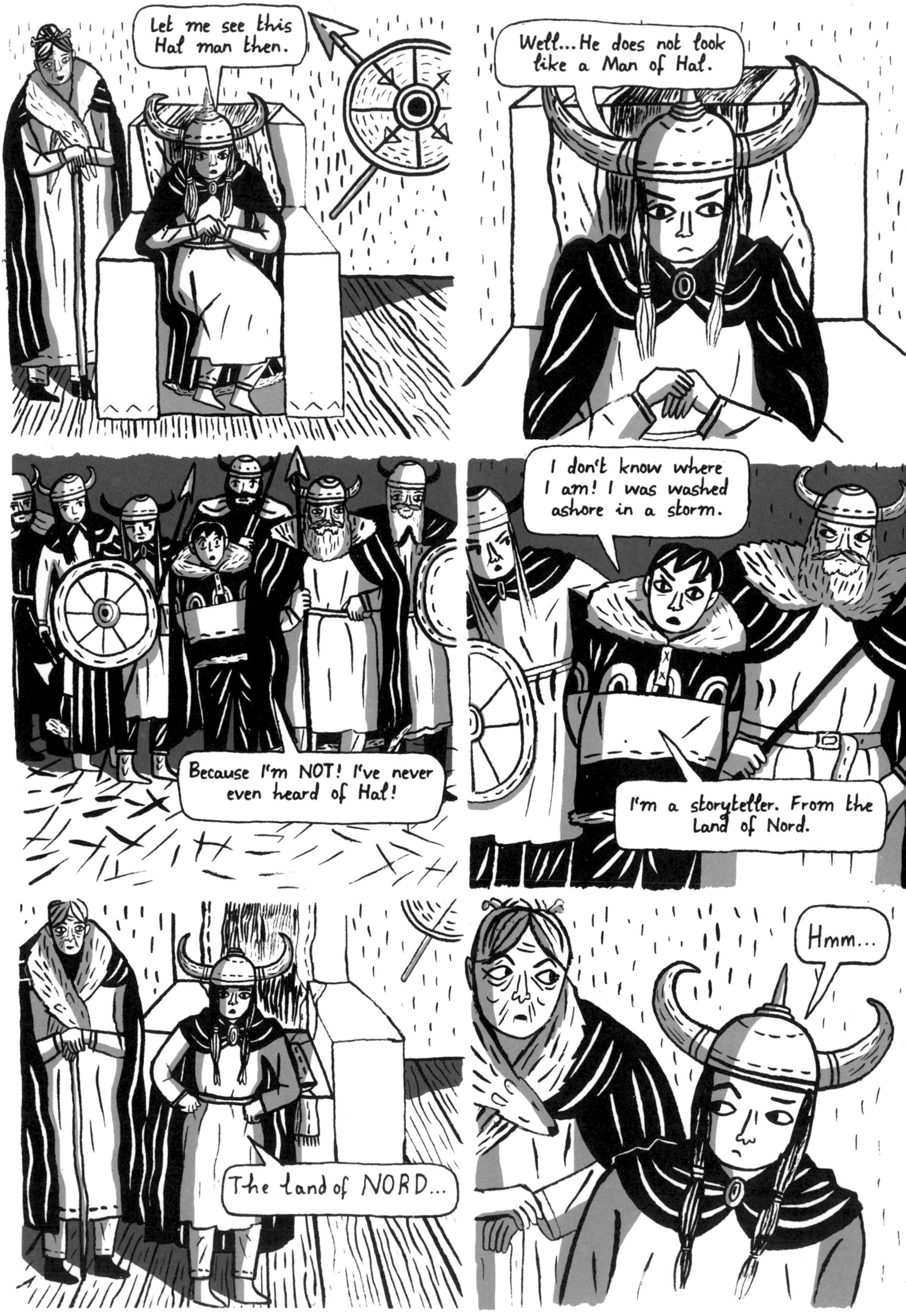
Let me see this Hal man then.
Well... He does not look like a Man of Hal.
Because I'm NOT! I've never even heard of Hal!
I don't know where I am! I was washed ashore in a storm.
I'm a storyteller. From the Land of Nord.
The land of NORD...
Hmm...

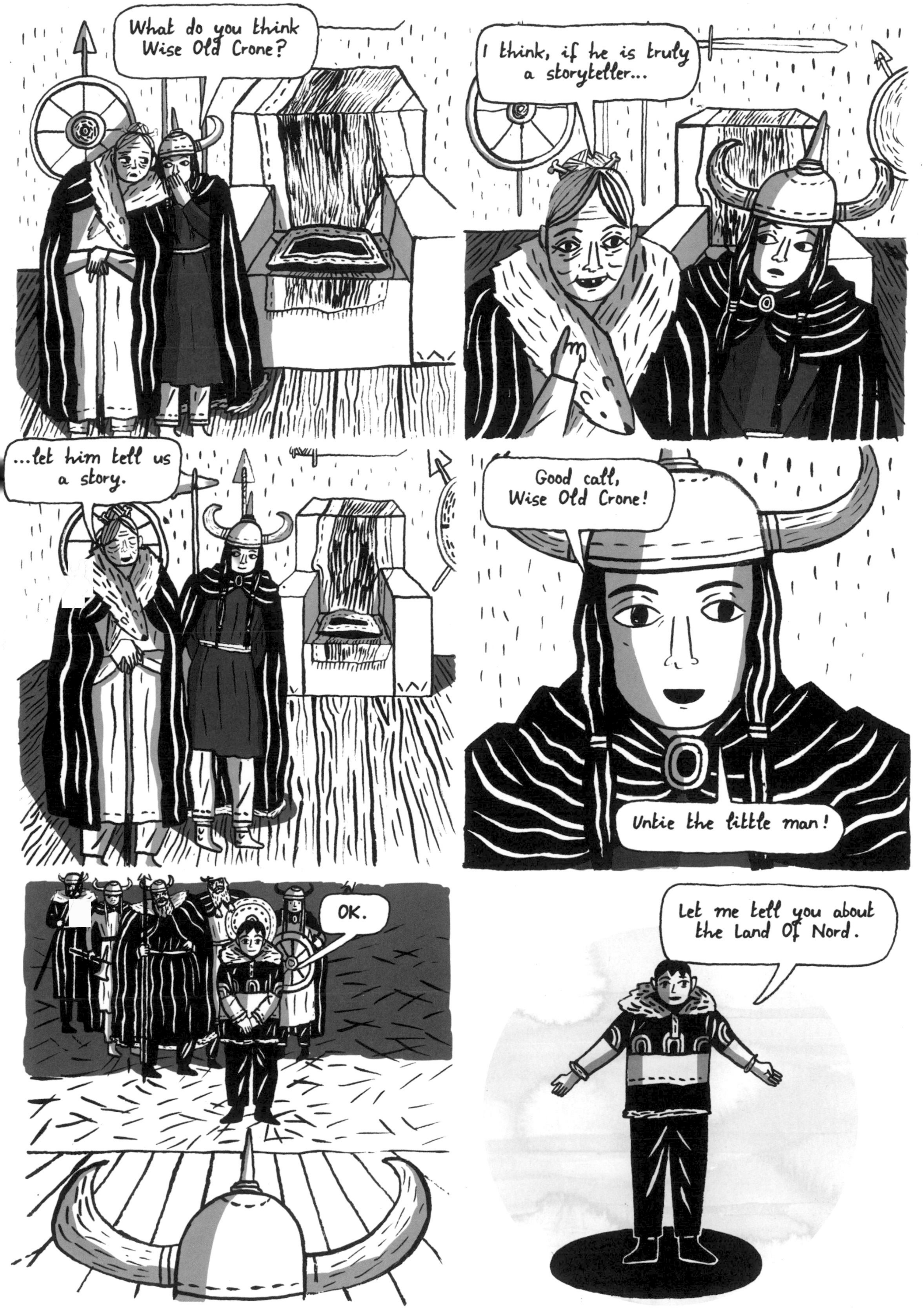
What do you think Wise Old Crone?
I think, if he is truly a storyteller...
...let him tell us a story.
Good call, Wise Old Crone!
Untie the little man!
OK.
Let me tell you about the Land Of Nord.

SUMMER AND

The Land of Nord in Summer is a sight like no other. For three months the sun never sets and the days stretch on and on. The Frozen Sea melts and the glaciers run with cold water and brilliant blue lakes are formed.

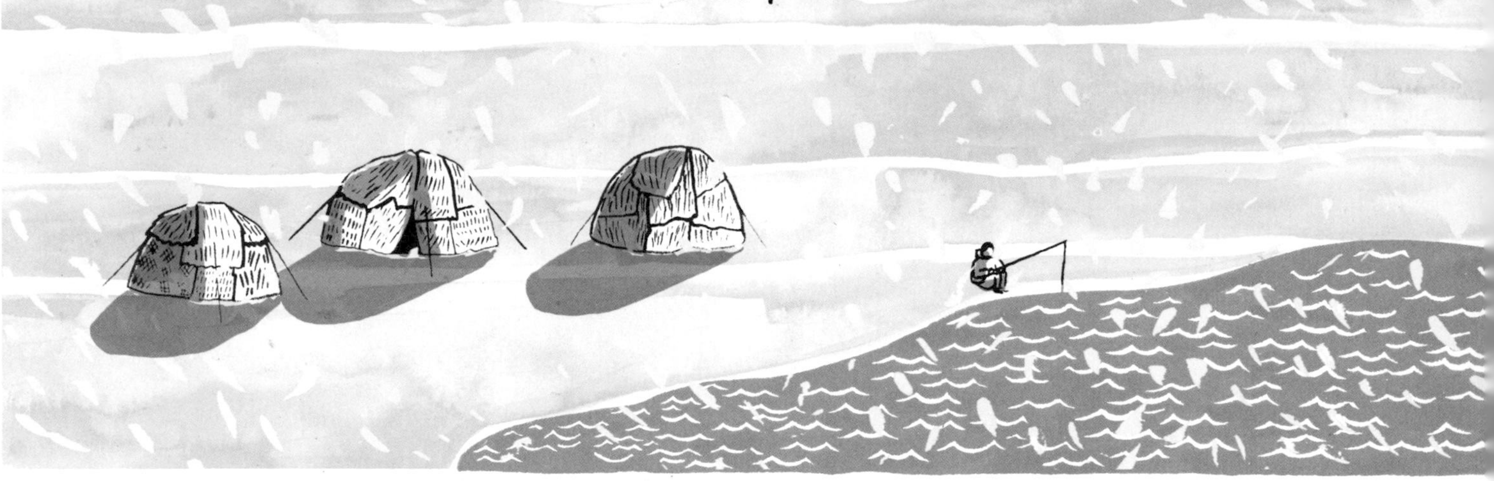

At the treeline the whiteness that has locked down the land is finally broken with green, and for those short, glorious months the people of Nord have plenty.

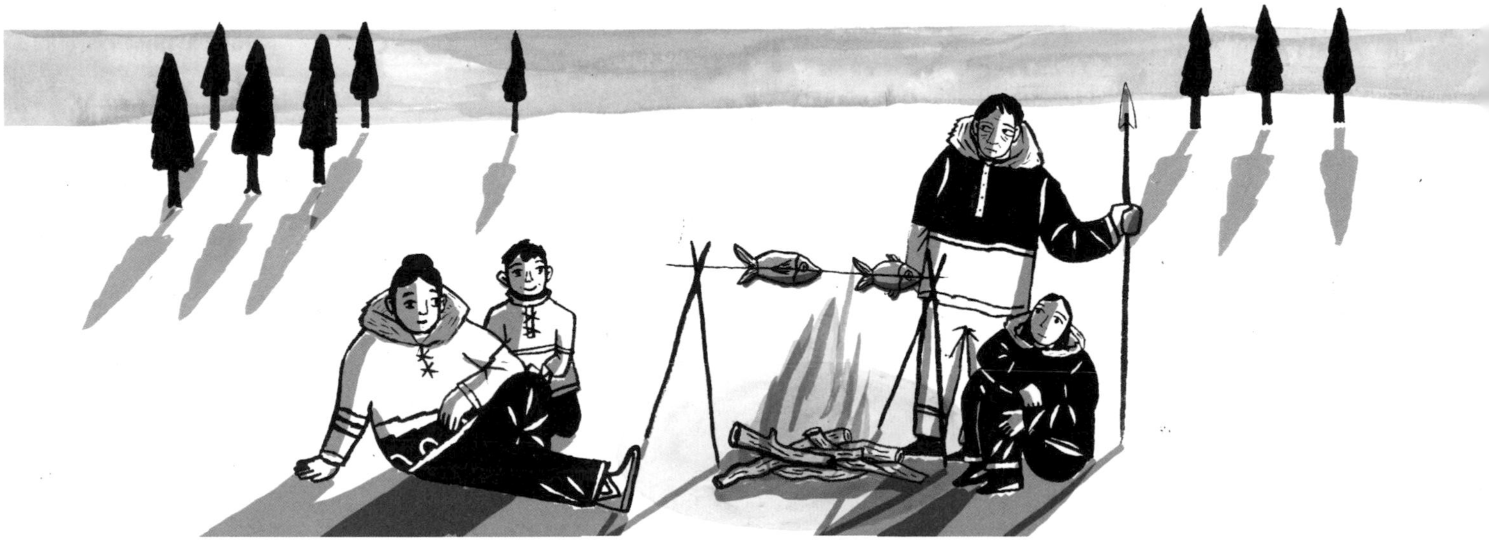

They hunt and fish, they dance and celebrate, clans that have been separated all winter come together marriages are made and children roam for miles across the tundra, playing and running and never being called in for bed.

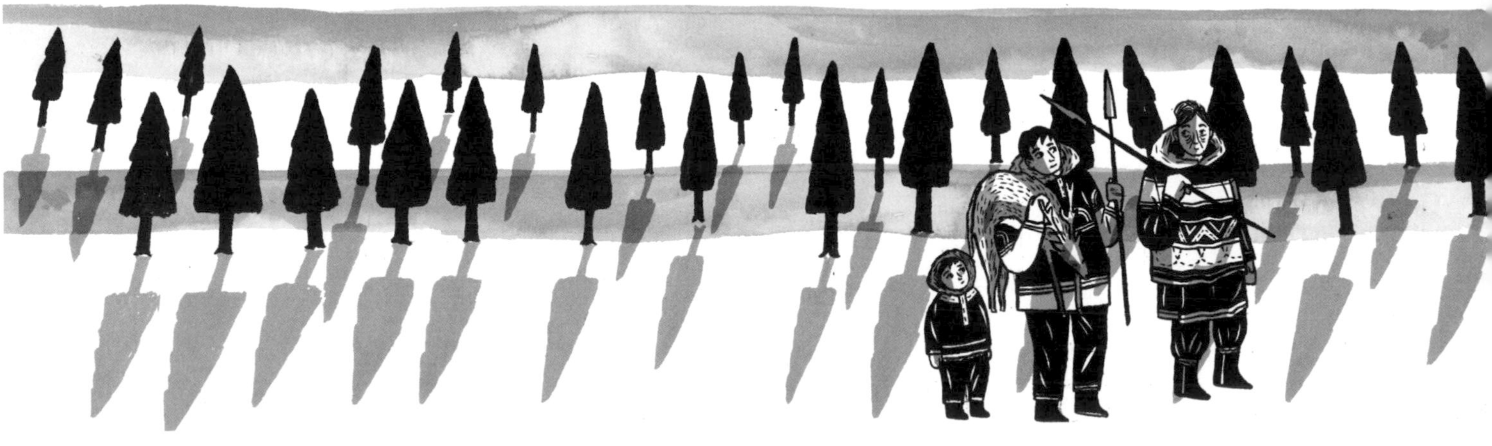

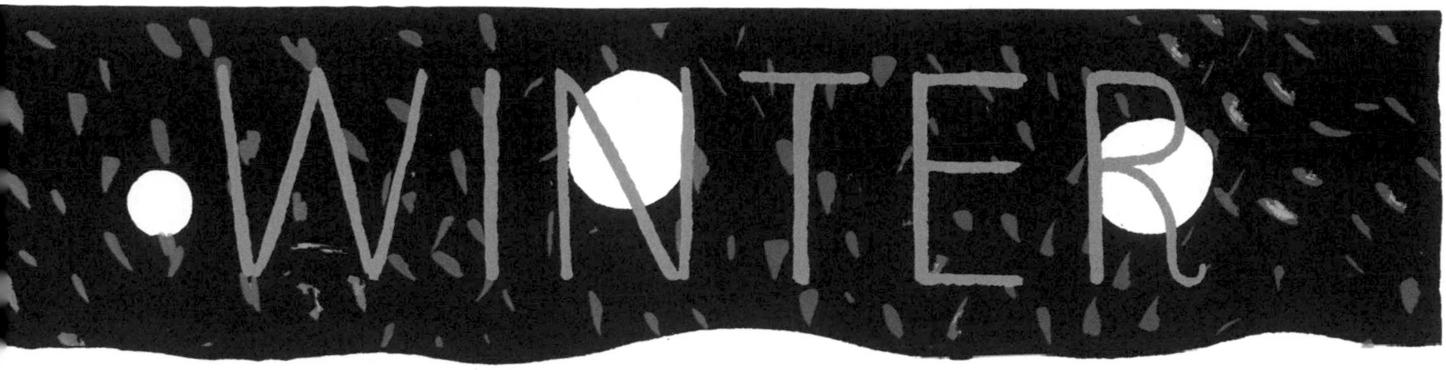
WINTER

But winter is harsh. The sun sets and it does not rise again, and darkness settles down, heavier even than the snow. Held fast in their ice houses and huts, wrapped in fur and pelt and hide, the people of Nord weather the winter as they have always done.

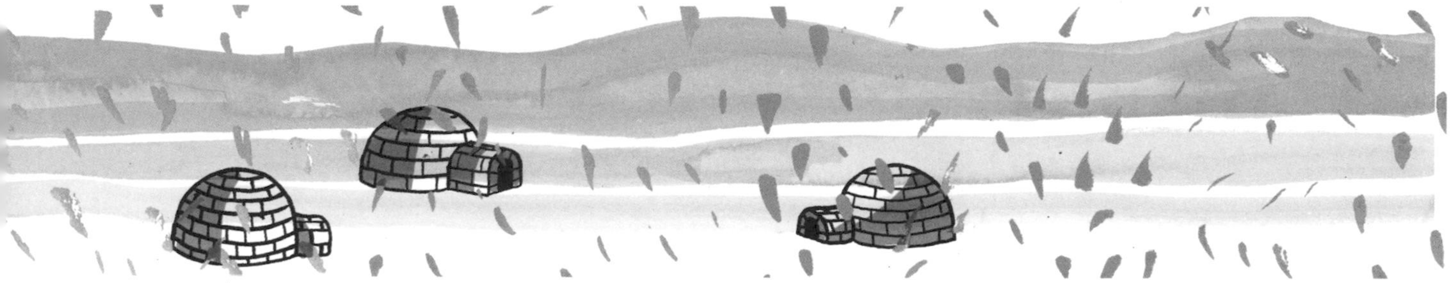

In that deep dark there are other dangers even worse than the fierce winds and the bitter bitter cold. There are packs of hungry wolves and great white bears, there are giant eagles and killer seals and things even darker, things from nightmares; quewls and ice spirits and the fiendish ghosts of men long dead.

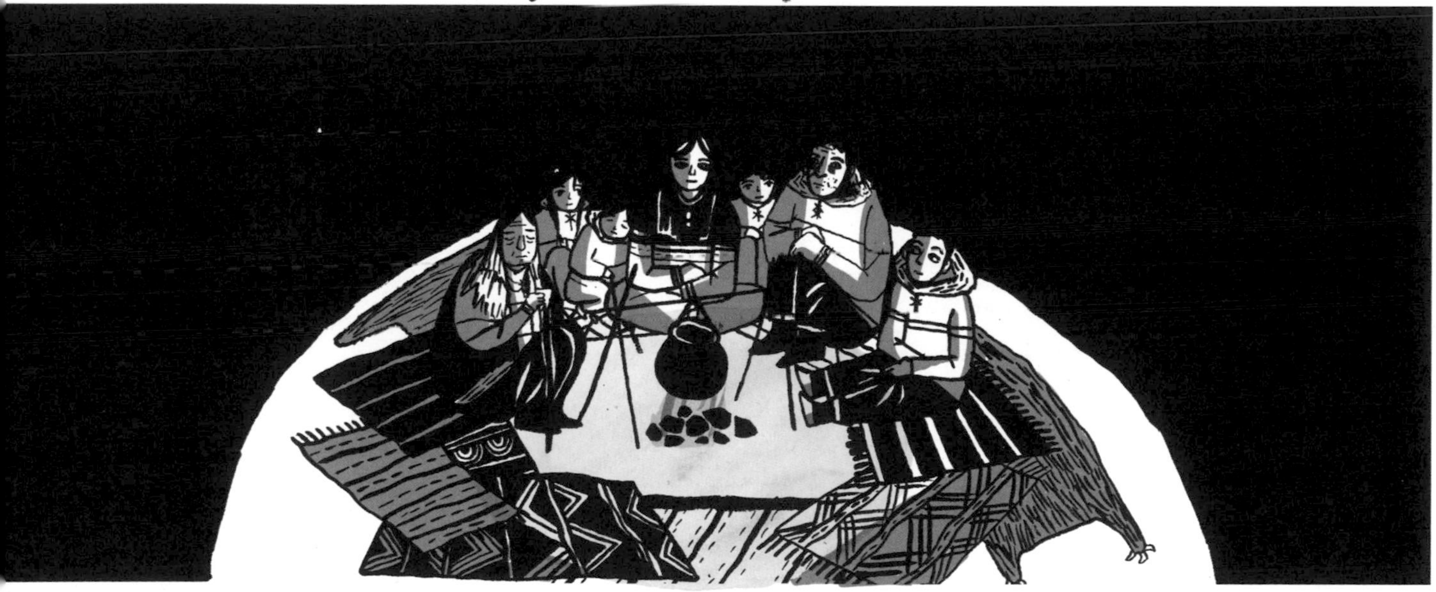

Winter is the time for stories, staying fast by the glow of fire. And outside, in the darkness, the stars are brighter than you can possibly imagine.

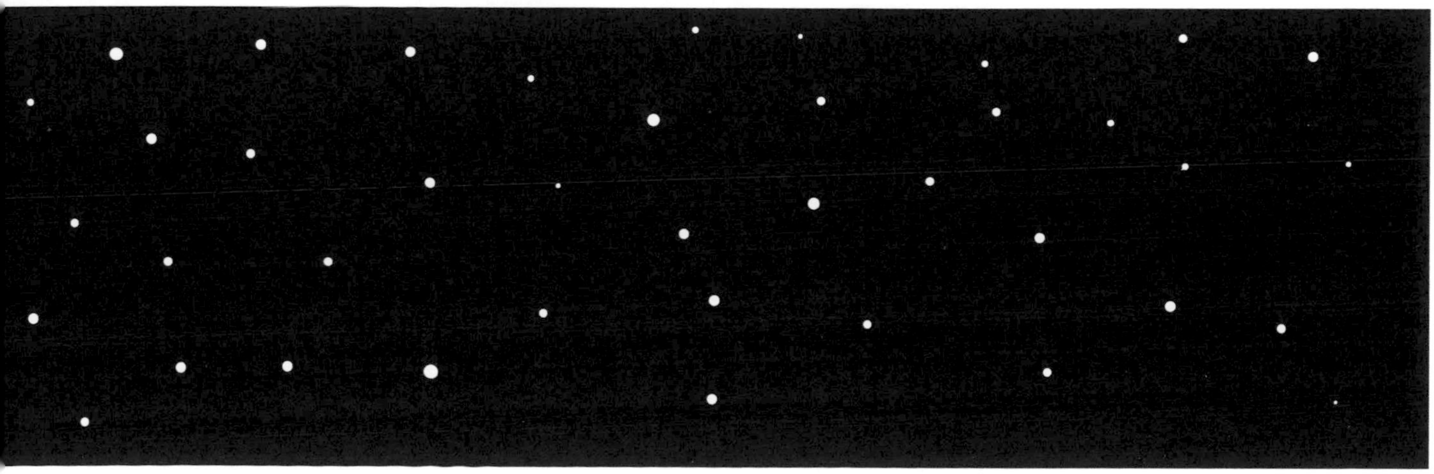

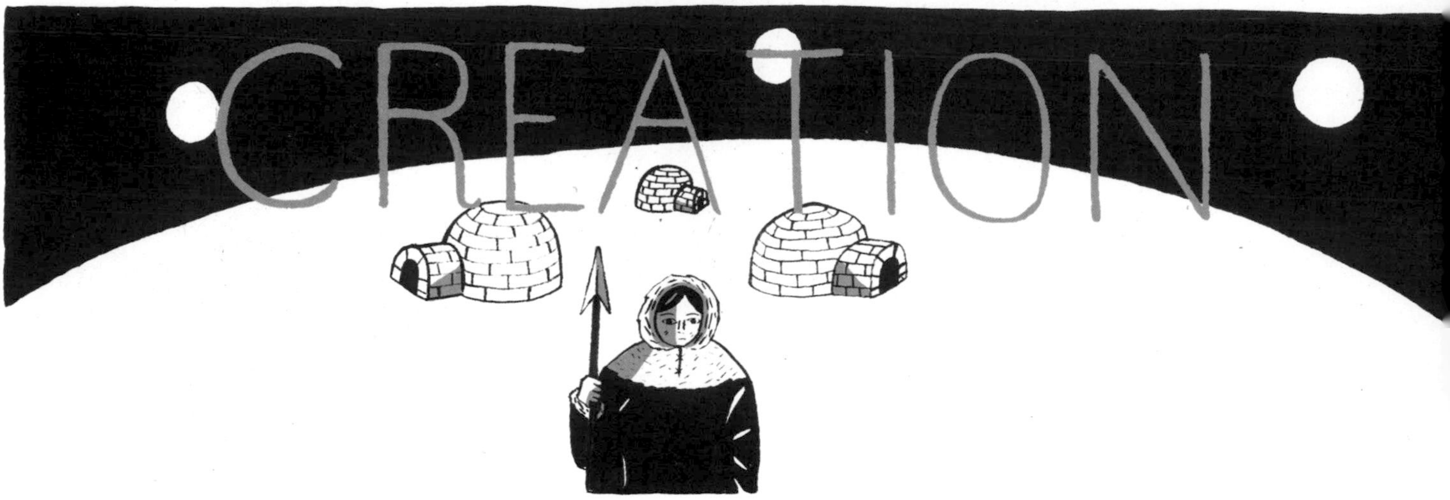
CREATION

The Nords believe that the Universe was created and exists in the mind's eye of the Eagle God BirdMan. Night occurs when the Eagle blinks. The long Nordic winter is when he sleeps.

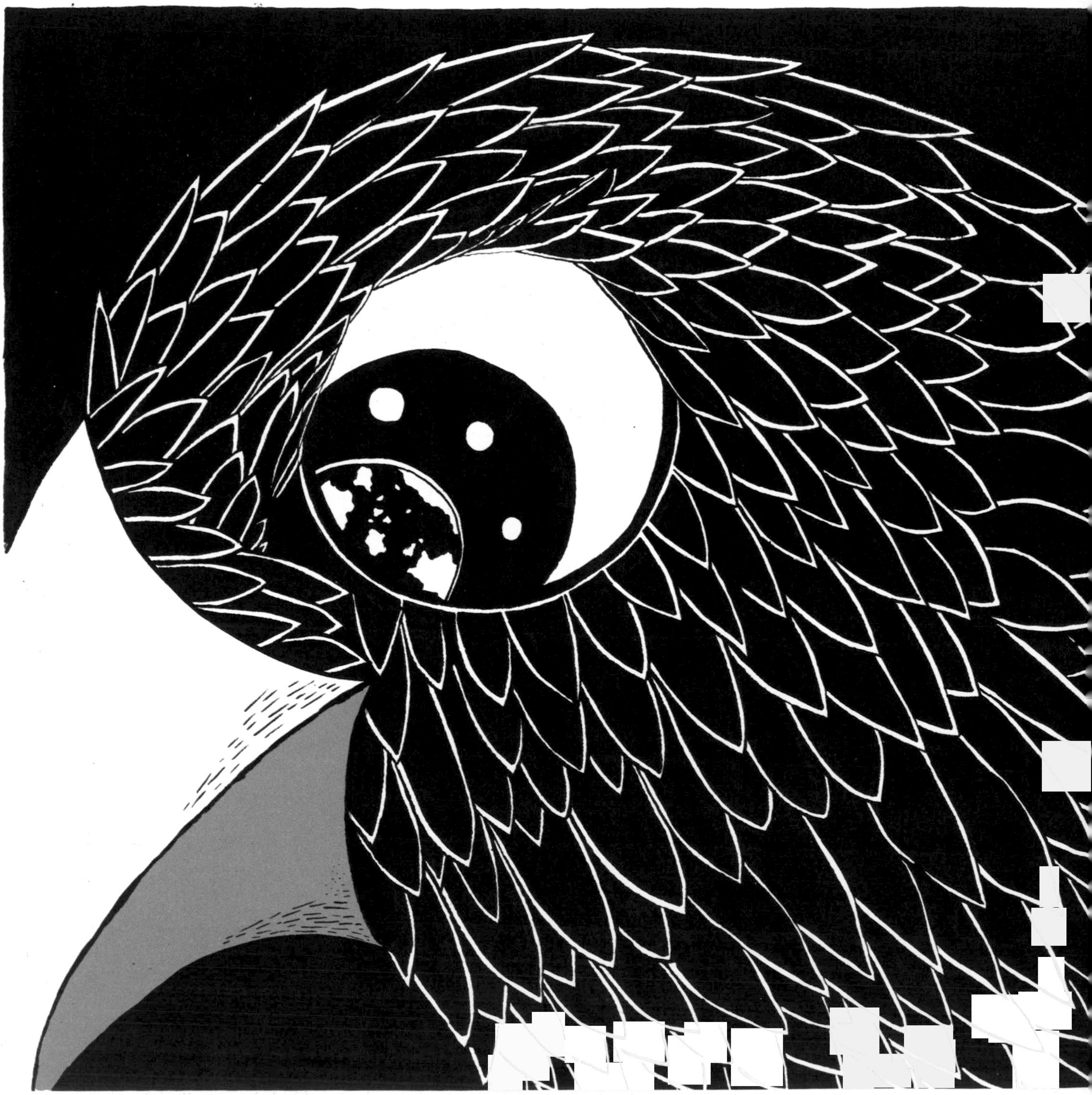

MEDICINE MAN

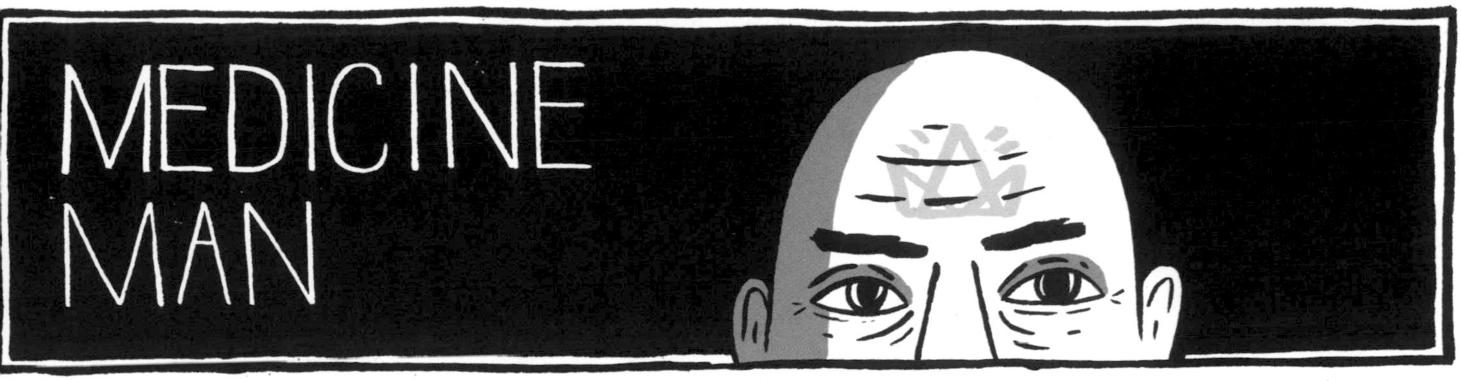

The Medicine Man is the most revered individual in Nord, and is referred to in all matters of importance and for ceremonial and festive days.

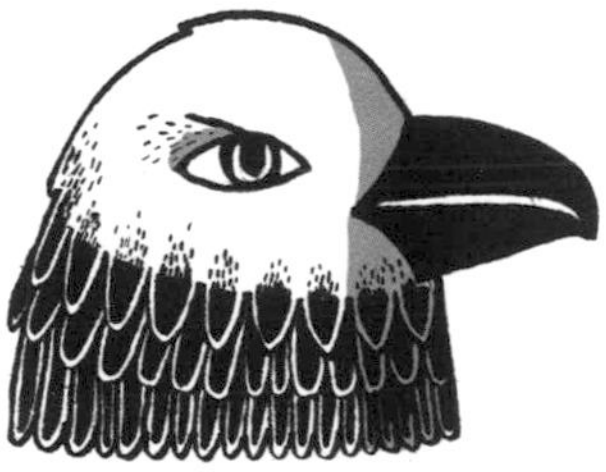

There is only one Medicine Man at any time. He is considered to be the human representative on Earth of BirdMan, the Master of the Universe.

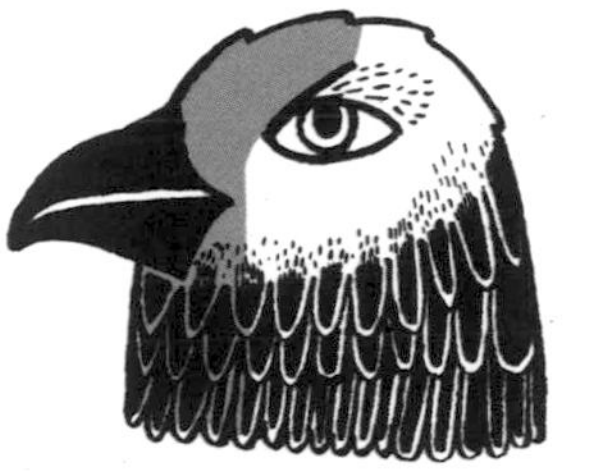

he Medicine Man is recognised astrological means, often as a ry young child, and is trained y the existing Medicine Man, ready to take over.

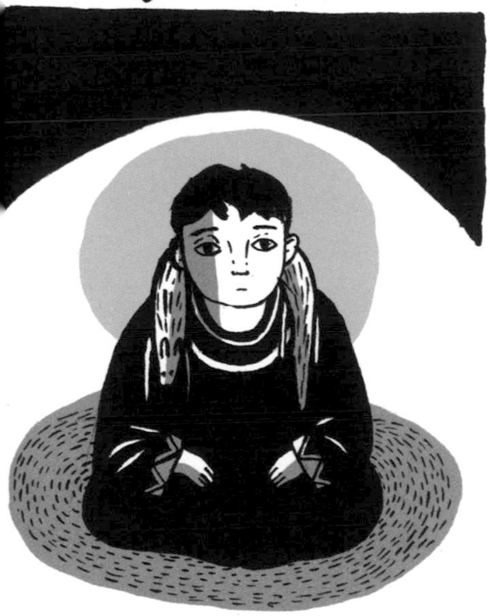

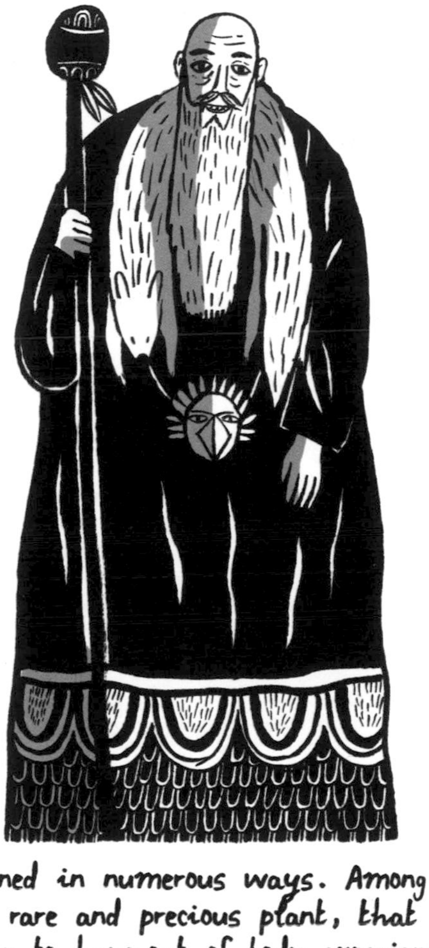

The Eagle God BirdMan is the Master of the Universe and his two children are the Ravens. They are represented by the symbol you see below, painted on the Medicine Man's forehead.

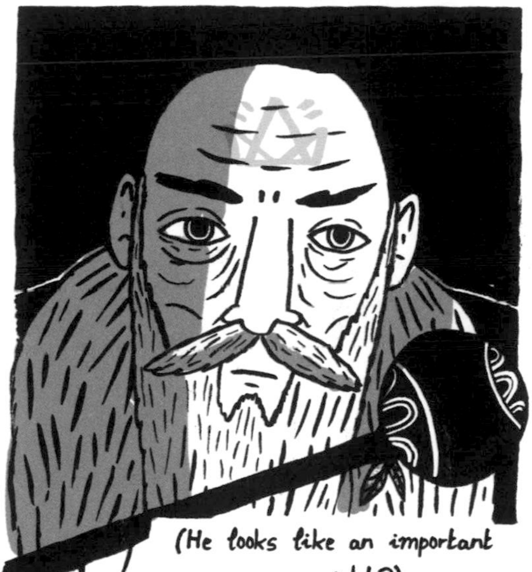

(He looks like an important guy, right?)

Medicine Men are wise and learned in numerous ways. Among other things they know how to prepare Northern Star. This is a rare and precious plant, that when prepared properly causes the user to have out of body experiences.

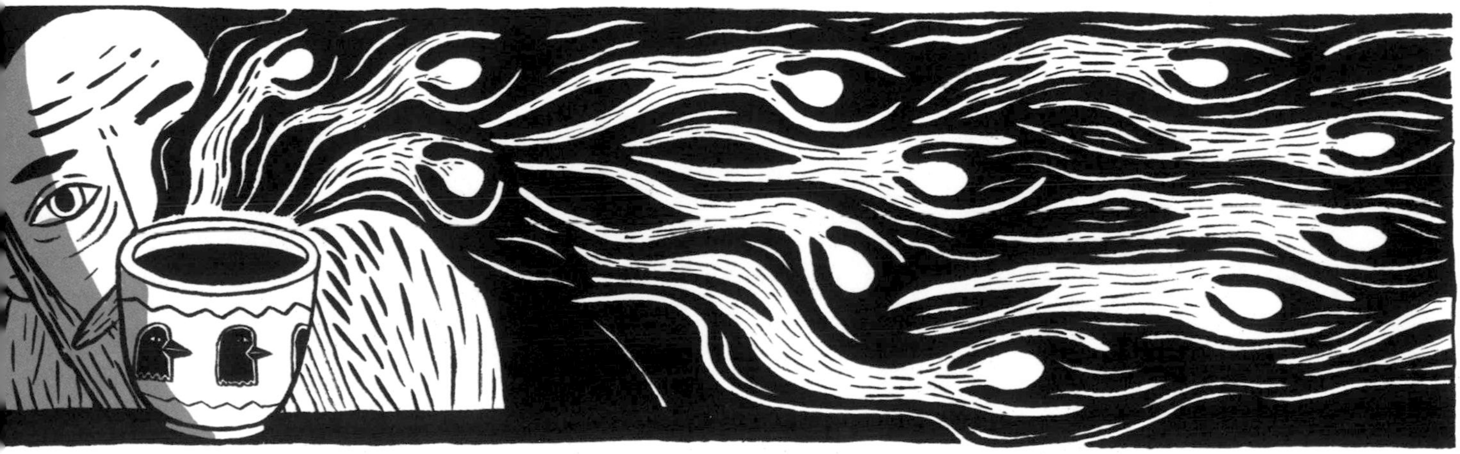

THE STORYTELLERS

Storytelling is one of the most important pastimes in Nord. Every clan has at least one storyteller, and every summer they criss-cross the land, swapping stories to tell through the long winter.

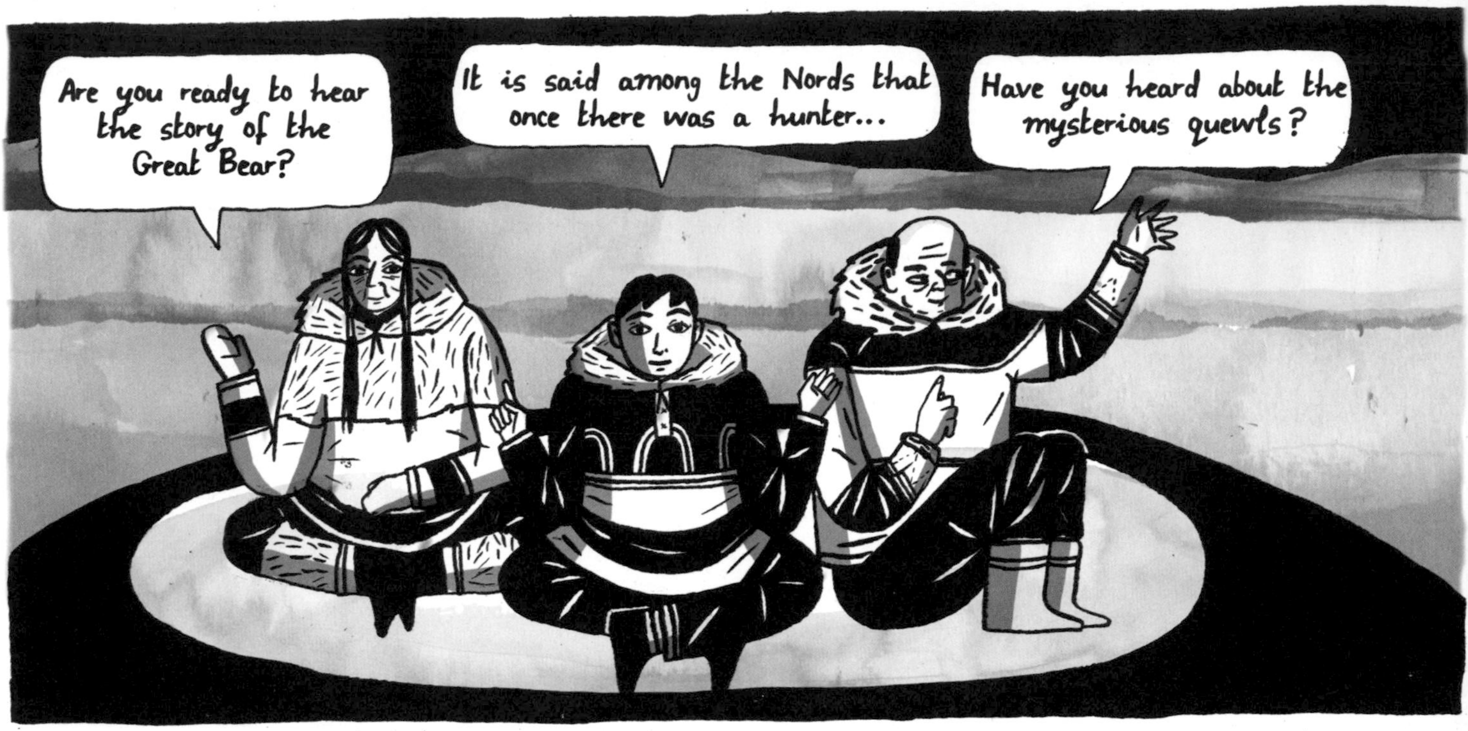
Are you ready to hear the story of the Great Bear?
It is said among the Nords that once there was a hunter...
Have you heard about the mysterious quewls?

The arrival of a storyteller is an extremely exciting event for a clan.

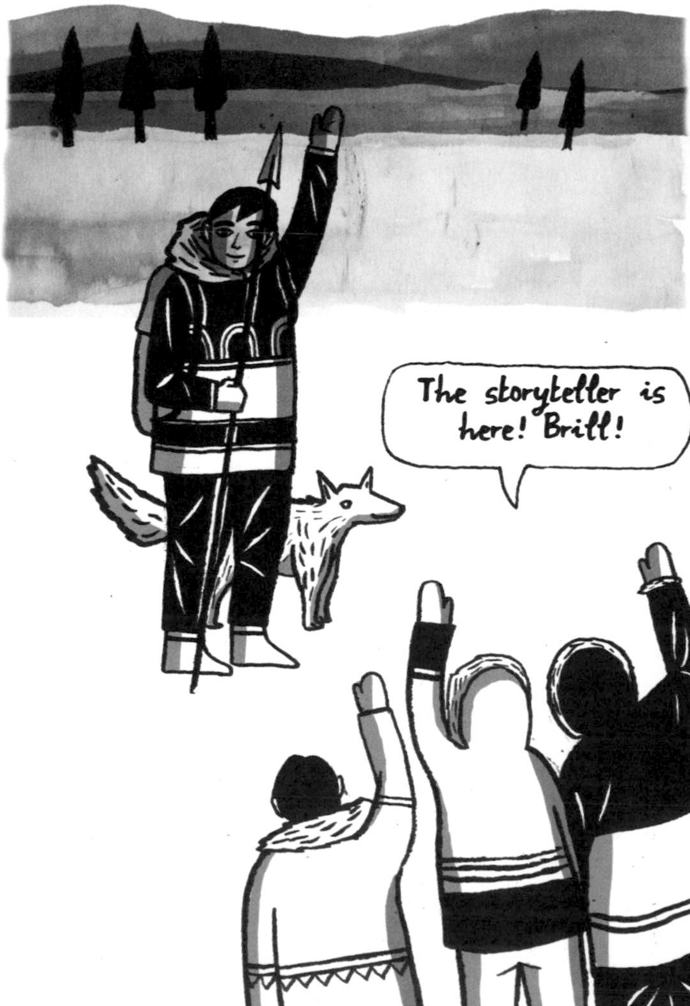
The storyteller is here! Brill!

Often villages and families would come together for the sole purpose of hearing the storytellers.

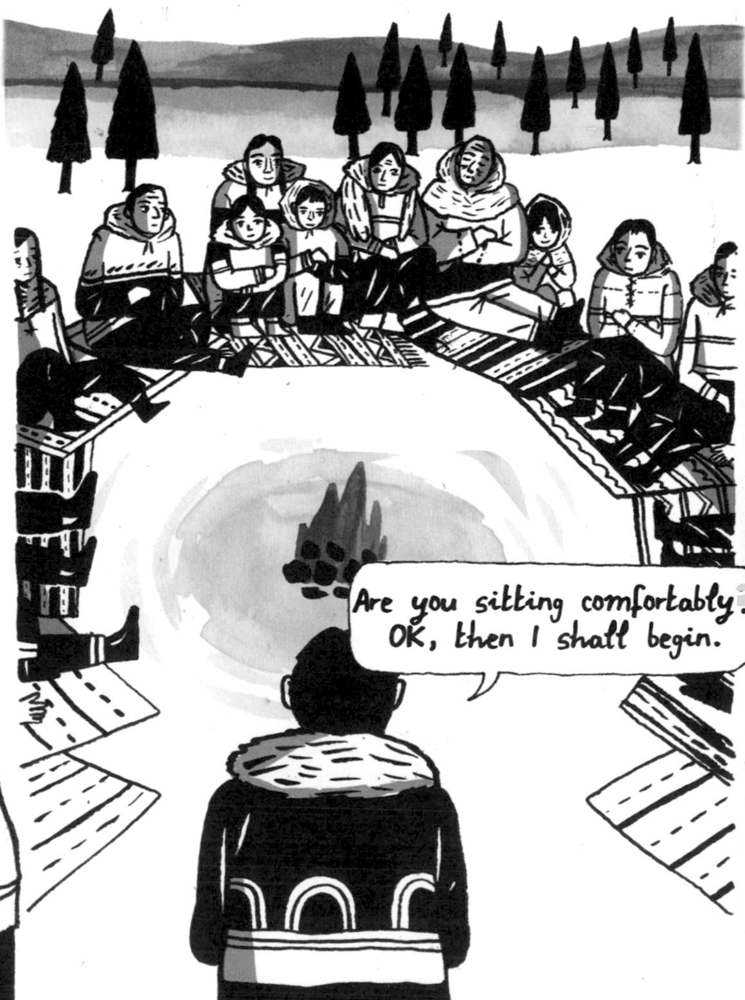
Are you sitting comfortably? OK, then I shall begin.

While the Medicine Man passes down the secrets of the snow and translates the whispers of the aurora, it is the storytellers who keep the legends of Nord alive.

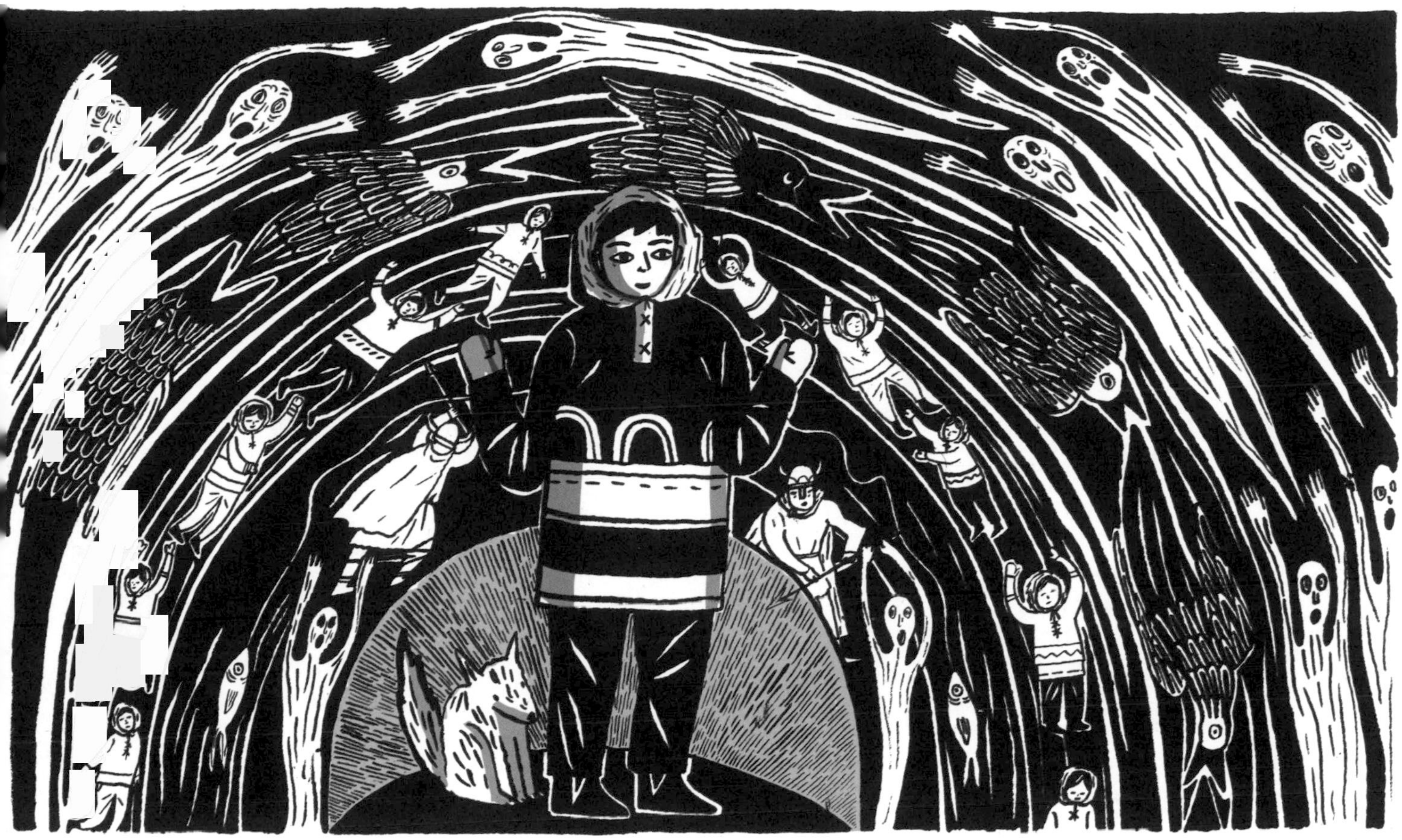

The best storytellers know all the old tales.

But also they can tell new ones...

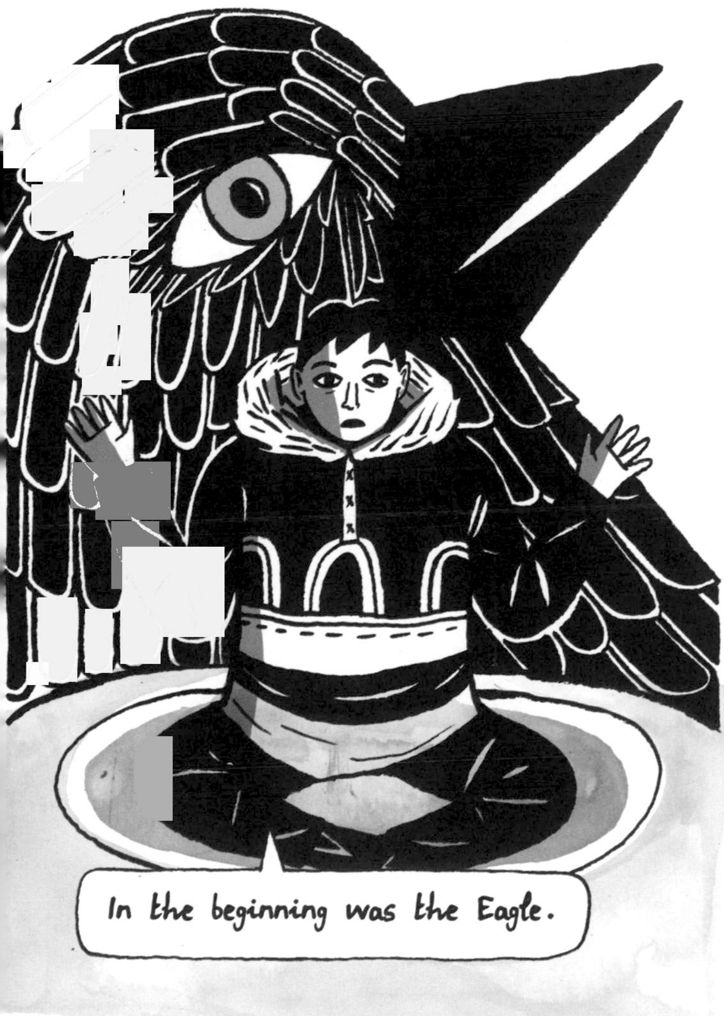
In the beginning was the Eagle.

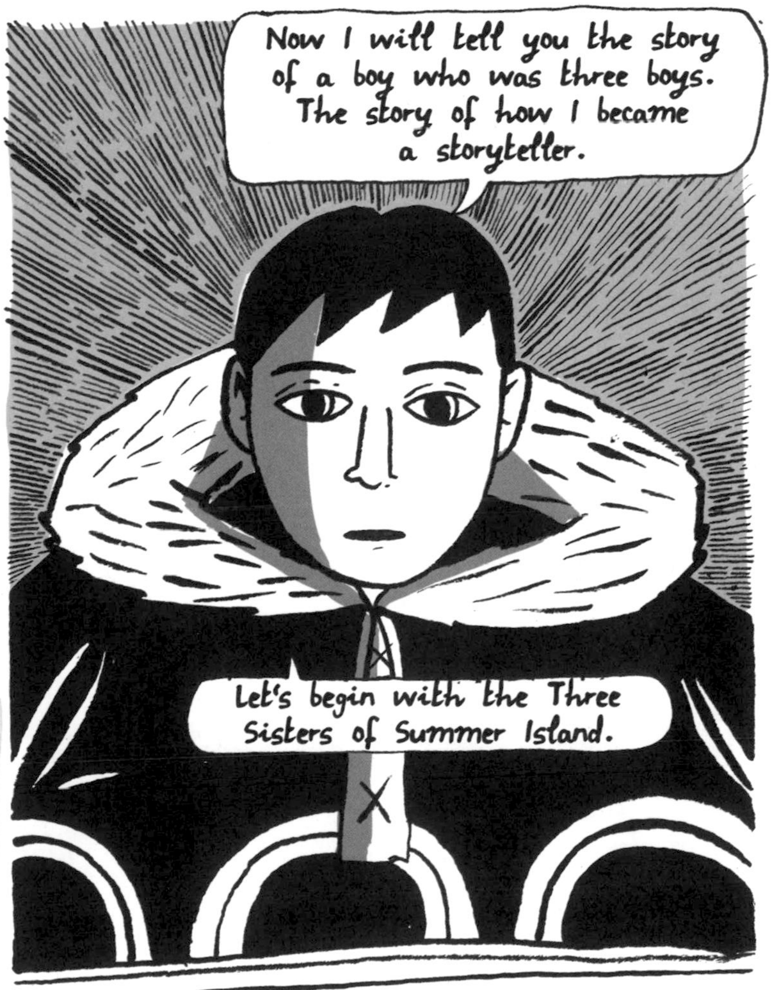
Now I will tell you the story of a boy who was three boys. The story of how I became a storyteller.
Let's begin with the Three Sisters of Summer Island.

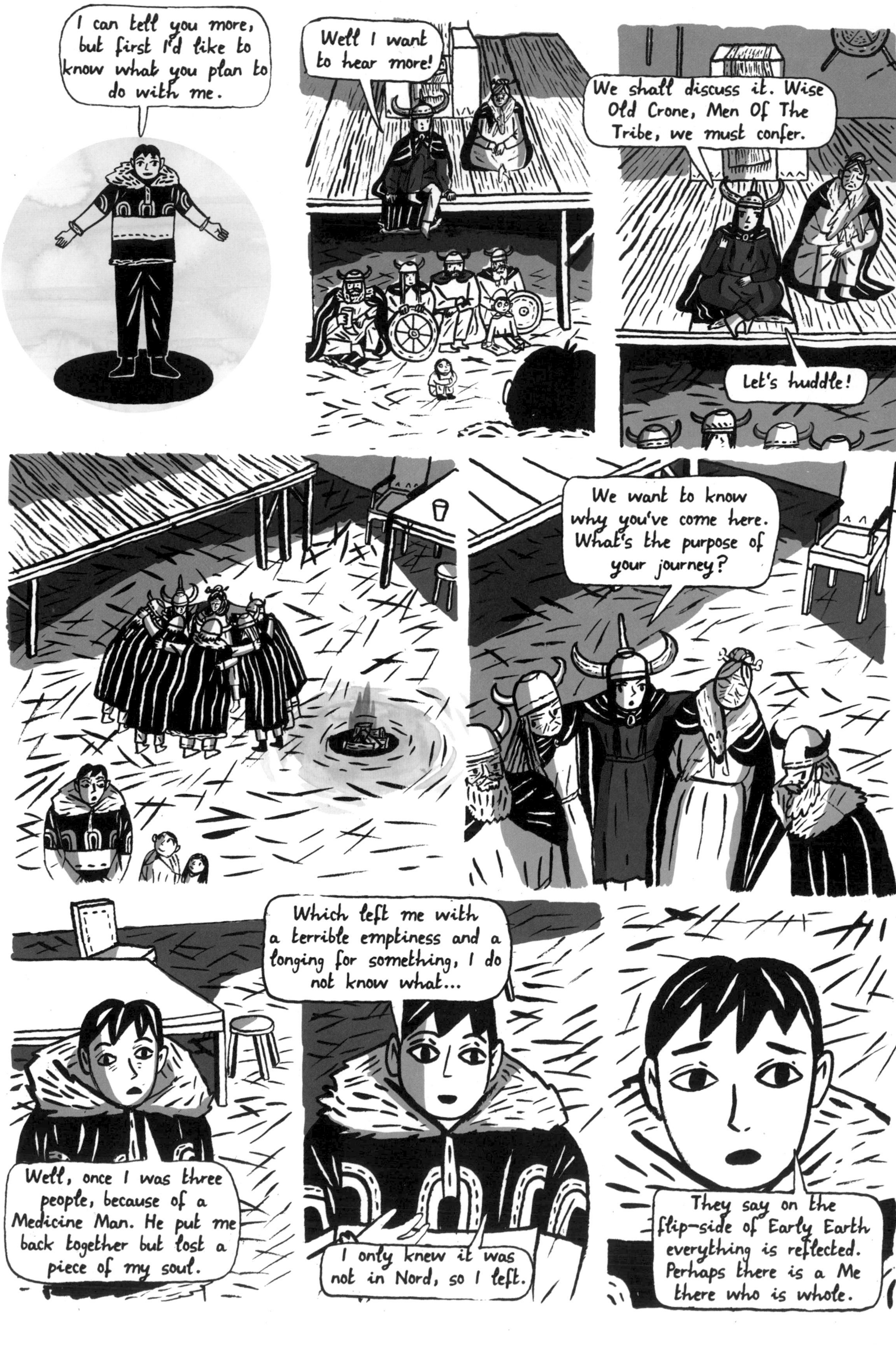
I can tell you more, but first I'd like to know what you plan to do with me.
Well I want to hear more!
We shall discuss it. Wise Old Crone, Men Of The Tribe, we must confer.
Let's huddle!
We want to know why you've come here. What's the purpose of your journey?
Well, once I was three people, because of a Medicine Man. He put me back together but lost a piece of my soul.
Which left me with a terrible emptiness and a longing for something, I do not know what...
I only knew it was not in Nord, so I left.
They say on the flip-side of Early Earth everything is reflected. Perhaps there is a Me there who is whole.

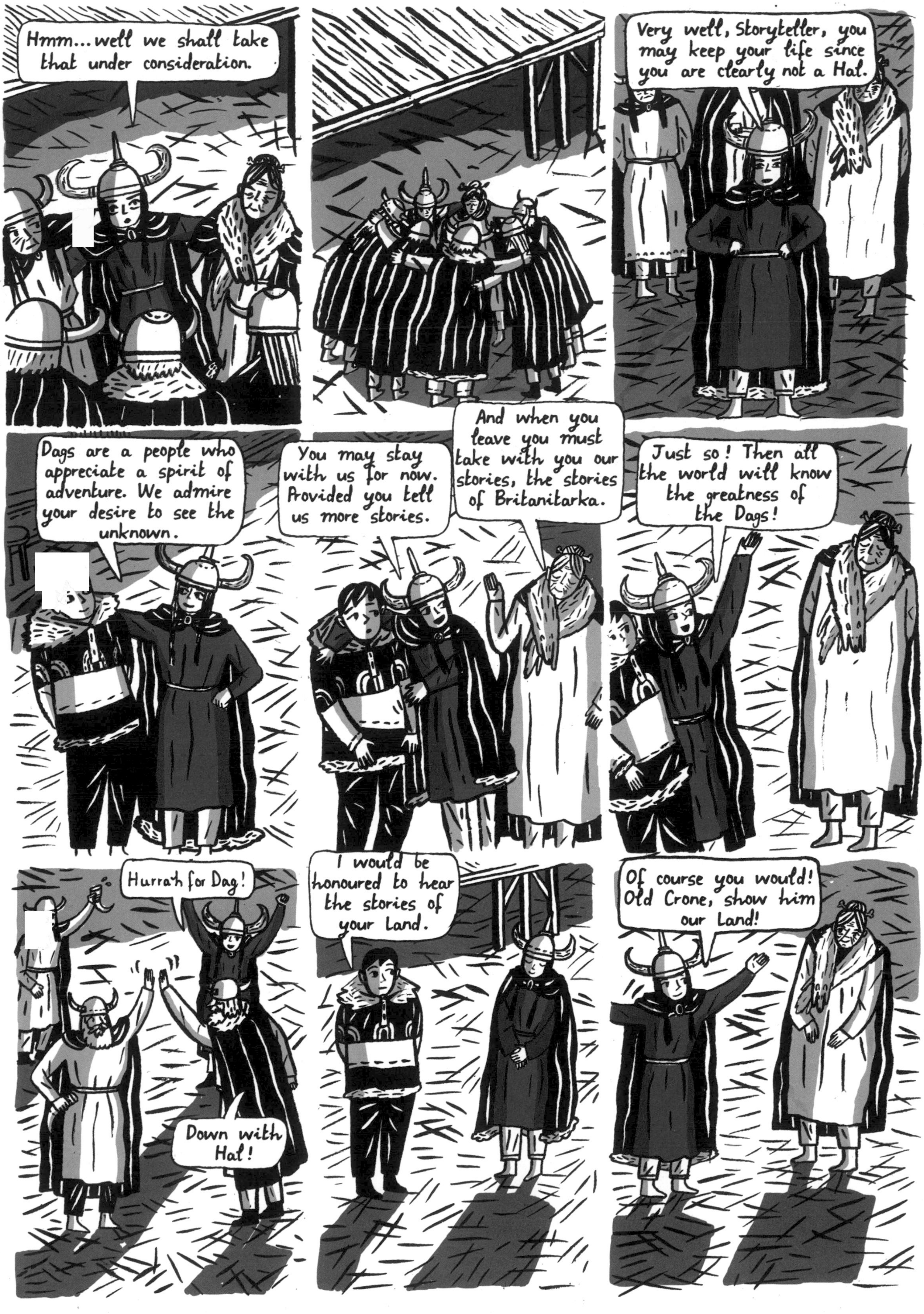
Hmm... well we shall take that under consideration.
Very well, Storyteller, you may keep your life since you are clearly not a Hal.
Dags are a people who appreciate a spirit of adventure. We admire your desire to see the unknown.
You may stay with us for now. Provided you tell us more stories.
And when you leave you must take with you our stories, the stories of Britanitarka.
Just so! Then all the world will know the greatness of the Dags!
Hurrah for Dag!
Down with Hal!
I would be honoured to hear the stories of your Land.
Of course you would! Old Crone, show him our Land!

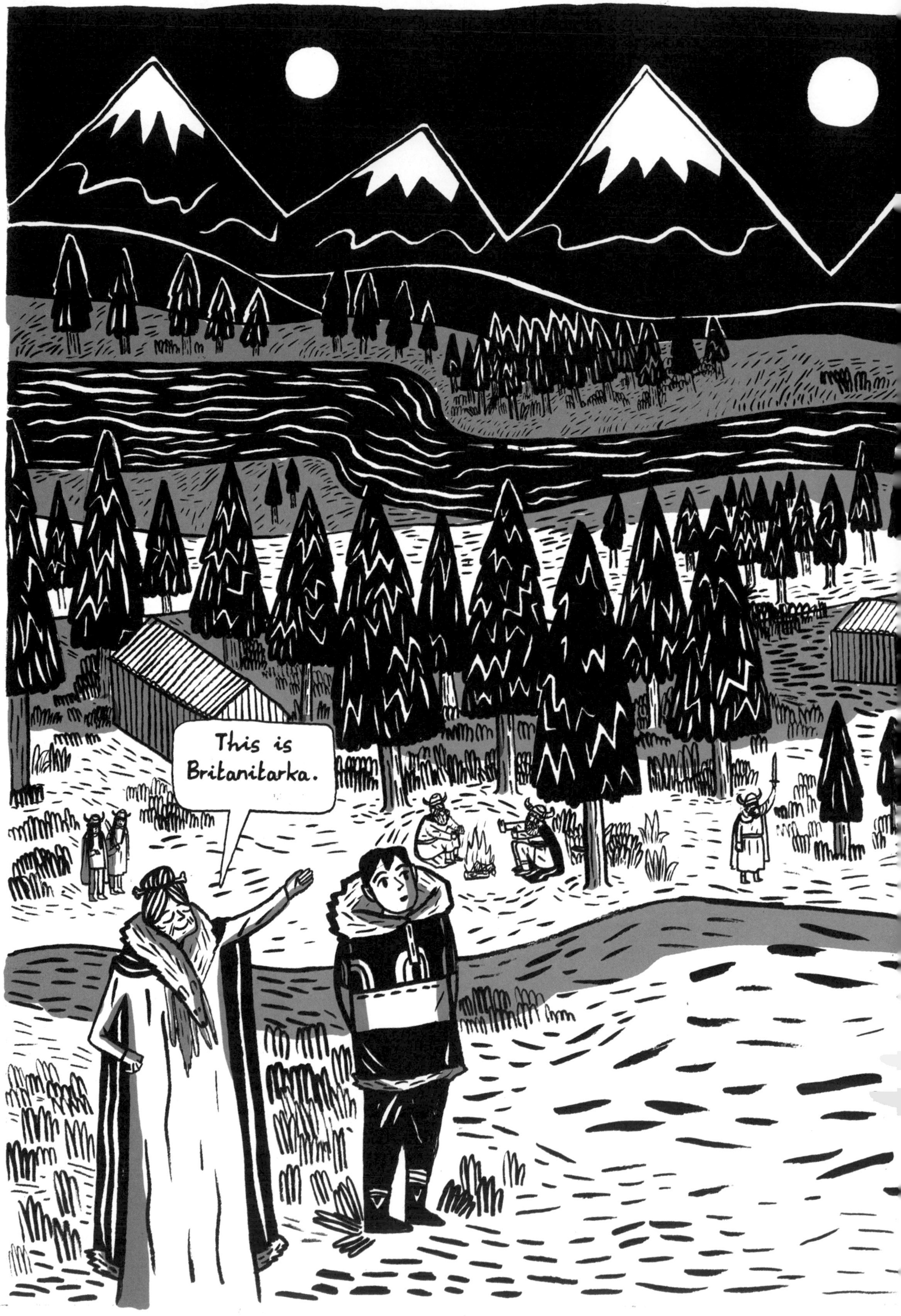
This is Britanitarka.

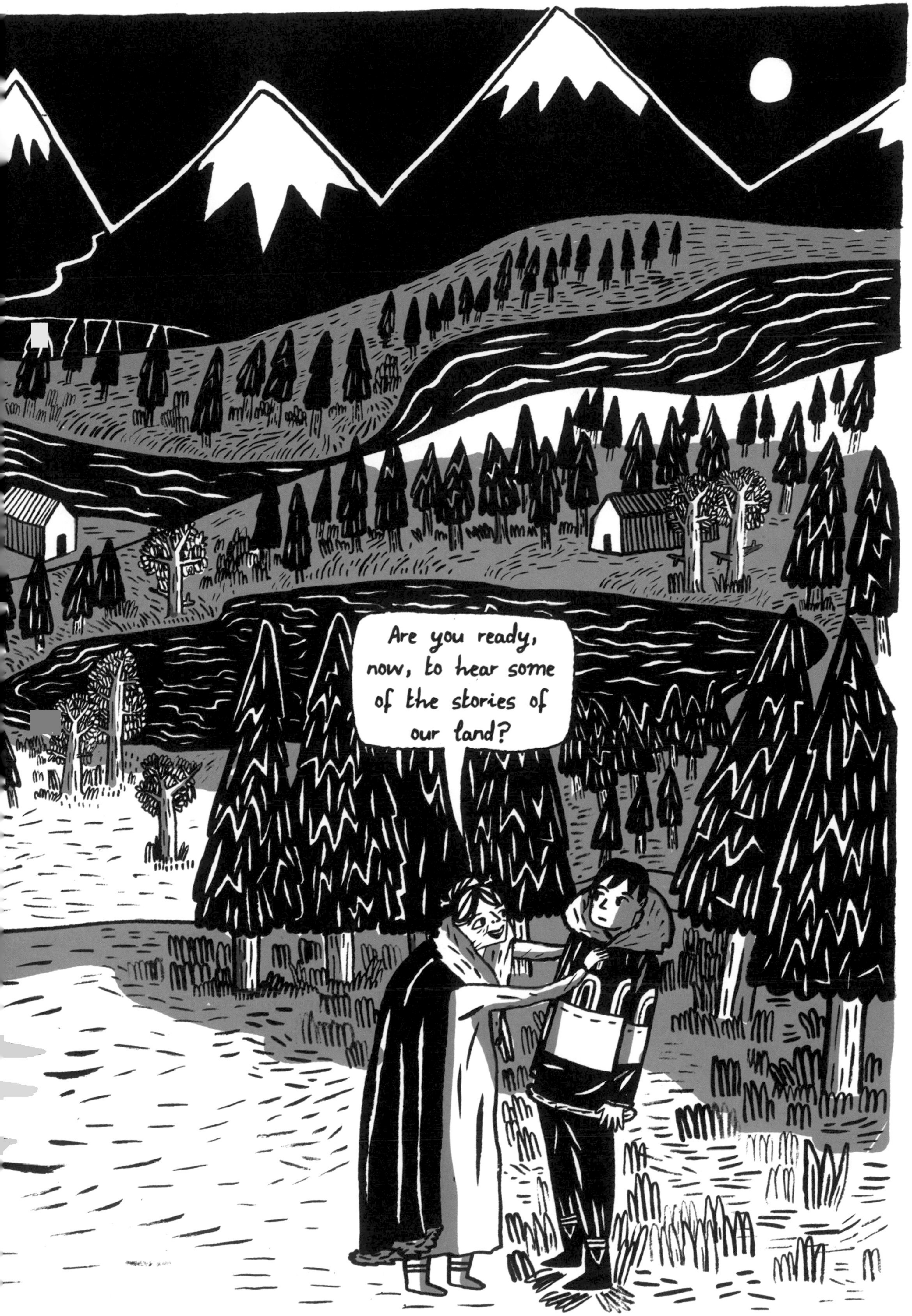
Are you ready, now, to hear some of the stories of our land?

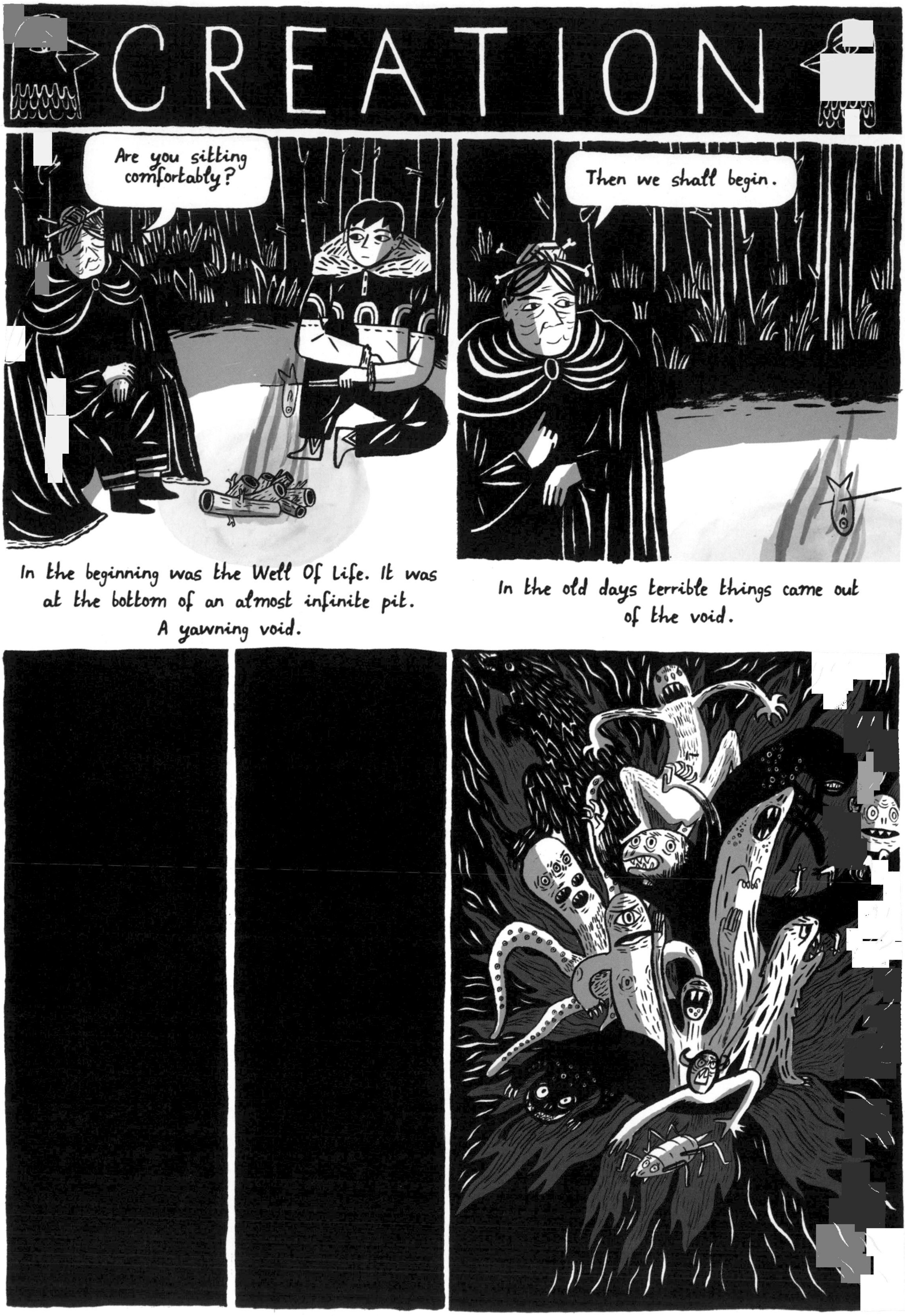
CREATION
Are you sitting comfortably?
Then we shall begin.
In the beginning was the Well Of Life. It was at the bottom of an almost infinite pit. A yawning void.
In the old days terrible things came out of the void.

But the God BirdMan and his children the Ravens forced the dark creatures back into the pit. And then they covered it with ice and snow.

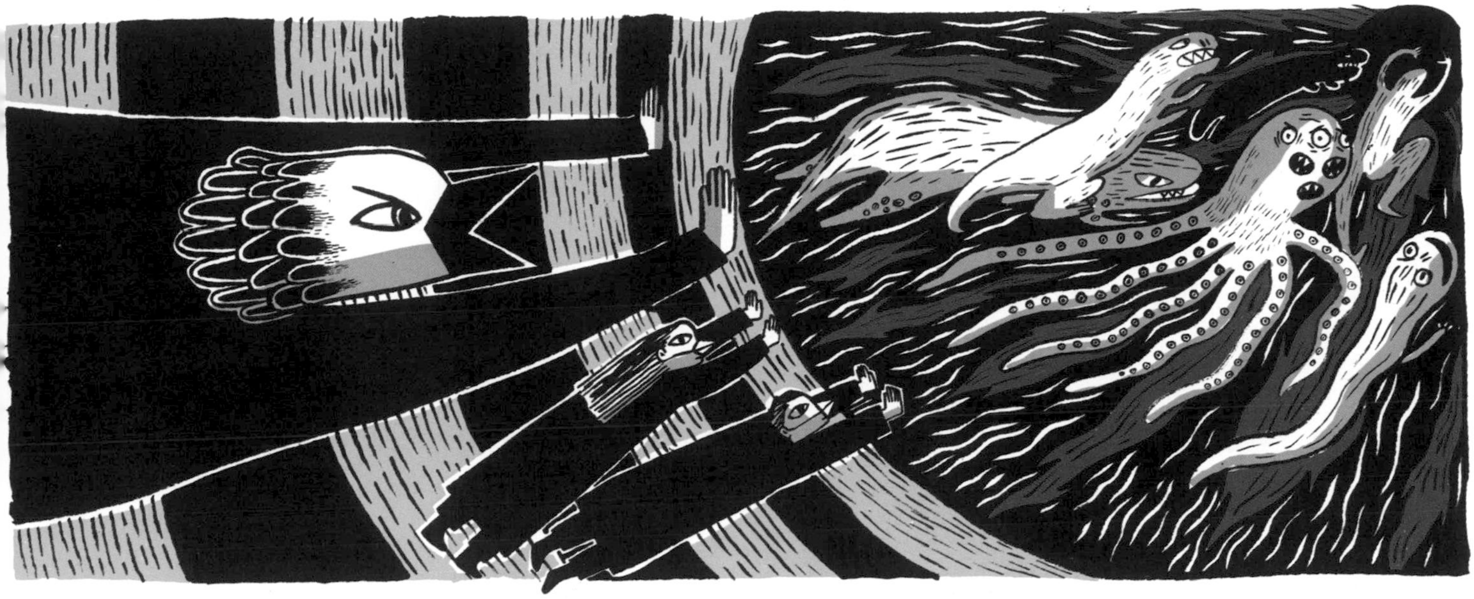

With clay from the well BirdMan made Early Earth.

With sparks from the well he made the stars.

A tall tree grew up to support the colossal weight of the sky.

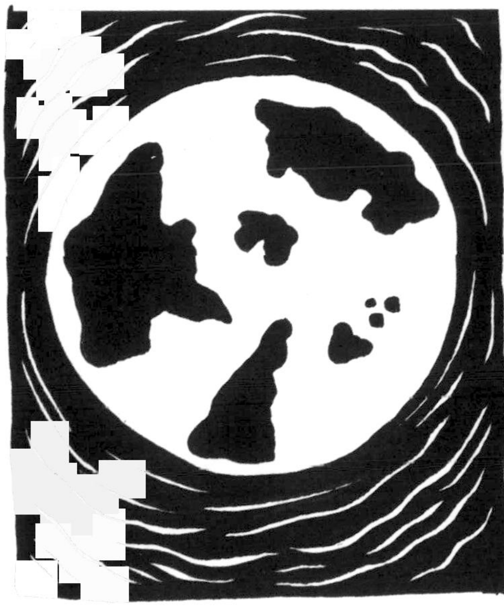

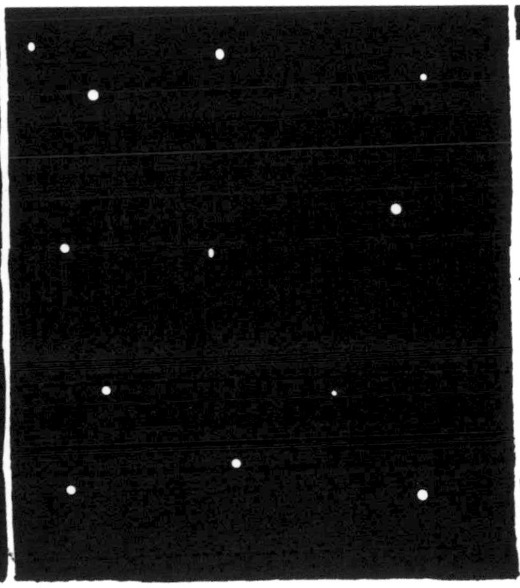

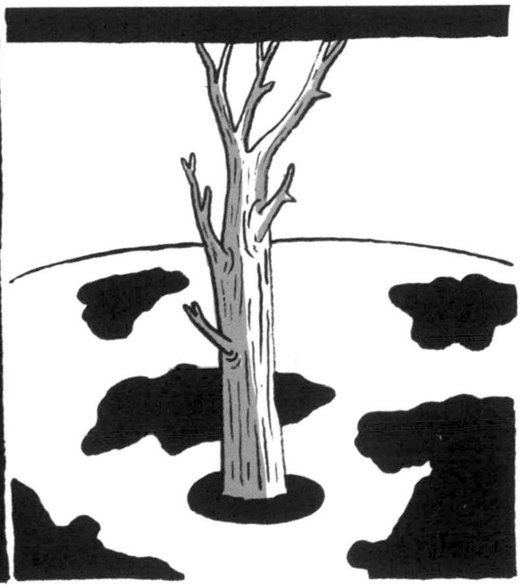

And then finally, when it was done BirdMan carved with wood from the tree the First Man and the First Woman. And the Ravens breathed life into them.

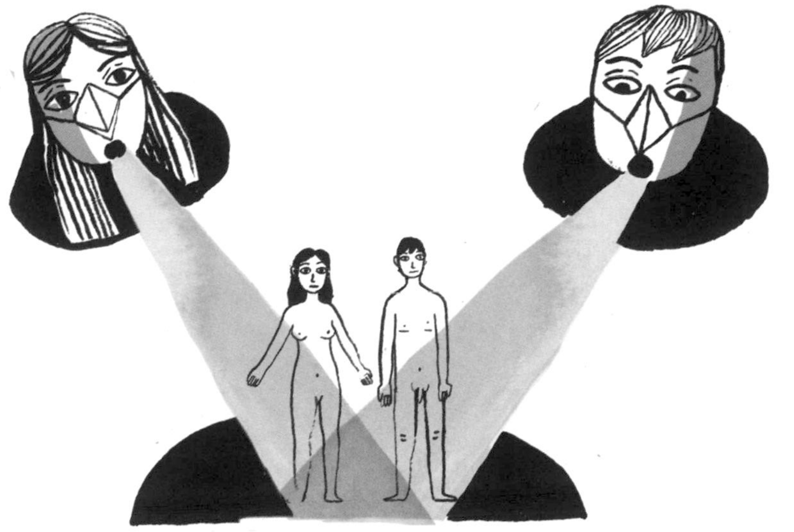

DAG AND HAL

After the Ravens had breathed life into the First Man and the First Woman, and set them free on the Earth, it was not long before they conceived a child.

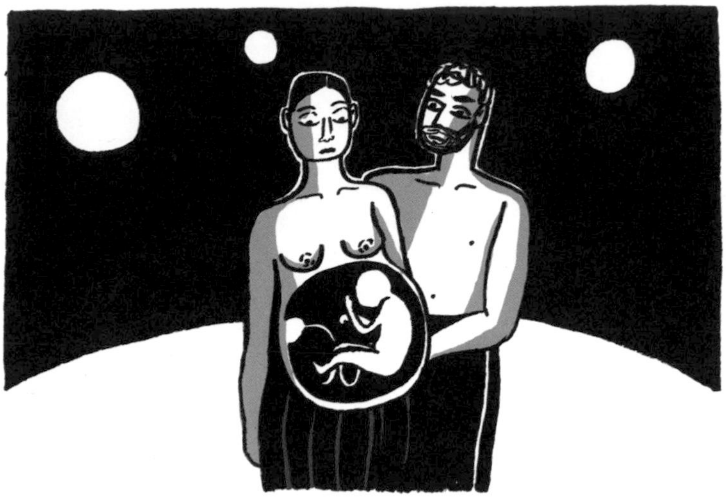

The child was born, and he was a boy. And they called him Dag.

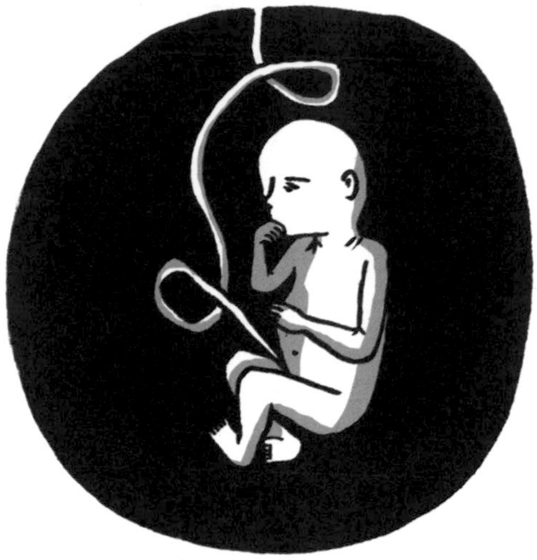

He was the first child to ever be born on Earth, and every first he had was a first that had never been before. He took his first step, he laughed his first laugh and everything (everything!) he did was a wonder and a marvel to his parents. They had never seen a child before, never been children themselves and so every milestone was a surprise.

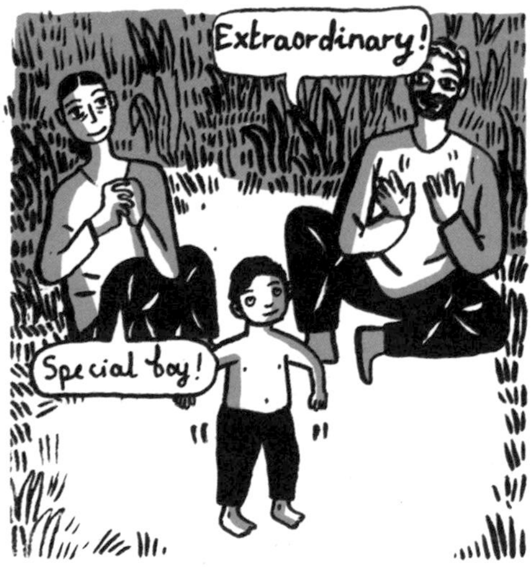
Extraordinary!
Special boy!

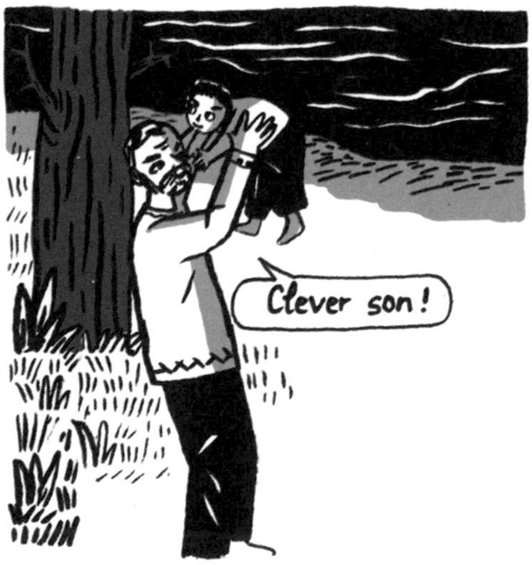
Clever son!

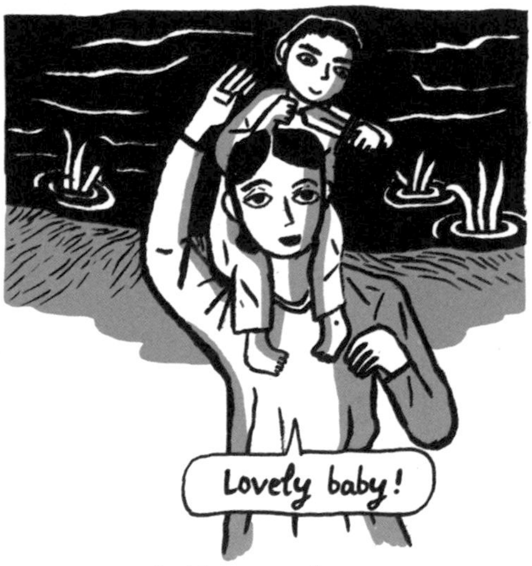
Lovely baby!

Dag grew up tall and dark and strong. He dug the earth and made wonderful things grow.

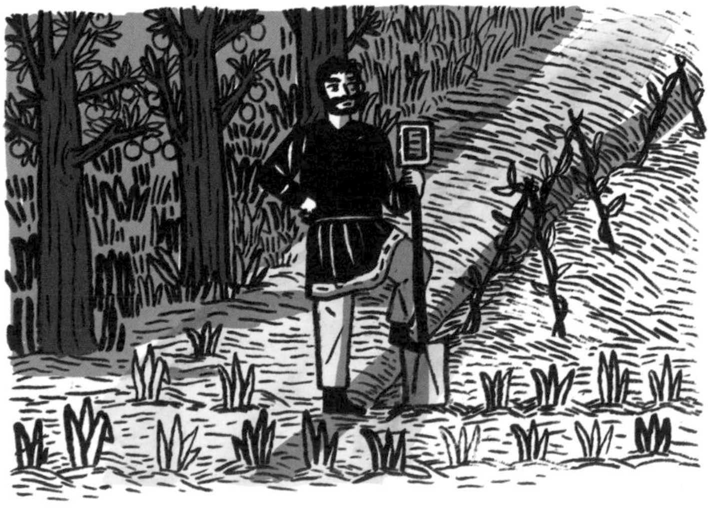

And so things were. And then Hal was born.

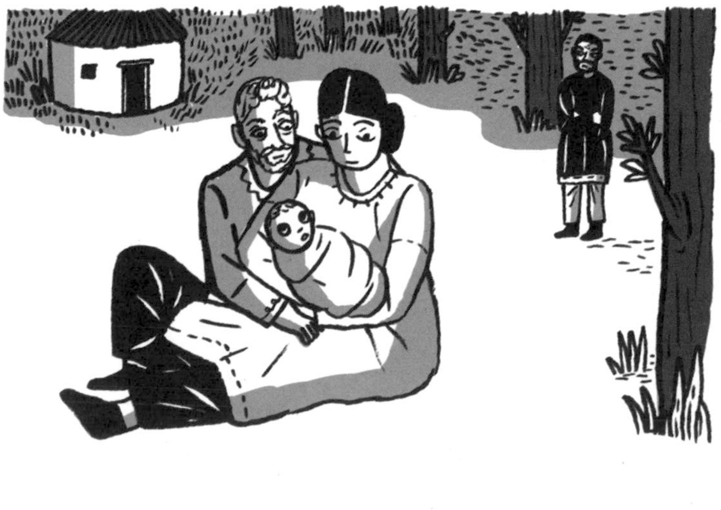

First Man and First Woman thought that all children would be like Dag. But in every way possible, Hal was different to Dag. He was small and swift and clever and gentle. And he was kinder than the sun. Dag did not understand his parents' delight in this new human.

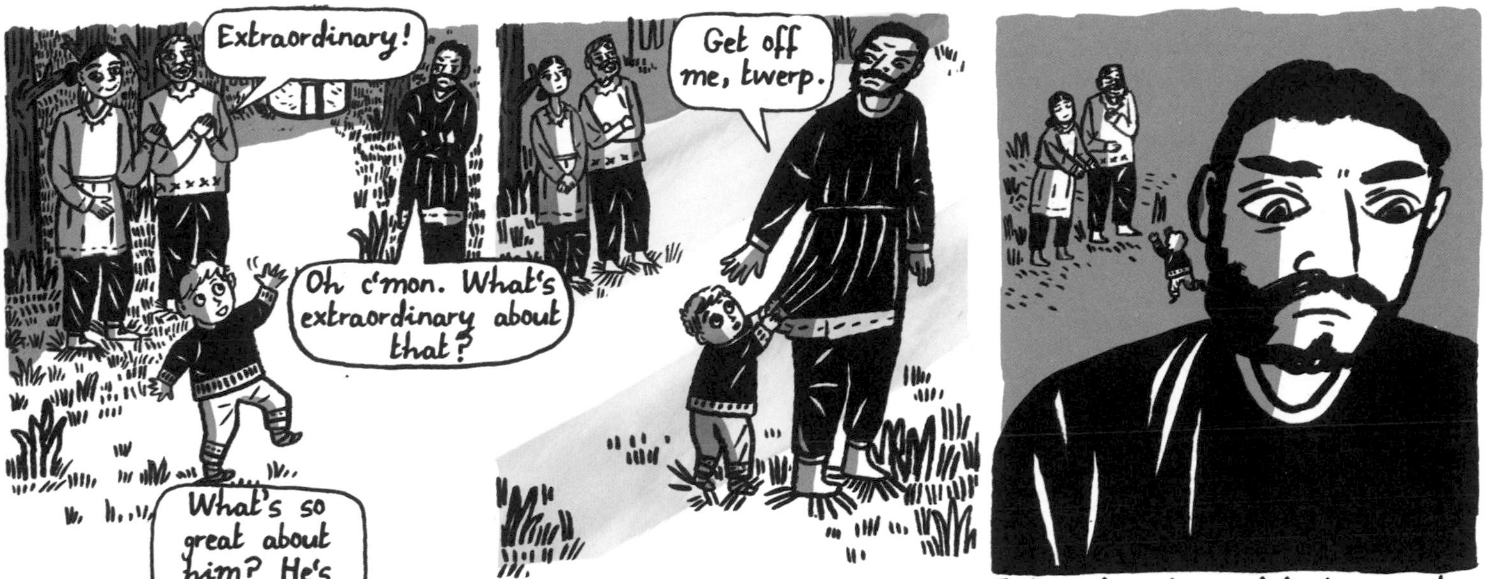
Extraordinary!
Oh c'mon. What's extraordinary about that?
Get off me, twerp.

But Hal just smiled, because he loved everyone and everything and his big brother most of all.

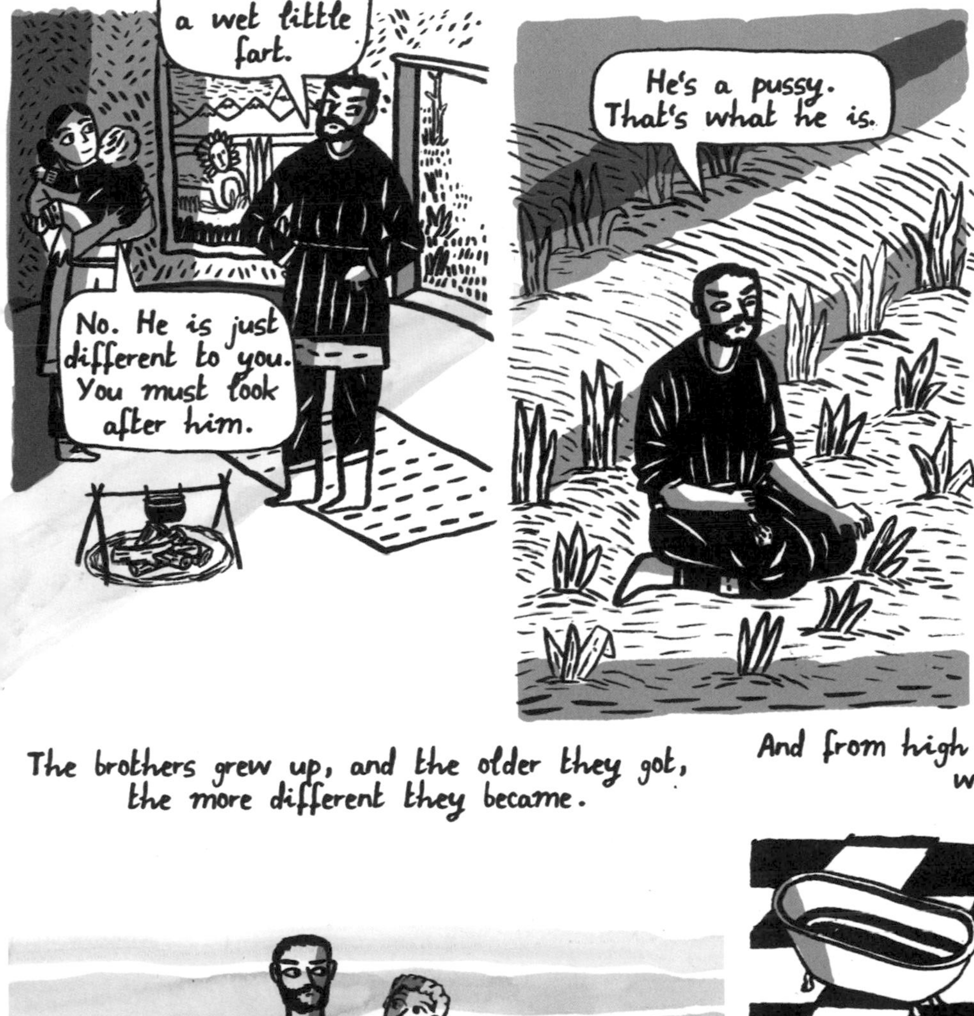
What's so great about him? He's a wet little fart.
No. He is just different to you. You must look after him.
He's a pussy. That's what he is.

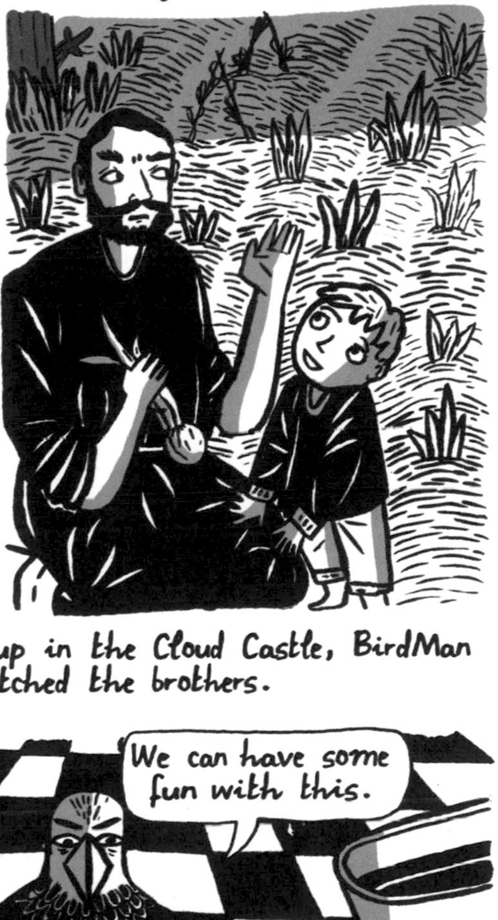

The brothers grew up, and the older they got, the more different they became.

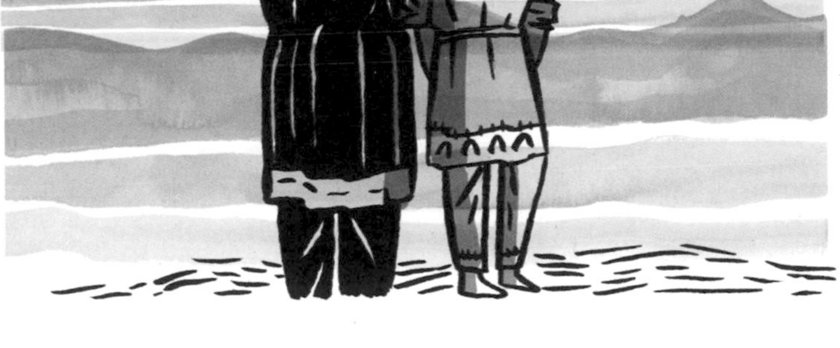

And from high up in the Cloud Castle, BirdMan watched the brothers.

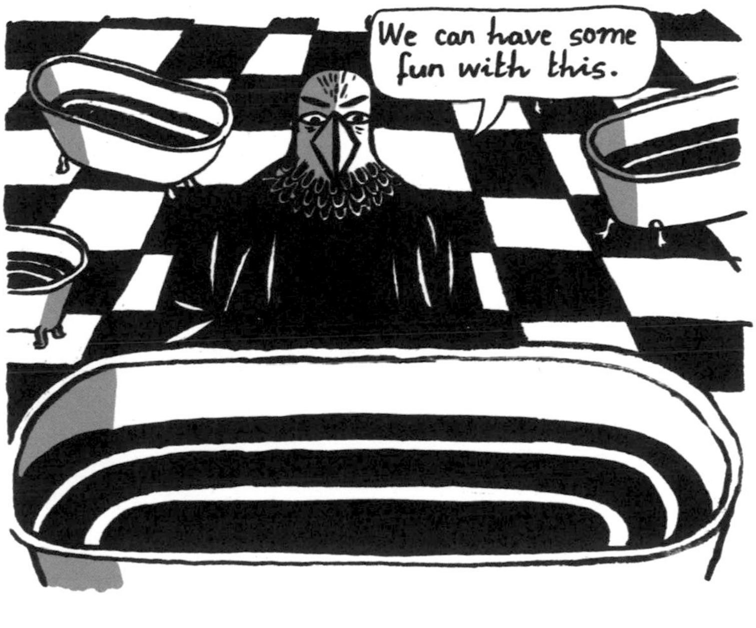
We can have some fun with this.

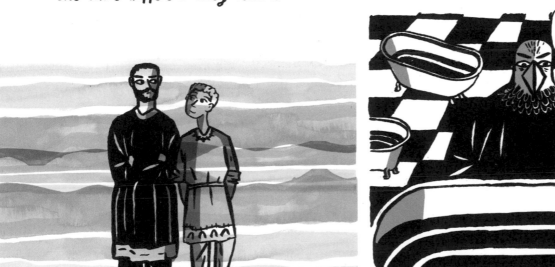

So BirdMan made Halla. She was the last human to be made by the Gods, and not conceived by natural means. She was to be the most beautiful girl that had ever been or ever was.

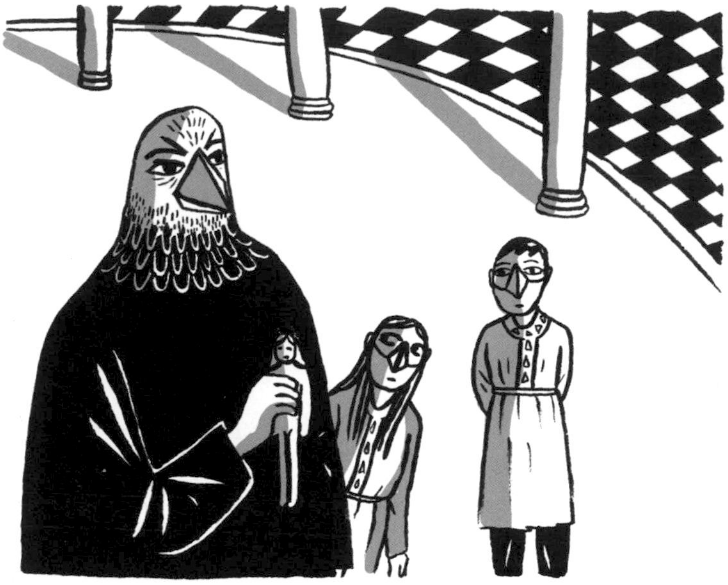

She was small and light and smiling and First Man and First Woman called her Halla, because she reminded them of their son Hal. Dag and Hal both fell in love with her, which of course was what BirdMan had intended.

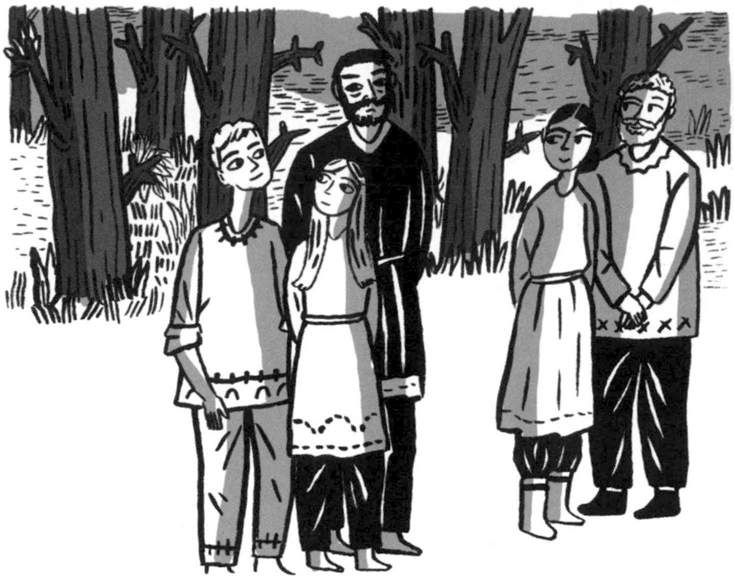

But Dag did not understand the churning in his gut or the quickening of his heart when he saw Halla. So he ignored her, and was rude and cold.

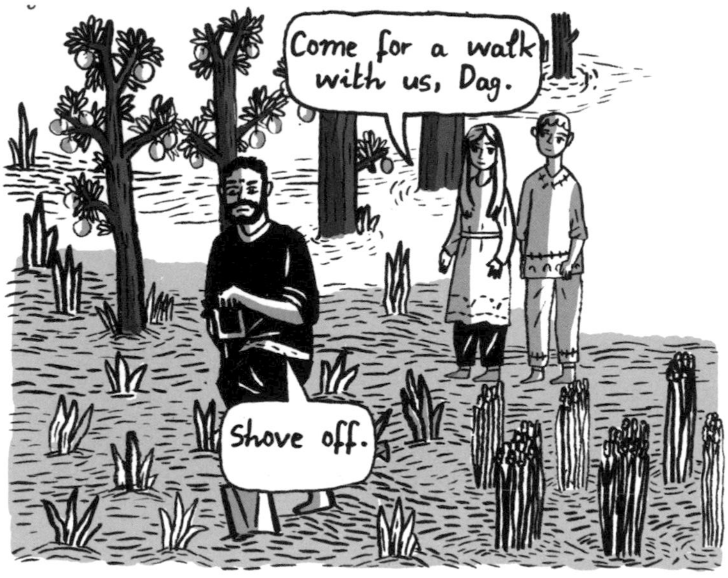
Come for a walk with us, Dag.
Shove off.

It was only when he came upon Hal and Halla kissing that he suddenly understood. He knew then what he wanted. But it was too late. Hal had got there first. And now they were in love.

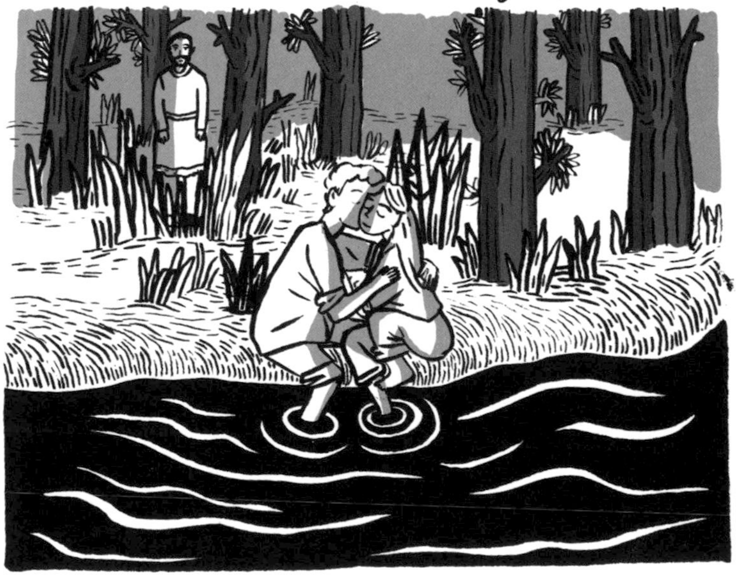

To Hal, it seemed that from the moment she had smiled her first smile, she was meant to be his partner. They were the first humans to fall in love. And it was glorious.

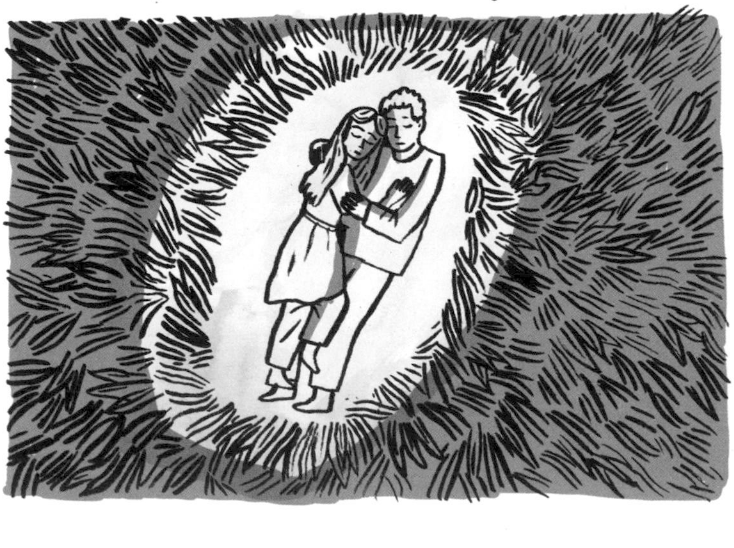

But Dag was jealous. He was the first human to ever feel jealousy. And it was terrible.

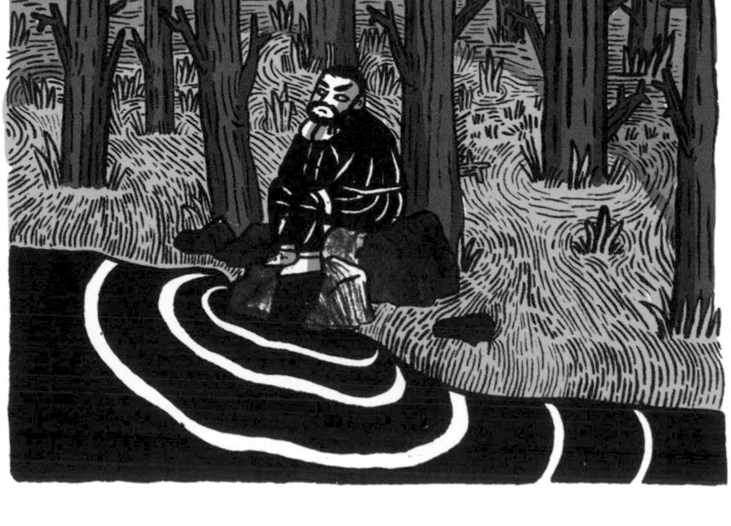

al and Halla were in love, but Dag loved Halla. And that was all there was to it.

Dag could not think why BirdMan had made only one woman, and why that woman had been intended for Hal. Hal was weaker, smaller, younger. In every way inferior to Dag.

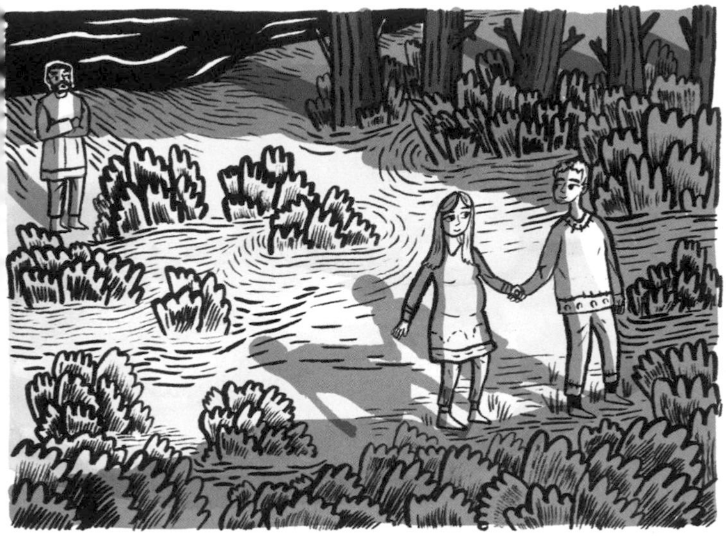

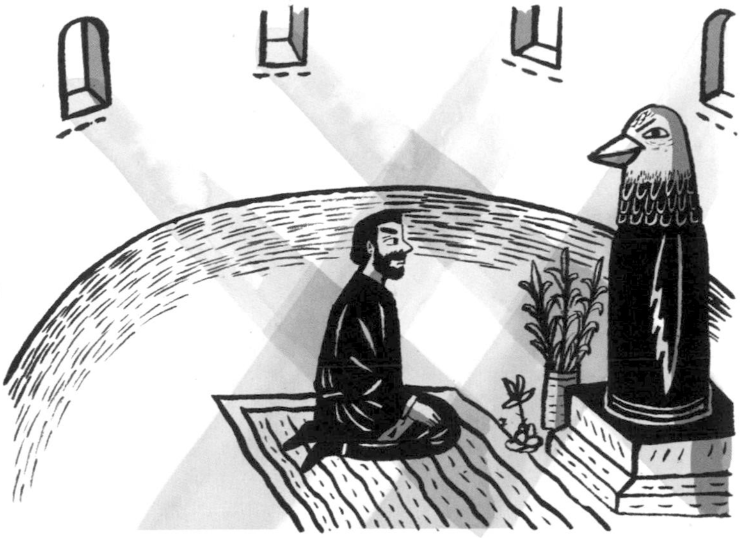

How was it possible that BirdMan had intended things thus? Surely something had gone seriously wrong. Halla must have been meant for Dag.

And once he had thought this thought, Dag believed it. He went to Hal and Halla, who by this point had had two children of their own.

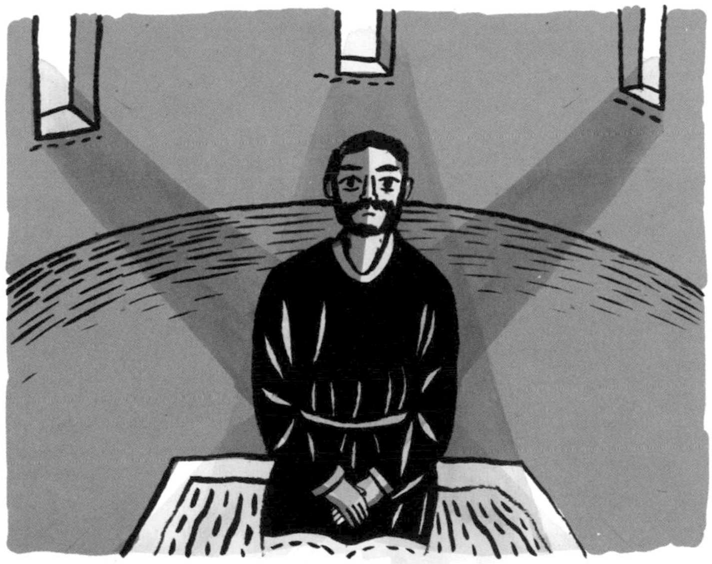

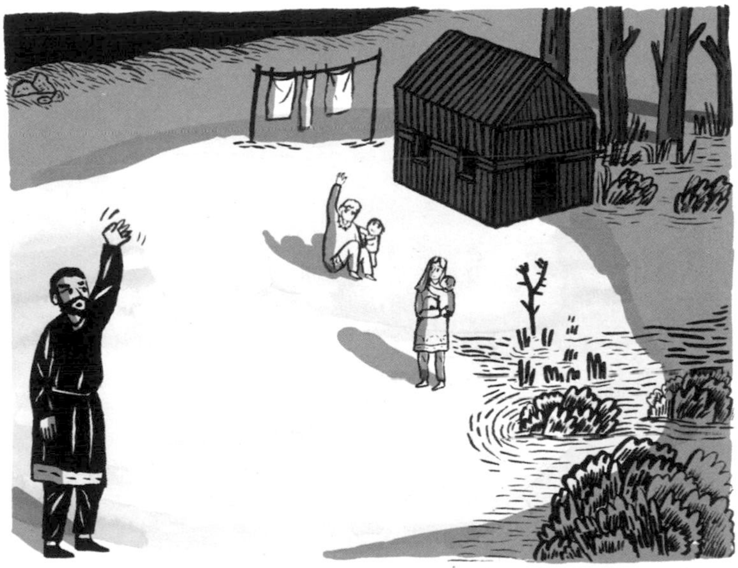

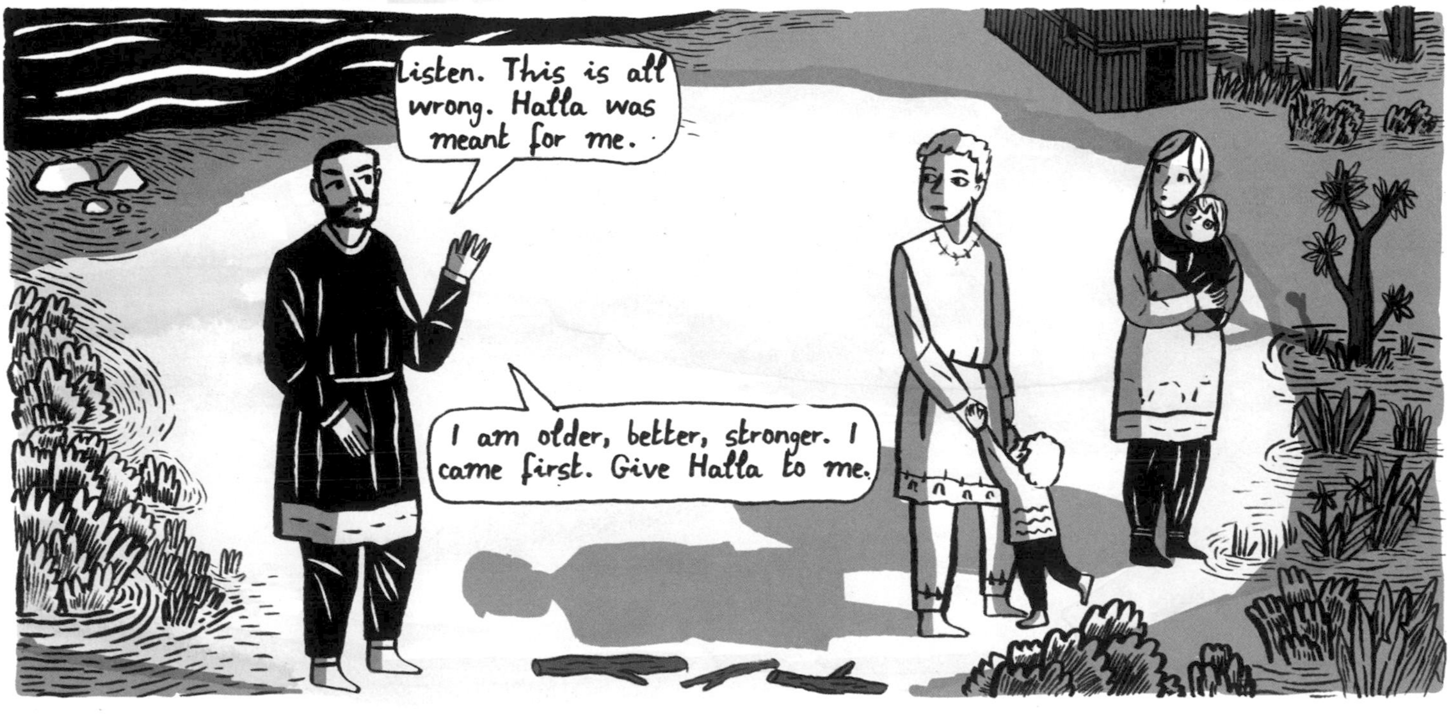
Listen. This is all wrong. Halla was meant for me.
I am older, better, stronger. I came first. Give Halla to me.

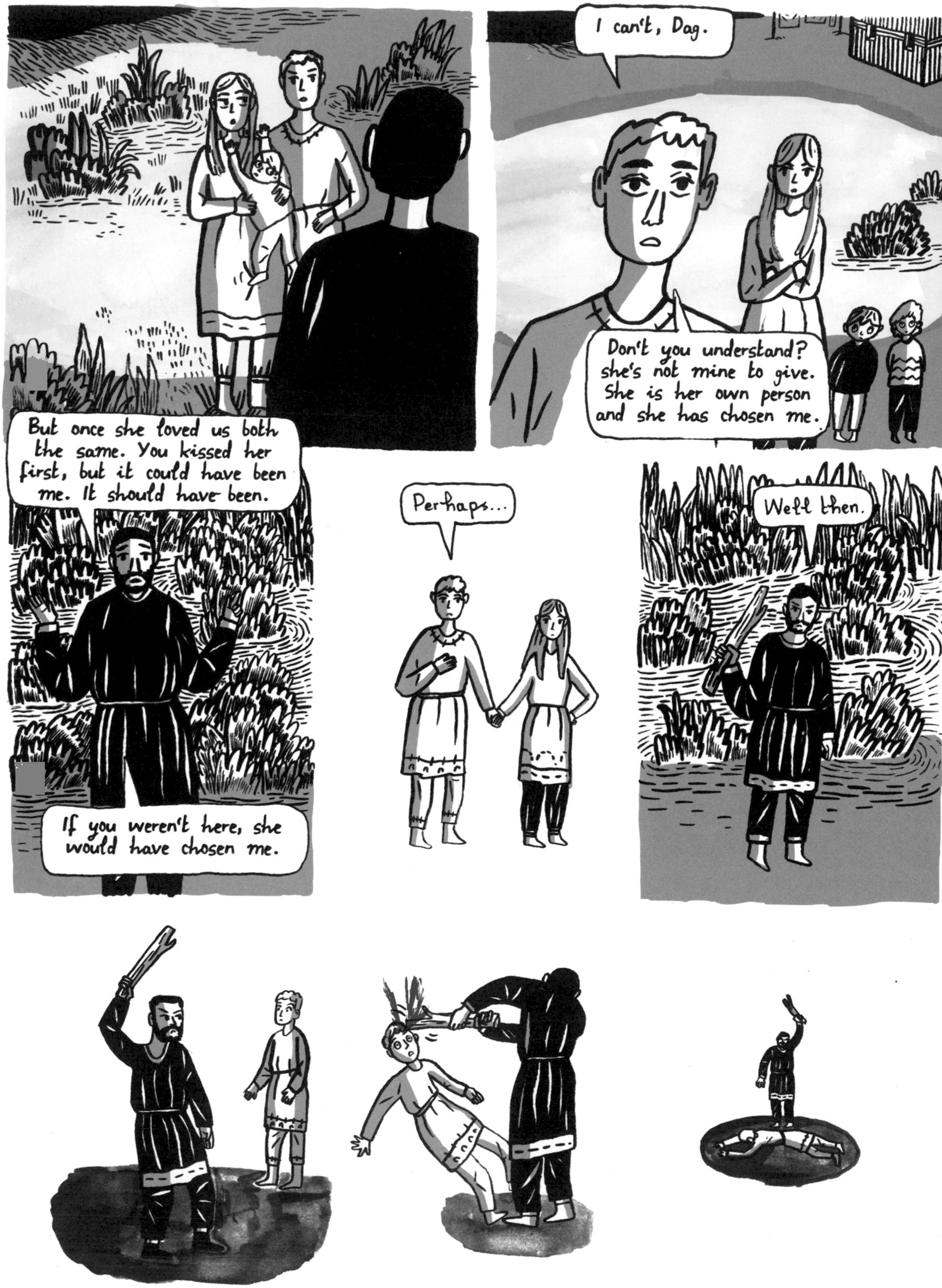
I can't, Dag.
Don't you understand? she's not mine to give. She is her own person and she has chosen me.
But once she loved us both the same. You kissed her first, but it could have been me. It should have been.
If you weren't here, she would have chosen me.
Perhaps...
Well then.

l was the first Human to die, and Dag was the rst human to kill another. And Halla? She was the first human to suffer a broken heart.

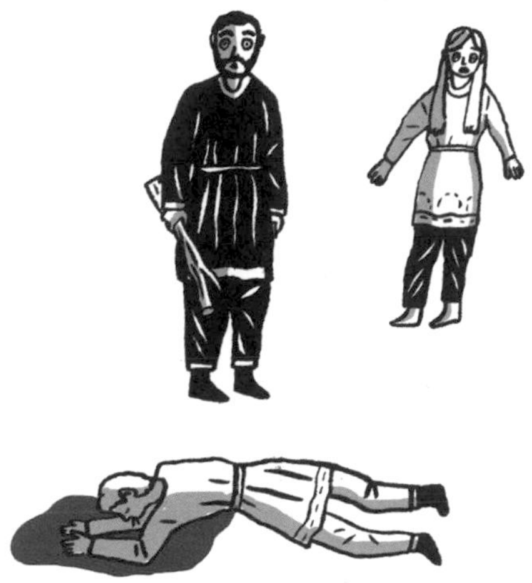

Dag took Halla against her will, and she bore him two children.

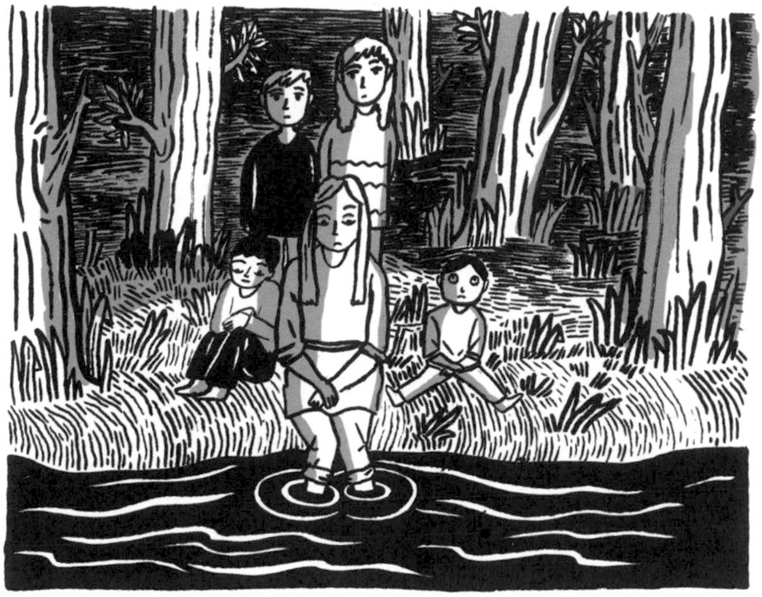

But she could never love Dag, as she once had. In fact, she hated him, and she died, eventually, of her broken heart.

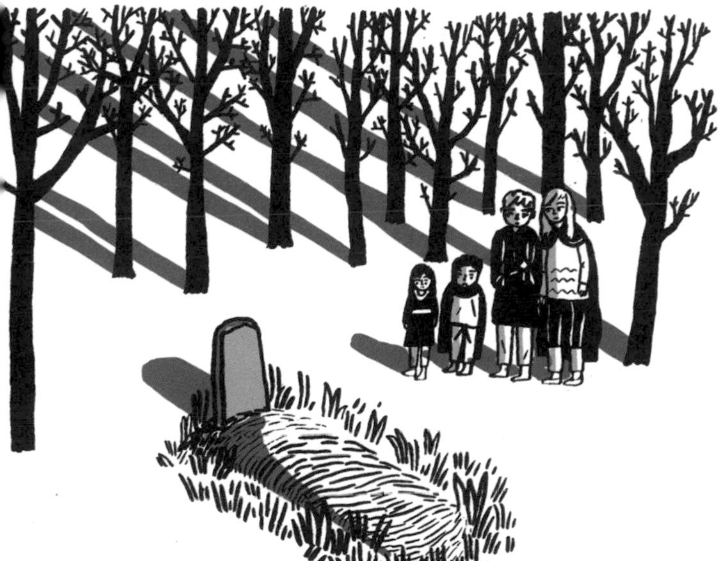

Dag mourned her, and he mourned Hal. He understood then, that death was permanent. He could never take it back.

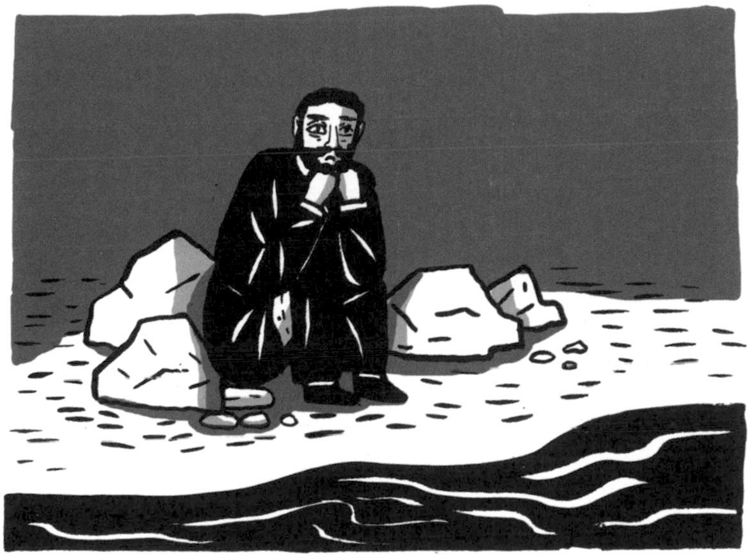

And that is how the first two clans of Britanitarka were formed. From the descendants of Dag and Hal. Other clans came later. But no two clans had a hatred and enmity as old and deep and fierce as that of the Dags and the Hals. Other clans formed alliances and made peace, but the Dags and Hals were ever and always at war.

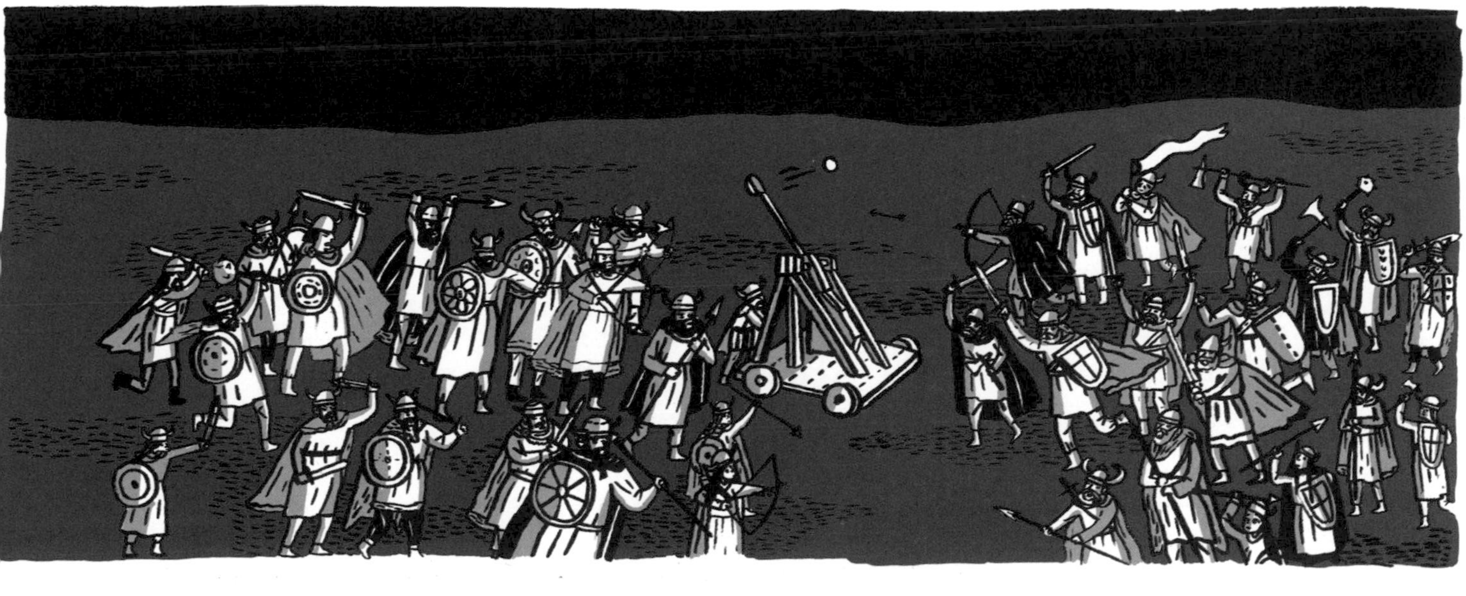

THE OLD LADY AND THE GIANT

Britanitarka is a harsh place. It is a place where the strong prevail and the weak are discarded. That is just how it is.

It is customary in Britanitarka that when a man or woman becomes old enough that they can no longer play an active role in the clan, they leave.

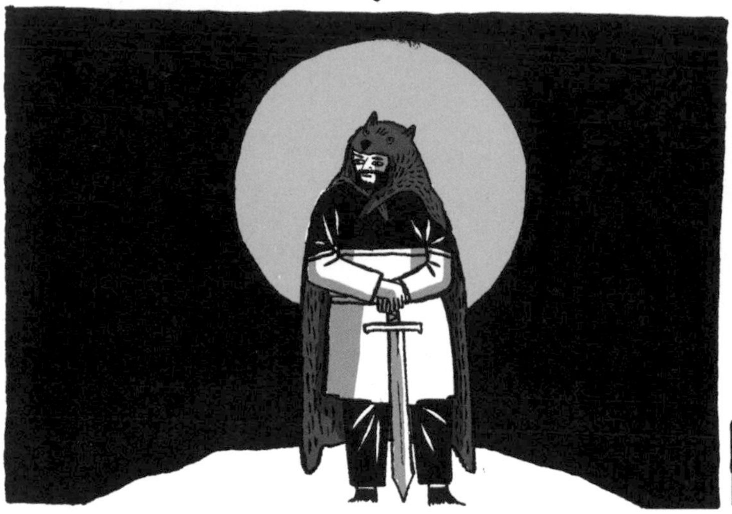

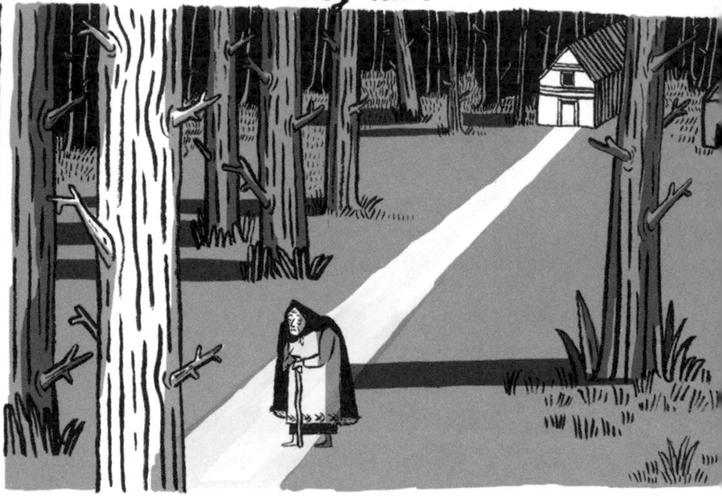

They will walk off one day into the cold mists of dawn, without a word to anyone, and go quietly off to die.

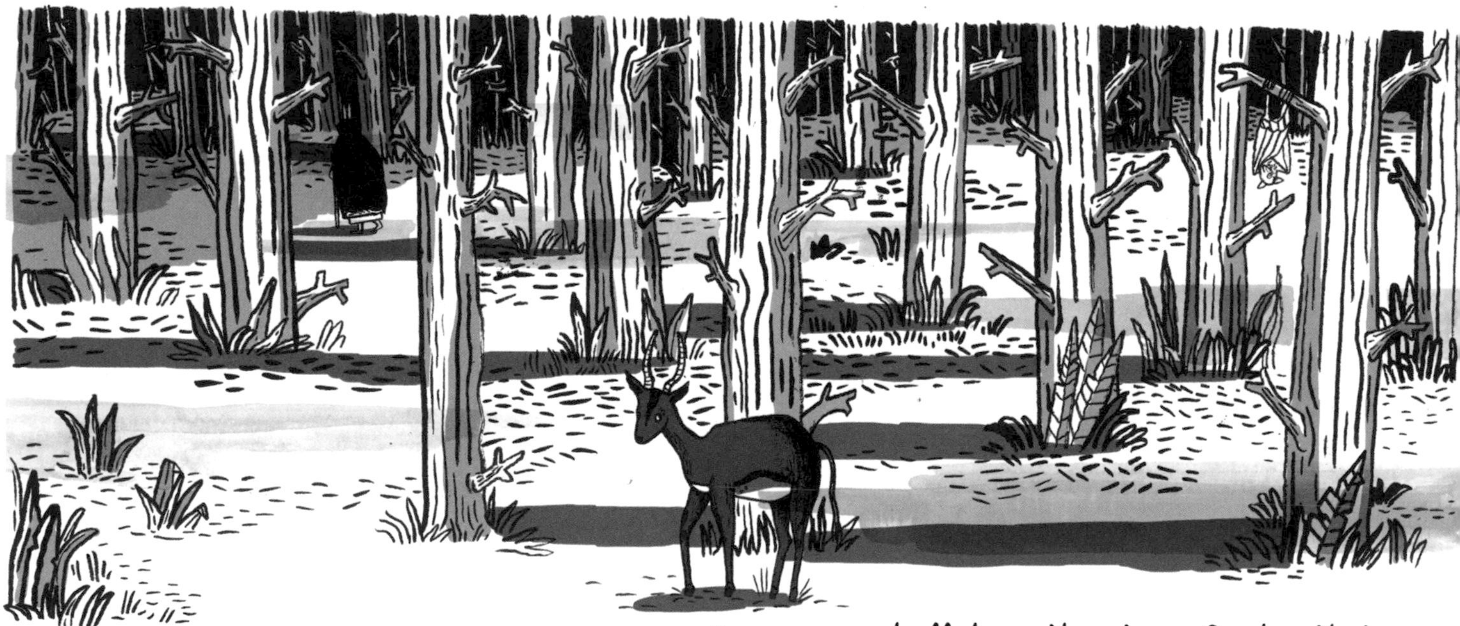

This is the way for all clans, except for the Dags.

So now we shall hear the story of why that is, and how one old lady of Dag caused this custom to be done away with.

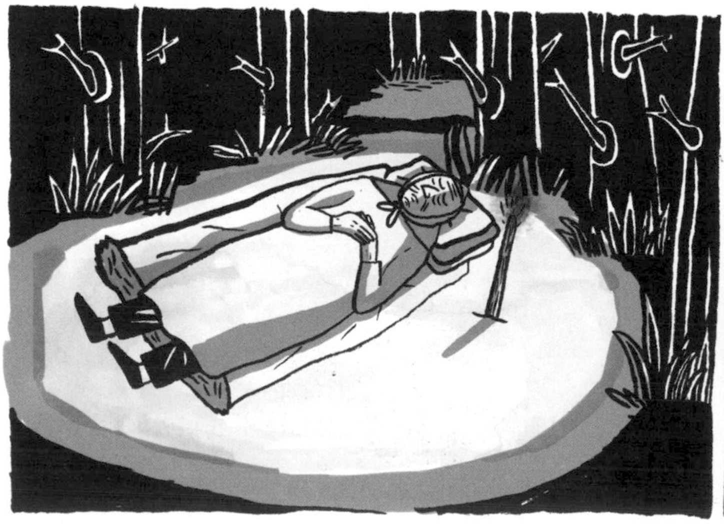

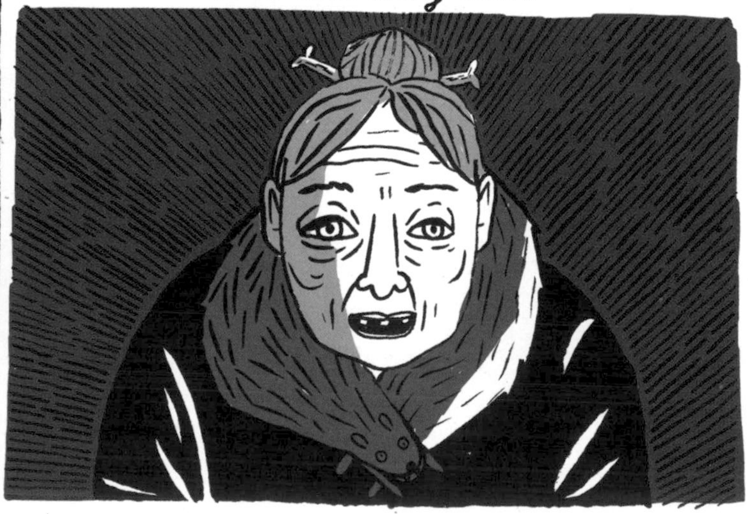

had been a long hard winter, and the Old Lady, who up until then had been the very picture of sprightliness, became suddenly frail. Her family observed that perhaps her time had come to make the walk.

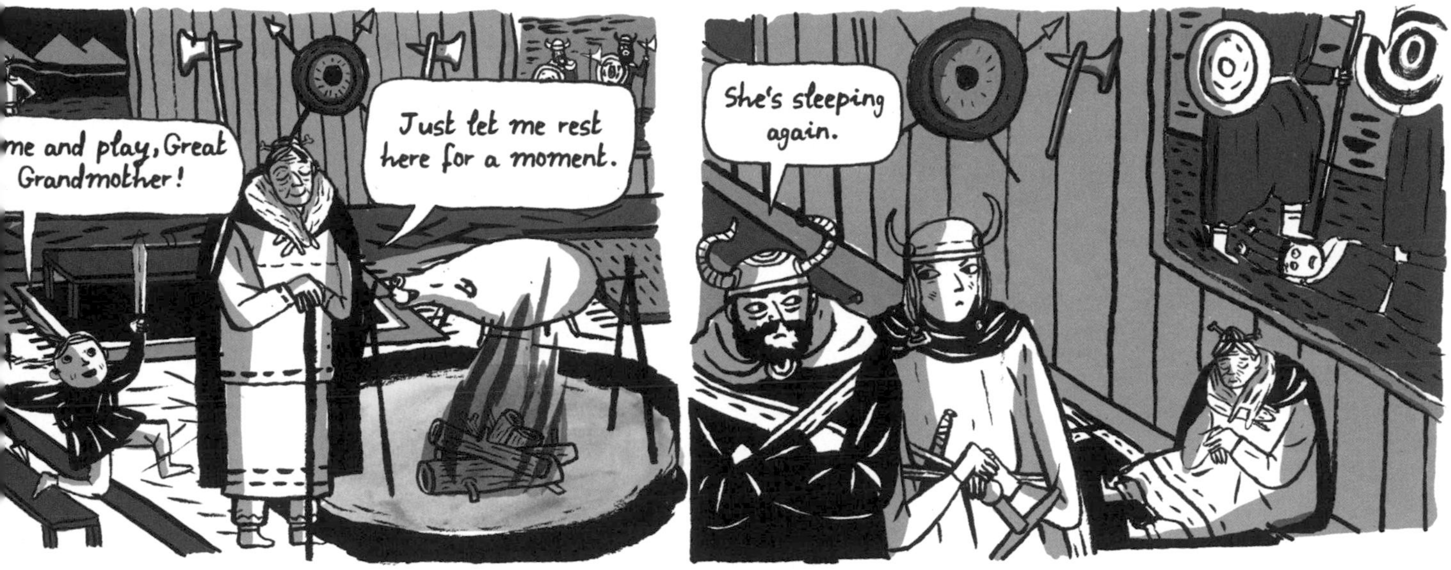
me and play, Great Grandmother!
Just let me rest here for a moment.
She's sleeping again.

Indeed, she slept all day, ate a great deal and told long rambling stories to whomever she could corner.

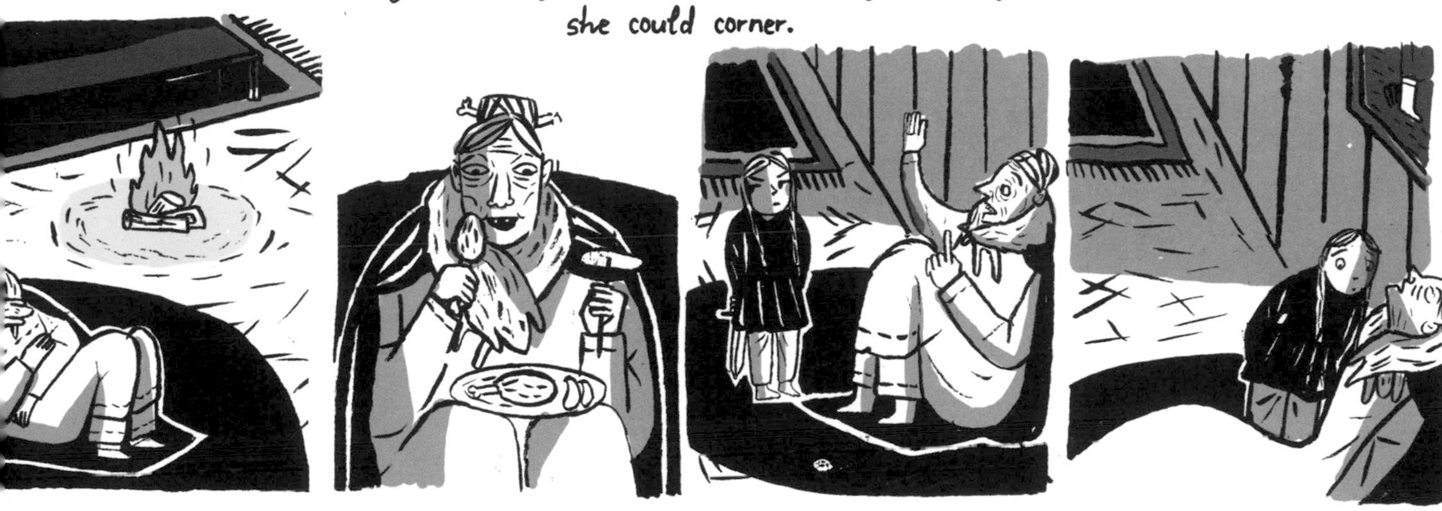

eemed as though she had not enjoyed herself so much in years and she seemed perfectly content to sleep and eat her way into old age.

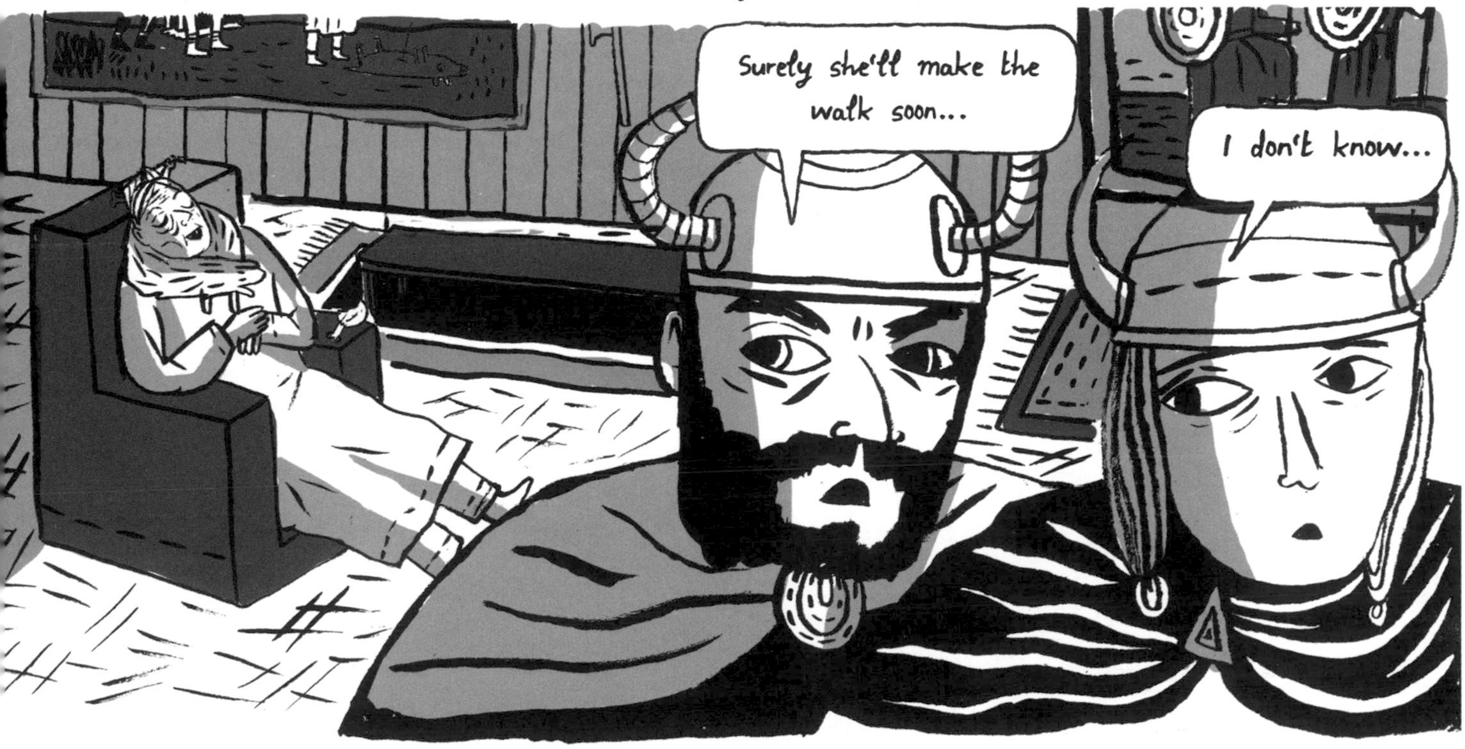
Surely she'll make the walk soon...
I don't know...

Winter ended but spring brought no mercy. For a giant had come down from the Cloud Mountain and was plaguing the villages.

The giant ate their crops, scared away what animals it had not already hunted and, worse still, carried off little children.

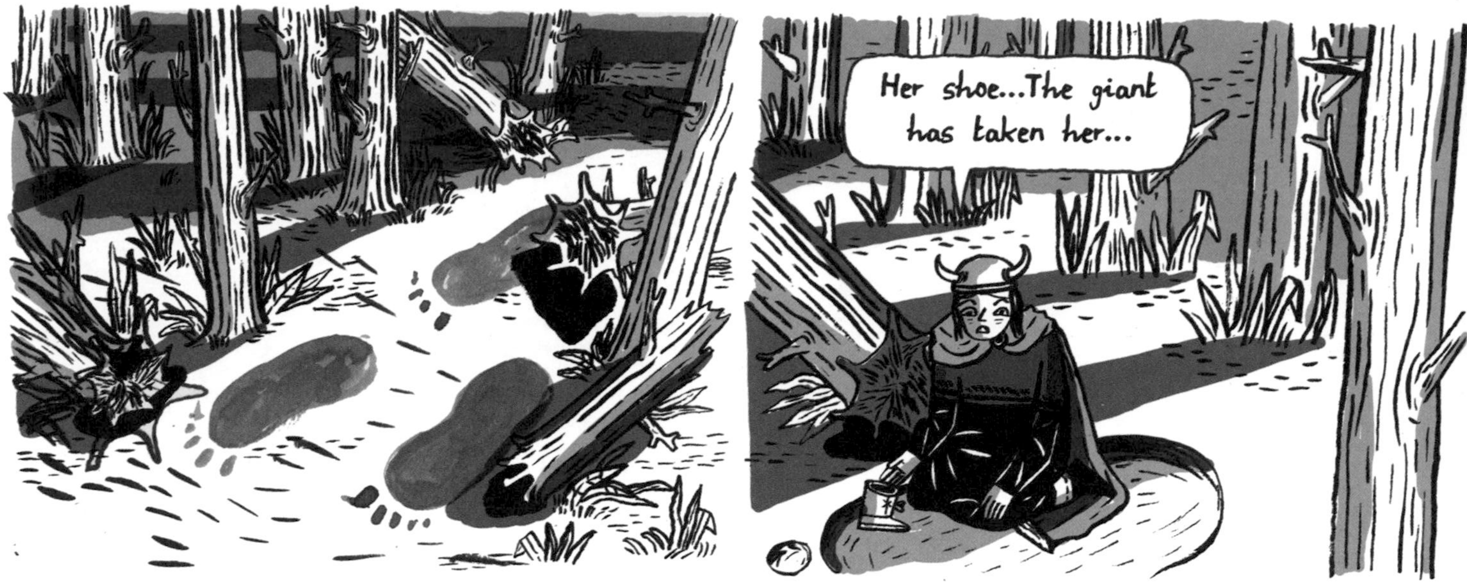
Her shoe...The giant has taken her...

This was no time for freeloaders.

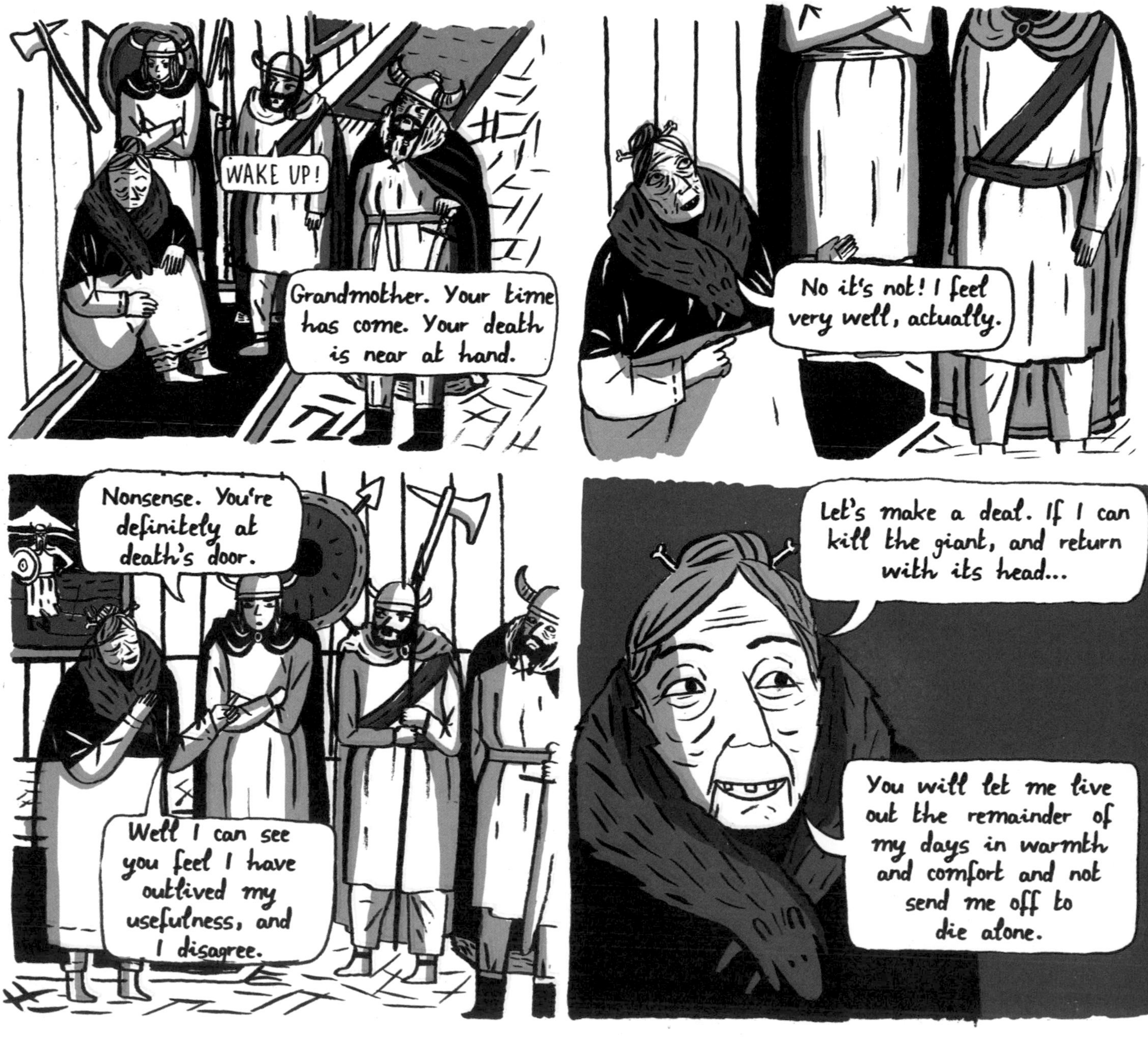
WAKE UP!
Grandmother. Your time has come. Your death is near at hand.
No it's not! I feel very well, actually.
Nonsense. You're definitely at death's door.
Well I can see you feel I have outlived my usefulness, and I disagree.
Let's make a deal. If I can kill the giant, and return with its head...
You will let me live out the remainder of my days in warmth and comfort and not send me off to die alone.

Well it seemed highly unlikely that a woman who could not walk ten paces without a stick could kill a twenty-foot giant. So they agreed.

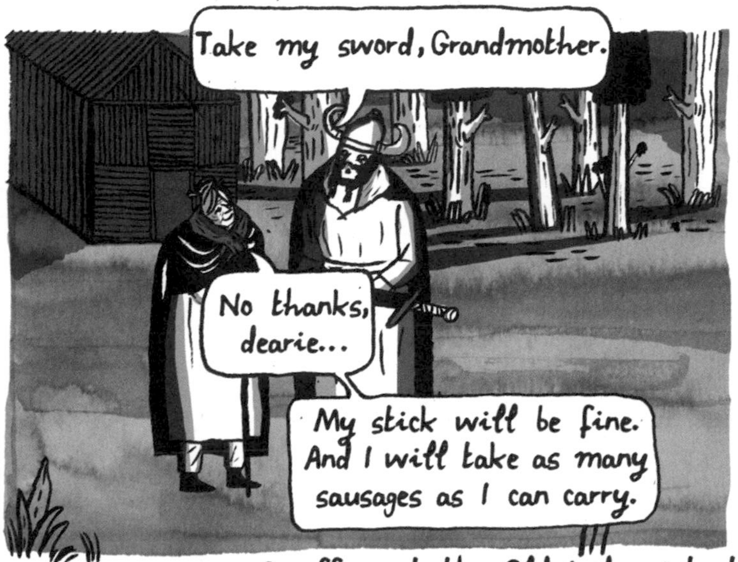

Take my sword, Grandmother.
No thanks, dearie...
My stick will be fine. And I will take as many sausages as I can carry.

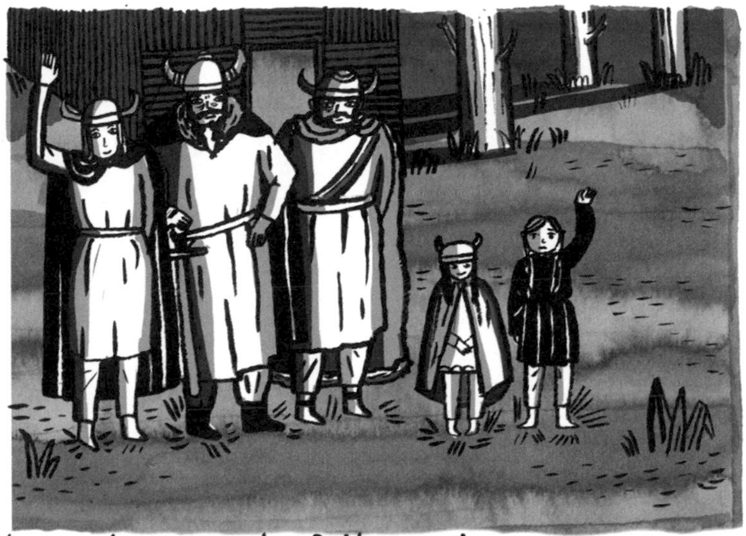

So off went the Old Lady, into the woods in search of the giant.

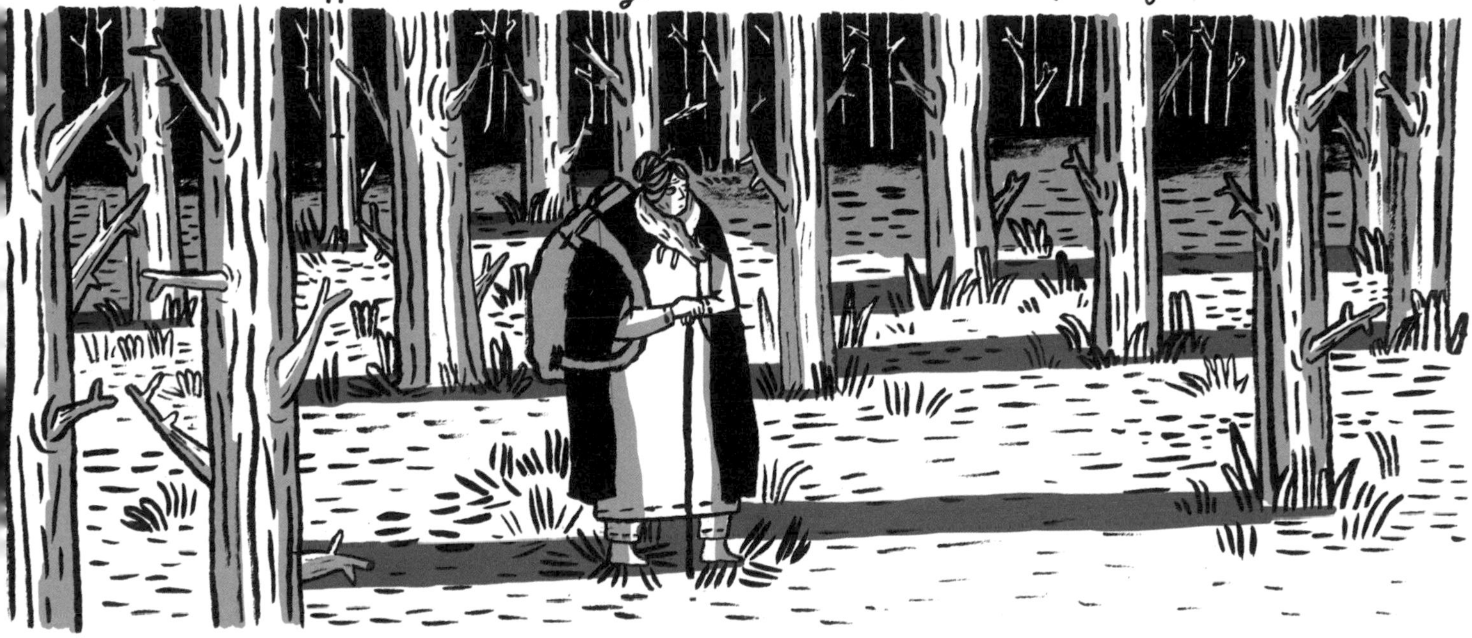

She walked until her legs could walk no further, and then she sat down and lit a fire. And waited.

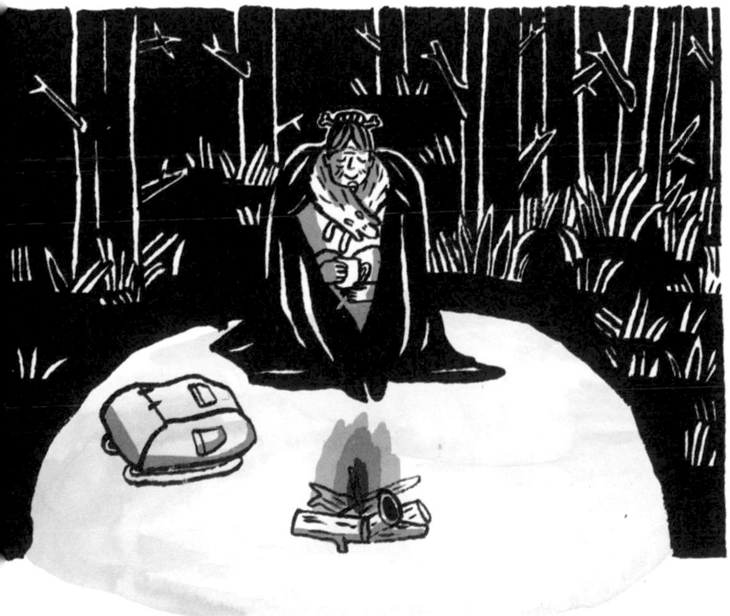

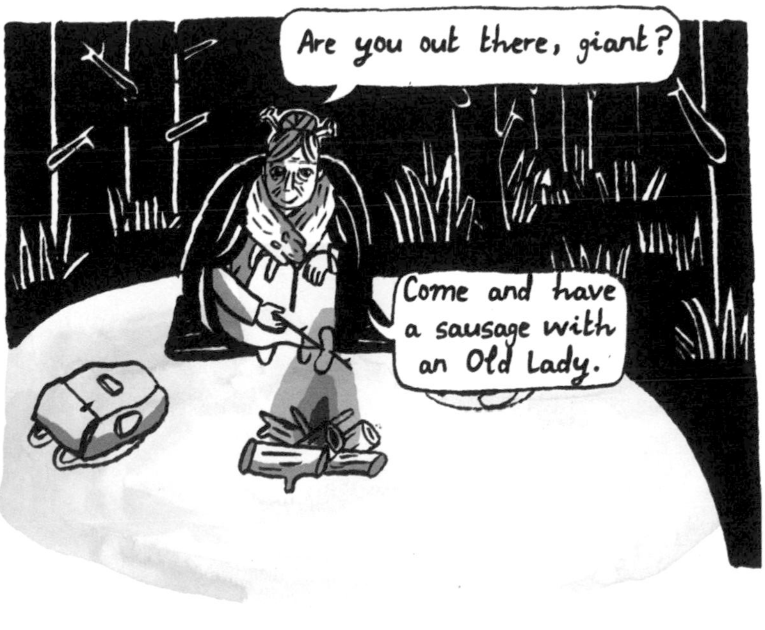

Are you out there, giant?
Come and have a sausage with an Old Lady.

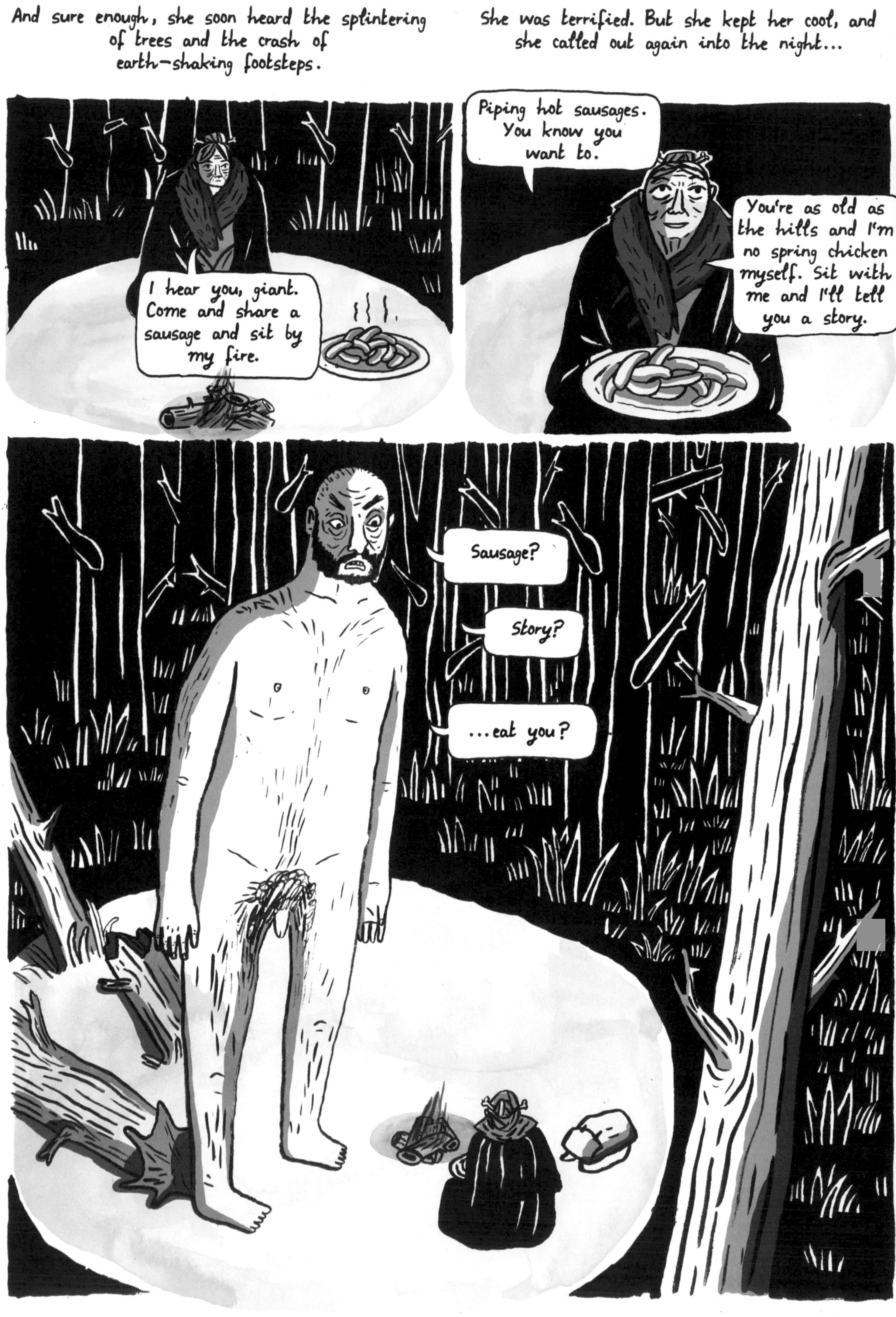
And sure enough, she soon heard the splintering of trees and the crash of earth-shaking footsteps.
I hear you, giant. Come and share a sausage and sit by my fire.
She was terrified. But she kept her cool, and she called out again into the night...
Piping hot sausages. You know you want to.
You're as old as the hills and I'm no spring chicken myself. Sit with me and I'll tell you a story.
Sausage?
Story?
...eat you?

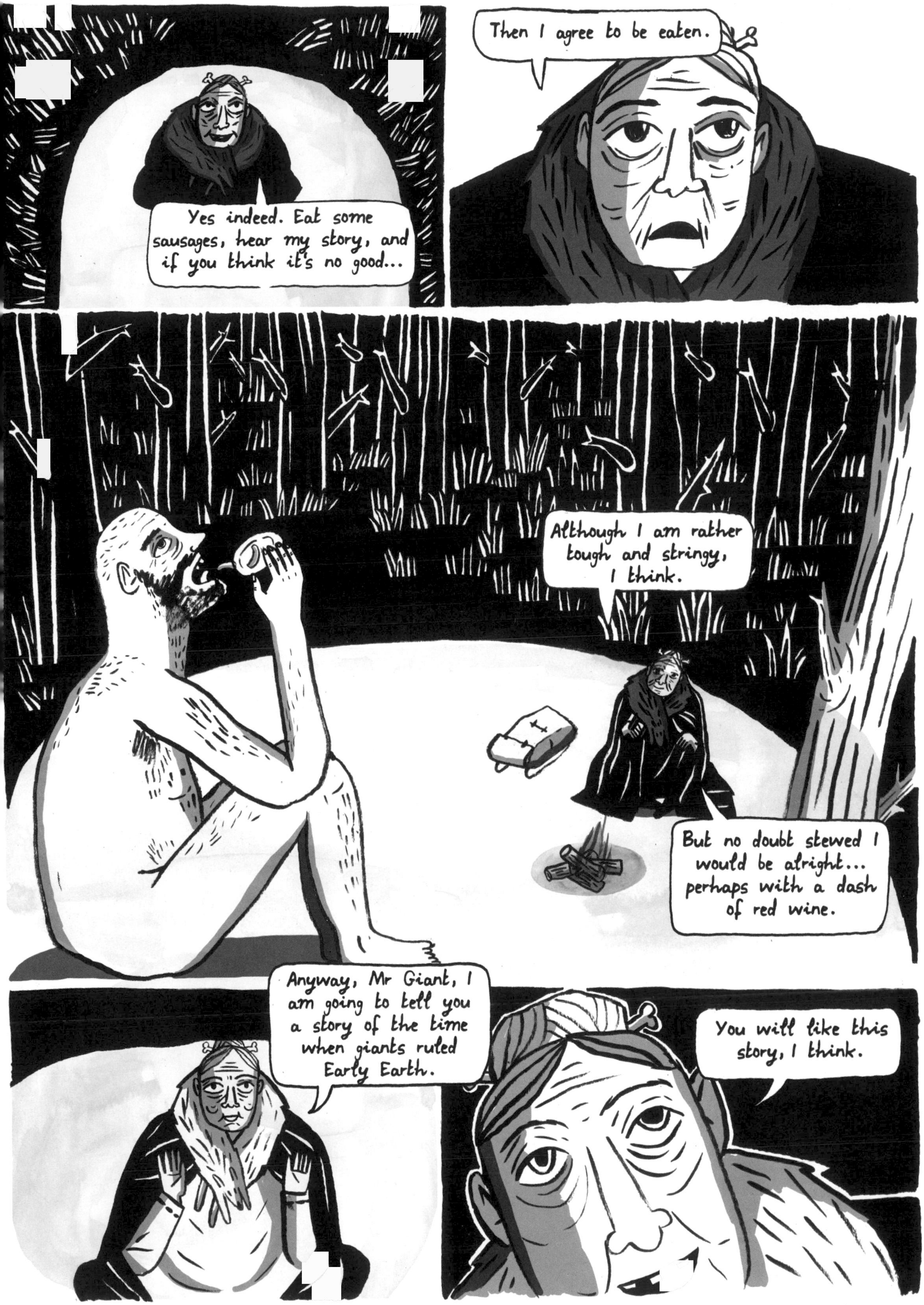
Yes indeed. Eat some sausages, hear my story, and if you think it's no good...
Then I agree to be eaten.
Although I am rather tough and stringy, I think.
But no doubt stewed I would be alright... perhaps with a dash of red wine.
Anyway, Mr Giant, I am going to tell you a story of the time when giants ruled Early Earth.
You will like this story, I think.

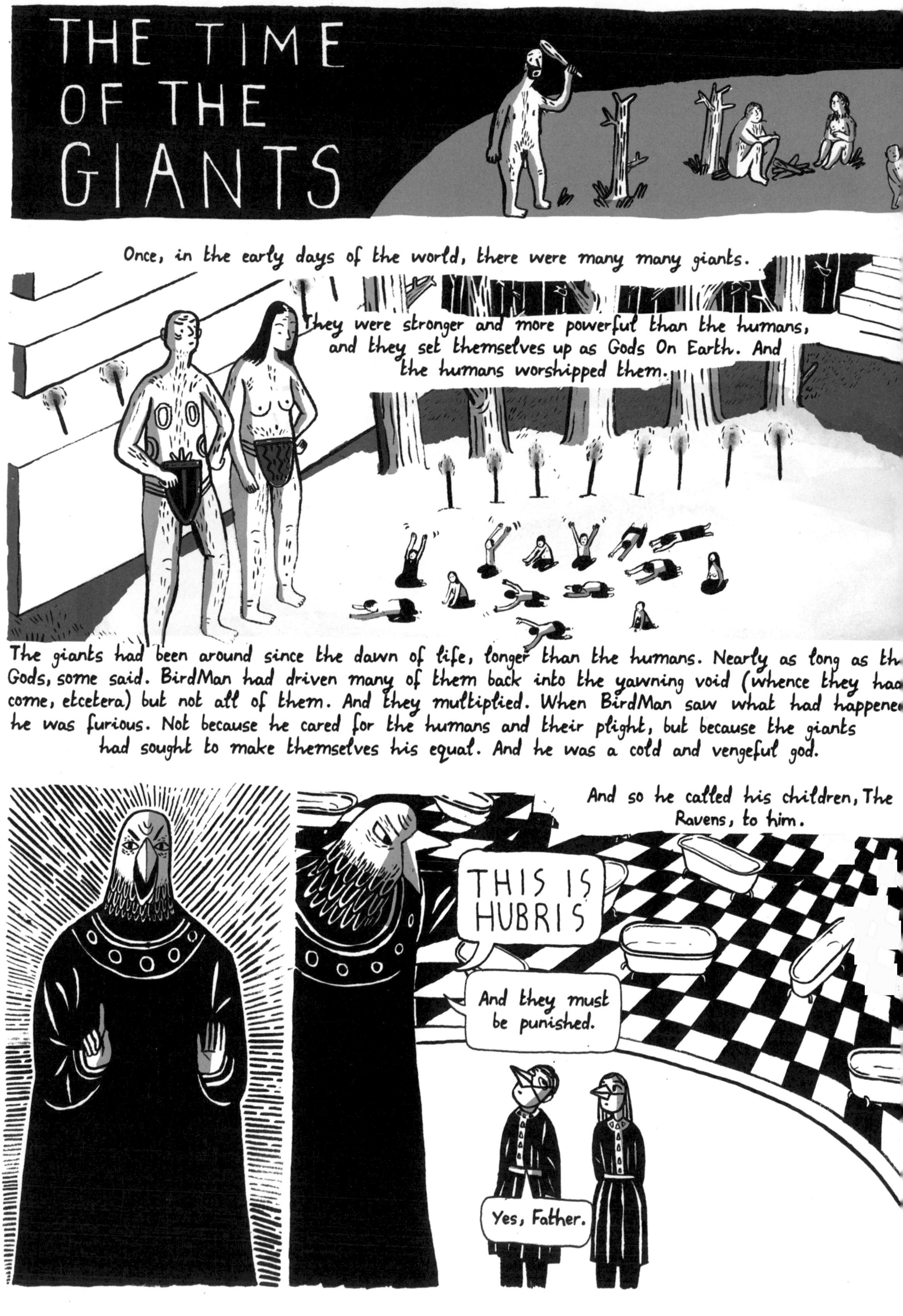
THE TIME OF THE GIANTS
Once, in the early days of the world, there were many many giants.
They were stronger and more powerful than the humans, and they set themselves up as Gods On Earth. And the humans worshipped them.
The giants had been around since the dawn of life, longer than the humans. Nearly as long as th
Gods, some said. BirdMan had driven many of them back into the yawning void (whence they ha
come, etcetera) but not all of them. And they multiplied. When BirdMan saw what had happene
he was furious. Not because he cared for the humans and their plight, but because the giants had sought to make themselves his equal. And he was a cold and vengeful god.
And so he called his children, The Ravens, to him.
THIS IS HUBRIS
And they must be punished.
Yes, Father.

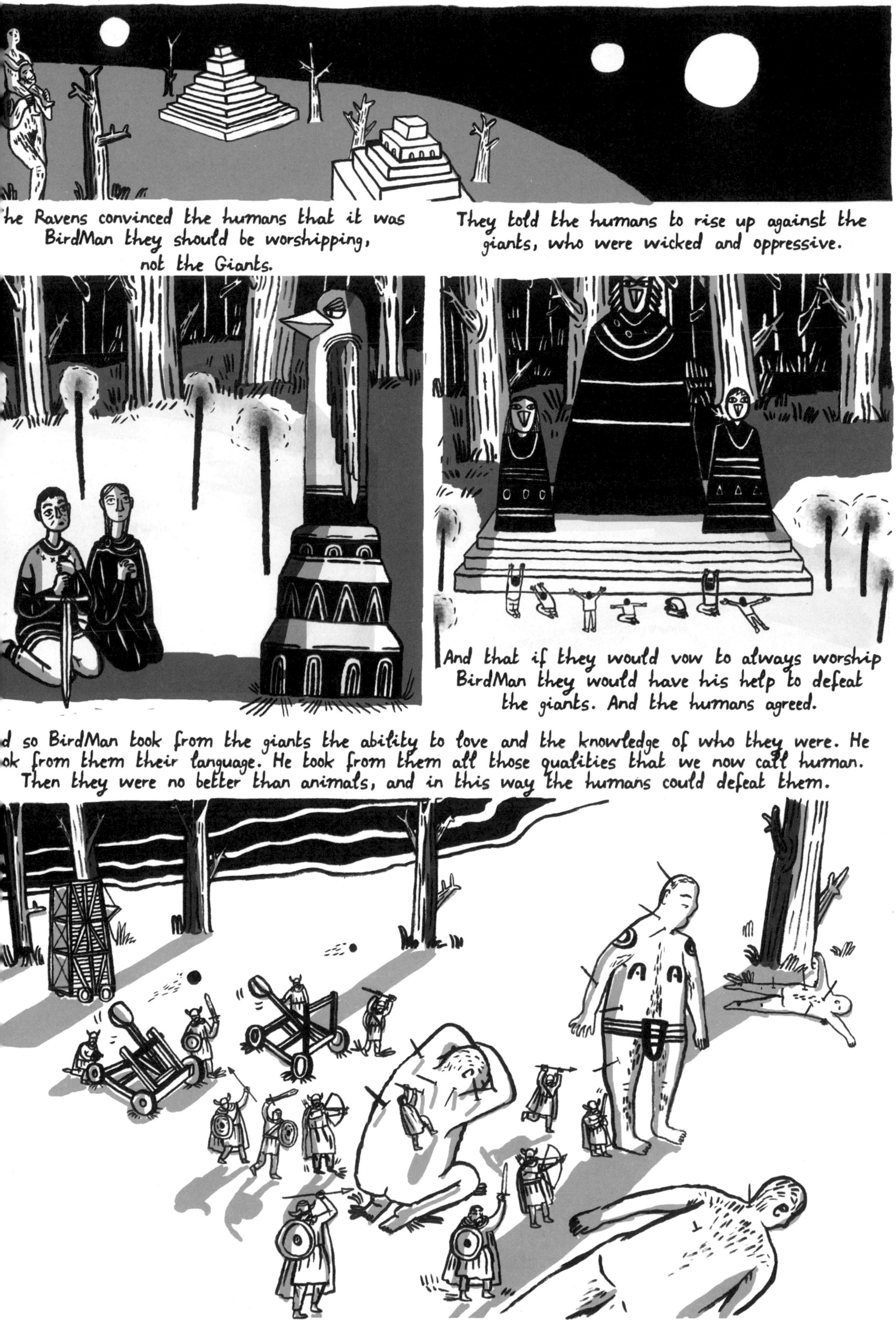
he Ravens convinced the humans that it was BirdMan they should be worshipping, not the Giants.
They told the humans to rise up against the giants, who were wicked and oppressive.
And that if they would vow to always worship BirdMan they would have his help to defeat the giants. And the humans agreed.
d so BirdMan took from the giants the ability to love and the knowledge of who they were. He ok from them their language. He took from them all those qualities that we now call human. Then they were no better than animals, and in this way the humans could defeat them.

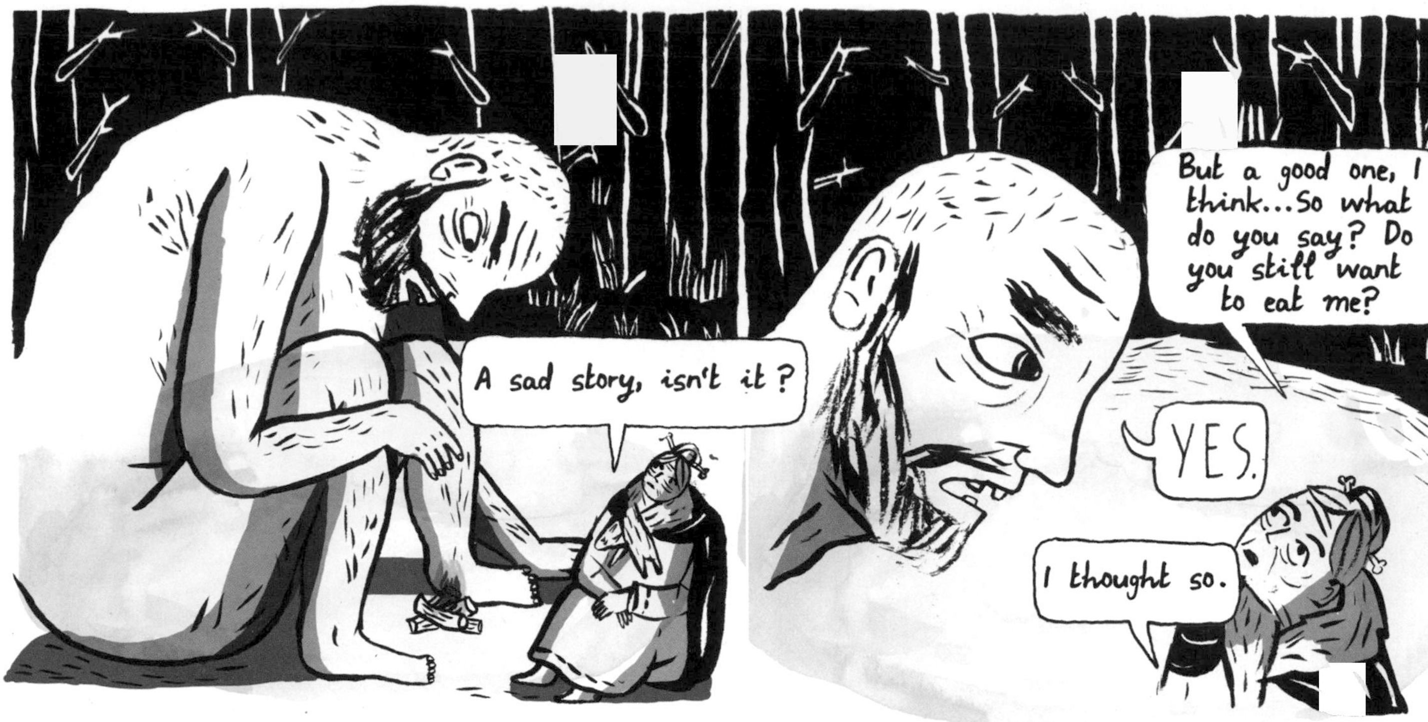
A sad story, isn't it?
But a good one, I think... So what do you say? Do you still want to eat me?
YES.
I thought so.

But as the giant reached forward to grasp her, his eyes rolled back in his head, and like a felled tree he crashed to the earth.

The clever Old Lady had stuffed the sausages full of a powerful sedative herb, and the story had kept him busy just long enough for it to take effect.

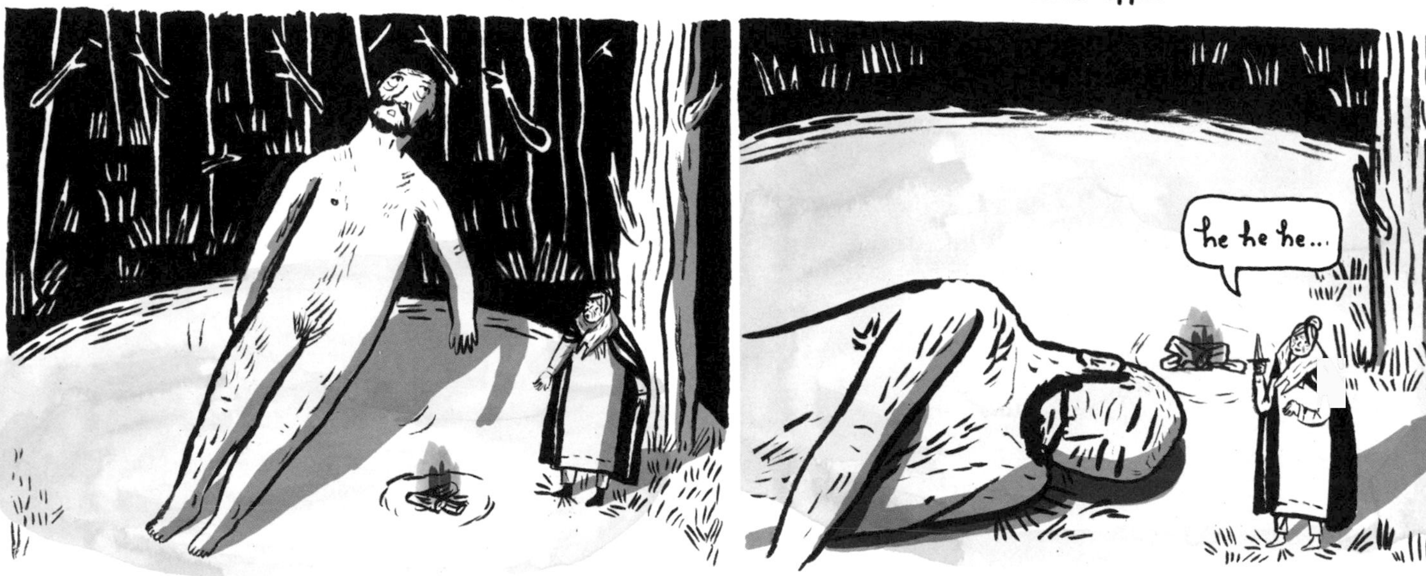
he he he...

And while he slept, using her little dagger, she began to carve off his head.

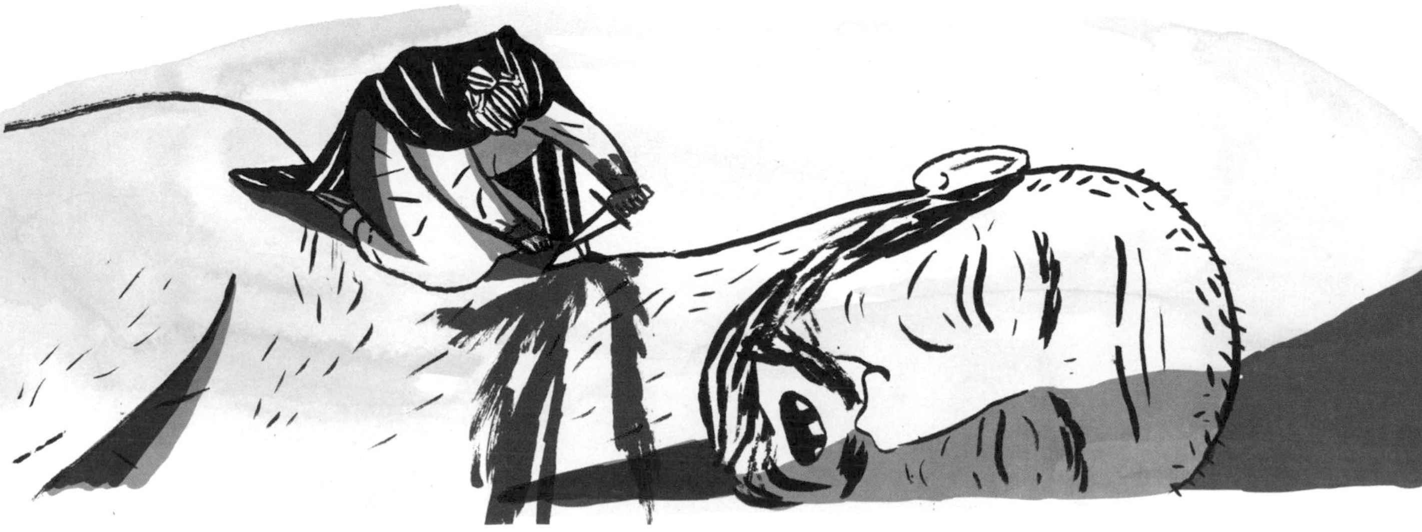

And then, drenched in his blood, she dragged it, step by arduous step, back to the village.

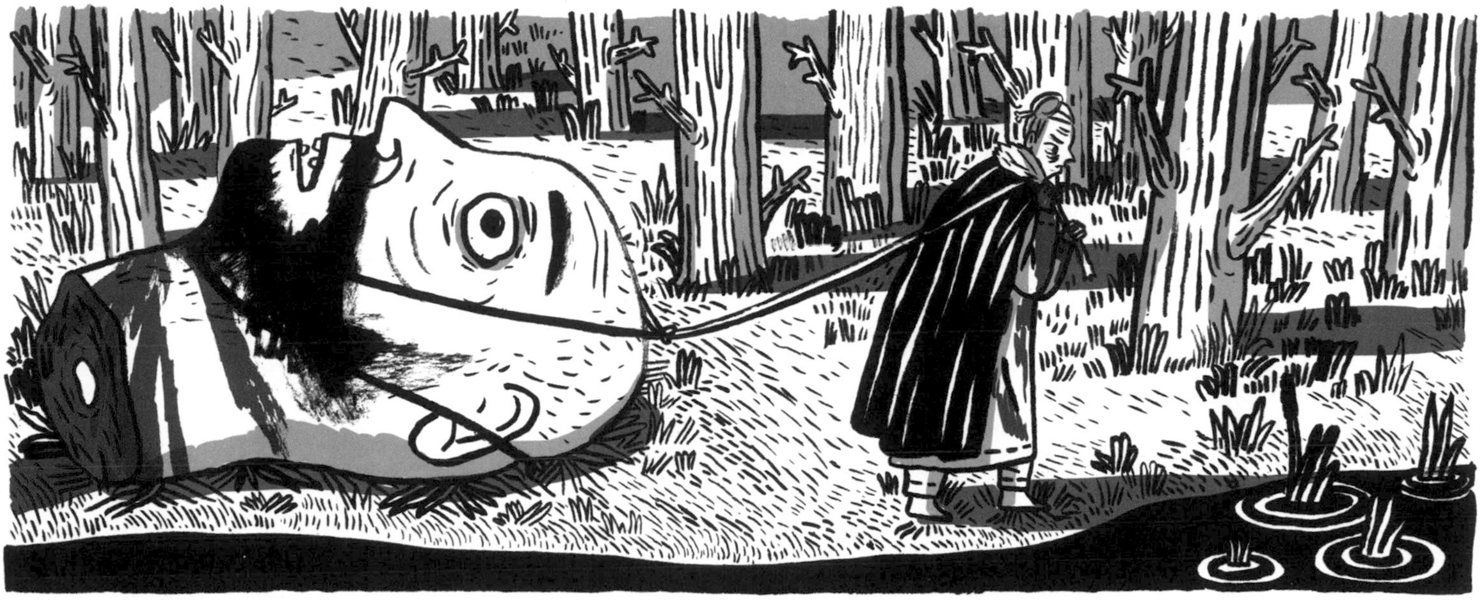

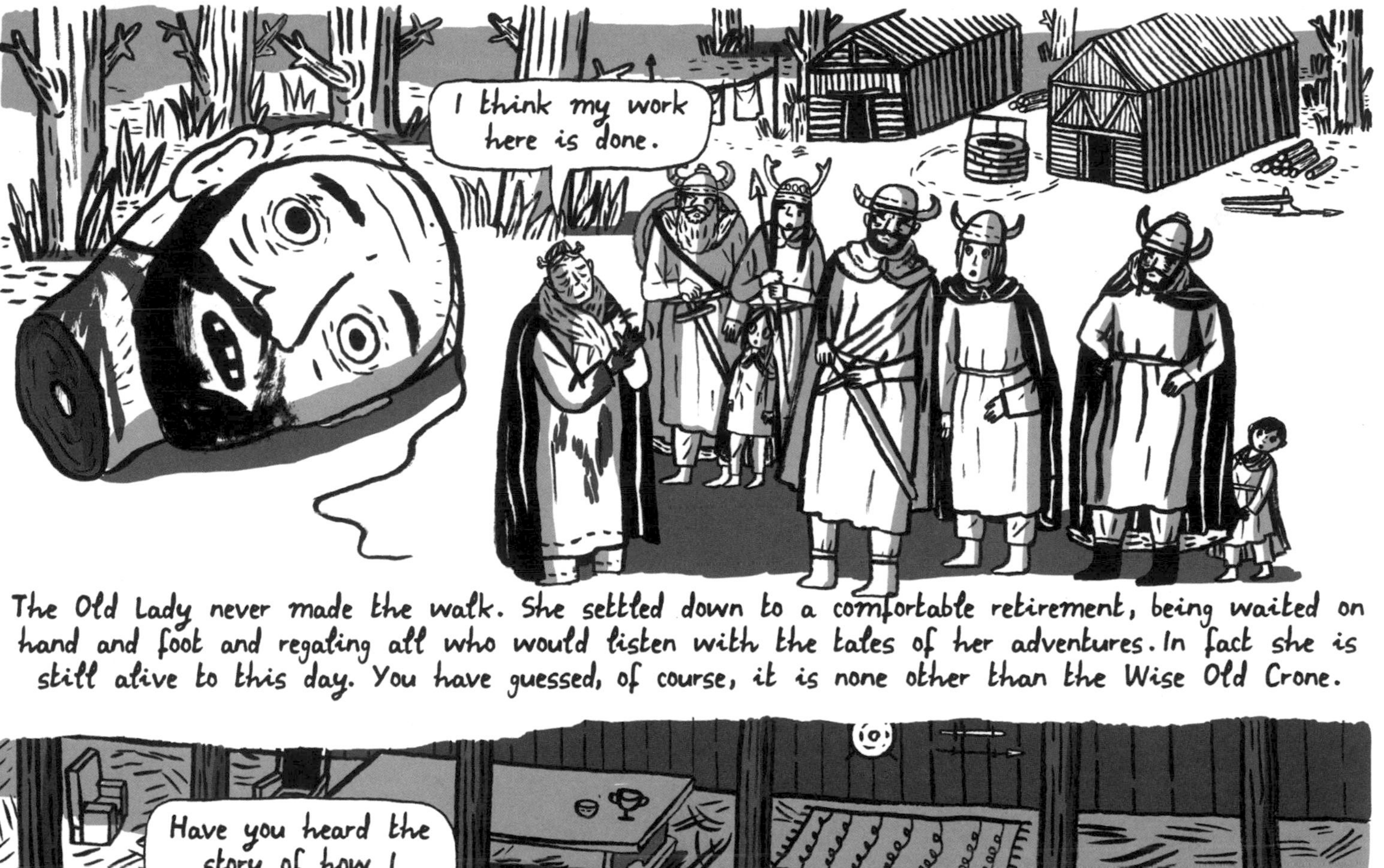
I think my work here is done.

The Old Lady never made the walk. She settled down to a comfortable retirement, being waited on hand and foot and regaling all who would listen with the tales of her adventures. In fact she is still alive to this day. You have guessed, of course, it is none other than the Wise Old Crone.

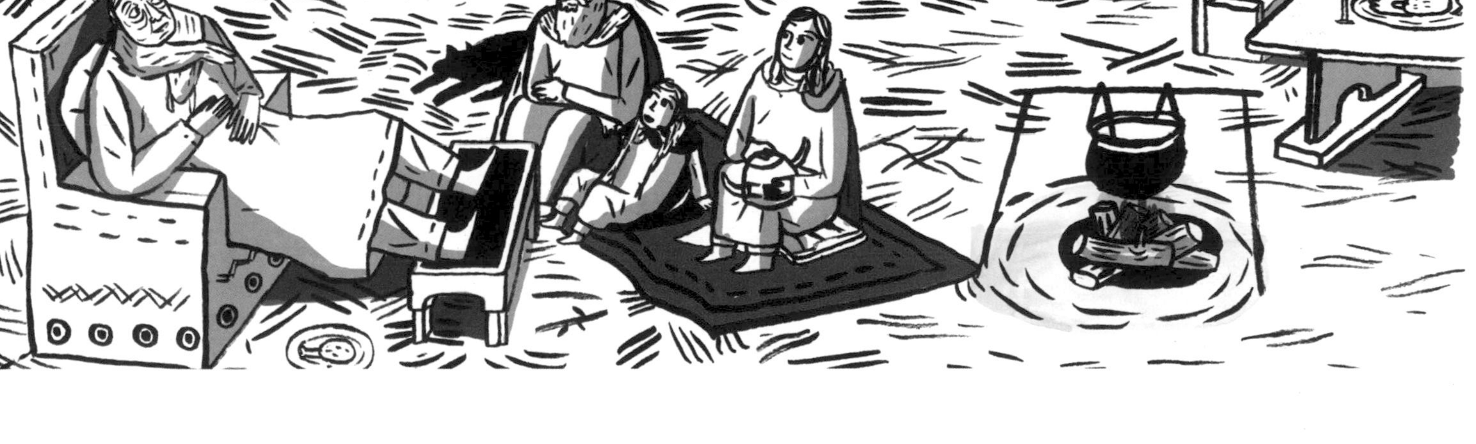
Have you heard the story of how I defeated the giant?

THE CHILDREN OF THE MOUNTAIN

Let me tell you of the Cloud Mountain. All year round its summit is tipped with snow and, more often than not, vanishing into the clouds. It is considered a holy mountain, because it is said that from its tip you can see the Cloud Castle where BirdMan dwells. But no one has ever reached the summit, so whether this is true, who can say?

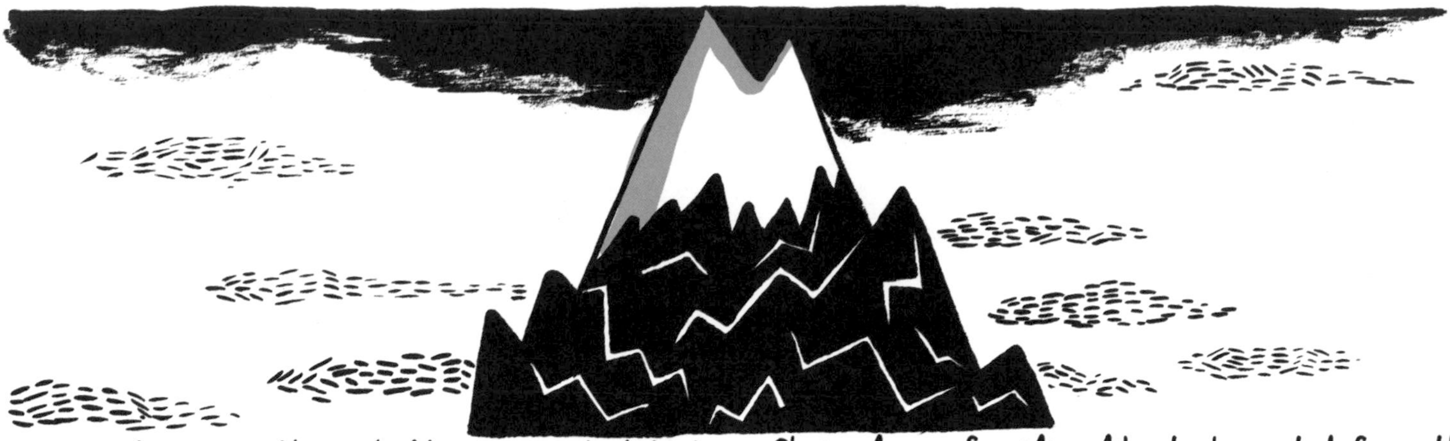

Every ten years three children are picked to be the Children of the Mountain. It is an honour above all other honours.

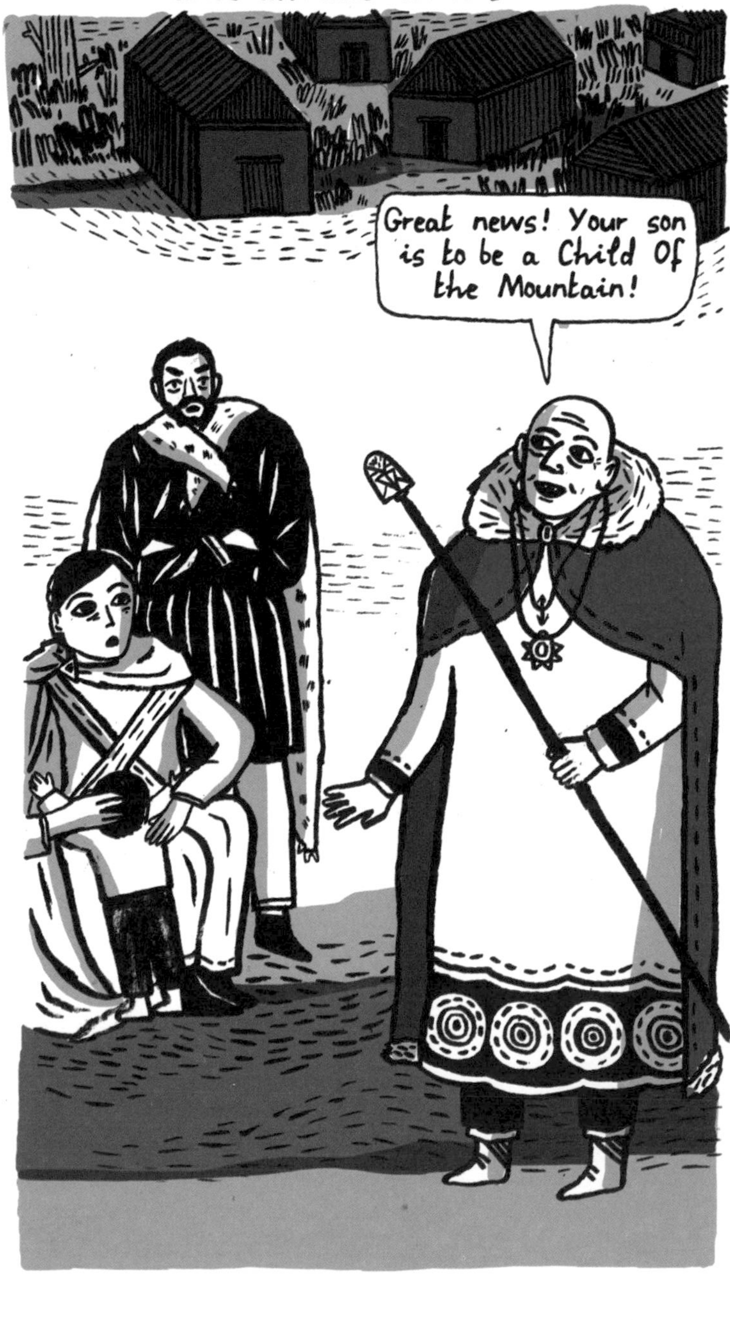

Great news! Your son is to be a Child Of the Mountain!

Obviously no families like to be parted from the children, but once the Necromancer has made hi selection that is that.

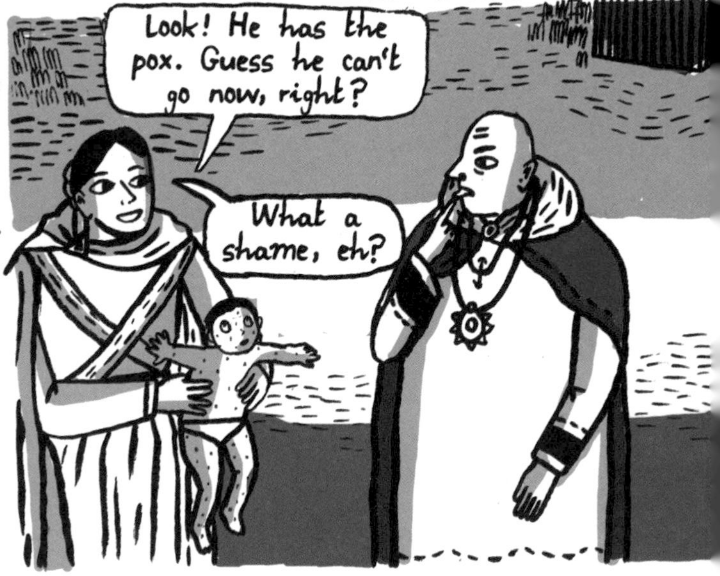

Look! He has the pox. Guess he can't go now, right?
What a shame, eh?

But you cannot fight the Will of BirdMan.

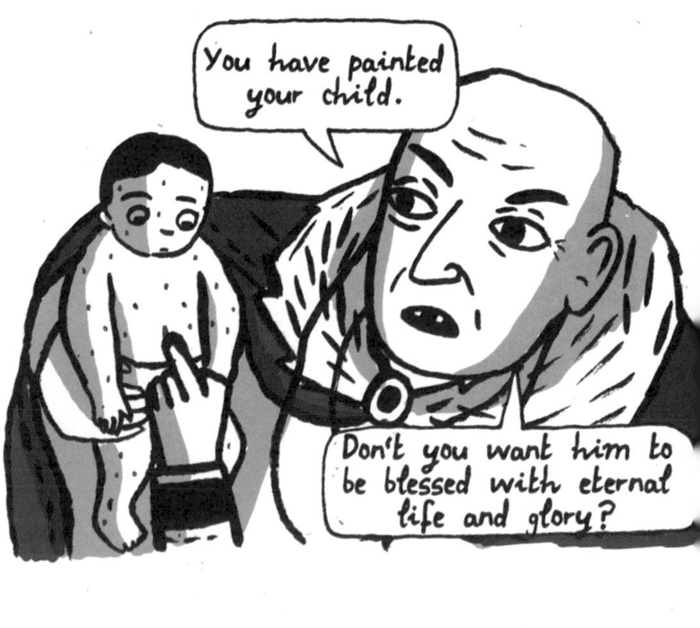

You have painted your child.
Don't you want him to be blessed with eternal life and glory?

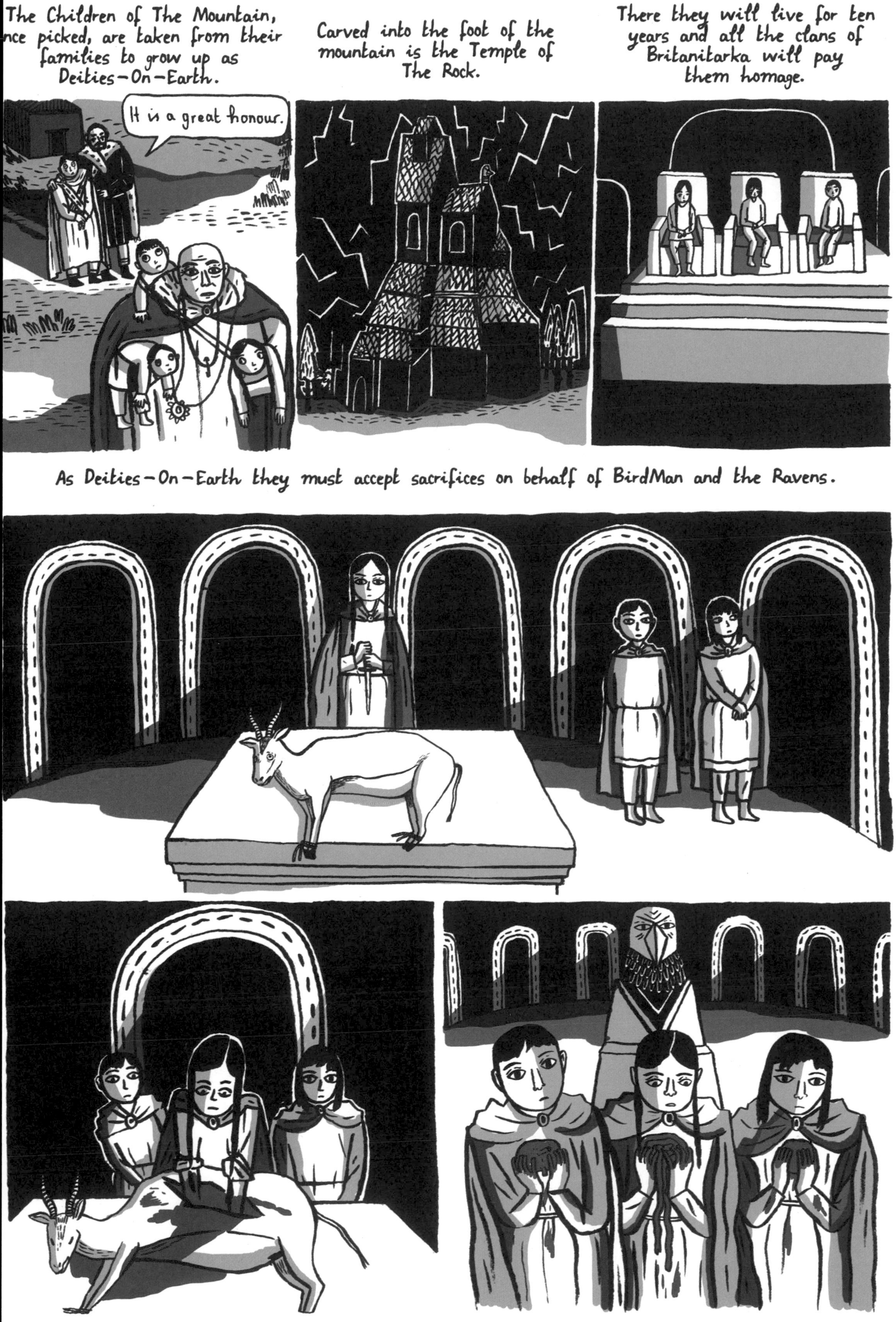
The Children of The Mountain, nce picked, are taken from their families to grow up as Deities-On-Earth.
It is a great honour.
Carved into the foot of the mountain is the Temple of The Rock.
There they will live for ten years and all the clans of Britanitarka will pay them homage.
As Deities-On-Earth they must accept sacrifices on behalf of BirdMan and the Ravens.

And then in the tenth year, on the eve of the Winter Solstice and the Great Wild Hunt, their day of Eternal Glory comes.

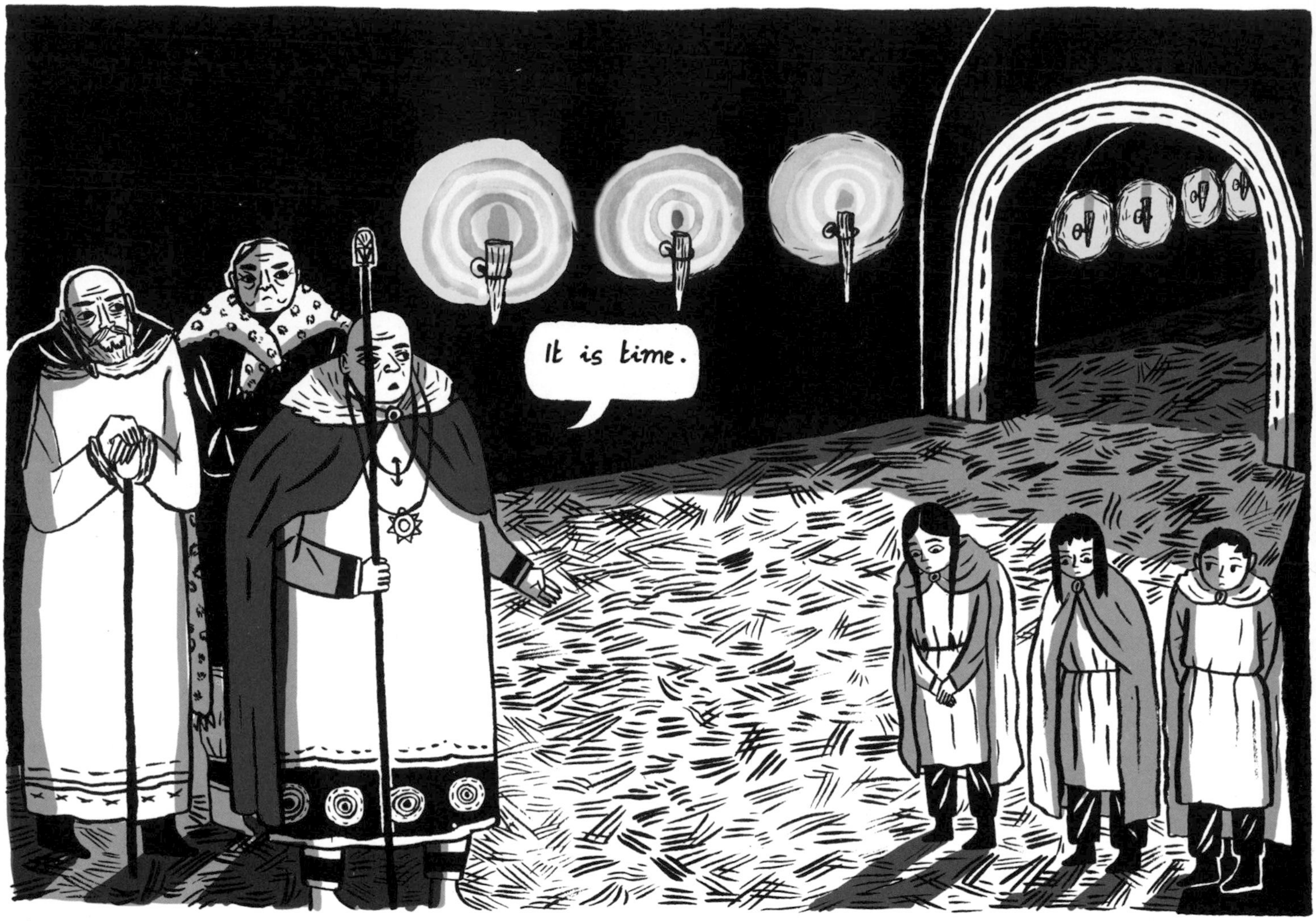
It is time.

They are dressed in the garments of adults, for their journey will be long, and by the time they reach the end they will be fully grown.

They are given provisions, amulets and weapons, everything they will need for the dangers ahead.

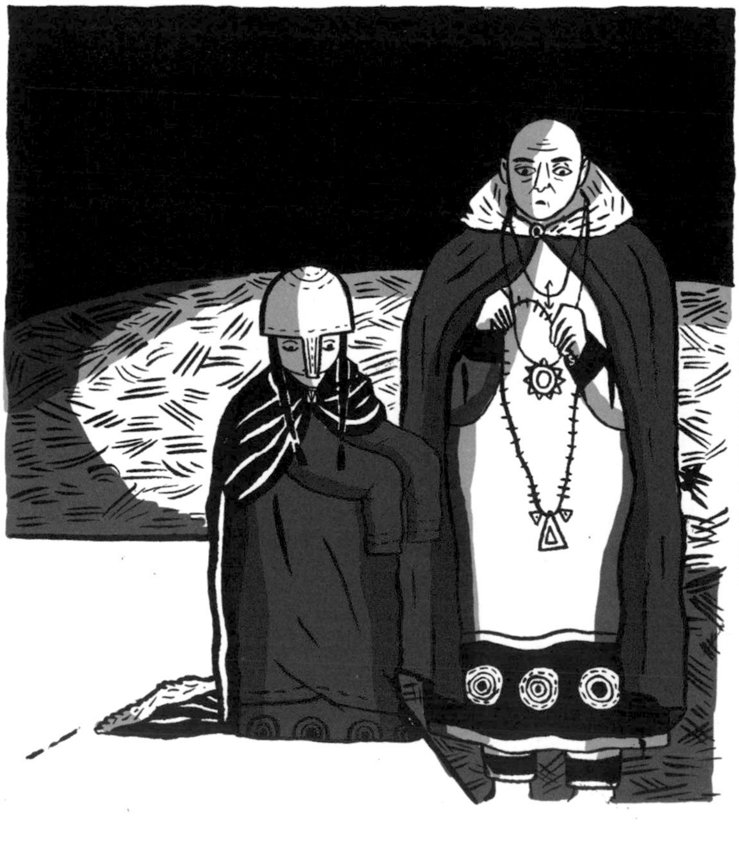

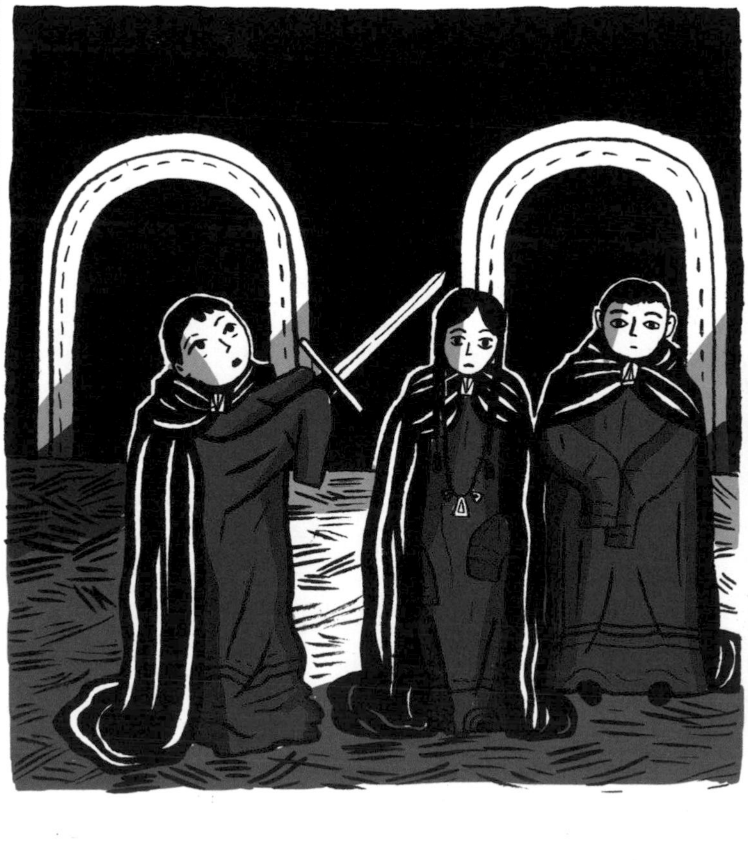

In the darkness of the longest night of the year, they are taken up the Cloud Mountain.

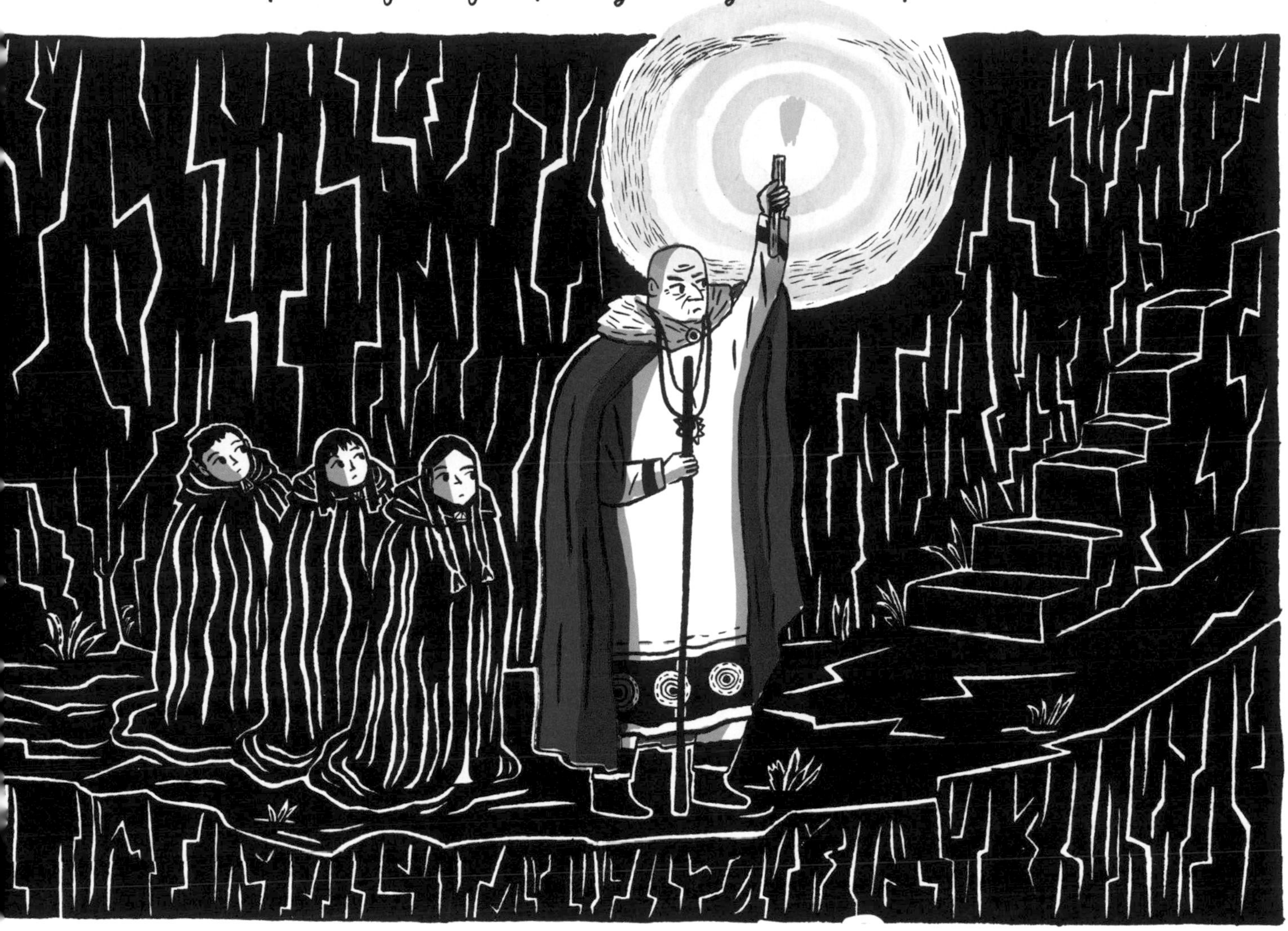

They are given a secret and holy potion to ease their journey into the Other World. It is a deadly potion that will stop their hearts beating. They will not wake up again in this life. Then the Gods will be appeased and the Great Wild Hunt can commence.

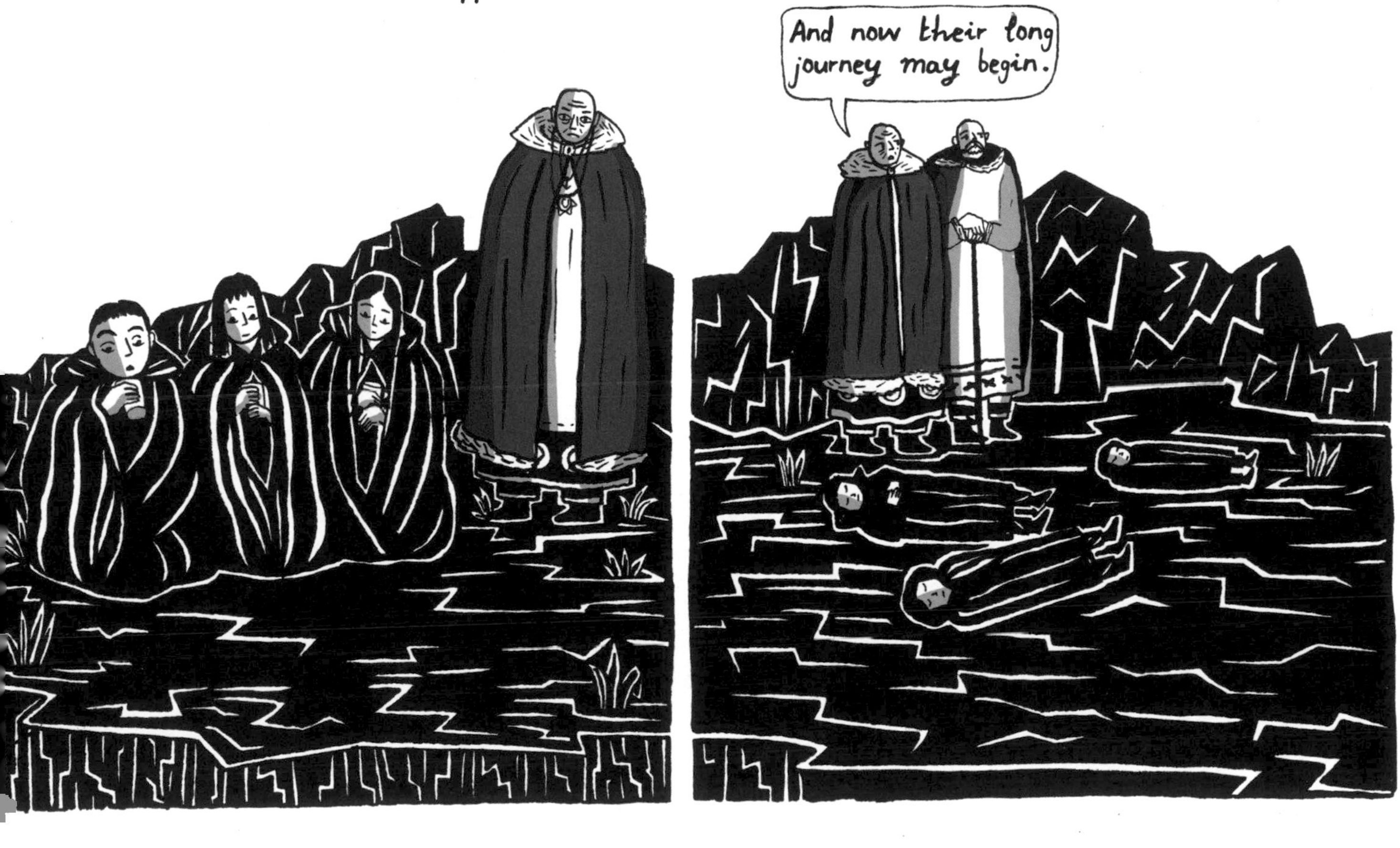
And now their long journey may begin.

THE LONG NIGHT

It was the night before the Great Wild Hunt, when the whole clan went out to hunt th elusive Giant Boar. They stayed up all night long, drinking and eating, and when dawn came the hunt would commence. The Storyteller was to be the first outsider to witness it

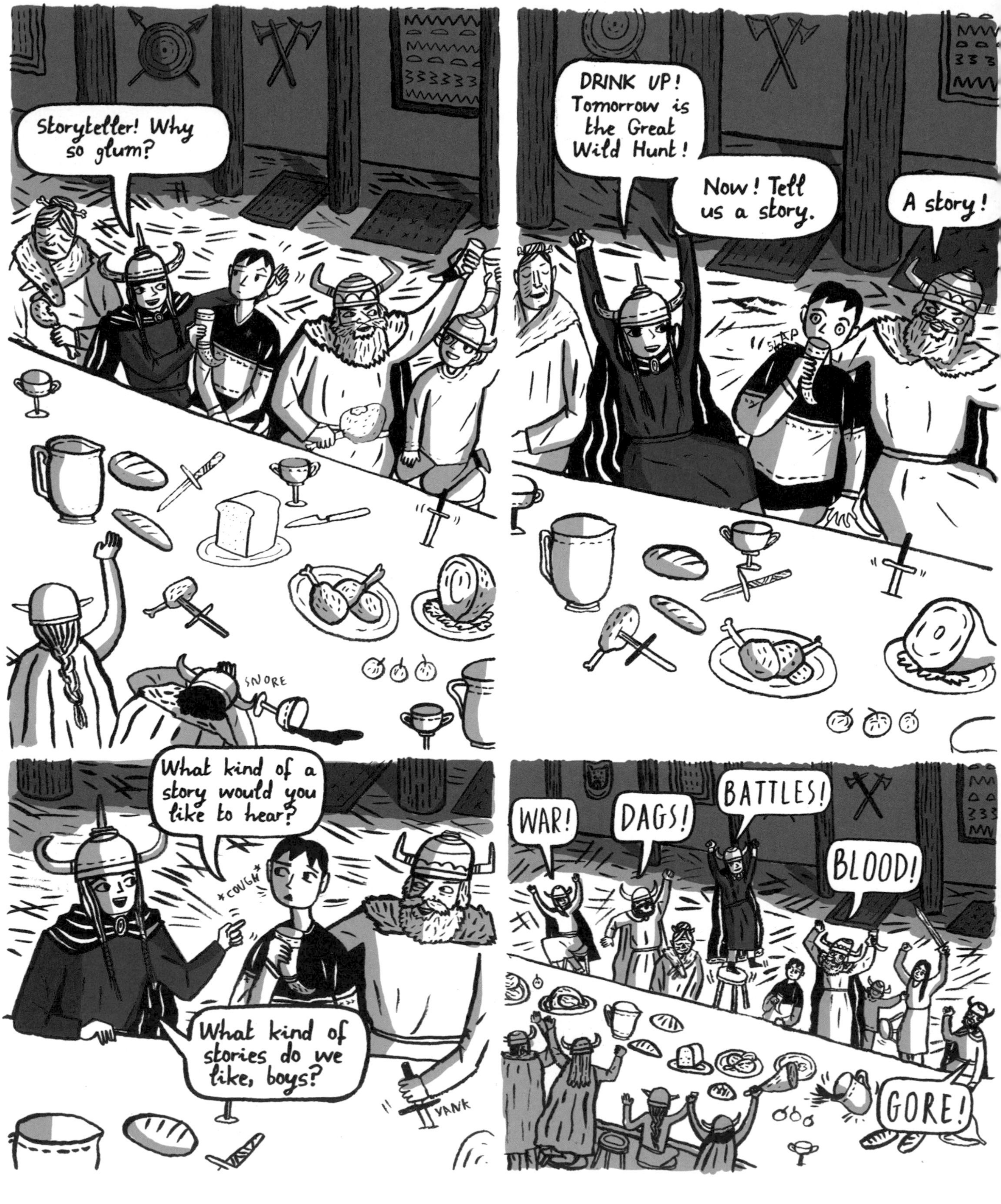

Storyteller! Why so glum?
SNORE
DRINK UP! Tomorrow is the Great Wild Hunt!
Now! Tell us a story.
A story!
SLAP
What kind of a story would you like to hear?
COUGH
What kind of stories do we like, boys?
YANK
WAR!
DAGS!
BATTLES!
BLOOD!
GORE!

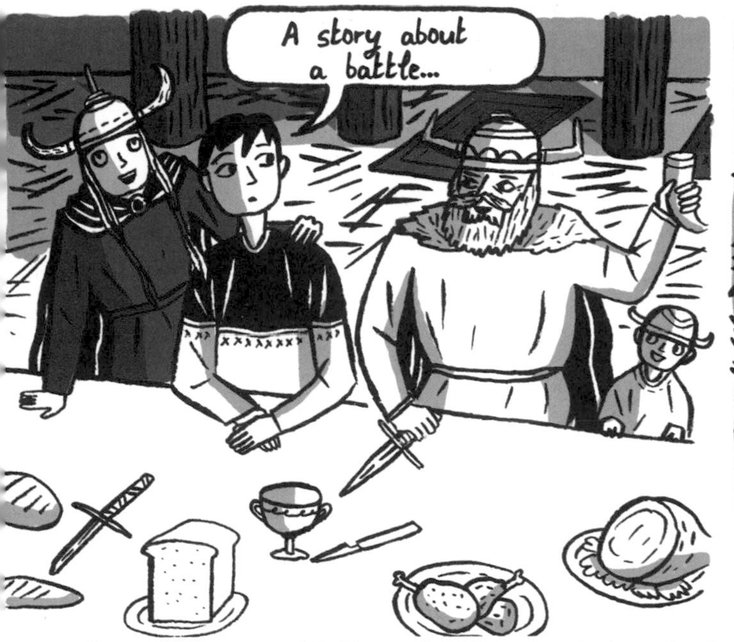
A story about a battle...

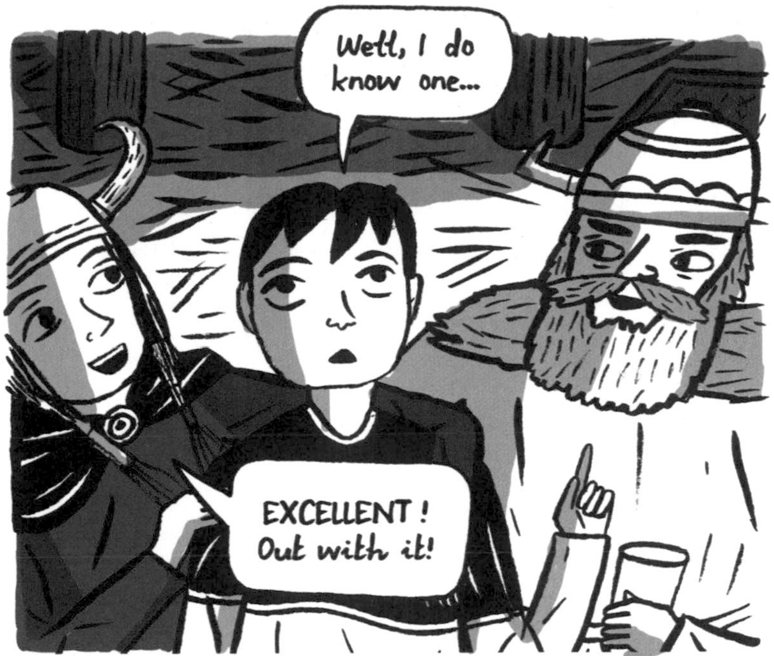
Well, I do know one...
EXCELLENT! Out with it!

Perhaps it was all the ale the Great Dag had been pouring him, or perhaps it was BirdMan's prophecy coming true; that his stories would be his undoing. Whatever it was, the Storyteller could not afterwards remember what had possessed him to tell such a story.

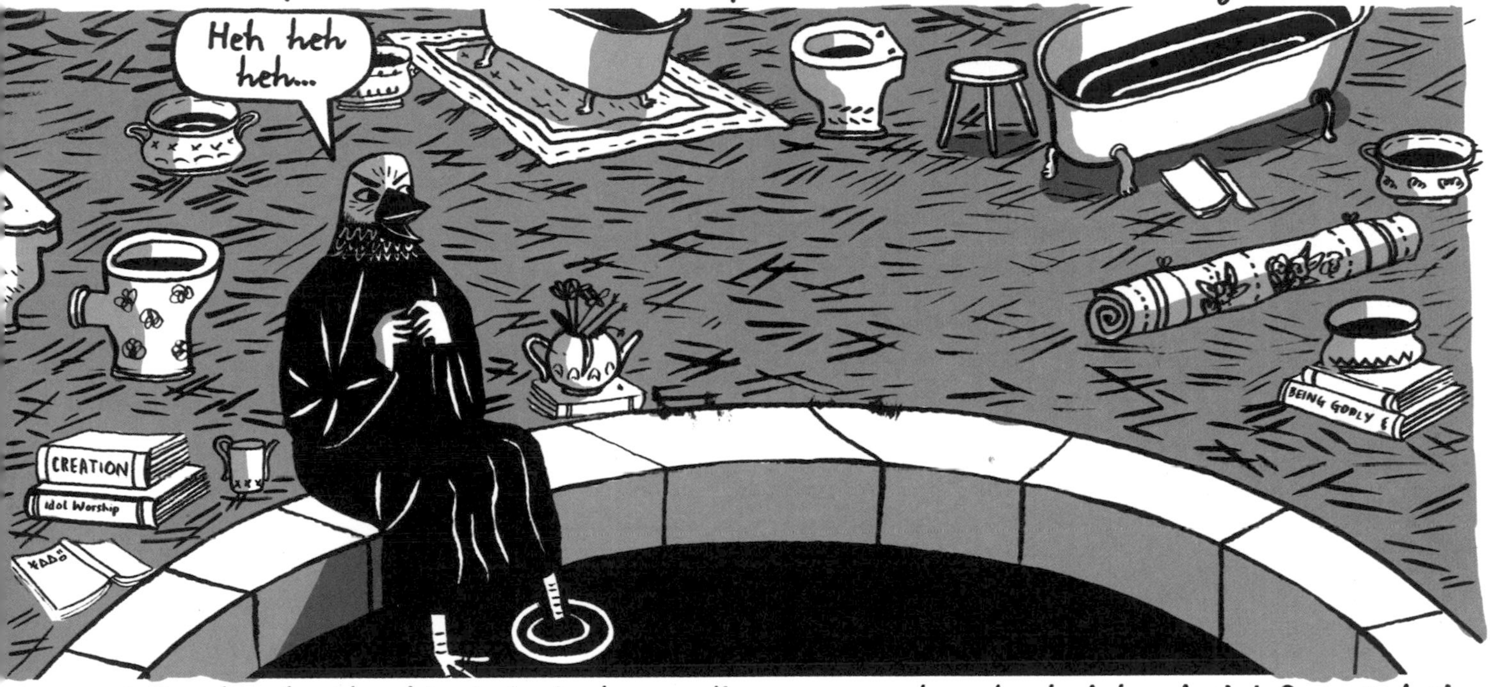
Heh heh heh...
CREATION
Idol Worship
BEING GODLY &

In fact, when he thought about it, he wasn't even sure where he had heard it before. And it certainly wasn't one of his best...

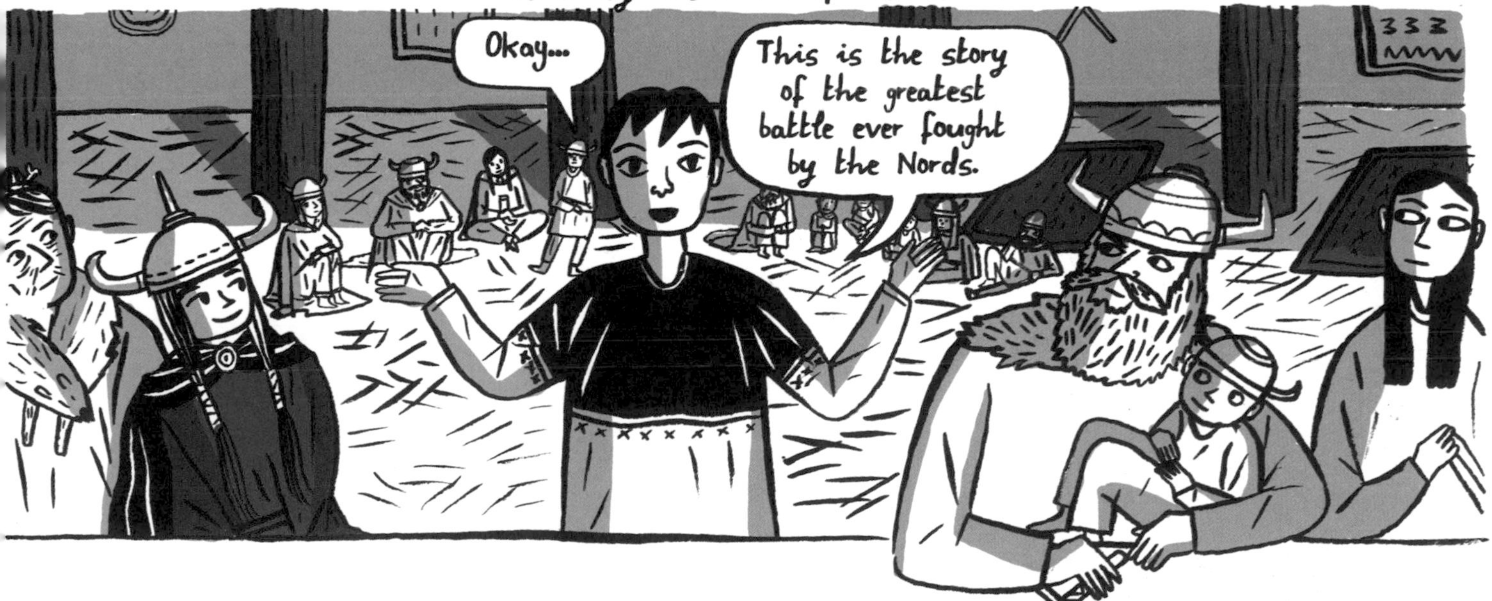
Okay...
This is the story of the greatest battle ever fought by the Nords.

DEAD TOWNS & GHOST MEN

The Nords say that one thousand years ago or more, ships of strangers arrived on the shores of thei land. They were pale of face and cold of eye, and they were warlike and savage.

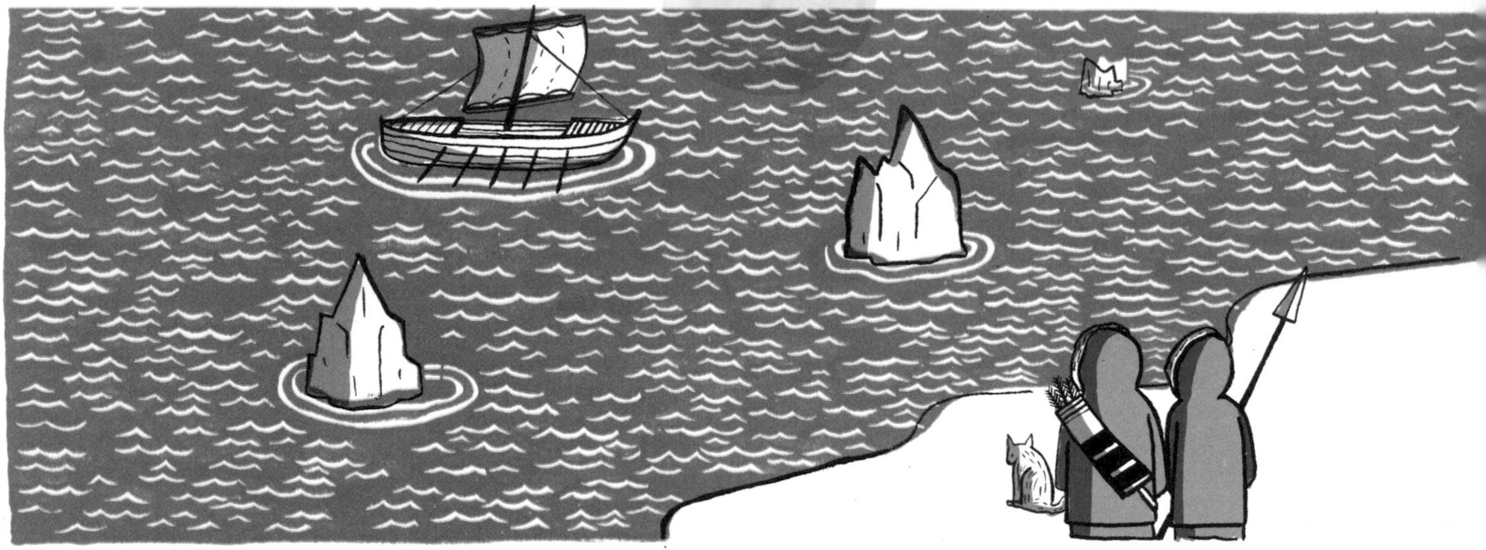

They plundered and rampaged and drove the Nords away from the coast, from the good hunting grounds, inland to the colder regions.

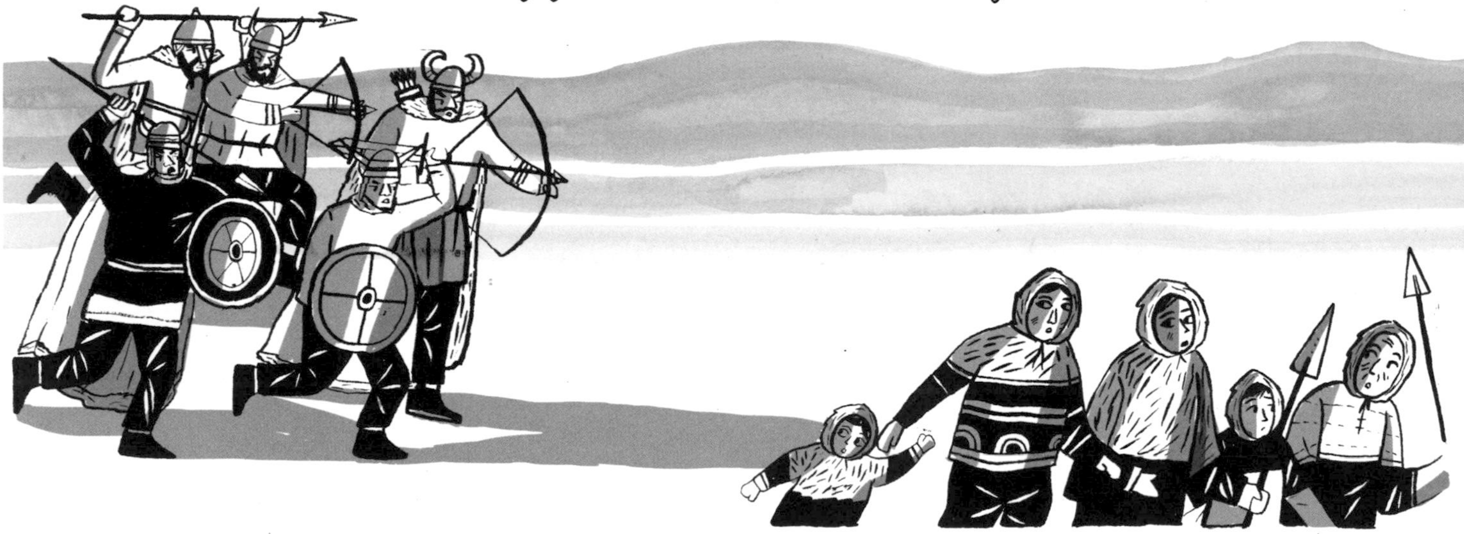

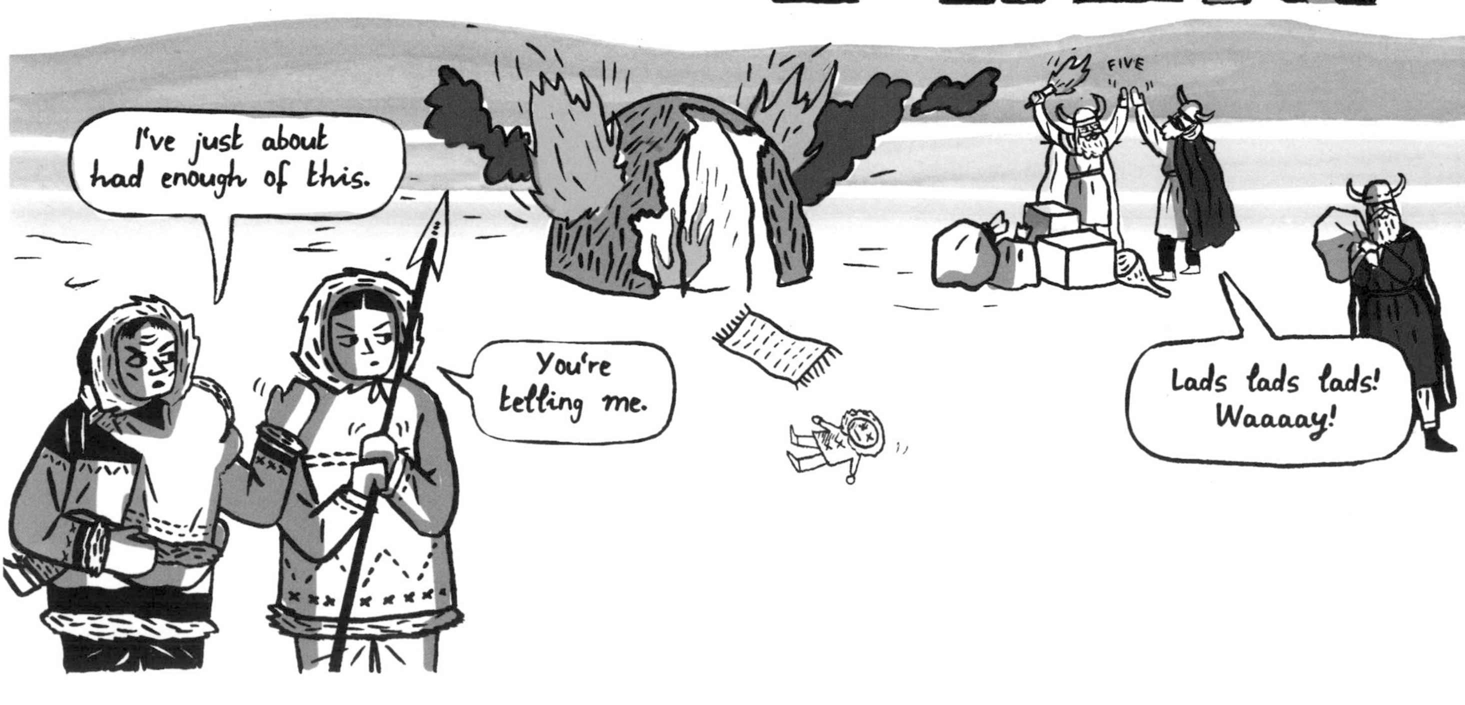
I've just about had enough of this.
FIVE
You're telling me.
Lads lads lads! Waaaay!

d so quietly and secretly the clans and families and villages of Nord began to plan and plot a great invasion to drive the Strangers from their land. The Strangers had better weapons, and were used to hting. But the Nords knew the land, and the land knew them. It was a bitter and terrible war, but in the end the Nords prevailed.

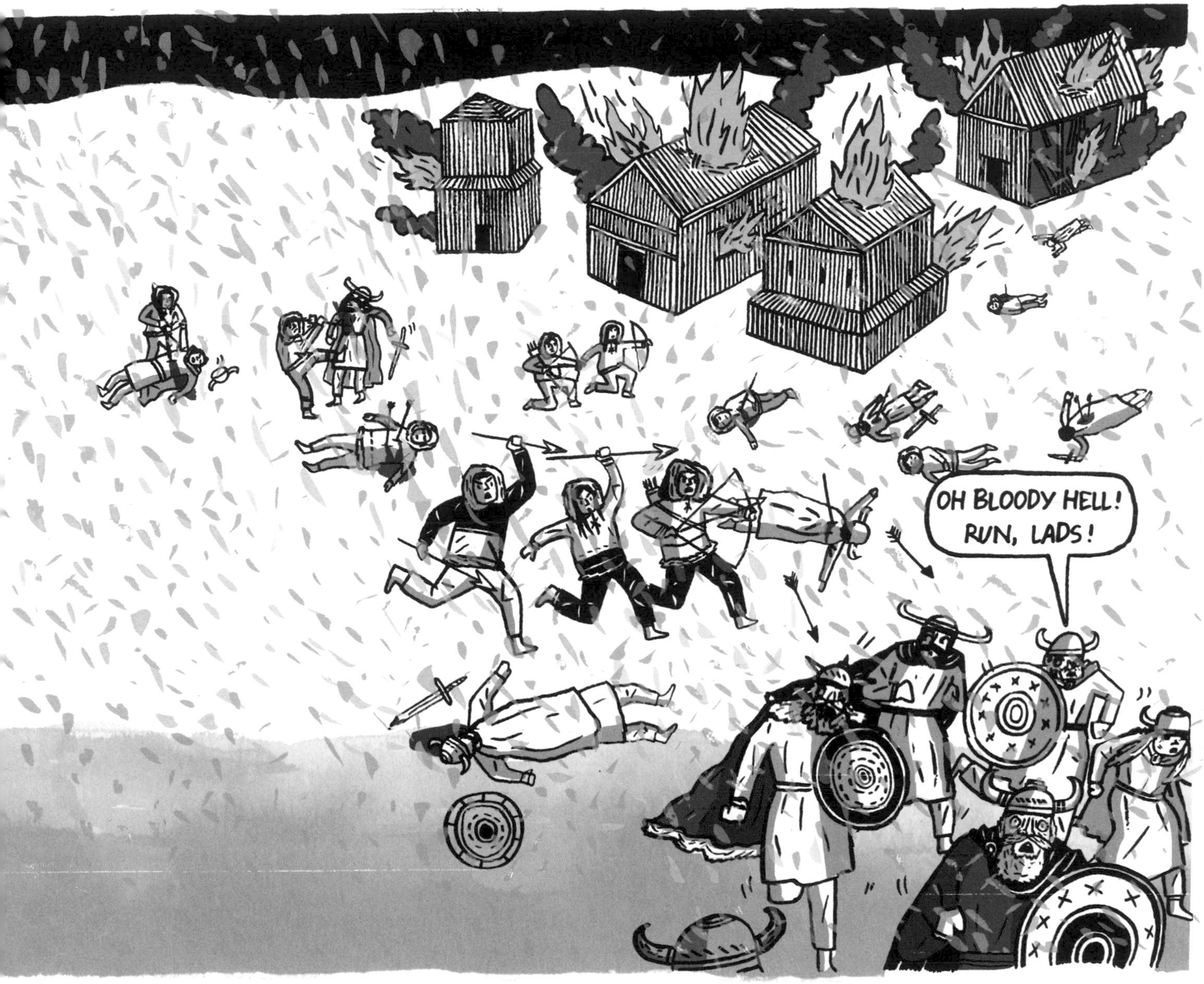
OH BLOODY HELL! RUN, LADS!

They drove the Strangers back to their boats and swore to kill them if they ever returned. The rangers sailed away, but winter came and trapped them fast in the ice. It was said that only one boat made it away from Nord. And that beneath the ice of the frozen sea the spirits of the cold-eyed, pale-faced strangers are still trapped.

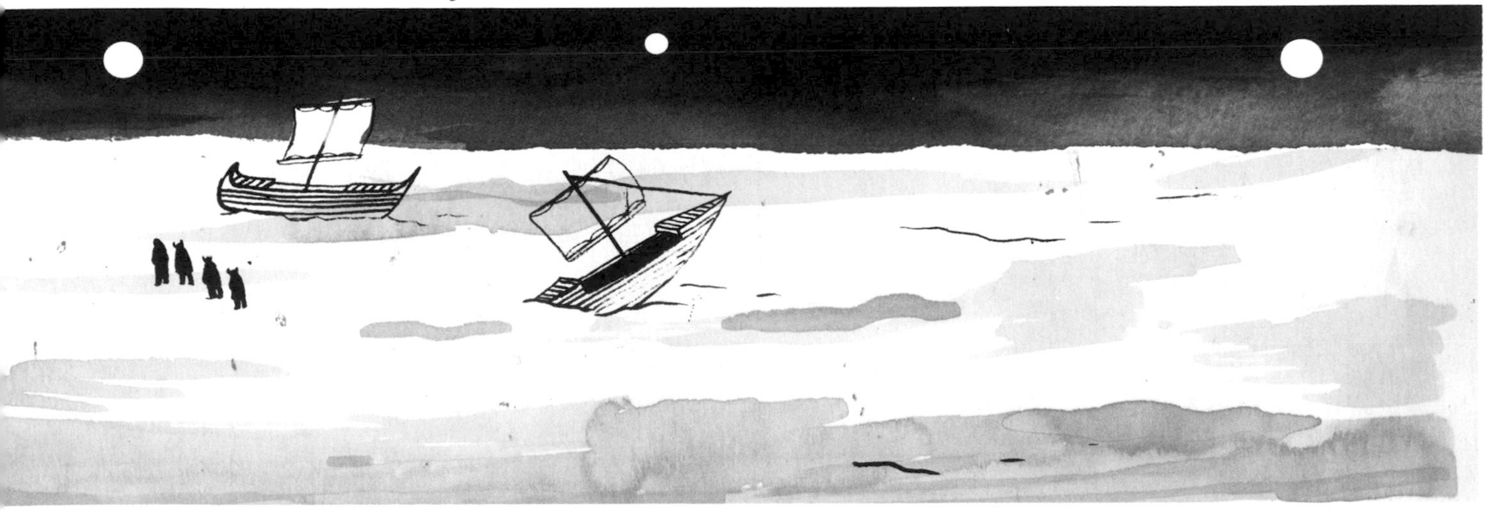

As he finished the story a terrible silence fell in the hall, and every eye was on him.
The Storyteller realised he had made a terrible mistake...

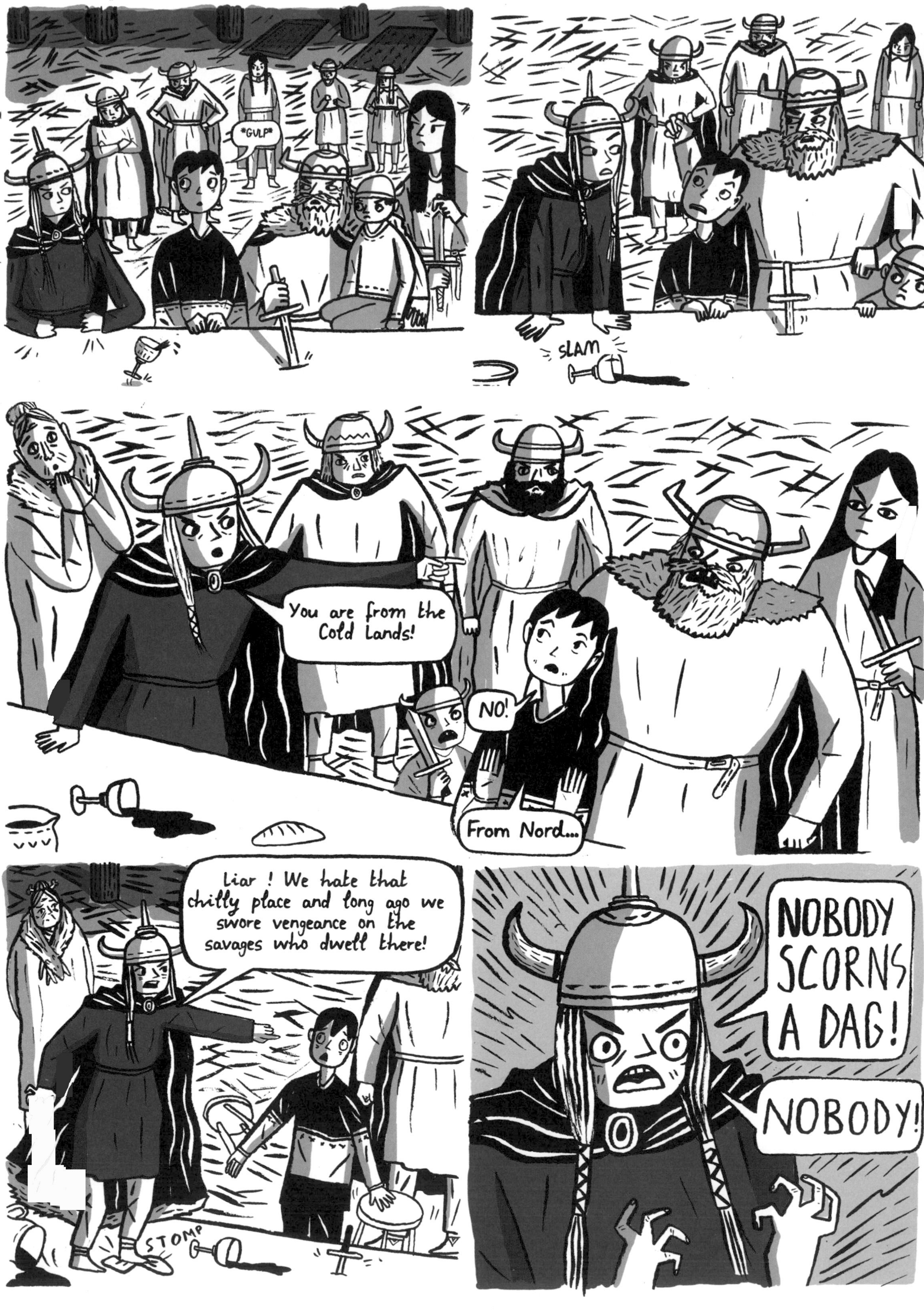
GULP
SLAM
You are from the Cold Lands!
NO!
From Nord...
Liar ! We hate that chilly place and long ago we swore vengeance on the savages who dwell there!
STOMP
NOBODY SCORNS A DAG!
NOBODY!

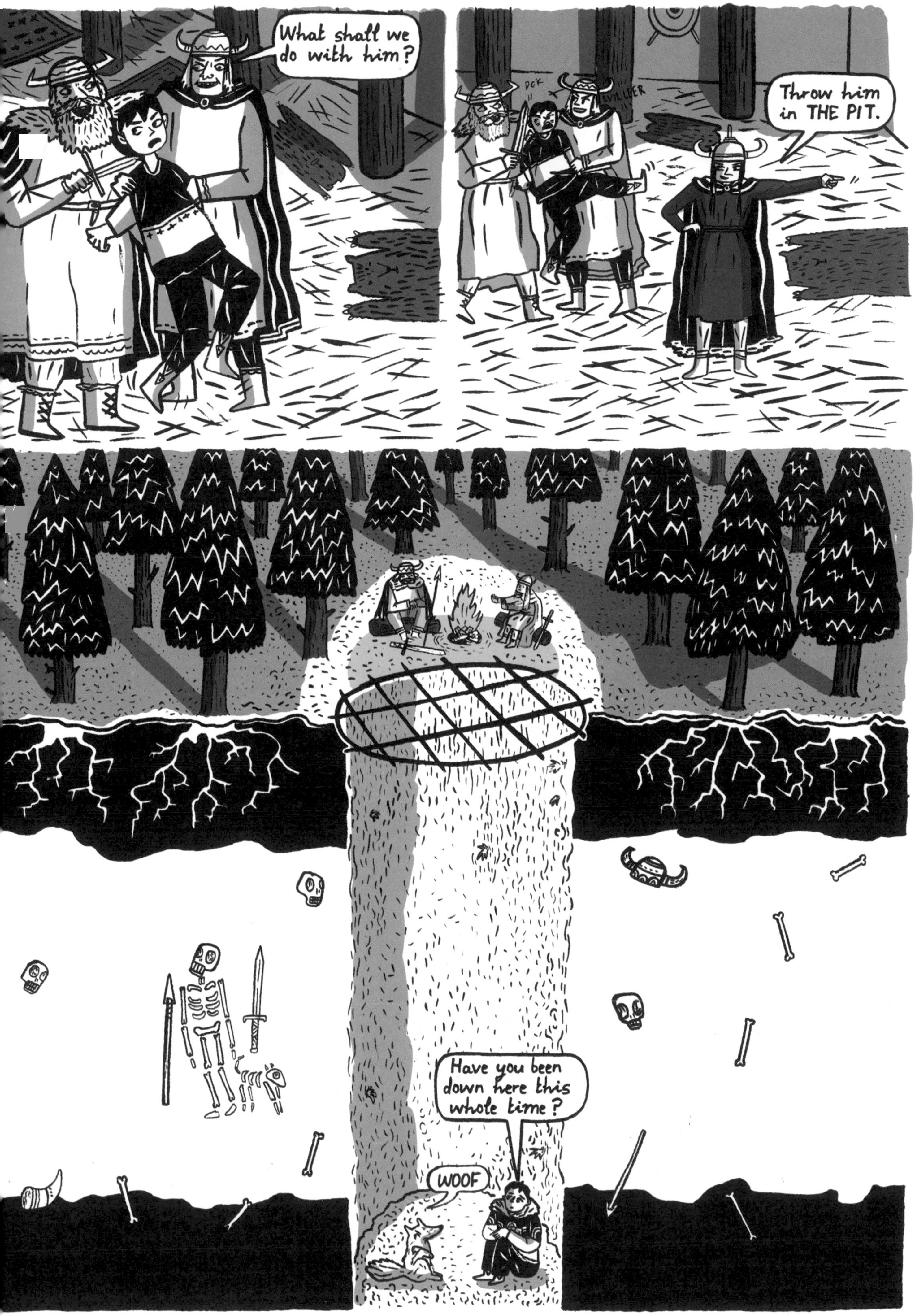
What shall we do with him?
Throw him in THE PIT.
Have you been down here this whole time?
WOOF

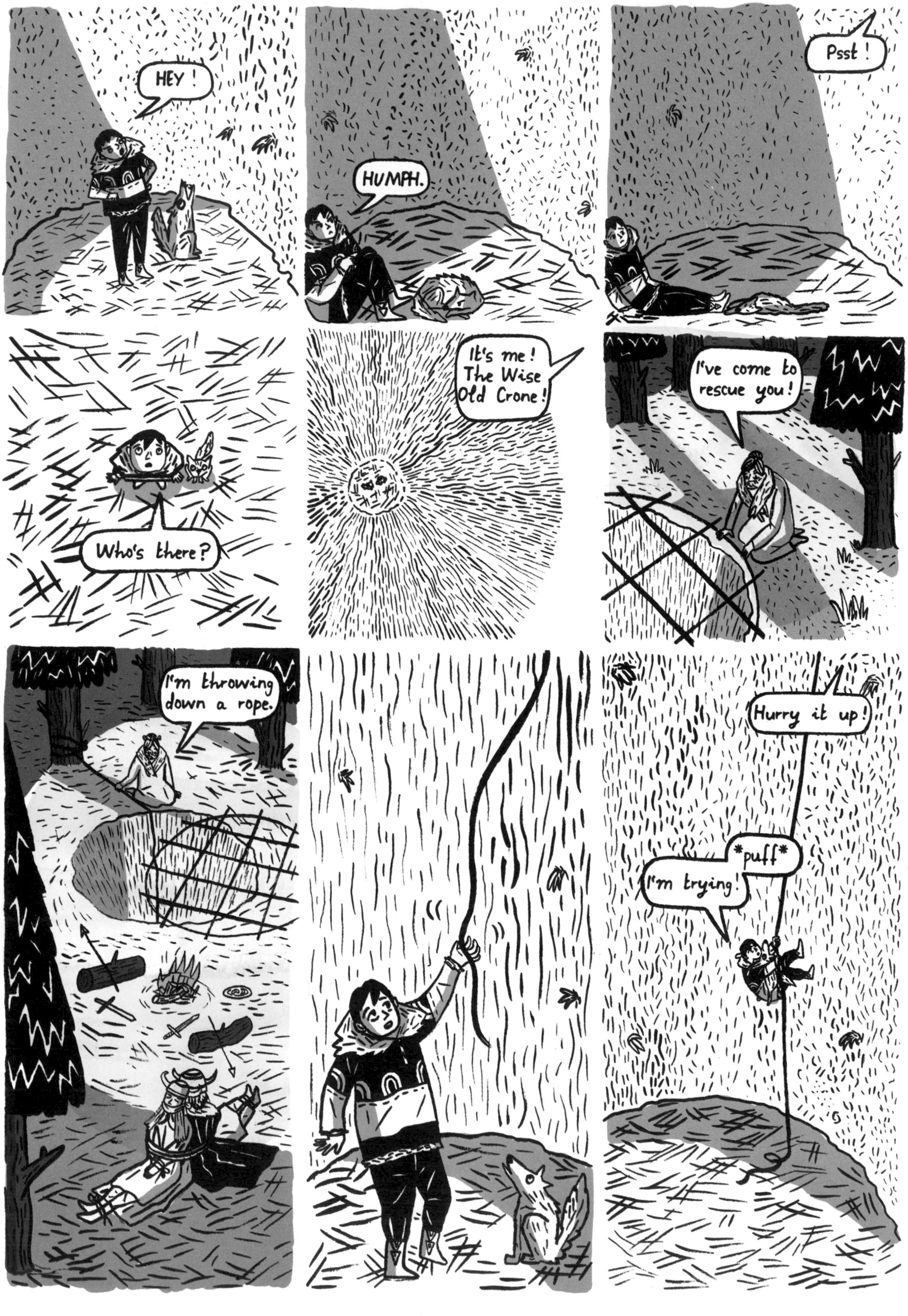
HEY!
HUMPH.
Psst!
Who's there?
It's me! The Wise Old Crone!
I've come to rescue you!
I'm throwing down a rope.
Hurry it up!
puff
I'm trying!

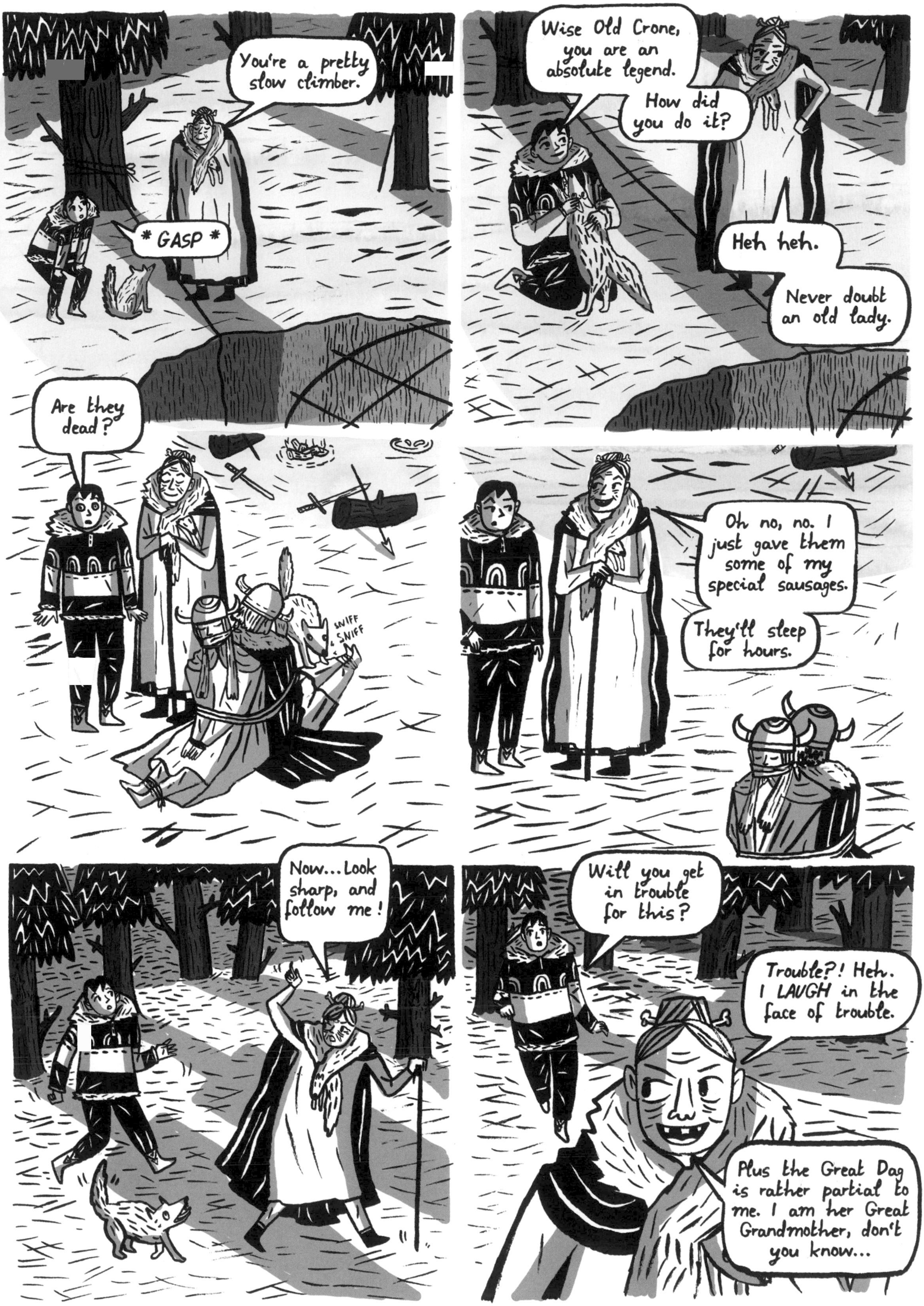
You're a pretty slow climber.
* GASP *
Wise Old Crone, you are an absolute legend.
How did you do it?
Heh heh.
Never doubt an old lady.
Are they dead?
SNIFF SNIFF
Oh no, no. I just gave them some of my special sausages.
They'll sleep for hours.
Now... Look sharp, and follow me!
Will you get in trouble for this?
Trouble?! Heh. I LAUGH in the face of trouble.
Plus the Great Dag is rather partial to me. I am her Great Grandmother, don't you know...

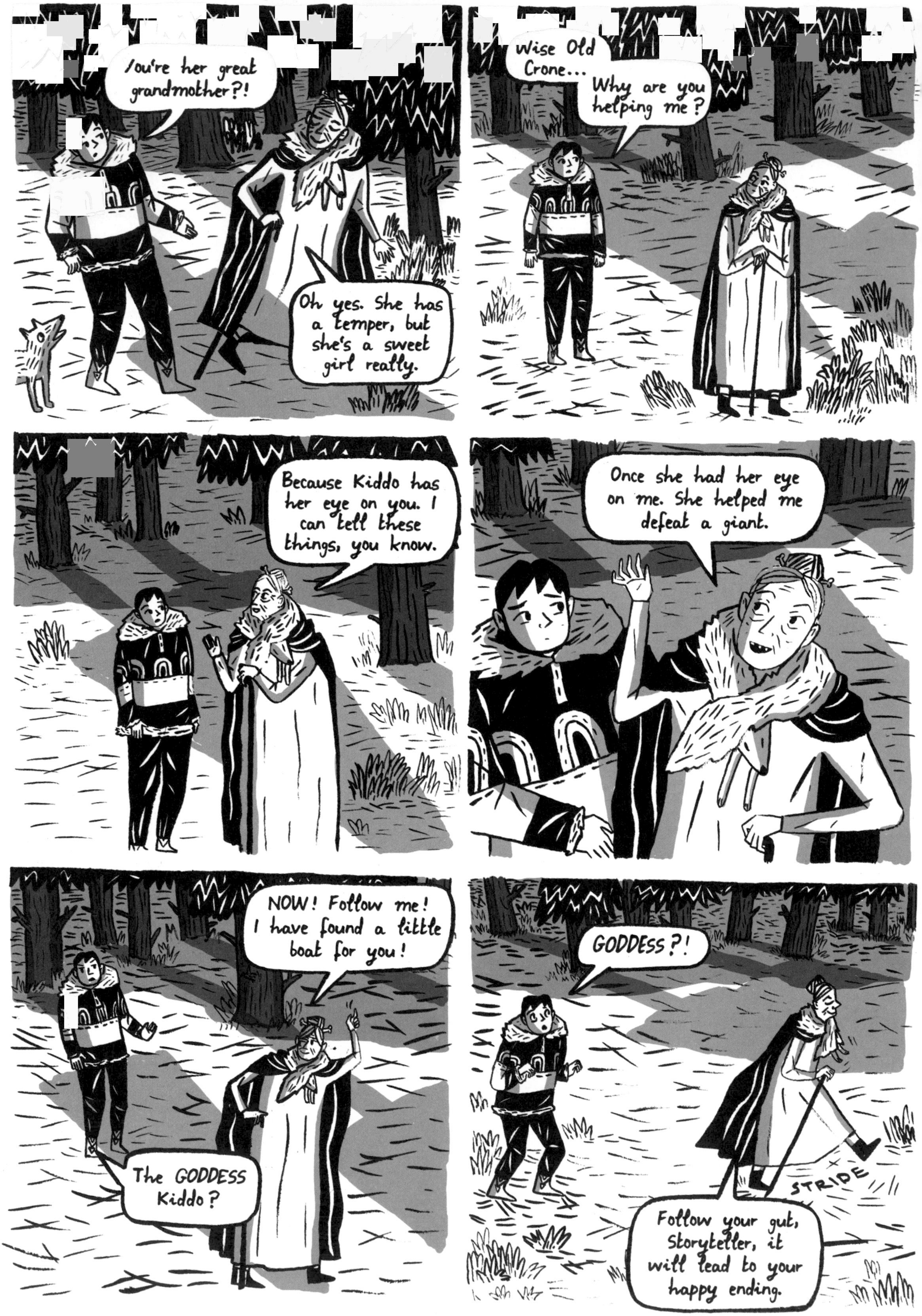
You're her great grandmother?!
Oh yes. She has a temper, but she's a sweet girl really.
Wise Old Crone...
Why are you helping me?
Because Kiddo has her eye on you. I can tell these things, you know.
Once she had her eye on me. She helped me defeat a giant.
NOW! Follow me! I have found a little boat for you!
The GODDESS Kiddo?
GODDESS?!
STRIDE
Follow your gut, Storyteller, it will lead to your happy ending.

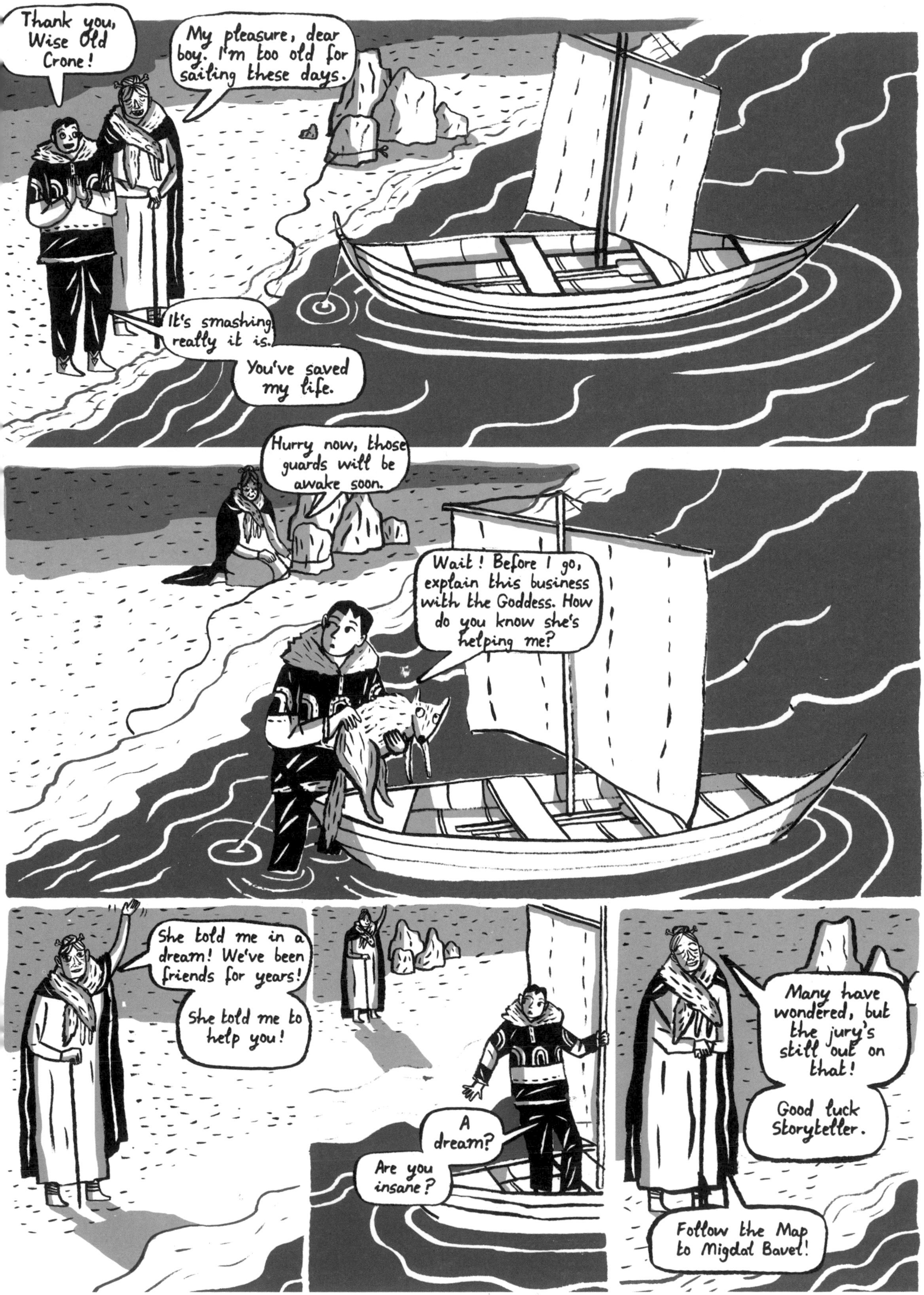
Thank you, Wise Old Crone!
My pleasure, dear boy. I'm too old for sailing these days.
It's smashing, really it is.
You've saved my life.
Hurry now, those guards will be awake soon.
Wait! Before I go, explain this business with the Goddess. How do you know she's helping me?
She told me in a dream! We've been friends for years!
She told me to help you!
A dream?
Are you insane?
Many have wondered, but the jury's still out on that!
Good luck Storyteller.
Follow the Map to Migdal Bavel!

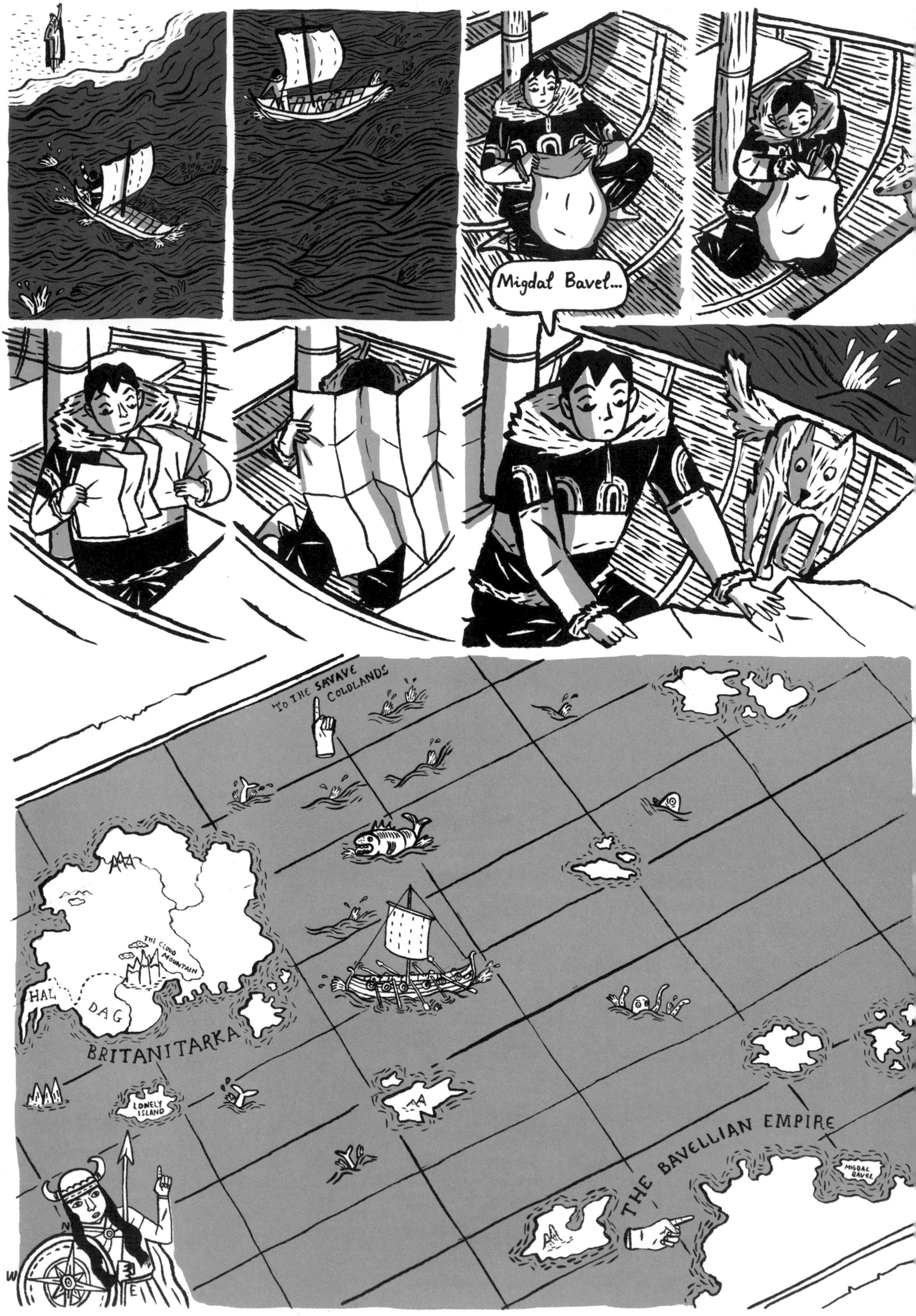
Migdal Bavel...
TO THE SAVAVE COLDLANDS
THE CLOUD MOUNTAIN
HAL
DAG
BRITANITARKA
LONELY ISLAND
THE BAVELLIAN EMPIRE
MIGDAL BAVEL
N
W
E

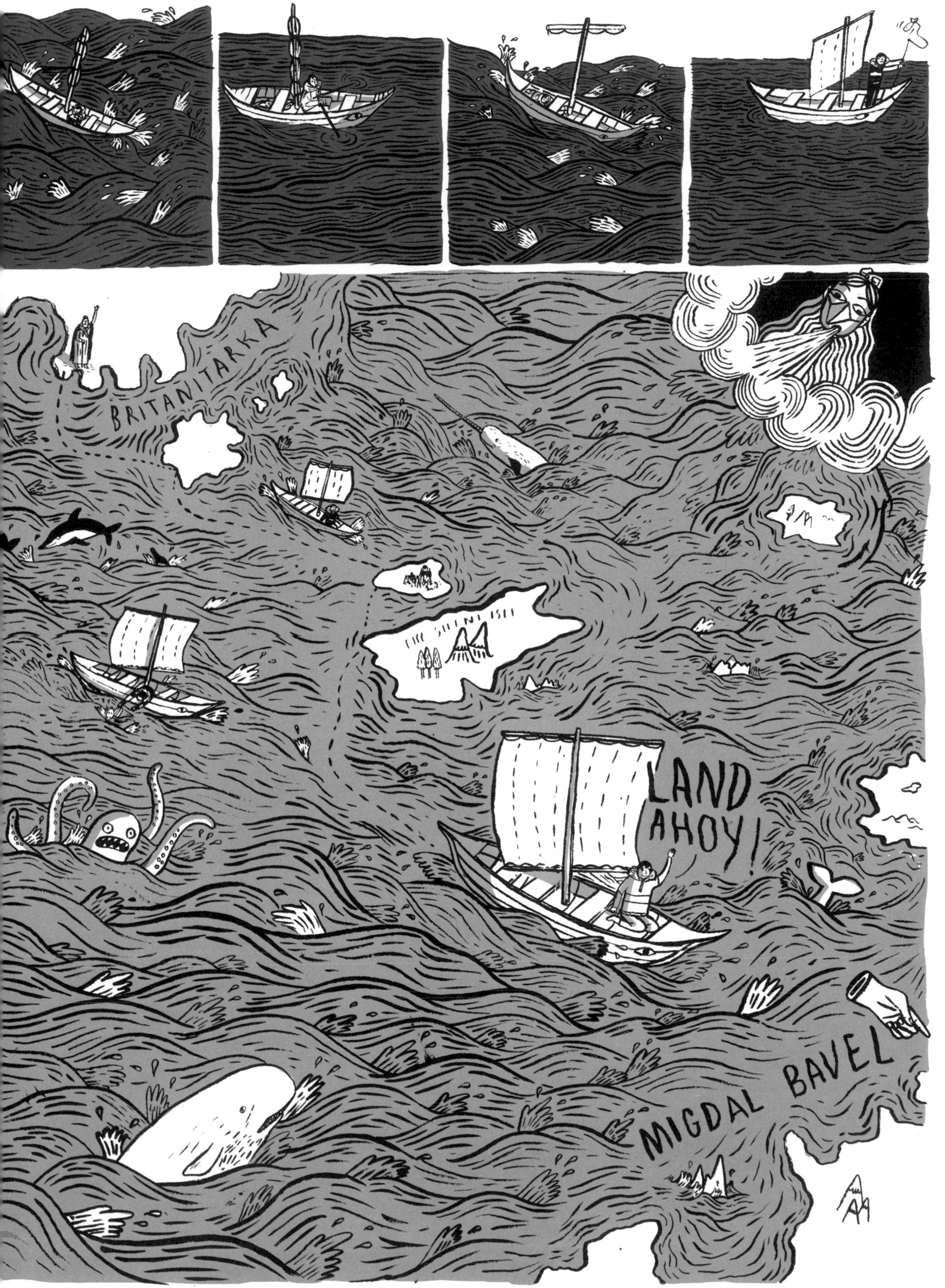
BRITANITARKA
LAND AHOY!
MIGDAL BAVEL

Part The Third:

MIGDAL BAVEL

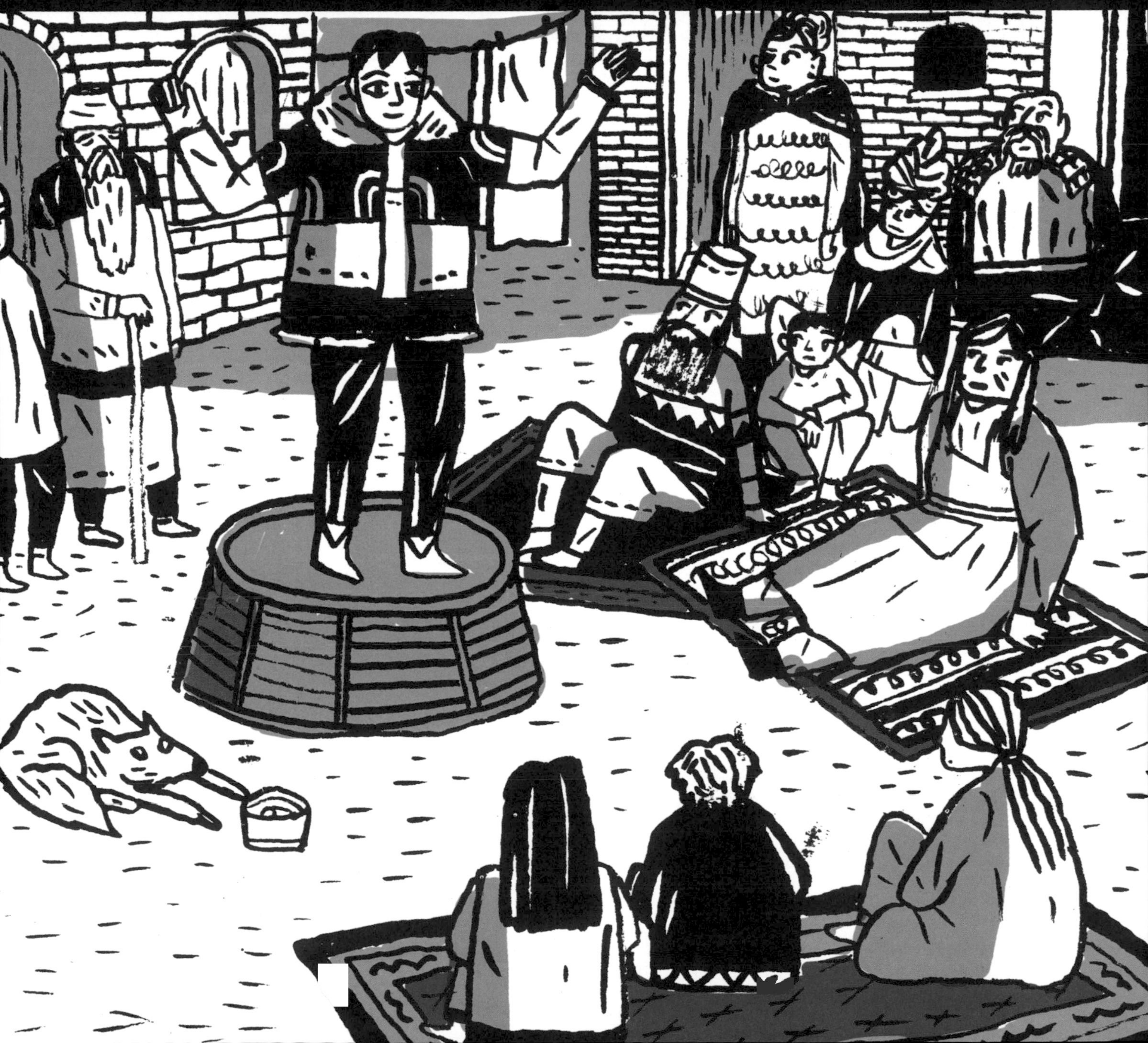

MIGDAL BAVEL

So we come to the next stop on our Storyteller's epic odyssey; The great city of Migdal Bavel. As he steered his little boat into the harbour, the storyteller got his first sight of what a city was. He had never seen so many buildings.

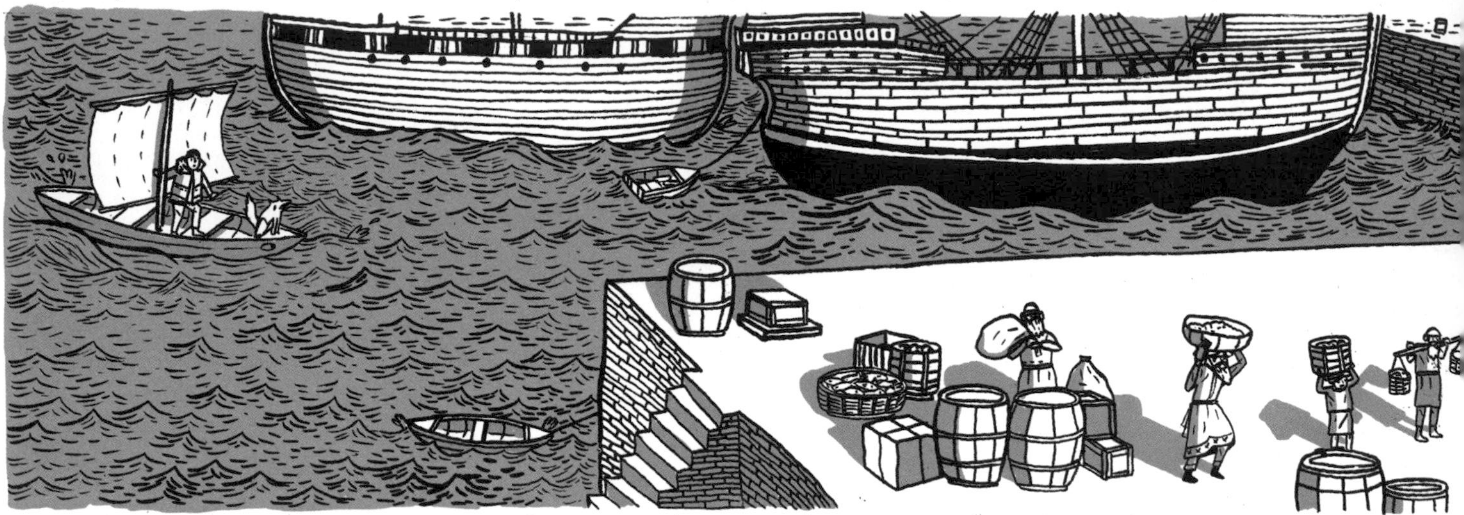

He had never seen so many people. Everywhere people. Teeming, jostling, shouting. In those vast crowds no one paid him any attention as he stepped ashore and looked around. He thanked his lucky stars once more for the Medicine Man's magic pebble.

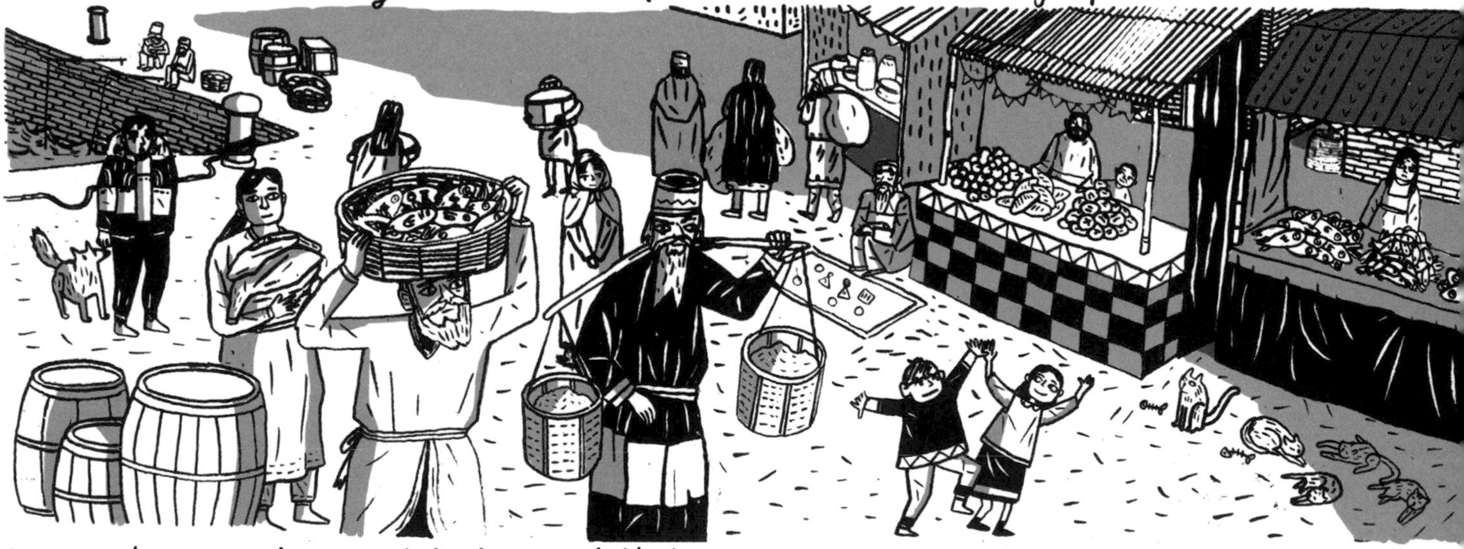

He was hungry and weary but it seemed that in this place, food could only be procured by swapping it for strange metal tokens.

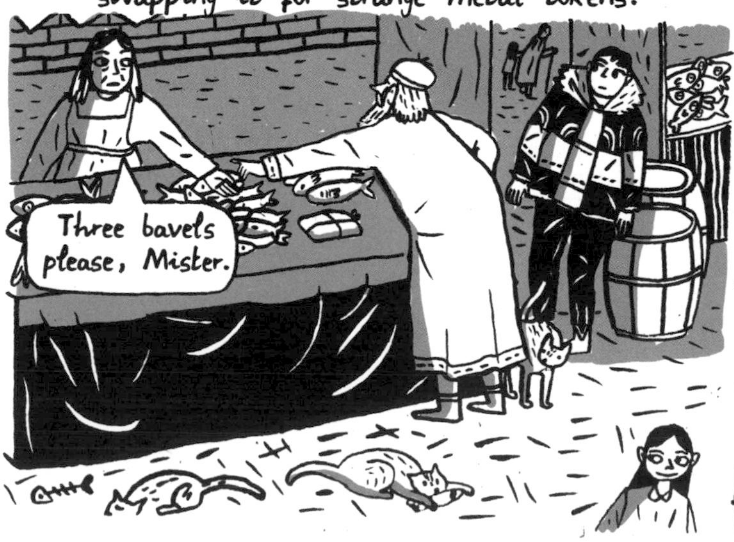
Three bavels please, Mister.

He had never seen anything like it before.

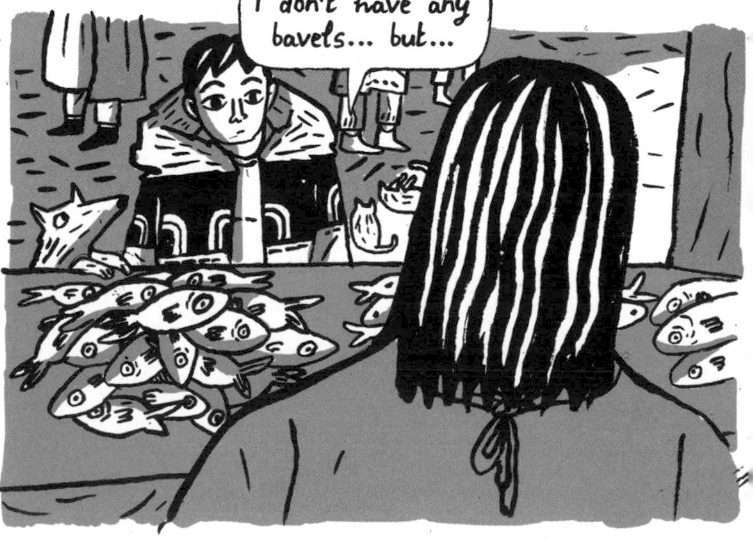
I don't have any bavels... but...

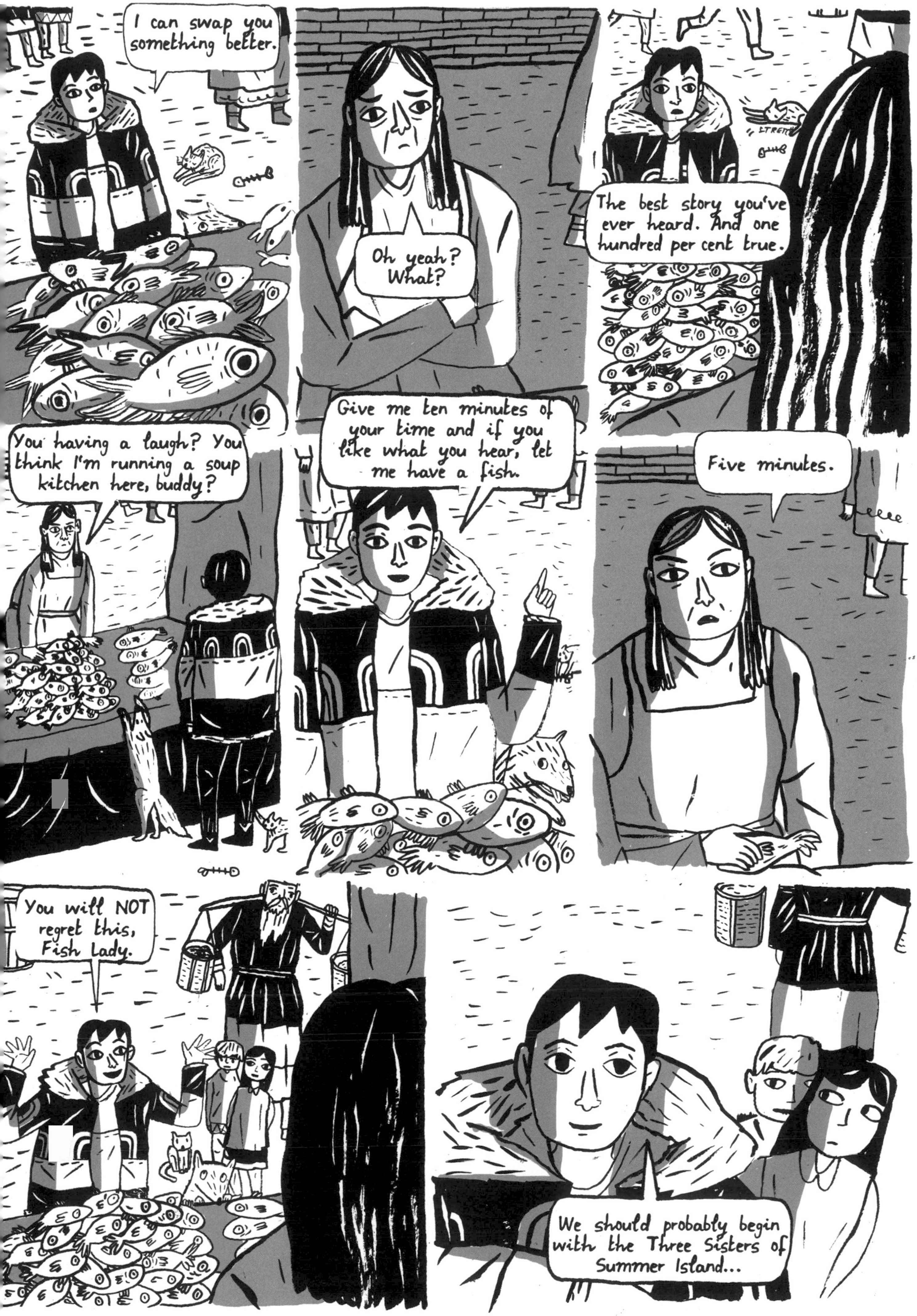
I can swap you something better.
Oh yeah? What?
The best story you've ever heard. And one hundred per cent true.
You having a laugh? You think I'm running a soup kitchen here, buddy?
Give me ten minutes of your time and if you like what you hear, let me have a fish.
Five minutes.
You will NOT regret this, Fish Lady.
We should probably begin with the Three Sisters of Summer Island...

Well obviously he wowed the Fish Lady. And by the next day he had wowed the rest of the market.

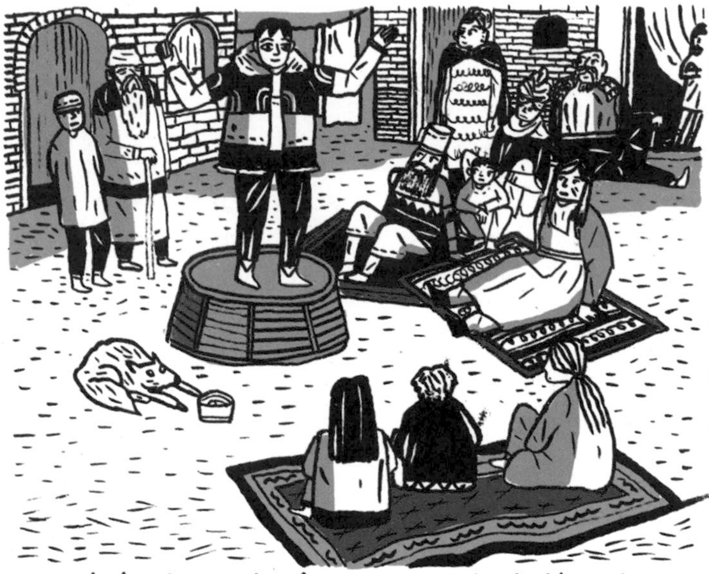

And pretty soon his stories were so popular that he never found himself without a hot meal. Every day the crowds who gathered to hear him talk grew larger and larger.

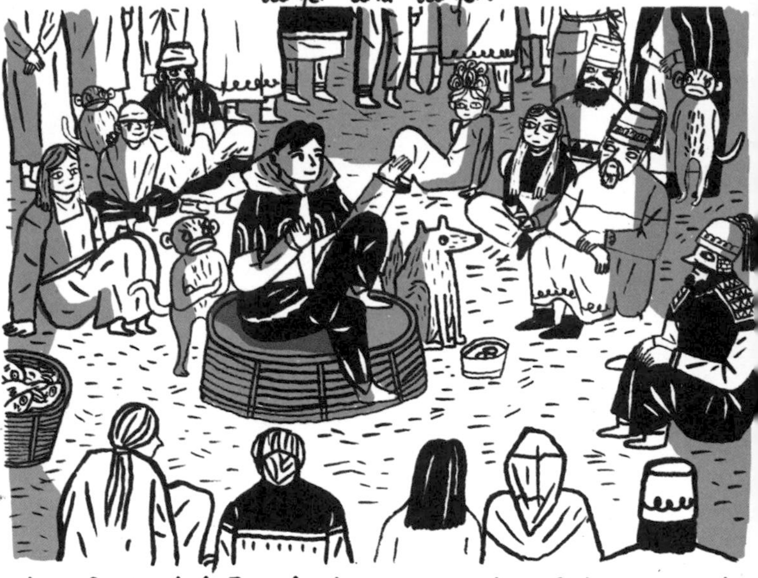

And he began to learn more about the strange city of Migdal Bavel. It was a city of towers and alleys and maze-like streets, of hidden courtyards and secret gardens. There were vast city walls patrolled by fearsome armoured guards and all over the city great buildings called Aviaries, in which black-clad monks called The Beaked Brothers worshipped BirdMan. The city was the heart of the Bavellian Empire which, the people said, stretched to the ends of the Earth.

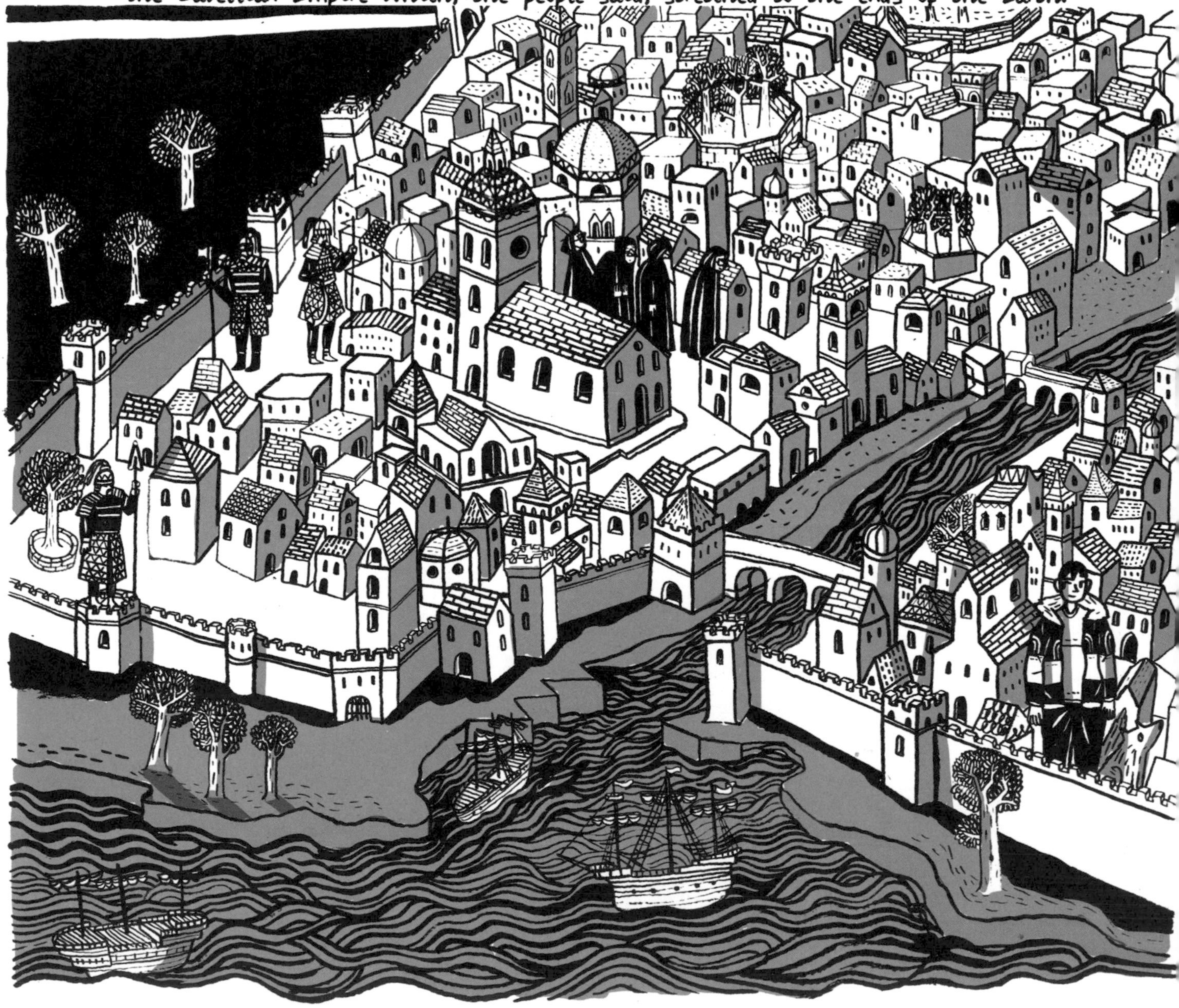

At the centre of the city, behind high walls, guarded by one thousand fearsome soldiers, lay the Palace Of Whispers, in which dwelt the Sun King himself.

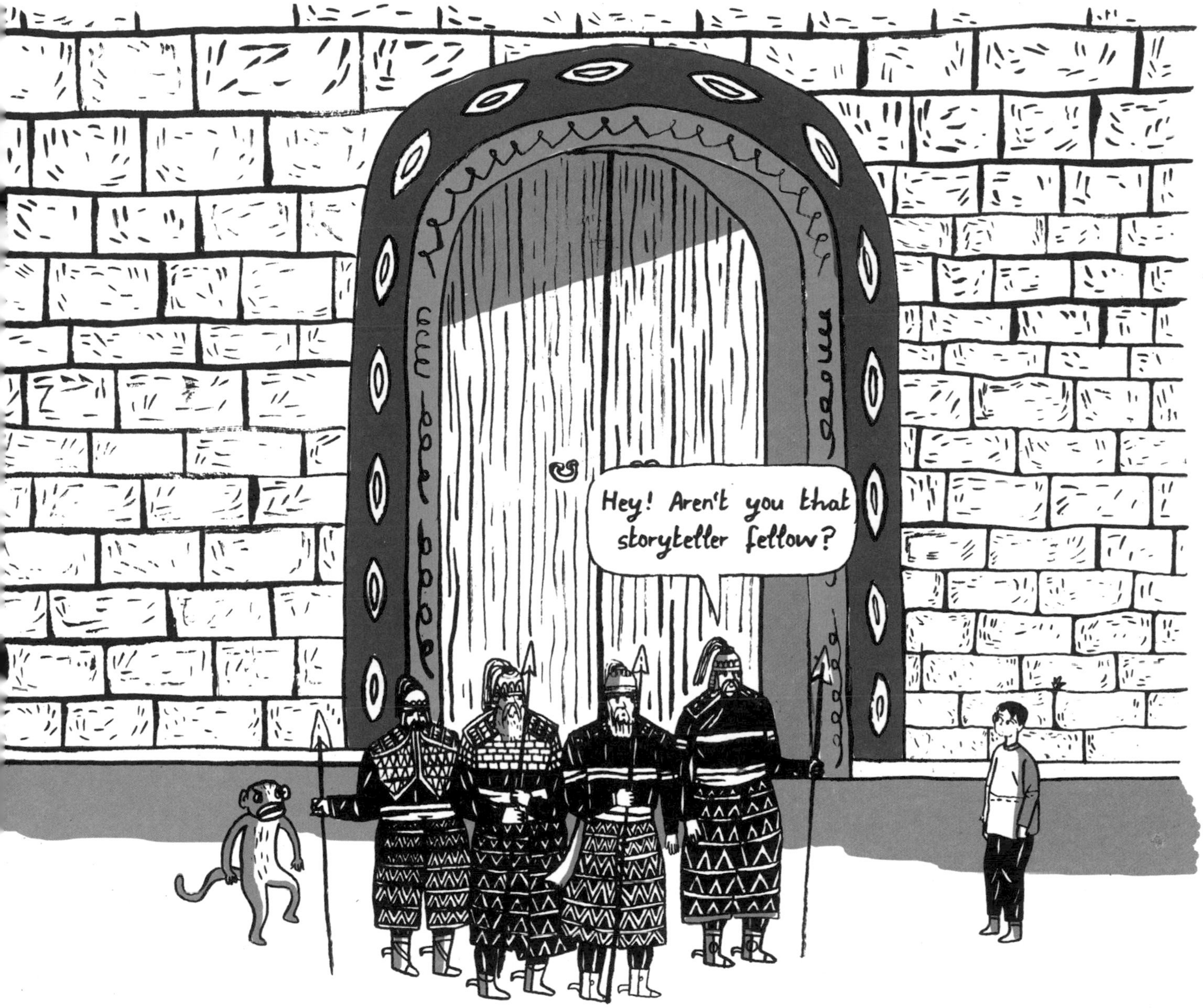
Hey! Aren't you that storyteller fellow?

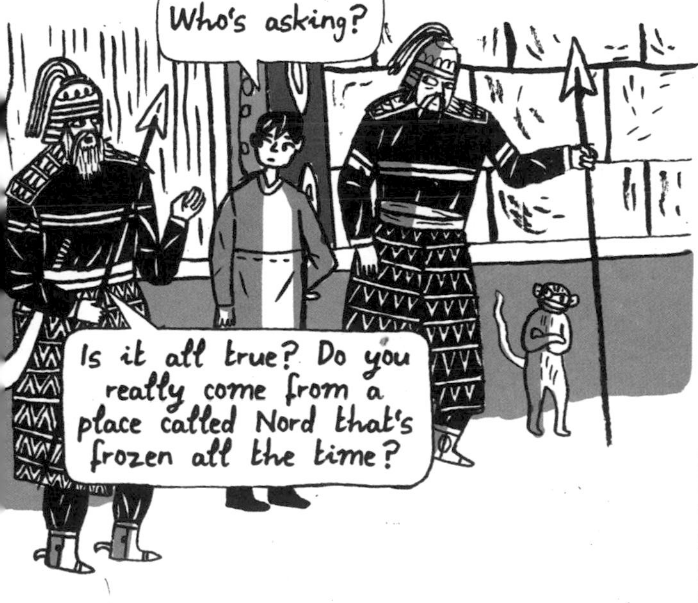
Who's asking?
Is it all true? Do you really come from a place called Nord that's frozen all the time?

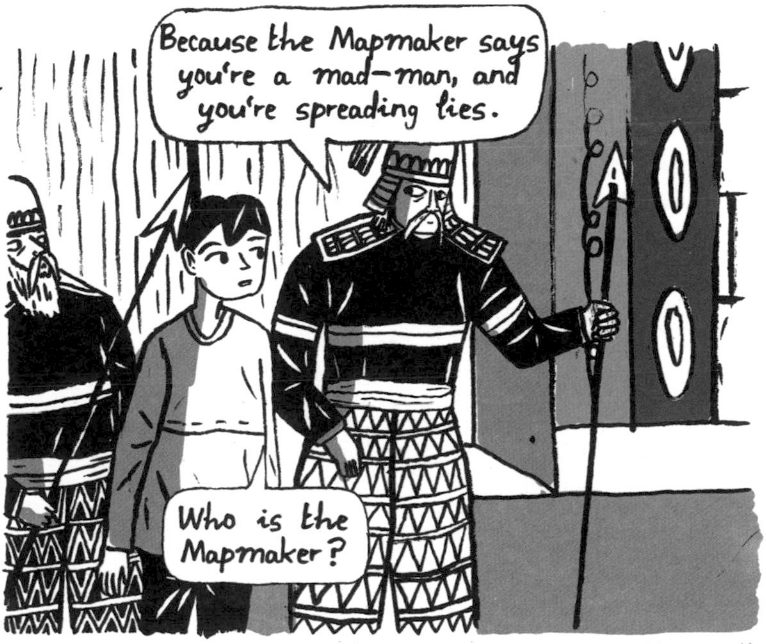
Because the Mapmaker says you're a mad-man, and you're spreading lies.
Who is the Mapmaker?

THE MAPMAKER OF MIGDAL BAVEL

The first map of Early Earth, the Bavellians say, was made by the famous cartographer Mancini Panini from his tower in the beautiful city of Migdal Bavel. It is generally agreed by explorers to be completely useless since it is almost entirely wrong on every level. But Mancini Panini was possessed of an excellent imagination and a steady and meticulous drawing hand, and so the maps can be valued as things of beauty.

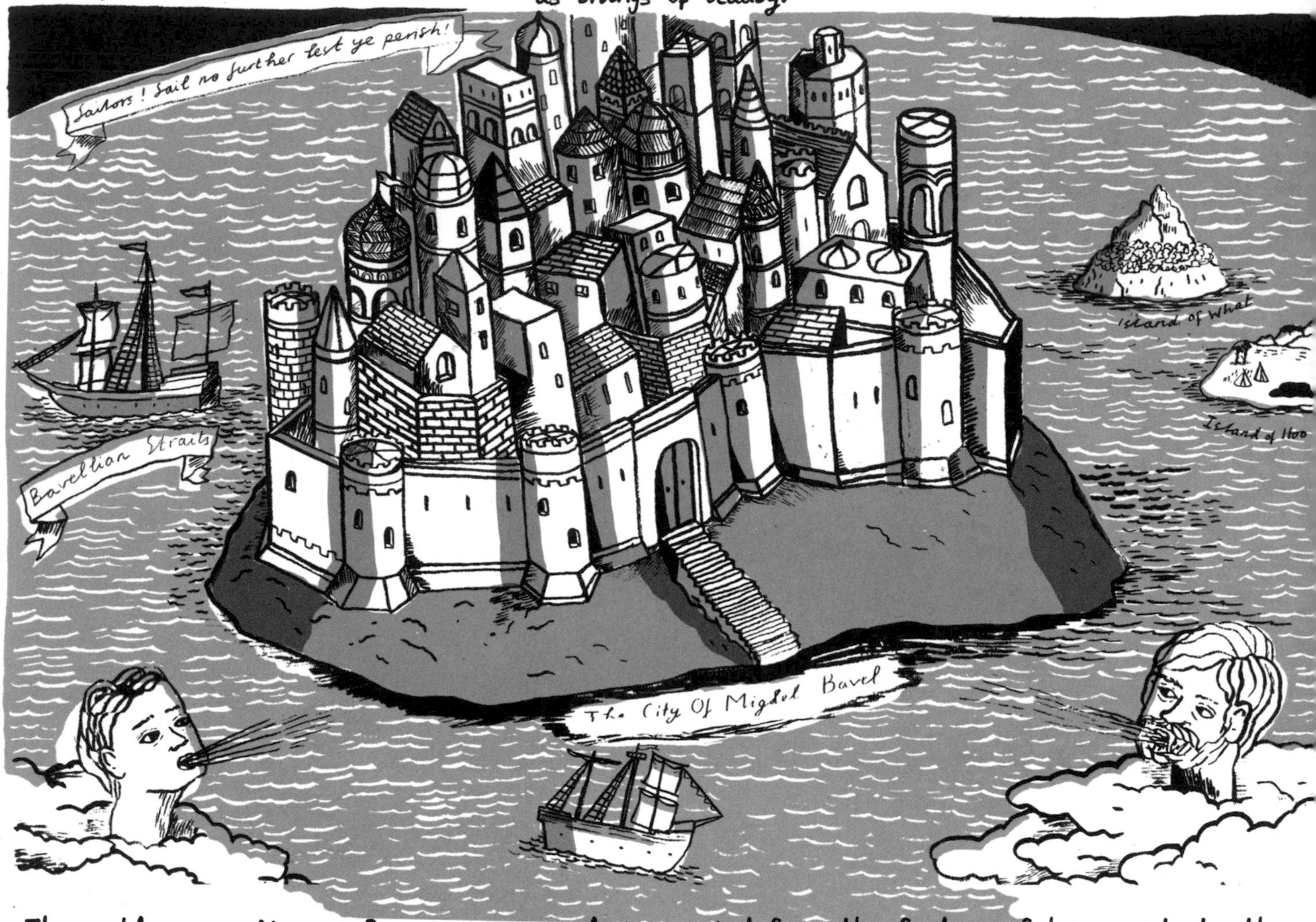
Sailors! Sail no further lest ye perish!
Island of What
Island of Hoo
Bavellian Strait
The City Of Migdal Bavel

The problem was Mancini Panini was severely agoraphobic, so everything he learnt came from his telescope.

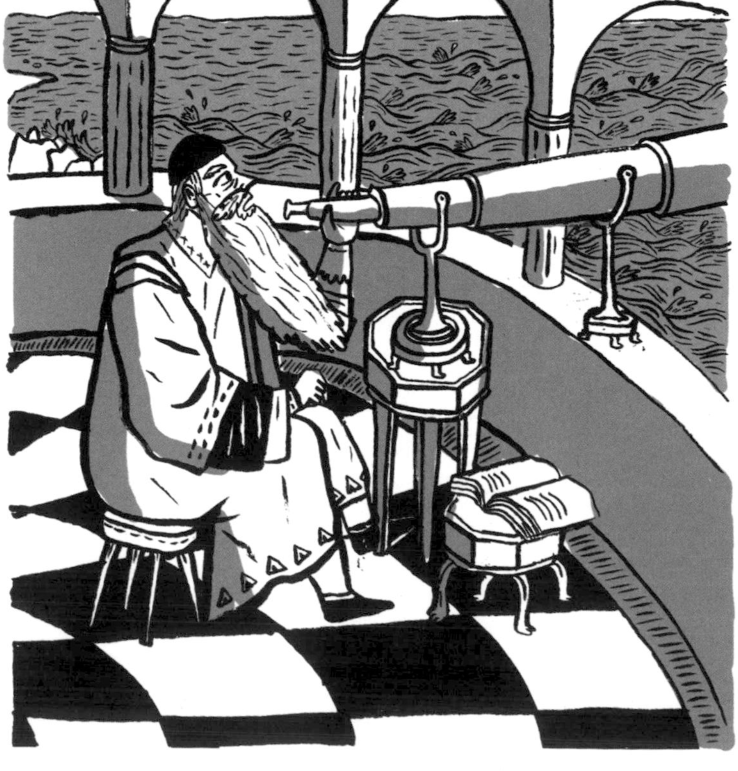

And from the findings of his assistants, three genius monkeys from the Island of What. He ha trained them himself and believed them to be o hundred per cent reliable.

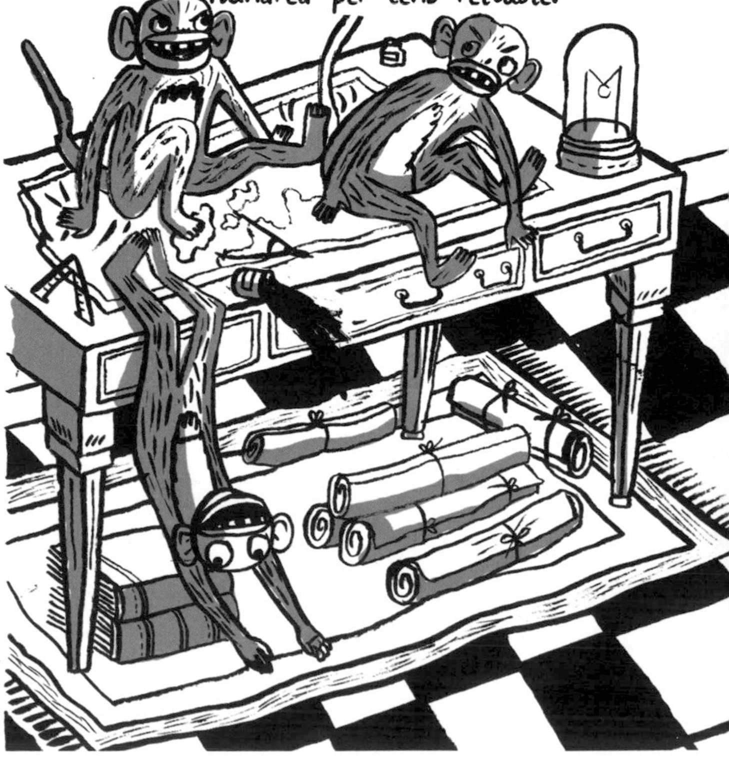

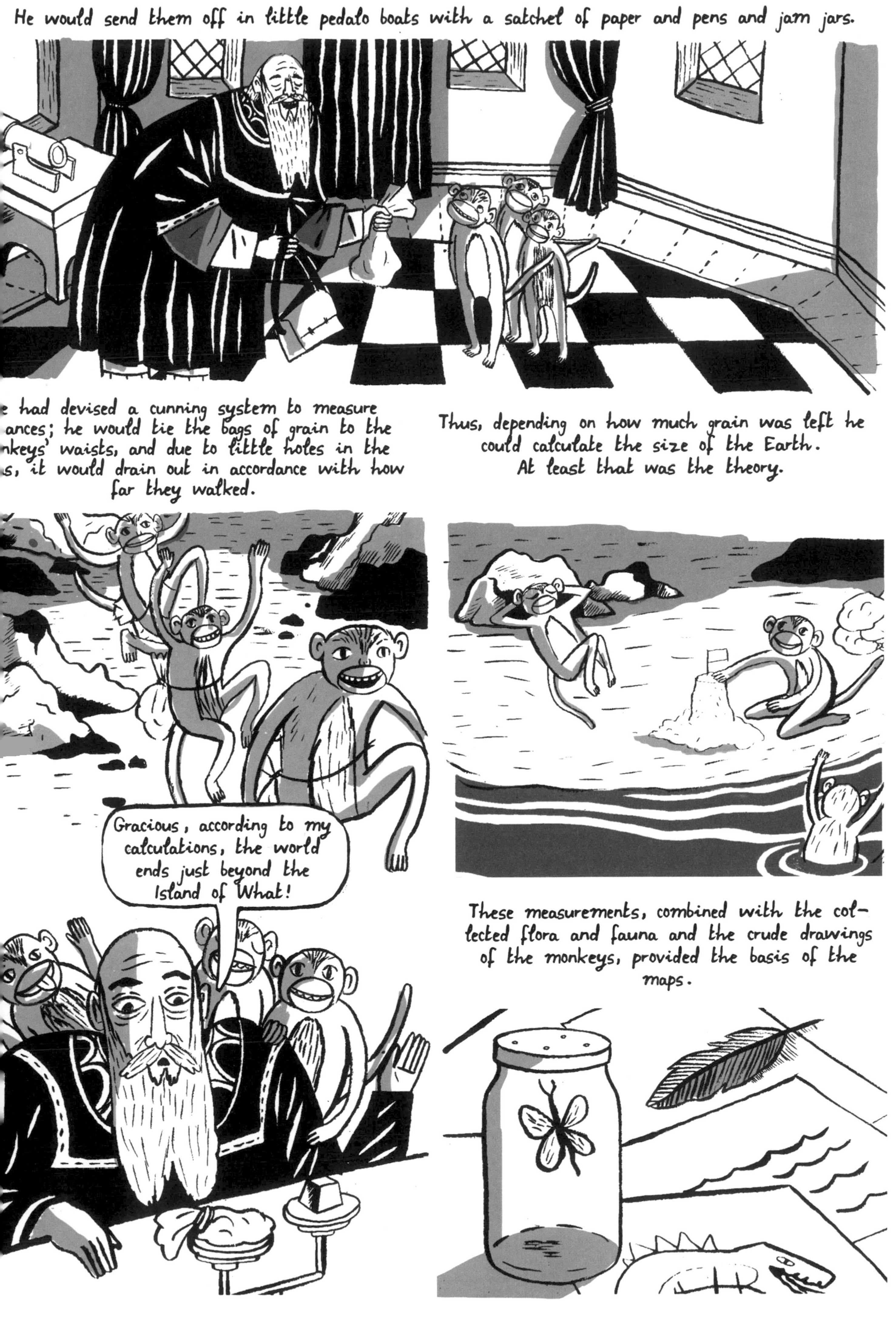
He would send them off in little pedalo boats with a satchel of paper and pens and jam jars.
e had devised a cunning system to measure ances; he would tie the bags of grain to the nkeys' waists, and due to little holes in the s, it would drain out in accordance with how far they walked.
Thus, depending on how much grain was left he could calculate the size of the Earth. At least that was the theory.
Gracious, according to my calculations, the world ends just beyond the Island of What!
These measurements, combined with the collected flora and fauna and the crude drawings of the monkeys, provided the basis of the maps.

The Mapmaker told the Bavellians that the city of Migdal Bavel was at the centre of the world. the northwest lay the savage lands of Britanitarka, to the north lay the Islands of Hoo, Wat and Wen. the west lay the island of Cos with its mysterious stone sculptures and east lay the Sea of Nowh

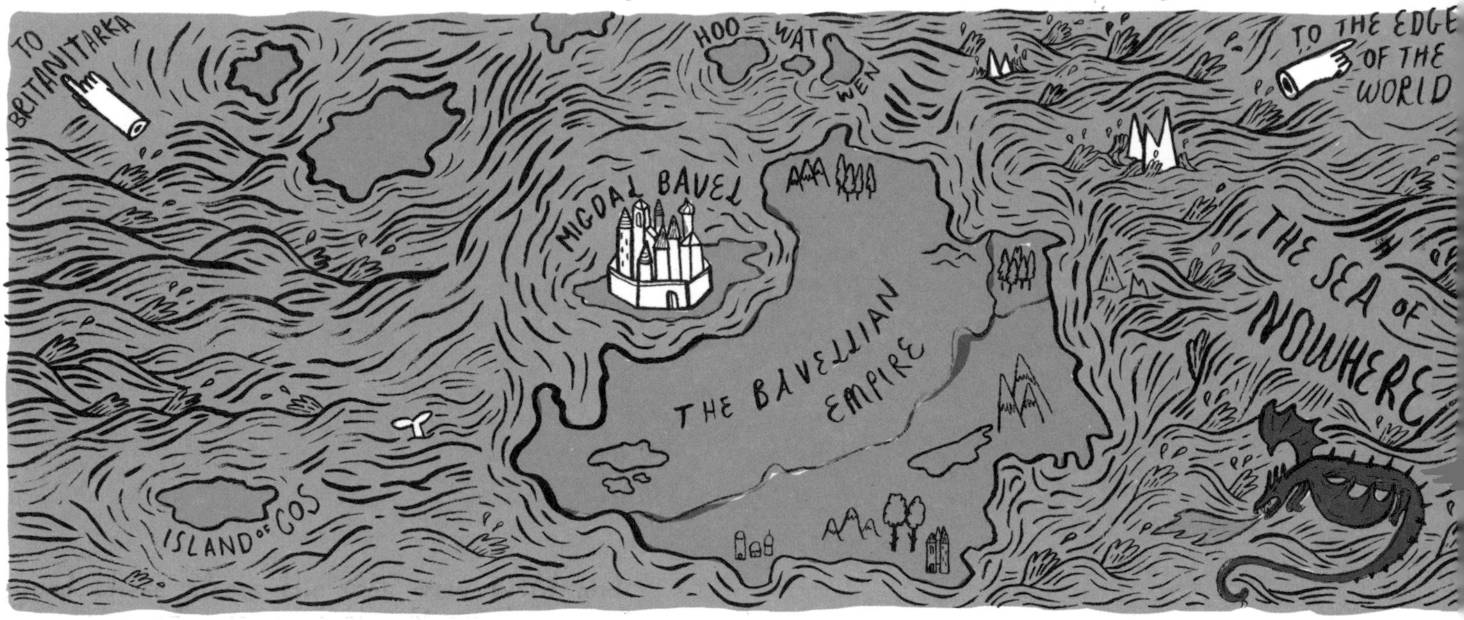
TO BRITANITARKA
HOO
WAT
WEN
TO THE EDGE OF THE WORLD
MIGDAL BAVEL
THE BAVELLIAN EMPIRE
THE SEA OF NOWHERE
ISLAND of COS

Beyond these places the seas grew wild and unpassable, so said the Mapmaker.

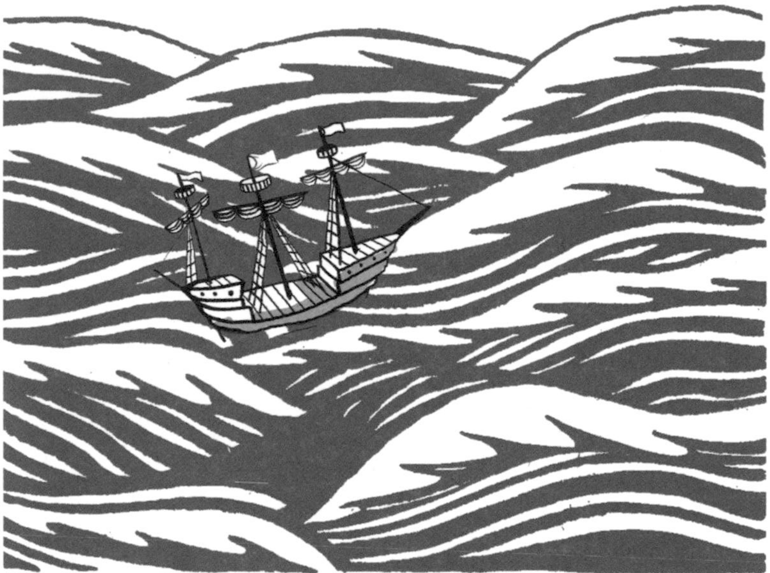

Terrible fire-breathing creatures wheeled and cawed in storm-drenched skies.

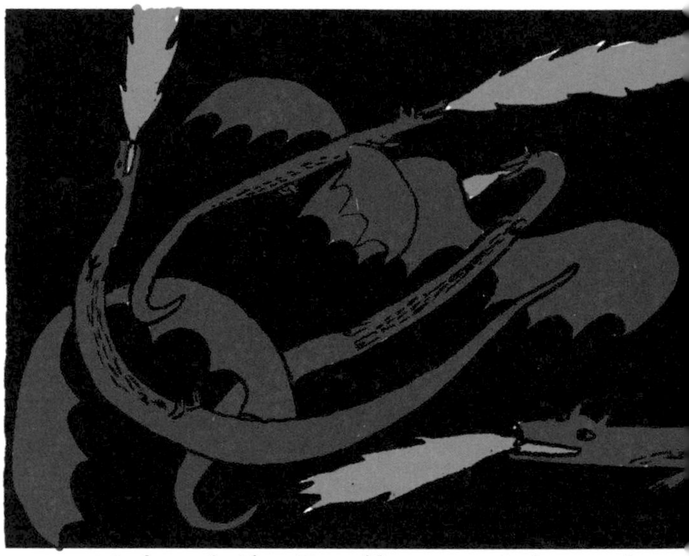

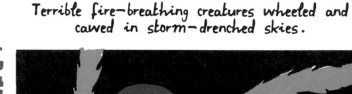

And then the flat disc of the world ended abruptly, and the ocean went tumbling off into nothingness.

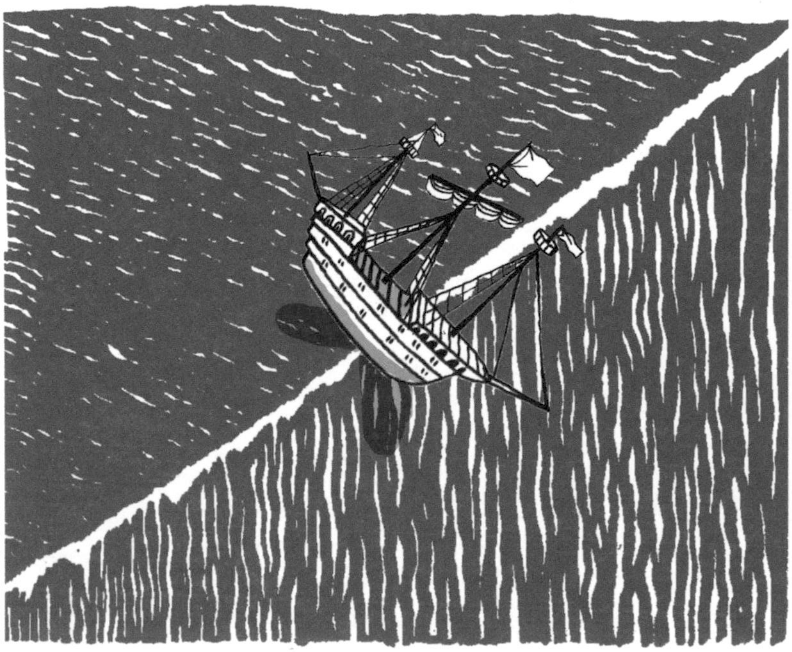

So believed the Bavellians, until one day stranger arrived in the harbour. He came in a bedraggled little boat, from a land far beyond edge of the world.

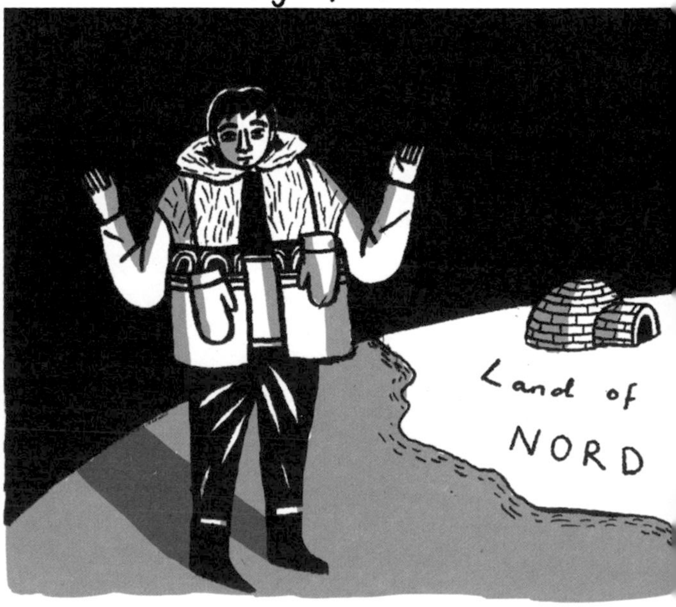
Land of
NORD

He told them of his land; of the frozen sea and the midnight sun. He told them of the places he had been and the places he imagined over the horizon. And before long word of the stranger spread, and the Sun King of Migdal Bavel himself demanded to hear the tales.

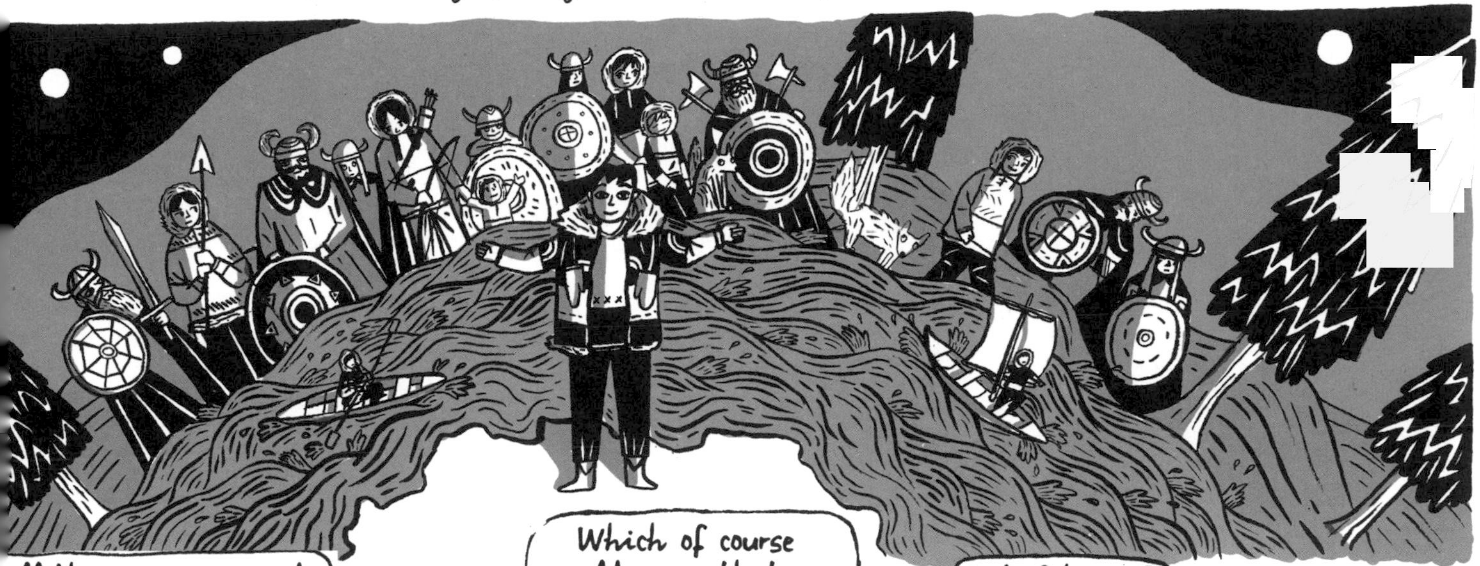

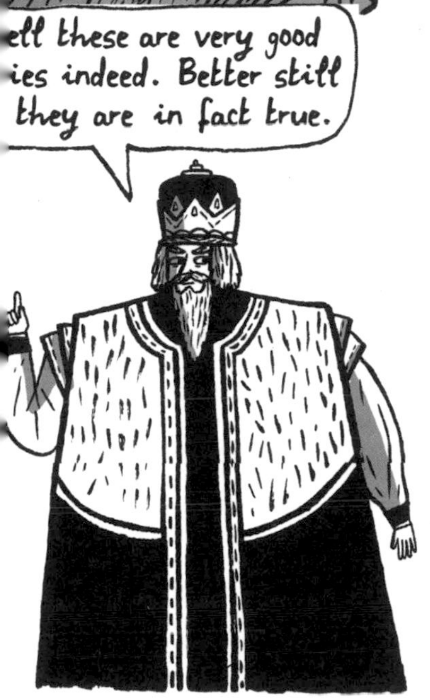
ell these are very good ies indeed. Better still they are in fact true.

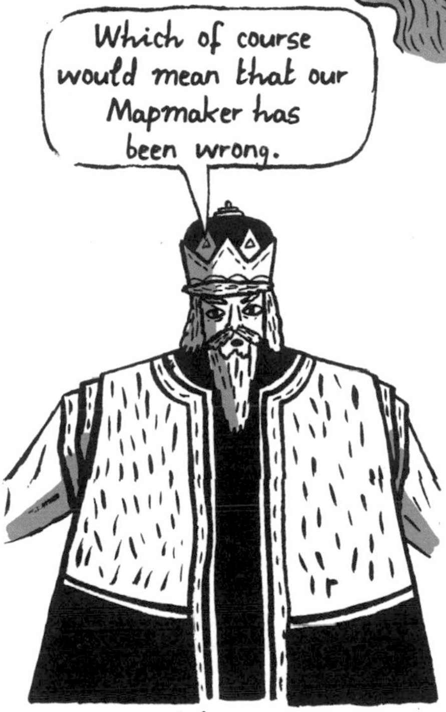
Which of course would mean that our Mapmaker has been wrong.

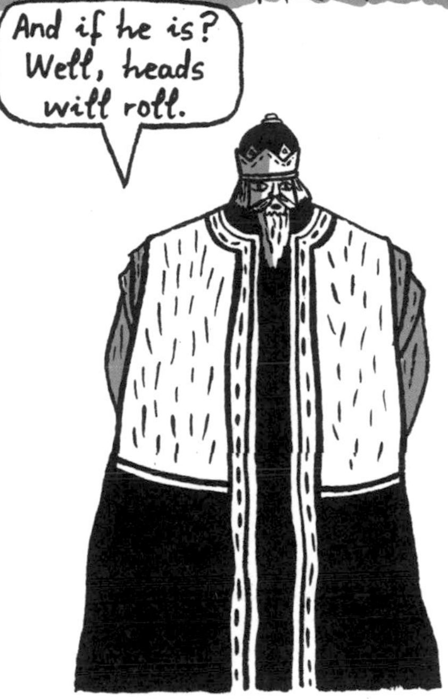
And if he is? Well, heads will roll.

e Mapmaker and the Genius Monkeys very quickly found themselves out of favour.

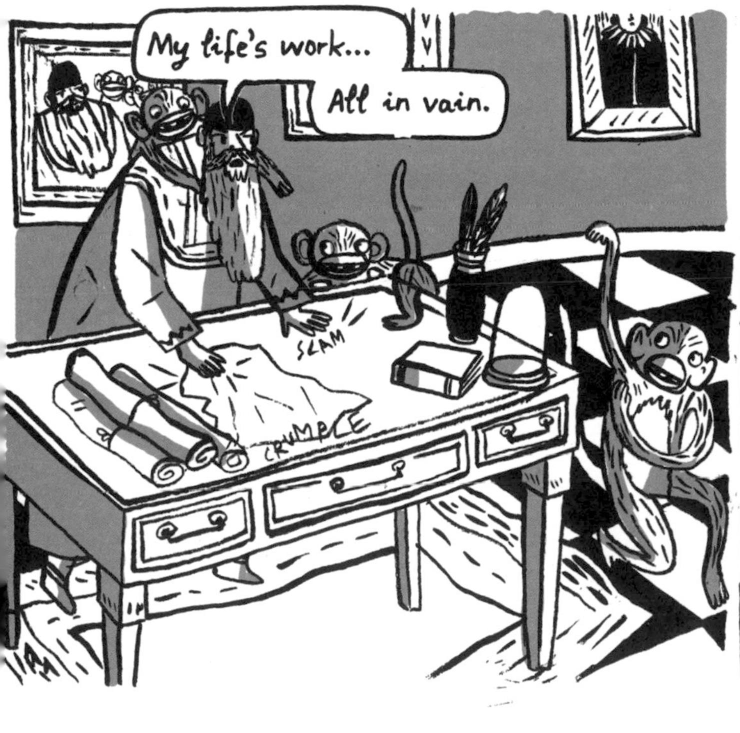
My life's work...
All in vain.
SLAM
CRUMPLE

Their maps, their beautiful maps, were all wrong.

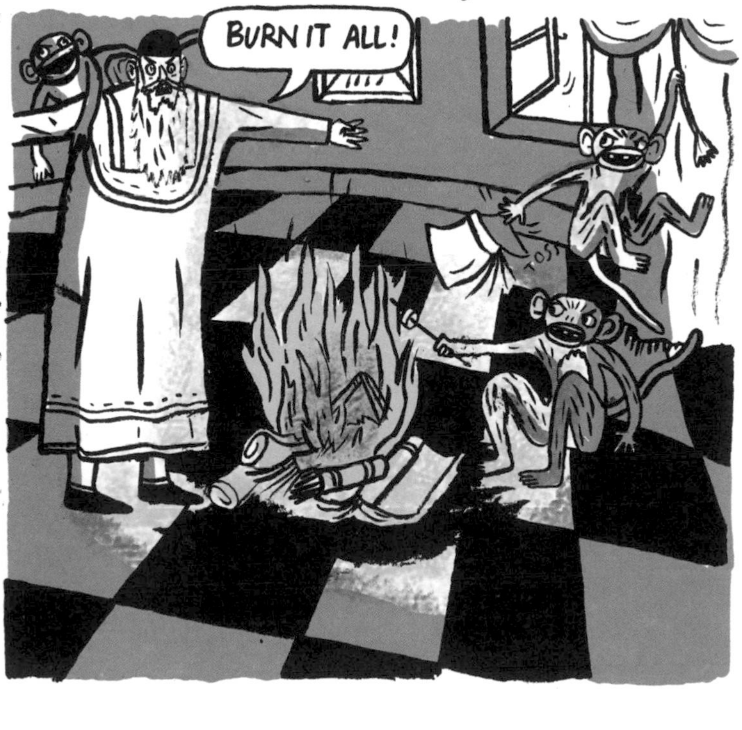
BURN IT ALL!

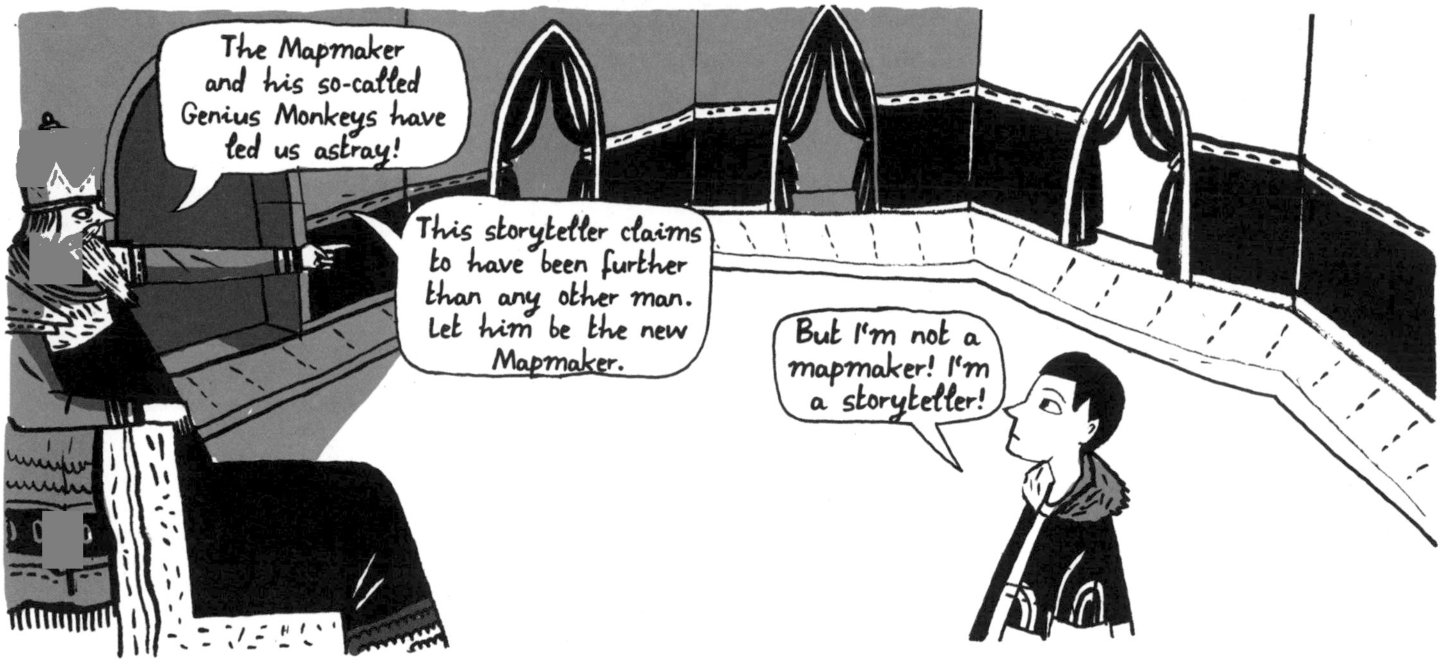
The Mapmaker and his so-called Genius Monkeys have led us astray!
This storyteller claims to have been further than any other man. Let him be the new Mapmaker.
But I'm not a mapmaker! I'm a storyteller!

Gaining the favour of the Sun King is notoriously hard, and losing it is notoriously easy. He has a huge staff of servants and advisors who take care of his every whim. He is never disobeyed.

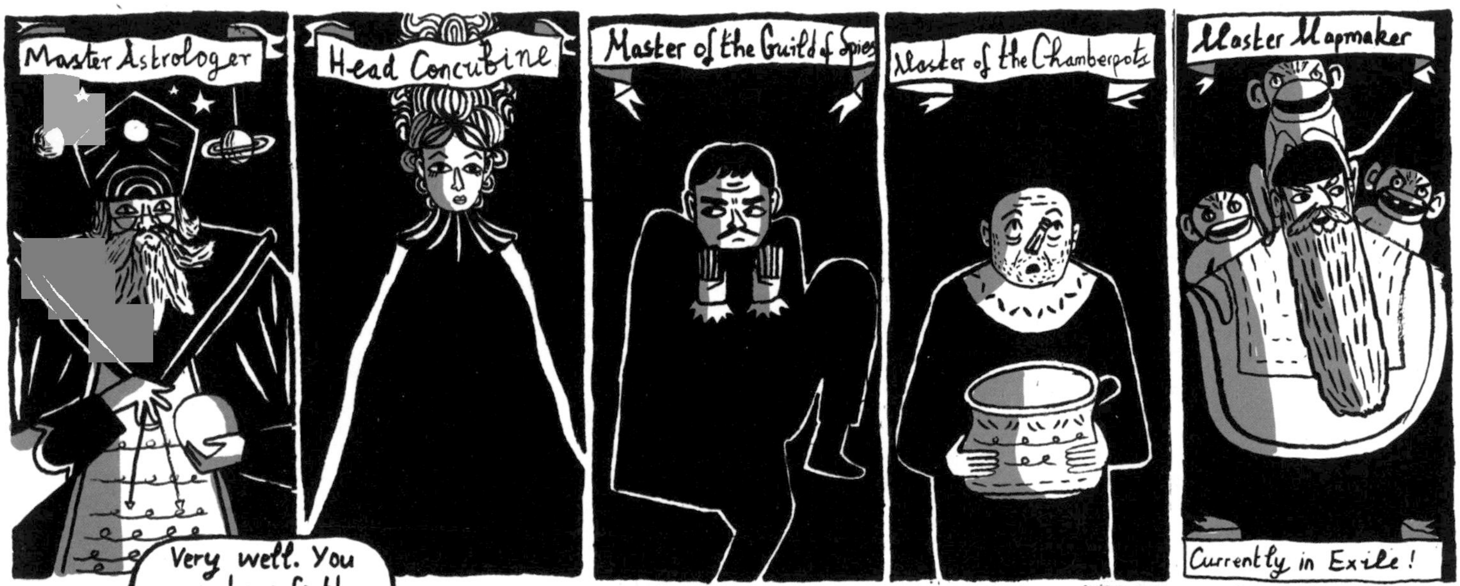
Master Astrologer
Head Concubine
Master of the Guild of Spies
Master of the Chamberpots
Master Mapmaker
Currently in Exile!

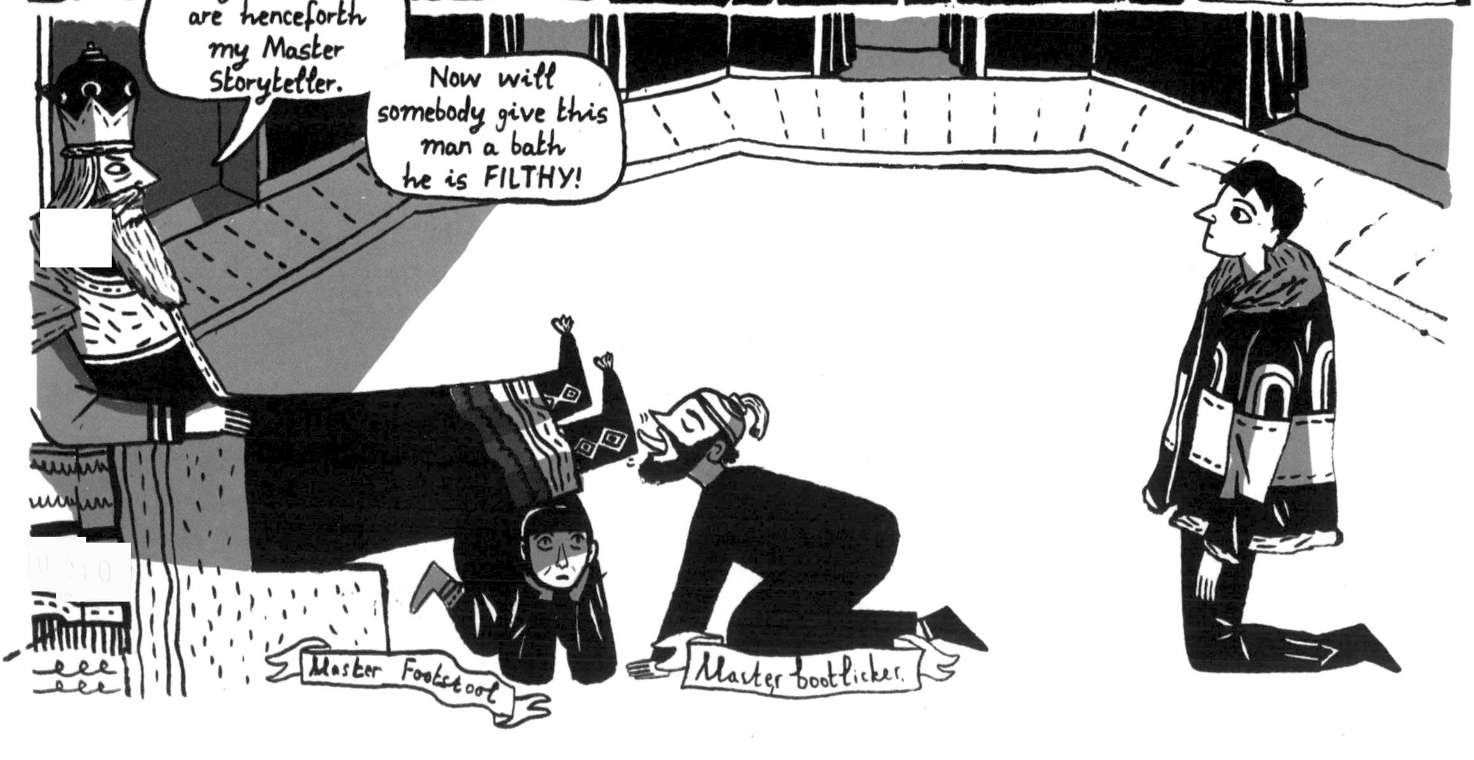
Very well. You are henceforth my Master Storyteller.
Now will somebody give this man a bath he is FILTHY!
Master Footstool
Master bootlicker.

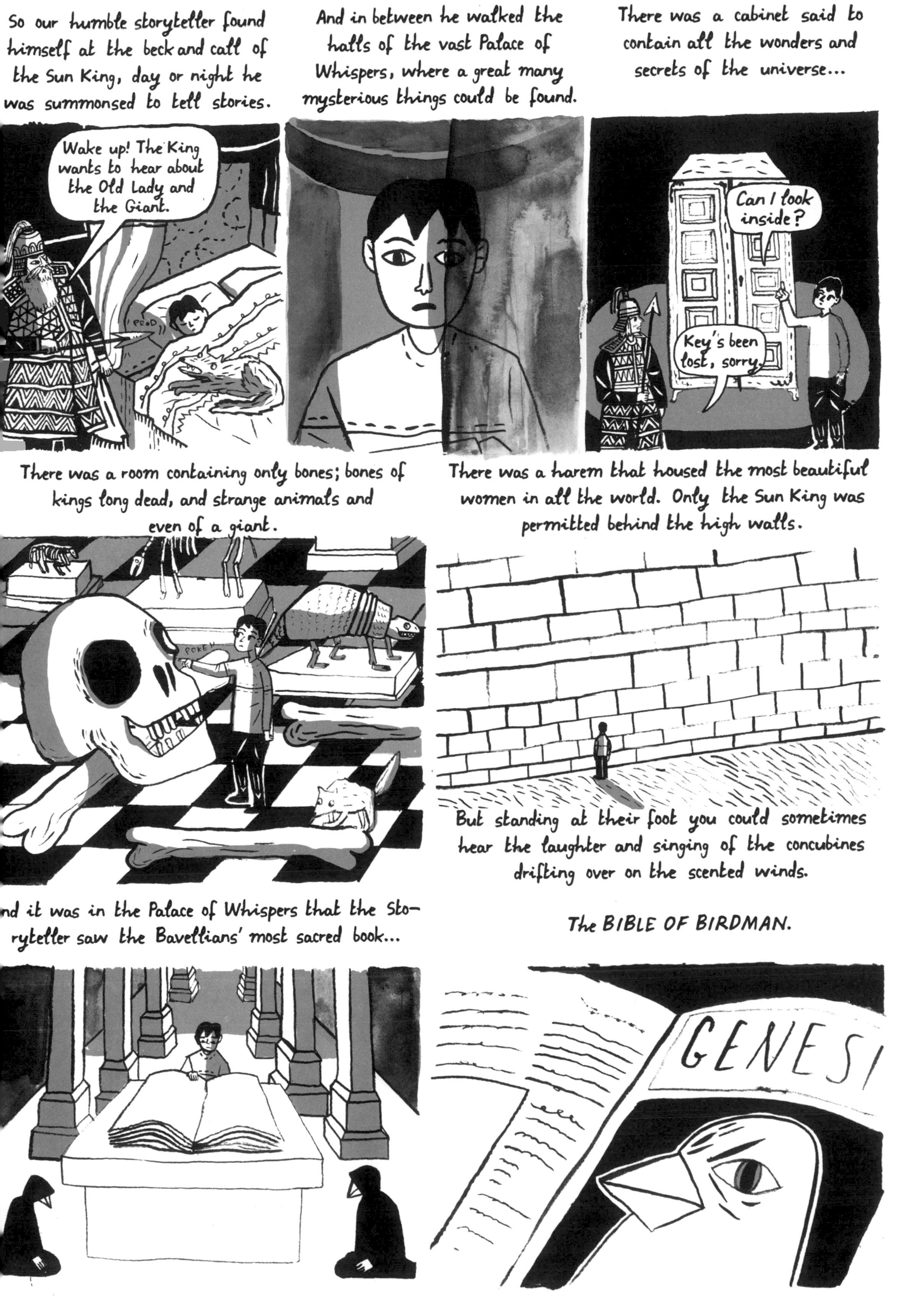
So our humble storyteller found himself at the beck and call of the Sun King, day or night he was summonsed to tell stories.
Wake up! The King wants to hear about the Old Lady and the Giant.
PROD
And in between he walked the halls of the vast Palace of Whispers, where a great many mysterious things could be found.
There was a cabinet said to contain all the wonders and secrets of the universe...
Can I look inside?
Key's been lost, sorry.
There was a room containing only bones; bones of kings long dead, and strange animals and even of a giant.
POKE
There was a harem that housed the most beautiful women in all the world. Only the Sun King was permitted behind the high walls.
But standing at their foot you could sometimes hear the laughter and singing of the concubines drifting over on the scented winds.
nd it was in the Palace of Whispers that the Storyteller saw the Bavellians' most sacred book...
The BIBLE OF BIRDMAN.
GENESI

THE BIBLE OF BIRD MAN

GENESIS

In the beginning there was nothing, only time. But since there was no one to count the time, there might as well have been nothing.

And then there was an egg. Don't ask how it got there, OK.

Every story has to have a beginning and this one begins with an egg, floating in an infinite, empty cosmos.

And from this egg came BIRDMAN. He was Top Cat, King God, Cosmic Architect.

He imagined a tree, and a tree was there. And so he sat in his tree, contemplating the mysteries of space and time.

He sat there for many millions of millennia, entertained always by the boundless possibilities of his infinitely powerful imagination.

And then? He laid an egg. In fact, two.

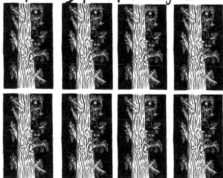

And from these eggs came his children, The Ravens. Kid and Kiddo.

For many millions of millennia, the three of them sat in the tree, in the empty cosmos, and contemplated the profound mysteries of space and time, and the nature of creation, and all sorts of things like that. But then something happened...

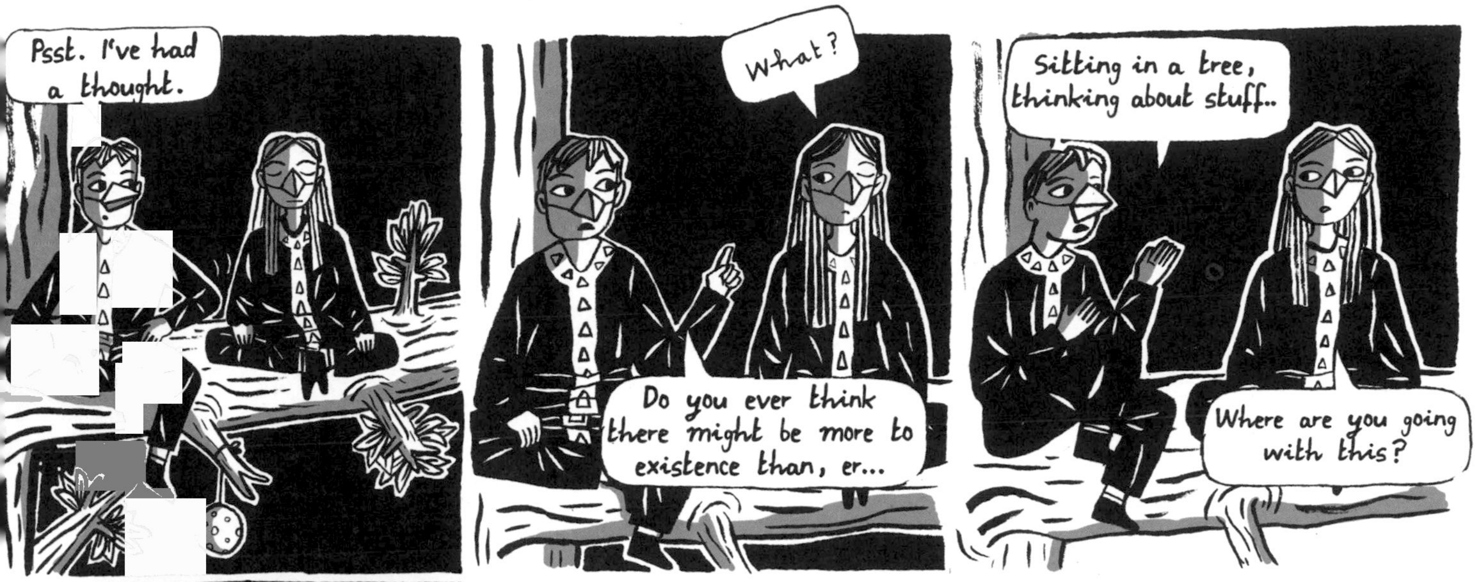

Psst. I've had a thought.
What?
Do you ever think there might be more to existence than, er...
Sitting in a tree, thinking about stuff..
Where are you going with this?

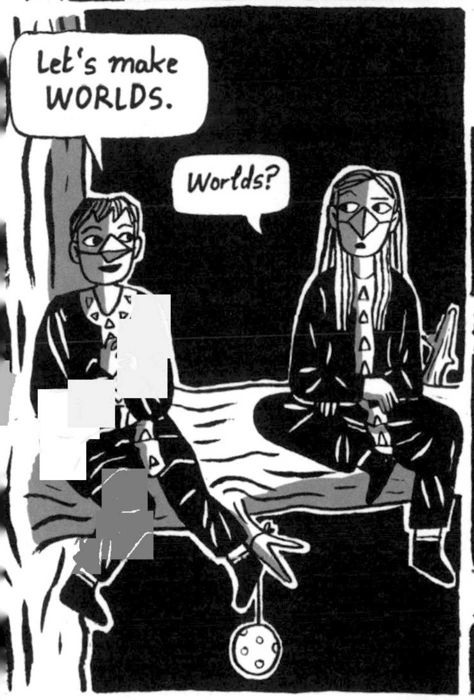

Let's make WORLDS.
Worlds?

So they went to BirdMan, and asked him for permission to create worlds. And he granted it, but on three conditions.

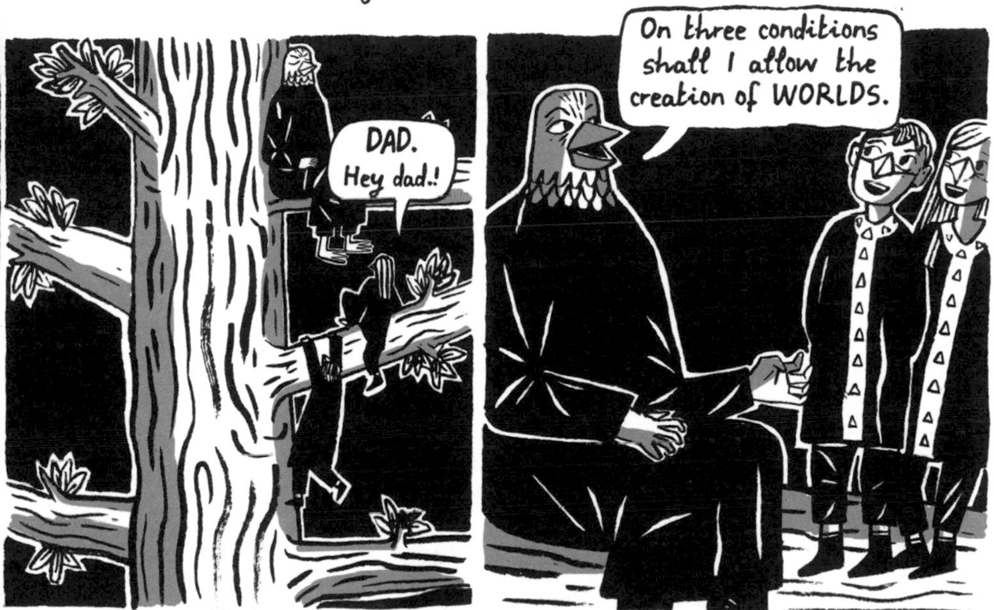

DAD. Hey dad.!
On three conditions shall I allow the creation of WORLDS.

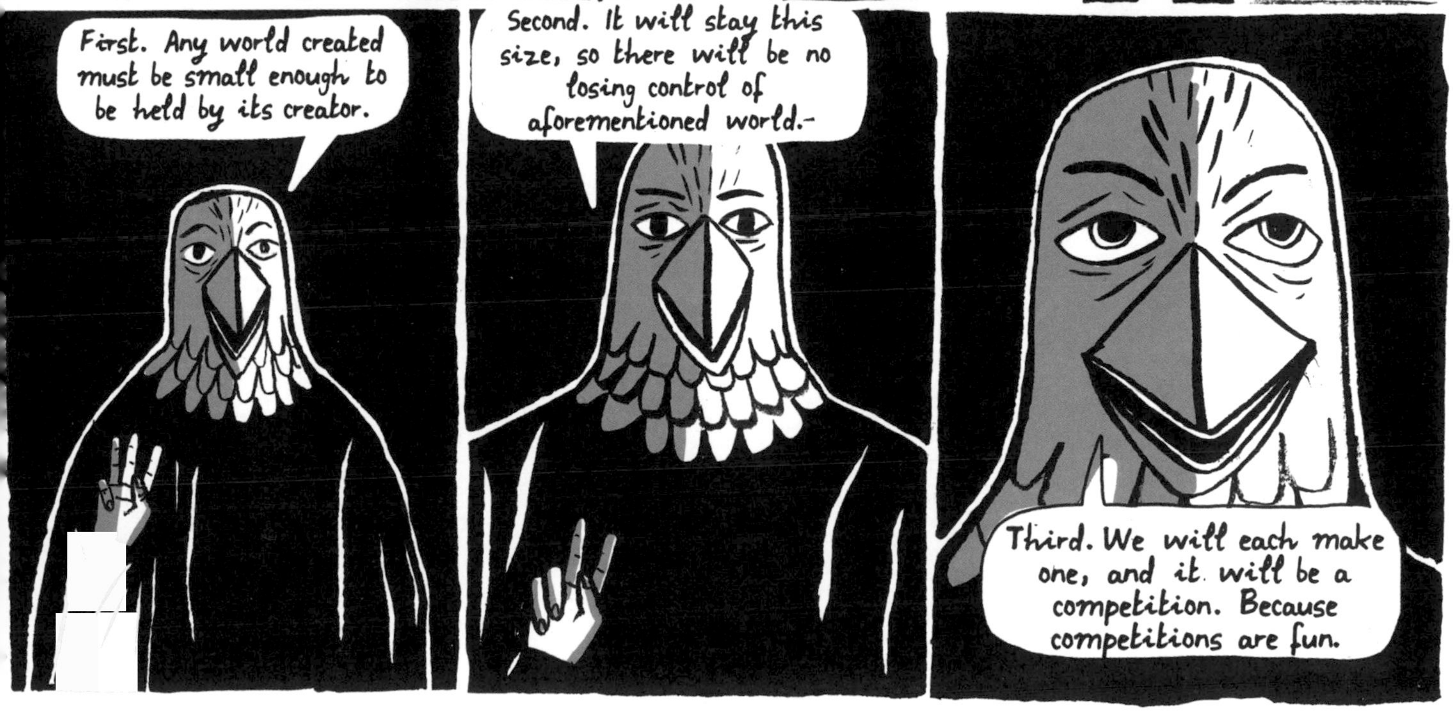

First. Any world created must be small enough to be held by its creator.
Second. It will stay this size, so there will be no losing control of aforementioned world.-
Third. We will each make one, and it will be a competition. Because competitions are fun.

So soon was the time to compare what they had made. Kid went first. He had a basin that h held in his hands. In the basin was an angel. The angel stood in a bowl of rubies, balanced on the back of a cow, perched on a fish, swimming in endless circles around the blue water. In the angel's tiny hands was another, tinier basin. In that basin was another angel. The angel was standing in a bowl of rubies, balanced on the back of a cow, perched on a fish...

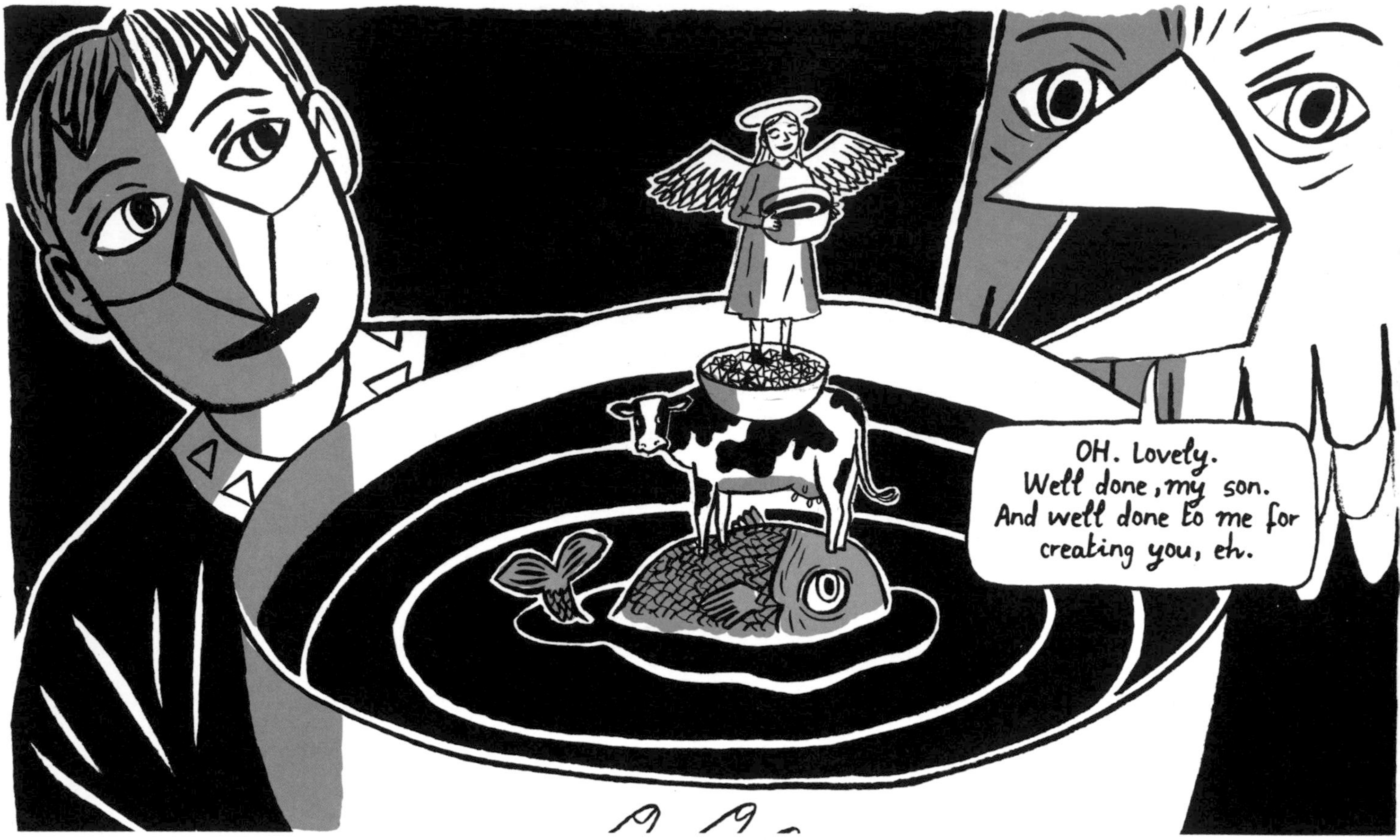
OH. Lovely. Well done, my son. And well done to me for creating you, eh.

Next BirdMan showed his world. Well he didn't exactly, because it was in his mind's eye. He invited his children to look into the inky depths of his pupil.

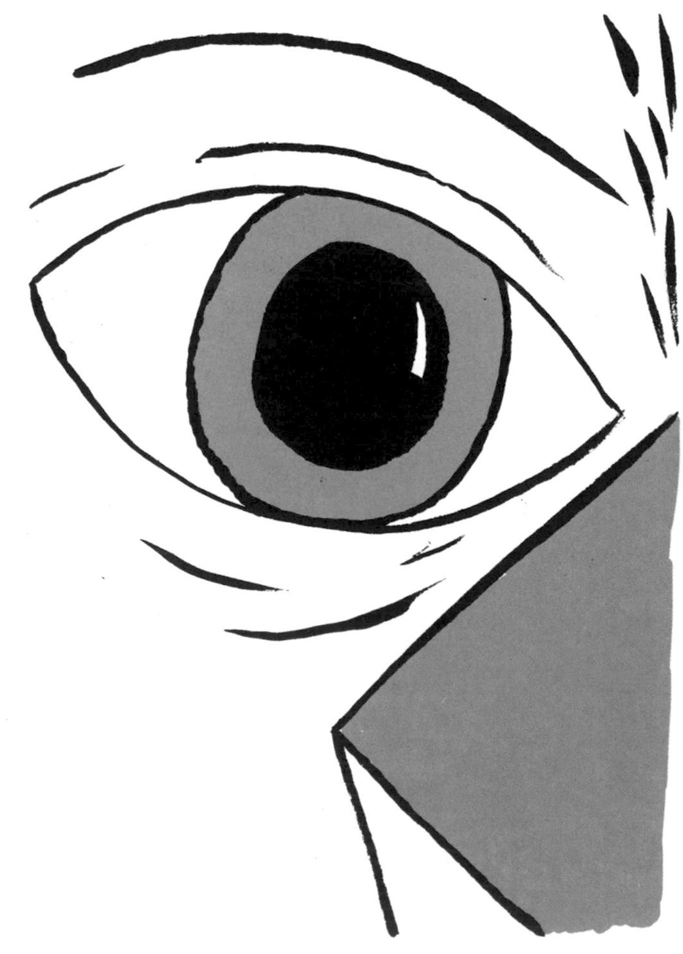

They were not impressed. They couldn't see anything.

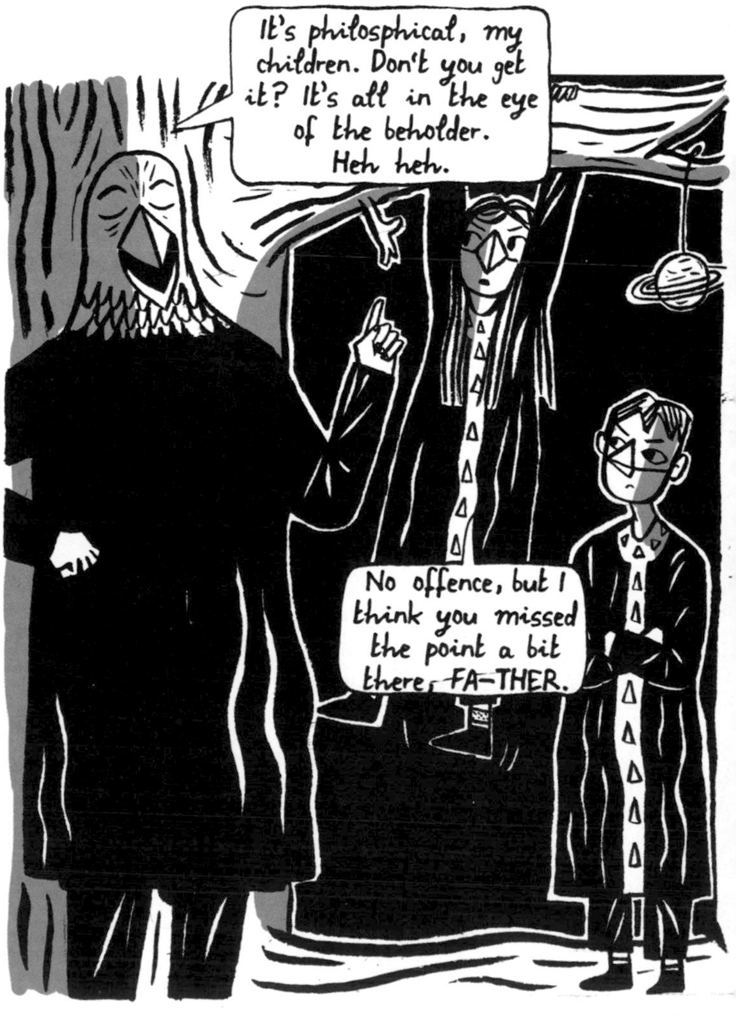
It's philosphical, my children. Don't you get it? It's all in the eye of the beholder. Heh heh.
No offence, but I think you missed the point a bit there, FA-THER.

n Kiddo showed her world. She was carrying it in her hair and it was a beautiful, complex world of gardens and rivers and mountains and forests. And best of all, tiny little creatures.

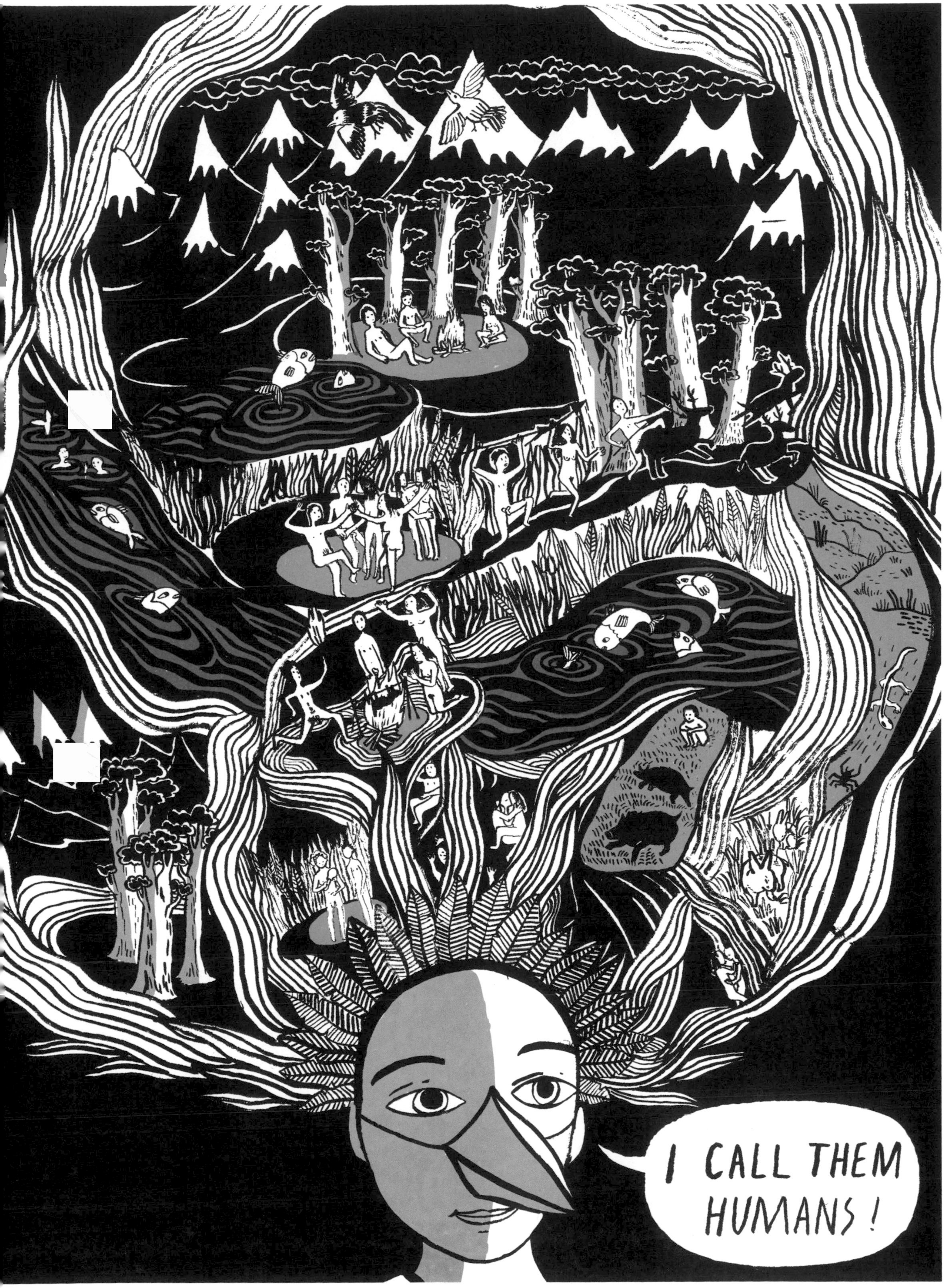
I CALL THEM HUMANS!

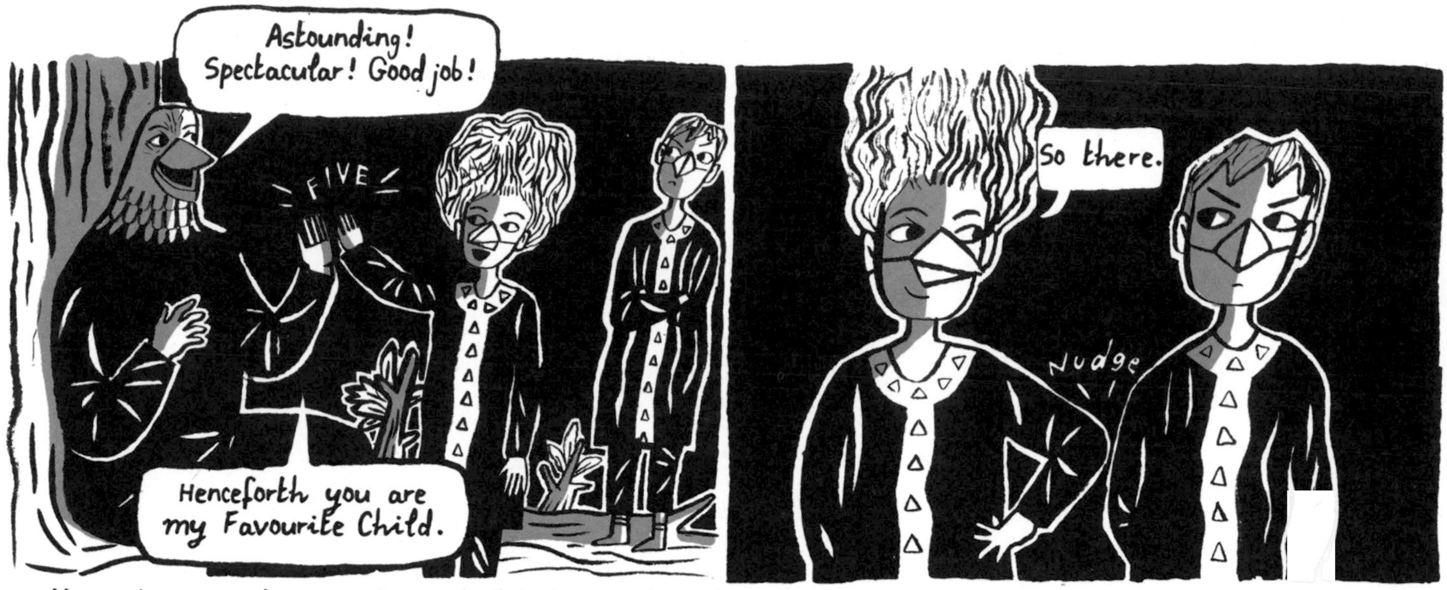
Astounding! Spectacular! Good job!
FIVE
Henceforth you are my Favourite Child.
So there.
Nudge

Well, Kid was jealous. And so whilst his sister slept, he crept up on her and cut off her hair. And as it fell from her head, it went tumbling away into the infinite cosmos, and as it fell it began to grow and to expand... Something was happening...

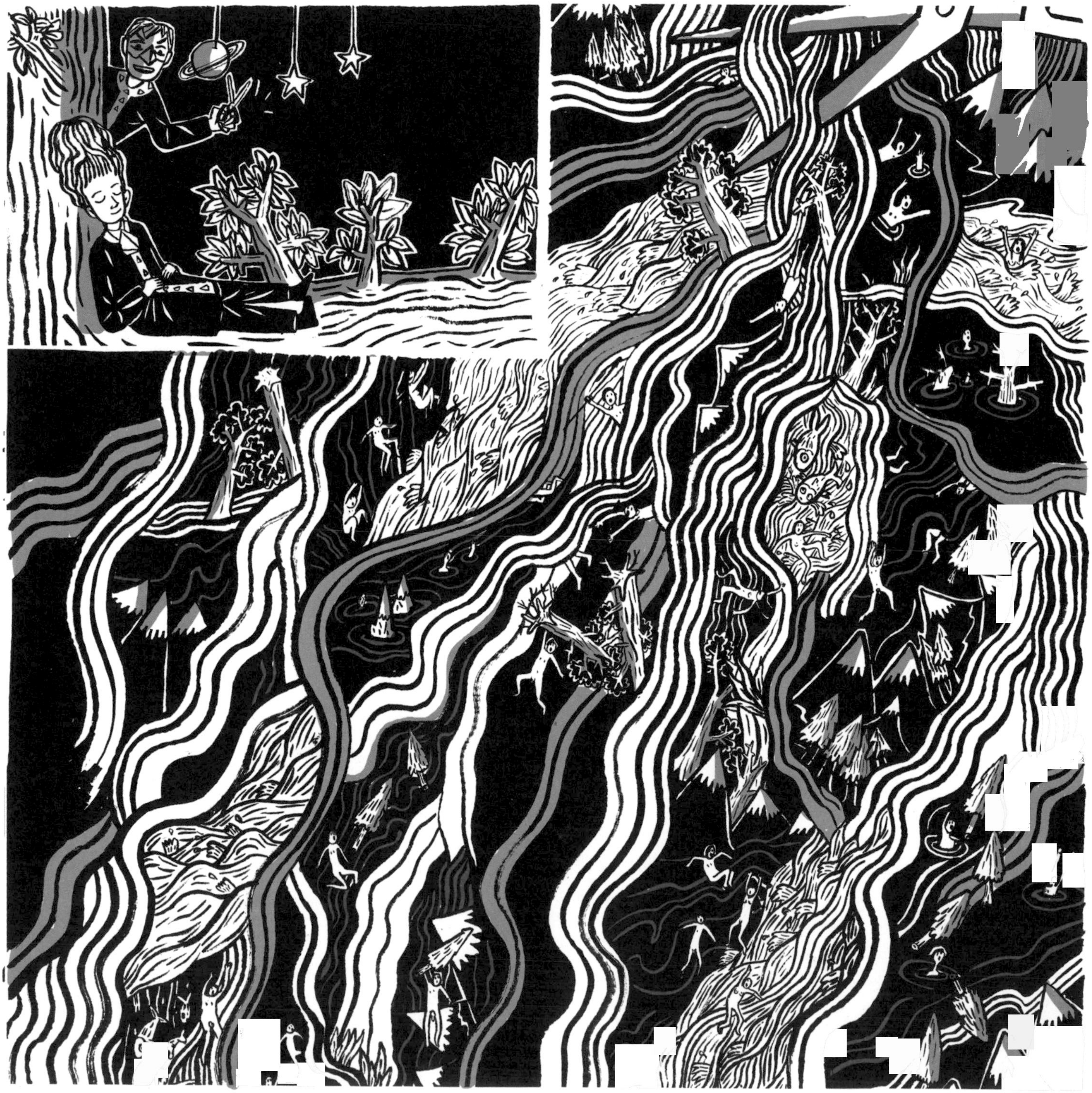

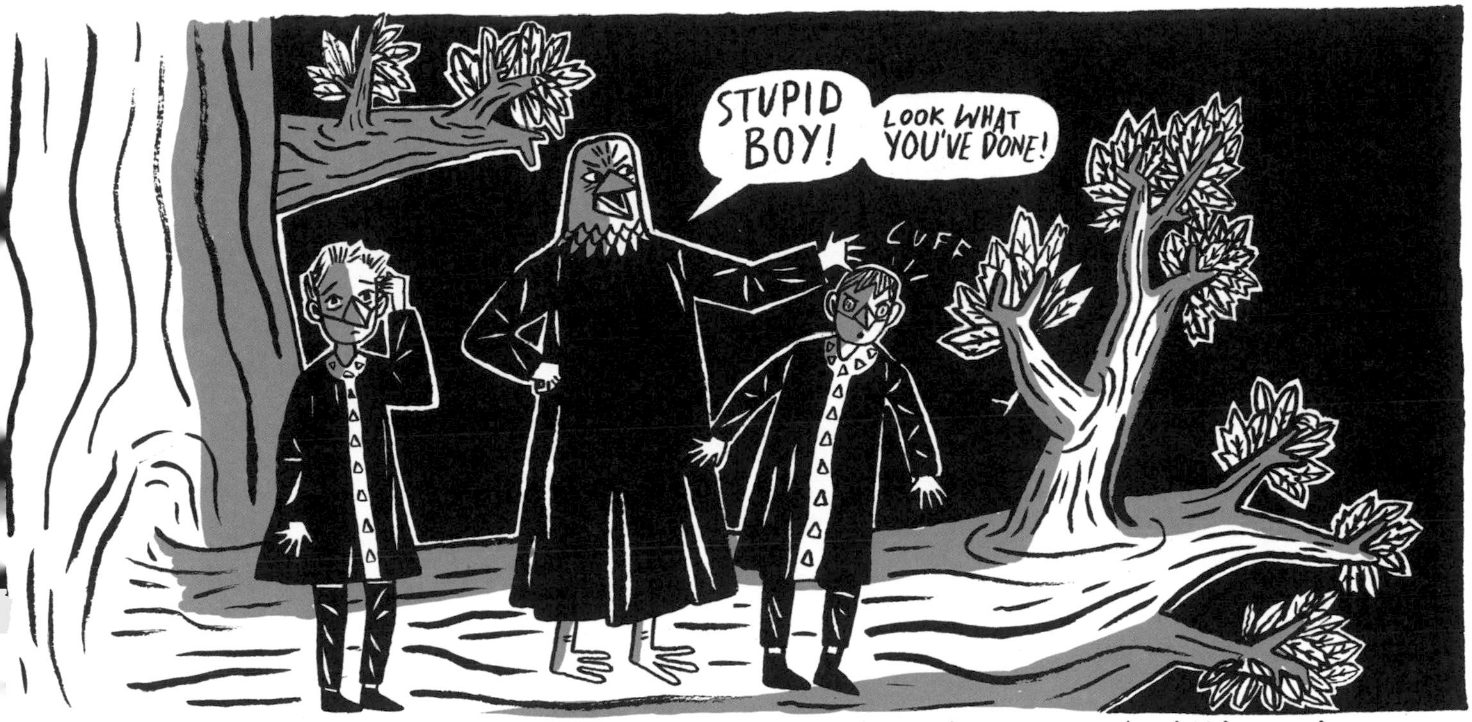
STUPID BOY!
LOOK WHAT YOU'VE DONE!
CUFF

Kiddo's world, so perfect in miniature, was growing before their eyes. The little people, the mountains, the rivers, the trees... all were shaping and forming and growing of their own accord. A world had been made.

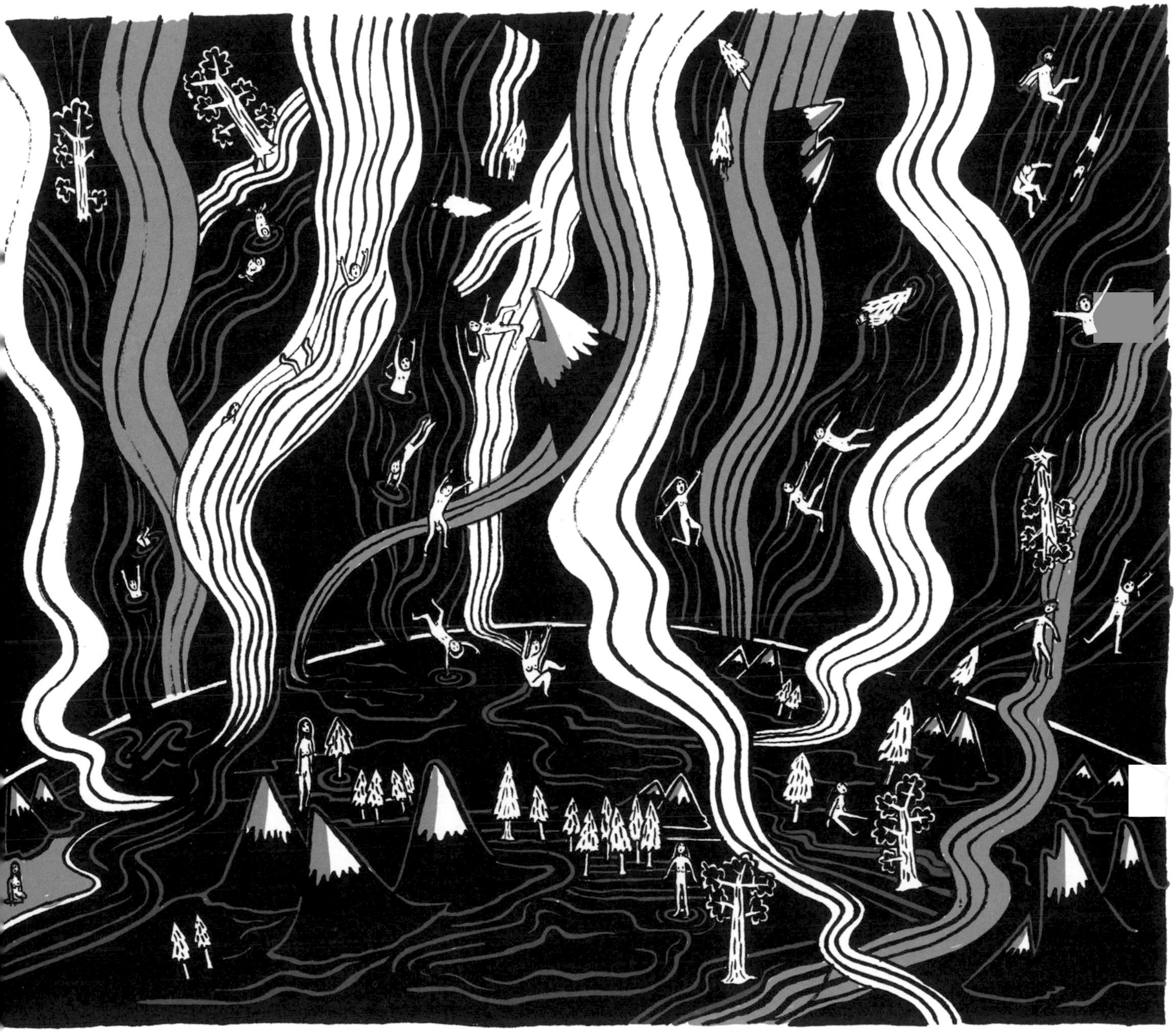

BIBLE OF BIRDMAN: BOOK OF KIDDO

THE GREAT FLOOD

After the world was made, the God BirdMan and his son Kid did not pay very much attention to it. They had more important things to think about.

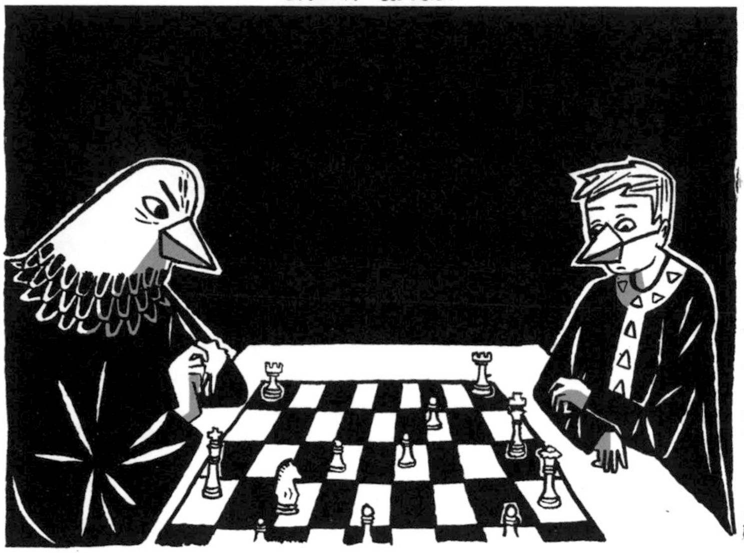

But Kiddo, she loved the world. She had made it, and she felt connected to it. To every atom and every organism.

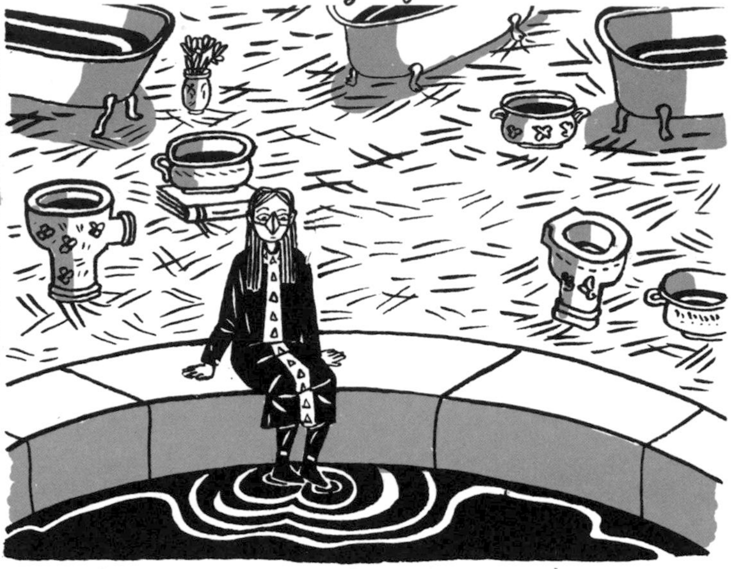

So BirdMan and Kid ignored Early Earth, instead doing much contemplation and thinking on a higher plane. But Kiddo spent more and more time on Earth, just walking around and watching her creations.

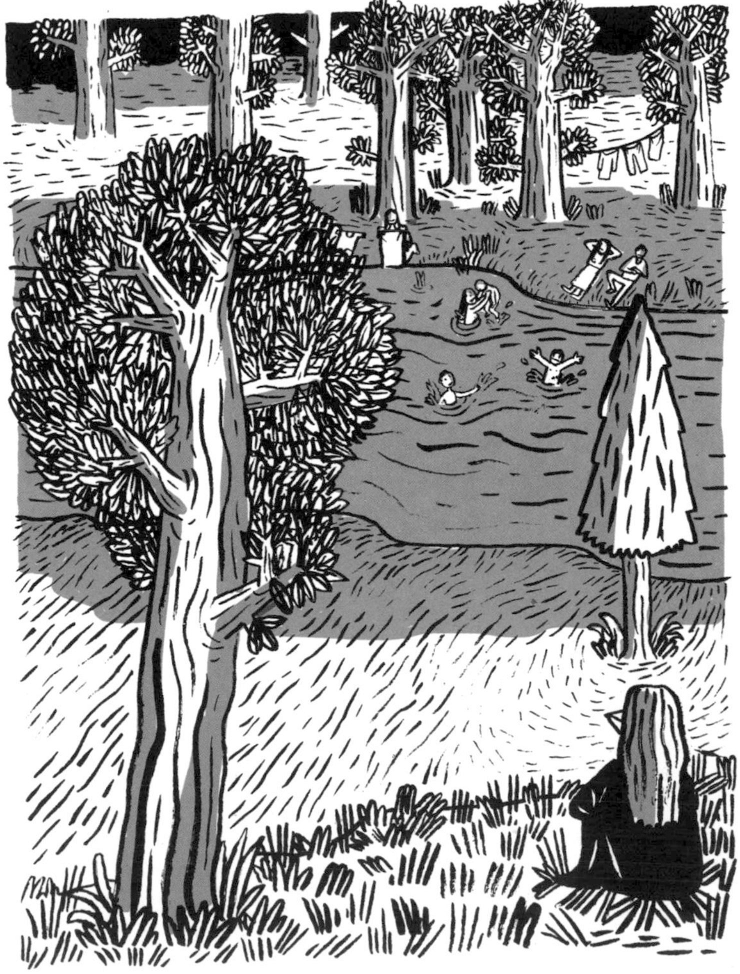

Now this story takes place back in the old days Early Earth, back when there were no cities and the world was a beautiful garden in which men and women just hunted and fished and had babie and loved and lived. And though they feared the Omnipotent BirdMan, it was Kiddo they worshippe most. Because they loved her, for she made them happy.

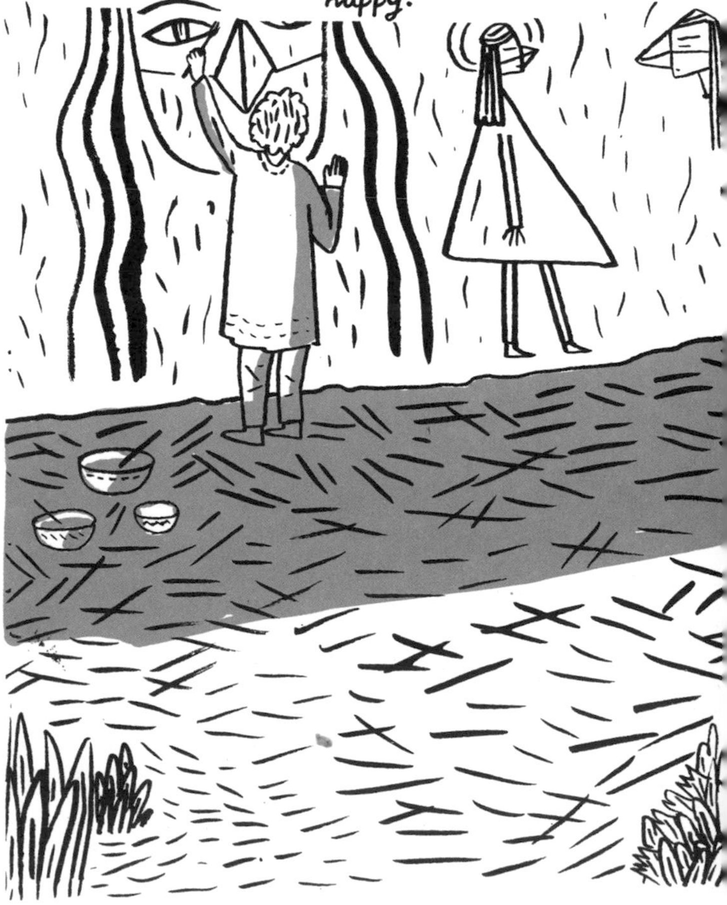

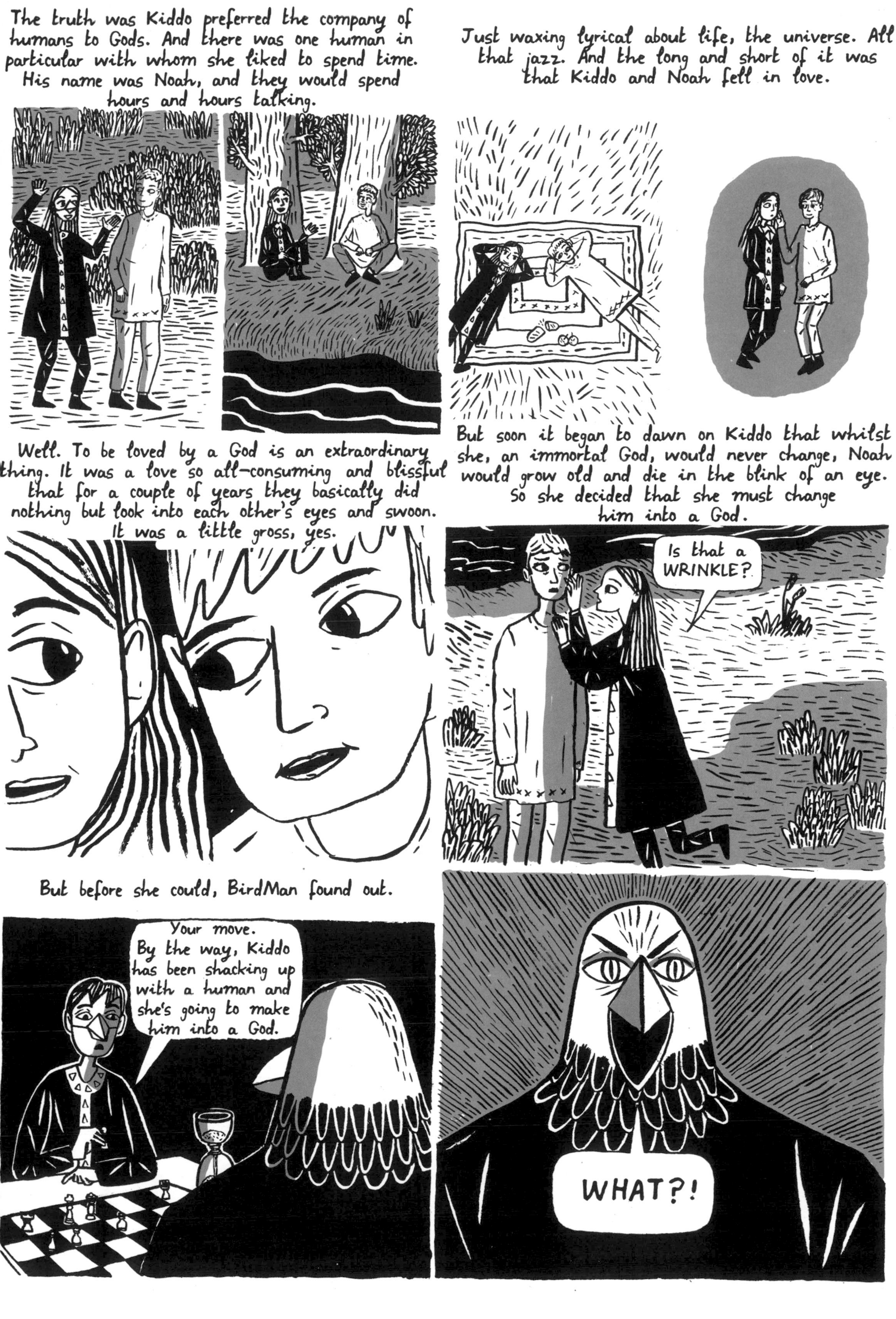
The truth was Kiddo preferred the company of humans to Gods. And there was one human in particular with whom she liked to spend time. His name was Noah, and they would spend hours and hours talking.
Just waxing lyrical about life, the universe. All that jazz. And the long and short of it was that Kiddo and Noah fell in love.
Well. To be loved by a God is an extraordinary thing. It was a love so all-consuming and blissful that for a couple of years they basically did nothing but look into each other's eyes and swoon. It was a little gross, yes.
But soon it began to dawn on Kiddo that whilst she, an immortal God, would never change, Noah would grow old and die in the blink of an eye. So she decided that she must change him into a God.
Is that a WRINKLE?
But before she could, BirdMan found out.
Your move. By the way, Kiddo has been shacking up with a human and she's going to make him into a God.
WHAT?!

He was beside himself, livid. Quite frankly he was hopping mad.

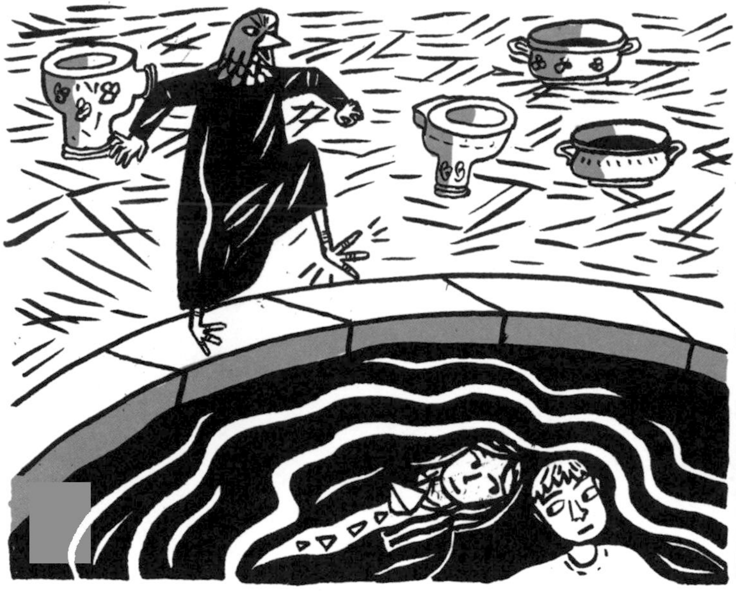

Nobody but he could create a GOD. Kiddo had gone too far.

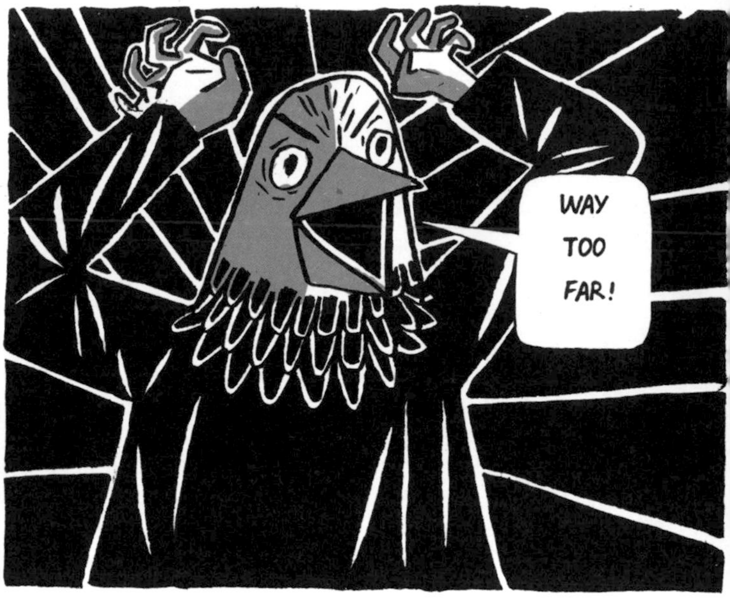
WAY TOO FAR!

So as punishment he decided he would destroy Earth. And since Noah lived on Earth, well...

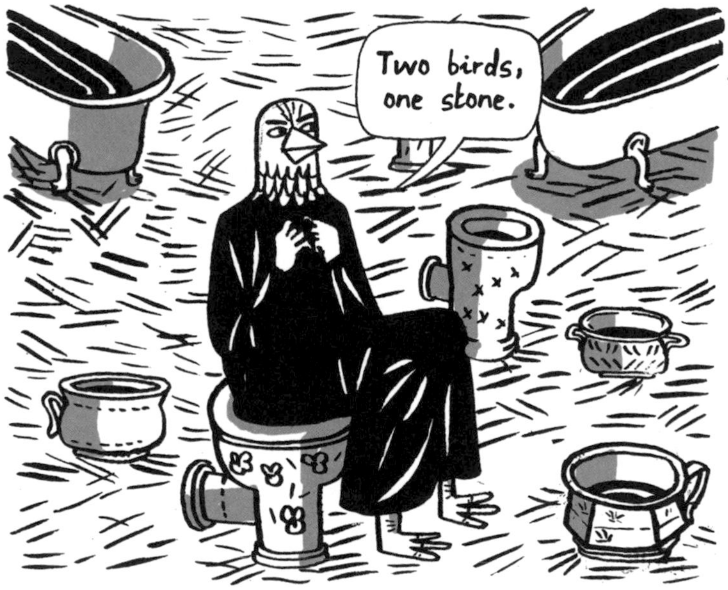
Two birds, one stone.

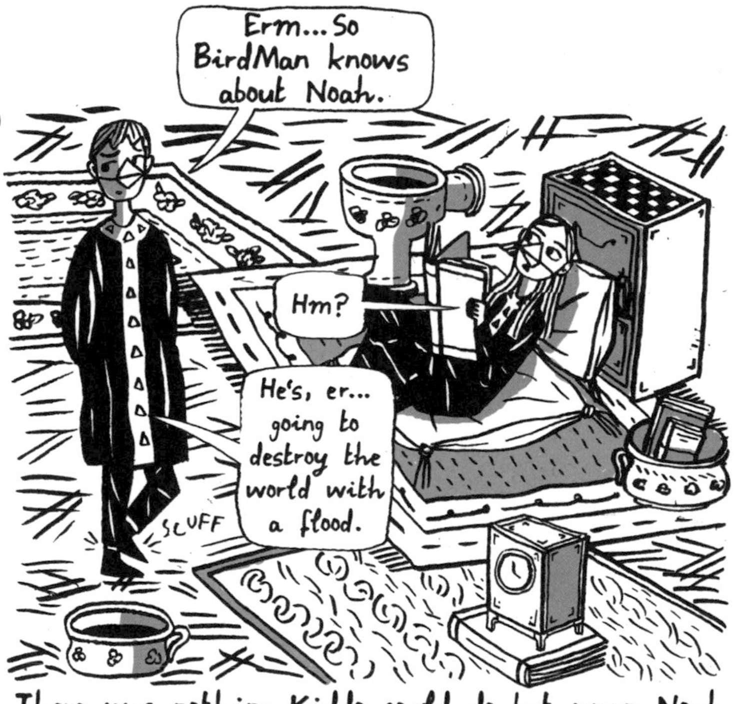
Erm...So BirdMan knows about Noah.
Hm?
He's, er... going to destroy the world with a flood.
SCUFF

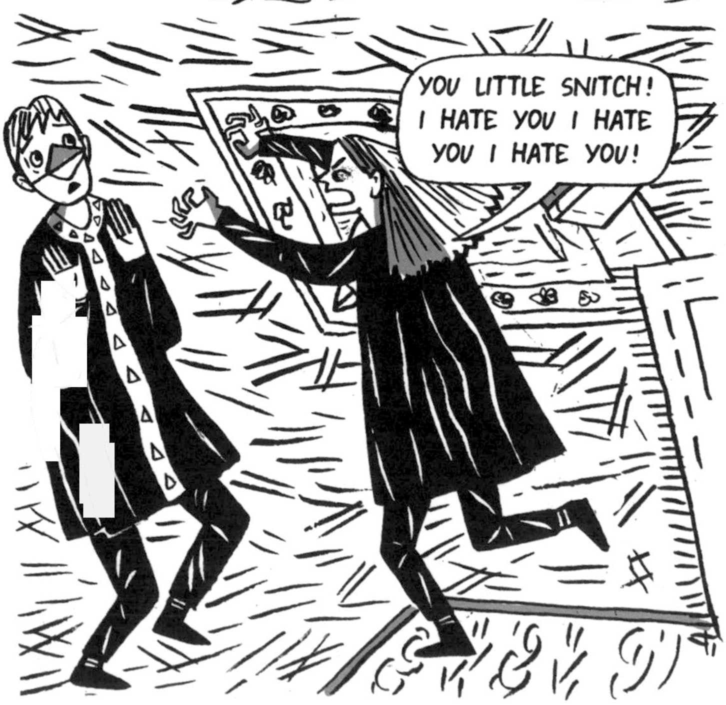
YOU LITTLE SNITCH! I HATE YOU I HATE YOU I HATE YOU!

There was nothing Kiddo could do but warn Noah. She told him to make an ark and take with him his family and friends and some animals, so that her world might continue after the flood.

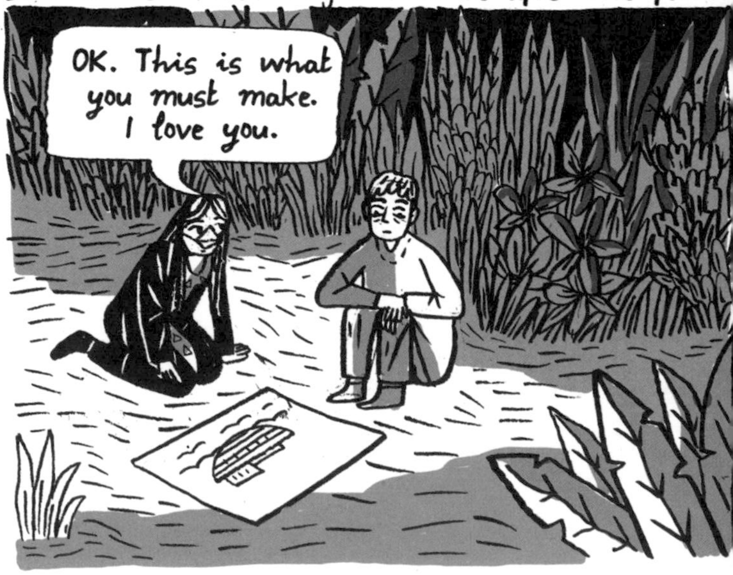
OK. This is what you must make. I love you.

Soon the ark was built, and a good thing too, for as Noah and the humans herded the animals on board, dark clouds were already gathering and the first cold drops of rain began to fall.

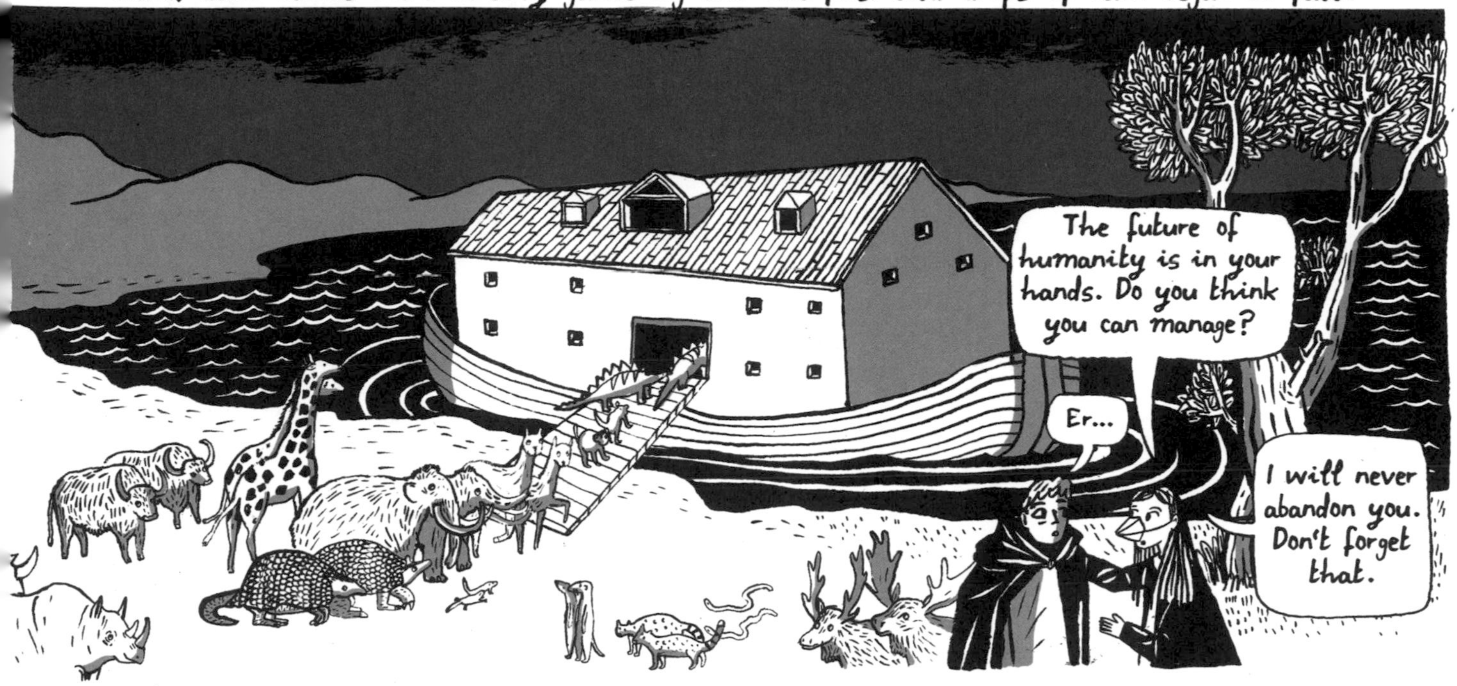
The future of humanity is in your hands. Do you think you can manage?
Er...
I will never abandon you. Don't forget that.

The rain began to come down harder and harder and dark clouds blacked out the sun, bringing on a terrible, endless night. The ark was a horrible place. It was cold and cramped and eerie and animal oises would fill the vessel at all times. High monkey shrieks and deep cat roars and the horrid uffling of nameless creatures. Noah and the other humans huddled together, and as time passed they began to wonder how and why Kiddo had forsaken them so.

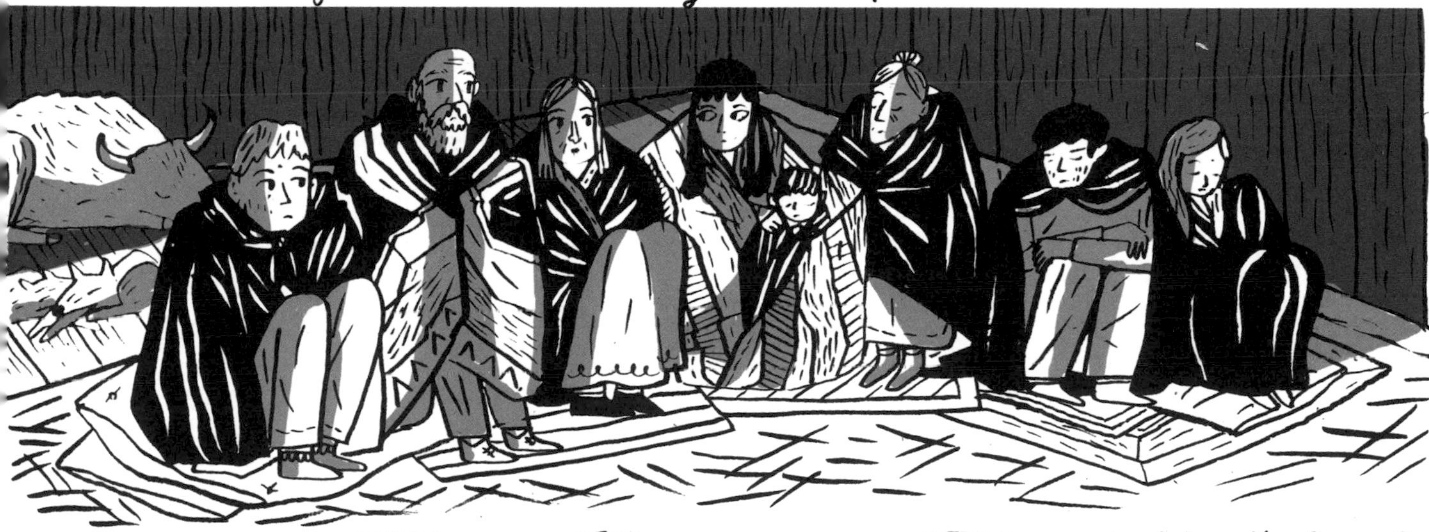

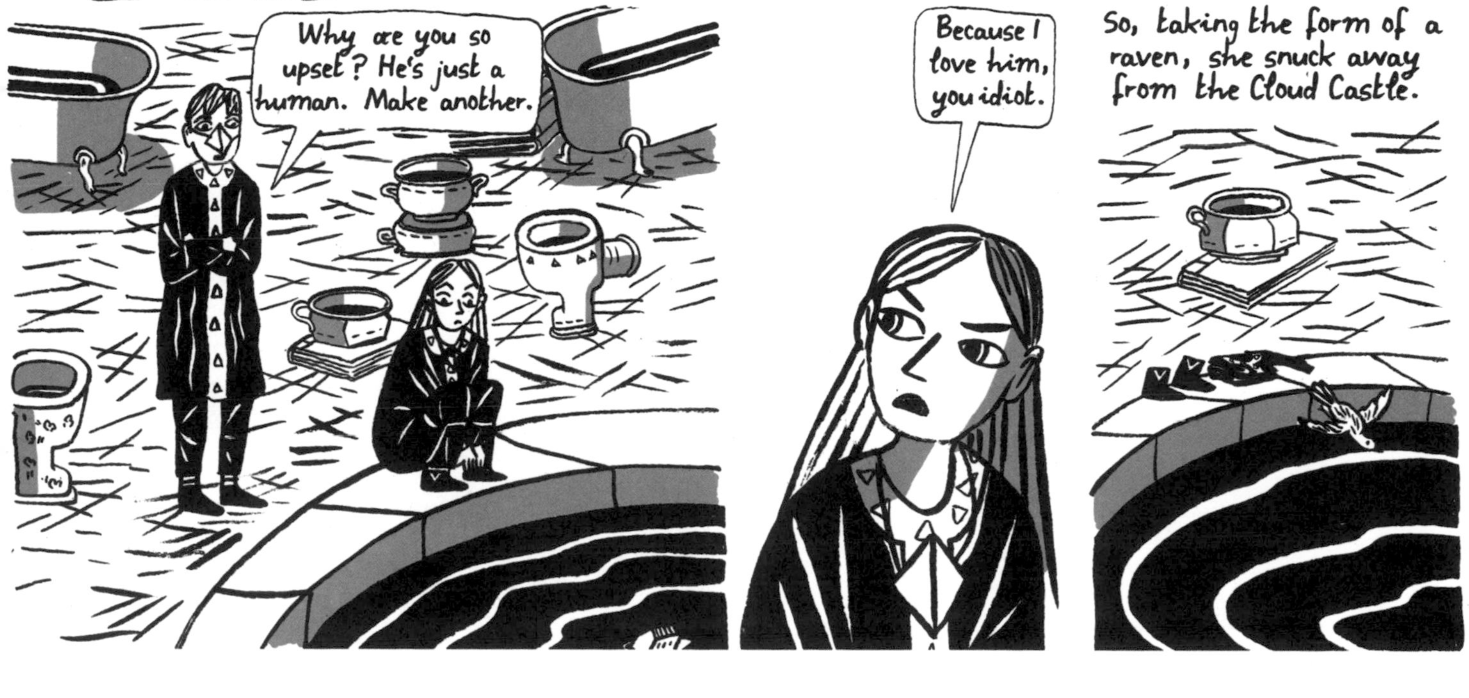
Why are you so upset? He's just a human. Make another.
Because I love him, you idiot.
So, taking the form of a raven, she snuck away from the Cloud Castle.

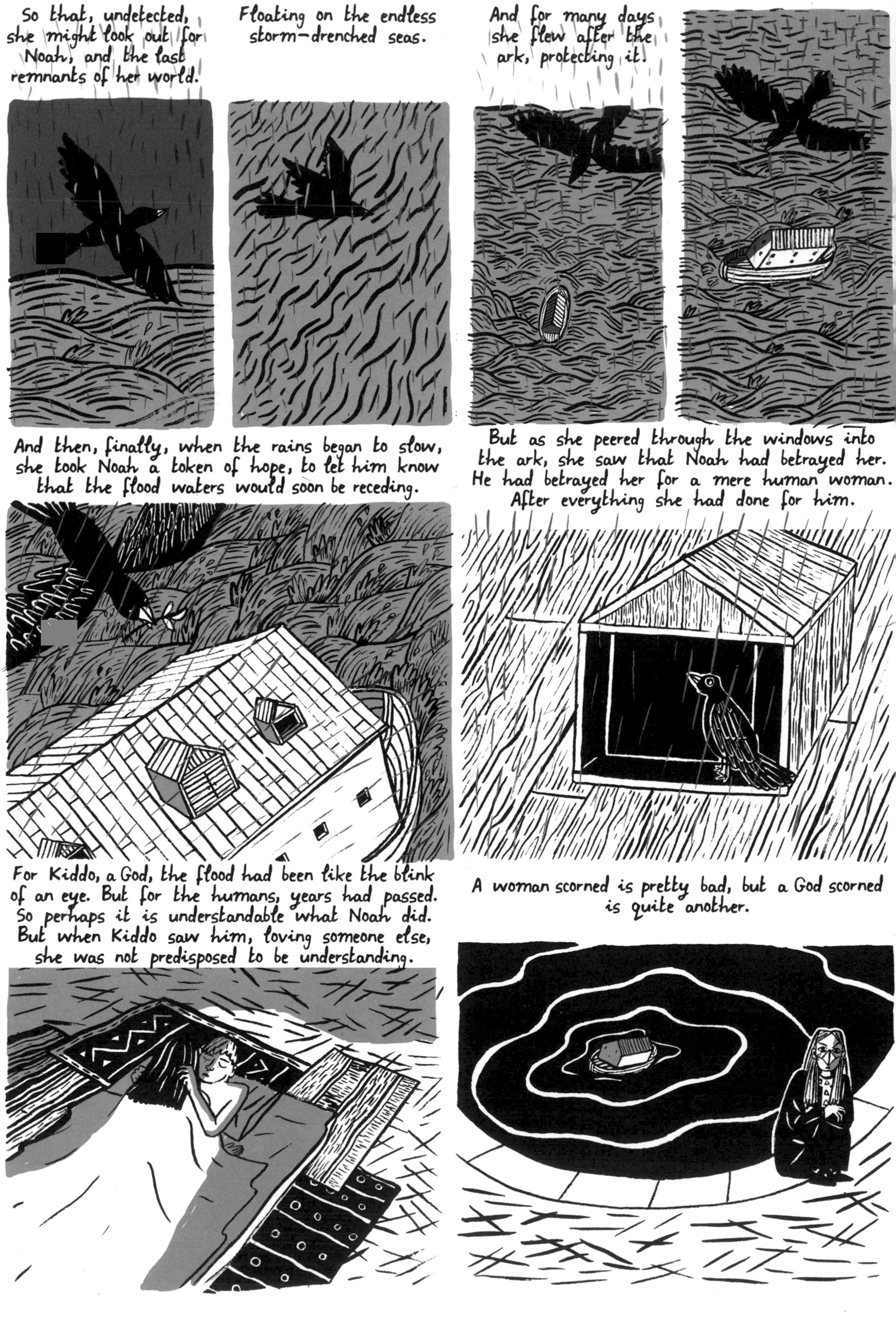
So that, undetected, she might look out for Noah, and the last remnants of her world.
Floating on the endless storm-drenched seas.
And for many days she flew after the ark, protecting it.
And then, finally, when the rains began to slow, she took Noah a token of hope, to let him know that the flood waters would soon be receding.
But as she peered through the windows into the ark, she saw that Noah had betrayed her. He had betrayed her for a mere human woman. After everything she had done for him.
For Kiddo, a God, the flood had been like the blink of an eye. But for the humans, years had passed. So perhaps it is understandable what Noah did. But when Kiddo saw him, loving someone else, she was not predisposed to be understanding.
A woman scorned is pretty bad, but a God scorned is quite another.

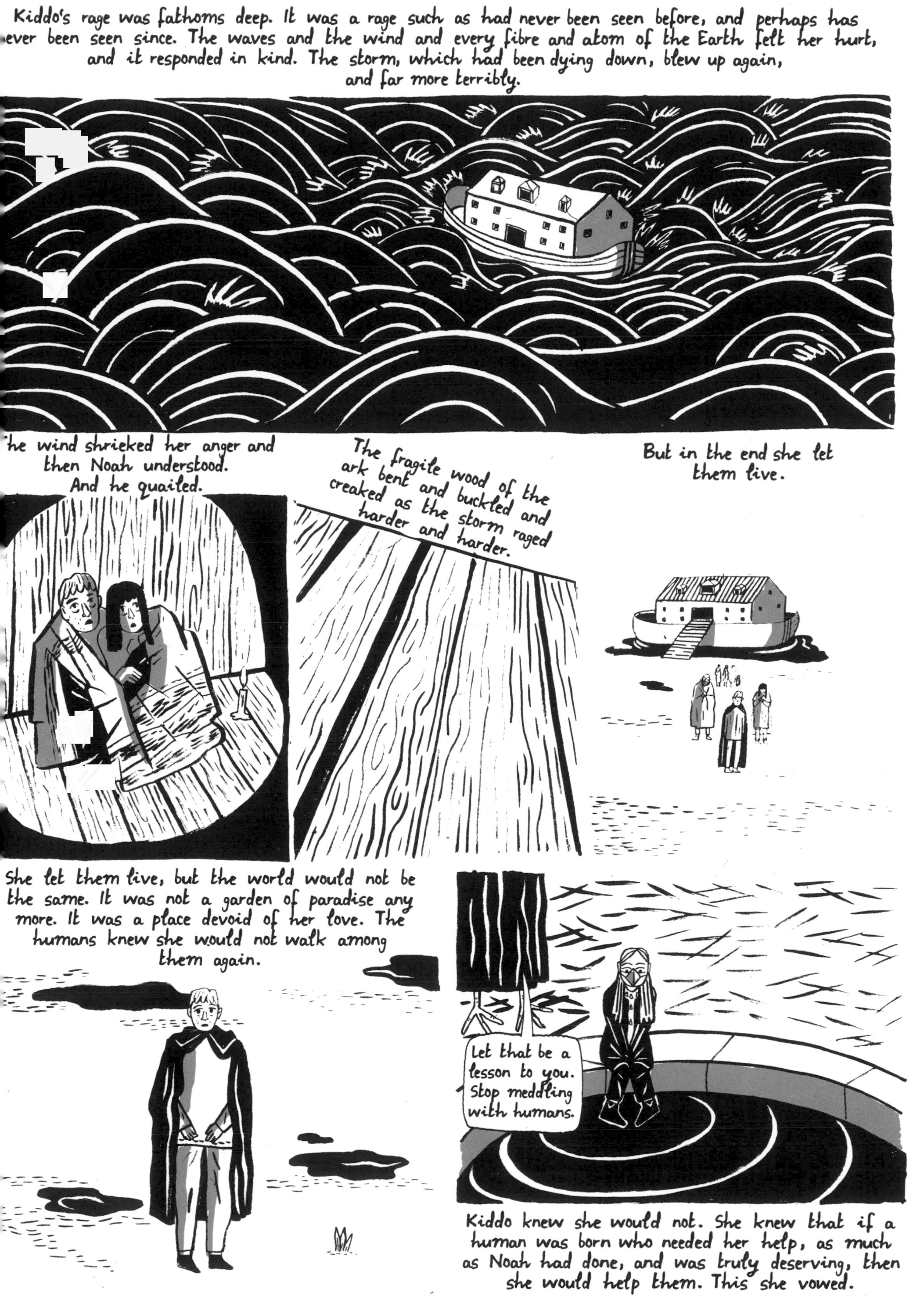
Kiddo's rage was fathoms deep. It was a rage such as had never been seen before, and perhaps has ever been seen since. The waves and the wind and every fibre and atom of the Earth felt her hurt, and it responded in kind. The storm, which had been dying down, blew up again, and far more terribly.
he wind shrieked her anger and then Noah understood. And he quailed.
The fragile wood of the ark bent and buckled and creaked as the storm raged harder and harder.
But in the end she let them live.
She let them live, but the world would not be the same. It was not a garden of paradise any more. It was a place devoid of her love. The humans knew she would not walk among them again.
Let that be a lesson to you. Stop meddling with humans.
Kiddo knew she would not. She knew that if a human was born who needed her help, as much as Noah had done, and was truly deserving, then she would help them. This she vowed.

THE TOWER OF MIGDAL BAVEL

Once, many years ago, the people of Migdal Bavel (or simply Bavel, as it was known then) began to build a tower. It was to be the tallest tower the world had ever seen. It was to reach the Cloud Castle. From all over the world people came to work on the great structure, for they wanted so much to look upon the faces of their creators. There had been a time, on Earth, before the Great Flood, when the Gods had walked among them. Now the humans yearned to see them again, in all their terrible glory.

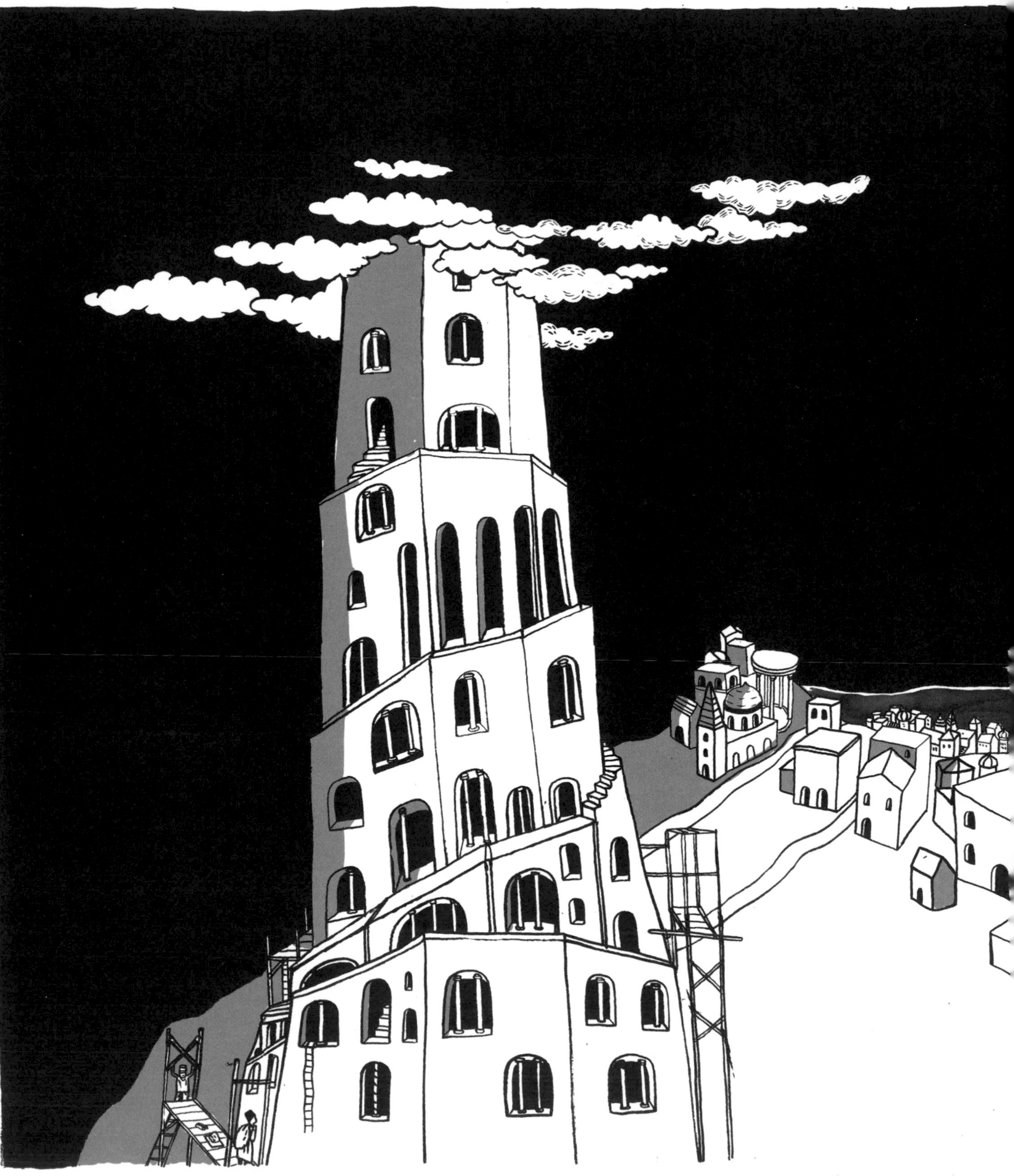

As more people flocked to work on the tower it grew higher, dwarfing the city below.

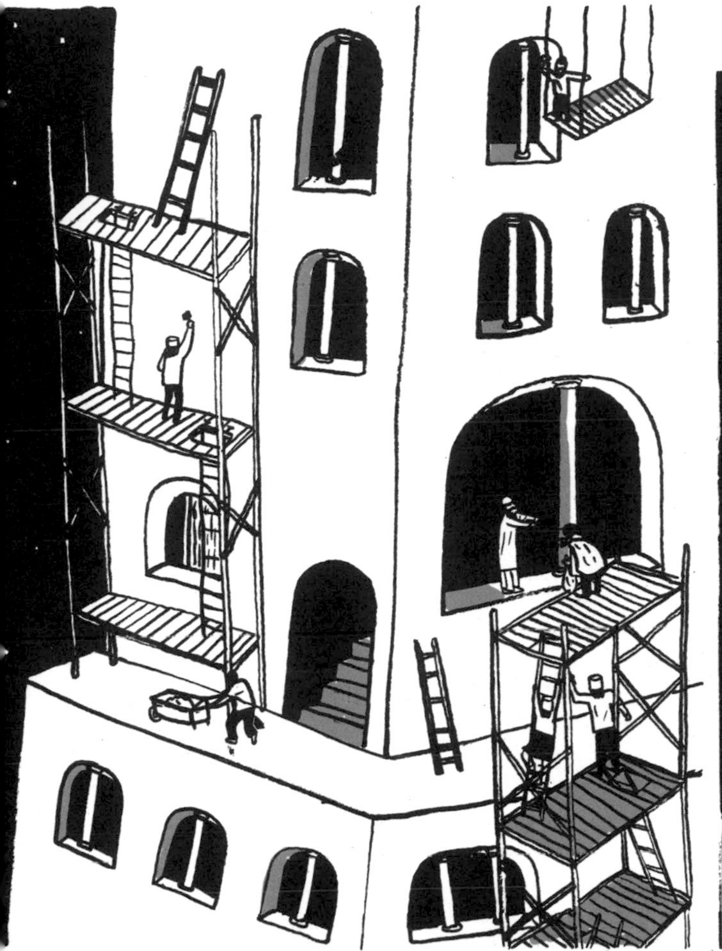

Every night they looked up into the stars and wondered how near they were to their Gods. Wondered if BirdMan could see them and their beautiful tower. He could. And he was not happy.

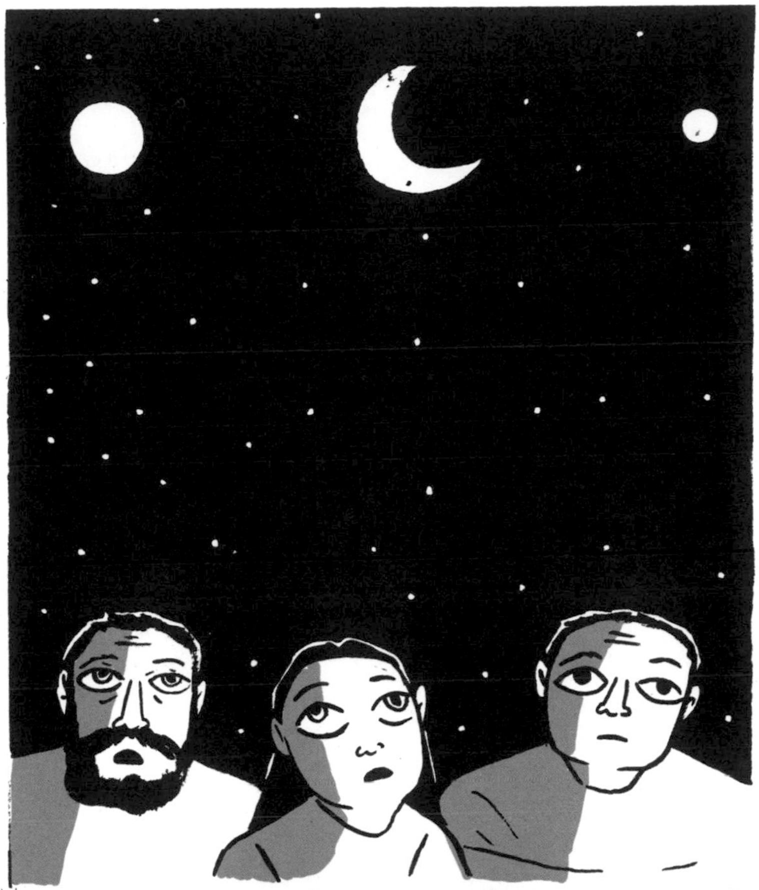

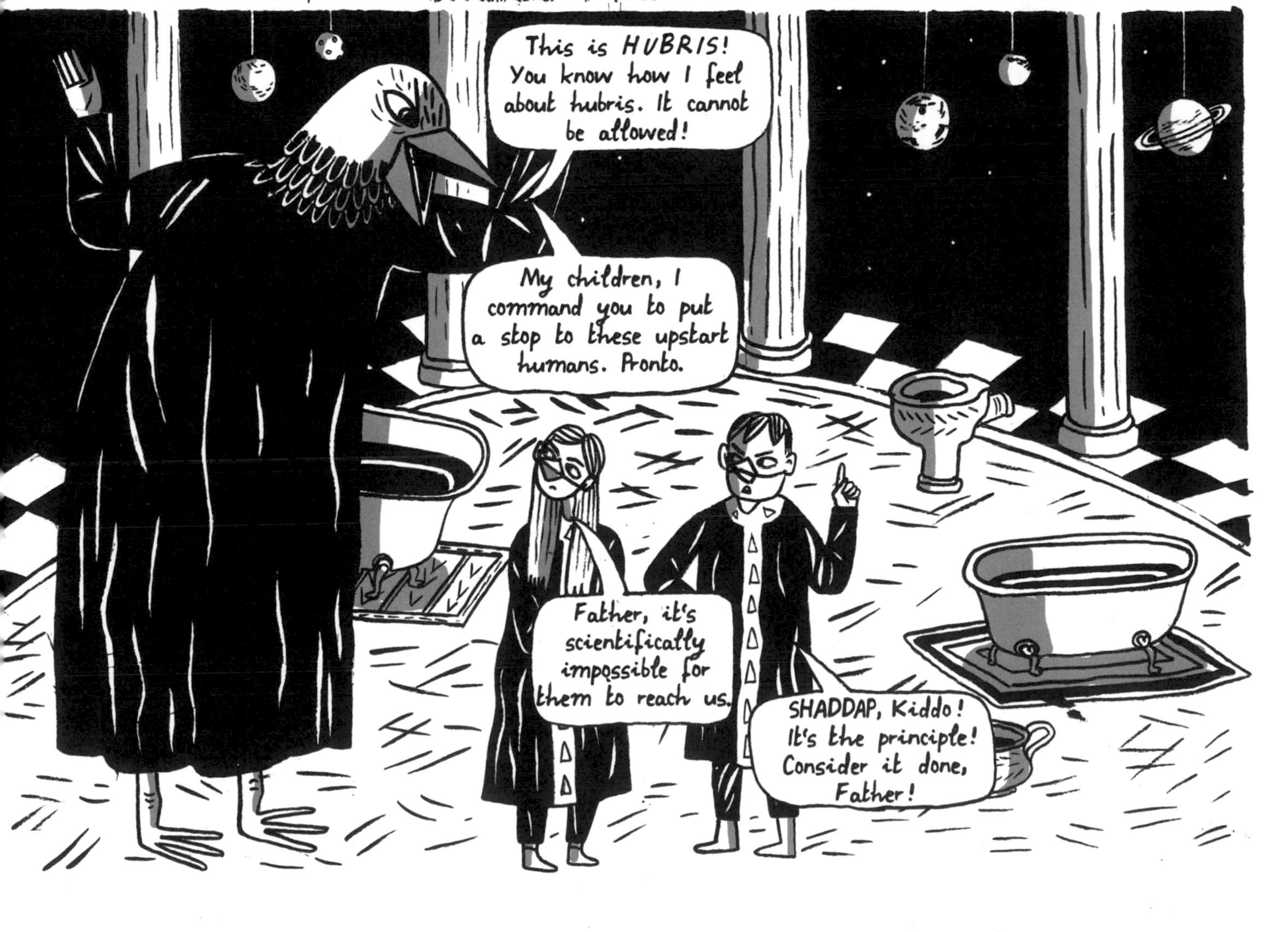
This is HUBRIS! You know how I feel about hubris. It cannot be allowed!
My children, I command you to put a stop to these upstart humans. Pronto.
Father, it's scientifically impossible for them to reach us.
SHADDAP, Kiddo! It's the principle! Consider it done, Father!

So the Ravens punished mankind for their preposterous tower. First they sent down fire and brimstone. But the tower was sturdy and well-built and it withstood the flames.

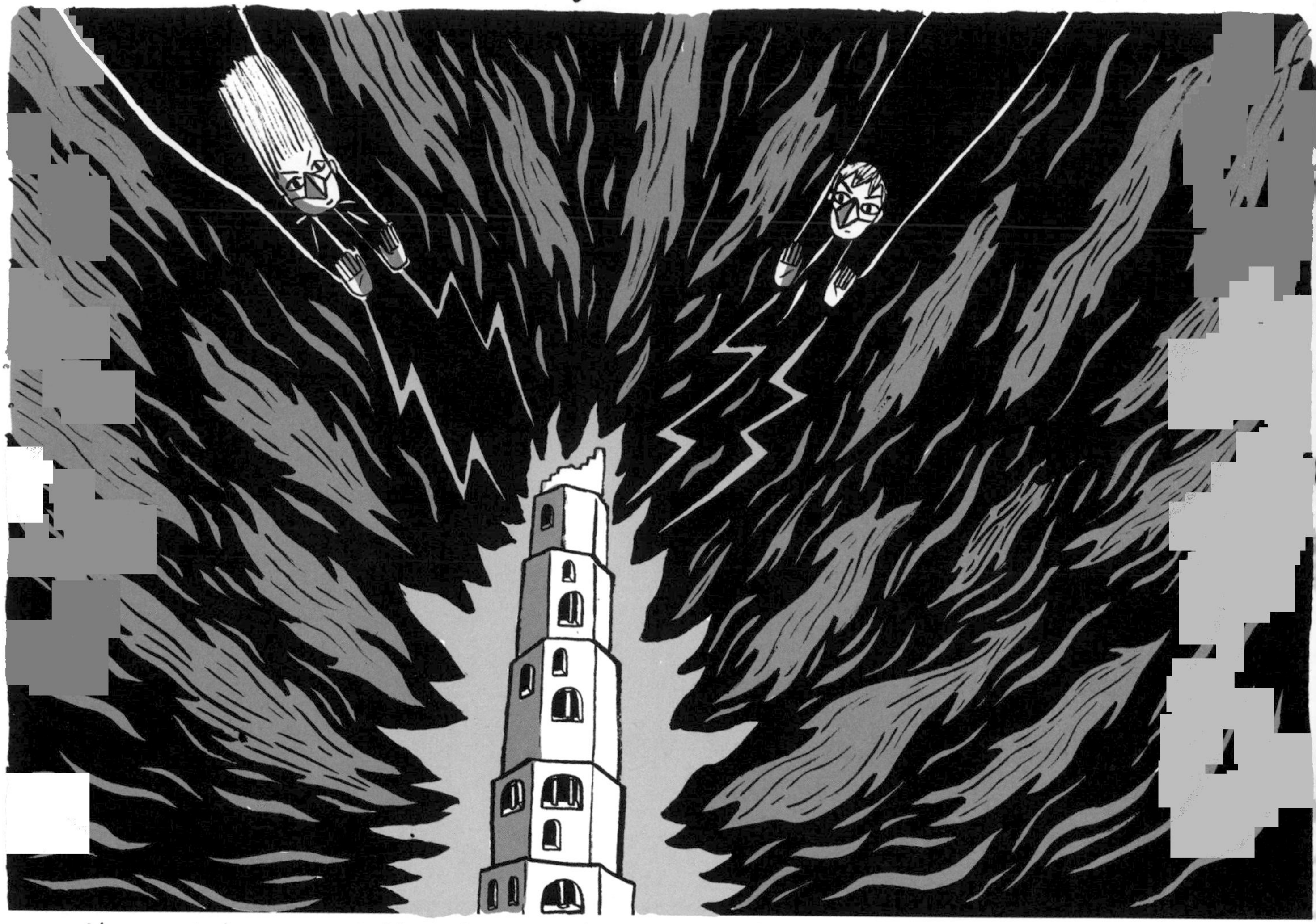

So they sent down a great flood (because floods, after all, are tried and tested) but the humans climbed the tower and were saved from the rising waters.

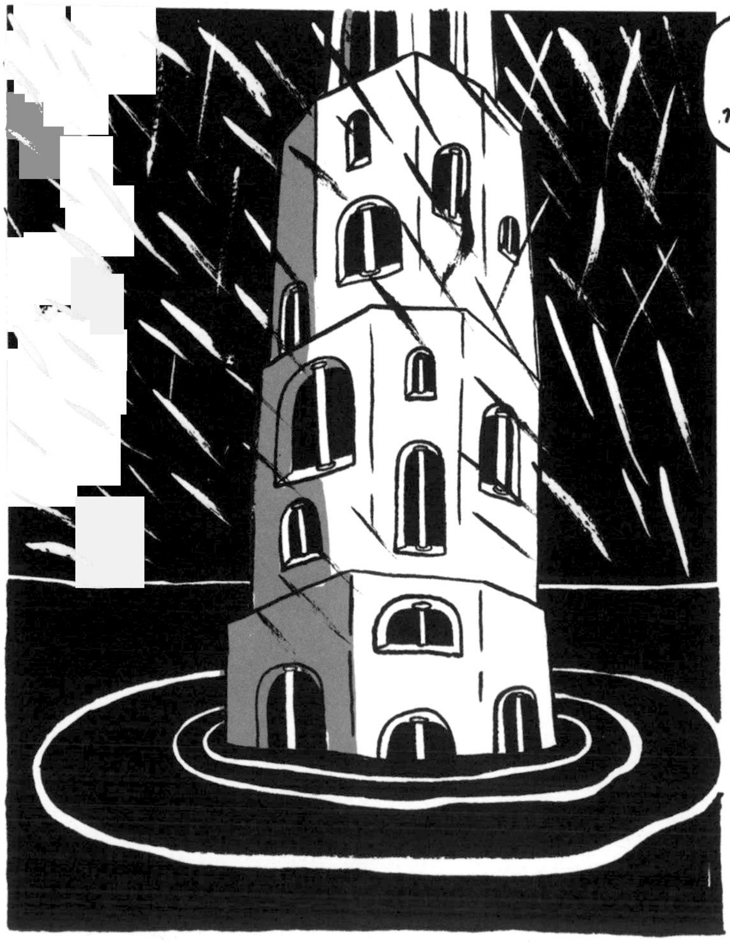

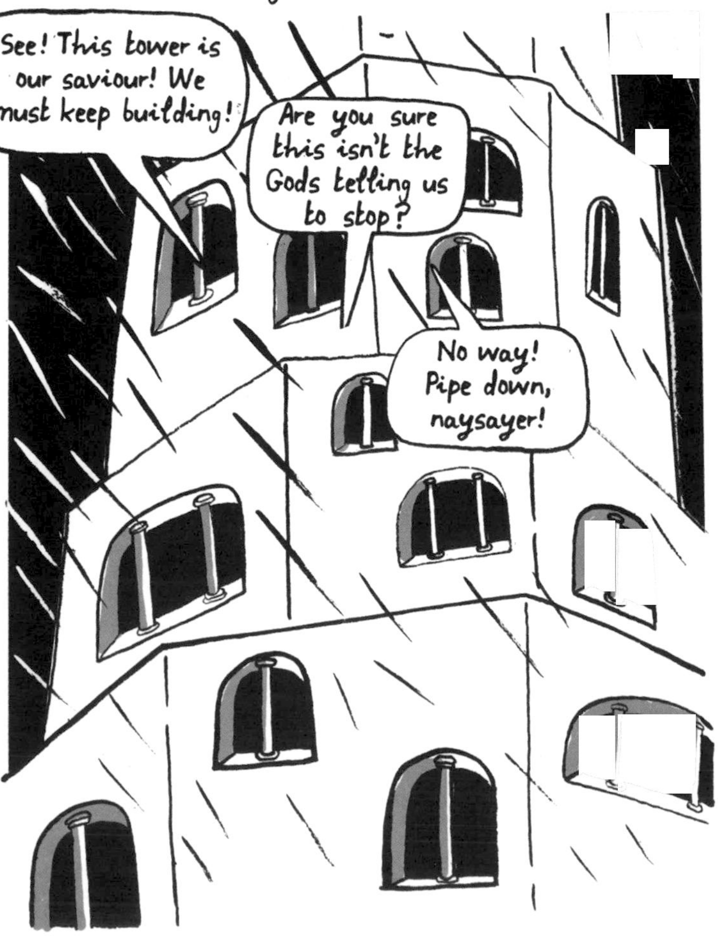
See! This tower is our saviour! We must keep building!
Are you sure this isn't the Gods telling us to stop?
No way! Pipe down, naysayer!

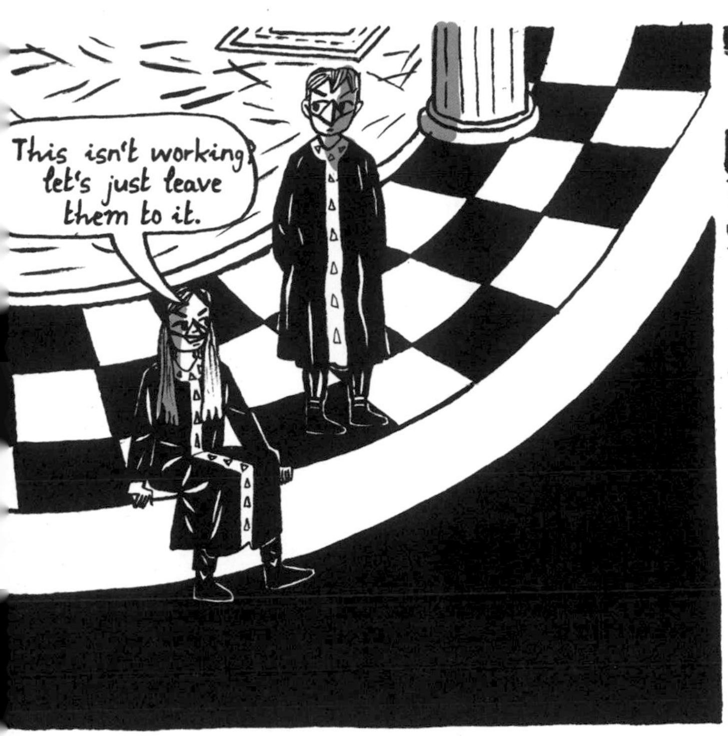
This isn't working, let's just leave them to it.

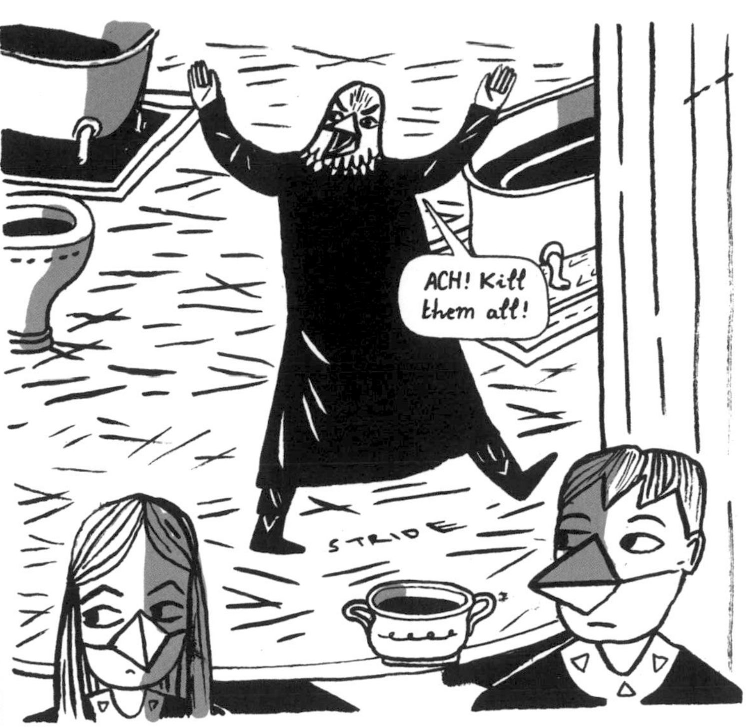
ACH! Kill them all!
STRIDE

But Kid had a different idea. At this point on Earth, there was only one language. But Kid took this language from them. Suddenly no one could understand each other. Building ceased immediately as husbands and wives, brothers and sisters and friends could no longer communicate. Where there had been only one language, suddenly there were multitudes.

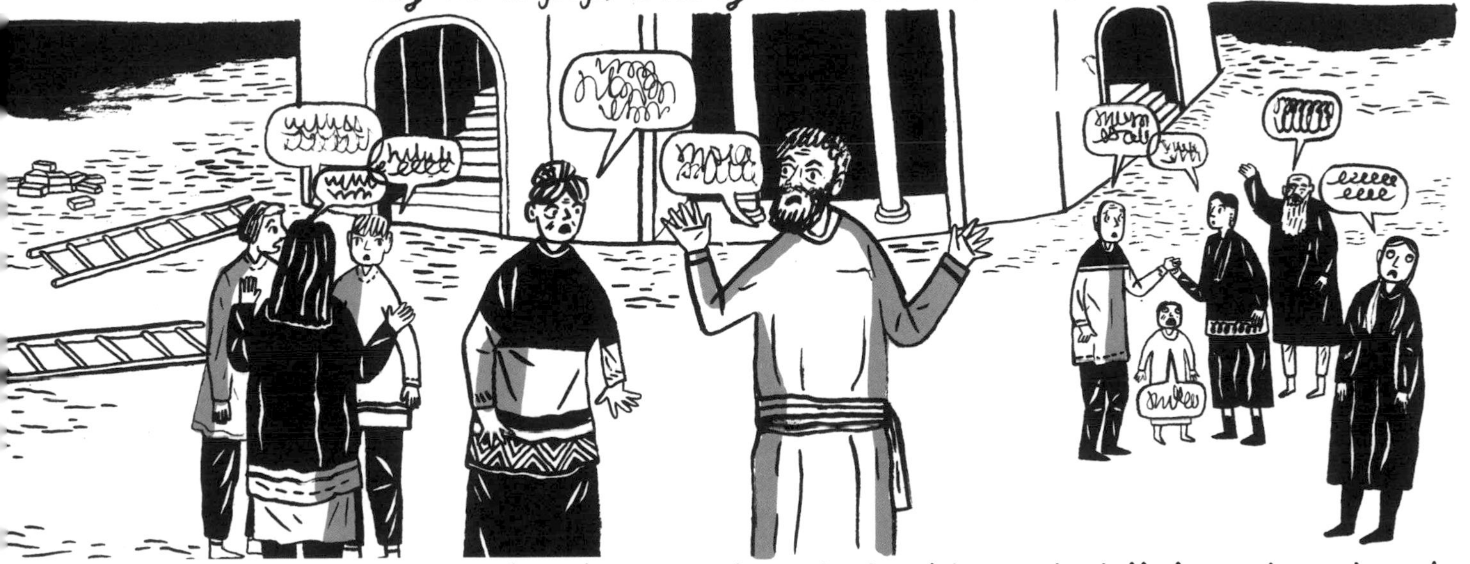

The tower crumbled and a great black lake formed in its foundations. It still lies, stagnant and dark, just outside the city, a reminder of the power of the Gods. And that is why the world is how it is; a place of discord and unrest, of misunderstandings and the conviction that some people are better than others.

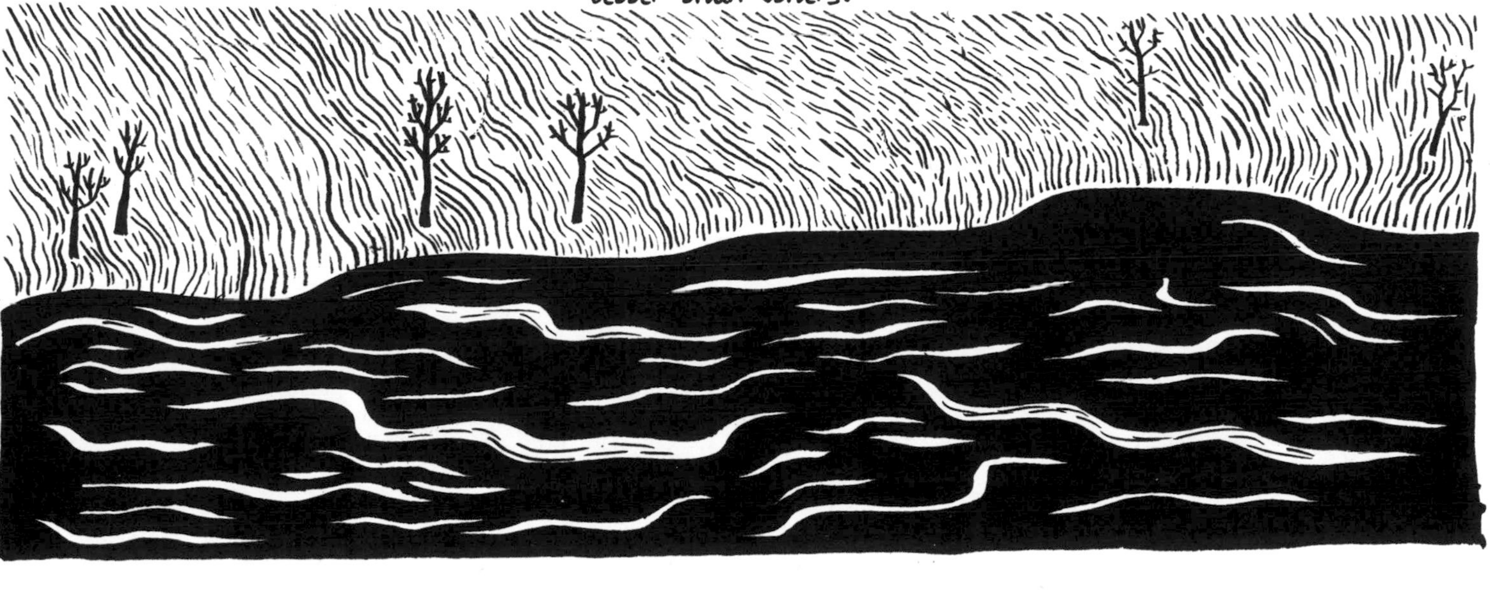

THE PALACE OF WHISPERS

There was no doubt that Migdal Bavel was a strange and beautiful city. But everywhere the Storyteller could see the influence of BirdMan.

And the BirdMan that the Bavellians worshipped seemed to be a cold God, both vengeful and ambivalent. The Storyteller knew he could not stay.

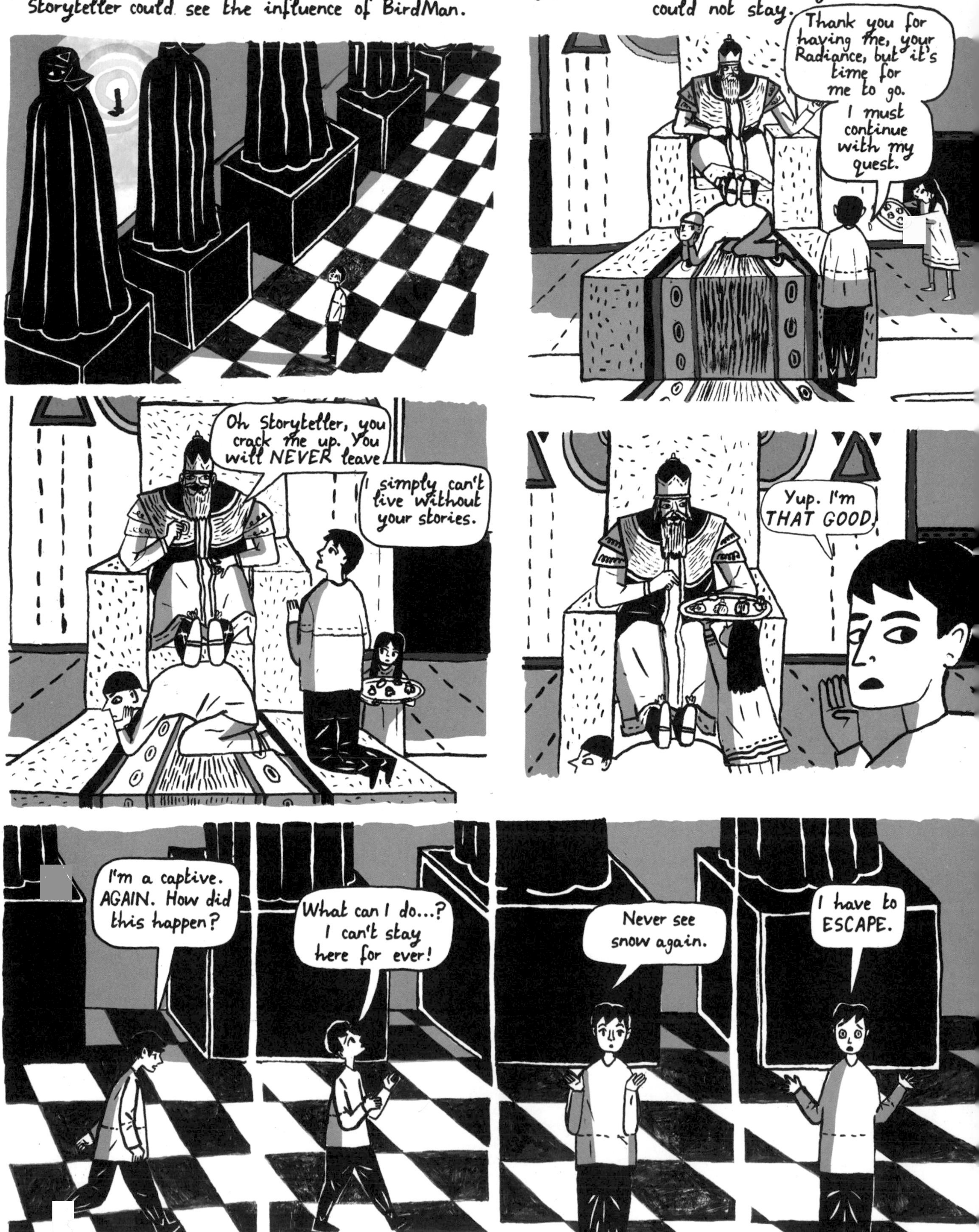
Thank you for having me, your Radiance, but it's time for me to go.
I must continue with my quest.
Oh Storyteller, you crack me up. You will NEVER leave.
I simply can't live without your stories.
Yup. I'm THAT GOOD.
I'm a captive. AGAIN. How did this happen?
What can I do...? I can't stay here for ever!
Never see snow again.
I have to ESCAPE.

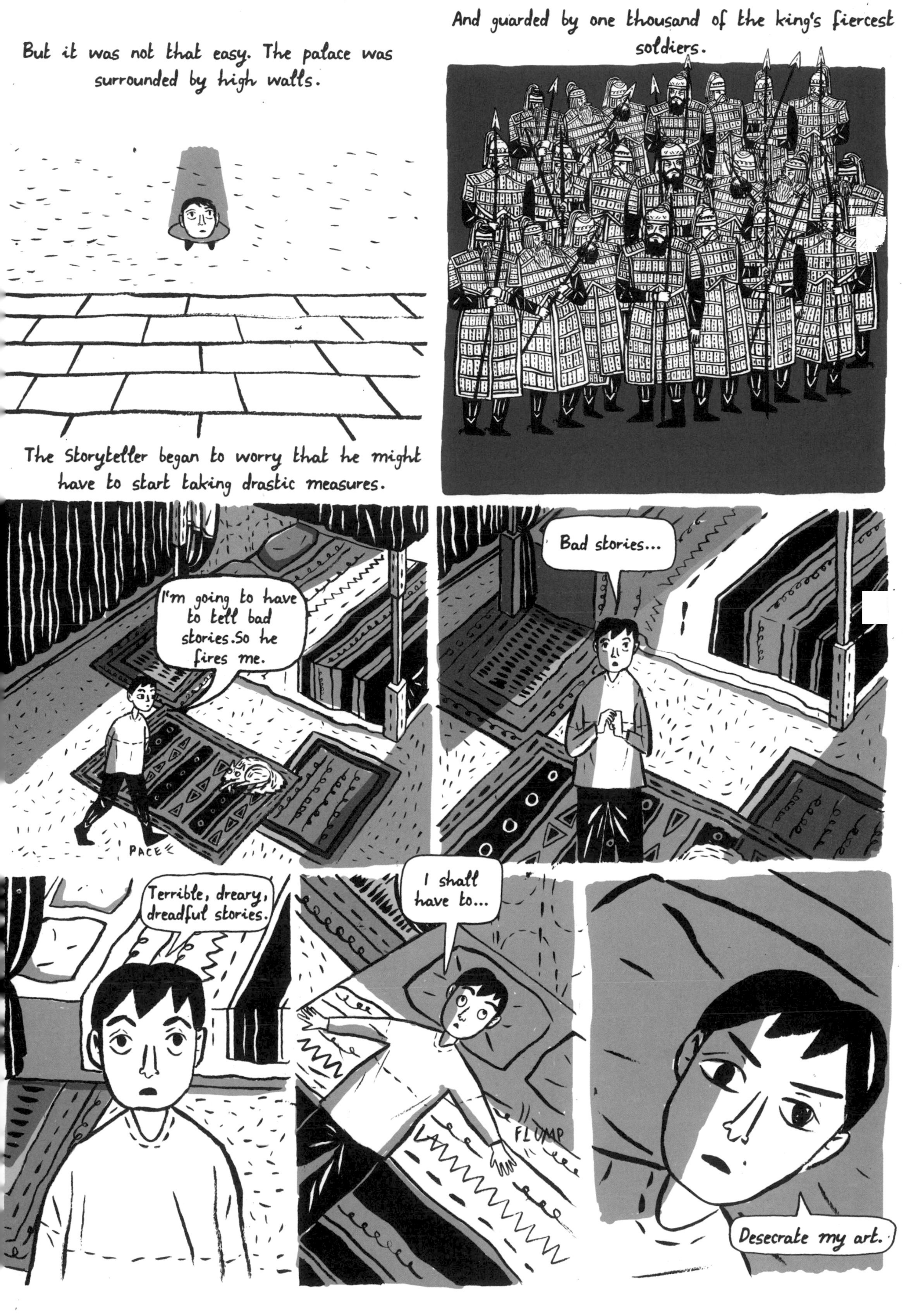
But it was not that easy. The palace was surrounded by high walls.
And guarded by one thousand of the king's fiercest soldiers.
The Storyteller began to worry that he might have to start taking drastic measures.
I'm going to have to tell bad stories. So he fires me.
PACE
Bad stories...
Terrible, dreary, dreadful stories.
I shall have to...
FLUMP
Desecrate my art.

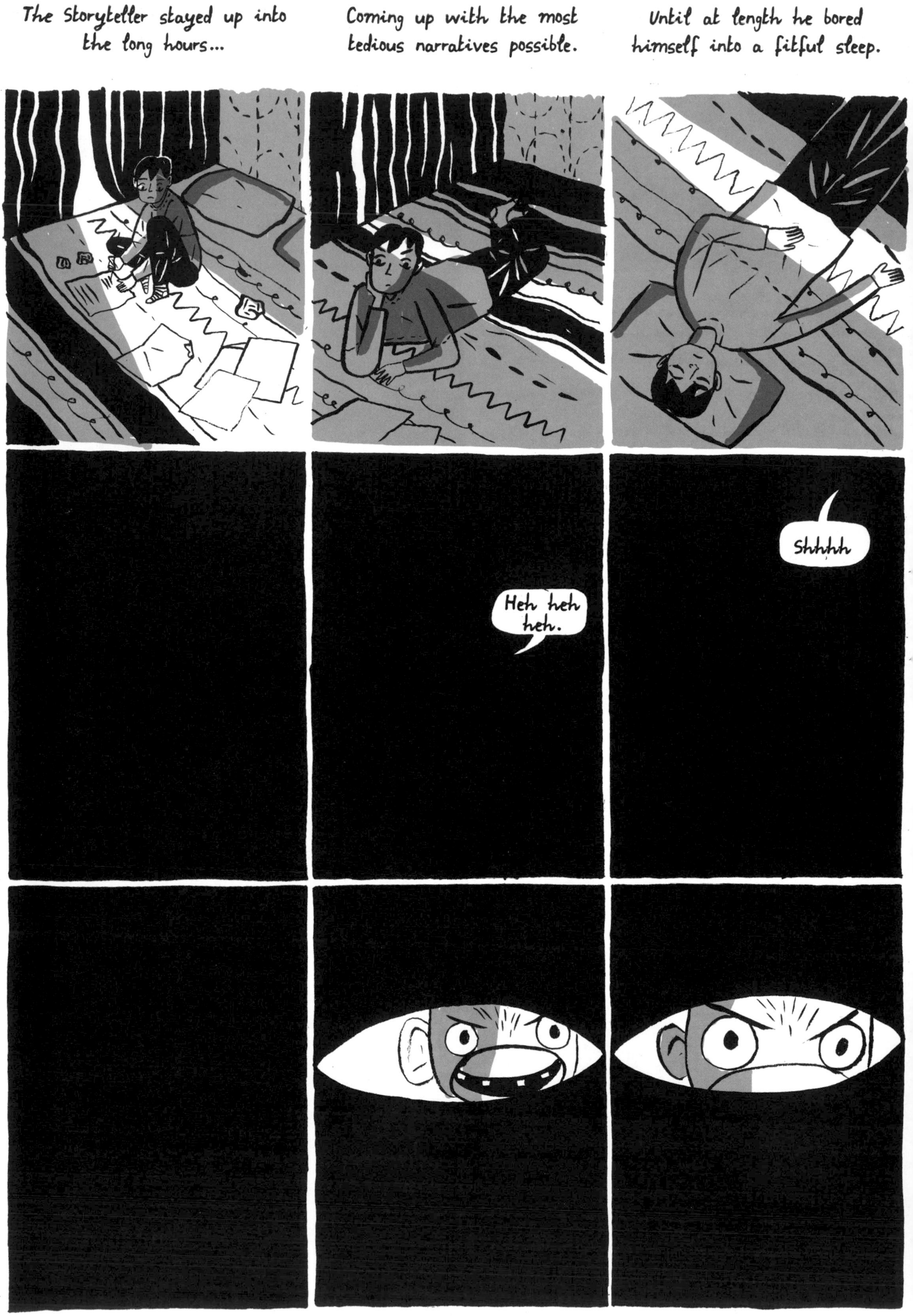
The Storyteller stayed up into the long hours...
Coming up with the most tedious narratives possible.
Until at length he bored himself into a fitful sleep.
Heh heh heh.
Shhhh

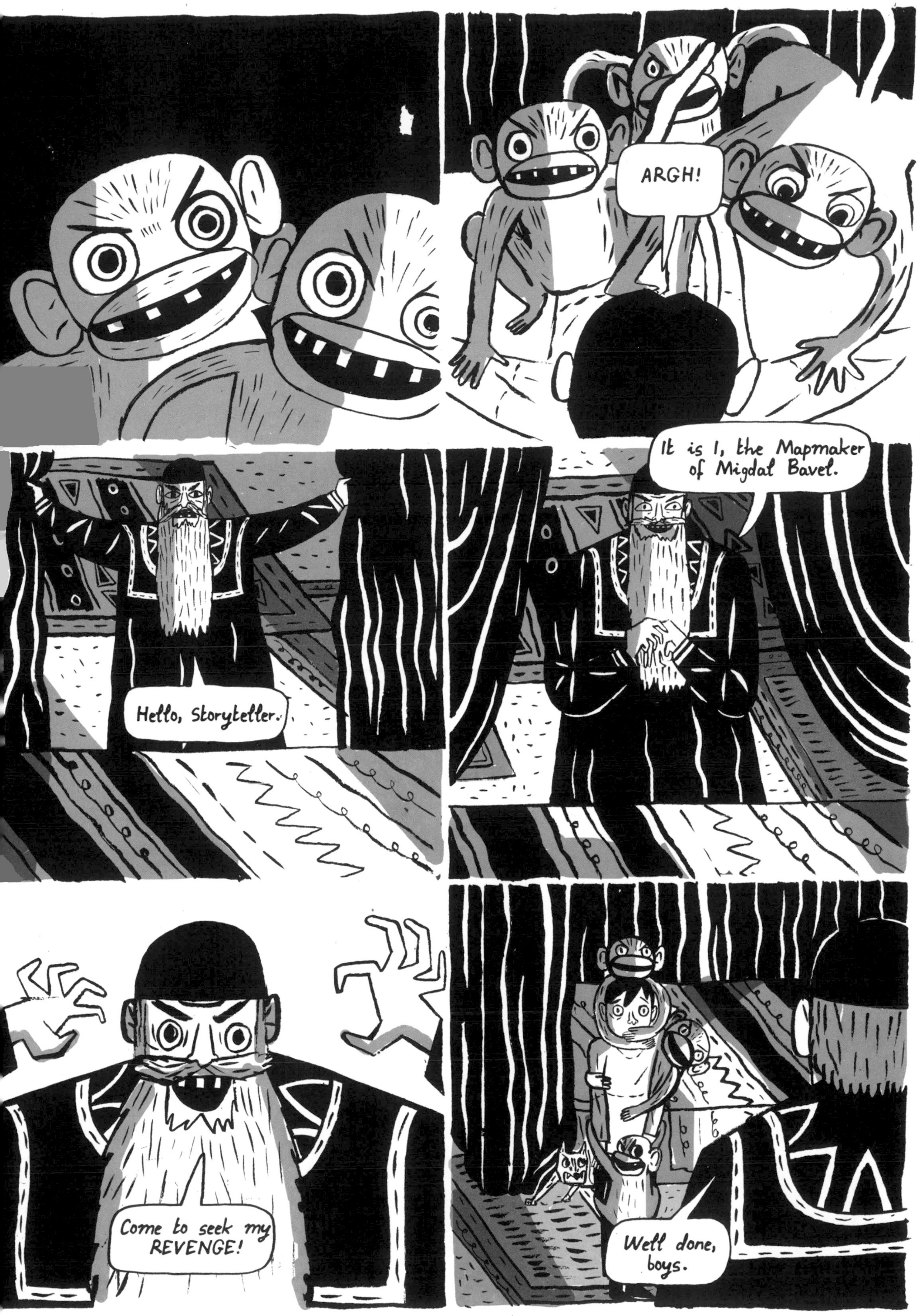
ARGH!
It is I, the Mapmaker of Migdal Bavel.
Hello, Storyteller.
Come to seek my REVENGE!
Well done, boys.

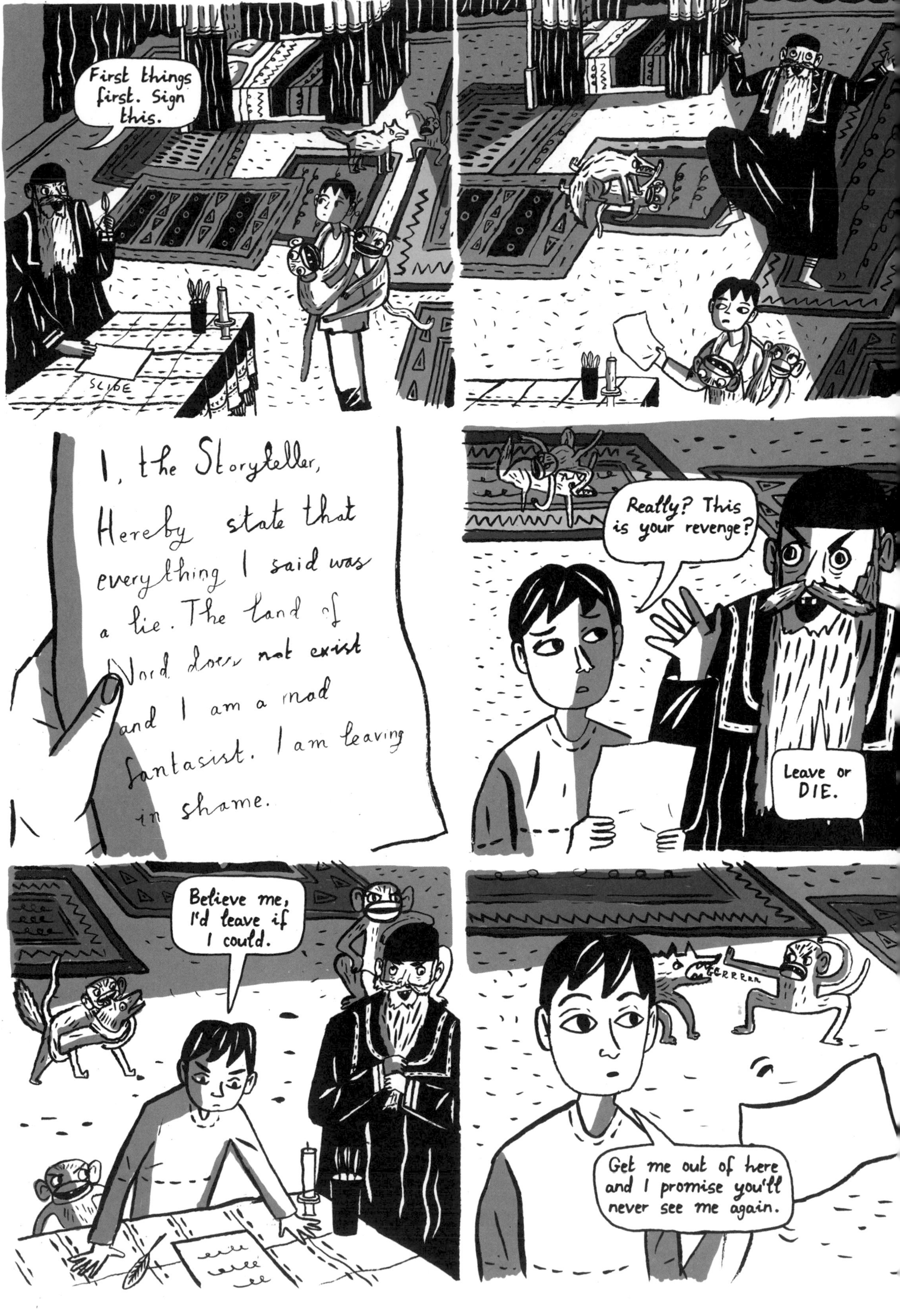

First things first. Sign this.
SLIDE
I, the Storyteller, Hereby state that everything I said was a lie. The land of Nord does not exist and I am a mad fantasist. I am leaving in shame.
Really? This is your revenge?
Leave or DIE.
Believe me, I'd leave if I could.
GRRRRRR
Get me out of here and I promise you'll never see me again.

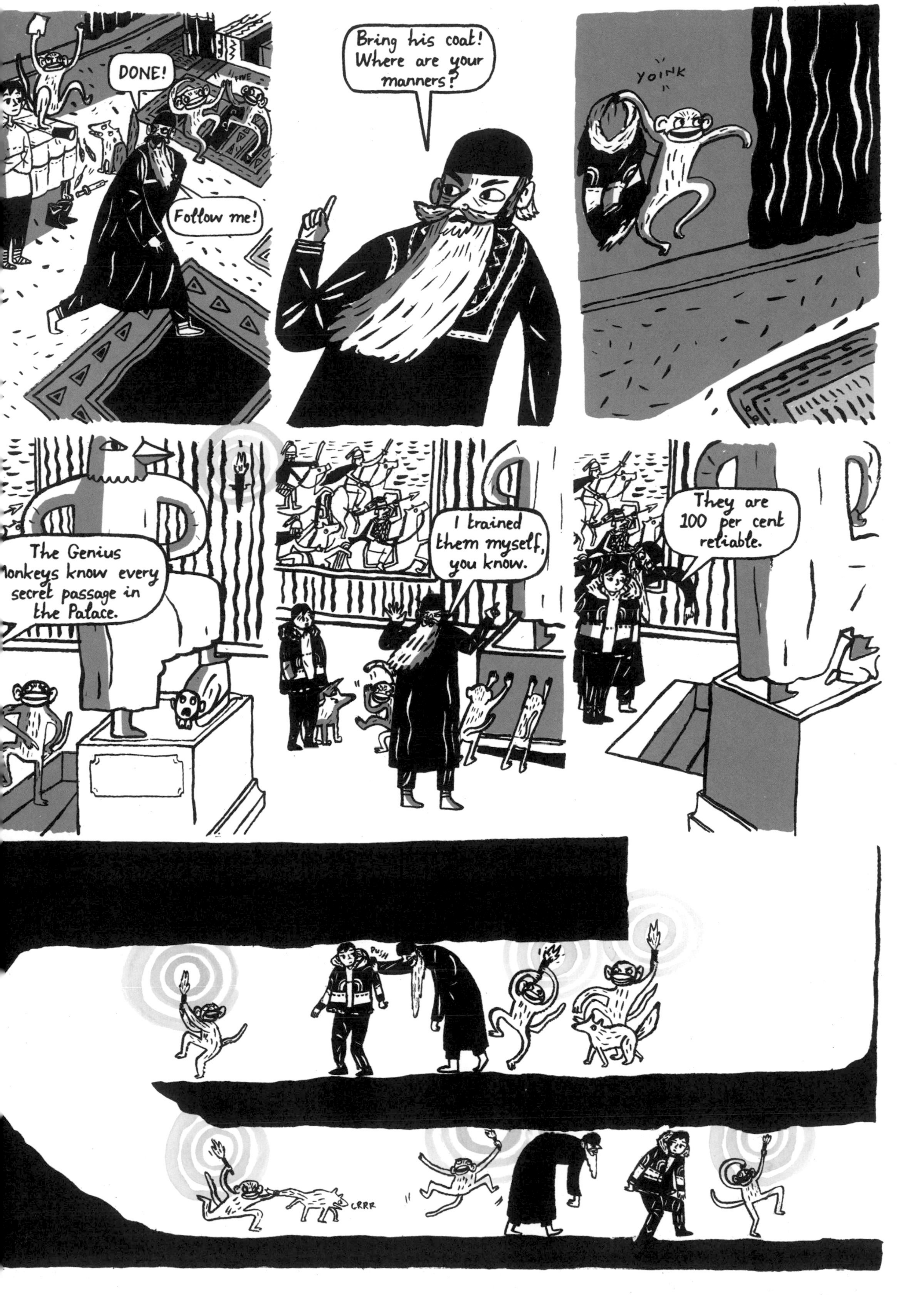
DONE!
FINE
Follow me!
Bring his coat! Where are your manners?
YOINK
The Genius Monkeys know every secret passage in the Palace.
I trained them myself, you know.
They are 100 per cent reliable.
PUSH
CRRR

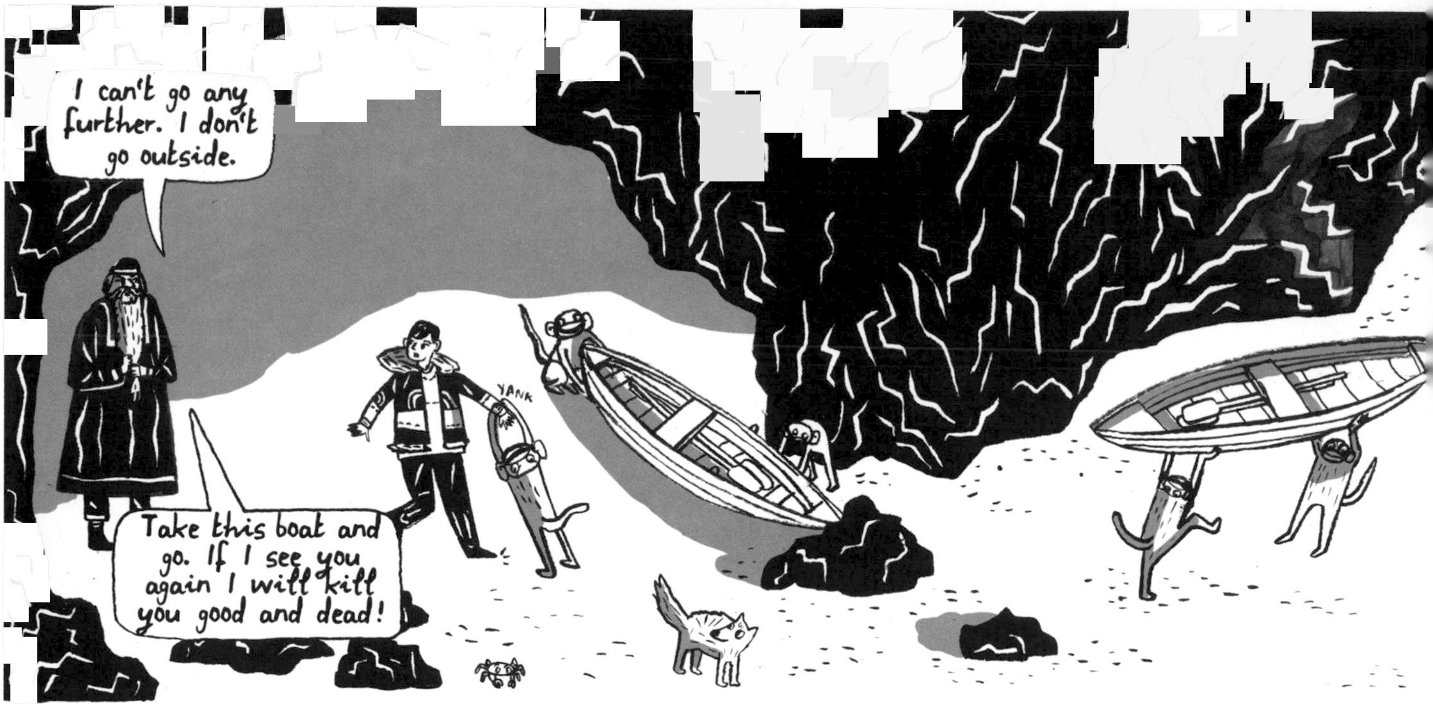
I can't go any further. I don't go outside.
YANK
Take this boat and go. If I see you again I will kill you good and dead!

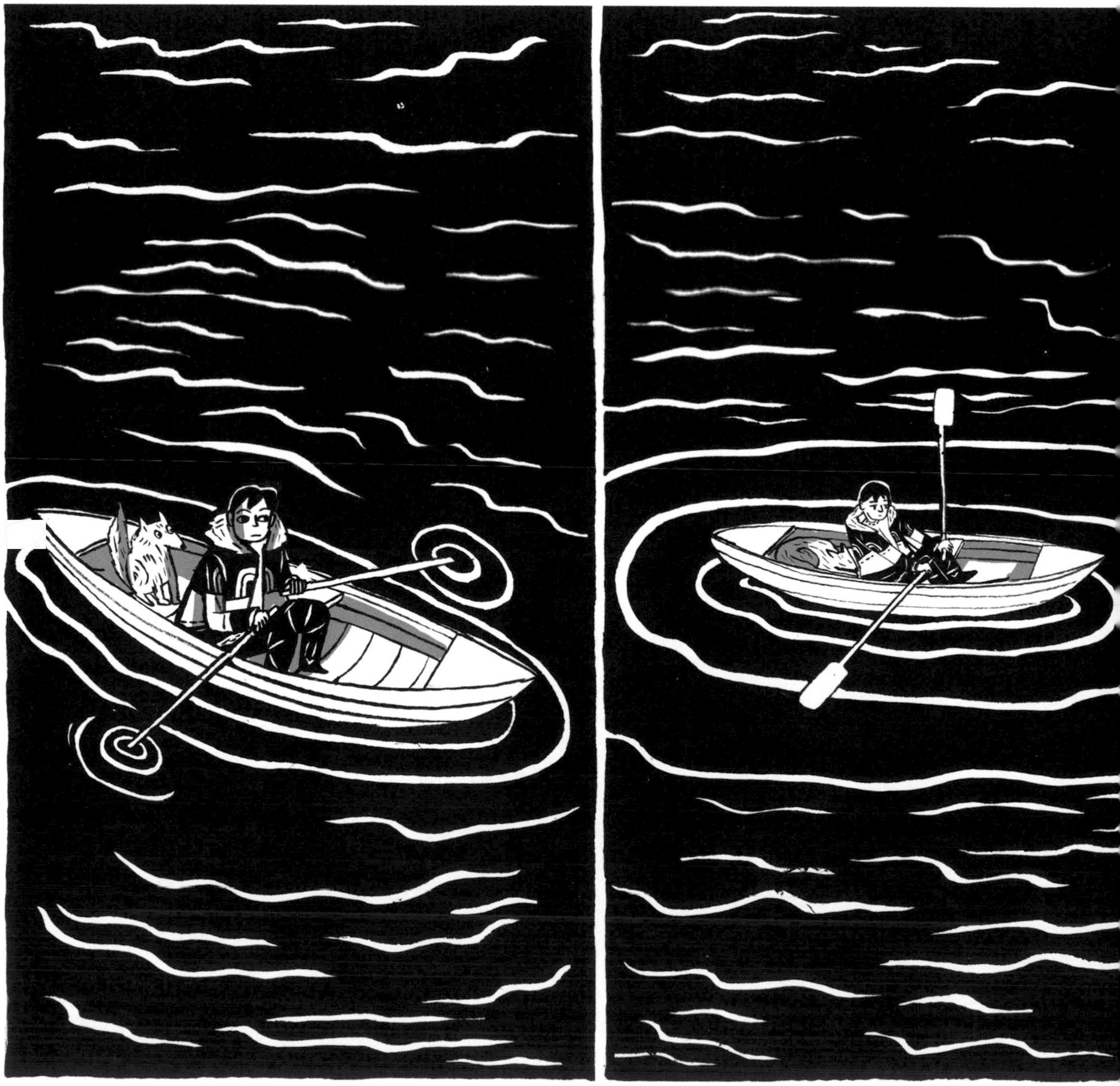

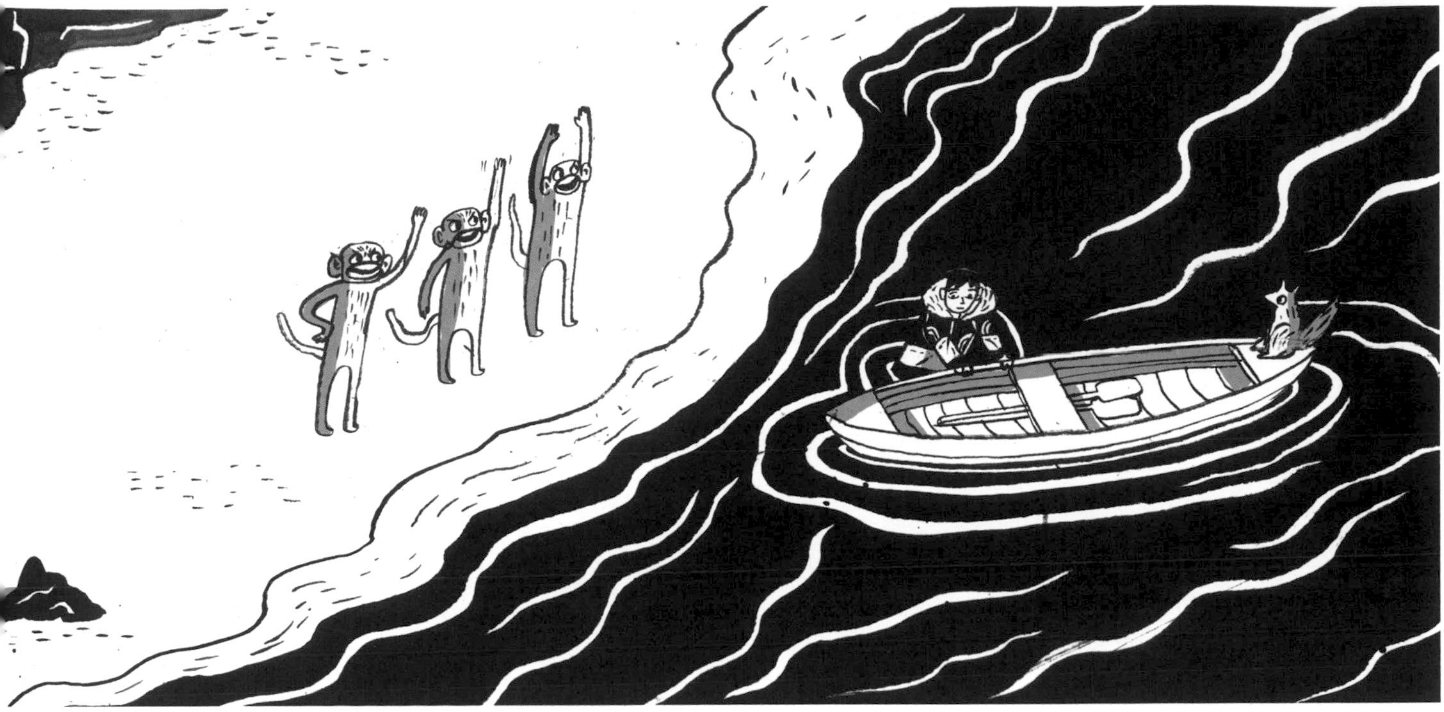

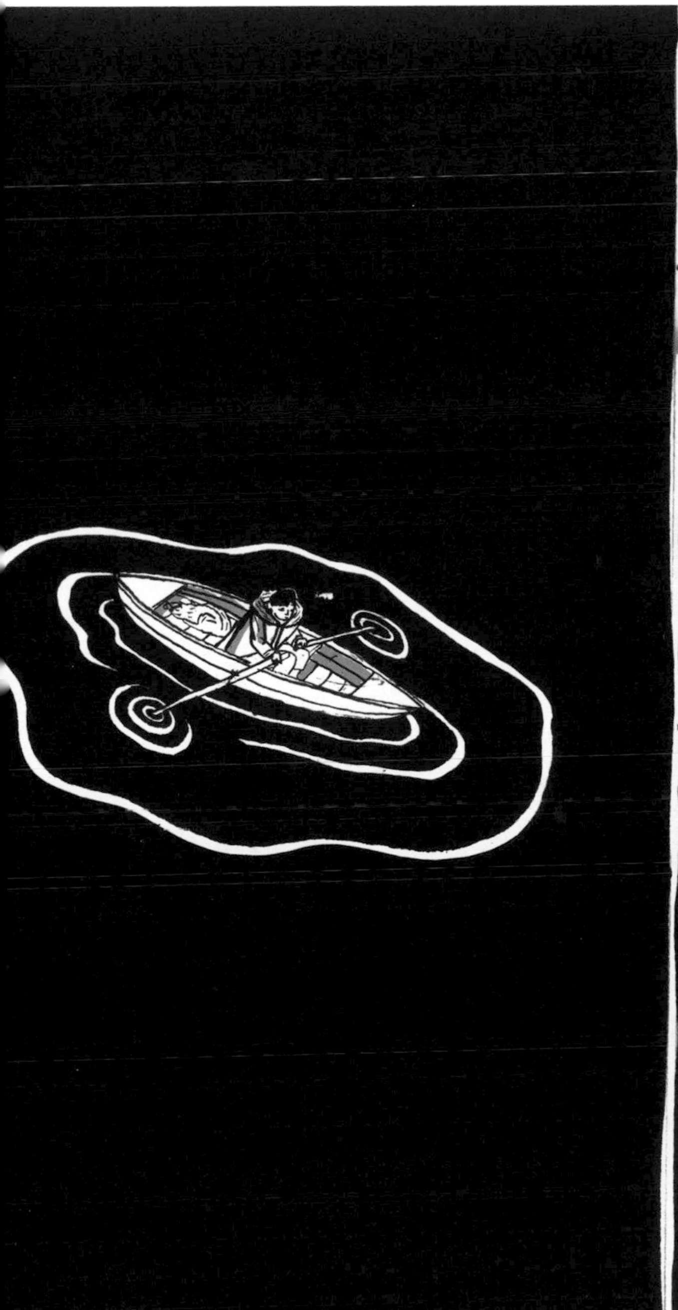

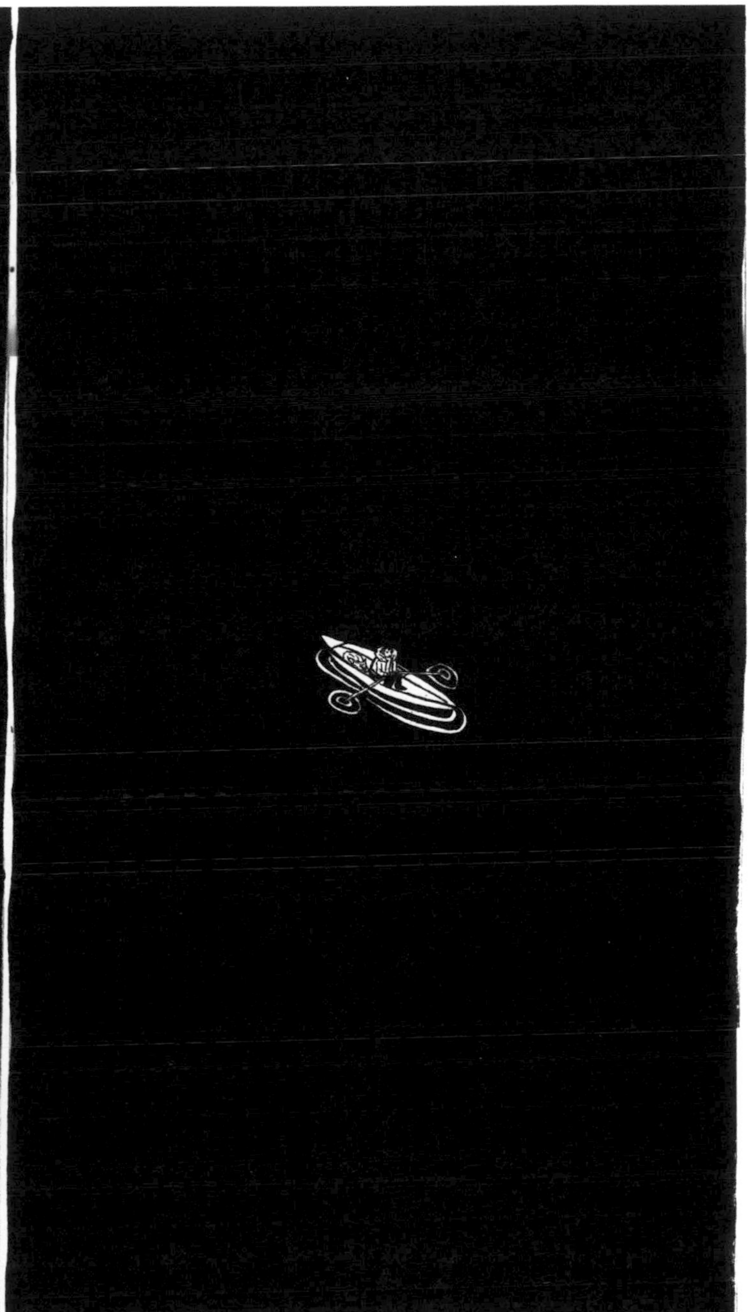

THE GODS # 2

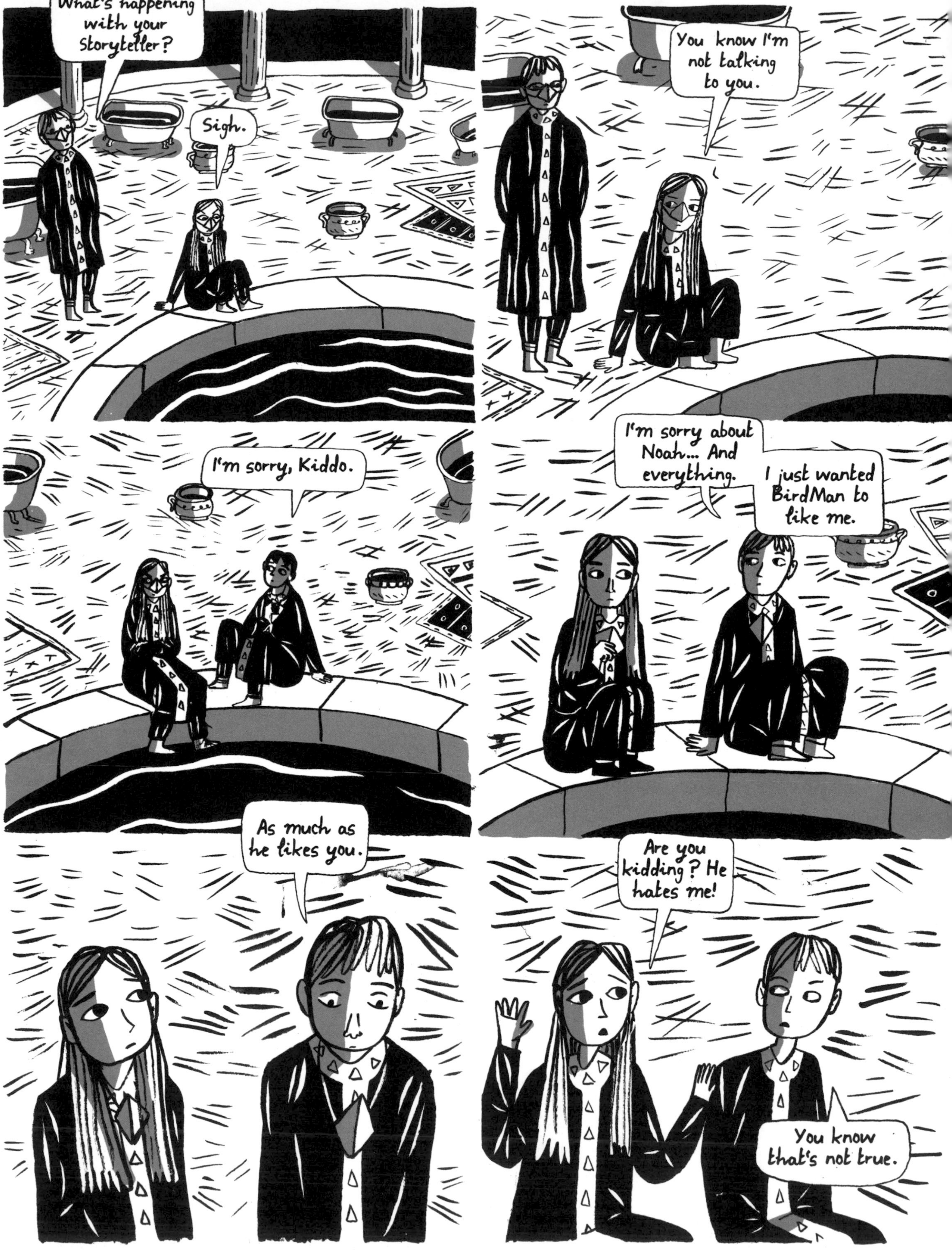

What's happening with your Storyteller?
Sigh.
You know I'm not talking to you.
I'm sorry, Kiddo.
I'm sorry about Noah... And everything.
I just wanted BirdMan to like me.
As much as he likes you.
Are you kidding? He hates me!
You know that's not true.

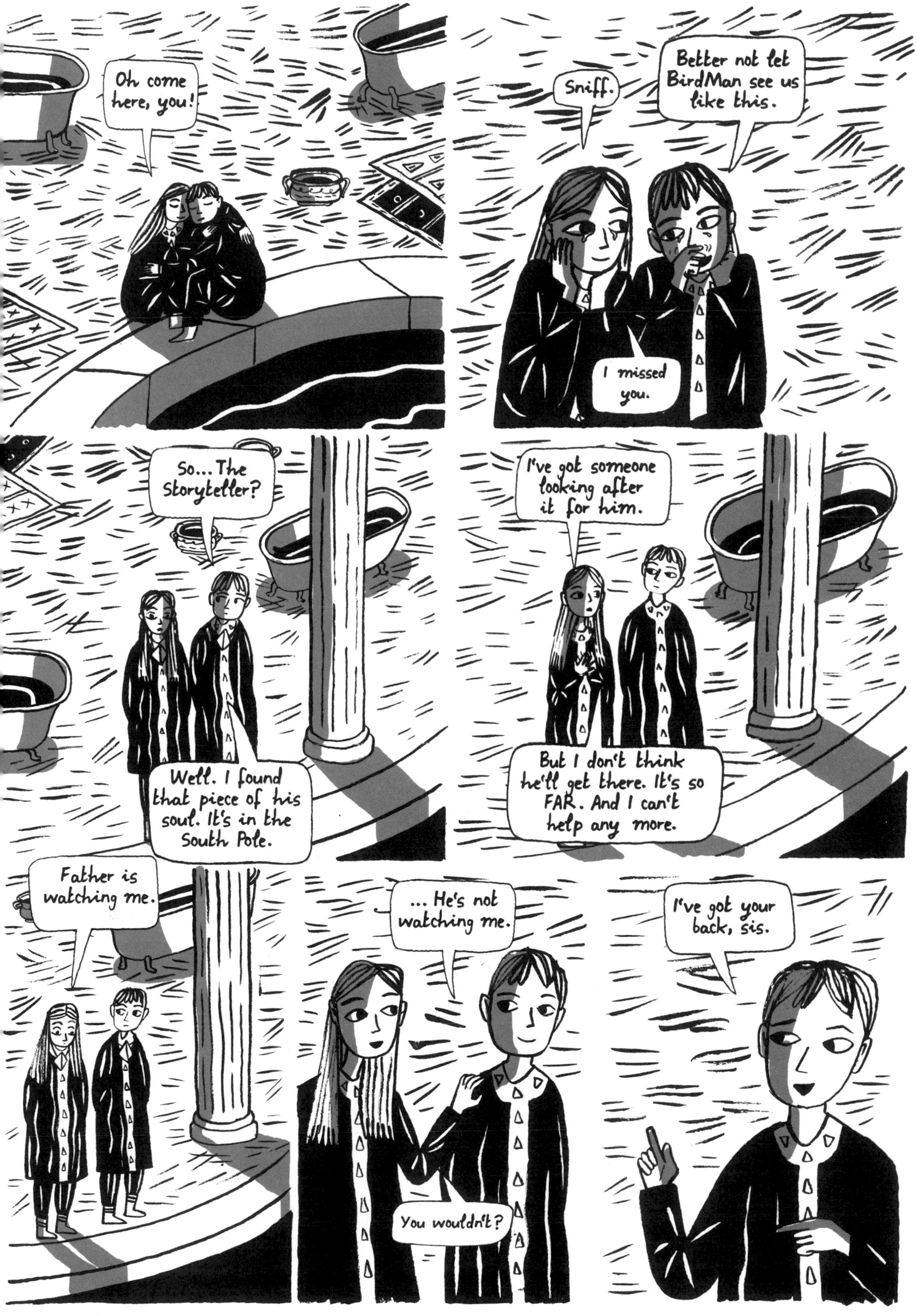
Oh come here, you!
Sniff.
Better not let BirdMan see us like this.
I missed you.
So... The Storyteller?
Well. I found that piece of his soul. It's in the South Pole.
I've got someone looking after it for him.
But I don't think he'll get there. It's so FAR. And I can't help any more.
Father is watching me.
... He's not watching me.
You wouldn't?
I've got your back, sis.

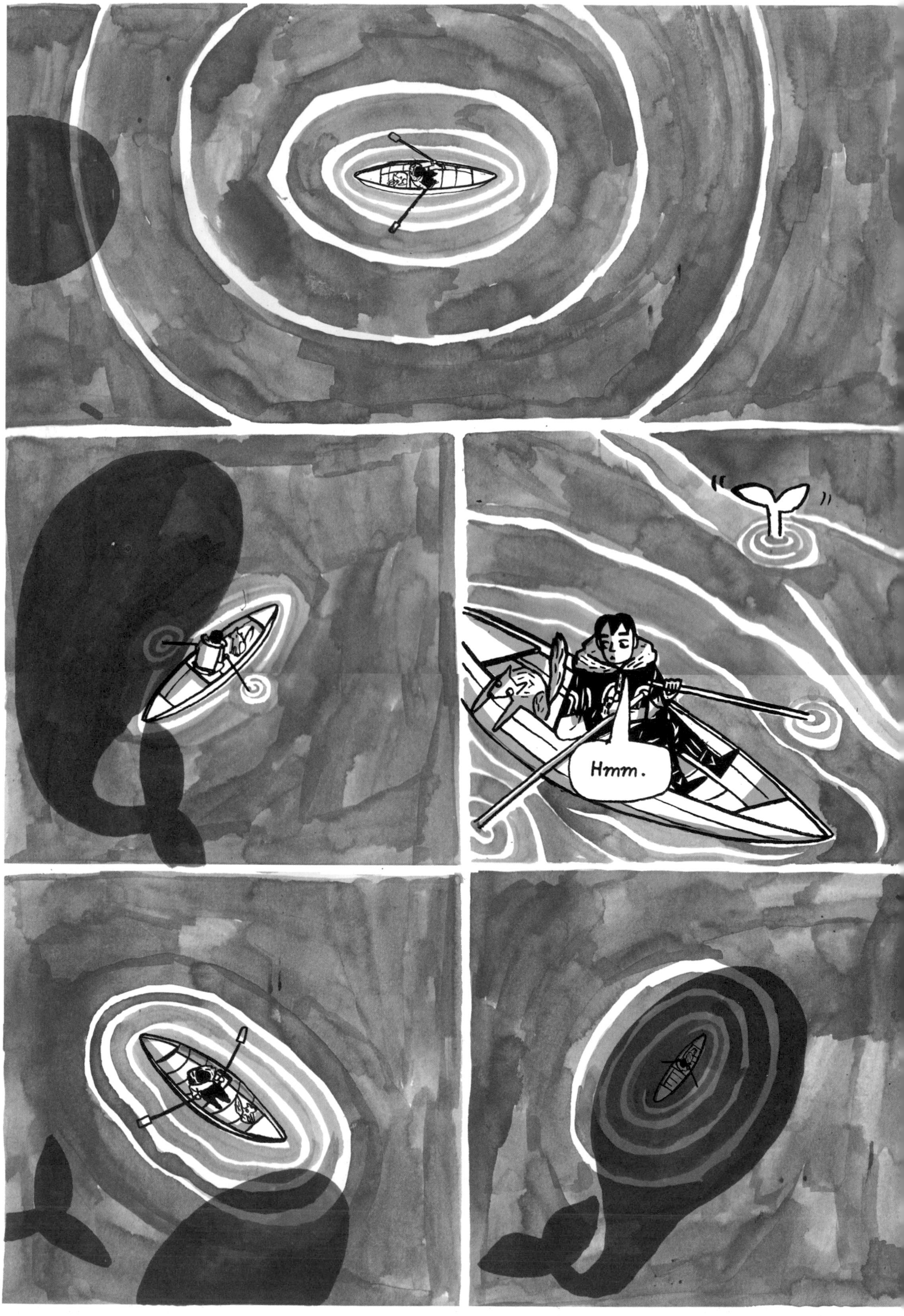
Hmm.

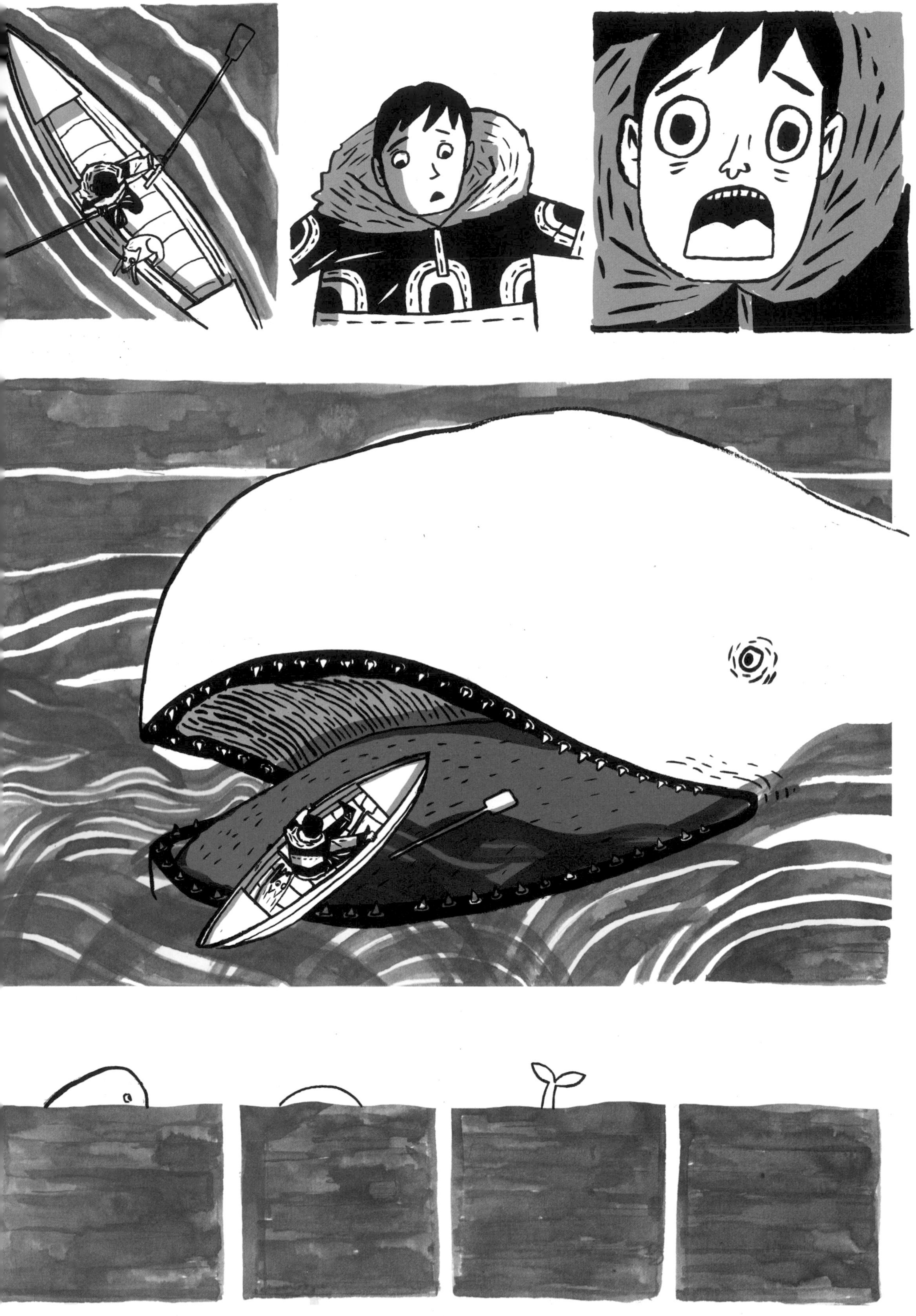

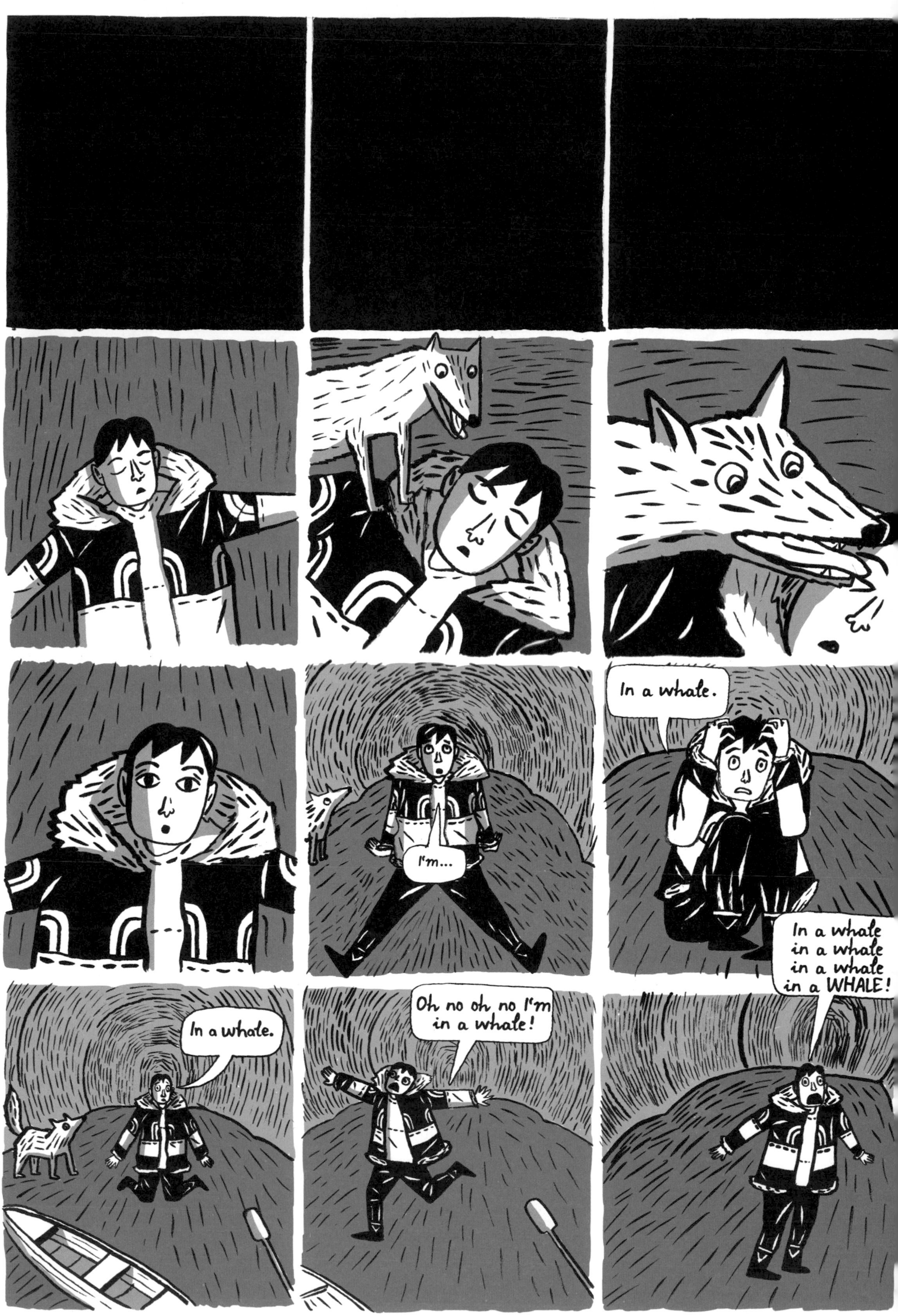
I'm...
In a whale.
In a whale.
Oh no oh no I'm in a whale!
In a whale in a whale in a whale in a WHALE!

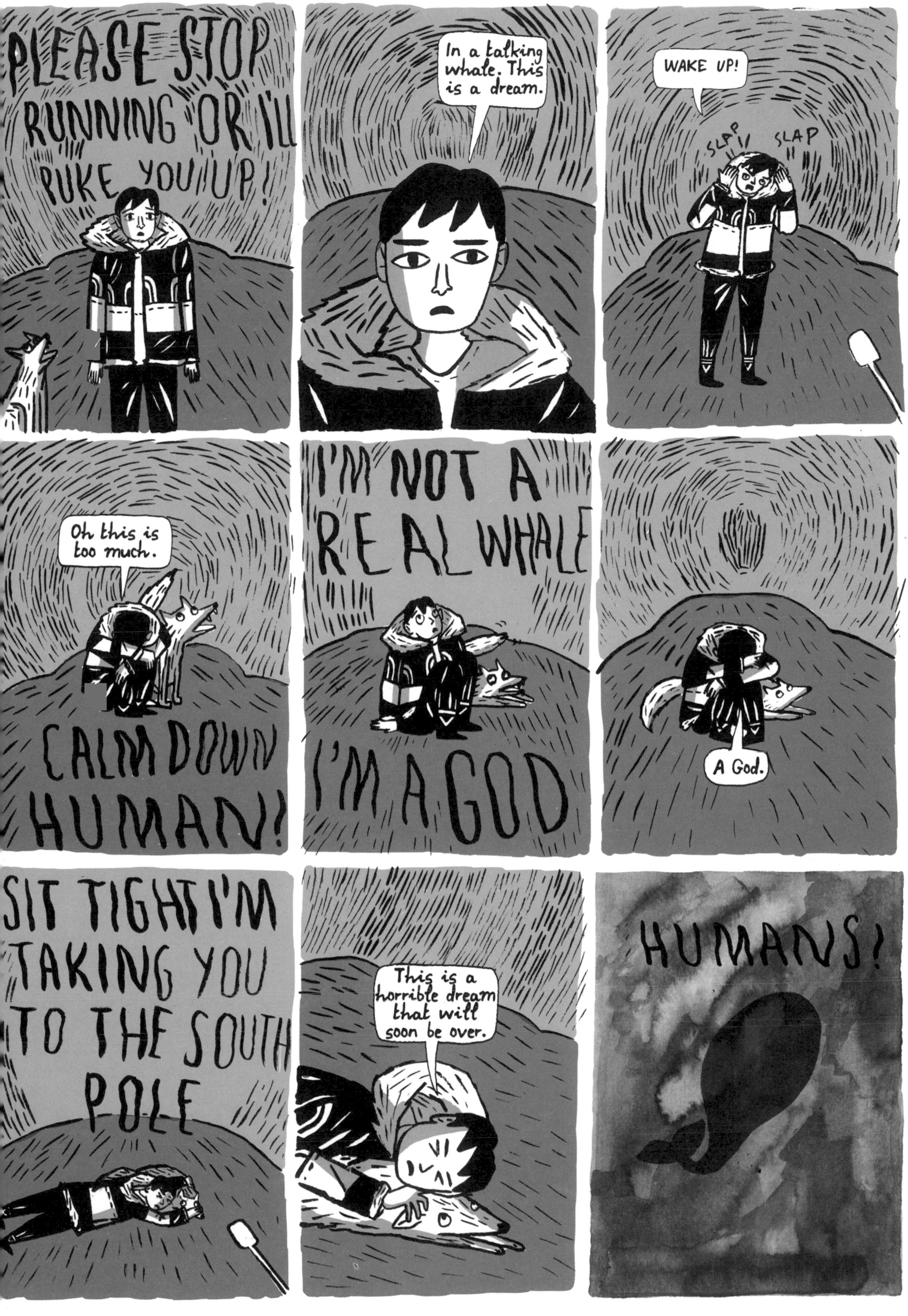
PLEASE STOP RUNNING OR I'LL PUKE YOU UP!
In a talking whale. This is a dream.
WAKE UP!
SLAP
SLAP
Oh this is too much.
CALM DOWN HUMAN!
I'M NOT A REAL WHALE
I'M A GOD
A God.
SIT TIGHT I'M TAKING YOU TO THE SOUTH POLE
This is a horrible dream that will soon be over.
HUMANS!

Part The Fourth:
The
SOUTH POLE

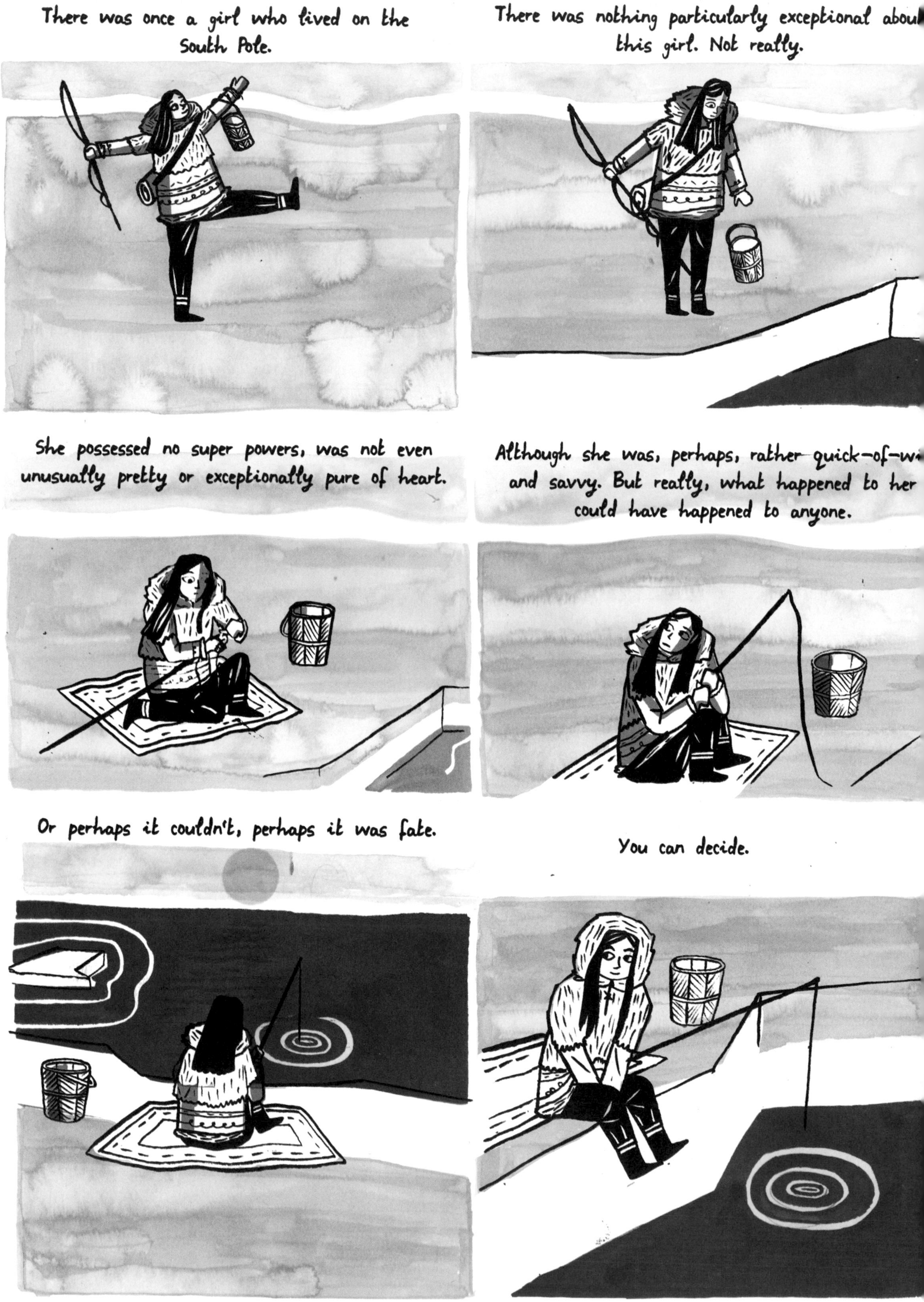
There was once a girl who lived on the South Pole.
There was nothing particularly exceptional abou
this girl. Not really.
She possessed no super powers, was not even unusually pretty or exceptionally pure of heart.
Although she was, perhaps, rather quick-of-w
and savvy. But really, what happened to her could have happened to anyone.
Or perhaps it couldn't, perhaps it was fate.
You can decide.

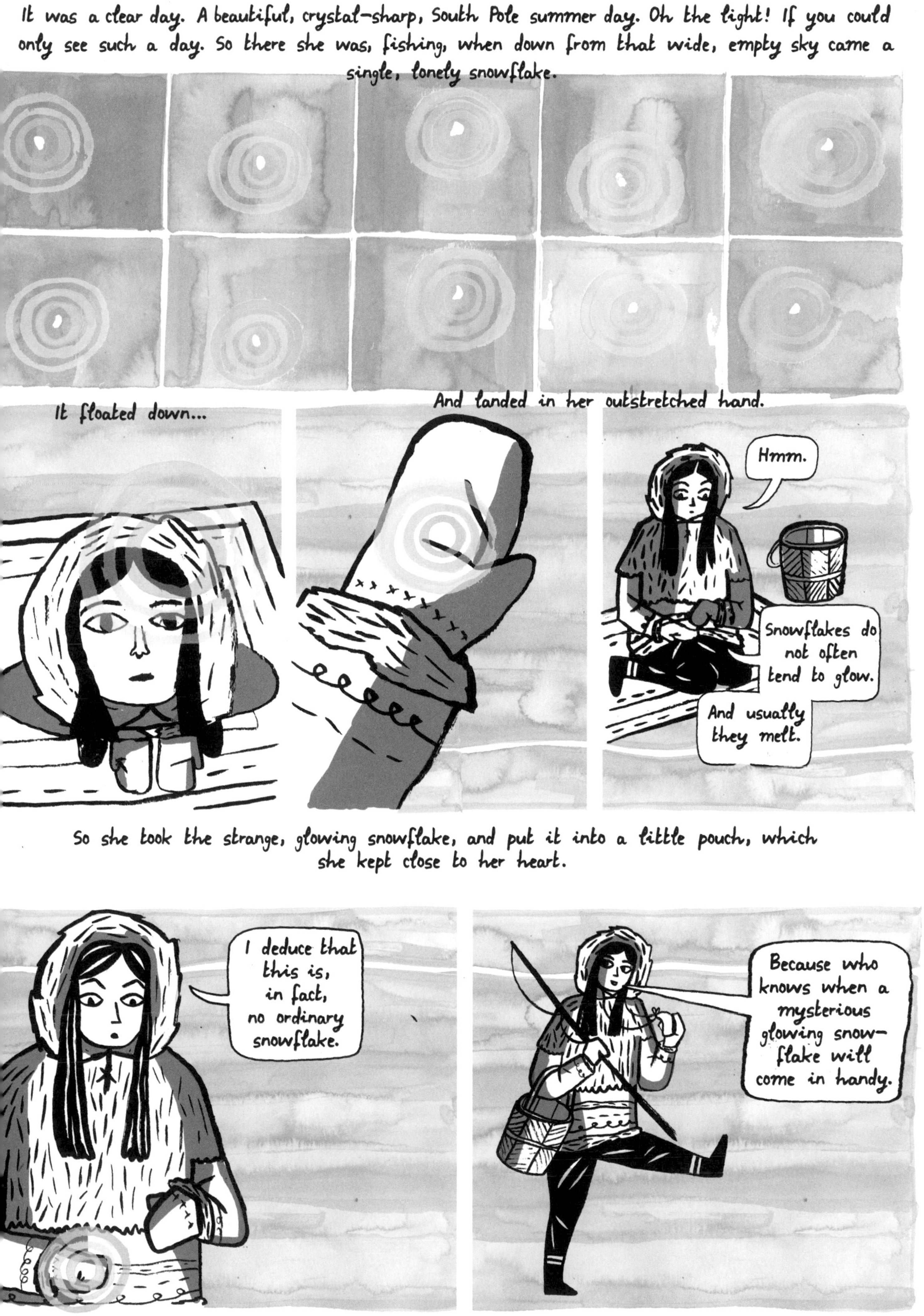
It was a clear day. A beautiful, crystal-sharp, South Pole summer day. Oh the light! If you could only see such a day. So there she was, fishing, when down from that wide, empty sky came a single, lonely snowflake.
It floated down...
And landed in her outstretched hand.
Hmm.
Snowflakes do not often tend to glow.
And usually they melt.
So she took the strange, glowing snowflake, and put it into a little pouch, which she kept close to her heart.
I deduce that this is, in fact, no ordinary snowflake.
Because who knows when a mysterious glowing snow-flake will come in handy.

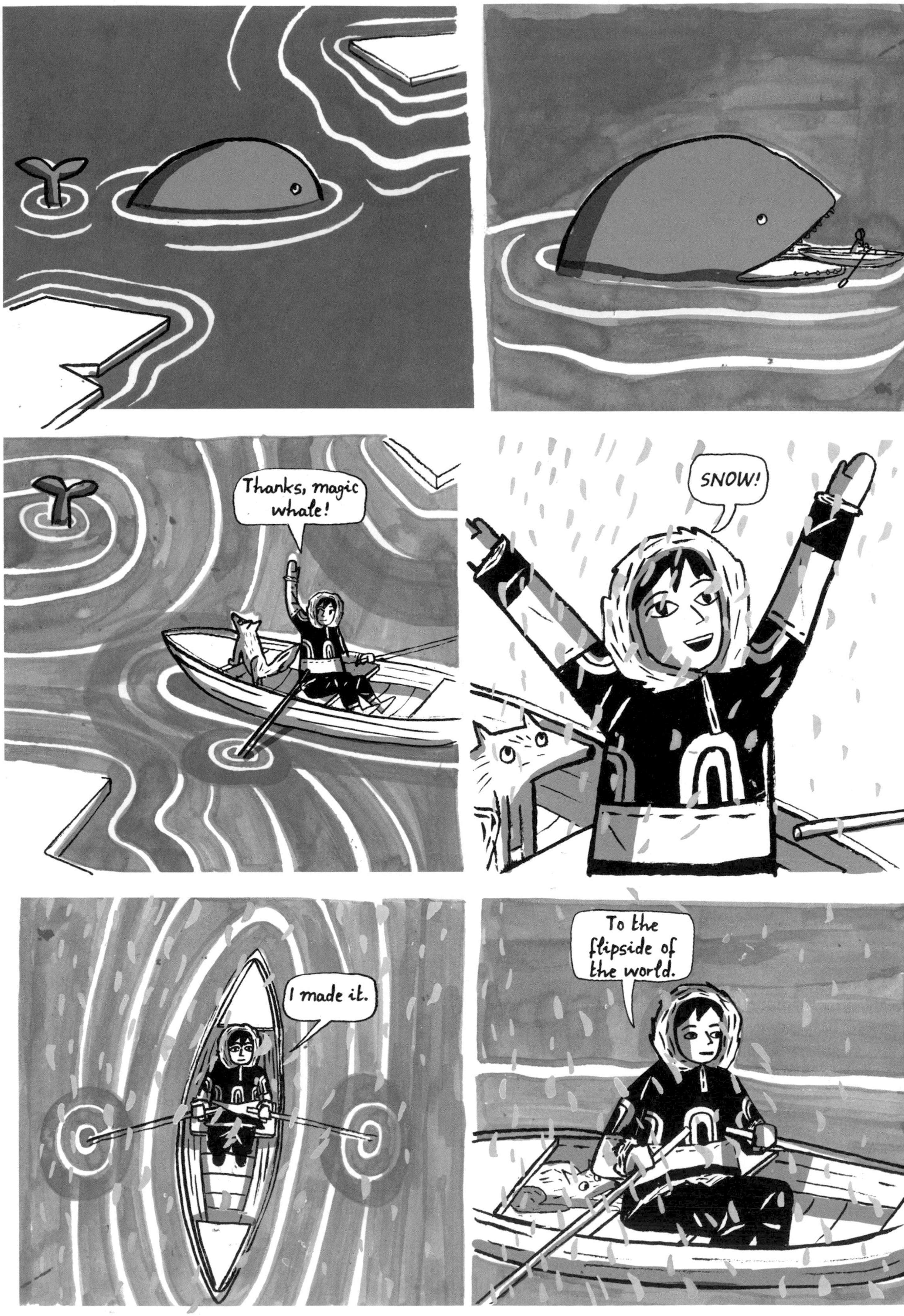
Thanks, magic whale!
SNOW!
I made it.
To the flipside of the world.

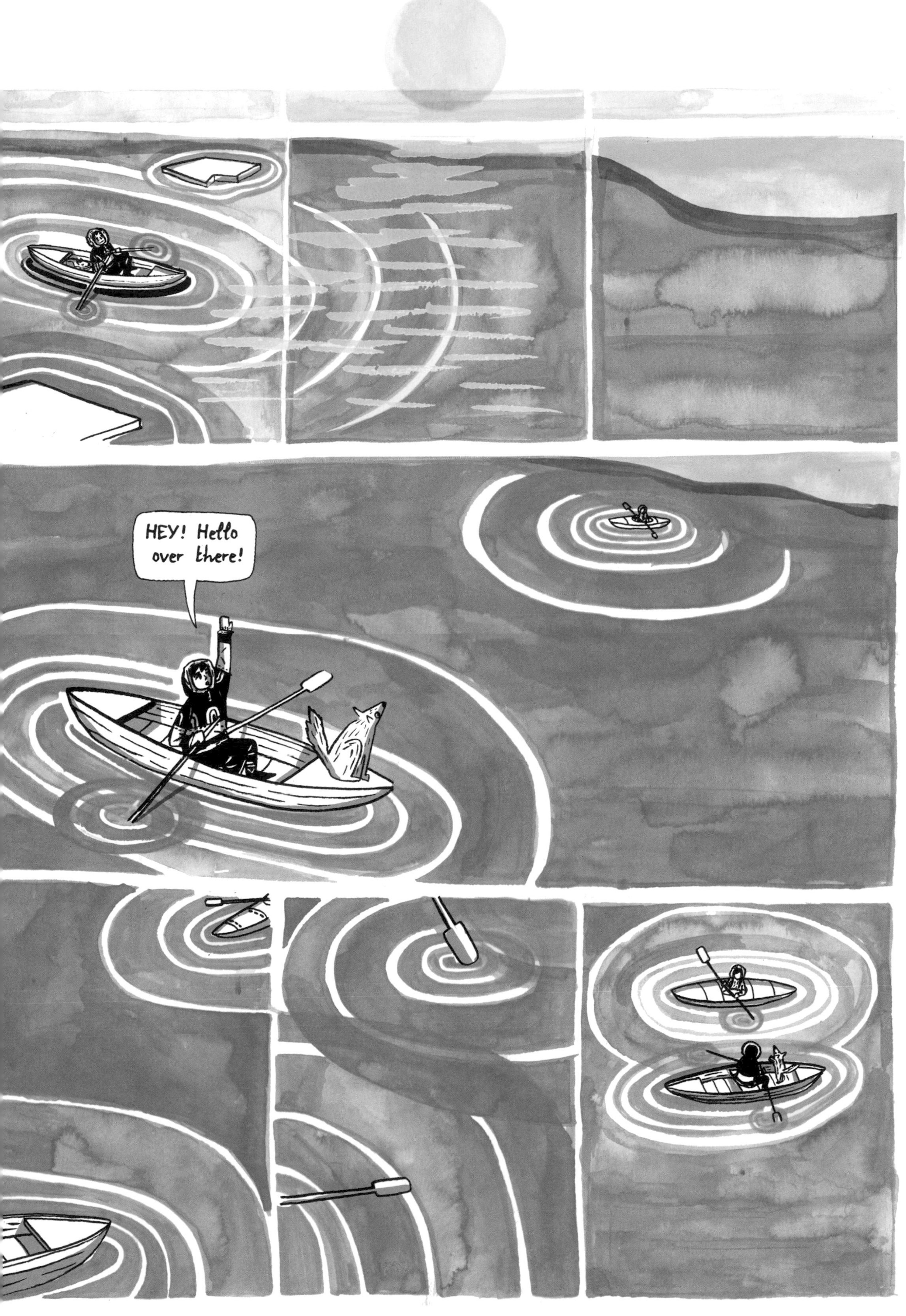
HEY! Hello over there!

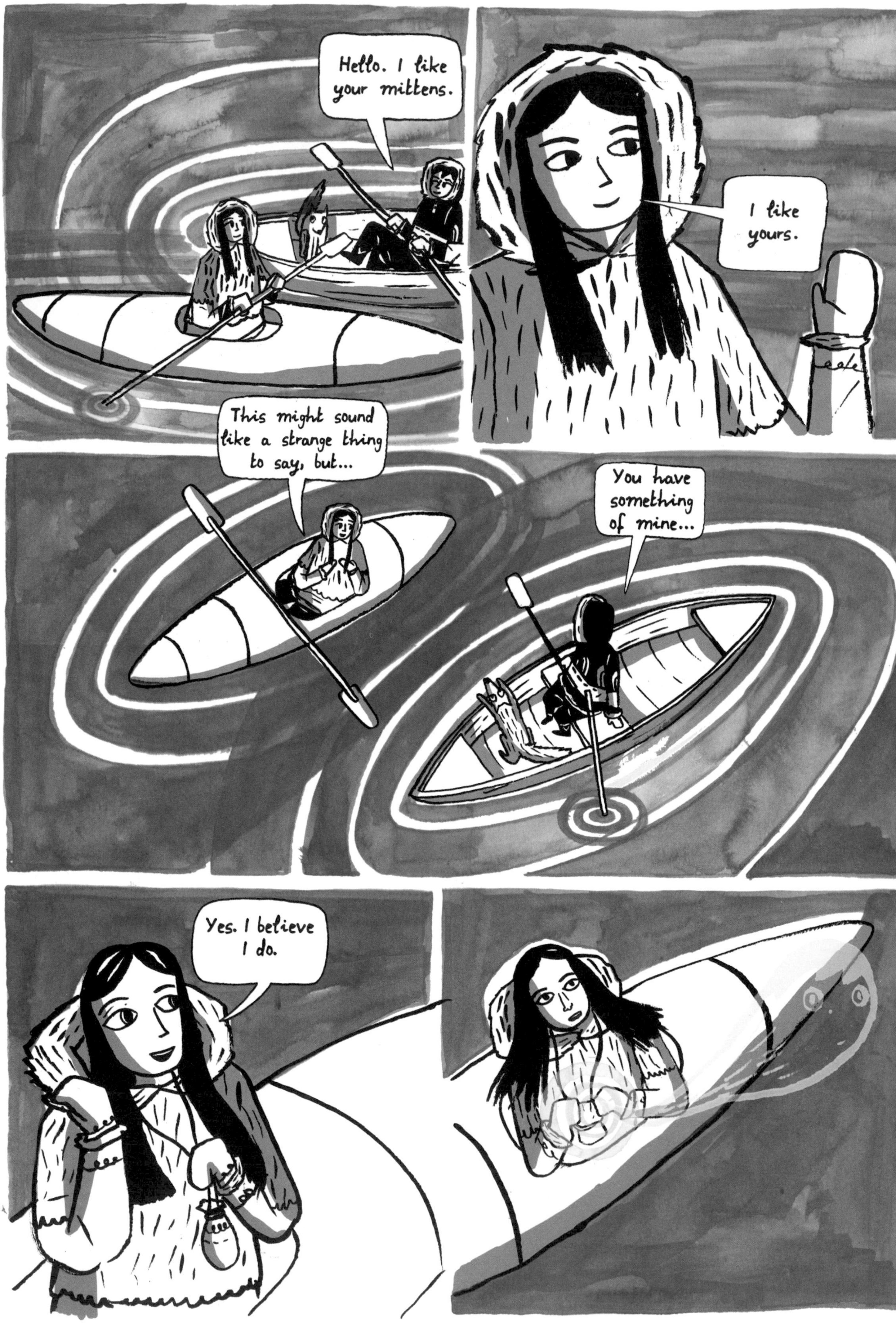

Hello. I like your mittens.
I like yours.
This might sound like a strange thing to say, but...
You have something of mine...
Yes. I believe I do.

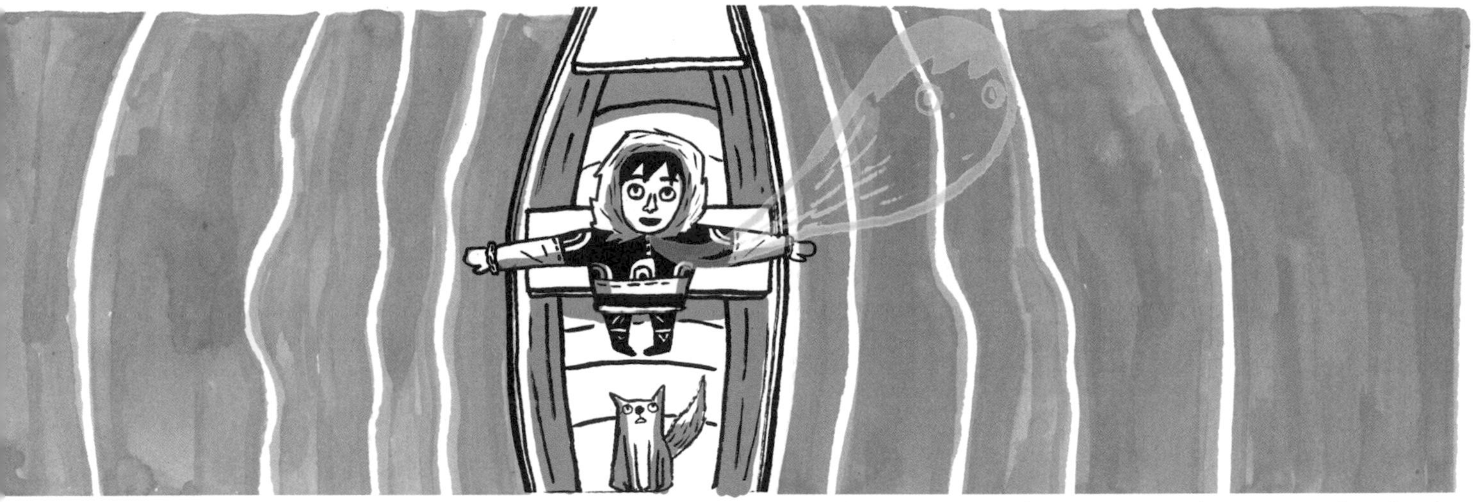

And as the little glowing snowflake landed on the Storyteller's outstretched tongue, he knew he had found what he had been looking for.

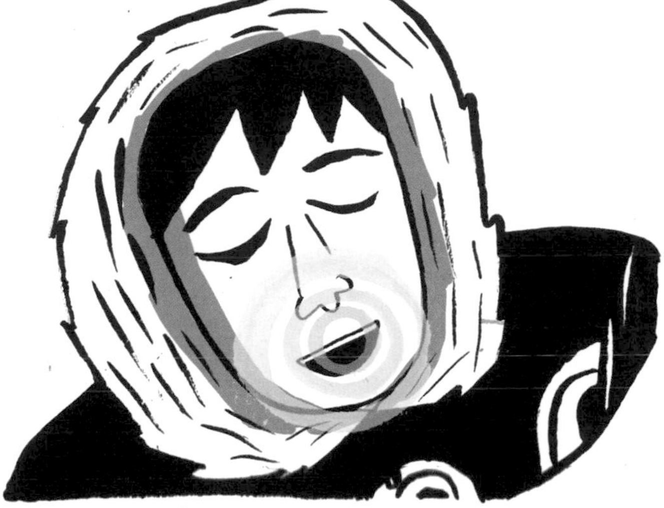

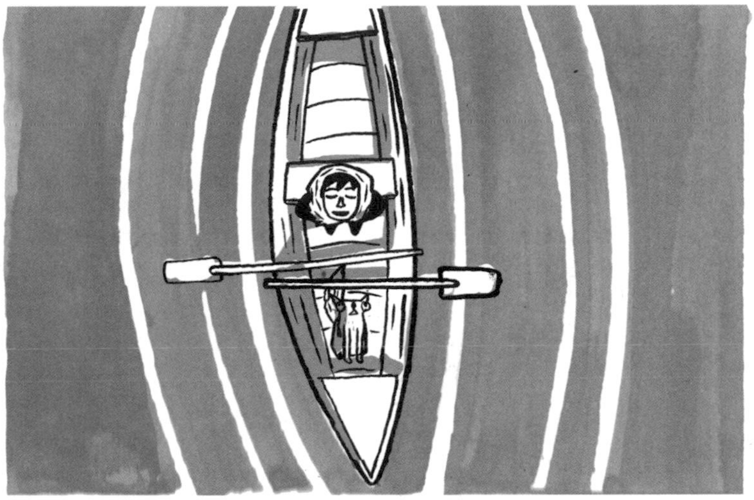

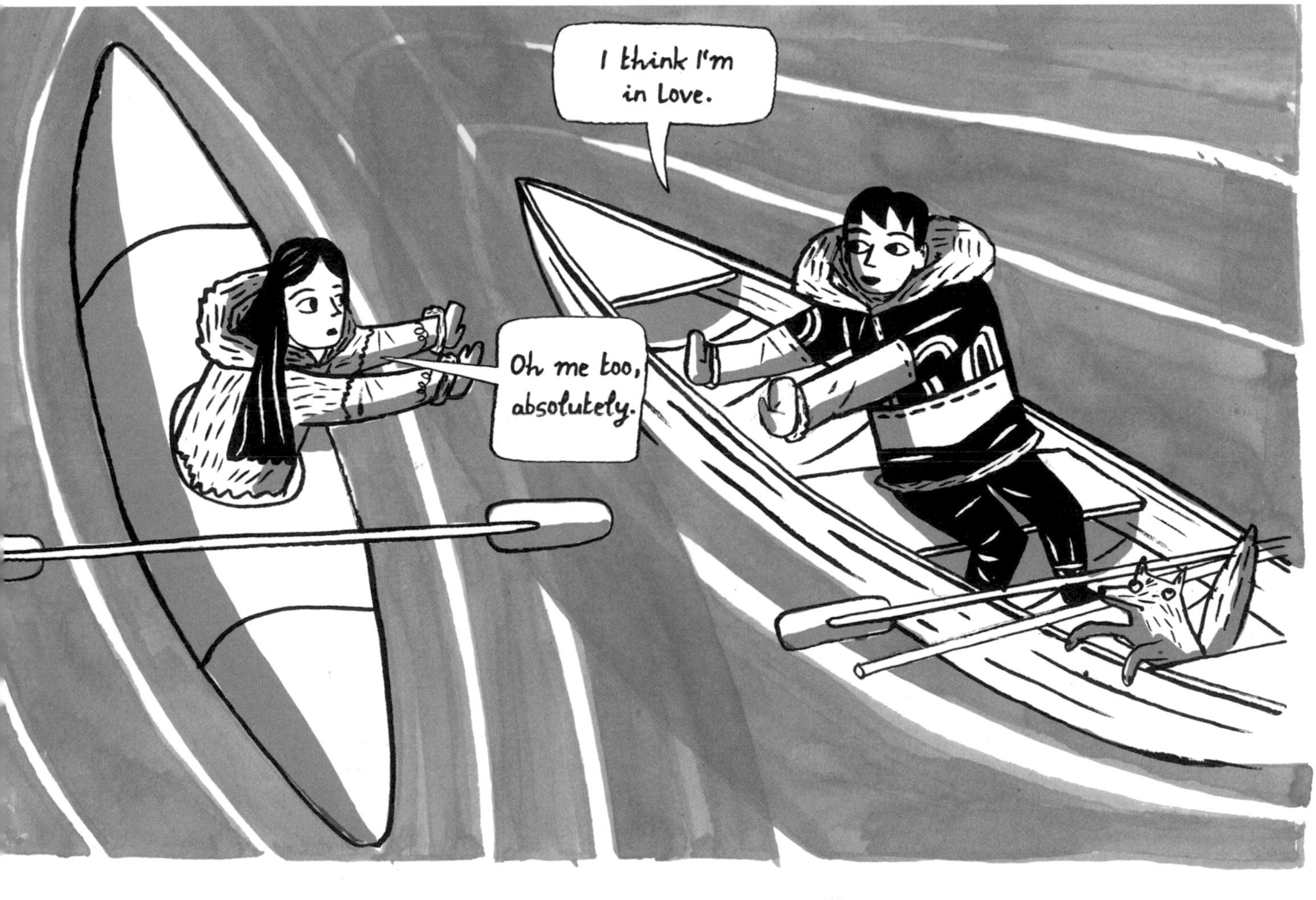
I think I'm in Love.
Oh me too, absolutely.

THE GODS #3

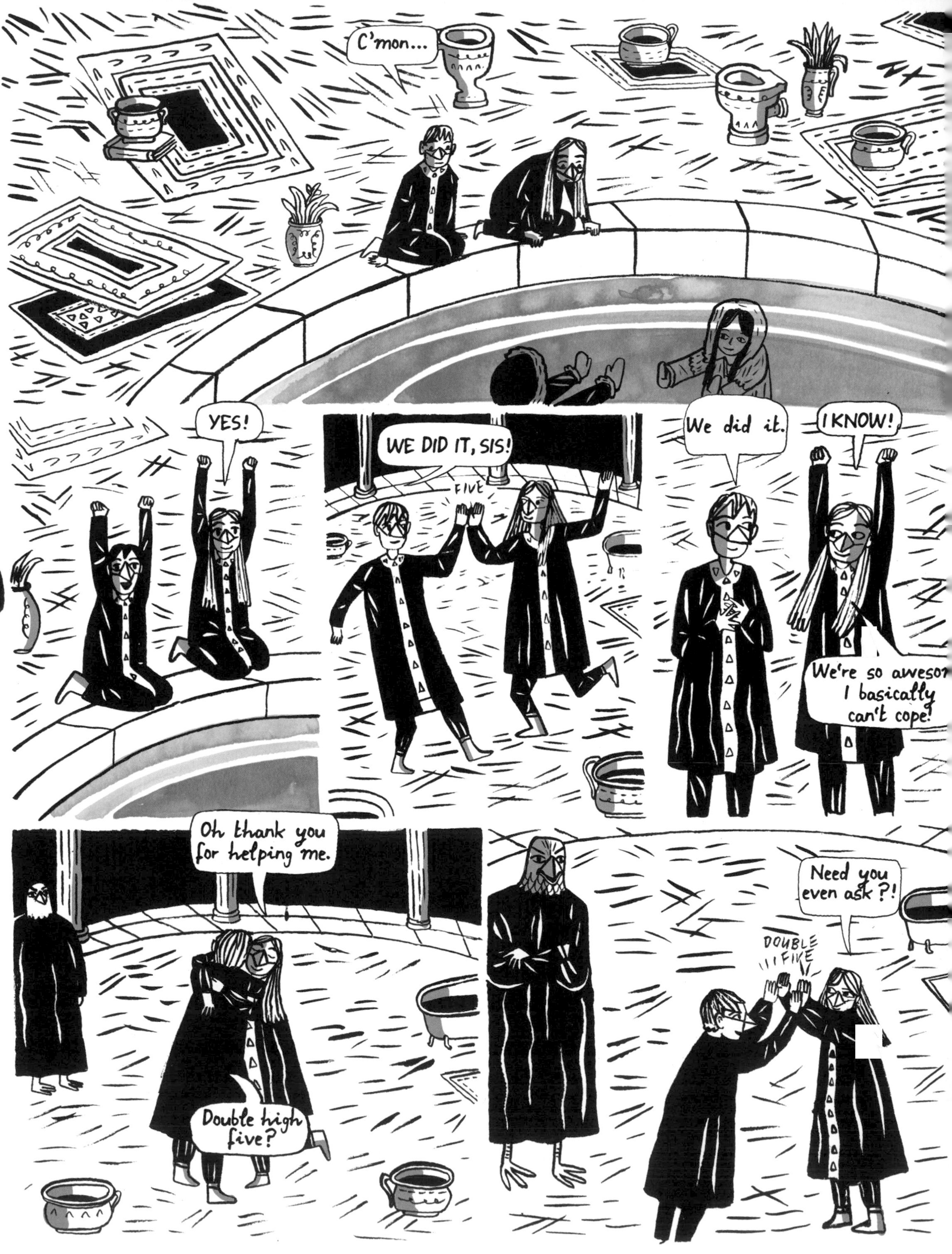

C'mon...
YES!
WE DID IT, SIS!
FIVE
We did it.
I KNOW!
We're so aweso
I basically
can't cope!
Oh thank you
for helping me.
Double high
five?
Need you
even ask?!
DOUBLE
FIVE

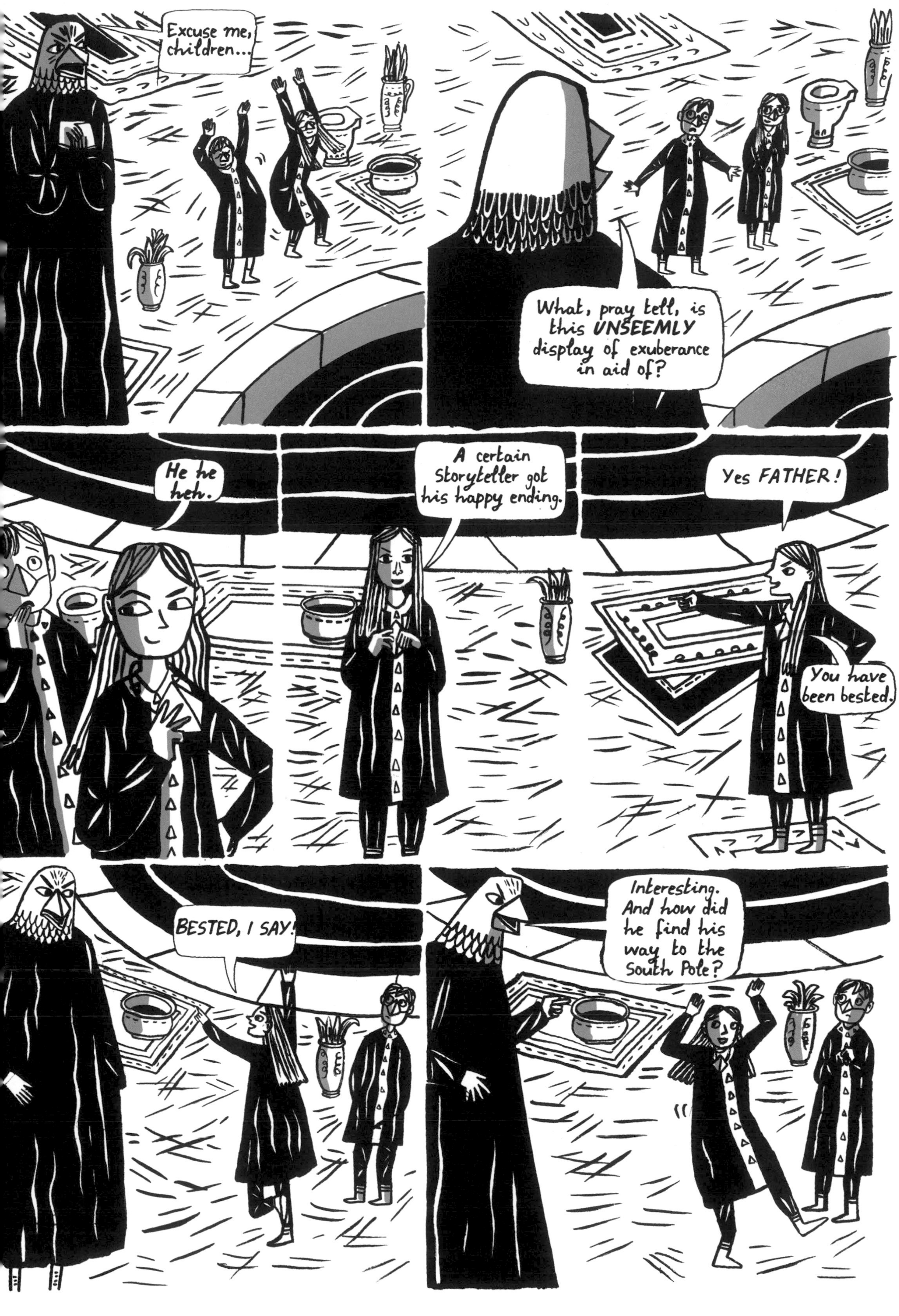
Excuse me, children...
What, pray tell, is this UNSEEMLY display of exuberance in aid of?
He he heh.
A certain Storyteller got his happy ending.
Yes FATHER!
You have been bested.
BESTED, I SAY!
Interesting. And how did he find his way to the South Pole?

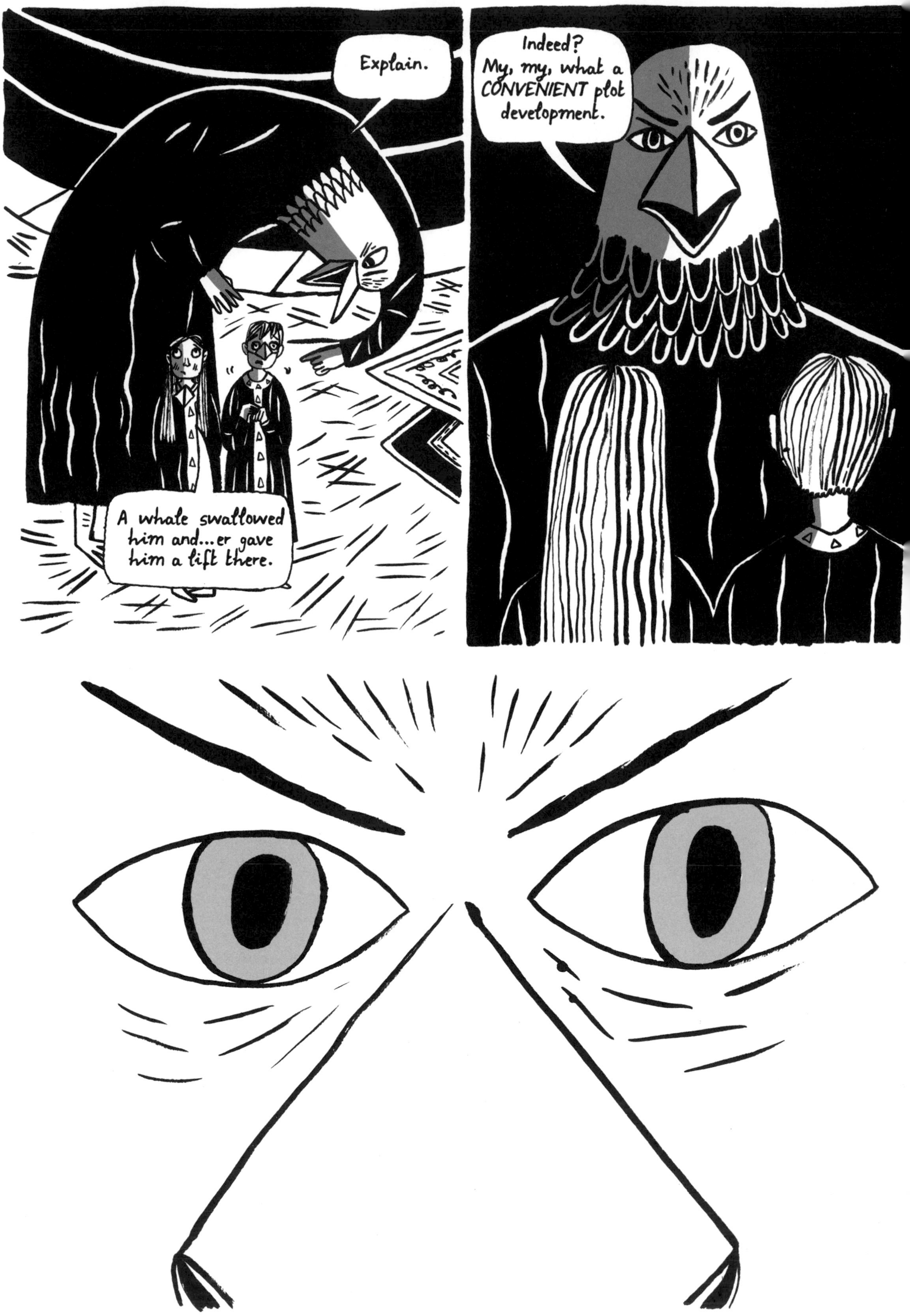
Explain.
A whale swallowed him and...er gave him a lift there.
Indeed? My, my, what a CONVENIENT plot development.

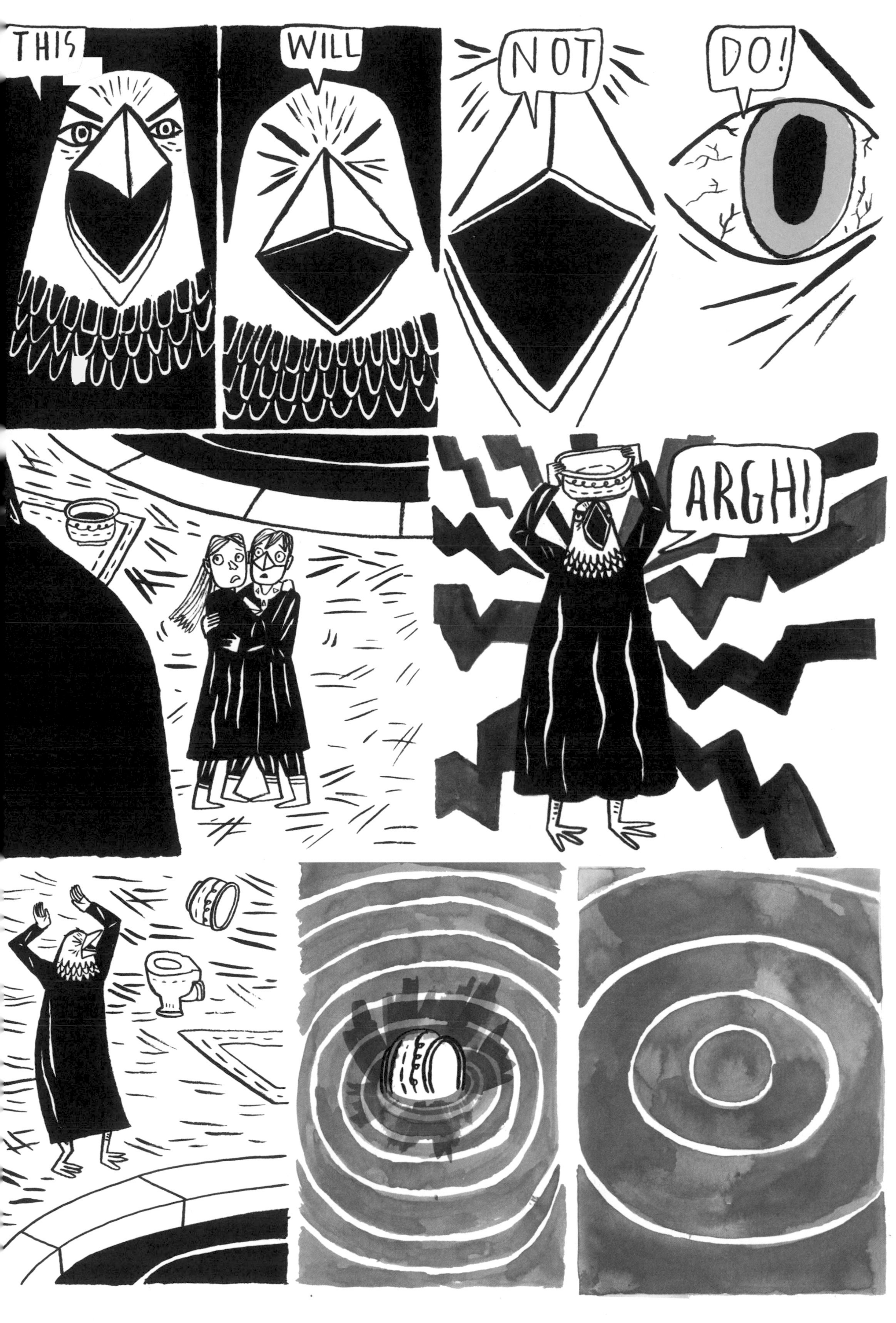
THIS
WILL
NOT
DO!
ARGH!

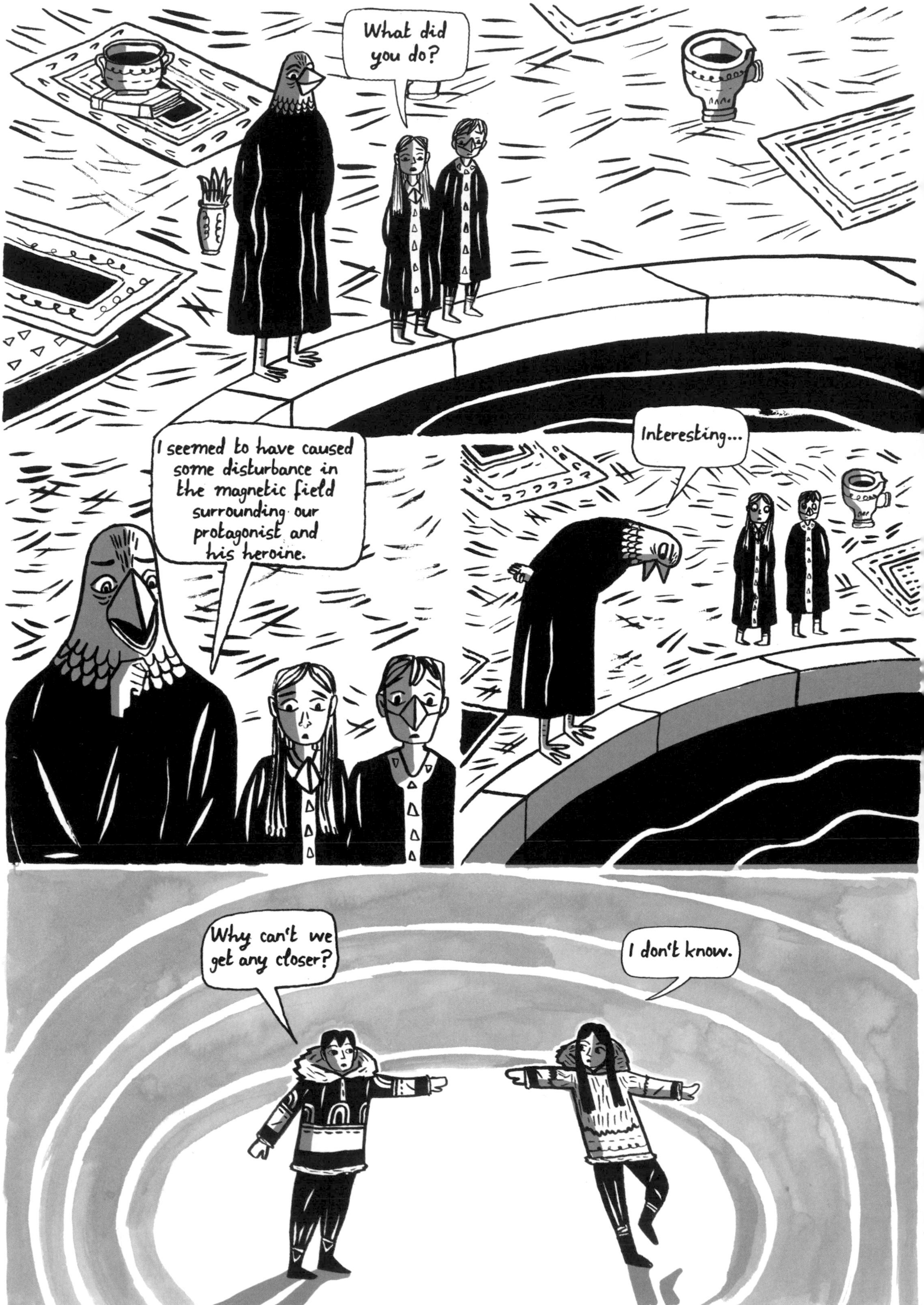
What did you do?
I seemed to have caused some disturbance in the magnetic field surrounding our protagonist and his heroine.
Interesting...
Why can't we get any closer?
I don't know.

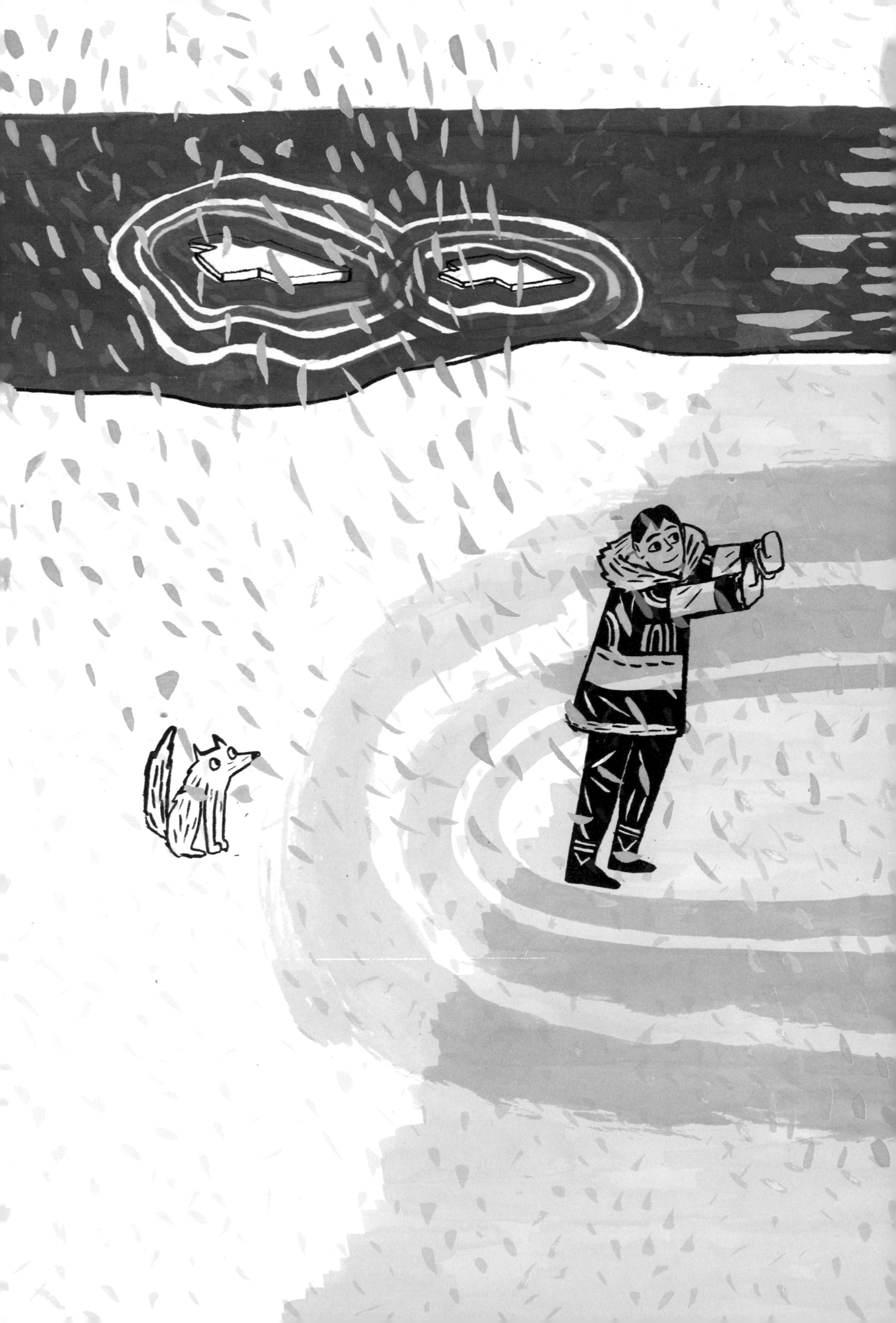

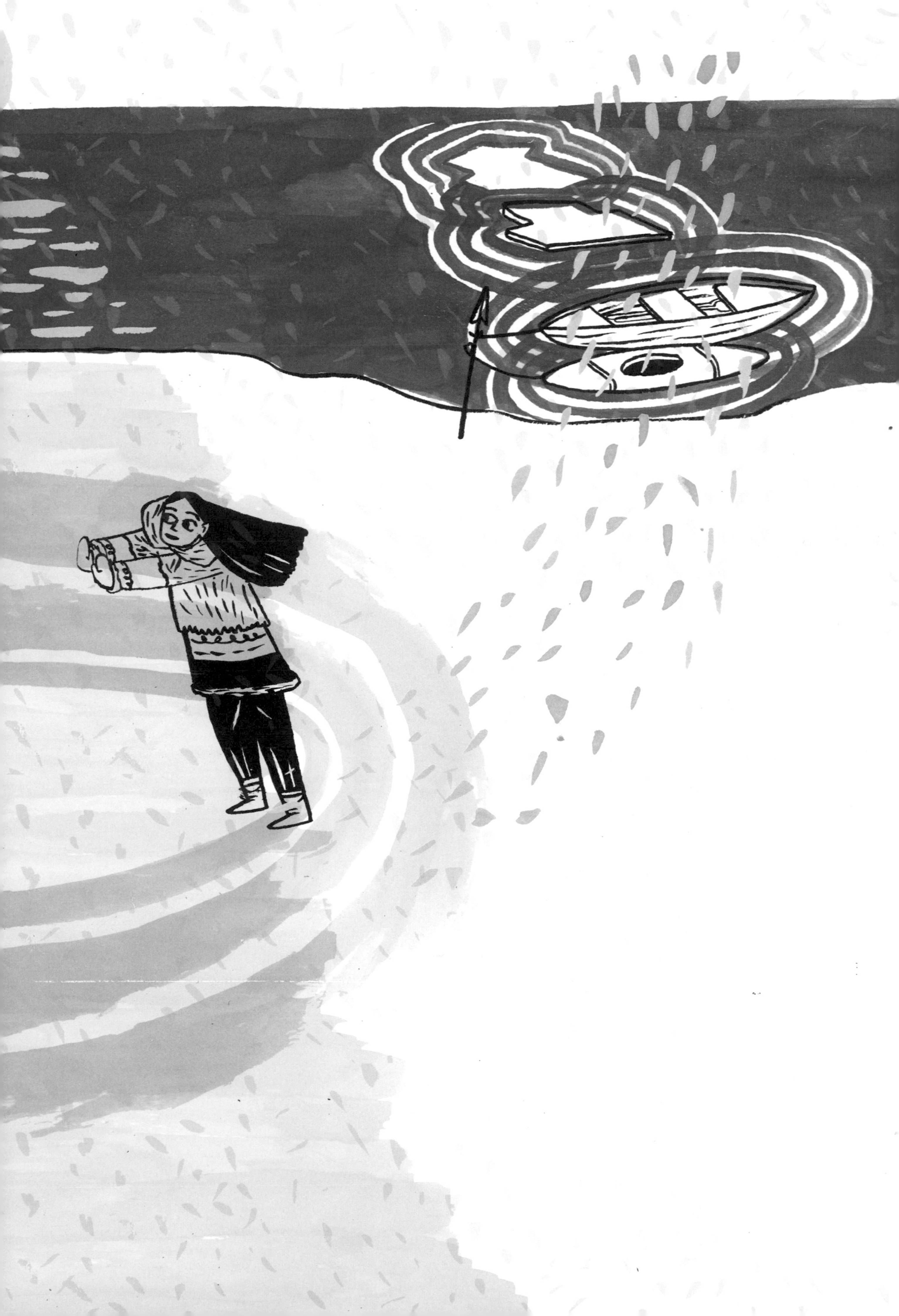

the days became weeks, and the weeks became years, and still the magnetic force did not relent. They spent hours staring into each other's eyes. And yet still they could not so much as brush fingertips.

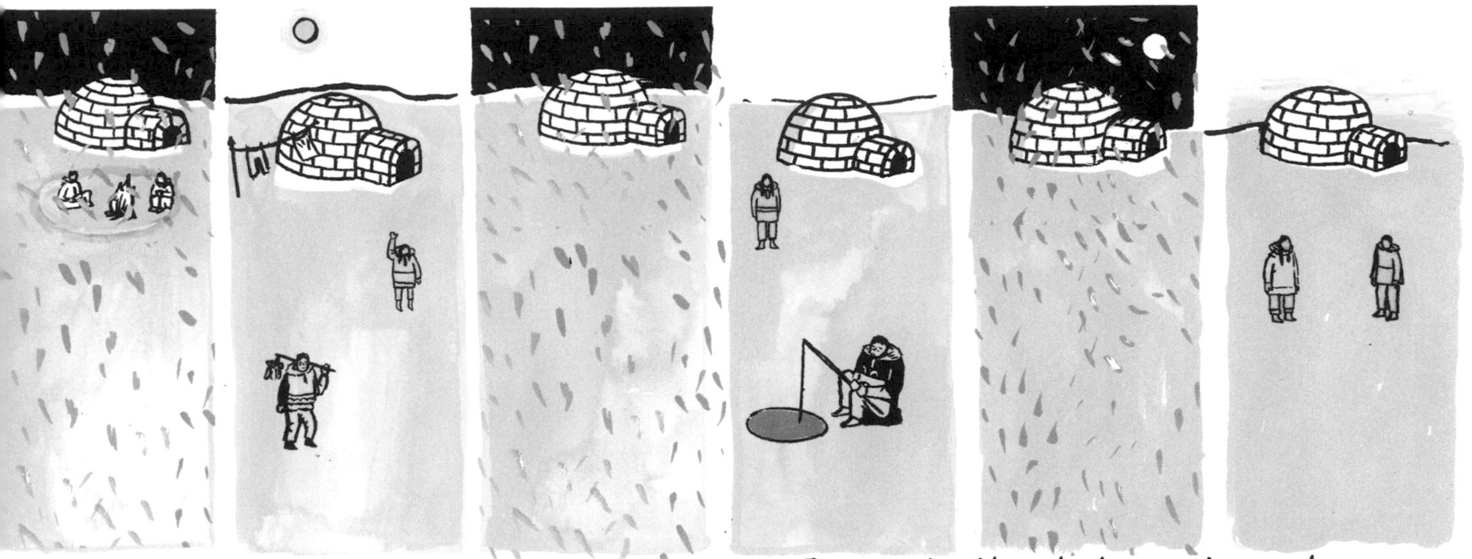

he strange thing was, that as the years went by hey simply loved each other more. But the more t grew, the fiercer the magnetic force became. By fifty they could not come within a metre of each other.

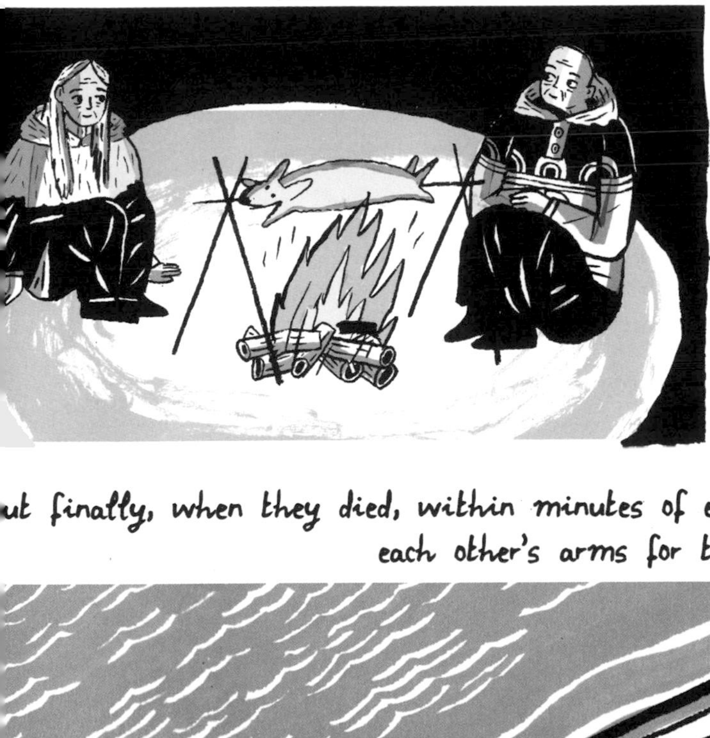

By seventy they had separate ice houses.

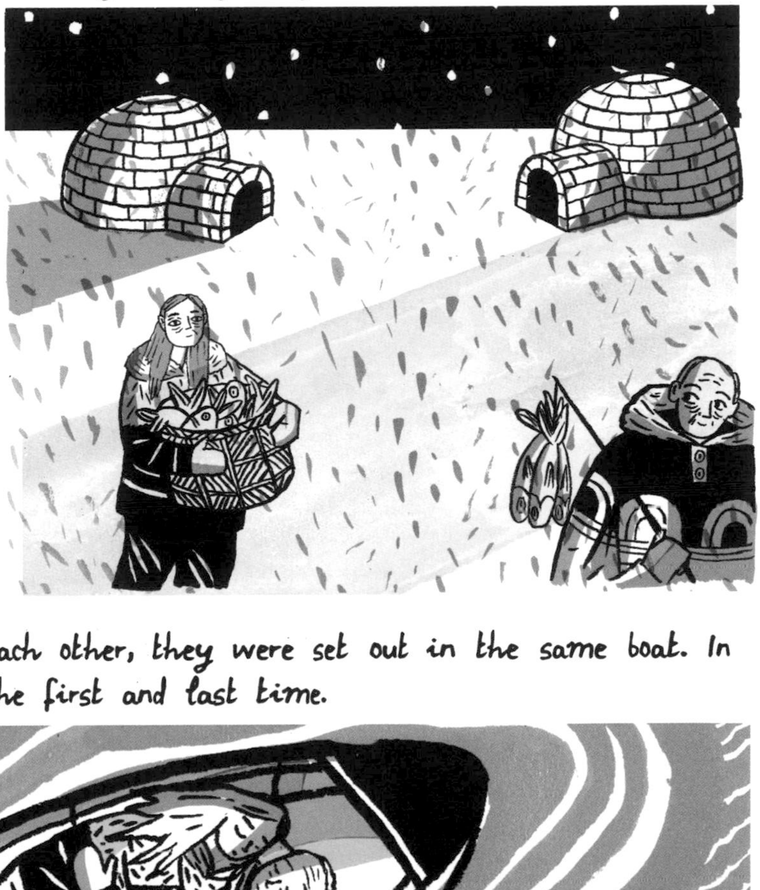

ut finally, when they died, within minutes of each other, they were set out in the same boat. In each other's arms for the first and last time.

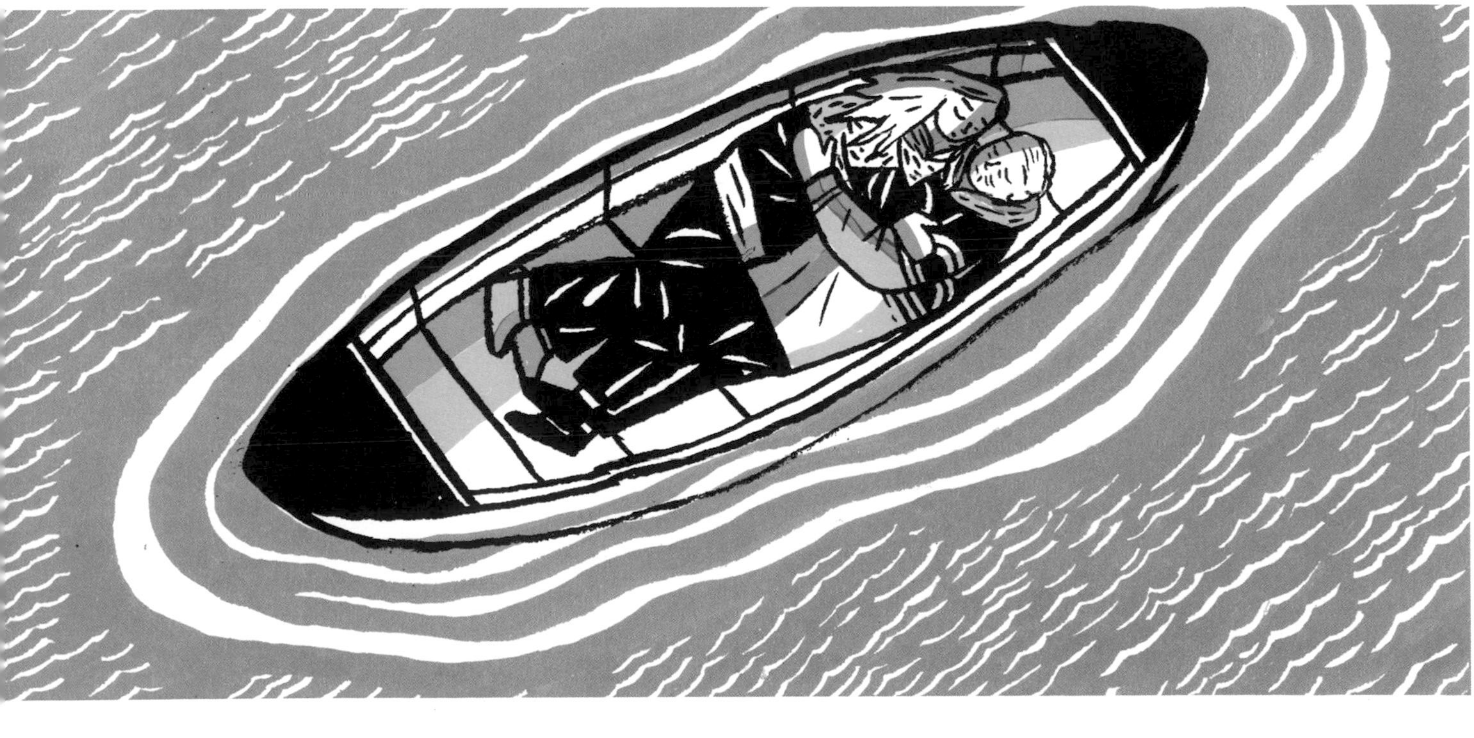

APPENDICES

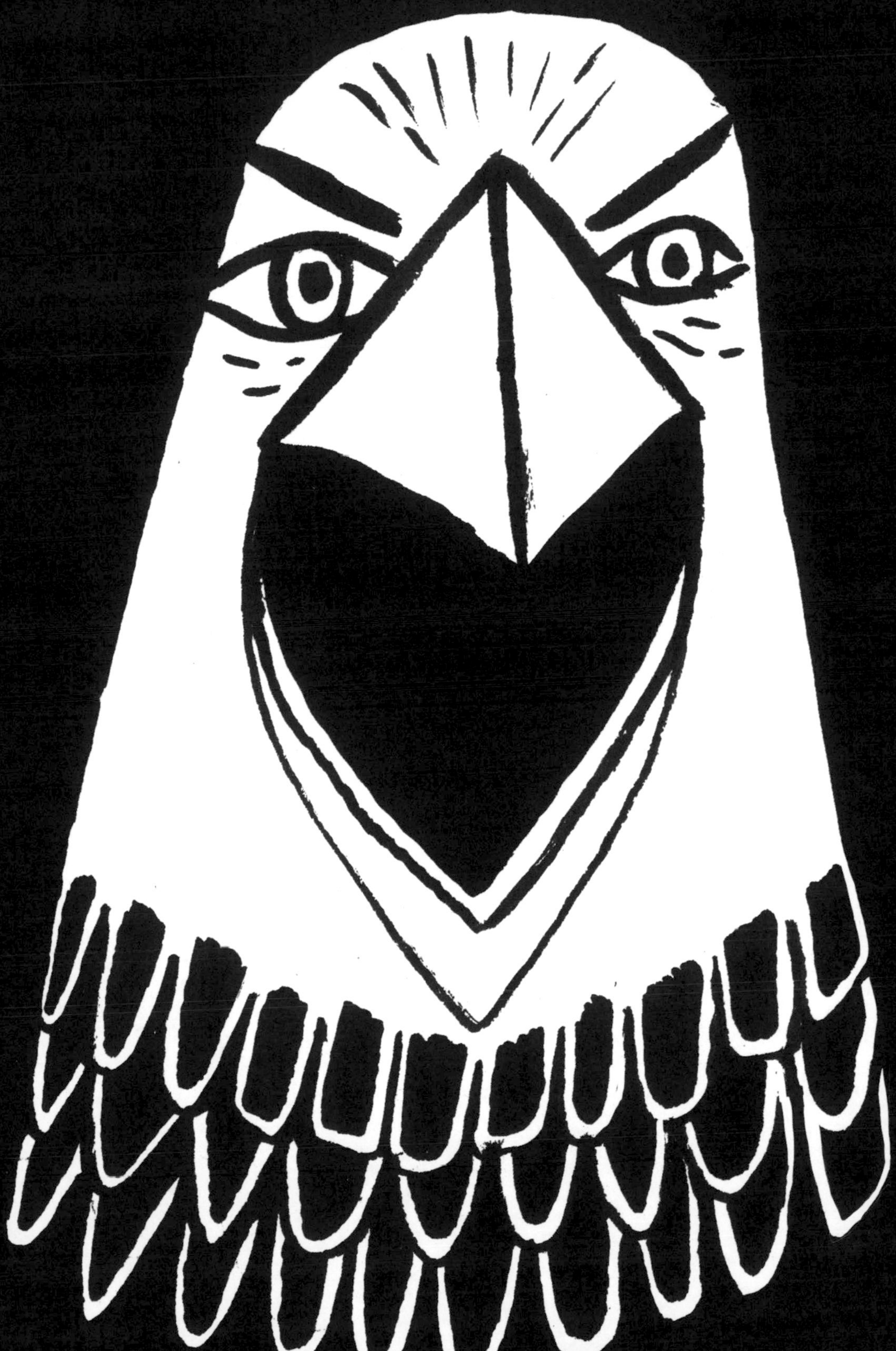

A BRIEF HISTORY OF TIME

Or some things you should know about Early Earth.

A long time after the Big Bang, but long before the Permian or Mesozoic Eras (when giant reptiles first began to swim about in the watery oceans of our planet) there is a little known segment of Earth's History.

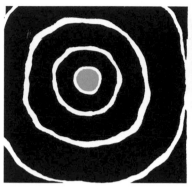   

This Era, this unrecorded time, is known to those who study it as EARLY EARTH. It is not an era that is taught in schools, and is believed by many to be as far-fetched as time travel or Martians. Believers are often considered to be mad-men or mavericks. But that, of course, is what people said about Galileo. So...long before the Permian Era, there were millions upon millions of years in which a whole different planet of living creatures evolved. In which civilised humanoids like us dominated a world of animals and plants not unlike the ones that populate our planet today.

These Early people had cities and languages and gods and writings. But all of this is gone now. For the planet then was a strange and volatile place, ever changing. As fast as the humans evolved so too did the Earth. It grew and grew, inflating like a balloon until the crusts of the land-masses started to crack like the surface of a nearly baked cake, and all the water that was boiling up in the centre of the planet came pouring out in a flood like no other, and every living creature on Earth was all but destroyed. It then expanded to ten or twenty times the size, until it looked roughly like the planet we know today, and a blank canvas once more.

Then came the watery years, and many Ice Ages, and cells and fishes and dinosaurs and reptiles and little mammals an bigger mammals and monkeys and finally us.

You would never have known that for millions of years another civilisation had flourished. That we had, in fact, been her before. No ruined cities, no buried pots, hardly even a fossilised bone remains to record the existence of this fantastic time But thanks to a series of incredible subterranean cave paintings, we have these stories. Stories of a time called Early Earth.

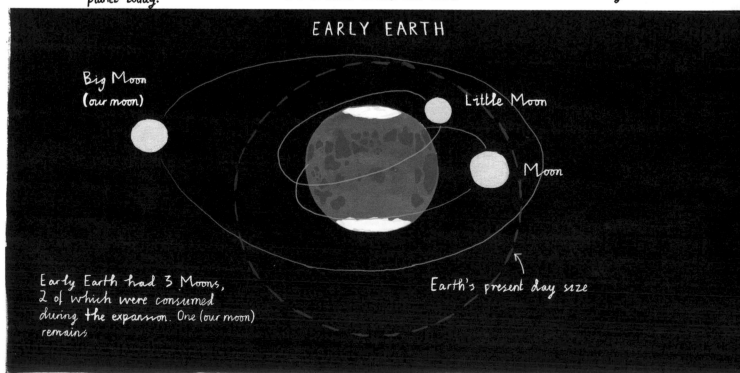

EARLY EARTH

Big Moon (our moon)

Little Moon

Moon

Earth's present day size

Early Earth had 3 Moons, 2 of which were consumed during the expansion. One (our moon) remains

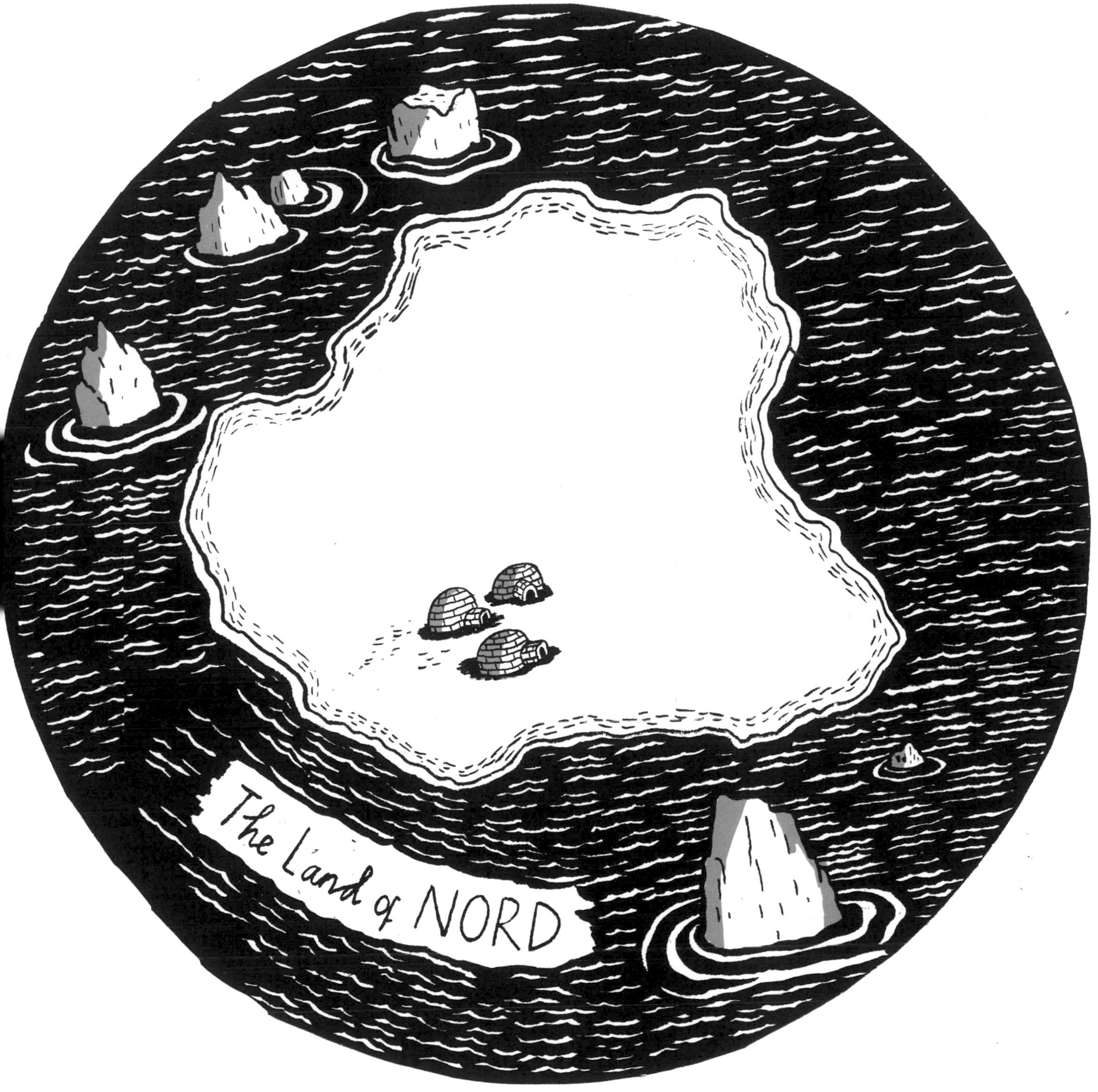
The Land of NORD

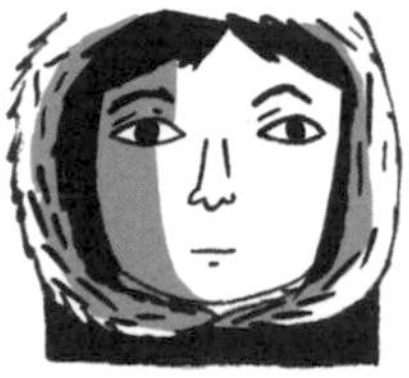

THE NORDS

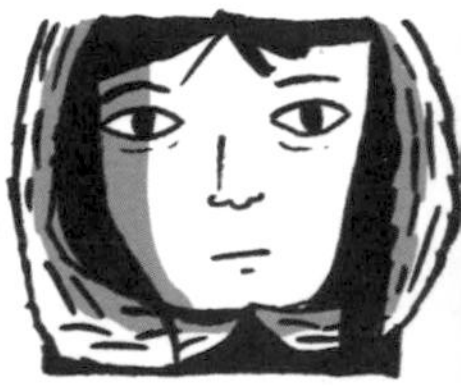

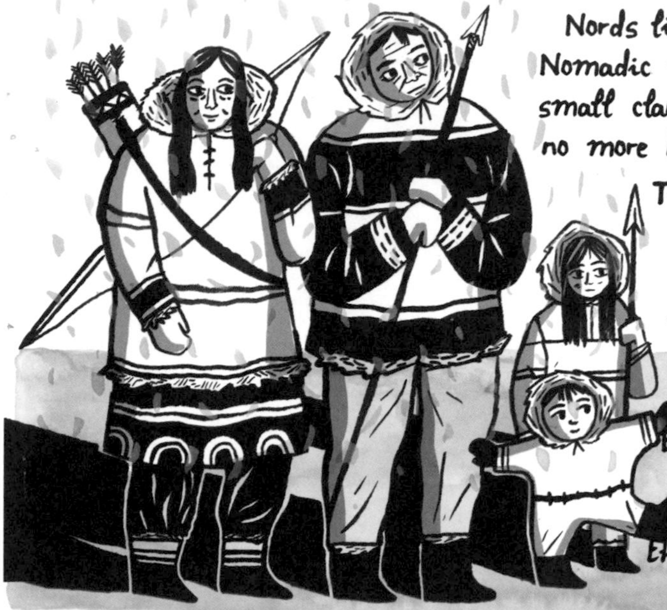

Nords live a hard, mostly Nomadic life. They dwell in small clans, family units of no more than twenty people. They hunt and live off the land, possessing an intuitive knowledge and respect of its subtleties. Even youngsters can recognise the one thousand and one varieties of snow.

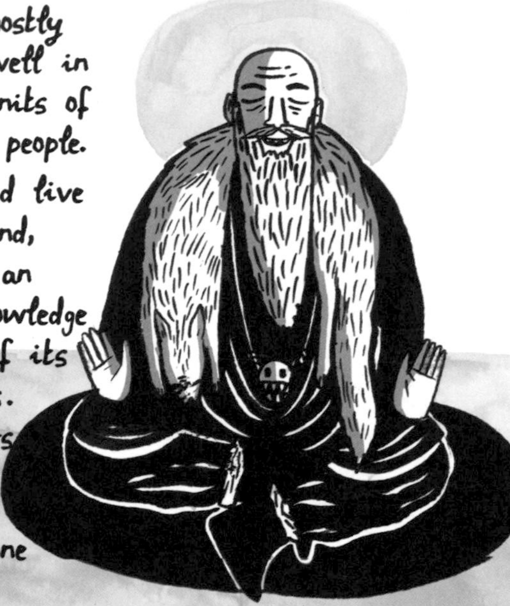

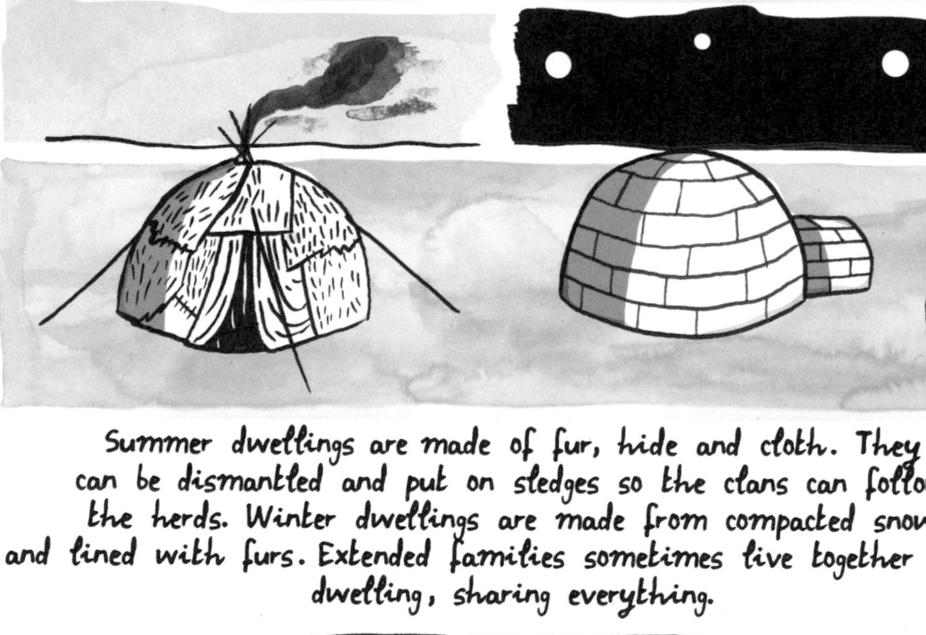

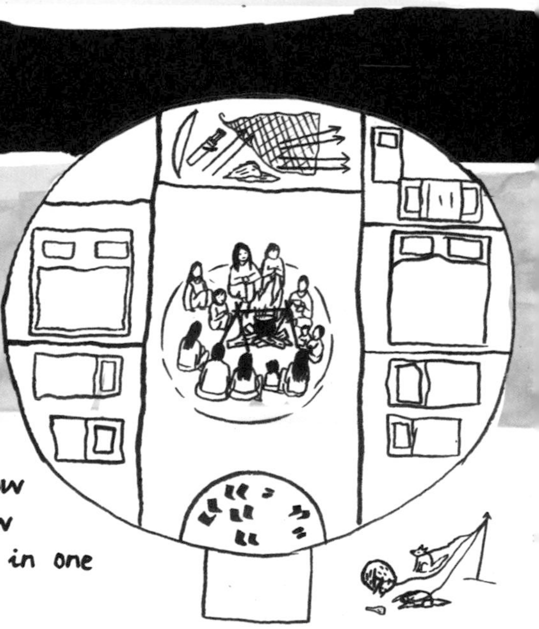

Summer dwellings are made of fur, hide and cloth. They can be dismantled and put on sledges so the clans can follow the herds. Winter dwellings are made from compacted snow and lined with furs. Extended families sometimes live together in one dwelling, sharing everything.

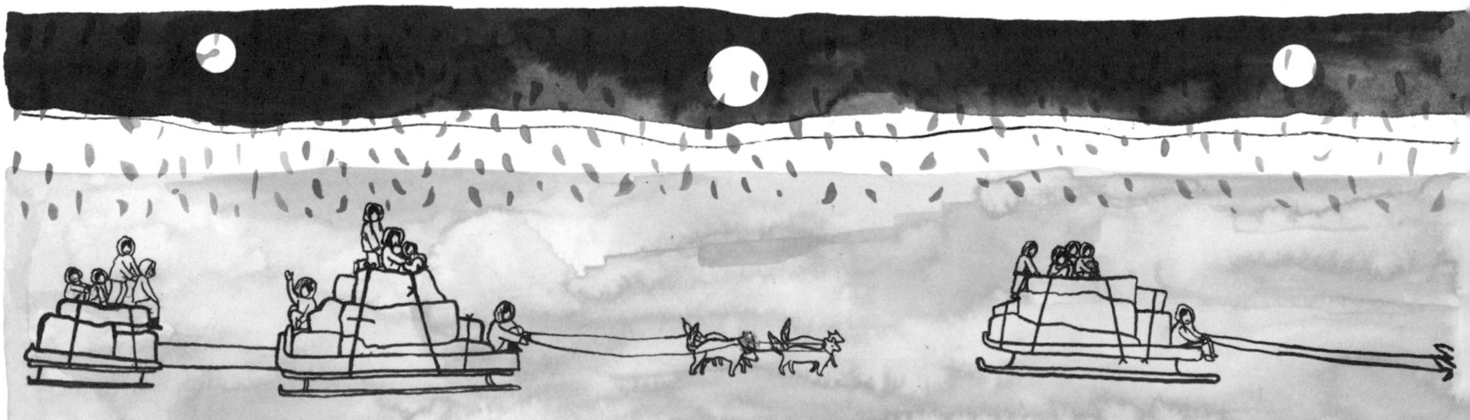

HUNTING AND FISHING

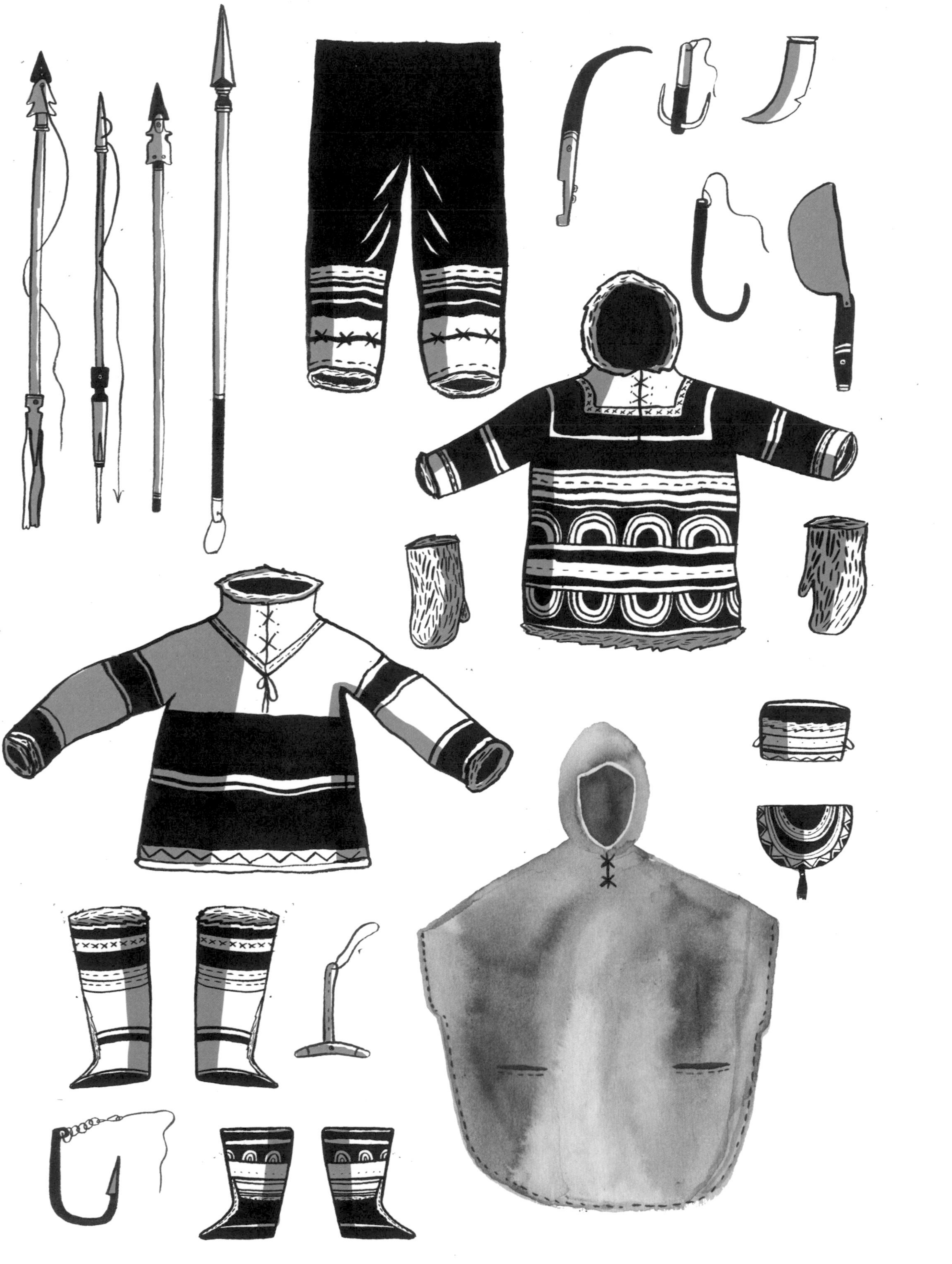

THE 1001 VARIETIES OF SNOW

The people of Nord have no one word for snow. But they have over one thousand words to describe its subtleties. There are words for every scent and texture, the way it might feel on the tip of your nose or look as it melts into the fur of your mittens and hardens into tiny crystals.

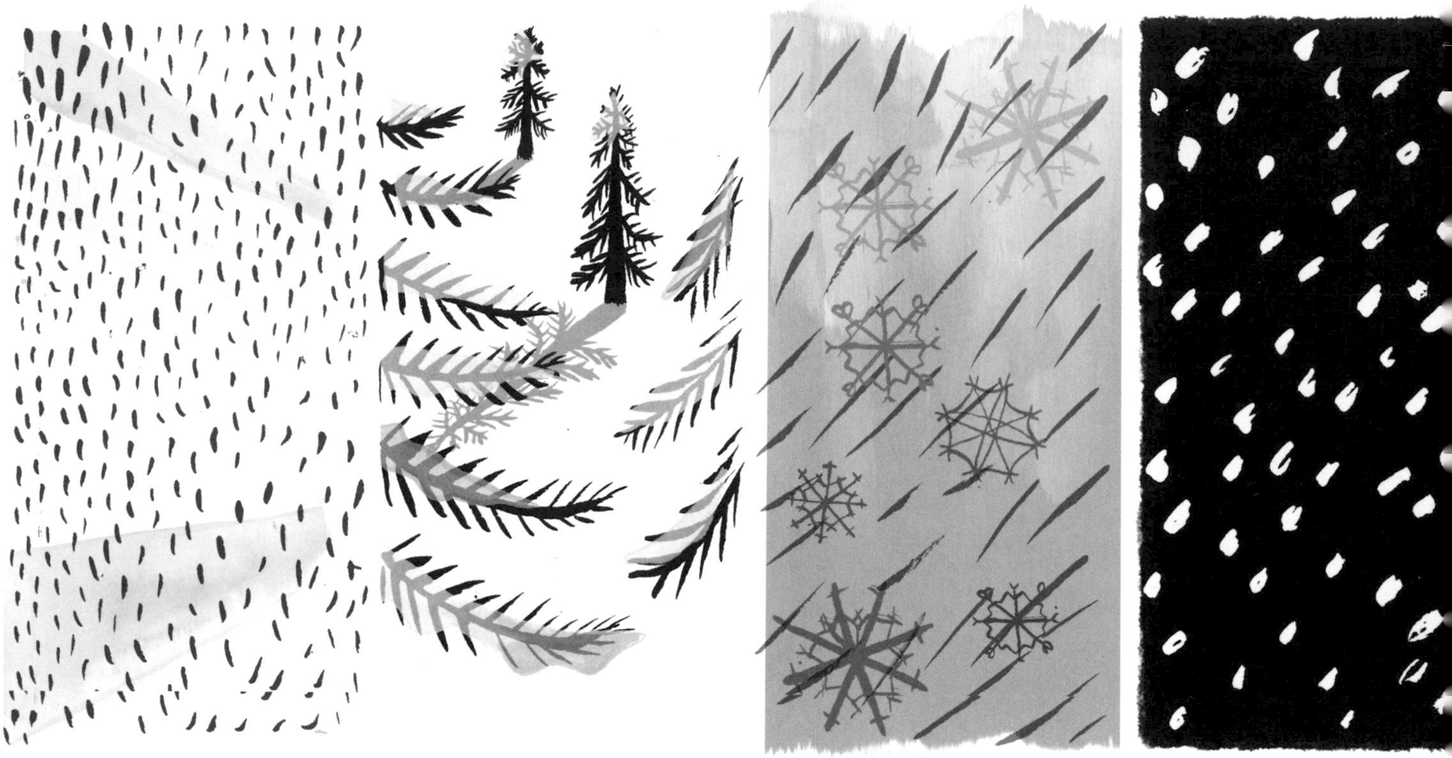

There is wet snow, powdery snow, gusting snow, downward-falling snow, horizontal-sleeting snow, flurries of snow that appear from nowhere even when the sky seems clear as a mirror.

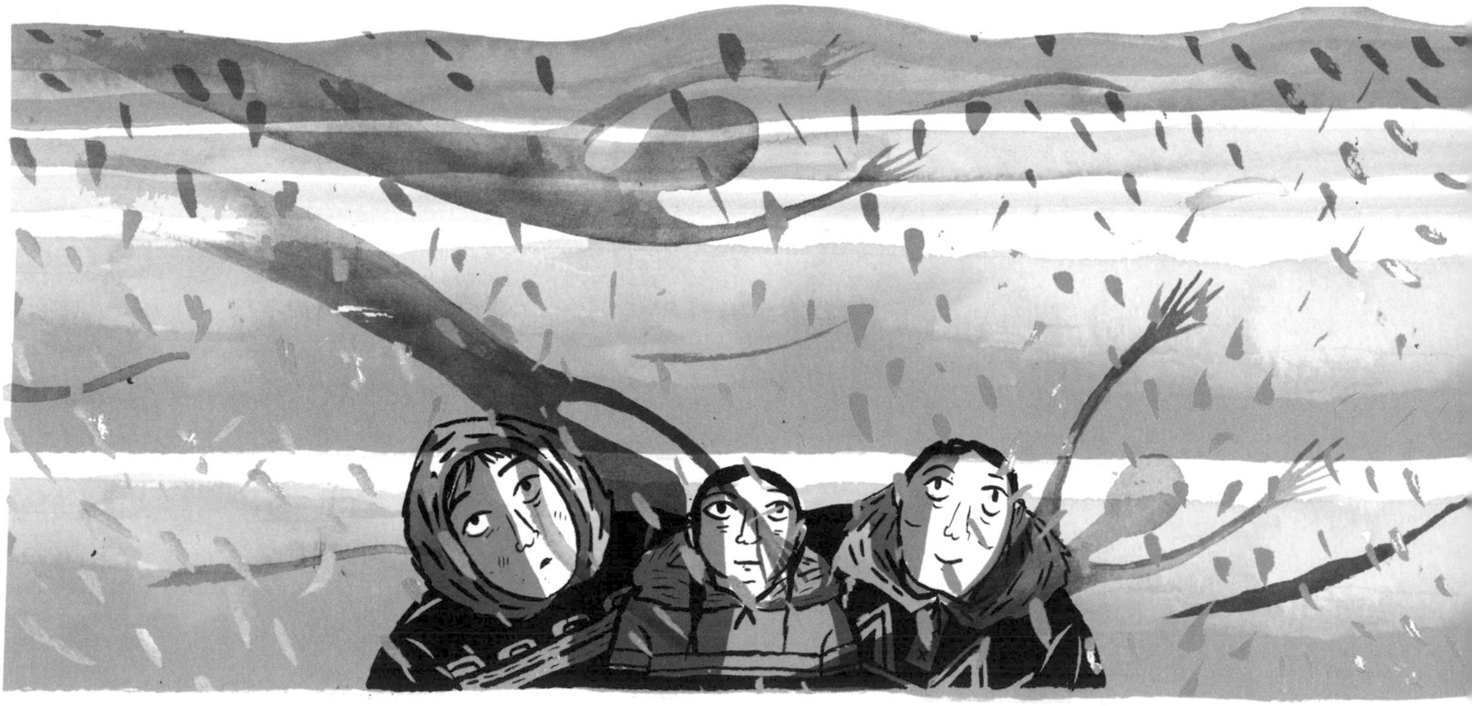

And the snow of Early Earth, well it has about it a certain magic that snow today does not. Th
people of Nord believe it whispers to them, it brings with it stories and ghosts and strange voices.

They have a complicated saying that likens snow to love. It is not easy to translate and relies eavily on a confusing similarity between the Nord word for love and the word used to describe the first snow fall of winter, a much anticipated event in the Nordish calendar.

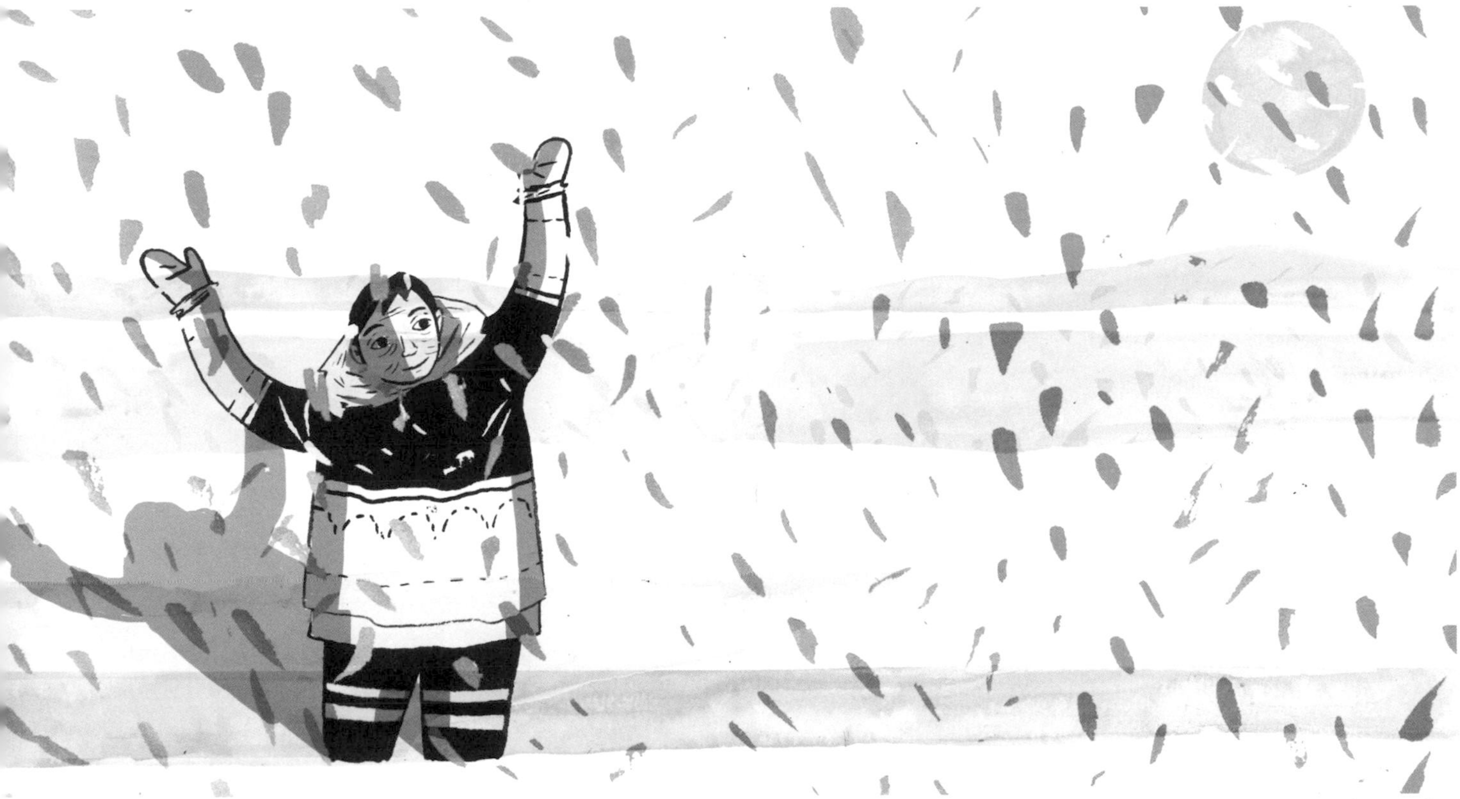

t speaks of the beauty and the harshness, of watching a perfect flake land on bare skin and melt way in an instant. Of the soft powder giving way underfoot and the creeping chill of ice in your bones turning your lips blue and your fingers black. Of terrible pain and delirious joy.

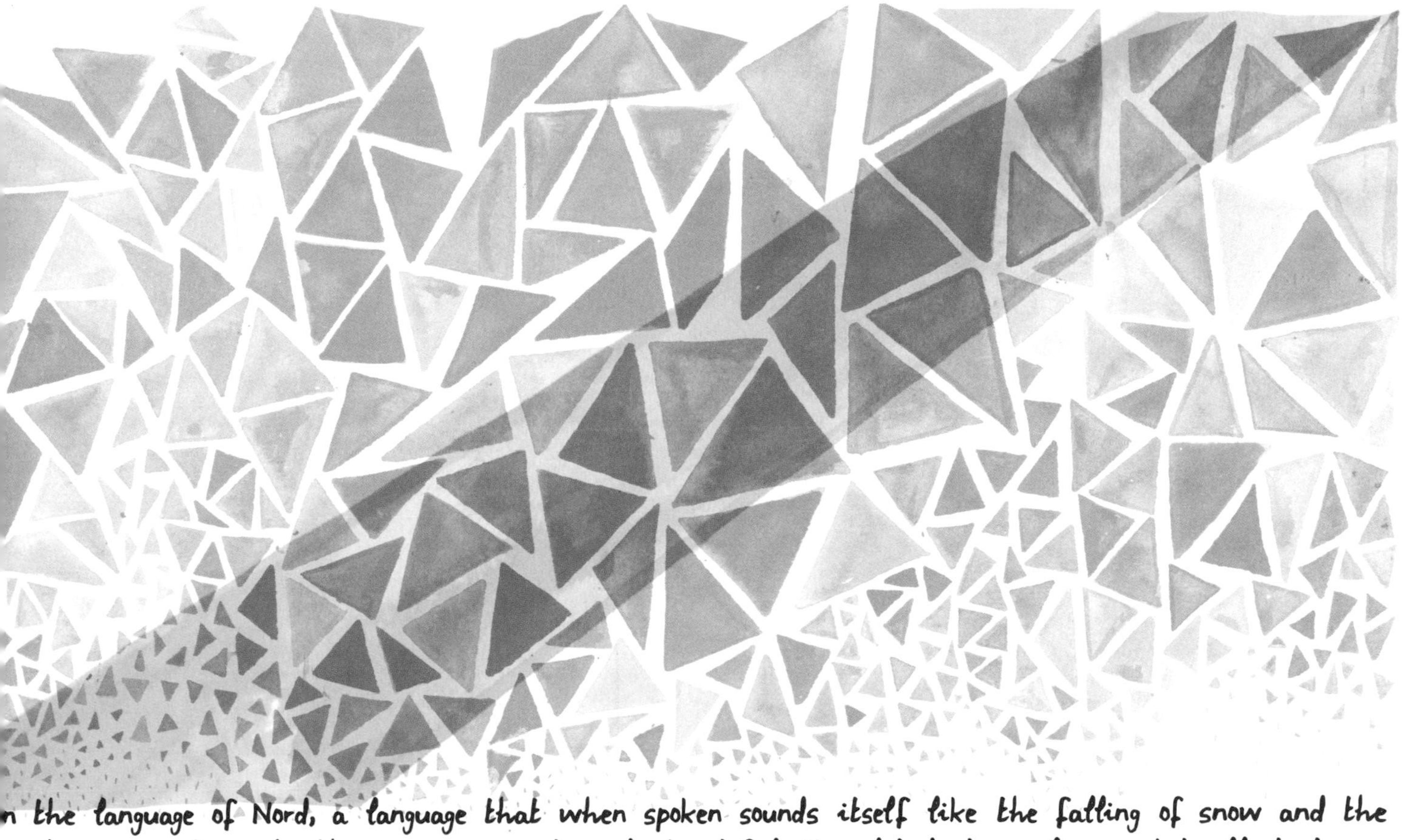

n the language of Nord, a language that when spoken sounds itself like the falling of snow and the whispering of winds, this saying is extremely beautiful. Translated it is clumsy, but illustrates, perhaps, how closely linked the Nords are to their land.

THE INVISIBLE HUNTER

Nannoo and Ian were hunters. They were born into the same clan and when they were children they shared their toys, later they shared their first kill and their first kiss and after that they never hunted apart again.

> Nice shot, Nannoo.

But as they grew older unhappiness came into their lives. It was as slow and creeping as winter, but it came all the same.

For years they waited, but no children came [to] them. Nannoo was consumed, she could think [of] nothing else. When she closed her eyes all sh[e] saw was babies.

> Why can't we have children?

> I don't know. I don't know.

And so she decided to ask BirdMan. She prayed for hours on end, for days, for weeks, for years.

Really, she prayed harder than any human h[as] ever prayed before (this was in the early days [of] creation, so not such a feat as you might imagine) In fact she finally prayed so hard th[at] BirdMan heard her.

> What the bloody h[ell] is that noise?

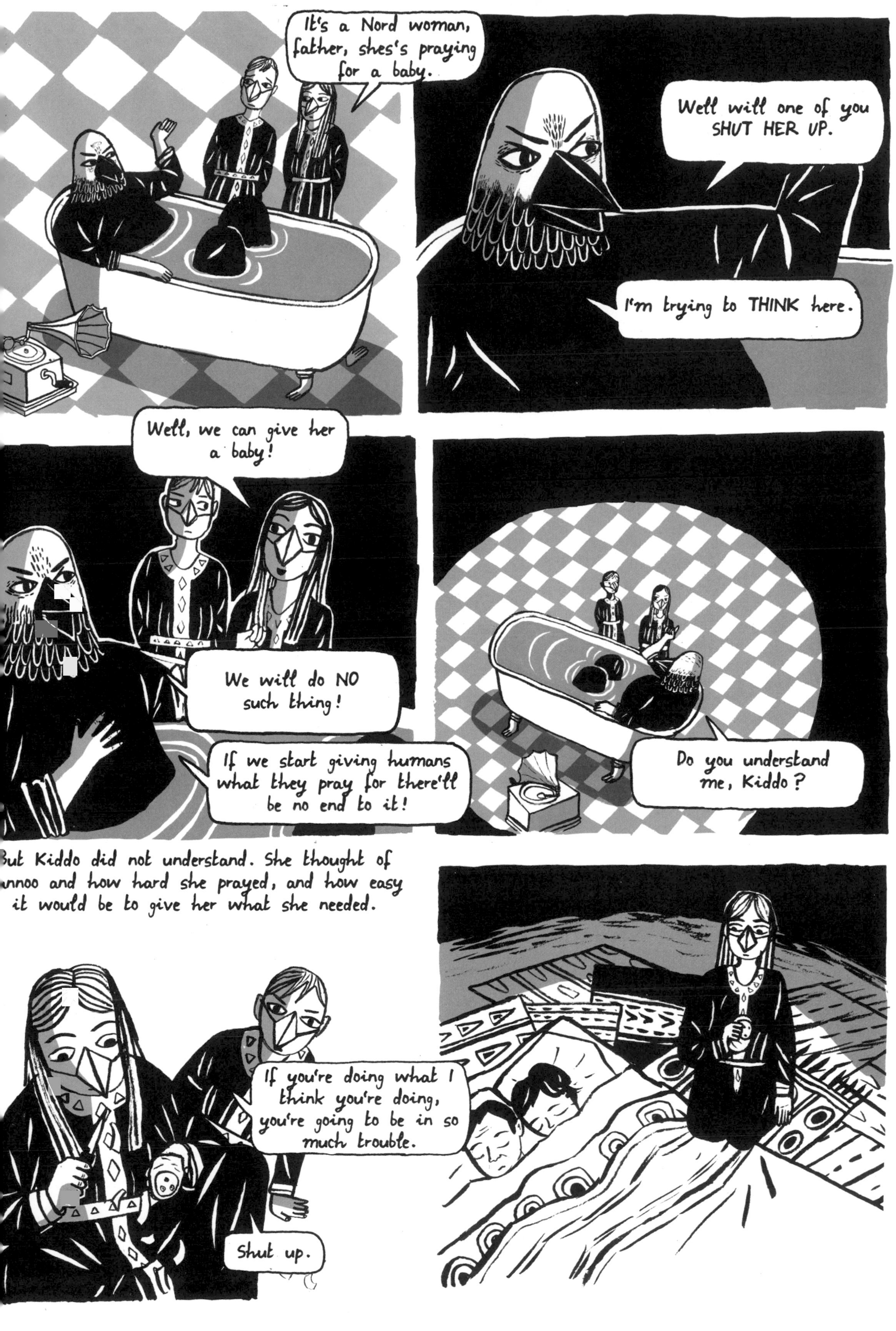
It's a Nord woman, father, shes's praying for a baby.
Well will one of you SHUT HER UP.
I'm trying to THINK here.
Well, we can give her a baby!
We will do NO such thing!
If we start giving humans what they pray for there'll be no end to it!
Do you understand me, Kiddo?
ut Kiddo did not understand. She thought of nnoo and how hard she prayed, and how easy it would be to give her what she needed.
If you're doing what I think you're doing, you're going to be in so much trouble.
Shut up.

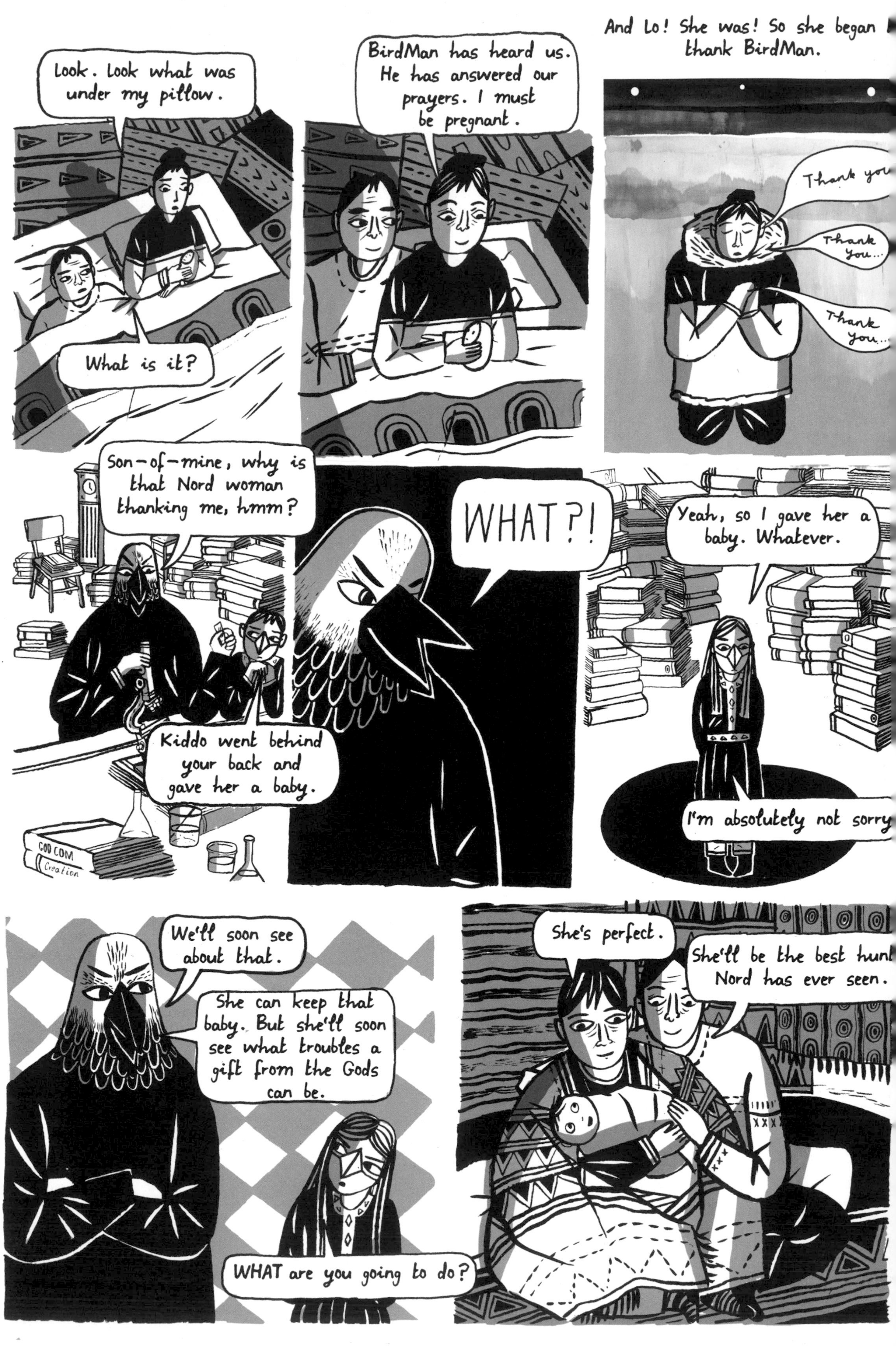
And Lo! She was! So she began to thank BirdMan.
Look. Look what was under my pillow.
What is it?
BirdMan has heard us. He has answered our prayers. I must be pregnant.
Thank you
Thank you...
Thank you...
Son-of-mine, why is that Nord woman thanking me, hmm?
Kiddo went behind your back and gave her a baby.
GOD COM
Creation
WHAT?!
Yeah, so I gave her a baby. Whatever.
I'm absolutely not sorry
We'll soon see about that.
She can keep that baby. But she'll soon see what troubles a gift from the Gods can be.
WHAT are you going to do?
She's perfect.
She'll be the best hunter Nord has ever seen.

From the outset, it was clear that she was no ordinary child. Almost as soon as she could crawl, she began to develop an uncanny ability to blend into her surroundings.

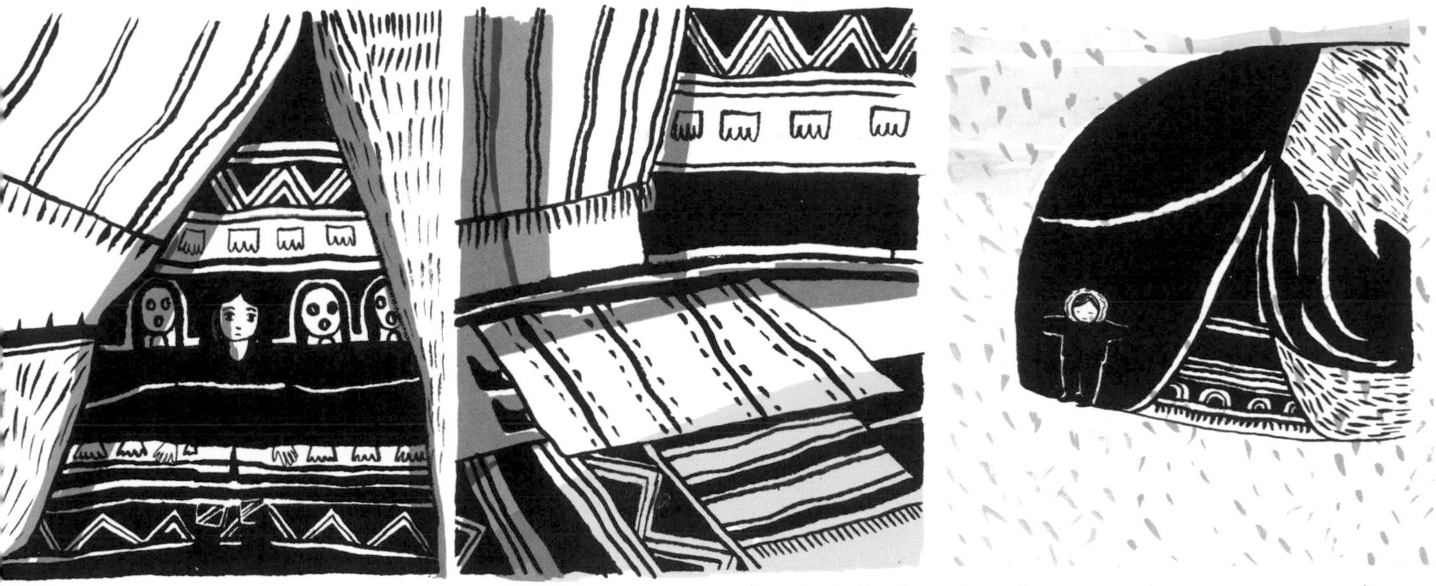

By the age of four this talent had developed into fully fledged invisibility.

She faded, day by day, until one morning her mother looked into her bed and found it empty.

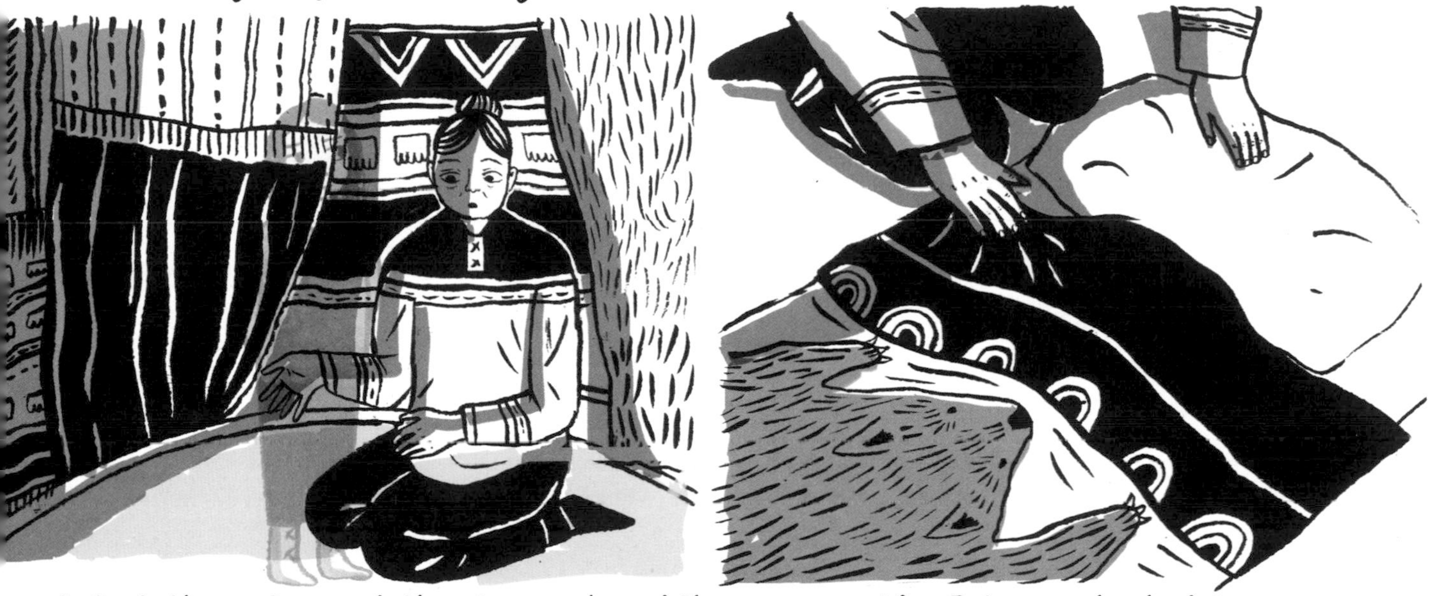

At first they got around this because her clothes were visible. But once she had been wearing something for an hour or so her invisibility started to rub off on it, so her family were always tripping over discarded garments.

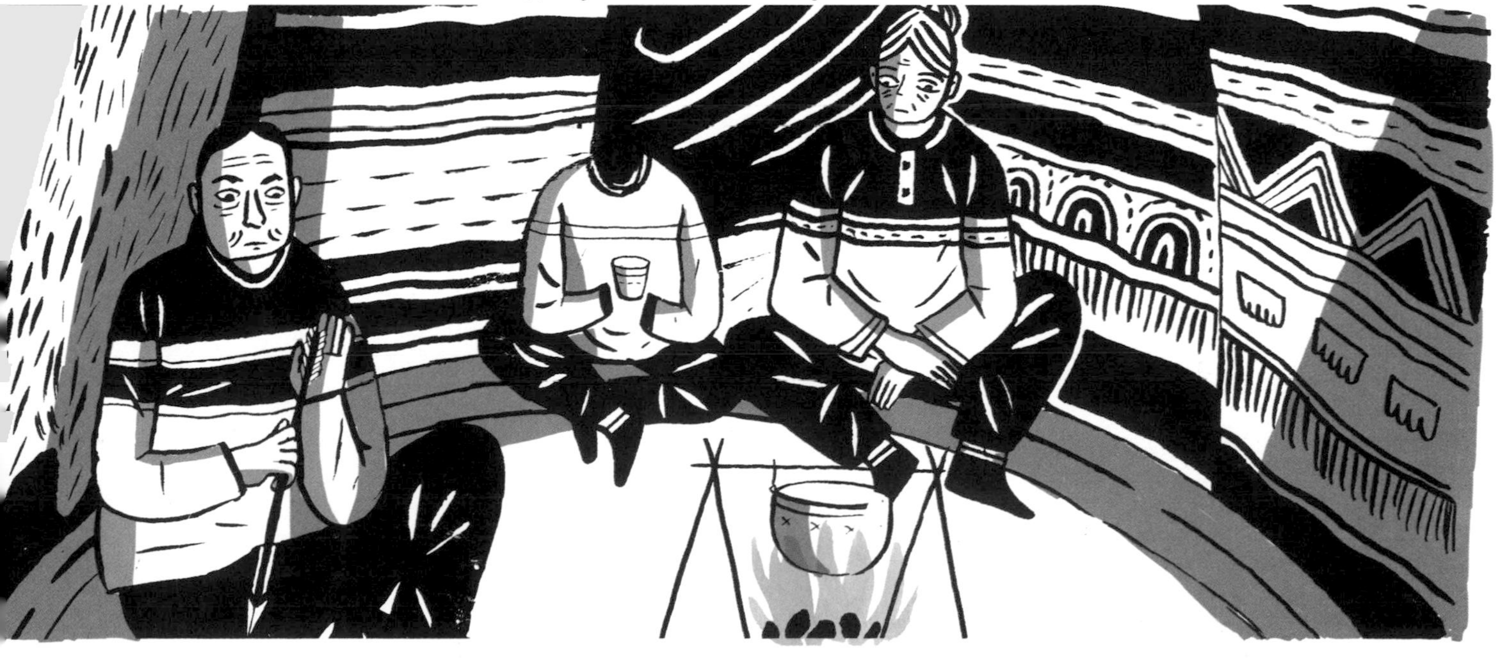

You might think that Nannoo and Lan would be worried by this. But they weren't. The truth was that occurrences of this kind were quite common in Nord. The Nords put it down to the close proximity of the Aurora.

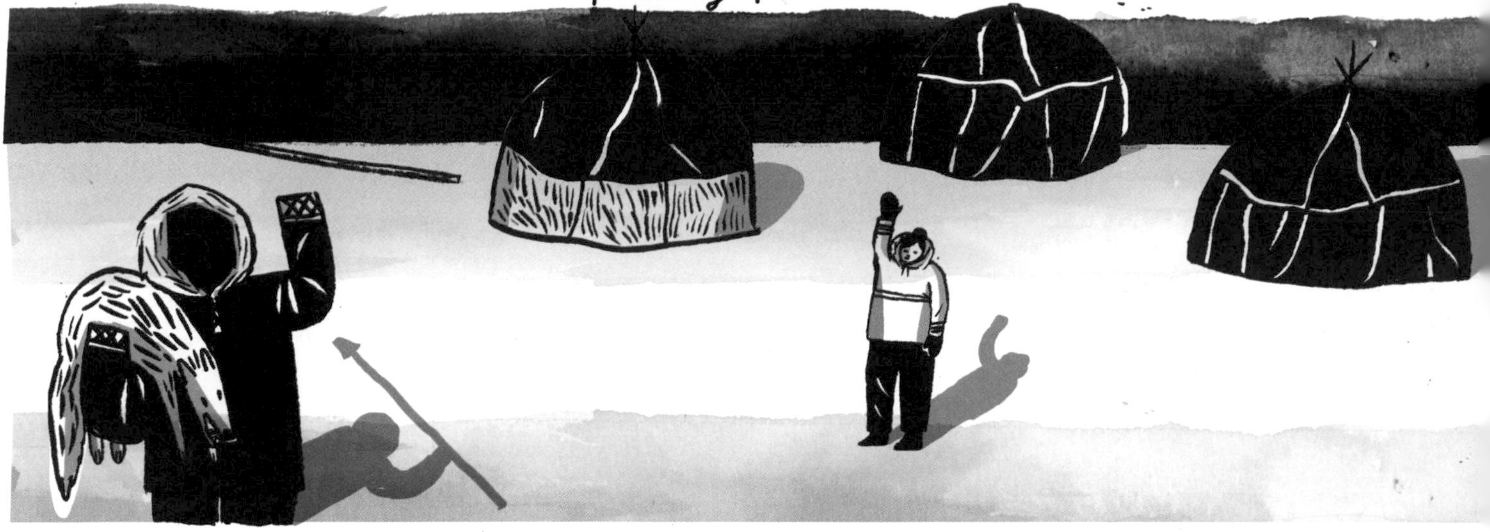

Anyway, it came in handy, for she became a better hunter day by day.

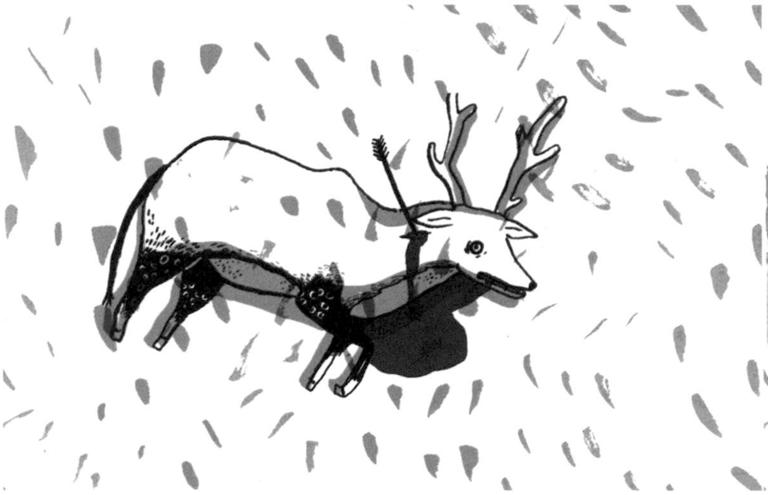

But being invisible, as you might imagine, is a lonely business, and she became more and more solitary.

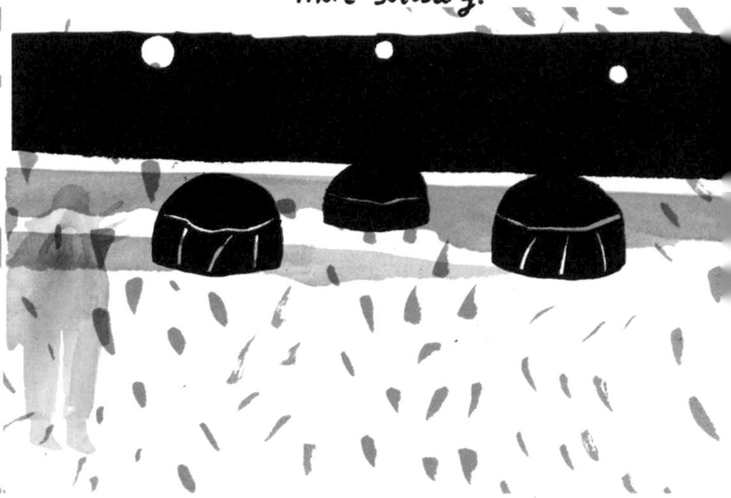

Until one day, when she was grown up, bigger but by no means less invisible, her family awoke to find her bed made and unrumpled. And outside, vanishing off into the distance, a set of footprints i the snow.

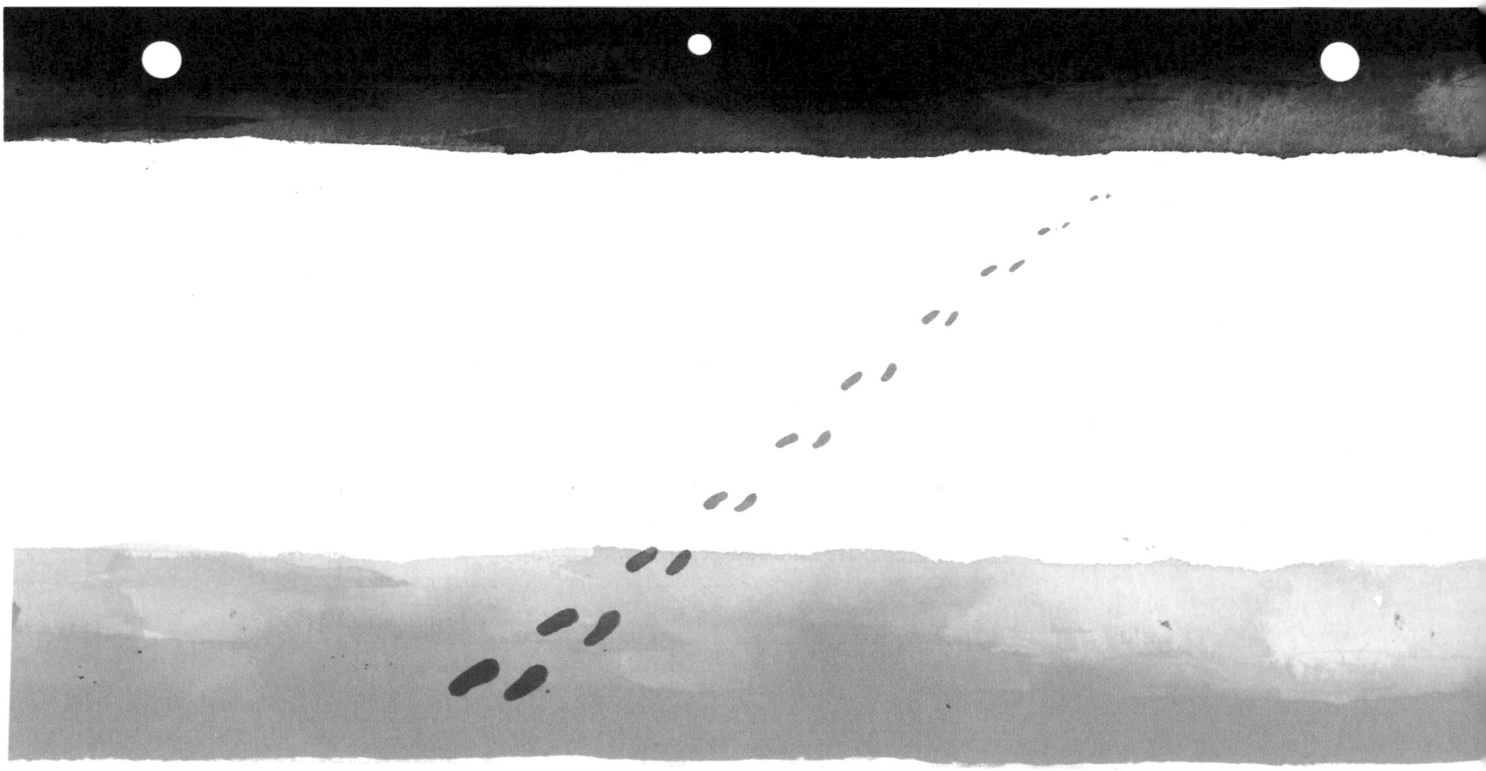

annoo watched the horizon, day ter day, hoping for a sign that her daughter might return.

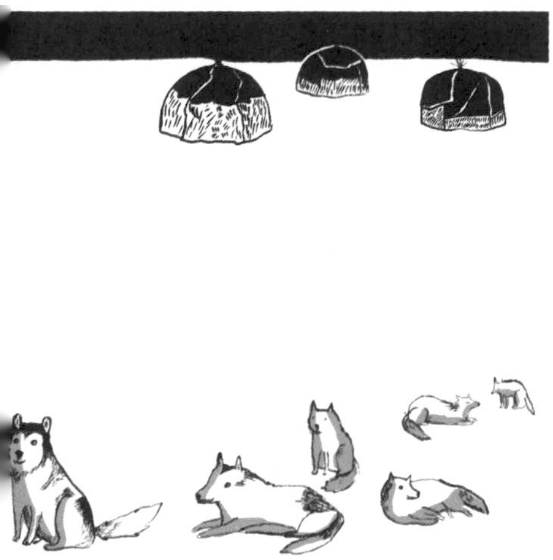

But though she never did, now and then there came a reminder that she had not forgotten them. A gift from the Invisible Hunter.

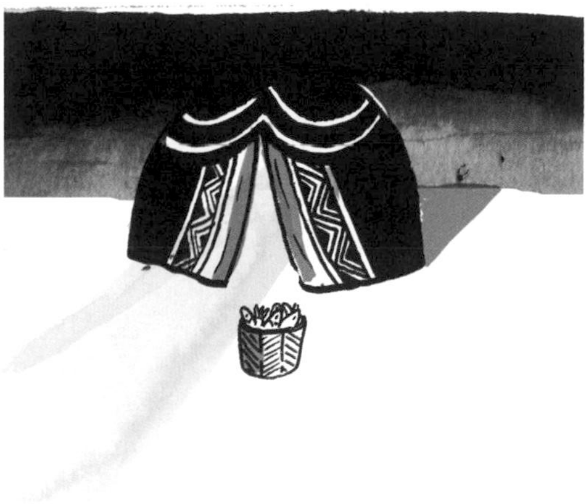

Lan had said their daughter would be the best hunter that the land of Nord had ever known. And that is what BirdMan had given them.

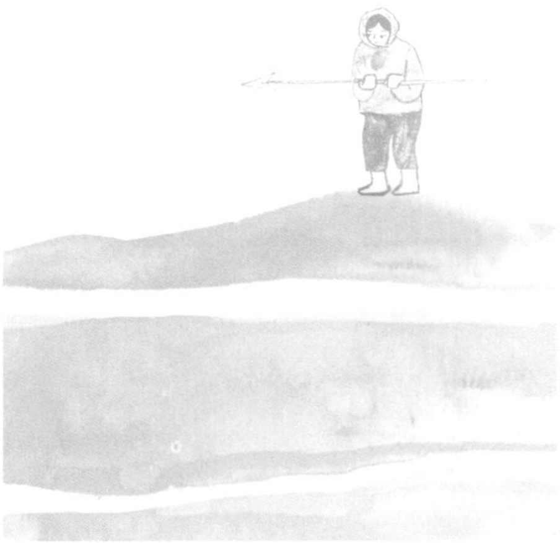

The Invisible Hunter is worshipped all over Nord now, even though it has been many generations since her footsteps have been seen in the snow. Every year, on the darkest day of midwinter, Nords leave gifts for each other, in honour of the Invisible Hunter.

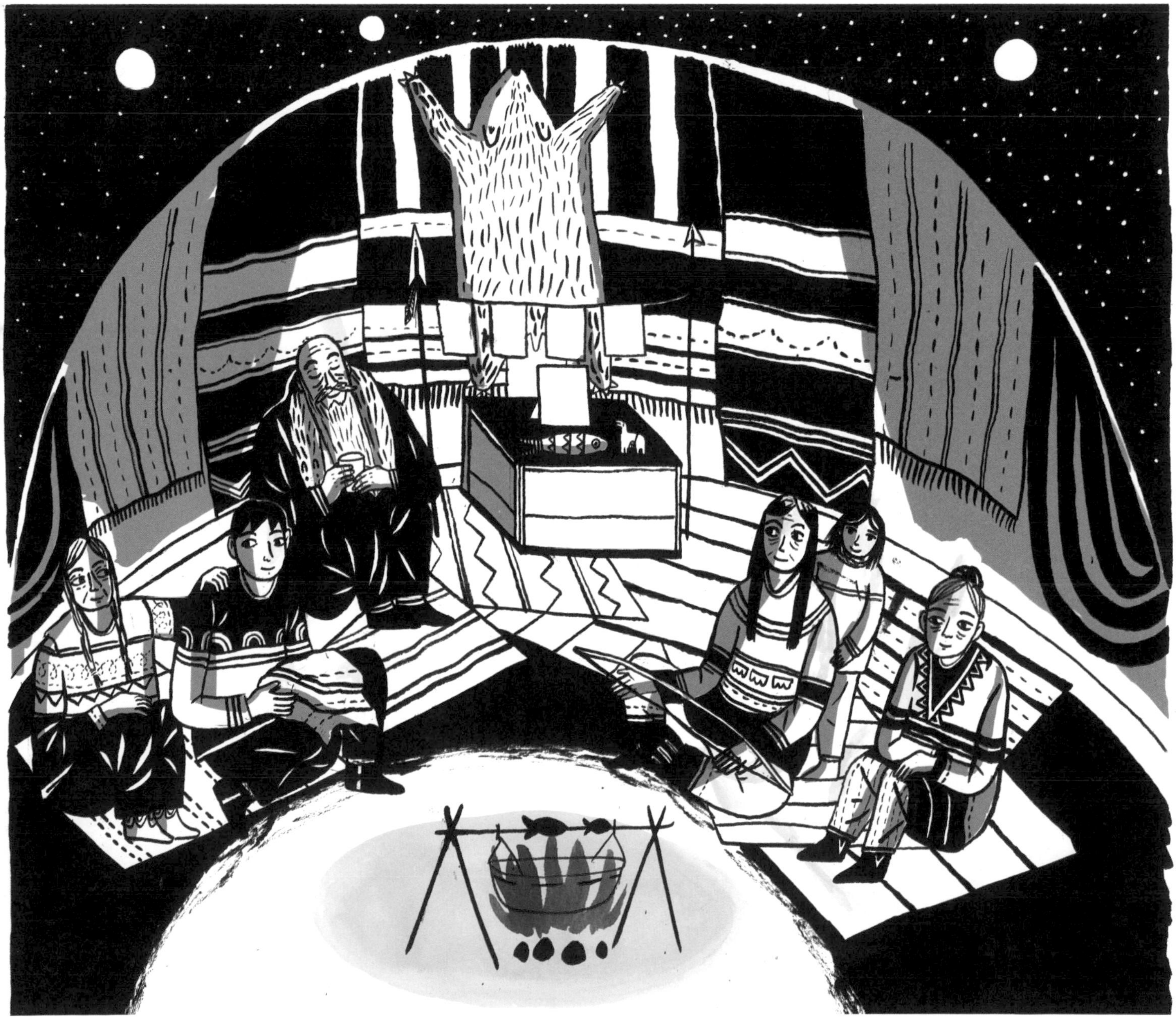

BRITANITARKA

Britanitarka is a land of tall trees and deep, black fjords. The people are proud and warlike and even the children are trained to fight. Britanitarkans give their babies wooden spears to play with, not rattles or dolls, and send them out to kill their first boar at age ten.

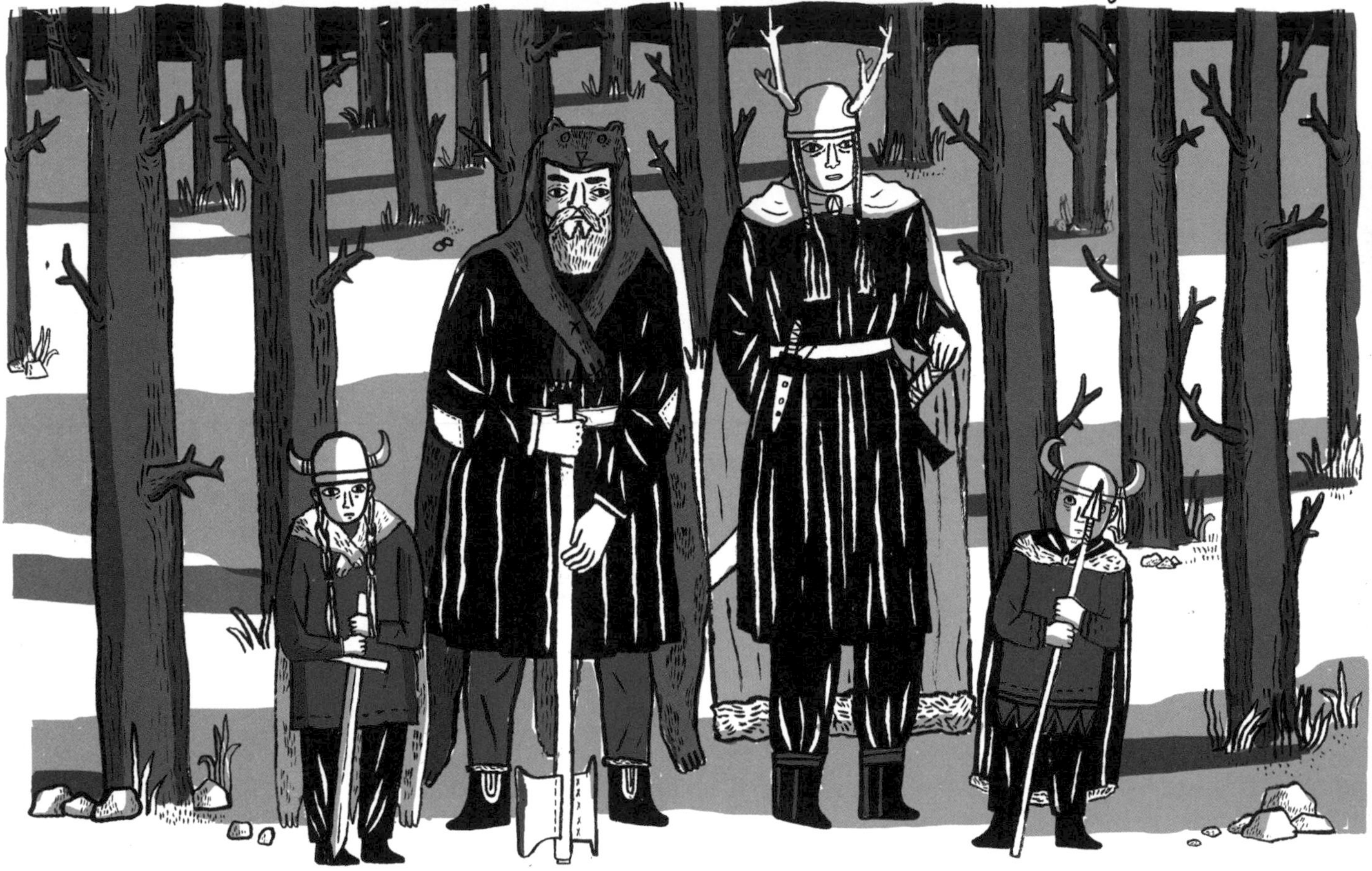

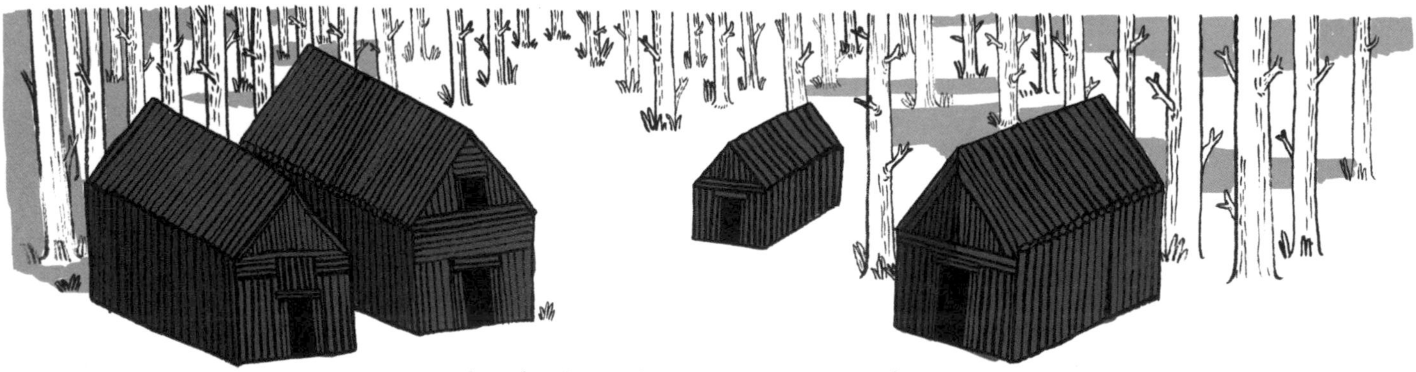

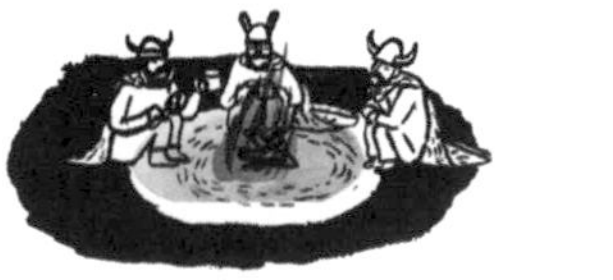

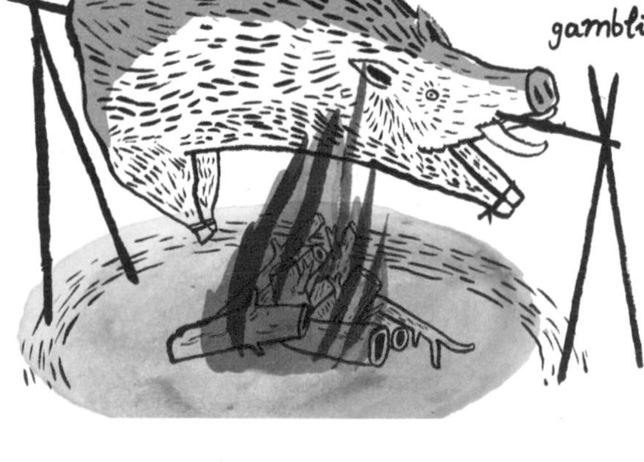

The land of Britanitarka is split into fourteen tribes, the oldest of whom are the Dags and Hals, who are always at war with one another. The other tribes are generally at war with someone too, since war is one of the favourite pastimes of Britanitarkans. As well as drinking ale and fighting they also like to play a gambling game with coloured wooden sticks. This has been the start of many clan wars.

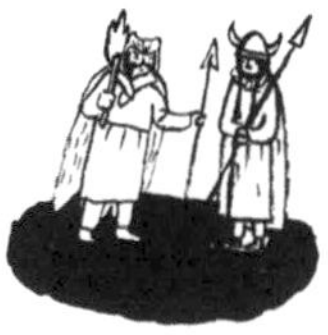

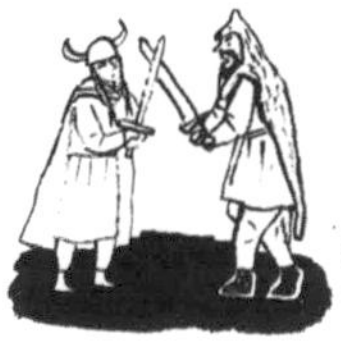

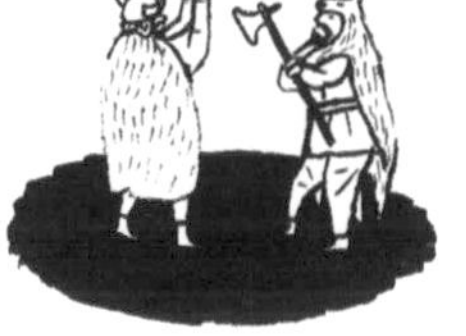

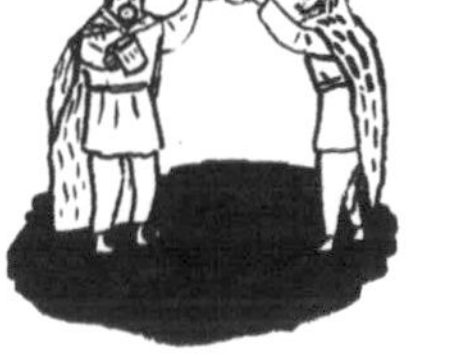

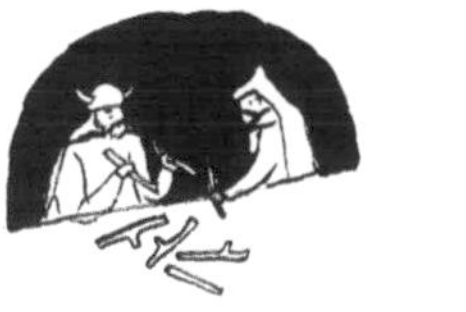

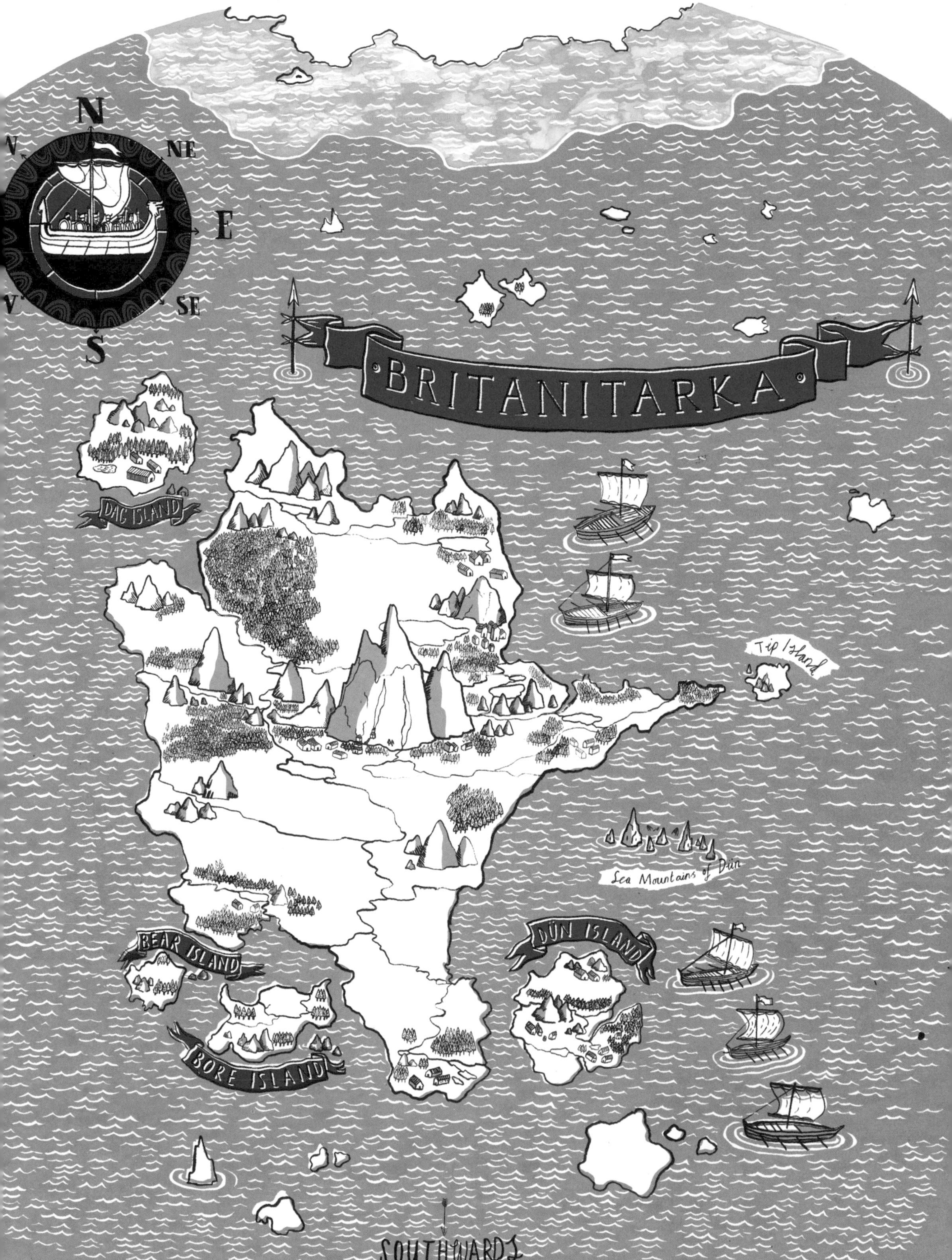
N
NE
E
SE
S
BRITANITARKA
DAG ISLAND
Tip Island
Sea Mountains of Dún
DÚN ISLAND
BEAR ISLAND
BORE ISLAND
SOUTHWARDS

BIRDS & BEASTS

FROM EARLY EARTH

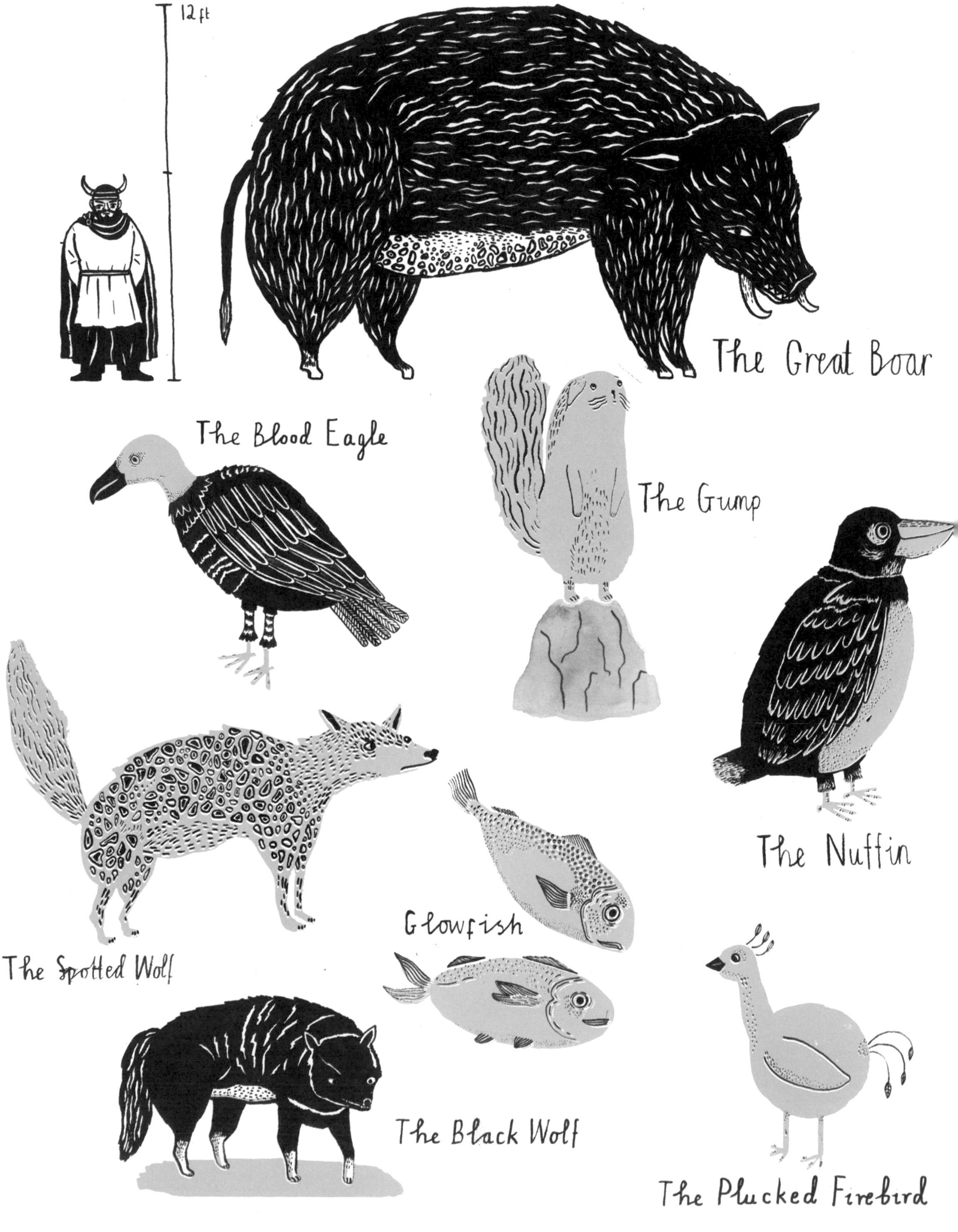
12 ft
The Great Boar
The Blood Eagle
The Gump
The Nuffin
The Spotted Wolf
Glowfish
The Black Wolf
The Plucked Firebird

The Moonstone

The most valuable piece in the treasury of Migdal Bavel is a stone that used to be the moon. It had been the fourth moon, the smallest, and one day it had dropped out of orbit. The Sun King, who had long wished to possess a Moon, saw it fall, right into the ocean.

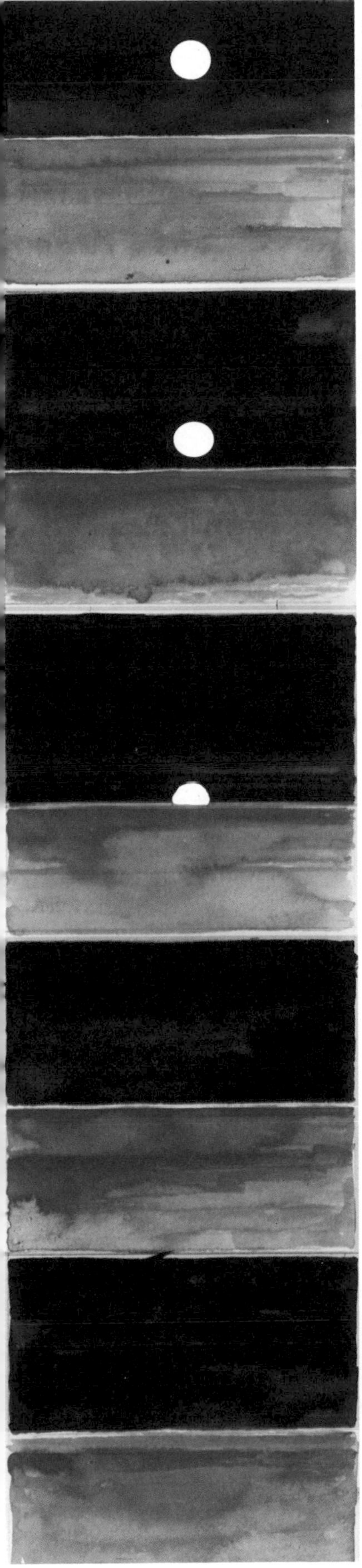

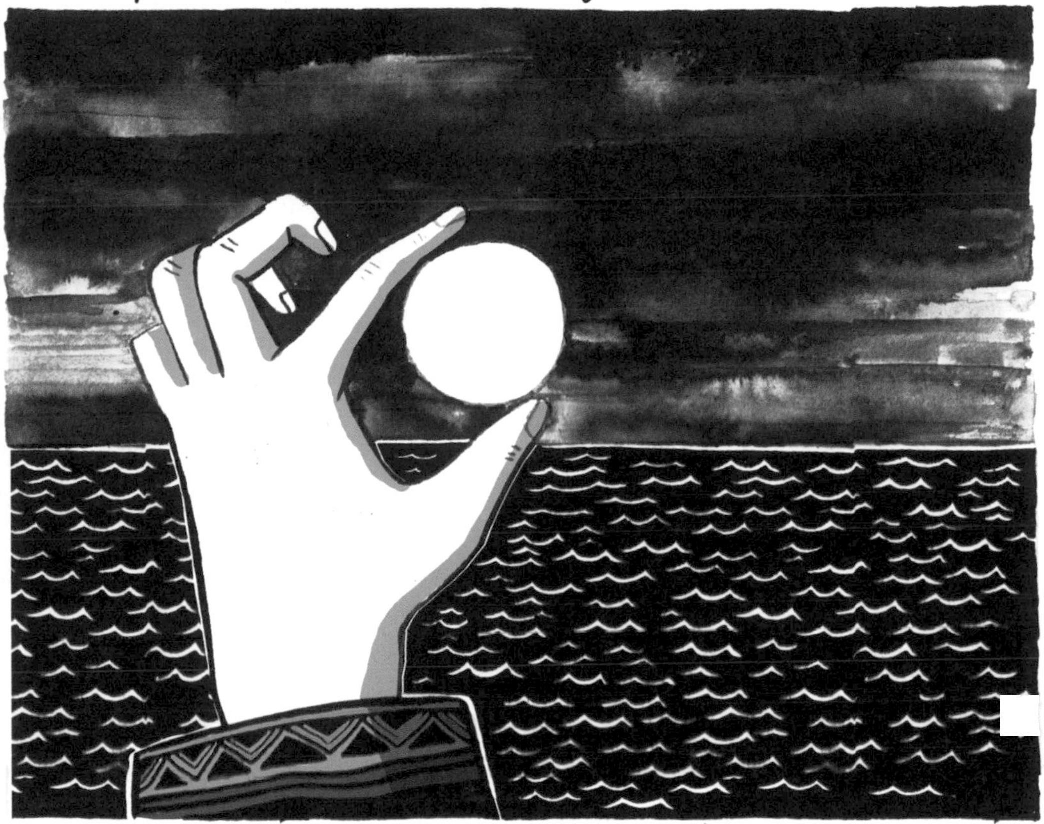

He ordered that the moon be fetched there and then. All the advisors and the army and the navy and the cleverest men in the city set to squabbling about how to get it.

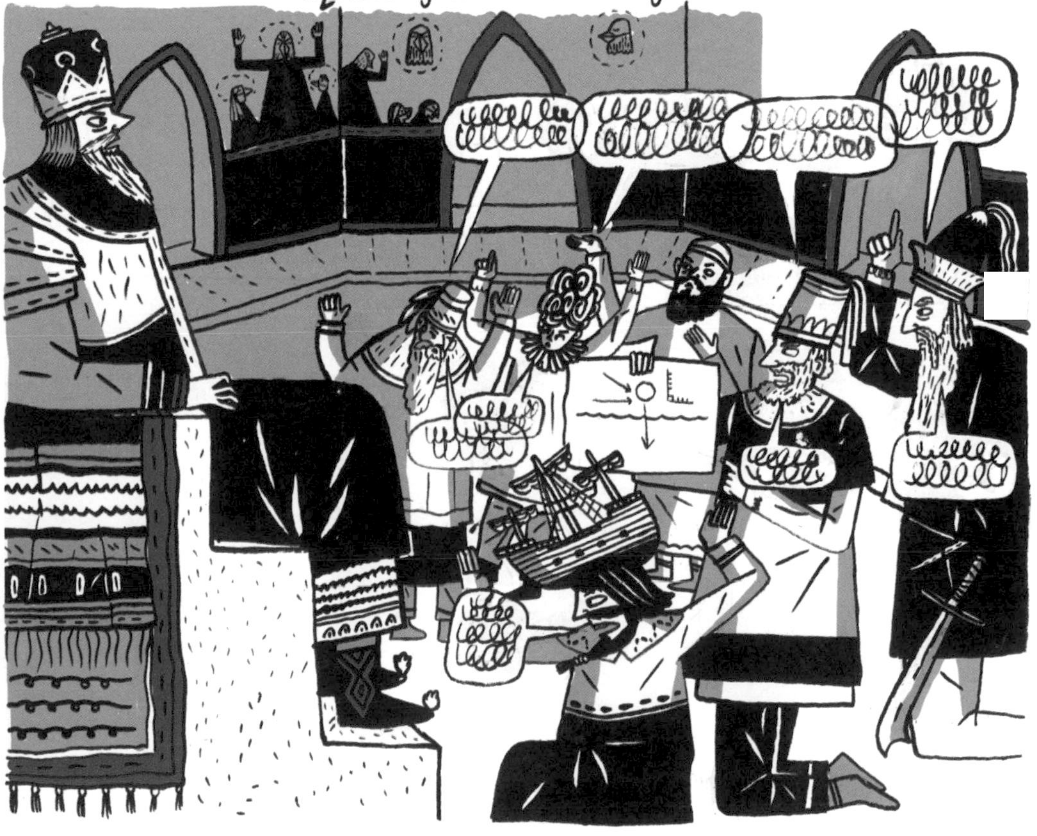

They were getting nowhere. But one day a fisherman came to the Palace with an extraordinary story.

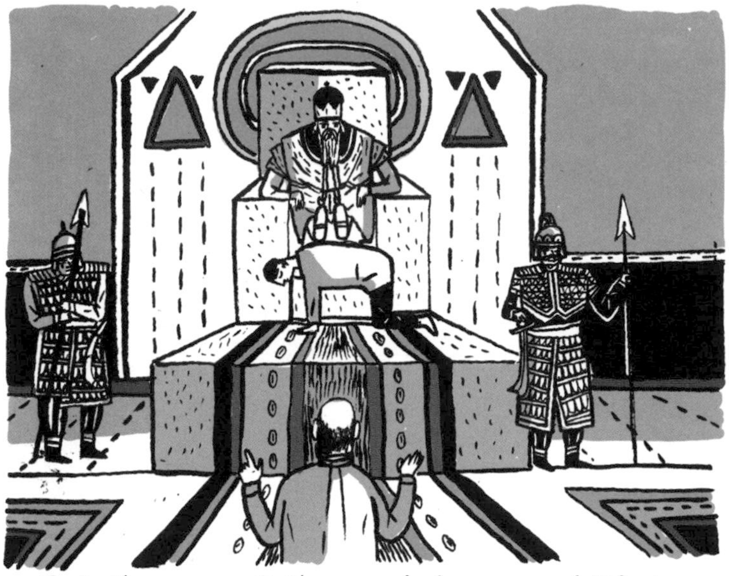

He had taken a group of pearl divers out in his fishing boat. It was a fine day and everything was quite usual.

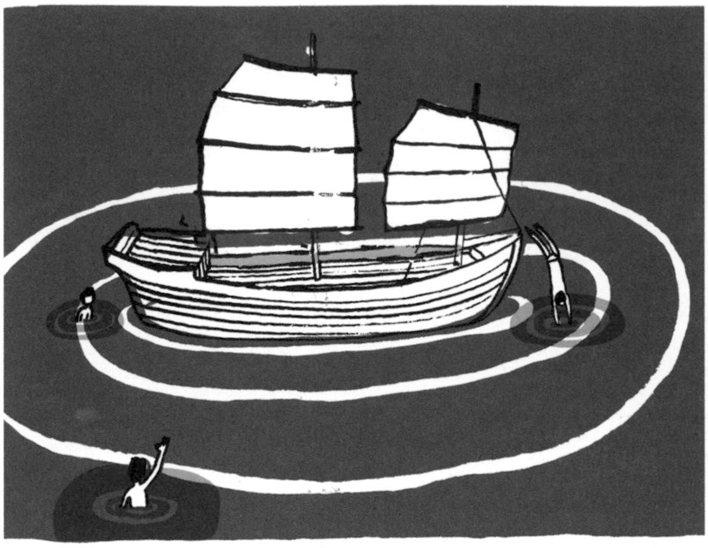

But then one of the pearl divers, a little boy who could swim like a fish, came to the surface coughing and gasping. He said he had found the moon and had put it in his mouth for safe keeping,

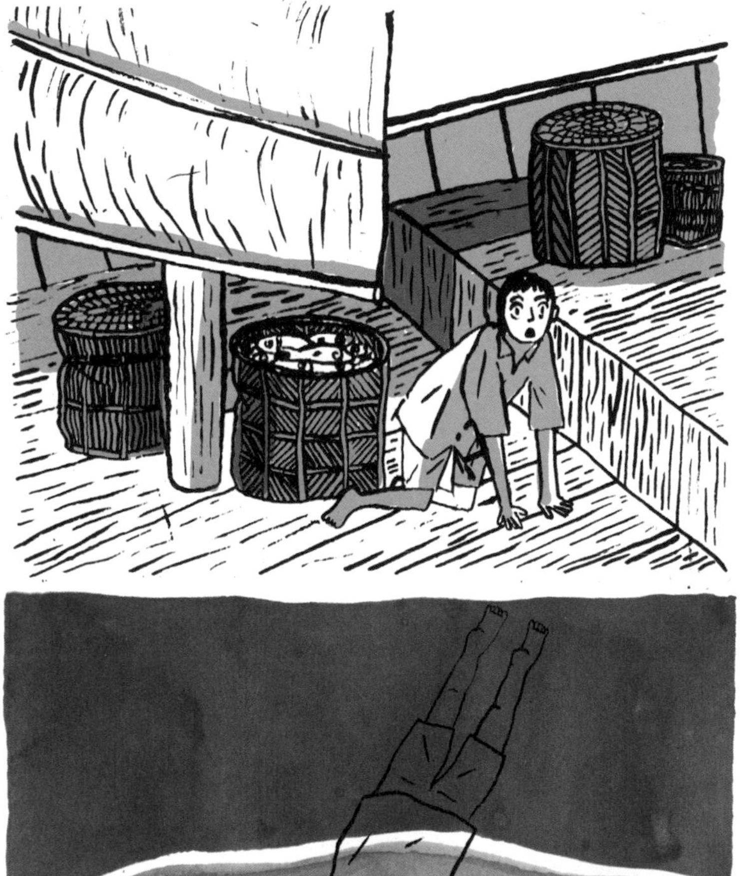

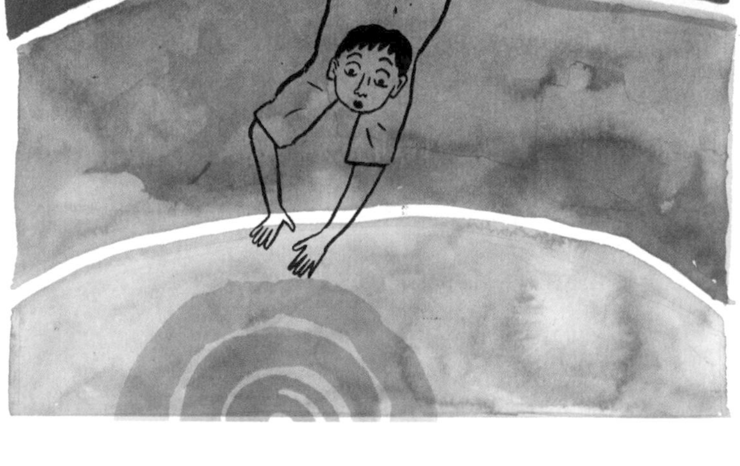

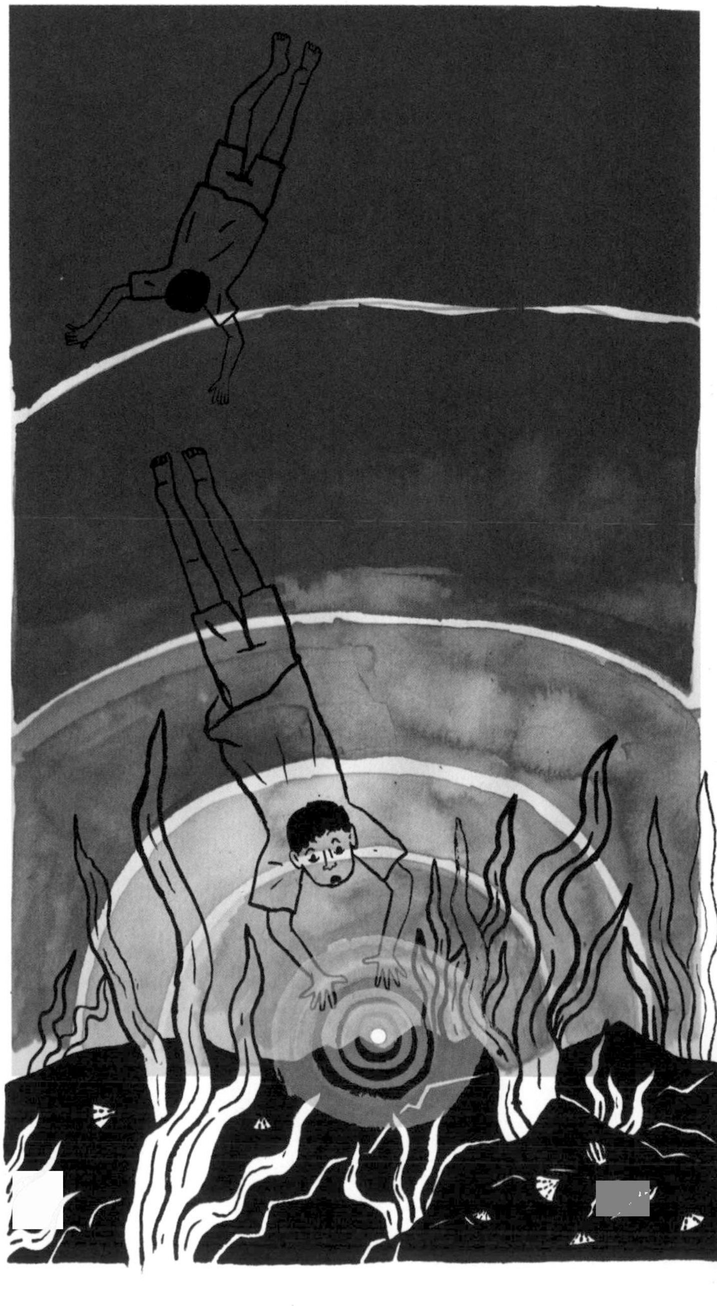

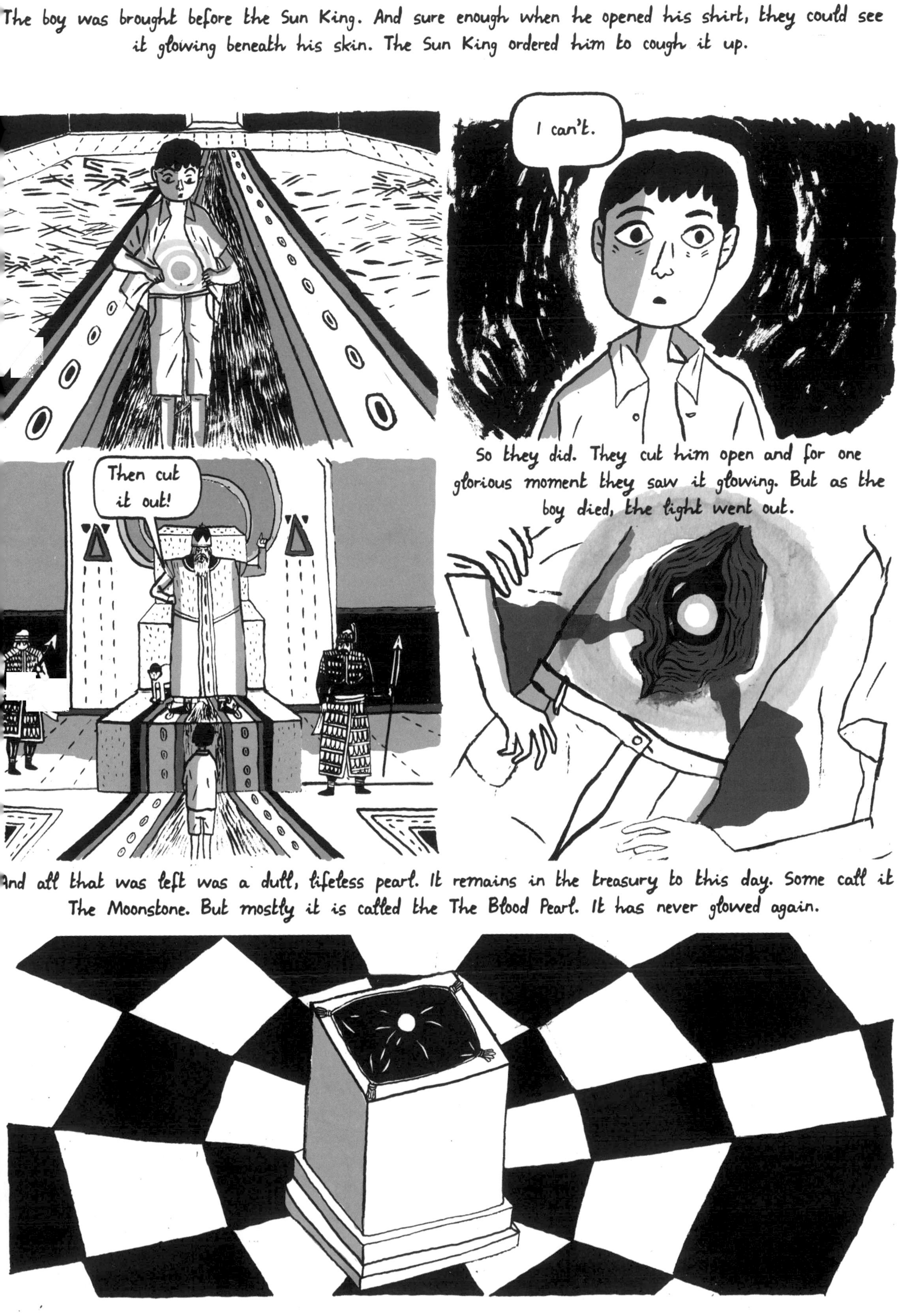
The boy was brought before the Sun King. And sure enough when he opened his shirt, they could see it glowing beneath his skin. The Sun King ordered him to cough it up.
I can't.
Then cut it out!
So they did. They cut him open and for one glorious moment they saw it glowing. But as the boy died, the light went out.
And all that was left was a dull, lifeless pearl. It remains in the treasury to this day. Some call it The Moonstone. But mostly it is called the The Blood Pearl. It has never glowed again.

THE PLUCKED FIREBIRD OF HOO

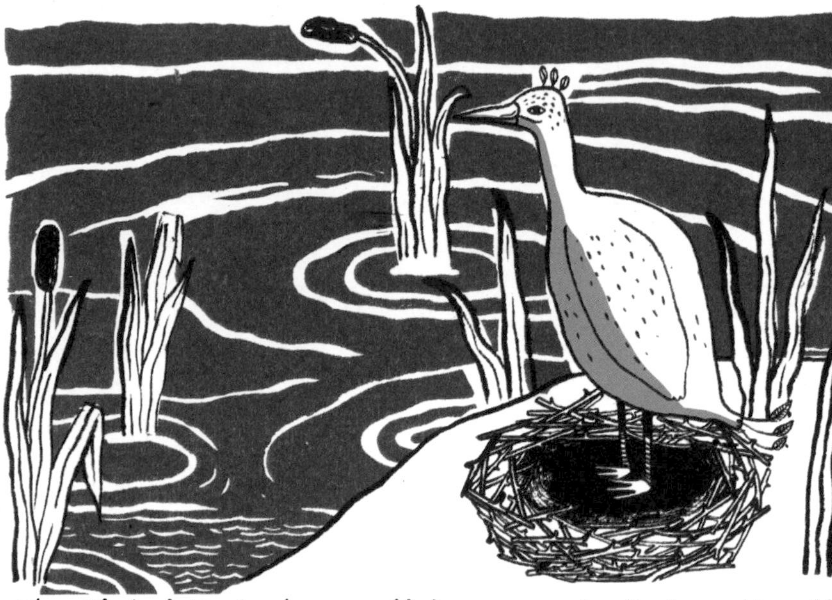

The Plucked Firebird, so called on account of its being almost entirely bald, is to be found nesting on the banks of the warm jungle rivers of Hoo.

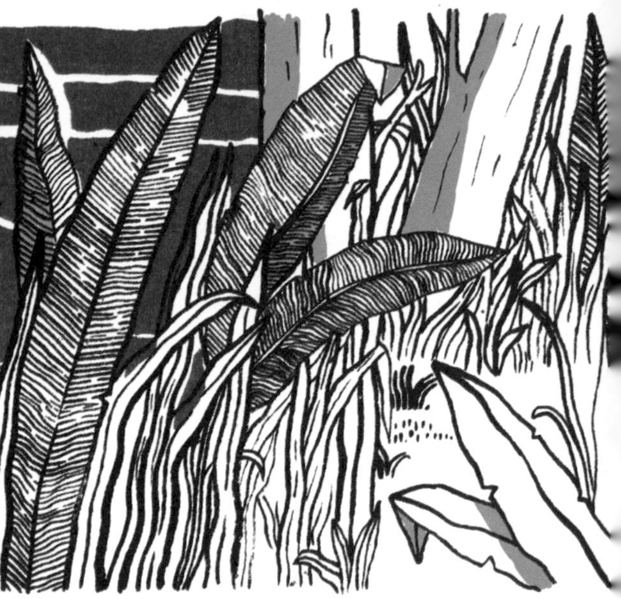

Hoo, the largest of the Ama-zin isles, is of course home to the May-May, a fierce tribe of warrior women.

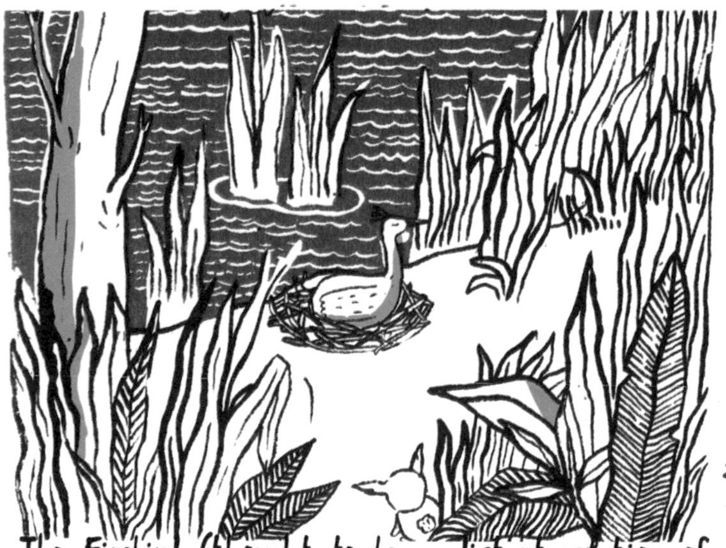

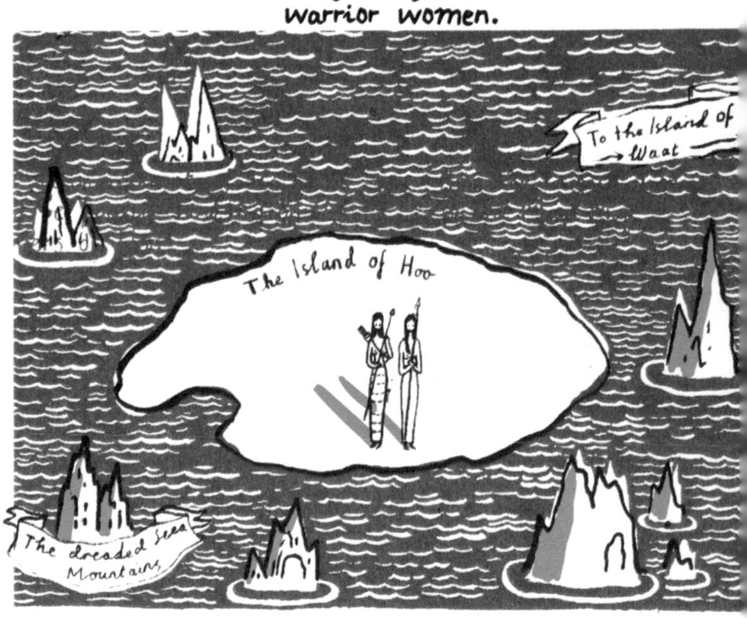
To the Island of Waat
The Island of Hoo
The dreaded Sea Mountains

The Firebird (thought to be a distant relation of the phoenix) is incredibly rare, being not only shy but also fragile. When agitated it will spontaneously combust, bursting into flames...

And roasting itself.

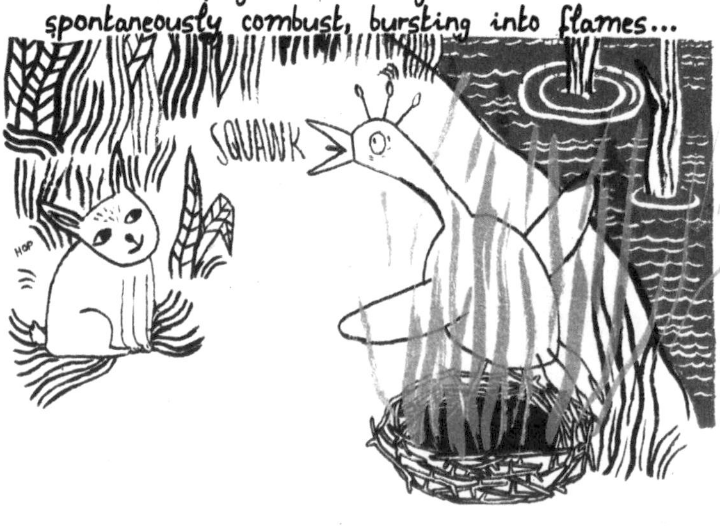
SQUAWK
HOP

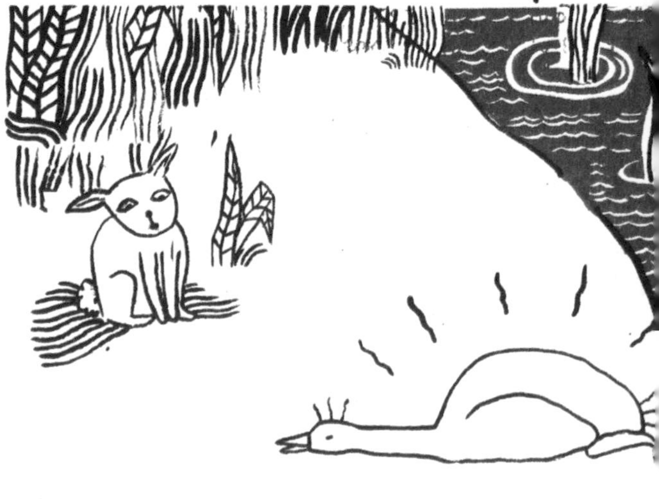

...ebirds mate for life but rarely produce offspring. This is because the excitement of mating tends to cause them to combust, bursting into flames and being consumed together. Poignant, but impractical from an evolutionary perspective.

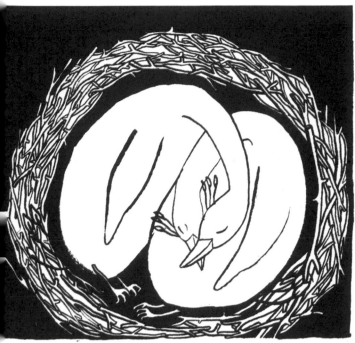

The plucked firebird is considered a great delicacy in Migdal Bavel. Poachers catch them with tranquilliser arrows.

They are kept sedated on the journey back and not woken up until they are brought to the table.

The City Of Migdal Bavel

Guests are then invited to wake the bird by throwing seasoning at it. Naturally the terrified creature bursts into flames, roasting before their eyes. It is then carved and served.

Thankfully this fate is not for many firebirds since the May-May deal harshly with any poachers they catch trespassing on Hoo.

They consider the firebirds most precious and to harm one is a heinous crime.

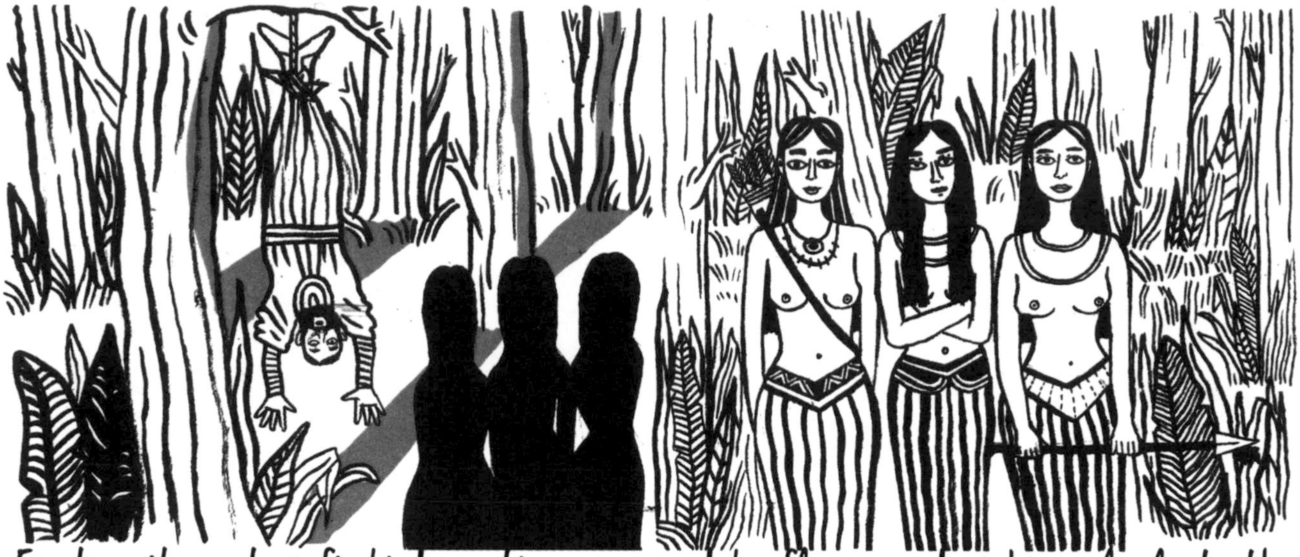

For to witness two firebirds mating, consumed by flames and sinking slowly to their deaths is a rare and beautiful thing. And the May-May know that for every firebird that ends its life on the Sun King's table, its mate will be waiting for it.

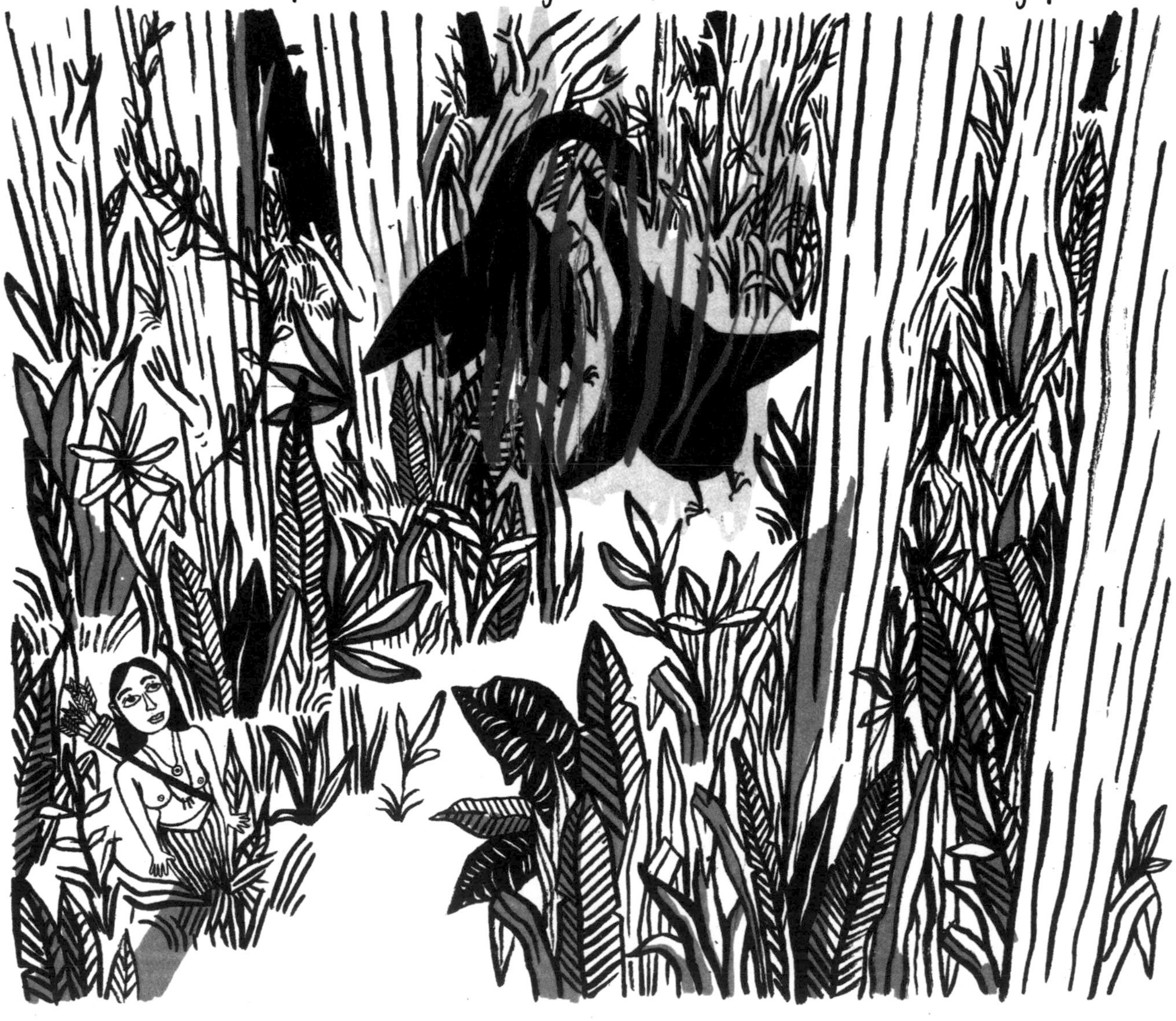

Thanks to Dan Berry for making me a font from my handwriting, and to Pete Dungey and Miles Gould at Oak for designing the front cover. Thank you to everyone at Jonathan Cape, particularly Dan Franklin and Neil Bradford. To Laura Tisdel, Kristin Cochrane, Katharina Dittes and Seth Fishman. Thank you to Simon Trewin at WME for making the whole thing happen.
Thanks to El, Em and RJV for always being on the other end of the phone.
And especially thanks to Mum, Dad and Im.

Published by Jonathan Cape 2013
2 4 6 8 10 9 7 5 3 1
Copyright © Isabel Greenberg 2013

First published in Great Britain in 2013 by Jonathan Cape
Random House, 20 Vauxhall Bridge Road,
London SW1V 2SA
www.vintage-books.co.uk
Addresses for companies within The Random House Group Limited can be found at:
www.randomhouse.co.uk/offices.htm
The Random House Group Limited Reg. No. 954009
A CIP catalogue record for this book is available from the British Library

ISBN 9780224097192

The Random House Group Limited supports the Forest Stewardship Council® (FSC®), the leading international forest-certification organisation. Our books carrying the FSC label are printed on FSC®-certified paper. FSC is the only forest-certification scheme supported by the leading environmental organisations, including Greenpeace. Our paper procurement policy can be found at:
www.randomhouse.co.uk/environment
Printed and bound in China by C&C Offset Printing Co., Ltd

The story 'The Mapmaker of Migdal Bavel' originally appeared in Solipsistic Pop 4. The story 'Genesis' originally appeared under the title 'Masters of the Universe' in
A Graphic Cosmogony, published by Nobrow Press.

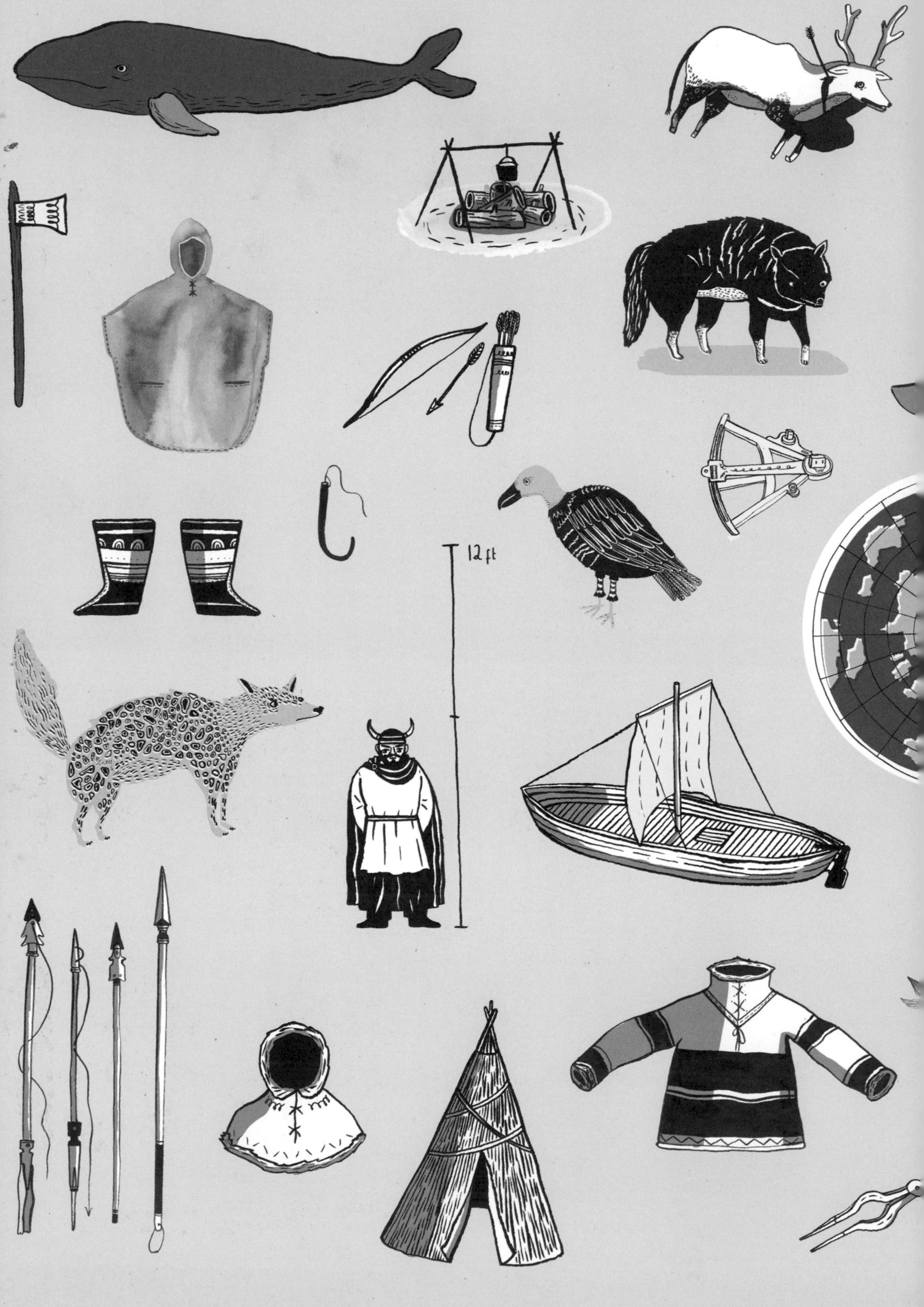
12 ft